Lecture Notes in Computer Science   11025

Commenced Publication in 1973
Founding and Former Series Editors:
Gerhard Goos, Juris Hartmanis, and Jan van Leeuwen

More information about this series at http://www.springer.com/series/7410

Joaquin Garcia-Alfaro · Jordi Herrera-Joancomartí
Giovanni Livraga · Ruben Rios (Eds.)

Data Privacy Management, Cryptocurrencies and Blockchain Technology

ESORICS 2018 International Workshops, DPM 2018
and CBT 2018, Barcelona, Spain, September 6–7, 2018
Proceedings

 Springer

Editors
Joaquin Garcia-Alfaro 🆔
Télécom SudParis
Evry
France

Giovanni Livraga 🆔
Università degli Studi di Milano
Crema
Italy

Jordi Herrera-Joancomartí 🆔
Enginyeria de la Informacio I de les Com
Universitat Autonoma de Barcelona
Bellaterra
Spain

Ruben Rios 🆔
Universidad de Málaga
Málaga
Spain

ISSN 0302-9743   ISSN 1611-3349 (electronic)
Lecture Notes in Computer Science
ISBN 978-3-030-00304-3   ISBN 978-3-030-00305-0 (eBook)
https://doi.org/10.1007/978-3-030-00305-0

Library of Congress Control Number: 2018953831

LNCS Sublibrary: SL4 – Security and Cryptology

This Springer imprint is published by the registered company Springer Nature Switzerland AG
The registered company address is: Gewerbestrasse 11, 6330 Cham, Switzerland

Foreword from the CBT 2018 Program Chairs

This volume contains the proceedings of the Second International Workshop on Cryptocurrencies and Blockchain Technology (CBT 2018) held in Barcelona during September 6–7, 2018, in conjunction with the 23rd European Symposium on Research in Computer Security (ESORICS) 2018.

In less than ten years, cryptocurrencies and blockchain technology have taken a central position in the IT world. The capitalization marked for cryptocurrencies is bigger than 300 billion dollars and other promising applications of blockchain technology range from personal identification and good tracking to distributed autonomous organizations. Since security is probably the main objective behind all such proposals, a careful analysis should be performed on those proposals before they reach the mass market. To that end, the CBT workshop aims to provide a forum for researchers in this area to carefully analyze current systems and propose new ones in order to create a scientific background for the solid development of this new area.

In response to the call for papers, we received 39 submissions that were carefully reviewed by the Program Committee (PC), comprising 19 members, and by additional reviewers. Each submission received at least three reviews. The PC selected seven full papers and eight short papers for presentation at the workshop. The selected papers cover aspects about smart contracts, second layer and off-chain transactions, transparency, performance, attacks, and privacy.

Furthermore, the workshop will be enhanced with a keynote talk sponsored by the Research Institute (cf. https://researchinstitute.io/), complemented by sponsoring from BART (Blockchain Advanced Research & Technologies), Inria Saclay, Institut Mines-Télécom, Universitat Autónoma de Barcelona, and SAMOVAR (URM 5157 of CNRS).

A special thank you goes to all the authors, who submitted papers to CBT 2018, as well as the PC and additional reviewers, who worked hard to review the submissions and discussed the final program. Last but not least, we would like to thank the ESORICS organizers, especially Sokratis Katsikas (ESORICS Symposium Steering Committee Chair), Miquel Soriano (ESORICS 2018 General Chair), Javier Lopez (ESORICS 2018 Program Chair), Josep Pegueroles-Valles (ESORICS 2018 Organization Chair), Marcel Fernandez and Jose Luis Muñoz Tapia (ESORICS 2018 Webmasters), for all their help and support during the organization of CBT 2018.

July 2018

Joaquin Garcia-Alfaro
Jordi Herrera-Joancomartí

Organization

2nd International Workshop on Cryptocurrencies and Blockchain Technology — CBT 2018

Program Committee Chairs

Joaquin Garcia-Alfaro	Institut Mines-Télécom, Télécom SudParis, France
Jordi Herrera-Joancomartí	Universitat Autònoma de Barcelona, Spain

Program Committee

Daniel Augot	Inria Saclay, France
Rainer Böhme	Universität Innsbruck, Austria
Joseph Bonneau	New York University, USA
Jeremy Clark	Concordia University, Canada
Ittay Eyal	Technion, Israel
Hannes Hartenstein	Karlsruher Institut für Technologie, Germany
Akira Kanaoka	Toho University, Japan
Ghassan Karame	NEC Research Institute, Germany
Shin'ichiro Matsuo	BSafe.network and Keio University, Japan
Patrick McCorry	University College London, UK
Sarah Meiklejohn	University College London, UK
Andrew Miller	University of Illinois, Urbana-Champaign, USA
Pedro Moreno Sanchez	Purdue University, USA
Jose Luis Muñoz Tapia	Universitat Politècnica de Catalunya, Spain
Guillermo Navarro	Universitat Autònoma de Barcelona, Spain
Cristina Pérez-Solà	Universitat Autònoma de Barcelona, Spain
Tim Ruffing	Saarland University, Germany
Roger Wattenhofer	ETH Zürich, Switzerland
Aviv Zohar	The Hebrew University, Israel

Steering Committee

Rainer Böhme	Universität Innsbruck, Austria
Joaquin Garcia-Alfaro	Institut Mines, France
Hannes Hartenstein	Karlsruher Institut für Technologie, Germany
Jordi Herrera-Joancomartí	Universitat Autònoma de Barcelona, Spain

Additional Reviewers

Sergi Delgado-Segura
Joan Bel
Carlos Dolader
Till Neudecker

Patrik Keller
Michael Fröwis
Felix Klaedtke
Juan Hernandez-Serrano

Foreword from DPM 2018 Program Chairs

This volume contains the proceedings of the 13th International Workshop on Data Privacy Management (DPM 2018), which was held in Barcelona, Spain, during September 6–7, 2018, in conjunction with the 23rd European Symposium on Research in Computer Security (ESORICS 2018).

The aim of DPM is to promote and stimulate international collaboration and research exchange in areas related to the management of privacy-sensitive information. This is a very critical and important issue for organizations and end users. It poses several challenging problems such as translation of high-level business goals into system-level privacy policies, administration of sensitive identifiers, data integration, and privacy engineering, among others.

In response to the call for papers, 36 submissions were received and each of them was evaluated on the basis of significance, novelty, and technical quality. The Program Committee, comprising 35 members, performed an excellent task and with the help of additional reviewers all submissions went through a careful anonymous review process (3 reviews per submission). The Program Committee's work was carried out electronically, yielding intensive discussions. Among the submitted papers, the Program Committee accepted 11 full papers (resulting in an acceptance rate of 30.5%) and 5 short papers for presentation at the workshop.

The success of DPM 2018 depends on the volunteering effort of many individuals, and there is a long list of people who deserve special thanks. We would like to thank all the members of the Program Committee and all the external reviewers for all their hard work in evaluating the papers in a short time window and for their active participation in the discussion and selection process. We are very grateful to all people who gave their assistance and ensured a smooth organization process: the DPM Steering Committee for the guidance and support in the organization of the workshop; Enrico Bacis for taking care of publicity; the ESORICS Symposium Steering Committee and its chair, Sokratis Katsikas, for all the arrangements that made the satellite events possible; Joaquin Garcia-Alfaro (ESORICS 2018 Workshop Chair), Miguel Soriano (ESORICS 2018 General Chair), and Josep Pegueroles (ESORICS 2018 Organization Chair) for their support in the workshop organization and logistics. We would also like to thank the keynote speakers for accepting our invitation and for their enlightening talks. We also express our gratitude for the support received from the UNESCO Chair in Data Privacy, sponsor of the workshop.

Last but certainly not least, our thanks goes to all the authors who submitted papers and to all the attendees of the workshop. We hope you find the program of DPM 2018 interesting, stimulating, and inspiring for your future research.

July 2018

Giovanni Livraga
Ruben Rios

Organization

13th International Workshop on Data Privacy Management — DPM 2018

Program Committee Chairs

Giovanni Livraga	Università degli Studi di Milano, Italy
Ruben Rios	Universidad de Málaga, Spain

Publicity Chair

Enrico Bacis	Università degli Studi di Bergamo, Italy

Program Committee

Ken Barker	University of Calgary, Canada
Jordi Castellà-Roca	Universitat Rovira i Virgili, Spain
Mauro Conti	University of Padua, Italy
Jorge Cuéllar	Siemens AG, Germany
Frederic Cuppens	Telecom Bretagne, France
Nora Cuppens	Telecom Bretagne, France
Sabrina De Capitani di Vimercati	Università degli Studi di Milano, Italy
José M. De Fuentes	Universidad Carlos III de Madrid, Spain
Roberto Di Pietro	Hamad Bin Khalifa University, Qatar
Josep Domingo-Ferrer	Universitat Rovira i Virgili, Spain
Carmen Fernandez-Gago	University of Málaga, Spain
Sara Foresti	Università degli Studi di Milano, Italy
Sebastien Gambs	Université du Québec à Montréal, Canada
Joaquin Garcia-Alfaro	Télécom SudParis, France
Marc Juarez	Katholieke Universiteit Leuven, Belgium
Christos Kalloniatis	University of the Aegean, Greece
Sokratis Katsikas	Giøvik University College in Norway, Norway
Hiroaki Kikuchi	Meiji University, Japan
Costas Lambrinoudakis	University of Piraeus, Greece
Maryline Laurent	Télécom SudParis, France
Wouter Lueks	École Polytechnique Fédérale de Lausanne, Switzerland

Fabio Martinelli   IIT-CNR, Italy
Chris Mitchell   Royal Holloway, University of London, UK
Guillermo Navarro-Arribas   Universitat Autònoma de Barcelona, Spain
David Nuñez   NuCypher, USA
Martín Ochoa   Universidad del Rosario, Colombia
Javier Parra-Arnau   Universitat Rovira i Virgili, Spain
Gerardo Pelosi   Politecnico di Milano, Italy
Silvio Ranise   FBK, Security and Trust Unit, Italy
Pierangela Samarati   Università degli Studi di Milano, Italy
Matthias Templ   Vienna University of Technology, Austria
Vicenç Torra   University of Skövde, Sweden
Yasuyuki Tsukada   Kanto Gakuin University, Japan
Lena Wiese   University of Göttingen, Germany
Melek Önen   EURECOM, France

Steering Committee

Josep Domingo-Ferrer   Universitat Rovira i Virgili, Spain
Joaquin Garcia-Alfaro   Télécom SudParis, France
Guillermo Navarro-Arribas   Autonomous University of Barcelona, Spain
Vicenç Torra   University of Skövde, Sweden

Additional Reviewers

Michael Bamiloshin   Zahra Pooranian
Alberto Blanco-Justicia   Sara Ricci
Lorena Cazorla   Andrea Saracino
Salimeh Dashti   Mina Sheikhalishahi
Lorena González Manzano   Mohammad Shojafar
Nicholas Mainardi   Aggeliki Tsohou
Katerina Mavroeidi   Katerina Vgena
David Pàmies Estrems

Contents

CBT Workshop: Smart Contracts

Succinctly Verifiable Sealed-Bid Auction Smart Contract.............. 3
  Hisham S. Galal and Amr M. Youssef

Blockchain-Based Fair Certified Notifications..................... 20
  Macià Mut-Puigserver, M. Magdalena Payeras-Capellà,
  and Miquel A. Cabot-Nadal

On Symbolic Verification of Bitcoin's SCRIPT Language.............. 38
  Rick Klomp and Andrea Bracciali

Self-reproducing Coins as Universal Turing Machine................ 57
  Alexander Chepurnoy, Vasily Kharin, and Dmitry Meshkov

**CBT Workshop: Second Layer, Off-chain Transactions
and Transparency**

Split Payments in Payment Networks........................ 67
  Dmytro Piatkivskyi and Mariusz Nowostawski

Payment Network Design with Fees 76
  Georgia Avarikioti, Gerrit Janssen, Yuyi Wang, and Roger Wattenhofer

Atomic Information Disclosure of Off-Chained Computations
Using Threshold Encryption................................. 85
  Oliver Stengele and Hannes Hartenstein

Contour: A Practical System for Binary Transparency 94
  Mustafa Al-Bassam and Sarah Meiklejohn

CBT Workshop: Consensus, Mining Pools and Performance

What Blockchain Alternative Do You Need? 113
  Tommy Koens and Erik Poll

Valuable Puzzles for Proofs-of-Work.......................... 130
  Colin Boyd and Christopher Carr

A Poisoning Attack Against Cryptocurrency Mining Pools.............. 140
  Mohiuddin Ahmed, Jinpeng Wei, Yongge Wang, and Ehab Al-Shaer

Using Economic Risk to Model Miner Hash Rate Allocation
in Cryptocurrencies.. 155
  George Bissias, Brian N. Levine, and David Thibodeau

CBT Workshop: Deadlocks, Attacks and Privacy

Avoiding Deadlocks in Payment Channel Networks 175
  Shira Werman and Aviv Zohar

Coloured Ring Confidential Transactions.......................... 188
  Felix Engelmann, Frank Kargl, and Christoph Bösch

Pitchforks in Cryptocurrencies: Enforcing Rule Changes Through
Offensive Forking- and Consensus Techniques (Short Paper)............ 197
  *Aljosha Judmayer, Nicholas Stifter, Philipp Schindler,
  and Edgar Weippl*

DPM Workshop: Privacy Assessment and Trust

Towards an Effective Privacy Impact and Risk Assessment
Methodology: Risk Analysis....................................... 209
  Majed Alshammari and Andrew Simpson

Privacy Risk Assessment: From Art to Science, by Metrics 225
  Isabel Wagner and Eerke Boiten

Bootstrapping Online Trust: Timeline Activity Proofs 242
  Constantin Cătălin Drăgan and Mark Manulis

DPM Workshop: Private Data and Searches

Post-processing Methods for High Quality Privacy-Preserving
Record Linkage 263
  Martin Franke, Ziad Sehili, Marcel Gladbach, and Erhard Rahm

δ-DOCA: Achieving Privacy in Data Streams....................... 279
  *Bruno C. Leal, Israel C. Vidal, Felipe T. Brito, Juvêncio S. Nobre,
  and Javam C. Machado*

Data Oblivious Genome Variants Search on Intel SGX 296
  Avradip Mandal, John C. Mitchell, Hart Montgomery, and Arnab Roy

DPM Workshop: Internet of Things

Developing GDPR Compliant Apps for the Edge 313
  Tom Lodge, Andy Crabtree, and Anthony Brown

YaPPL - A Lightweight Privacy Preference Language for Legally
Sufficient and Automated Consent Provision in IoT Scenarios   329
   Max-R. Ulbricht and Frank Pallas

PrivacyGuard: Enforcing Private Data Usage with Blockchain
and Attested Execution   345
   Ning Zhang, Jin Li, Wenjing Lou, and Y. Thomas Hou

DPM Workshop: Privacy and Cryptography

A Performance and Resource Consumption Assessment of Secret
Sharing Based Secure Multiparty Computation   357
   Marcel von Maltitz and Georg Carle

Privacy-Preserving Trade Chain Detection   373
   Stefan Wüller, Malte Breuer, Ulrike Meyer, and Susanne Wetzel

FHE-Compatible Batch Normalization for Privacy Preserving
Deep Learning   389
   Alberto Ibarrondo and Melek Önen

DPM Workshop: Future Internet

A General Algorithm for *k*-anonymity on Dynamic Databases   407
   Julián Salas and Vicenç Torra

On Security of Anonymous Invitation-Based System   415
   Naoto Yanai and Jason Paul Cruz

Probabilistic Metric Spaces for Privacy by Design Machine Learning
Algorithms: Modeling Database Changes   422
   Vicenç Torra and Guillermo Navarro-Arribas

Lifelogging Protection Scheme for Internet-Based Personal Assistants   431
   David Pàmies-Estrems, Nesrine Kaaniche, Maryline Laurent,
   Jordi Castellà-Roca, and Joaquin Garcia-Alfaro

Author Index   441

CBT Workshop: Smart Contracts

Succinctly Verifiable Sealed-Bid Auction Smart Contract

Hisham S. Galal[✉] and Amr M. Youssef

Concordia Institute for Information Systems Engineering,
Concordia University, Montréal, QC, Canada
h_galal@encs.concordia.ca

Abstract. The recently growing tokenization process of digital and physical assets over the Ethereum blockchain requires a convenient trade and exchange mechanism. Sealed-bid auctions are powerful trading tools due to the advantages they offer compared to their open-cry counterparts. However, the inherent transparency and lack of privacy on the Ethereum blockchain conflict with the main objective behind the sealed-bid auctions. In this paper, we tackle this challenge and present a smart contract protocol for a succinctly verifiable sealed-bid auction on the Ethereum blockchain. In particular, we utilize various cryptographic primitives including zero-knowledge Succinct Non-interactive Argument of Knowledge (zk-SNARK), Multi-Party Computation (MPC), Public-Key Encryption (PKE) scheme, and commitment scheme for our approach. First, the proving and verification keys for zk-SNARK are generated via an MPC protocol between the auctioneer and bidders. Then, when the auction process starts, the bidders submit commitments of their bids to the smart contract. Subsequently, each bidder individually reveals her commitment to the auctioneer using the PKE scheme. Then, according to the auction rules, the auctioneer claims a winner and generates a proof off-chain based on the proving key, commitments which serve as public inputs, and their underlying openings which are considered the auctioneer's witness. Finally, the auctioneer submits the proof to the smart contract which in turn verifies its validity based on the public inputs, and the verification key. The proposed protocol scales efficiently as it has a constant-size proof and verification cost regardless of the number of bidders. Furthermore, we provide an analysis of the smart contract design, in addition to the estimated gas costs associated with the different transactions.

Keywords: Ethereum · Smart contract · Sealed-bid auction
zk-SNARK

1 Introduction

The unprecedented growing deployment of assets on Ethereum has created a remarkable market for assets exchange [1] which imposes a high demand for various trading tools such as verifiable and secure auctions. Auctions are platforms

© Springer Nature Switzerland AG 2018
J. Garcia-Alfaro et al. (Eds.): DPM 2018/CBT 2018, LNCS 11025, pp. 3–19, 2018.
https://doi.org/10.1007/978-3-030-00305-0_1

for vendors to advertise their assets where interested buyers deposit competitive bids based on their own monetary valuation. Commonly, the auction winner is the bidder who submitted the highest price, however, there are a variety of other rules to determine the winner. Additionally, auctions have also been known to promote many economic advantages for the efficient trade of goods and services. According to [18], there exist two types of sealed-bid auctions: (i) First-price sealed-bid auctions (FPSBA) where the bidders submit bids in sealed envelops to the auctioneer. Subsequently, the auctioneer solely opens them to determine the winner who submitted the highest bid, and (ii) Vickrey auctions, which are similar to FPSBA with the exception that the winner pays the second highest bid instead.

Arguably, the main objective behind concealing the losing bids in sealed-bid auctions is to prevent the use of bidders' valuations against them in future auctions. Therefore, bidders are motivated to cast their bids without worrying about the misuse of their valuations. Nonetheless, when auctioneers collude with malicious bidders, the aforementioned advantage is easily broken. Consequently, the auctioneer has to be trusted to preserve bids' privacy and to correctly claim the auction winner. Therefore, various constructions of sealed-bid auctions utilize cryptographic protocols to ensure the proper and secure implementation without harming the privacy of bids.

Ethereum is the second most popular blockchain based on its market capitalization that exceeds $53 billion USD as of May 2018 [4]. Ethereum allows running decentralized applications in a global virtual machine environment known as Ethereum Virtual Machine (EVM) [28] without depending on any third-party. From a practical viewpoint, the EVM is a large decentralized computer with millions of objects (known as smart contracts) that can maintain an internal database, execute code, and interact with each other. As a result, the EVM substantially simplifies the creation of blockchain applications on its platform rather than building new application-specific blockchain from scratch.

The code executed in the EVM is commonly known as a smart contract which lies dormant and passive until its execution is triggered by transactions. It inherits strong integrity assurance from the blockchain, even its creator cannot modify it once it has been deployed. In Ethereum, computation is expensive as transactions are executed and verified by the full-nodes on Ethereum network. Therefore, Ethereum defines a gas metric to measure the computation efforts and storage cost associated with transactions. In other words, each transaction has a fee (i.e., consumed gas) that is paid by the transaction's sender in Ether (Ethereum currency). With the help of the consensus protocol, the smart contract is also guaranteed to execute precisely as its code dictates. Although many other blockchains such as Bitcoin [24] offer the capability to run smart contracts, they are often very limited to a specific set of instructions. Conversely, the instructions on EVM theoretically allow running any Turing-complete program. However, there is a block gas limit that defines the maximum amount of gas that can be consumed by all transactions combined in a single block. The current block gas limit is around is 8-million gas as of May 2018 [2]. Therefore, smart contracts cannot include very expensive computations that exceed the block gas limit.

In addition, despite the flexible programming capability in Ethereum smart contracts, they still lack transactional privacy. In fact, the details of every transaction executed in the smart contract are visible to the entire network. Moreover, these details are eventually stored in the Ethereum blockchain which also gives the ability to review past transactions as well. Consequently, the lack of transactional privacy is a major challenge towards the deployment of sensitive financial applications. Usually, individuals and organizations prefer to preserve the privacy of their transactions. For example, an organization may not want to post how much it spent on the purchase of some arbitrary assets.

Our contribution, we present a protocol for a sealed-bid auction smart contract that utilizes a set of cryptographic primitives to provide the following properties:

1. **Bids' Privacy.** The submitted bids are not visible to competitors during the bidding phase of the auction in the presence of malicious adversaries.
2. **Posterior privacy.** The losing bids are not revealed to the public assuming a semi-honest auctioneer.
3. **Bids' Binding.** Bidders cannot deny or change their bids once they are committed.
4. **Public Verifiability.** Any individual can verify the correctness of the auction winner proof.
5. **Fairness.** Rational parties are obligated to follow the proposed protocol to avoid being financially penalized.
6. **Non-Interactivity.** The smart contract, on behalf of the bidders, verifies the auction winner proof submitted by the auctioneer.
7. **Scalability.** The verification cost of the auction winner is nearly constant regardless of the number of bidders.

We have also created an open-source prototype for a Vickrey auction smart contract and made it available on Github [1] for researchers and community to review it. The rest of this paper is organized as follows. Section 2 provides a review of privacy-preserving protocols and sealed-bid auctions on the blockchain. In Sect. 3, we present the cryptographic primitives and tools utilized in designing the proposed Vickrey auction smart contract. Then, In Sect. 4, we provide the design of the auction contract together with an analysis of the estimated gas cost of relevant transactions. Finally, we present our conclusions and suggestions for future work in Sect. 5.

2   Related Work

Our proposal depends on utilizing zk-SNARK and distributed ledger (blockchain) technology to build an efficient (i.e., succinct proof with a relatively small verification cost) sealed-bid auction on Ethereum. Therefore, we

---

[1] https://github.com/hsg88/vickreyauction.

provide a review of state-of-the-art research papers that utilize zk-SNARK in building different cryptographic protocols on the blockchain, besides to papers that provide solutions to building sealed-bid auctions on top of blockchains.

A variety of privacy-preserving protocols are built on top of blockchain technology [5,10,11,15–17,19,20,22]. They combine cryptocurrency with cryptographic primitives such as MPC protocols, commitment schemes, and ZK proofs to achieve fairness in different adversary models. In a nutshell, initially, the protocol participants locks an arbitrary amount of cryptocurrency in an escrow smart contract. Subsequently, they proceed to engage in the various steps of the protocol. Finally, once the protocol reaches its final state, the escrow smart contract refunds the deposits back to the honest participants. Consequently, financially rational participants are obligated to adhere to the protocol rules in order to avoid the financial penalty.

One prominent example of the privacy-preserving protocol that has been deployed on Bitcoin is Zero-Knowledge Contingent Payment [22]. It allows a buyer and a seller to fairly trade an arbitrary digital good in exchange for bitcoins payment. Fairness is achieved without the need for a trusted party. In essence, by the end of the protocol, either the exchange completes with every participant receiving what they are expecting, or none of the participants gains an advantage over another one. Despite the limited flexibility of Bitcoin scripting language, the authors managed to provide a solution by depending on *hash-lock* transactions that allow someone to pay an arbitrary amount of bitcoins to anyone who can provide a preimage x such that $y = $ SHA-256(x), for a publicly known value y. We describe a simple version of ZKCP for the sake of illustration purposes. Suppose that a seller Bob wants to trade a digital item p in exchange for v bitcoins. First, Bob encrypts the item p using a symmetric encryption algorithm to obtain $c = Enc_x(p)$ using a key x. Then, Bob computes the hash value of the key $y = $SHA-256$(x)$. Subsequently, he sends (c, y) along with a ZK proof that claims $c = ENC_k(p)$ and $y = $SHA-256$(x)$. After that, if Alice is interested in that item, she creates a *hash-lock* transaction to pay v bitcoins to anyone who reveals the preimage x such that $y = SHA256(x)$. Finally, Bob receives the payment v bitcoins by revealing x which also means that Alice can decrypt c to get the digital good p.

Campanelli et al. [15] took a step further to propose Zero-Knowledge Contingent Service Payments (ZKCSP) on top of Bitcoin. The main goal is to permit a fair exchange of services and payments over the Bitcoin blockchain. The authors argue that previous constructions of ZKCP [22] are not suitable for the exchange of digital service and payments. They utilized zk-SNARK proof systems [7] to build practical proofs for complex arguments. As an example, they built a prototype for Proofs of Retrievability (PoR) where a client Bob has stored some data on a cloud server and he wants to verify whether the server still keeps and stores his data correctly. In this case, the server offers a digital service rather than a digital good where the server's owner Alice wants to be certain that there is a payment at the end of successful verification of PoR. Moreover, Bob does not want to pay in advance. Therefore, ZKCSP tackles this situation. Also, ZKCSP can be viewed to be more general than ZKCP as it allows for the trade of goods as well as services.

On the area of smart contract frameworks, Kosba et al. [17], presented Hawk, a framework for writing smart contracts that preserves the privacy of financial transactions on the blockchain. The main advantage is to allow programmers without knowledge of cryptographic protocols to build a secure and privacy-preserving smart contract. To this end, the framework includes a compiler that utilizes various cryptographic primitives in generating the smart contracts. A Hawk program source code is composed of public and private parts. The public part is responsible for the logic that does not deal with the sensitive data or the money flow. On the other hand, the private part is responsible for hiding the information about data and input currency units. The compiler translates the Hawk program into three pieces that define the cryptographic protocol between users, manager, and the blockchain nodes. Up to our knowledge, the framework has not been released yet and we could not find a deployed smart contract on Ethereum blockchain built by Hawk.

On the subject of sealed-bid auctions, Blass and Kerschbaum [11] proposed *Strain*, a protocol to build sealed-bid auctions, on top of blockchain technology, that preserve bids privacy against malicious participants. Strain uses a two-party comparison protocol to compare bids between pairs of bidders. Then, the comparison's outcome is submitted to the blockchain which serves as a secure bulletin board. Additionally, since bidders initially submit commitments to their bids, Strain utilizes ZK proof to verify that the submitted comparison's result corresponds to the committed bids. Furthermore, Strain uses reversible commitment scheme such that a group of bidders can jointly open the bid commitment. The objective of this scheme is to achieve fairness against malicious participants who prematurely abort or deviate from the protocol. As the authors reported in their work, Strain has an obvious flaw that reveals the order of bids, similar to Ordered Preserving Encryption (OPE). Furthermore, running protocols involving MPC on blockchain is not efficient due to extensive computations and the number of rounds involved. Meanwhile, our protocol does not suffer from Strains flaws, and it utilizes zk-SNARK to generate a proof that can be efficiently verified with a feasible cost on Ethereum.

Furthermore, Galal and Youssef [16] presented a protocol for running sealed-bid auctions on Ethereum. The protocol ensures the public verifiability, privacy of bids, and fairness. Initially, bidders submit Pedersen commitments of their bids to a smart contract. Subsequently, they reveal their commitments individually to the auctioneer using RSA encryption. Finally, the auctioneer determines the winning bid and claims the winner of the auction. There are two major issues in this protocol. First, for each losing bid, the auctioneer has to engage into a set of interactive commit-challenge-verify protocol to prove that the winning bid is greater than the losing bid. In other words, the number of interactions is proportional to the number of bidders. Second, current techniques for generating a secure random number on blockchains are not proven to be secure due to miners' influence; therefore, the random numbers used in a commit-challenge-verify proof can be compromised. The approach proposed in our paper overcomes these challenges by utilizing zk-SNARK which requires a single proof-verification for the whole auction process. Moreover, it is a non-interactive protocol that does not require random numbers to be generated on the blockchain.

3   Preliminaries

In this section, we briefly introduce the cryptographic primitives that are utilized in the design of our proposed protocol for the sealed-bid auction smart contract.

3.1   Commitment Scheme

Recall that in sealed-bid auctions, the bidders initially submit their bids in sealed envelops for a fixed period of time. Then, the auctioneer opens these envelopes to determine the winner. In other words, we need a tool to hide the bids temporarily, yet with the ability to reveal them later. This task can be easily fulfilled by a cryptographic primitive known as commitments schemes. Typically, a commitment scheme involves two parties: a sender (Alice) and a receiver (Bob). Additionally, it provides two security properties, namely, hiding and binding. Simply, let us denote for an abstract commitment scheme by the public algorithm $c = Com(x, r)$ which takes a value x, a random r, and produces a commitment c. In the reveal phase, Alice simply reveals the values x' and r', then Bob checks whether these two values produces the same original commitment c. The hiding property implies that it is infeasible for Bob to learn the value x given the commitment c. Likewise, the binding property implies that it is infeasible for Alice to reveal with different values x' and r' that produces the same commitment c. such that when Alice commits to an arbitrary value x and sends the commitment c to Bob. Although there are commitment schemes with strong security properties (e.g., information-theoretic hiding) such as Pedersen commitment, we instead use a relaxed one based on collision-resistant hash function due to its flexible integration with zk-SNARK.

To be precise, we choose SHA-256 to be the public algorithm for our commitment scheme. In order for Alice to commit to a bid x, she sends to Bob the commitment $c = $ SHA-256(s) where $s = (x||r)$, r is a k-bit randomness, and $||$ denotes the concatenation operation. Later on, to decommit c, she sends the value s' to him. Subsequently, Bob verifies that $c = $ SHA-256(s'). Then, on successful verification, he strips off the least significant k-bits from s' to recover the bid x.

3.2   zk-SNARK

ZK-SNARK is essentially a non-interactive zero-knowledge (NIZK) proof system. There are several constructions of zk-SNARK especially in the field of verifiable computations. In this paper, we follow the construction proposed by Sasson et al. [9] to verify computations compatible with Von Neumann architecture.

More precisely, to verify the correctness of the auctioneer's computations in determining the auction's winner.

Typically, any NIZK proof system about NP-language L consists of the following three main algorithms:

1. **Key generation:** $crs \leftarrow K(1^\lambda, L)$ which takes a security parameter λ, a description of the language L, and outputs the common reference string crs.
2. **Proof generation:** $\pi \leftarrow P(crs, s, w)$ which takes a crs, a statement s, a witness w such that $(s, w) \in L$, and outputs a proof π.
3. **Proof verification:** $\{0, 1\} \leftarrow V(crs, \pi, s)$ which takes a proof π, the previously generated crs, a statement s, and outputs 0 or 1 to denote accept or reject.

In general, any NIZK proof is simply a bulk of data that can be verified at any time without prior interactions between the prover and the verifier. A key requirement though is the proper generation of common reference string (CRS). If there is any trapdoor in the generation of CRS, then the prover is able to generate a fraudulent proof. Likewise, a malicious verifier can exploit the trapdoor to extract information about the witness. Therefore, the generation of CRS is of utmost importance to the security of NIZK proof. The zk-SNARK construction [9] provides the following security properties:

1. **Perfect Completeness.** An honest prover with a valid witness can always convince an honest verifier. More formally, given $(s, w) \in L, crs \leftarrow K(1^\lambda, L), \pi \leftarrow P(crs, s, w)$, then $V(crs, \pi) = 1$.
2. **Computational Soundness.** A polynomial-time adversary can convince a verifier that an invalid statement is true with a negligible probability. More formally, given $crs \leftarrow K(1^\lambda, L), \pi \leftarrow A(crs, s), s \notin L$, then $Pr[V(crs, \pi, s) = 1] \approx 0$.
3. **Computational Zero-Knowledge.** It is computationally infeasible for any polynomial-time adversary to reveal any information about the witness from the proof. More formally, there exists a simulator $S = (K\prime, P\prime)$ that outputs a transcript that is computationally indistinguishable from the one produced by (K, P) in a proof π without knowing a witness.
4. **Succinctness.** A NIZK is said to be succinct if an honestly generated proof has $Poly(\lambda)$- bits and the verification algorithm $V(crs, \pi, s)$ runs asymptotically in $O(|s| \cdot Poly(\lambda))$.

Recall that the key generation algorithm in zk-SNARK takes as an input a representation of the language L. Therefore, we want to find a suitable representation for the auction winner problem. Sasson et al. [9] proposed a general-purpose circuit generator that takes a C-code and translates it into an arithmetic circuit. Simply, arithmetic circuits are acyclic graphs with wires and mathematical operation gates as edges and node, respectively [23]. More precisely, an arithmetic circuit is a function $C : \mathbb{F}^m \times \mathbb{F}^n \to \mathbb{F}^l$ which essentially takes $(m + n)$-inputs and generates l-outputs. The arithmetic circuit C is said to have a valid assignment tuple $(a_1, ..., a_N)$ where $N = m + n + l$ when $C(a_1, ..., a_{x+y}) = (a_{x+y+1}, ..., a_N)$.

4   Auction Contract Design

In this section, we present the protocol for running a Vickrey auction as a smart contract on top of Ethereum. Our protocol is composed of six phases, where the first two phases are responsible for initializing the zk-SNARK proof system, while, the remaining four phases deal with the auctioning process itself.

4.1   Arithmetic Circuit Generation

Recall that before we can use the first algorithm in zk-SNARK, namely key generation, we need an arithmetic circuit that represents the function we want to provide a proof about its correct execution. Practically, creating an arithmetic circuit for complex arguments is a tedious and error-prone task, especially when the arguments involve operations that are intrinsically depending on logical operators such as the comparison operation and SHA-256 transformation. For this reason, we utilize the general-purpose circuit generator [3,9] to translate a program code into an arithmetic circuit.

Arguably, using a general-purpose arithmetic circuit generator often yields an inefficient circuit with a large number of gates. However, the computation problem of Vickrey auction, as shown in Algorithm 1, is not complex to the degree we worry about the performance of the generated circuit. Moreover, it is reported in [9] that the size of the generated arithmetic circuits scales additively rather than multiplicatively with respect to the size of the translated code.

Algorithm 1. Find highest and second-highest bids and verify commitments

---

1: **function** AUCTION(C, U, V)
2:    $highest \leftarrow 0, secondHighest \leftarrow 0, status \leftarrow 0, i \leftarrow 0$
3:    $success \leftarrow true$
4:    **while** $i < N$ **do**   ▷ N is the constant number of bidders
5:       **if** $C[i] \neq$ SHA-256($U[i], V[i]$) **then**   ▷ check if commitment is valid
6:          $success \leftarrow false$
7:          return [success, highest, secondHighest]
8:       **end if**
9:       **if** $highest < bid$ **then**
10:          $secondHighest \leftarrow highest$
11:          $highest \leftarrow bid$
12:       **end if**
13:       $i \leftarrow i + 1$
14:    **end while**
15:    $success \leftarrow true$
16:    return [success, highest, secondHighest]
17: **end function**

While the auctioneer might be tempted to omit commitments to let a colluding bidder win the auction, doing so will result in a failed verification by the smart contract. In other words, the algorithm does not check whether the auctioneer supplies all commitments as part of the public inputs. On the other hand, the verification which is carried out by the smart contract does supply all commitments. As a consequence, there will be a difference between the public parameters used by the auctioneer to generate the proof, and the public parameters used by the smart contract to verify the proof. Therefore, the verification will fail, and the auctioneer will be penalized if he cannot supply a valid proof that uses the same public parameters as the smart contract.

4.2   Generation of CRS

The outputs of the CRS generation algorithm are the proving and verification keys which are used by the prover and verifier, respectively. It is a mandatory requirement in any NIZK proof system including zk-SNARK to ensure the proper generation of CRS in order to preserve the zero-knowledge and soundness properties. Commonly, the CRS is usually generated by a trusted party. However, this is against the whole premise of the blockchain as a decentralized platform that does not require a trusted party. Moreover, it is sufficient to generate the CRS only one-time as long as the problem statement does not change. In other words, we can initially generate the CRS for the Vickrey auction. Then, we can utilize the resultant CRS in multiple Vickrey auctions.

To avoid the need for a trusted party, various MPC protocols have been proposed to generate the CRS. Bowe et al. [13] presented an MPC protocol to generate CRS for the Zcash cryptocurrency. For the sake of simplicity, let us consider that the CRS is composed of a single element $s \cdot g$ where $s \in \mathbb{F}_p^*$ and g is the generator for a group $\mathbb{G}$ written in the additive notation. Consider that, a prover Alice and a verifier Bob want to generate the CRS such that none of them has knowledge of its discrete log. The protocol runs as follows:

1. Alice chooses a uniform number $s_1 \in \mathbb{F}_p^*$ and sends the element $s_1 \cdot g$ to Bob.
2. Bob chooses a number $s_2 \in \mathbb{F}_p^*$ and sends the element $s_2 s_1 \cdot g$ to Alice.
3. Finally, Alice and Bob use the element $s_2 s_1 \cdot g$ as the CRS.

The problem with this simple protocol is that Bob can maliciously choose s_2 in a way that affects the final output of s. Therefore, the authors in [8,13] proposed a pre-commitment step where each participant first picks a secret number s_i then sends a commitment to it. Later on, they follow the same steps as above but with providing a ZK proof that they used the same secret number corresponding to their commitments. A major problem with this protocol is that the pre-commitment step requires a pre-selection of participants. Moreover, there is an overhead with generating the commitments and verifying the associated ZK proofs.

We follow the MPC protocol for CRS generation in [14] for a number of reasons. First, it does not require a pre-selection of parties to participate in the MPC protocol. Therefore, instead of trusting a specific group of people with the generation of the CRS, any individual can actively join to be assured that a valid CRS is generated even when the rest of participants are malicious. Second, It is more scalable and efficient than the previous construction as it is only a two-round protocol. The basic idea is to use random beacons to eliminate the step of pre-commitment in [13]. Fortunately, Ethereum is the second most popular blockchain, which implies that a large number (i.e., more than 51%) of the miners in the network are reasonably assumed to act honestly. Therefore, we can leverage the blockchain itself as a source of random beacons [12] without worrying about the influence of malicious miners. Hence, the MPC protocol for CRS generation proceeds as follows:

1. Alice chooses a uniform number $s_1 \in \mathbb{F}_p^*$ and sends the element $s_1 \cdot g$ to Bob.
2. Similarly, Bob chooses a uniform number $s_2 \in \mathbb{F}_p^*$ and sends the element $s_2 s_1 \cdot g$ to the smart contract.
3. A beacon s_3 is read from the blockchain, and the element $s_3 s_2 s_1 \cdot g$ is used as CRS.

Assuming that no malicious miner can affect the beacon s_3 in a way that makes finding the discrete log of $s_3 s_2 s_1.g$ an easy problem, then we can safely say that the generated CRS has no trapdoor that compromises the security of a zk-SNARK proof. We also note that it is an optional task for the bidders to participate in the CRS generation. In other words, the integration of the random beacon in the MPC protocol is sufficient to ensure that the auctioneer cannot control the trapdoor of the generated CRS. Obviously, the achieved security is much stronger when at least one honest bidder participates in the MPC protocol.

1. T_1, T_2, T_3 define the periods using block numbers for the following phases: commitments of bids, opening the commitments, and proof generation and verification, respectively. Note that, T refers to the current block number.
2. N is the maximum number of bidders.
3. F defines the financial deposit of ethers to guarantee fairness against financial rational malicious participants.
4. A_{pk} is the auctioneer's public key of an asymmetric encryption scheme.
5. $Vkey$ is the verification key part of the generated CRS.

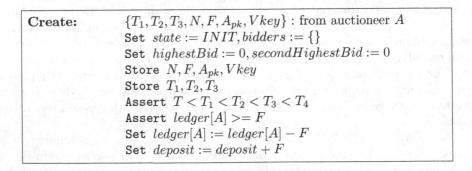

Fig. 1. Pseudocode for Vickrey auction smart contract constructor

4.3   Smart Contract Deployment

The auctioneer deploys the smart contract that runs the Vickrey auction on top of Ethereum. The deployment is basically a transaction that carries the compiled EVM bytecode as a payload and triggers the execution of the constructor. The constructor is responsible for initializing the state of variables in the smart contract. In Fig. 1, we show a pseudocode to illustrate the initialization of the state variables based on the parameters received from the auctioneer.

4.4   Submission of Bids

In this phase, the bidders create transactions to pay F-ethers and submit commitments of their bids as described in Sect. 3 to the function Bid which stores the commitments on the smart contract as shown in Fig. 2.

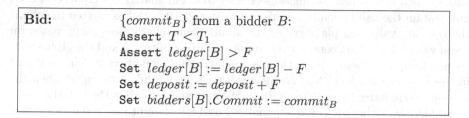

Fig. 2. Pseudocode for the submission of bid commitment

We also note that at the end of this phase, if the number of the submitted commitments is less than the maximum number of bidders N, then the auctioneer has to submit the remaining number of commitments with an underlying bid value equals to zero. The reason behind this step is due to technical limitation in the general-purpose arithmetic circuit generator [9]. More precisely, the translated code is not allowed to have loops with variable number of iterations, so we have to fix the loop counter to the maximum number of bidders N. Basically, the circuit generator flattens and unrolls the loop iterations, therefore, the number of iterations has to be known in advance.

4.5   Opening the Commitments

In this phase, each bidder B_i encrypts the pair (x_i, r_i) by the public key A_{pk}, where x_i is the bid value, and r_i is a random number. Then, the ciphertext is sent to the function Open on the smart contract as shown in Fig. 3.

Arguably, paying for a transaction that stores the ciphertext on the smart contract seems to be an unnecessary task at the first glance. However, we chose to store the ciphertext rather than sending them off-chain to the auctioneer so we can avoid the following attack scenario. Suppose a malicious auctioneer pretends that an arbitrary bidder Bob has not submitted a ciphertext of the correct

```
Open:          {ciphertext_B} from a bidder B:
               Assert T_1 < T < T_2
               Assert B ∈ bidders
               Set bidders[B].Ciphertext := ciphertext_B
```

Fig. 3. Pseudocode for the Open function

opening values of his associated commitment. In this case, Bob has no chance of denying this false claim. However, if Bob's ciphertext is stored on the smart contract, then the transaction that carried Bob's ciphertext of his commitment's opening values sufficiently defeats this false claim. Furthermore, as it is shown in the pseudocode Fig. 3, the ciphertext is stored in a mapping $bidders[Bob]$ as part of a structure that also contains the sealed-bid (commitment) with senders address as a key. When the auctioneer tries to claim that Bob's ciphertext does not contain the valid openings of his commitment, then Bob is alerted to submit the opening values as plaintext to the smart contract. Subsequently, based on these values, the smart contract recomputes the commitment and the ciphertext, then it compares them against the commitment and ciphertext which are stored in the mapping $bidders[Bob]$. In the case, they are found to be equal, then the protocol terminates by penalizing the auctioneer and refunding the initial deposit to all bidders. Otherwise, Bob is penalized and his commitments and ciphertext are discarded from further processing steps.

4.6 Proof Generation and Verification

In this phase, the auctioneer reads the ciphertext stored on the smart contract and decrypts them off-chain. As a result, the auctioneer has a knowledge of the necessary witness (i.e., openings of commitments), highest-bid, and second-highest bid to generate a proof. Hence, the auctioneer creates a transaction to pass the highest and second-highest bids as part of the public inputs, and the generated proof as shown in Fig. 4.

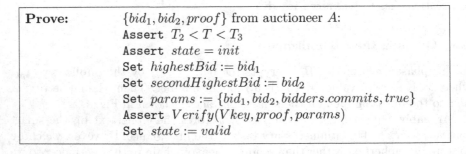

```
Prove:         {bid_1, bid_2, proof} from auctioneer A:
               Assert T_2 < T < T_3
               Assert state = init
               Set highestBid := bid_1
               Set secondHighestBid := bid_2
               Set params := {bid_1, bid_2, bidders.commits, true}
               Assert Verify(Vkey, proof, params)
               Set state := valid
```

Fig. 4. Pseudocode for the Reveal function

The function `Verify` checks the validity of the submitted proof based on the verification key $Vkey$ and the public inputs *params*. It utilizes the precompiled contracts EIP-196 [27] and EIP-197 [26] to perform the necessary elliptic-curve pairing operations required for zk-SNARK proof verification [9]. Finally, it returns a boolean output to indicate whether to accept the proof or reject it.

Once the verification of zk-SNARK proof has passed successfully, the auctioneer creates a transaction to finalize the auctioning process. Basically, the auctioneer reveals to the smart contract the openings associated with the auction winner commitment as shown in Fig. 5. Then, the smart contract checks whether the winner's bid value equals to the highest bid, and it also checks that the commitment of the opening values is equivalent to one of the previously submitted commitments by the bidders. Finally, the smart contract determines the address associated with the auction winner, and it begins to refund the deposit F to the losing bidders and the auctioneer. However, the winner deposit is not refunded until she fulfills the payment of the second-highest bid.

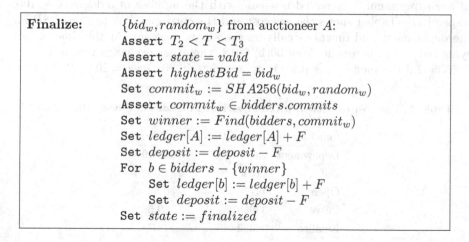

Finalize:	$\{bid_w, random_w\}$ from auctioneer A:
	`Assert` $T_2 < T < T_3$
	`Assert` $state = valid$
	`Assert` $highestBid = bid_w$
	`Set` $commit_w := SHA256(bid_w, random_w)$
	`Assert` $commit_w \in bidders.commits$
	`Set` $winner := Find(bidders, commit_w)$
	`Set` $ledger[A] := ledger[A] + F$
	`Set` $deposit := deposit - F$
	`For` $b \in bidders - \{winner\}$
	    `Set` $ledger[b] := ledger[b] + F$
	    `Set` $deposit := deposit - F$
	`Set` $state := finalized$

Fig. 5. Pseudocode for the Finalize function

As shown in Fig. 6, there is one more function in the smart contract called *Dispute*. The objective of this function is to counter a possible malicious behavior by the auctioneer. Let us assume the auctioneer refuses to carry out the proof generation and verification task. This will certainly result in a permanent lock of the deposits paid by the bidders. Therefore, any bidder can call this function that checks if the *state* variable on the smart contract is still equal to *init* after the block number T_3 has been mined, then it refunds the deposits back to the bidders. Consequently, only the auctioneer ends up being financially penalized since there is no way to refund his deposit.

```
Dispute:        Assert T > T₃
                Assert state = init
                For b ∈ bidders
                    Set ledger[b] := ledger[b] + F
                    Set deposit := deposit − F
```

Fig. 6. Pseudocode for the Dispute function

4.7 Gas Cost Analysis

We have implemented a prototype for the proposed protocol and smart contract, We have also made it open-source and published it on Github repository [2]. To experiment with our prototype, we have created a local Ethereum blockchain using the *Geth* client version 1.8.10. The genesis file that is responsible for the initialization of the local blockchain contains the following attribute in order to support the pre-compiled contracts EIP-196 and EIP-197: { "*byzantiumBlock*" : *0* }. In our experiment, we created test-case with the number of bidders $N = 100$, respectively. Table 1 shows the gas cost and the corresponding price in *USD* for the deployment and functions calls on the smart contract. At the time of carrying out our experiment, May 30th, 2018, the ether exchange rate is 1 ether = 583\$ and the median gas price is approximately 20 *Gwei* = 20×10^{-9} ether.

Table 1. Gas cost associated with the various functions in the smart contract

Function	Transaction cost	Price
Deployment	1346611	15.70
Bid	115583	1.35
Open	44176	0.52
Prove	3395077	39.58
Finalize	92362	1.07
Dispute	47112	0.55

The smart contract deployment cost is a little bit expensive as it involves the deployment of helper contracts and libraries that are responsible for verifying zk-SNARK proof. However, this cost can be significantly reduced if the helper contracts and libraries are already deployed beforehand. Also, the cost of the *Prove* function is constant due to the fixed cost of the elliptic-curve operations performed during the verification of the zk-SNARK proof. Arguably, this cost might be not convenient for relatively cheap auctioned assets. However, our work scales much better and more efficiently than previous auctions constructions on blockchain [11,16,25].

---

[2] https://github.com/hsg88/VickreyAuction.

Although we mimic the real-world behavior of sealed-bid auctions where the auctioneer gains knowledge of the sealed-bids, we still guarantee a verifiable computation of the auction winner. One may argue that the auctioneer may abuse the information she gained in future auctions to increase her revenues. We are currently investigating the integration of Trusted Execution Environment (TEE) such as Intel Software Guard eXtensions (SGX) into our protocol. Briefly speaking, the role of the auctioneer is replaced by a code that runs inside an enclave that protects it from modification and prevents disclosure of its state by the operating system or any other application. Hence, it provides the confidentiality of data which the blockchain lacks. Additionally, the enclave can issue proof which is also known as *attestation* of computation correctness.

4.8   Checking for Potential Security Bugs

The Vickrey auction smart contracts are implemented in Solidity which is the de-facto programming language for writing smart contracts on Ethereum. Due to the sensitive nature of the smart contracts especially when they involve operations to send or receive money, we have to properly assess their security before deployment. Recall that, once a smart contract is deployed, there is no way to modify it to patch a bug. Therefore, we utilize security analysis tools to check for potential bugs such as the famous *Re-entry* [6] bug found in DAO smart contracts that eventually caused hard-fork on Ethereum to mitigate the attack. Precisely, we use Oyente[3] [21] to ensure that the Vickrey auction smart contract does not contain any vulnerabilities to known critical security issues. The results from running Oyente on the Vickrey auction protocol are shown in Fig. 7. Also, we have utilized unit-testing to detect errors in the Solidity code, and the applied tests are included in the repository for further inspection by the community.

5   Conclusions

In this paper, we showed how zk-SNARK can be utilized to build Vickrey auction on top of Ethereum blockchain. The proposed protocol achieves many desirable properties such as bids privacy where the information about the bids is kept hidden from competitors. Additionally, the auction smart contract, on behalf of the bidders verifies the correctness of the auction winner claimed by the auctioneer. Moreover, the proposed protocol is scalable as the cost of the verification transaction is constant regardless of the number of bidders. Furthermore, the proposed protocol is in the favor of bidders with relatively low-processing power devices, since there are only two simple interactions with the smart contract involving the submission of commitments of bids, and revealing the underlying openings. For future work, we will investigate other approaches applicable to the blockchain where we can also protect the privacy of bids from all parties including the auctioneer by integrating TTE into our protocol. More precisely, we are

---

[3] We used the online Oyente tool available on https://oyente.melon.fund.

browser/ballot.sol:Auction	
EVM Code Coverage:	15.4%
Callstack Depth Attack Vulnerability:	False
Re-Entrancy Vulnerability:	False
Assertion Failure:	False
Timestamp Dependency:	False
Parity Multisig Bug 2:	False
Transaction-Ordering Dependence (TOD):	False

Fig. 7. Results from running Oyente online tool on the smart contract

exploring the feasibility of alternative approaches to building sealed-bid auction on top of the Enigma protocol [29]. Additionally, we will continue improving our prototype and apply formal verification techniques on our code to detect potential flaws and vulnerabilities.

References

1. Digital assets in ethereum blockchain. https://tokenmarket.net/blockchain/ethereum/assets/
2. Ethereum gaslimit history (2018). https://etherscan.io/chart/gaslimit
3. Python-based system for zk-snark based verifiable computations and smart contracts (2018). https://github.com/Charterhouse/pysnark
4. Top 100 cryptocurrencies by market capitalization (2018). https://coinmarketcap.com
5. Andrychowicz, M., Dziembowski, S., Malinowski, D., Mazurek, L.: Secure multiparty computations on bitcoin. In: IEEE Symposium on Security and Privacy (SP), pp. 443–458. IEEE (2014)
6. Atzei, N., Bartoletti, M., Cimoli, T.: A survey of attacks on ethereum smart contracts (SoK). In: Maffei, M., Ryan, M. (eds.) POST 2017. LNCS, vol. 10204, pp. 164–186. Springer, Heidelberg (2017). https://doi.org/10.1007/978-3-662-54455-6_8
7. Ben-Sasson, E., Chiesa, A., Genkin, D., Kfir, S., Tromer, E., Virza, M.: libsnark (2014). https://github.com/scipr-lab/libsnark
8. Ben-Sasson, E., Chiesa, A., Green, M., Tromer, E., Virza, M.: Secure sampling of public parameters for succinct zero knowledge proofs. In: IEEE Symposium on Security and Privacy (SP), pp. 287–304. IEEE (2015)
9. Ben-Sasson, E., Chiesa, A., Tromer, E., Virza, M.: Succinct non-interactive zero knowledge for a von neumann architecture. In: USENIX Security Symposium, pp. 781–796 (2014)

10. Bentov, I., Kumaresan, R.: How to use bitcoin to design fair protocols. In: Garay, J.A., Gennaro, R. (eds.) CRYPTO 2014. LNCS, vol. 8617, pp. 421–439. Springer, Heidelberg (2014). https://doi.org/10.1007/978-3-662-44381-1_24
11. Blass, E.-O., Kerschbaum, F.: Strain: A secure auction for blockchains. Cryptology ePrint Archive, Report 2017/1044 (2017). https://eprint.iacr.org/2017/1044
12. Bonneau, J., Clark, J., Goldfeder, S.: On bitcoin as a public randomness source. IACR Cryptology ePrint Archive 2015, 1015 (2015)
13. Bowe, S., Gabizon, A., Green, M.D.: A multi-party protocol for constructing the public parameters of the pinocchio zk-snark. Technical report, TR 2017/602, IACR (2017)
14. Bowe, S., Gabizon, A., Miers, I.: Scalable multi-party computation for zk-snark parameters in the random beacon model (2017)
15. Campanelli, M., Gennaro, R., Goldfeder, S., Nizzardo, L.: Zero-knowledge contingent payments revisited: attacks and payments for services. In: Proceedings of the 2017 ACM SIGSAC Conference on Computer and Communications Security, pp. 229–243. ACM (2017)
16. Galal, H., Youssef, A.: Verifiable sealed-bid auction on the ethereum blockchain. In: International Conference on Financial Cryptography and Data Security, Trusted Smart Contracts Workshop. Springer (2018)
17. Kosba, A., Miller, A., Shi, E., Wen, Z., Papamanthou, C.: Hawk: the blockchain model of cryptography and privacy-preserving smart contracts. In: IEEE Symposium on Security and Privacy (SP), pp. 839–858. IEEE (2016)
18. Krishna, V.: Auction Theory. Academic Press (2009)
19. Kumaresan, R., Bentov, I.: Amortizing secure computation with penalties. In: Proceedings of the 2016 ACM SIGSAC Conference on Computer and Communications Security, pp. 418–429. ACM (2016)
20. Kumaresan, R., Vaikuntanathan, V., Vasudevan, P.N.: Improvements to secure computation with penalties. In: Proceedings of the 2016 ACM SIGSAC Conference on Computer and Communications Security, pp. 406–417. ACM (2016)
21. Luu, L., Chu, D.-H., Olickel, H., Saxena, P., Hobor, A.: Making smart contracts smarter. In: Proceedings of the 2016 ACM SIGSAC Conference on Computer and Communications Security, pp. 254–269. ACM (2016)
22. Maxwell, G.: Zero knowledge contingent payment (2011). https://en.bitcoin.it/wiki/Zero_Knowledge_Contingent_Payment. Accessed 05 Jan 2016
23. Mayer, H.: zk-snark explained: Basic principles (2016). https://blog.coinfabrik.com/wp-content/uploads/2017/03/zkSNARK-explained_basic_principles.pdf
24. Nakamoto, S.: Bitcoin: a peer-to-peer electronic cash system (2008)
25. Snchez, D.C.: Raziel: private and verifiable smart contracts on blockchains. Cryptology ePrint Archive, Report 2017/878 (2017). https://eprint.iacr.org/2017/878
26. Reitwiessner, C., Buterin, V.: Elliptic curve pairing operations (2017). https://github.com/ethereum/EIPs/blob/master/EIPS/eip-197.md
27. Reitwiessner, C., Buterin, V.: Elliptic curve point addition and scalar multiplication operations (2017). https://github.com/ethereum/EIPs/blob/master/EIPS/eip-196.md
28. Wood, G.: Ethereum: a secure decentralised generalised transaction ledger. Ethereum Proj. Yellow Paper 151, 1–32 (2014)
29. Zyskind, G., Nathan, O., Pentland, A.: Enigma: decentralized computation platform with guaranteed privacy. arXiv preprint arXiv:1506.03471 (2015)

Blockchain-Based Fair Certified Notifications

Macià Mut-Puigserver[✉], M. Magdalena Payeras-Capellà,
and Miquel A. Cabot-Nadal

Dpt. de Ciències Matemàtiques i Informàtica, Universitat de les Illes Balears,
Ctra. de Valldemossa, km 7,5., 07122 Palma, Spain
{macia.mut,mpayeras,miquel.cabot}@uib.es

Abstract. Lots of traditional applications can be redefined thanks to
the benefits of Blockchain technologies. One of these services is the provision of fair certified notifications. Certified notifications is one of the
applications that require a fair exchange of values: a message and a non-
repudiation of origin proof in exchange for a non-repudiation of reception evidence. To the best of our knowledge, this paper presents the first
blockchain-based certified notification system. We propose two solutions
that allow sending certified notifications when confidentiality is required
or when it is necessary to register the content of the notification, respectively. First, we present a protocol for Non Confidential Fair Certified
Notifications that satisfies the properties of strong fairness and transferability of the proofs thanks to the use of a smart contract and without
the need of a Trusted Third Party. Then, we also present a DApp for
Confidential Certified Notifications with a smart contract that allows a
timeliness optimistic exchange of values with a stateless Trusted Third
Party.

Keywords: Blockchain · Fair certified notifications · Smart contract
Confidentiality · Fairness · Cryptocurrencies · Certified electronic mail

1 Introduction

Blockchain technology provides an unalterable system of data registry that
enables new solutions for a wide range of traditional applications. One of these
traditional services that could benefit of the distinctive features of blockchain is
the provision of certified notifications, that is, a service that allows a sender to
prove that she has sent a message to a receiver or set of receivers. Thus, certified
notification services provide evidence that a receiver has access to a message
since a specific date/time. Certified notifications, along with other electronic
services, such as electronic signature of contracts, electronic purchase (payment
in exchange for a receipt or digital product) or certified mail, require a fair
exchange of items between two or more users. In order to create protocols that
allow carrying out these exchanges and, at the same time, maintain the security

© Springer Nature Switzerland AG 2018
J. Garcia-Alfaro et al. (Eds.): DPM 2018/CBT 2018, LNCS 11025, pp. 20–37, 2018.
https://doi.org/10.1007/978-3-030-00305-0_2

of communications, there are solutions that fall into the generic pattern named *fair exchange of values*. A fair exchange always provides an equal treatment of all users, and, at the end of each execution, either each party has the element she wishes to obtain from the other party, or the exchange has not been carried out successfully for no one (any party has received the expected item). In a typical notification case, the element to be exchanged is the message along with non-repudiation proof of origin and reception.

Fair exchange protocols proposed so far usually use TTPs [12,13,20], which are responsible for resolving any conflict that arises as a result of interrupted exchanges or fraud attempts. In addition to that, these protocols normally use non-repudiation mechanisms in order to generate evidence that proves the behavior of the actors of the protocol. Currently, with the advent of the blockchain technology and smart contracts, TTPs can be replaced or complemented by this new know-how, which opens a range of new possibilities to find effective solutions to the electronic versions of the protocols that fulfil the generic pattern of fair exchange of values. A method for designing new fair exchanges by means of the Bitcoin network is to motivate parties to complete the protocol in order to assure fairness by using a bond or a monetary penalty for dishonest parties [4,10,15].

In addition to that, the Ethereum blockchain and its cryptocurrency Ether offers an even richer functionality set than conventional cryptocurrencies such as bitcoin, since they support smart contracts in a fully distributed system that could lead, as we will see in this paper, to enable fair exchanges of tokens without the involvement of a TTP (since smart contracts are self-applied and reduce the need for trusted intermediaries or reputation systems that decrease transaction risks). This new technology allows us to define transactions with predetermined rules (written in a contract) in a programmable logic that can guarantee a fair exchange between parties with an initial mutual distrust. This feature prevents parties from cheating each other by aborting the exchange protocol and discharges the need for intermediaries with the consequent reduction of delays and commissions for their services.

The revealing power of the blockchain is further enhanced by the fact that blockchains naturally incorporate a discrete notion of time, a clock that increases each time a new block is added. The existence of a trusted clock/register is crucial to achieve the property of fairness in the protocols. This feature can make the cryptography model in the blockchain even more powerful than the traditional model without a blockchain where the fairness is very difficult to guarantee without the intervention of a TTP.

This paper aims to show how the blockchain technology and the smart contracts can introduce a new paradigm to deal with the fair exchange problem. By using this technology, we can reduce or even remove the role of the TTPs inside such protocols. As far as we know, there are no previous works that deals with blockchain-based fair certified notifications and smart contracts. Previous studies on fairness using blockchain focus on fair purchase operations between a product (or a receipt) in exchange of cryptocurrencies (usually bitcoin) [3,5,6,11].

[16] uses a smart contract for the resolution of a purchase operation while [1] uses smart contracts and trusted execution environments to guarantee the fair exchange of a payment and the result of an execution.

We present two Blockchain-based Systems for Fair Certified Notifications, the first proposal allows a non-confidential fair exchange of a notification message for a non-repudiation of reception token with no involvement of any TTP. The second one allows a confidential fair exchange of a notification for a non-repudiation of reception token. It has the optimistic intervention of a stateless TTP.

2 Ideal Properties of a Fair Certified Notification System.

Some requirements for fair exchange were stated in [2], and re-formulated in [21]:

1. **Effectiveness.** If two parties behave correctly, the exchange will take place and all parties will receive the expected items.
2. **Fairness.** After completion of a protocol run, either each party receives the expected item or neither party receives any useful information about the others item. The fairness is *weak* if, by the end of the execution, both parties have received the expected items or if one entity receives the expected item and another entity does not, the latter can get evidence of this situation.
3. **Timeliness.** At any time, during a protocol run, each party can unilaterally choose to terminate the protocol without losing fairness.
4. **Non-repudiation.** If an item has been sent from party A to party B, A can not deny origin of the item and B can not deny receipt of the item.
5. **Verifiability of Third Party.** If the third party misbehaves, resulting in the loss of fairness for a party, the victim can prove this fact in a dispute.

We can add, to this set of properties, some other interesting properties for the case of certified notifications.

6. **Confidentiality.** Only the sender and the receiver of the notification know the contents of the certified message.
7. **Efficiency.** An efficient protocol uses the minimum number of steps that allow the effective exchange or the minimum cost.
8. **Transferability of evidence.** The proofs generated by the system can be transferred to external entities to prove the result of the exchange.
9. **State Storage.** If the TTP that can be involved in the exchange is not required to maintain state information then the system is *stateless*.

Some of the above properties cannot be achieved in the same protocol. The authors of [9] enumerate the incompatibilities among the ideal features. Some examples are Weak Fairness and Transferability of Evidence, Stateless TTP and timeliness and Verifiability and transparenvy of the TTP. in this paper we will see that in a protocol that offers weak fairness a party cannot transfer the evidence to an arbiter since the other party could have contradictory evidence.

3   State of the Art of Fair Certified Notification Protocols

Fair certified notification follows the pattern of fair exchange of values. This kind of exchange does not have a definitive and standardized solution in its electronic version. The notifications can be done using electronic mail and, until now, several proposals have been presented for this service. However, it is not required that the certified notifications use electronic mail, as it will be discussed in this paper. A certified notification includes an exchange of elements between the sender and the receiver; the sender has to send a message to the receiver, then the receiver is able to read it and, in exchange, the receiver has to send a proof of reception to the sender.

To overcome reluctances between the parties and to assure fairness, almost all the existing proposals use a TTP. This trusted third party can play and important role, participating in each exchange or a more relaxed role in which the TTP is only active in case of arising a dispute between the parties (optimistic protocols).

Due to the incompatibility among some of the properties and the difficulty to achieve simultaneously some other properties, we can find protocols that solve the exchange in an efficient way with an optimistic TTP although achieving only weak fairness [7], other systems focused in the achievement of specific features as the transferability of evidences [14], the verifiability of the TTP [17], the avoidance of the selective rejection based on the identity of the sender [19], the flexibility to allow the delivery to multiple receivers [8] or the reduction of the volume of state information that the TTP must maintain [18].

This paper proposes the use of blockchain-based technologies and the Ethereum ecosystem to implement a DApp for certified notifications in a decentralized way. This proposal does not require the use of electronic mail and, depending on the desired application, it does not requiere neither the use of a TTP to guarantee the fairness of the exchange. As far as we know, there are no proposals to solve the problem of certified notification using blockchain-based technologies. Only some papers about fair payments, very recently, refers to fair exchange protocols over blockchain [5, 16].

4   Conceptual Design of Two Blockchain-Based Systems for Fair Certified Notifications

In this section we will analyse the possibilities of the use of blockchain-based technologies to provide a DApp for fair certified notifications reducing the involvement of trusted third parties compared with traditional approaches. We present a high level description of two solutions (the details of them will be presented in Sects. 6 and 7, respectively). One of them is well suited for those notifications that do not require the confidentiality of the message (or even it is required that the message can be public and accessible to everybody). The other solution allows the message to be hidden to others than the receiver. As it is showed in the descriptions, in the first approach there is no need of a TTP in any step of the exchange nor in a dispute resolution phase while in the second proposal the TTP will be involved only in the dispute resolution phase (optimistic protocol). Moreover, it is not required that this TTP stores information of the state of any transaction.

4.1 Non-confidential Notifications Without TTP

In this first proposal we consider that confidentiality is not required or even not desired. The sender executes the first step of the protocol using the DApp to register the hash of the notification message on the blockchain. At this point, the receiver does not have access to the message, although the transaction remains stored in the blockchain due to the fact that the registered value is the hash of the message and not the message itself.

The sender will make a new transaction including the message in a third step, provided that the receiver would have made a previous transaction manifesting his desire to receive the notification.

The protocol for non-confidential certified notifications works as follows:

1. The sender, originator of the message, uses the smart contract to publish in the blockchain the hash of the notification message. Other parameters of this transaction are the address of the receiver and the deadline for the notification to be completed. Moreover, a deposit can be required in this step. The amount will be included in the transaction.
2. The receiver, if he accepts the reception of the notification, publishes a message expressing his will.
3. Finally, before the expiration of the deadline, the sender can execute the *finish* procedure to publish the message. As a consequence, the smart contract publishes the non-repudiation proof. If the execution of the exchange requires a deposit, the smart contract returns the amount to the sender.

After the deadline, if the three steps have not been executed properly, the state of the exchange is not *finish* and then both parties can access a function in the smart contract to request the cancellation of the transferred elements.

(a) Cancellation of reception, requested by the receiver if the sender does not publish the message when the receiver has accepted the notification.
(b) Cancellation of delivery, requested by the sender, if the receiver has not accepted the notification.

In both cases, the smart contract checks the identity of the user and the deadline. The smart contract generates a transaction to point out that the notification has been cancelled. In the first case, the sender will not receive the refund of the deposit (this way, the deposit is useful to motivate the sender to finish the exchange before the deadline).

Since the message is included in a transaction, it will be registered in the blockchain, so the notification in this case is not confidential. This protocol is executed entirely over Ethereum, so no off-chain communication between the parties is required. This way, there is no need of communication channels between the parties.

4.2   Optimistic Confidential Notifications with Stateless TTP

This second proposal has been designed taking into account those notifications that require confidentiality. That is, the blockchain has to preserve the fairness of the exchange but the message cannot be stored in a publicly accessible block. The main difference with the first proposal is that in this case the protocol allows an optimistic exchange, that is, the exchange can be executed completely without the intervention of the TTP nor the blockchain. Another important feature is that this proposal does not require a deadline and can be finished at any moment. A stateless TTP can be used to resolve the disputes that can arise between the parties.

The proposed protocol for confidential fair certified notifications is based in the protocol described in [7], an optimistic protocol in three steps with a trusted third party that is involved only in case of disputes between the parties. In [7] both parties can contact the TTP who maintains state information. The three steps of [7] are:

1. The sender A encrypts the message M with a simmetric key K, producing a ciphertext c. The key K is encripted with the public key of the TTP (it means that the TTP, who knows the correspondent private key, can decrypt it), producing K_t. A third element h_A is the signature of A on the concatenation of the hash of ciphertext c and K_t, part of the evidence of Non-Repudiation of Origin for B. Then A sends the triplet c, k_t and h_A.
2. B sends h_B, a signature of B on the concatenation of the hash of ciphertext c and k_t, evidence of Non-Repudiation of Receipt for B, to A.
3. A sends k_A, the key K enciphered with the private key of A, second part of the Non-Repudiation of Origin evidence for B.

During this three steps protocol the parties exchange the Non-Repudiation proofs together with elements that are useful in case of interruption of the exchange. These elements, as K_t, are managed by the TTP during a dispute resolution subprotocol. The execution of the dispute resolution subprotocol can be requested by both A and B contacting the TTP.

In this new blockchain-based solution, the originator A and the recipient B will exchange messages and non-repudiation evidences directly. Only as a last resort, in the case they cannot get the expected items from the other party, the smart contract or the TTP would be invoked, by initiating the *cancel* or *finish* functions. In comparison with the protocol described in [7], in the blockchain-based solution the role of the TTP has been reduced. The sender will never contact the TTP. The TTP will answer only requests from the receiver B by accessing to the smart contract that has been deployed. The TTP is totally stateless and, in any case, it stores information about the state of any exchange.

The protocol for confidential certified notifications works as follows: The parties, A (the sender) and B (the receiver) will execute a direct exchange in three steps, using the DApp (the details of it will be presented in Sect. 7).

1. A sends an encrypted message to B using a session key. Moreover, A also sends an element to B that could be useful in case of dispute, that is, if A

does not follow the steps of the protocol (i.e.: the session key encrypted with the public key of the TTP). The TTP is the responsible of the deployment of the smart contract that will manage the exchange.

2. B sends the non-repudiation proof.
3. A sends the key to decipher the message.

If some party does not follow the protocol, the exchange can be resolved as follows:

   (a) If A does not receive the element of step 2., she can send a request to the smart contract. If the state of the notification is 'Created' (nor 'Cancelled' neither 'Finished'), then the state will be changed to 'Cancelled', indicating that the notification has not been performed successfully.
   (b) If B does not receive the message in step 3, B will contact the TTP providing the received elements in step 1 together with the non-repudiation of reception proof. The TTP will access the smart contract to check the state of the notification. If the notification has not been cancelled, the TTP will publish in the blockchain a non-repudiation of reception proof and the required elements for B to obtain the confidential message.

5   Smart Contracts Development Settings

In order to deploy smart contracts on the blockchain there are some frameworks that help the developer manage the deployment on the network. To develop the DApp we have interacted with the console of the Node JS platform[1]. This modular platform provides us with the necessary components to develop, test and deploy decentralized applications such as smart contracts. Functionalities provided by Node JS are implemented by independent modules and packages. In this way, we use NPM (Node Package Manager[2]) to easily install/uninstall, configure and update the different modules and software packages of the platform (called third-party modules).

An important configuration file is *package.json*. This is a JSON format file that is stored in the application root folder. This file provides the specific aspects to manage the module dependencies that the application requires. For instance, the file states information like our application name, module versions (name and version together work as an identifier that is assumed to be unique), license, directories, version control repository and so on. Keeping in mind this structure, a smart contract ready to deploy will be stored inside a folder within the solidity file that specifies the code of our application, the *package.json* and the node modules folder with all the necessary packages. Inside the root directory we have two more significant files: *compile.js* and *deploy.js*. Both are javascript files that, while compile.js specifies the requirements to compile the smart contract and the statement to compile it, the *deploy.js* file defines the tools used to deploy the smart contract. In order to deploy the smart contract, we need to have a connection to the Ethereum blockchain and to sign a transaction.

---

[1] https://nodejs.org/en.

[2] https://www.npmjs.com/.

We have deployed the smart contract on the Rinkeby testnet[3]. Rinkeby is the main Ethereum blockchain testnet that behaves similarly to the real Ethereum blockchain. We can acquire Rinkeby Ether for our account from a faucet[4]. Of course, before acquiring Ether we need to have an account that we can manage with an Ethereum wallet. For this reason, we have installed the Metamask[5] add-on in our browser. Metamask is an Ethereum browser that allows us to interact with the blockchain and to run Ethereumm DApps. Metamask also implements an Ether wallet that enables to sign blockchain transactions.

Therefore, the deploy.js file makes a call to the compile.js file to compile the contract and then specifies the web3 connection (i.e. the bridge to the blockchain) and the account needed to sign the transaction in order to deploy the contract. For this reason, we introduced the *HDWalletProvider* from Truffle[6] to handle the connection to the Ethereum network and sign the transaction. We have to give our private key from the Metamask wallet to the *HDWalletProvider* so as to sign the transactions.

However, to avoid setting up our own blockchain node, we have used the Infura Ethereum node cluster[7]. This service enables us to run our transaction on the blockchain without needing to establish our own blockchain node. To work with this cloud-based Ethereum client we just need to sign up and then we are provided with a token that enables us to connect to the Ethereum network (with this service we can use the main Ethereum network, Rinkeby, Kovan or Ropsten). The result of the execution of the deploy.js file is the address of the new deployed smart contract.

At this point, we can easily interact with our deployed contract by using Remix[8]. Remix is a browser-based solidity compiler that also supports testing and debugging smart contracts. To run transactions on Remix we just have to select the environment (Web3 Provider), our Ethereum account and the address where the smart contract is deployed. The Metamask will always ask us confirmation before signing any transaction on the blockchain. Remix will show the transaction in pending mode until it is validated.

In addition to that, we also have tested our smart contracts locally. Ganache[9] implements a personal blockchain made by the Ethereum development of smart contracts that runs in local. Besides, Ganache also simulates an Ethereum Virtual Machine (EVM). After launching Ganache in our computer, a list with the private and public key from ten recently created accounts is reported at the node console in order to use them as test bank (each account has 100 ether in its balance). Now, Ganache is ready to be used to deploy, run and test smart contracts without using any public network. In Fig. 1 we have depicted our development configuration.

---

[3] https://www.rinkeby.io.
[4] https://faucet.rinkeby.io/.
[5] https://metamask.io.
[6] http://truffleframework.com.
[7] https://infura.io.
[8] https://remix.ethereum.org.
[9] http://truffleframework.com/ganache/.

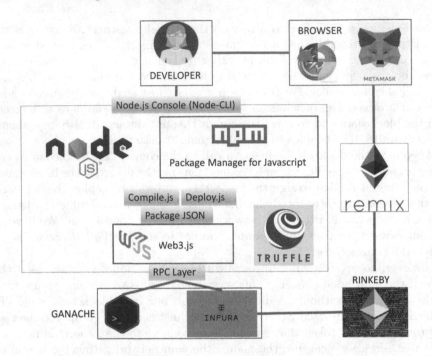

Fig. 1. Smart Contract Development Architecture

6 Development of the Non-Confidential Blockchain-Based Fair Certified Notifications Protocol Without TTP

6.1 Smart Contract

We have designed and implemented the smart contract for non-confidential notifications. For this proposal, a new instance of the smart contract will be created by the sender and it will manage all the steps of the exchange. It has been programmed using Solidity[10] and it has been deployed over an Ethereum network. Ethereum addresses have been assigned to both the sender A and the receiver B. Both A and B will interact with the blockchain using Web3.js interfaces (Fig. 4).

Figure 3 shows the smart contract that manages the non-confidential notifications. The constructor of the smart contract includes variables to store the addresses of the sender and the receiver, the hash of the notification message, the instant of execution of the first step of the exchange and the value of the execution period (the deadline). The contract includes five functions: to initiate the notification (the constructor), to accept a notification, to deliver the message, to cancel the exchange and to inquiry about the state of the exchange. The certified notification is created by the sender, who specifies the receiver, the hash of the message and the maximum duration of the exchange. The smart contract also has an attribute to store the content of the message.

---

[10] https://solidity.readthedocs.io/en/v0.4.21/.

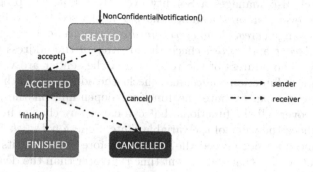

Fig. 2. Possible states of the exchange in the Non-Confidential Notifications Protocol.

```solidity
pragma solidity ^0.4.24;

contract Notification {
    address public sender; // Parties involved
    address public receiver;
    bytes32 public messageHash; // Message
    string public message;
    uint public term; // Time limit (in seconds)
    uint public start; // Start time
    enum State {created, cancelled, accepted, finished } // Possible states
    State public state;

    event StateInfo( State state );

    constructor (address _sender, address _receiver, bytes32 _messageHash, uint _term)
    public payable {
        require (msg.value>0); // Requires sender deposits minimum 1 wei (>0 wei)
        sender = _sender;
        receiver = _receiver;
        messageHash = _messageHash;
        start = now; // now = block.timestamp
        term = _term;
        state = State.created;
        emit StateInfo(state);
    }
    function accept() public {
        require (msg.sender==receiver && state==State.created);
        state = State.accepted;
        emit StateInfo(state);
    }
    function finish(string _message) public {
        require(now < start+term); // It's not possible to finish after deadline
        require (msg.sender==sender && state==State.accepted);
        require (messageHash==keccak256(_message));
        message = _message;
        sender.transfer(this.balance); // Sender receives the refund of the deposit
        state = State.finished;
        emit StateInfo(state);
    }
    function cancel() public {
        require(now >= start+term); // It's not possible to cancel before deadline
        require((msg.sender==sender && state==State.created) ||
                (msg.sender==receiver && state==State.accepted));
        if (msg.sender==sender && state==State.created) {
            sender.transfer(this.balance); // Sender receives the refund of the deposit
        }
        state = State.cancelled;
        emit StateInfo(state);
    }
}
```

Fig. 3. Smart Contract for the Non-Confidential Notifications Protocol.

The contract also manages a Solidity event to follow the progress of the exchange. This event *stateInfo* allows the parties to see the evolution of the state of the exchange (*created, accepted, finished* or *cancelled*).

Functions *Accept* and *Finish* check the identity of the address that throws the transaction. The address of the receiver and the sender are verified before updating the state. Function *Cancel* also checks the addresses. In this case, both sender and receiver can execute the function, depending on the state of the exchange. Moreover, all the functions that can cause any change in the state of the exchange check the value of the variable *State*. Function *Finish* requires that the present time does not exceed the deadline before executing its code. Also, function *Cancel* verifies that the current time is greater than the deadline before carrying on with the execution of it.

The smart contract will manage the publication on the blockchain of all the values of the required variables to maintain the fairness of the exchange following the protocol described in Sect. 4.1.

6.2   Properties

The non-confidential certified notifications protocol allows the fair exchange of a message and non-repudiation proofs. The main properties achieved by the protocol are analyzed in this section.

- **Strong Fairness.** *A* will not receive the non-repudiation proof of reception provided by the smart contract unless she executes the transaction to register the message in the blockchain (case *State=finished*). On the other hand, *B* will not have access to the message unless he executes the transaction to accept the notification (*State=Accepted*). At any moment, the smart contract does not generate alternative cancellation or finalization proofs that could create any situation where one of the parties can have contradictory proofs (leading the exchange to weak fairness), as can be seen in Fig. 3.
- **Total absence of TTP. Substitution by an smart contract.** This proposal does not require an external party acting as a TTP. The parties execute the functions of the smart contract creating the associate transactions and there is no need of dispute resolution.
- **Transferability of the proofs.** Since the parties cannot obtain contradictory proofs in any way, the generated proofs can be presented as evidence to an external entity. Moreover, its transferability is easy, since the results of the exchange are stored in the blockchain. Due to the immutability of the blockchain, the content of the notification cannot be modified so the system provides integrity to the notification. The moment that the notification takes place can be derived from the timestamp of the block where the transaction is included.
- **Weak Timeliness.** The protocol is not asynchronous. If one of the parties delays its intervention in the exchange, the other party will not be able to resolve it until the deadline. However, after the deadline both parties can request the finalization of the exchange. Moreover, the protocol wants to

motivate the sender to conclude the exchange before the timeout blocking an amount of money in the smart contract. This amount will only be refunded to the sender if she concludes before the deadline.

– **Non Repudiation.** The protocol achieves non-repudiation of origin together with non-repudiation of receipt after the execution of the exchange. A cannot deny having sent the message since there is a transaction on the blockchain from her address containing the message and another one related with the same message including the address of the receiver and the hash of the message. B cannot deny having received the notification since there is a transaction from his address in the blockchain accepting the reception of the message and the *State* of the exchange is *Finished*, so the message is publicly accessible in the blockchain.

7   Development of the Confidential Blockchain-Based Fair Certified Notifications Protocol

7.1   Smart Contract

We have designed and implemented a DApp that allows the optimistic exchange between the parties and a smart contract for the resolution of disputes. The smart contract has been programmed in Solidity and deployed over the Ethereum network (see Sect. 5). Ethereum addresses have been assigned to the sender A, the receiver B and the TTP. In comparison with the protocol described in [7], the role of the TTP has been reduced. The sender will never contact the TTP. The TTP will answer only requests from the receiver B by accessing to the smart contract that has been deployed. The TTP is totally stateless and, in any case, it stores information about the state of any exchange. Both A and B can interact with the blockchain if it is necessary through the Web3.js interface. For this reason, we have also designed a web service where the web client can connect using TLS protocol. This web service is used the off-chain communication exchanges between sender and recipient described in the protocol. In order to implement the cryptographic operations, we have used Stanford Javascript Crypto Library[11]. This enables us to use AES for the symmetric encryption operation, EC-ElGammal for the asymmetric encryption operations and ECDSA for the signature functions. However, the implementation of a PKI and the secure exchange of public keys are beyond the scope of this work. Figure 5 shows the smart contract that will manage the possible disputes between the parties after the execution of the exchange described in Sect. 4.2 for confidential notifications. This smart contract is deployed by the TTP, who defines the identities of the sender and the receiver. The smart contract manages the variable *state* in order to keep track of the state of each exchange (Fig. 2).

The event *stateInfo* allows the tracking of the evolution of each exchange state. The function *Cancel* checks the identity of the address that throws the transaction, which must be the address of the sender, together with the value

---

[11] http://bitwiseshiftleft.github.io/sjcl/.

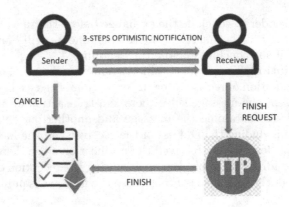

Fig. 4. Interaction between the actors.

of the variable *state*. This function can be executed only by the sender. The function *Finish* checks the identity of the party that sends the transaction, that is, the TTP, together with the value of the variable *state*. The TTP will execute this function if it receives a request from the receiver. The smart contract is responsible for the publication in the blockchain of the values of the elements used to maintain the fairness of the exchange following the protocol described in Sect. 4.2. In function *Finish*, if the conditions are fulfilled, the smart contract publishes in the blockchain both the non repudiation of reception proof (hB) and the session key encrypted with B's public key (hBt).

7.2 Properties

The main properties achieved by the confidential certified notifications protocol are analysed in this section.

- **Weak Fairness.** The protocol does not allow that any of the parties receive the expected item if the other party does not receive it. However, the intervention of the TTP can lead to a situation in where one of the parties possesses contradictory evidence. A malicious A can have the non-repudiation proof received directly from B and also the cancellation proof generated by the smart contract after a cancellation request from A. For these reason, the fairness will be weak and the generated proofs are non transferable. Comparing this feature with the version of the protocol without blockchain, this protocol does not require that the arbitrator consults both parties to resolve the final state of the exchange. It is enough to check one of the parties and then match this version with the contents of the blockchain.
- **Optimistic.** The parties can finalize the exchange without the need to contact with a TTP or execute any function of the smart contract. If the parties do not follow the protocol and the execution of the smart contract is required, the gas necessary for its operation would be reduced compared with the protocol for non-confidential notifications protocol.

```
pragma solidity ^0.4.11;

contract ConfidentialNotifications {

    //Parties involved
    address sender;
    address receiver;
    address ttp;

    string hB; //NRR proof
    string hBt; //Intervention proof

    //Possible states
    enum State { created, cancelled, finished }
    State public state;

    function ConfidentialNotification (address _sender, address _receiver){
        ttp = msg.sender;
        sender = _sender;
        receiver = _receiver;
        state = State.created;
    }


    event stateInfo(
        State state
    );

    function Cancel() returns (string) {
        if(msg.sender==sender){
            if(state==State.created){
                state=State.cancelled;
                //return abort token
                stateInfo(state);
            }else if (state == State.finished){
                return hB;
            }
        }
    }

    function Finish(string _hB, string _hBt) returns (State) {
        if (msg.sender==ttp){
            if(state==State.cancelled){
                return state;
            }else{
                hB=_hB;
                hBt=_hBt;
                state=State.finished;
            }
        }
    }

    function getState() returns (string){
        if(state==State.cancelled) return "cancelled";
        if(state==State.created) return "created";
        if(state==State.finished) return "finished";
    }
}
```

Fig. 5. Smart Contract for Confidential Notifications.

– **Stateless TTP.** When the TTP is involved in the exchange, it can resolve the exchange through the use of the smart contract. The TTP does not need to store any kind of state information of the exchange.
– **Timeliness.** The parties can finish the exchange at any moment accessing the smart contract (sender A) or contacting the TTP (receiver B). The duration of the resolution will depend of the block notification treatment. The protocol can assume that the transactions are valid immediately (zero confirmation) or wait until the block is confirmed in the chain (fully confirmation).
– **Non repudiation.** The protocol achieves non-repudiation of origin together with non-repudiation of receipt after the execution of the three step exchange

or the finalization using the smart contract. A cannot deny having sent the message since B has the element received in the third step or the state of the smart contract is *Finished*. B cannot deny having received the notification since A has the elements sent by B in the second step of the protocol.

- **Confidentiality.** If the exchange is finished through the execution of the three step exchange protocol, then no other entity is involved in the exchange, and the message remains confidential. If the TTP is involved or the functions of the smart contract are executed, then the TTP will process the received elements and will make a transaction including the element that will allow B to decrypt the message but the plain message is not included in the transaction so it will not be included in a block of the blockchain to preserve the confidentiality.

8   Comparison and Conclusions

Previous solutions for fair certified notifications are mainly based on the intervention of a TTP that acts as an intermediary between sender and receiver. In this model of fair exchange, both parties obtain the expected item from the other or neither obtains what was expected. That is, either the issuer has received a non-repudiation of reception evidence and the recipient has received the message, or neither party obtains the desired item, the TTP can intervene to guarantee the fairness of the exchange if some participant misbehaves.

This paper presents two alternatives for sending certified notifications on a blockchain-based fairness. On the one hand, the first solution (see Sect. 6) allows users to send non-confidential notifications, the new DApp supports the sending and receiving of certified messages and guarantees the fairness of the exchange without requiring the intervention of any TTP to guarantee the security properties of the exchange since the actions of the different actors are recorded in the blockchain and, in the event that any actor does not fulfil the protocol, the smart contract will generate the corresponding evidence to preserve fairness. This proposal also preserves the properties of limited Timeliness (involved parties can be certain that the protocol will be completed at a certain finite point in time [16]), Transferability of proofs and Non-repudiation as it is stated in Sect. 6.2.

On the other hand, the second solution (see Sect. 7) is a fair exchange protocol that allows users to send confidential notifications and introduce an optimistic TTP (its intervention is only required if a party does not fulfil the protocol) to guarantee fairness. Thanks to the usage of a blockchain and a smart contract, the TTP can be stateless (i.e. the TTP does not need to store the state of the exchange regarding any protocol execution because all the information of each exchange is stored in the blockchain by using the smart contract). This solution assures the fair exchange (weak fairness, see Sect. 7.2). Like the first solution, this proposal also preserves Timeliness and Non-repudiation properties. However, Transferability of proofs is not strictly provided because anyone who want to verify the correctness of the exchange not only has to check the provided evidence by the parties but also has to check the blockchain. Table 1 compares

Table 1. Comparasison of Properties

Property	Non Confidential Notifications	Confidential Notifications
Non-repudiation	YES	YES
Fairness	STRONG	WEAK
Timeliness	LIMITED	YES
Effectiveness	YES	YES
TTP	NO	OPTIMISTIC/STATELESS
Evidence Transferibility	YES	NO
Confidentiality	NO	YES

Table 2. GAS per execution of the Non-Confidential Contract.

	Non-Confidential Notifications
Deployment	1086913
Accept	43644
Finish	59835
Cancel (created)	53011
Cancel (accepted)	30443

Table 3. GAS per execution of the Confidential Contract.

	Confidential notifications
Deployment	800433
Finish (Cancelled)	26388
Finish	88387
Cancel	44698
Cancel (Finished)	24772

the properties of both solutions while Tables 2 and 3 present the gas required for the execution of each function, for both protocols.

9 Future Work

There are some points to be studied to improve the proposed protocols. Thus, as further works we are going to:

- Test the smart contracts on real-like networks, checking confirmation delay time of transactions and possible undesired effects caused by these delays. Also we would like to obtain and evaluate an accurate register of the performance of our smart contracts in these real-like scenarios.
- Modify smart contracts to allow them to manage more than just one notification. This can be done with a contract that can create notification structs or

other new contracts that represent a notification exchange, and storing them into an array.
- Modify the confidential notification smart contract so that the TTP can create a main contract, and from this, multiples notifications can be created by the senders.
- Improve the use of events. Users can receive notifications, but they need the address of the smart contract in order to be subscribed to them. For this reason, the subscription to events can be also improved using only one smart contract that manages multiple notifications.
- In Tables 2 and 3 we have evaluated the necessary amount of gas to execute the contracts. However, we have left for further works a deeper analysis in order to find possible improvements to the code so as to reduce the commissions paid for using the blockchain.

The systems presented in this article show different sets of properties, so the choice of one system will depend basically on the needs of each exchange. As a future work, it is proposed to reformulate the system of confidential notifications to achieve strong fairness. The use of the blockchain for the diffusion of each of the executed steps and the full confirmations will be the element used to obtain this property.

Acknowledgments. This work has been partially financed by AccessTur TIN2014-54945-R AEI/FEDER UE and the network Consolider ARES TIN2015-70054-REDC projects.

References

1. Al-Bassam, M., Sonnino, A., Król, M., Psaras, I.: Airtnt: Fair Exchange Payment for Outsourced Secure Enclave Computations, CoRR, volume abs/1805.06411 (2018)
2. Asokan, N., Shoup, V., Waidner, M.: Asynchronous protocols for optimistic fair exchange. In: Proceedings of the IEEE Symposium on Research in Security and Privacy, pp. 86–99, Oakland, CA, May 1998
3. Barber, S., Boyen, X., Shi, E., Uzun, E.: Bitter to better — how to make bitcoin a better currency. In: Keromytis, A.D. (ed.) FC 2012. LNCS, vol. 7397, pp. 399–414. Springer, Heidelberg (2012). https://doi.org/10.1007/978-3-642-32946-3_29
4. Bentov, I., Kumaresan, R.: How to use bitcoin to design fair protocols. In: Garay, J.A., Gennaro, R. (eds.) CRYPTO 2014. LNCS, vol. 8617, pp. 421–439. Springer, Heidelberg (2014). https://doi.org/10.1007/978-3-662-44381-1_24
5. Delgado-Segura, S., Perez-Sola, C., Navarro-Arribas, G., Herrera-Joancomarti, J.: A fair protocol for data trading based on Bitcoin transactions. Future Gener. Comput. Syst. (2017)
6. Ethan H., Baldimtsi, F., Alshenibr, L., Scafuro, A., Goldberg, S.: TumbleBit: An Untrusted Tumbler for Bitcoin-Compatible Anonymous Payments. In: Network and Distributed System Security Symposium (NDSS) (2017)
7. Lluís Ferrer-Gomila, J., Payeras-Capellà, M., Huguet i Rotger, L.: An efficient protocol for certified electronic mail. In: Goos, G., Hartmanis, J., van Leeuwen, J., Pieprzyk, J., Seberry, J., Okamoto, E. (eds.) ISW 2000. LNCS, vol. 1975, pp. 237–248. Springer, Heidelberg (2000). https://doi.org/10.1007/3-540-44456-4_18

8. Ferrer-Gomila, J.L., Payeras-Capellá, M., Huguet-Rotger, L.: A realistic protocol for multi-party certified electronic mail. In: Chan, A.H., Gligor, V. (eds.) ISC 2002. LNCS, vol. 2433, pp. 210–219. Springer, Heidelberg (2002). https://doi.org/10.1007/3-540-45811-5_16

9. Ferrer-Gomilla, J., Onieva, J., Payeras-Capellà, M., Lopez, J: Certified electronic mail: properties revisited. Comput. Secur. **29**(2), 167–179 (2010)

10. Goldfeder, S., Bonneau, J., Gennaro, R., Narayanan, A.: Escrow protocols for cryptocurrencies: how to buy physical goods using bitcoin. In: Kiayias, A. (ed.) FC 2017. LNCS, vol. 10322, pp. 321–339. Springer, Cham (2017). https://doi.org/10.1007/978-3-319-70972-7_18

11. Heilman, E., Baldimtsi, F., Goldberg, S.: Blindly signed contracts: anonymous on-blockchain and off-blockchain bitcoin transactions. In: Clark, J., Meiklejohn, S., Ryan, P.Y.A., Wallach, D., Brenner, M., Rohloff, K. (eds.) FC 2016. LNCS, vol. 9604, pp. 43–60. Springer, Heidelberg (2016). https://doi.org/10.1007/978-3-662-53357-4_4

12. Huang, Q., Yang, G., Wong, D., Susilo, W.: A new efficient optimistic fair exchange protocol without random oracles. Int. J. Inf. Secur. **11**(1), 53–63 (2012). ISSN 1615–5270

13. Huang, Q., Wong, D.S., Susilo, W.: P^2OFE: privacy-preserving optimistic fair exchange of digital signatures. In: Benaloh, J. (ed.) CT-RSA 2014. LNCS, vol. 8366, pp. 367–384. Springer, Cham (2014). https://doi.org/10.1007/978-3-319-04852-9_19

14. Kremer, S., Markowitch, O.: Selective receipt in certified e-mail. In: Rangan, C.P., Ding, C. (eds.) INDOCRYPT 2001. LNCS, vol. 2247, pp. 136–148. Springer, Heidelberg (2001). https://doi.org/10.1007/3-540-45311-3_14

15. Küpçü, A., Lysyanskaya, A.: Usable optimistic fair exchange. In: Pieprzyk, J. (ed.) CT-RSA 2010. LNCS, vol. 5985, pp. 252–267. Springer, Heidelberg (2010). https://doi.org/10.1007/978-3-642-11925-5_18

16. Liu, J., Li, W., Karame, G., Asokan, N.: Towards Fairness of Cryptocurrency Payments. In: IEEE Security and Privacy (2017)

17. Mut-Puigserver, M., Ferrer-Gomila, J., Huguet-Rotger, L.: Certified e-mail protocol with verifiable third party. In: Proceedings of the 2005 IEEE International Conference on e-Technology, e-Commerce and e-Service, pp. 548–551 (2005)

18. Onieva, J., Zhou, J., Lopez, J.: Enhancing certified email service for timeliness and multicast. In: Fourth International Network Conference, pp. 327–335 (2004)

19. Payeras-Capellà, M., Mut-Puigserver, M., Ferrer-Gomila, J., Huguet-Rotger, L.: No Author Based Selective Receipt in an Efficient Certified E-mail Protocol. In: PDP 2009, pp. 387–392 (2009)

20. Shao, Z.: Fair exchange protocol of Schnorr signatures with semi-trusted adjudicator. Comput. Electric. Eng. (2010)

21. Zhou, J., Deng, R., Bao, F.: Some remarks on a fair exchange protocol. In: Imai, H., Zheng, Y. (eds.) PKC 2000. LNCS, vol. 1751, pp. 46–57. Springer, Heidelberg (2000). https://doi.org/10.1007/978-3-540-46588-1_4

On Symbolic Verification of Bitcoin's SCRIPT Language

Rick Klomp[✉] and Andrea Bracciali

Computing Science and Mathematics, University of Stirling, Stirling, UK
{Rick.Klomp,Andrea.Bracciali}@stir.ac.uk

Abstract. Validation of Bitcoin transactions rely upon the successful execution of scripts written in a simple and effective, non-Turing-complete by design language, simply called SCRIPT. This makes the validation of *closed* scripts, i.e. those associated to actual transactions and bearing full information, straightforward. Here we address the problem of validating *open* scripts, i.e. we address the validation of redeeming scripts against the whole set of possible inputs, i.e. under which general conditions can Bitcoins be redeemed? Even if likely not one of the most complex languages and demanding verification problems, we advocate the merit of formal verification for the Bitcoin validation framework. We propose a symbolic verification theory for *open* SCRIPT, a verifier toolkit, and illustrate examples of use on Bitcoin transactions. Contributions include (1) a formalisation of (a fragment of SCRIPT) the language; (2) a novel symbolic approach to SCRIPT verification, suitable, e.g. for the verification of newly defined and non-standard payment schemes; and (3) building blocks for a larger verification theory for the developing area of Bitcoin smart contracts. The verification of smart contracts, i.e. agreements built as transaction-based protocols, is currently a problem that is difficult to formalise and computationally demanding.

1 Introduction

The Bitcoin framework [15] enables monetary transactions of a virtual currency amongst untrusted individuals. The construction relies on a novel interpretation of distributed consensus for the validation of a decentralised ledger recording the Bitcoin transactions. Interestingly, the validation of transactions's in terms of their correctness, e.g. no double spending and proper ownership of the virtual coins, is demanded to the successful execution of cryptography-fenced scripts associated to transactions. Replicated execution of scripts is supported by a network of peers, whose consensus guarantees the validity of transactions.

R. Klomp and A. Bracciali —This research has been partially supported by The DataLab, UK, and partially informed by collaborations within COST Action IC1406 cHiPSet research network. Authors would like to thank Flavio Pizzorno for interesting feedback on the work. Andrea Bracciali is a Research Affiliate to the UCL Centre for Blockchain Technologies.

© Springer Nature Switzerland AG 2018
J. Garcia-Alfaro et al. (Eds.): DPM 2018/CBT 2018, LNCS 11025, pp. 38–56, 2018.
https://doi.org/10.1007/978-3-030-00305-0_3

Striving for correctness, robustness and efficiency in such an unconventional and constrained execution model, the scripting language SCRIPT has been designed according to minimality principles, e.g. it is not Turing complete, has no recursion, cycles or procedure calls, has an execution cost proportional to the length of the code, and "dangerous" operations like multiplication are not allowed. However, even if most transactions exploit standard payment schemes based on simple scripts believed to be robust, free and more complex payment schemes are allowed, new standard schemes can be introduced, and, interestingly, a whole area of protocols and smart contracts based on transactions are being developed [6,14].

Despite the apparent simplicity of SCRIPT, complex behavior is expressible through payment schemes wherein multiple transactions are linked. Such a scenario calls for formal verification of critical scripts validating financial transactions, which in the case of Bitcoin alone have a market cap of about 100B USD (2018 - about half the GDP of a country like Greece). Other approaches have been proposed, e.g. [8,9] amongst others, based on correctness by construction/specification. However we believe that having a formal validation of the consequences of a SCRIPT program is valuable in itself.

The general validation scheme is composed by two scripts, an *input script* in charge of providing data and credential to authorise the transaction, and an *output script*, whose structure defines the validation scheme and is in charge of checking that the data provided do actually enable the transaction. The two scripts communicate by means of a shared stack. The input script is executed first.

We address the problem of the *satisfiability of "open" output scripts*, i.e. under which general conditions an input script exists capable of providing the right information to let the output script successfully terminate and the transition be validated?

Although the simulation and execution of closed scripts present no problems and many tools and simulators are available, we observe that verification frameworks for satisfiability of open scripts are not so widespread and we believe that there are opportunities for further research in the area.

We introduce a symbolic verification framework which simulates the execution of an output script accumulating minimal constraints, akin to a lazy evaluation approach, for its successful termination. This helps, intuitively speaking, with possibly infinite datasets, e.g. integers, or cryptographic secrets that may become further specified as the execution proceeds. For each successful symbolic evaluation, returned constraints, if satisfiable, specify one (or more) input scripts that redeem the transaction.[1] This is true "up to cryptography": a possible constraint could require an inverse image of a hash. Deciding at which extent constraints can be fulfilled defines different possible attacker's models (but this is scope for future work). In this paper, the most general set of constraints is

---

[1] More precisely, constraints specify the required state of the stack for successful termination, after the execution of the input script. If constraints are satisfiable, a trivial input script pushing expected data on the stack always exists.

returned, e.g. including a request for cryptographic secrets, which could be fulfilled by a very powerful attacker, able for instance to guess certain keys.

The contributions of this paper are:

(1) a (yet to be completed, but including major constructs) formal description of the SCRIPT language, which has otherwise been mostly presented informally and by code releases. We have focussed on salient features for the correctness of validation, often digging in the code for clarity;

(2) the novel, to the best of our knowledge, symbolic framework allowing us to derive a correct and (ongoing research) complete specification of all the possible, and possibly unintended, ways to redeem transactions. Beyond the simplicity by construction of SCRIPT, complex "non-standard" payment scheme can and have been provided, worth being clearly analysed. Besides, new payment schemes can be defined and accepted as standard by the community, for instance to overcome existing limitations, similarly to P2PkH improving over the P2Pk scheme (i.e. revealing the hashed public key instead of the public key itself of the Bitcoin's owner in the output script). In such cases, a clear understanding of the implications of the scheme in use and the novel ones is desirable;

(3) valid transactions are being used to define more articulated protocols in the context of *smart contracts* over the Bitcoin blockchain, e.g. self-enforcing agreements in the form of executable code [16]. We envisage the framework here presented as a building block of a larger verification framework aimed at the extra level of complexity introduced by smart contracts, whose verification is currently a difficult to formalise and computationally demanding open research problem. It is worth reminding how this area is prone to "simple", and supposedly well-understood, security failures, which easily lead to consistent financial loss, e.g. for a different scripting language the recent overflow-based case of the Parity wallet [13].

In this paper we introduce the symbolic verification framework, SCRIPT ANALYSER, an open source application supporting the presented symbolic verification, and discuss two examples of non-standard transactions that appeared in the Bitcoin blockchain, which are slightly more complex than a typical standard payment scheme, and, we believe, illustrate how the proposed symbolic verification can support a better understanding of the solidity of Bitcoin's validation machinery.

For the sake of space, while we strived for a comprehensive presentation, a fully formal presentation is demanded to a forthcoming extended paper.

2 Bitcoin's Blockchain and Transactions

A quick review of the most relevant aspects of the design of Bitcoin are recapped here. The interested reader is referred to the SOK paper [10] for details.

The Bitcoin blockchain consists of a data structure implementing a distributed ledger. This can be understood, informally speaking, as an append only, and therefore immutable, list of blocks of data maintained by a peer-2-peer network. The blockchain is freely accessible and anyone can be a node

(Bitcoin is a permission-less blockchain). Each node stores an identical copy of the ledger. Main innovation is that the ledger is *decentralised*, i.e. the responsibility for certifying the correctness of the ledger is shared amongst all the nodes, no one being in charge, and guaranteed by a cryptographically-supported distributed consensus, currently the *proof-of-work*. The whole network guarantees correctness, and at least half of the computational power in the network is needed in order to alter the ledger.

The ledger records payments amongst accounts, i.e. addresses, based on PKI: the address can be derived from the public key and the private key is used to prove ownership of the address and the crypto-money therein.

Transactions move Bitcoins from one address to another. Each transaction has potentially multiple *inputs*, i.e. it draws Bitcoins from multiple addresses, and delivers the drawn Bitcoins over potentially multiple *outputs*, i.e. pays multiple recipient addresses. Once moved into an address, Bitcoins are redeemable by a suitable subsequent transaction. Each input of a subsequent redeeming transaction needs to provide suitable credential in order to "spend" Bitcoins. This is done by an *input script*, or *SigScript*, whose execution provides credentials, which are then validated by the *output script* associated to the output of the previous transaction. The format of the output script is, in principle, free, although a few standard output scripts are commonly used. The successful execution of the input and then the *unspent* Bitcoin's output script makes the transaction valid and it can be recoded on the ledger.

Bitcoin architecture uses *hash functions*, i.e. a mapping from an unbounded domain to a fixed domain, which is straightforward to compute but practically impossible to invert. A hash is often used to prove properties or validate a piece of information. Addtionally, *digital signatures* are used, based on public key cryptography. A signature, used to *validly* sign a message, proves that the signer authorized the message. Alteration of the message invalidates the signature. Generating a valid signature is straightforward when owning the private key, and generally infeasible otherwise. Verifying the validity of the combination of signature, public key and message is straightforward.

3   Related Work

Delmonino et al. [12], and Bartoletti and Pompianu [7], empirically analyse common patterns in designs of smart contracts. The authors show that some of the design patterns, though they are commonly applied, are actually undesired practices due to high odds of bug introducement. Increased risk of faults in (smart) contracts decreases their trustworthiness, as any fault possibly enables unexpected side effects (e.g. enabling a malicious party to claim, i.e. steal, honestly invested currency). As such, these results highlight the importance of improving smart contract design and verification practices.

Delgado-Segura et al. [11] present a tool (STATUS) for analysing Bitcoin's set of unspent transaction outputs (or UTXO). They present results from running this tool on the UTXO at block 491,868 of Bitcoin's blockchain (appended at October 26th, 2017). The UTXO was introduced to improve efficiency of validating new transactions. STATUS's main purpose is to analyse efficiency of the UTXO implementation approach, whereas our work aims to enable verification of certain properties of output scripts.

Andrychowicz et al. [6] introduce some interesting smart contracts and show through application of formal models that they are applicable in Bitcoin's ledger. In [5] they extend on this with a framework that captures the possible interaction sequences that may occur following a smart contract. Specifically, their approach enables automatic security verification by manually modeling the smart contract using timed automata. We propose a method which possibly enables automatically deriving a model, e.g. expressed in timed automatas, from only the output scripts of transactions. A generated model may then be further analysed, e.g. automatically following the approach in [6].

Lande and Zunino [14] propose a formal model to express smart contracts. They then use this formal model to survey and compare the smart contracts currently employed via Bitcoin's ledger. Furthermore, they propose designing Bitcoin scripts using a high level language DSL that can guarantee security. We on the other hand attempt to derive security properties directly from scripts. Ultimately our goals, to increase quality of smart contracts, are similar however.

Bartoletti and Zunino [8] present BitML, a high level DSL for designing smart contracts that are applicable through Bitcoin's ledger. The symbolic expressions that form an instance of BitML are easier to analyse than a Bitcoin's SCRIPT instance. Furthermore, they show that these BitML instances can be compiled to Bitcoin scripts.

Bhargavan et al. [9] propose verifying smart contracts written in Solidity (Ethereum's [17] primary smart contract language), by first either compiling Solidity code to F*, or decompiling EVM (Ethereum's virtual machine) bytecode to F*. It is then possible to verify whether the F* smart contract variant meets certain criteria by embedding these criteria into F*'s type and effect system.

4   SCRIPT - A Fragment of

The script programming language consists of a stack-based programming language, called SCRIPT. It is not Turing-complete by design. It does not allow for cycles and has a restricted set of instructions. Furthermore, complexity of SCRIPT is also limited by transaction fees that are typically proportional to the space occupied by a transaction in a block, and hence to the length of its scripts. *Successful execution* reverts to termination, leaving the stack in a *true* state.

We provide here an informal description of the semantics of the language. Full details on the language can be found, e.g., in [1] by directly inspecting the source code of the Bitcoin Core client, or in [3] where the semantics of SCRIPT's instructions are informally described following the Core client's implementation.

The fragment of SCRIPT considered in this paper is described next, starting from the syntax in Fig. 1. A program S in SCRIPT is either a sequence of stack operations (*cmd*) or the terminated program ◇. Trailing and prefixed ◇ are generally omitted or absorbed, respectively. Commands manipulate dynamically typed data on the stack, with automated type coercion. According to the execution model, operations are sequentially executed and may alter the stack by popping/pushing data. Operations may *fail* on missing data and mismatching or non-coercible types, causing a *runtime error*, immediately stopping the execution in a *failed* state. For instance, OP_RETURN fails by default, while ADD fails if there are not two integers on top of the stack. The script *succeeds* if all the operations are successfully executed, i.e. they do not fail, *and* the (top of the) stack is *true*.

Commands are represented by mnemonic codes in Fig. 1, while SCRIPT actually uses numeric opcodes. Some other abstractions have been introduced in the syntax that simplify the semantic presentation without altering its correctness - an example is the treatment of IF statements. The Bitcoin Core client provides fine tuning flags, mostly affecting the set of possible checks during the execution of scripts, which may affect the semantics[2]. Furthermore, we assume that arguments specifying the amount of provided signatures and the amount of provided public keys to the multiple signatures operation are constants in the output script.

Constants operations push data on the stack, e.g. OP_TRUE or OP_n which push the values *True* and n, and never fail.

$$S ::= cmd; S \mid \diamond$$

$cmd ::=$ OP_FALSE | OP_TRUE | OP_n	*constants*
IF S | IFE $S \circ S$ | VERIFY | OP_RETURN |	*flow control*
DUP | PUSH d | DROP | SWAP |	*stack ops*
ADD | SUB | SIZE | WITHIN |	*aritmetic ops*
EQ | LT | LTE | GT | GTE | AND | OR |	*boolean ops*
CHKSIG | CHKMSIG | HASH256 | HASH160	*crypto ops*

$$d ::= bs \mid Bool \mid int \mid key$$

Fig. 1. The syntax of SCRIPT.

Flow control includes a branching command IF S, representing the conditional execution of the program S if the top stack value is true (it is popped when checked). SCRIPT would actually write it as the sequence IF; S; ENDIF. Analogously for the if-then-else construct IFE. Branching constructs may fail on empty stack when testing the condition, or, in our representation, because one of the commands in S fails. VERIFY pops the stack and then fails if the

---

[2] In this paper we refer to the settings where flags MANDATORY_SCRIPT_VERIFY_FLAGS and SCRIPT_VERIFY_DERSIG are enabled and all other flags are disabled.

popped top of the stack was not true. OP_RETURN fails and, as a side effect, allows a limited amount of data to be recorded in the transaction, and hence permanently stored in the blockchain.

Stack operators work as expected. DUP, SWAP and DROP fail on empty stack. PUSH adds data on the stack.

SCRIPT operates on a stack with a 520-byte word. A *byte stream bs* is a sequence of bytes such that $|bs| \in [0, 520]$ ($|_-|$ is the length in bytes of a type), with ϵ the empty *bs* - which, e.g., can be successfully popped from the stack. bs_i represents a byte stream of length i, e.g. the result of a fixed-dimension hash operation.

A *boolean (Bool)* is a sequence of bytes with $|Bool| \in [0, 520]$ and 0, -0 and ϵ representing *False*.[3] An *integer (int)* is a 32-bit signed integer with $|int| \in [0, 4]$. $\top$ is the most generic type ($|\top| \in [0, 520]$). A *key (key)* is a sequence of bytes such that $|key| \in [9, 73]$. A public key *pk* can only be such that $|pk| = 65$ or $|pk| = 33$ (in the latter it is in compressed format). Some operations may have further requirements on keys, which will be modelled in the corresponding semantic rules[4] [5]. The type hierarchy is represented by (the transitive closure of) the following diagram, with solid lines for *being subtype of* and dotted ones representing allowed coercions under the constraint that bytestring lengths are respected, e.g. $b \in Bool$ can be successfully used as an integer only if $|b| \leq 4$. $\top$, *bs* and *Bool* are actually equivalent, while *int* and *key* disjoint. We introduced separate type entities for readability, and this hierarchy might be useful for more strictly typed variants of SCRIPT.

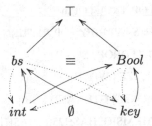

A type B can be automatically coerced to a type A $(A \rhd B)$:

$$\frac{|Bool| \leq 4}{int \rhd Bool}\ \textbf{B2i} \qquad \frac{|\top| \leq 4}{int \rhd \top}\ \textbf{T2i} \qquad \frac{|bs| \leq 4}{int \rhd \top bs}\ \textbf{bs2i} \qquad \frac{|bs| \in \{33, 67\}}{key \rhd bs}\ \textbf{bs2k}$$

---

[3] Although there are multiple values equal to *false* and multiple values equal to *true*, the Bitcoin Core client always *instantiates* these as ϵ and [0x01] respectively. Our symbolic verifier assumes the same representations.

[4] It is important to remark here that some type definitions, and other features, may depend on how the Bitcoin client is initialised. For instance, checking the dimension of a key depends on an initialisation parameter. We assume in this paper that the checking is done. We defer the verification against different possible initialisations to future work, noting that it must be addressed as different settings can affect correctness in different ways.

[5] Some operations may be more restrictive on the length of accepted keys, as well as their format. We will model this in the specific rules defining such operations, as appropriate. See Sect. 5.2.

Arithmetical operators ADD and SUB pop two *int* values from the stack and push the result r. It is worth noting that over/underflow may cause $|r| = 5$, which may cause a subsequent type error, and the choice of some constants may be implementation-dependent, e.g. 0 can be ϵ, 0_4, 0_3, -0_4, ... Arithmetical operators fail on lack of data or type error, e.g. an incoercible bs_{10}.

Boolean operators work similarly, as expected, and fail on lack of data on the stack (any data can be interpreted as a boolean). VERIFY pops a boolean value from the stack, and verifies that it is equal to *true*. If this constraint is not met evaluation of the SCRIPT fails. It is worth remarking here that some operators amongst those that push a boolean result to the stack have a _VERIFY variant, the so-called *verify operators*, such as EQ_VERIFY, CHKSIG_VERIFY. These variants are semantically equivalent to appending VERIFY after the original operator. For example, EQ_VERIFY is semantically equivalent to EQ;VERIFY.

Cryptographic operators check signatures, multi-signatures and push computed hash values to the stack. CHKSIG pops a signature s_k and a public key p_k from the stack, and checks if s_k is a valid signature of p_k combined with the hash of (part of) the transaction's data. It pushes the result of this check, i.e. *true* or *false*, to the stack. The non-VERIFY variant fails on lack of data and on type error. Note that performing CHKSIG without a VERIFY does not enforce prior operations (including those defined by the input script) to reach a matching signature check. This is only enforced when the result of CHKSIG is constrained to *true* by a subsequent VERIFY operation. CHKMSIG checks the validity of a list of signatures against a list of public keys. First, an integer n_{sk} is popped, defining the number of provided signatures. Then n_{sk} signatures (sks) are popped. Similarly, an integer n_{pk} determining the number of provided public keys and n_{pk} public keys (pks) are popped. As a result, CHKMSIG pushes *true* to the stack if each signature is valid for a public key combined with the hash of (part of) the transaction, i.e. $\forall sk \in sks.\exists pk \in pks$ such that CHKSIG on (sk, pk) is *true*[6]. Otherwise, *false* is pushed to the stack. The non-VERIFY variant fails on lack of data and on type error. HASH operators pop a value from the stack and push the hash of this value to the stack. Hashes fail on lack of data.

Locktime operators add time constraints to redeeming Bitcoins. We mention them here for the sake of a more complete overview of SCRIPT but do not address them in this work.

Example 1. The SCRIPT program

$$DUP;DROP;DROP;DUP$$

requires a top element in the stack, duplicates it, then pops the two copies, and then requires the presence of a second element initially on the stack and duplicates it.

---

[6] With the added note that matching public keys must be provided in the same order as the signatures they match with. Additionally, each provided public key can at most be matched with one signature.

Example 2. As an example of an unredeemable output script, consider the program

$$\text{PUSH 0xFB15AC2030FB; ADD}$$

ADD will require two *int* values, one of which must be pushed to the stack by the input script. However, regardless of what stack is left by the input script, ADD will always fail on type error as the first value it pops (originating from the PUSH operation in the output script) is of type bs_6, which cannot be coerced to *int*.

5   Symbolic Evaluation of SCRIPT Programs

Given the SCRIPT code of an output script, its execution is simulated from an empty stack. Required data on the initial stack for a successful computation is defined via a lazy approach returning the weakest constraints on data for successful termination.

5.1   The Execution Stack Model

A *symbolic stack* SK is an infinite (in both directions) list of indexed typed data, with indexes in $[-\infty, \infty]$ that uniquely identify a position and a datum in the stack:

$$[\ldots d_{i+1}, d_i, d_{i-1} \ldots]$$

$d_i = (x_i, t)$, with x_i a variable used to accumulate constraints on the expected data in the $i - th$ position, and t a type.

Two extra indexes associated to SK delimit the segment of significant data in SK: the *head index* h identifies the current top of the stack, and the *floor index* f denotes the first available position where data can be provided by the input script, that is the first position below the current bottom of the significant segment in SK. Initially, each d_i is undefined (and irrelevant) and $h = 0$ and $f = 0$, i.e. the top element is at position 0 and the first position where the input script could have provided data for operations in the output script is also 0. Such "inital" state is called the *empty stack* and denoted as SK_ϵ. Note that f can only decrease. Each command may further specify requirements on data by accumulating constraints on the associated variable. At the end of the computation, data of interest will be represented by the constraint store associated to the variables in $(f, 0]$, i.e. the data required to be provided by the input script for successful termination of the output script, if any. Symbolic expressions exp in the stack consist of constants d, variables x_i, operations $op \in \{+, -, <, \leq, =, \geq, >, \wedge, \vee\}$:

$$exp ::= exp \text{ op } exp \mid x_i \mid d \mid \text{hash } exp \mid \text{sig } exp \text{ } exp \mid \text{multisig } [exp] \text{ } [exp] \mid \text{size } exp$$

Table 1. An example of symbolic stack (**left**) and the input types (ty^1, ty^2, ty^3) and result type (ty^r) for some SCRIPT operators (**right**).

Instruction	ST	ST'
DUP;POP;POP;DUP	2 1 $h, f, 0$ -1	2 $h, 1$ x_0 0 x_0 $f, -1$
DUP;POP;POP;DUP	2 1 $h, 0$ x_0 $f, -1$	2 $h, 1$ 0 $h, f, -1$

OP	ty^1_{op}	ty^2_{op}	ty^3_{op}	ty^r_{op}
ADD SUB	Int	Int	-	$bs_{[0..5]}$
LT LTE GT GTE	Int	Int	-	Bool
SIZE	$\top$	-	-	Int
WITHIN	Int	Int	Int	Bool
EQ	$\top$	$\top$	-	Bool
AND OR	Bool	Bool	-	Bool
HASH256	$\top$	-	-	bs_{32}

Example 3. Considering informally the computation of the output script from Example 1, Table 1(left) shows the effect of command execution on SK. Each row shows the transformation from ST to ST', with ST the symbolic state prior to, and ST' the symbolic state post the symbolic computation of the in bold printed command.

5.2 Symbolic Simulation of SCRIPT Computations

The possible symbolic executions of an output script S are defined by a symbolic transition system, whose states represent the computation still to be executed and the current state of the associated symbolic state. Commands operate on typed data, type errors cause a *runtime error*, which stops the execution in a *failed* state, modelled here as standard as a non-terminal state (not $\diamond$) with no outgoing transitions. Table 1(right) reports examples of typed operations.

Definition 1. A *symbolic state* for a SCRIPT program S is a tuple (S, SK, h, f), with SK a symbolic stack and h and f its head and floor indexes.

Definition 2. A *symbolic transition system* for a SCRIPT program S is a relationship between symbolic states, and a constraint store Γ, written as

$$\Gamma \vdash (S_1, SK_1, h_1, f_1) \to (S_2, SK_2, h_2, f_2)$$

and read as Γ justifies the transition from (S_1, SK_1, h_1, f_1) to (S_2, SK_2, h_2, f_2). Γ is a *constraint store* over the variables $x_{f_2+1}, \ldots, x_{-1}, x_0$. $\to$ is the *transition relation* amongst states. Both Γ and $\to$ are defined by the *structural operation semantics* rules in Figs. 2, 3 and 4.

Γ may contain constraints like $\{(x_i, int), x_i \le 100\}$: x_i is an integer variable whose value must be less than 100. We use juxtaposition of constraint stores for their union. For the sake of space we do not enter in the details of the definition of the constraint language and solver, as they are standard techniques over the domain of interest.

$\Gamma \vdash (S_1, SK_1, h_1, f_1) \rightarrow (S_2, SK_2, h_2, f_2)$ reads as *the program S_1 with the stack (SK_1, h_1, f_1) can do a computation step, transform the stack into (SK_2, h_2, f_2), and become the program S_2, under the conditions in Γ.* The intended use of transactions is to define Γ through the semantic rules for a computation step of a given S_1 and (SK_1, h_1, f_1).

The union of the Γs along a computation made of several steps defines the *minimal* requirements on the initial stack to make that computation happen. Such a union for a *successful* execution trace defines one (or more) of the possible outputs of the *input script* that makes the transition redeemable. It is important to remark that one condition for success is that the top of the stack holds true. In order to validate such condition we

1. add a VERIFY operation at the end of the *output script* under consideration, which will cause the constraint $e_h = True$ to be added to Γ - see Fig. 3, and
2. resolve successful termination as Γ satisfiability (and script's termination).

Definition 3. Let SK_ϵ be the empty stack. A *successful trace* for a program S is a finite sequence

$$\Gamma_0 \vdash (S, SK_\epsilon, 0, 0) \rightarrow (S_1, A_1) \ldots \Gamma_n \vdash (S_{n-1}, A_{n-1}) \rightarrow (\diamond, SK_n, h_n, f_n)$$

with A_i symbolic stacks, and such that $\Gamma_0 \ldots \Gamma_{n-1}$ (i.e. the union of Γ_i over the trace) is satisfiable.

Γ satisfiability means that there exists an assignment γ such that $\Gamma\gamma$, i.e. the grounding of Γ through γ, is consistent. Interestingly, γ defines $x_{f+1}, \ldots, x_0$, the stack variables that have been identified by Γ and need to be to instantiated by the *input script*.

Rules in Fig. 2a model auxiliary operations ($\xrightarrow[x_f]{pop}$) transforming symbolic stacks, hereafter ranged over by $A, B, C, \ldots$. These operations are used by many of the other semantics rules and may define constraints for the constraint store. Worth noting the rule *s_pop*: data is expected (to have been provided by the input script) but the stack is empty: a new symbolic variable x_f is allocated in the first available position on the stack, i.e. f, and added to Γ with $\top$, i.e. no requirements, as type.

Rules for constants and stack ops are straightforward, examples are in Fig. 2b (with d *is_a* t expressing that d is of type t).

Arithmetic and boolean ops follow a common scheme: data are popped from the stack and, if types are correct, the respective computation is pushed to the stack in symbolic expression syntax. Figure 2c shows the scheme for the operations that take two arguments, most of which are defined in Table 1. Similar schemes for operations that take less, or more, arguments follow analogously.

Flow control is described in Fig. 3. Rule *seq* is the core of a small-step semantics: a sequence of commands is unfolded one at the time. *ite_t* checks the value popped from the stack: if it is, or can be assumed to be a *Bool* according to type

$$\frac{h = f}{\{(x_f, \top)\} \vdash (SK, h, f) \xmapsto[\ (x_f, \top)\ ]{pop} (SK, h-1, f-1)} \text{ s\_pop} \qquad \frac{h > f}{\emptyset \vdash (SK, h, f) \xmapsto[\ SK[h]\ ]{pop} (SK, h-1, f)} \text{ pop}$$

$$\frac{}{\emptyset \vdash (SK, h, f) \xmapsto[\ (e,t)\ ]{push} (SK[(e_{h+1}, t)], h+1, f)} \text{ push}$$

(a) Stack semantics rules

$$dis\_a\ t \qquad \frac{\Gamma \vdash A \xmapsto[\ (d,t)\ ]{push} B}{\Gamma \vdash (\text{PUSH } d, A) \to (\diamond, B)} \text{ d-push} \qquad \frac{\Gamma \vdash A \xmapsto{pop} B}{\Gamma \vdash (\text{DROP}, A) \to (\diamond, B)} \text{ drop}$$

$$\frac{\Gamma_1 \vdash A \xmapsto[(e,t)]{pop} B \quad \Gamma_2 \vdash B \xmapsto[(e,t)]{push} C \quad \Gamma_3 \vdash C \xmapsto[(e,t)]{push} D}{\Gamma_1 \Gamma_2 \Gamma_3 \vdash (\text{DUP}, A) \to (\diamond, D)} \text{ dup} \qquad \frac{\Gamma \vdash A \xmapsto[(i, \text{BS}_1)]{push} B}{\Gamma \vdash (\text{OP\_}i, A) \to (\diamond, B)} \text{ op n}^7$$

$$\frac{\Gamma_1 \vdash A \xmapsto[(e_1,t_1)]{pop} B \quad \Gamma_2 \vdash B \xmapsto[(e_2,t_2)]{pop} C \quad \Gamma_3 \vdash C \xmapsto[(e_1,t_1)]{push} D \quad \Gamma_4 \vdash D \xmapsto[(e_2,t_2)]{push} E}{\Gamma_1 \Gamma_2 \Gamma_3 \Gamma_4 \vdash (\text{SWAP}, A) \to (\diamond, E)} \text{ swap}$$

(b) Constants and stack ops

$$\frac{\Gamma_1 \vdash A \xmapsto[(e_1,t_1)]{pop} B \quad \Gamma_2 \vdash B \xmapsto[(e_2,t_2)]{pop} C \quad \begin{matrix} ty_{op}^1 \triangleright t_1 \\ ty_{op}^2 \triangleright t_2 \end{matrix} \quad \Gamma_3 \vdash C \xmapsto[(e_1 \ op \ e_2, ty_{op}^r)]{push} D}{\Gamma_1 \Gamma_2 \Gamma_3 \vdash (op, A) \to (\diamond, D)} \text{ 2arg-ops}$$

(c) Arithmetic & Boolean ops

Fig. 2. Semantic rules I. (With $n \in [1..16]$)

coercion rules, then ITE reduces to its *if* branch under the (minimal) assumptions that the type is a *Bool* and the value is *True*. Note that, as a general rule, a type error prevents that application of the rule, not allowing termination and therefore a successful trace. ite_f follows straightforwardly, as well as the omitted rules for IF, and the (only) one for VERIFY - not *Bool* or *false* prevent termination.

The crypto ops are in Fig. 4. $h256$ (and the omitted $h160$) describes the hashing of the top value in the stack. Similarly, *chksig* pops a signature and a public key and pushes a symbolic expression of validating the (signature, public key, transaction message) pair. Analogously, *chkmsig* pops a number n_{sk}, pops n_{sk} signatures, pops a number n_{pk}, pops n_{pk} public keys, pops 1 irrelevant value[7] and pushes a symbolic expression of validating the multiple signatures with multiple public keys to the stack.

---

[7] This is conforming to the Bitcoin Core client, which contains a bug resulting in this additional stack entry to be popped from the stack.

$$\frac{\Gamma \vdash (cmd, SK_1, h_1, f_1) \rightarrow (\diamond, SK_2, h_2, f_2)}{\Gamma \vdash (cmd; S, SK_1, h_1, f_1) \rightarrow (S, SK_2, h_2, f_2)} \ seq$$

$$\frac{\Gamma \vdash A \xmapsto[(e,t)]{pop} B \qquad Bool \triangleright t}{\Gamma\{t \, is \, Bool\}\{e = True\} \vdash (\text{IFE } S_t \circ S_f; S, \ A) \rightarrow (S_t; S, \ B)} \ ite_t$$

$$\frac{\Gamma \vdash A \xmapsto[(e,t)]{pop} B \qquad Bool \triangleright t}{\Gamma\{t \, is \, Bool\}\{e = False\} \vdash (\text{IFE } S_t \circ S_f; S, \ A) \rightarrow (S_f; S, \ B)} \ ite_f$$

$$\frac{\Gamma \vdash A \xmapsto[(e,t)]{pop} B \qquad Bool \triangleright t}{\Gamma\{t \, is \, Bool\}\{e = True\} \vdash (\text{VERIFY}, A) \rightarrow (\diamond, B)} \ ver$$

Fig. 3. Semantic rules II

Theorem 1 (Soundness). *Let*

$$\Gamma_0 \vdash (S, SK_\epsilon, 0, 0) \rightarrow (S_1, A_1) \ldots \Gamma_n \vdash (S_{n-1}, A_{n-1}) \rightarrow (\diamond, SK_n, h_n, f_n)$$

be a successful trace for the script S, i.e. $\Gamma_0 \ldots \Gamma_{n-1}$ is satisfiable.

Then there exist a script I and an assignment γ such that $\Gamma\gamma$ is consistent, and the execution of I from the empty stack provides the stack $X\gamma = [x_{(f_n+1)}, \ldots, x_0]$ and the actual execution of $I; S$ is successful from the empty stack.

Proof. Sketch! We prove the stronger result: if

$$\Gamma_0 \vdash (S_0, \mathbf{SK_0}, \mathbf{h_0}, \mathbf{f_0}) \rightarrow (S_1, SK_1, h_1, f_1) \ldots \Gamma_n \vdash (S_{n-1}, A_{n-1}) \rightarrow (\diamond, SK_n, h_n, f_n)$$

$$\frac{\Gamma_1 \vdash A \xmapsto[(e,t)]{pop} B \qquad \Gamma_2 \vdash B \xmapsto[(hash(e), BS_{32})]{push} C}{\Gamma_1 \Gamma_2 \vdash (\text{HASH256}, A) \rightarrow (\diamond, C)} \ h256$$

$$\frac{\Gamma_1 \vdash A \xmapsto[d_{pk}]{pop} B \qquad \Gamma_2 \vdash B \xmapsto[d_{sk}]{pop} C \qquad \Gamma_3 \vdash C \xmapsto[(Sig \ d_{sk} \ d_{pk}, Bool)]{push} D}{\Gamma_1 \Gamma_2 \Gamma_3 \vdash (\text{CHKSIG}, A) \rightarrow (\diamond, D)} \ chksig$$

$$\frac{\Gamma_1 \vdash A \xmapsto[n_{pk}]{pop} B \qquad \qquad \Gamma_3 \vdash C \xmapsto[n_{sk}]{pop} D \qquad \qquad \Gamma_5 \vdash E \xmapsto[-]{pop} F}{\Gamma_2 \vdash B \xmapsto[pks]{pops \ n_{pk}} C \quad \Gamma_4 \vdash D \xmapsto[sks]{pops \ n_{sk}} E \quad \Gamma_6 \vdash F \xmapsto[(MultiSig \ sks \ pks, Bool)]{push} G}{\Gamma_1 \Gamma_2 \Gamma_3 \Gamma_4 \Gamma_5 \Gamma_6 \vdash (\text{CHKMSIG}, A) \rightarrow (\diamond, G)} \ chkmsig$$

Fig. 4. Semantic rules III

is a successful trace then exists I such that $I; S_0$ is successful starting from a ground instance SK_0, $f_0 \leq 0$ and $h_0 = |SK_0| - f_0$, according to Γ. By induction on the trace length n:

Case $n = 1$. S_0 consists of the added VERIFY operation (S was initially empty), the only constraint is that I is able to provide an $x_h = True$ value on the stack, which define $I = \text{OP\_TRUE}$, and trivially $I; S_0$ is successful.

Case $n \Rightarrow n + 1$. For each single semantic rule r that can be applied to S, let us consider the step

$$\Gamma_0 \vdash (S_0, SK_0, h_0, f_0) \to (S_1, SK_1, h_1, f_1)$$

By construction a successful trace for S_1 of length $n - 1$ exists (it goes to $\diamond$ and $\Gamma_1 \dots \Gamma_n$ is satisfiable if Γ_0 is), and by induction I' exists such that $I'; S'$ is successful. Depending on the rule r applied, it is possible to show that I exists, such that $I; S$ is successful.

Case $r = d - push$. We take SK_1 as the stack after the execution of PUSH d from (SK_0, h_0, f_0). By induction, since a successful trace exists for (S_1, SK_1, f_1, h_1) of length $n - 1$, then I' exists such that $I'; S_1$ is successful from (S_1, SK_1, f_1, h_1), with SK_1 equal to SK_0 with on top the pushed datum d, and $f_1 = f_0$ and $h_1 = h_0 + 1$.

It follows that $I'; \text{PUSH d}; S_1$ is successful from (SK_0, h_0, f_0), indeed we will have a suitable ground instance of SK_0 (given that Γ is satisfiable) after the concrete computation of I', the execution of PUSH d will yield (a ground instance of) SK_1 from which we know that S_1 is successful.

Case $r = dup$. We take SK_1 as the stack after the execution of DUP from (SK_0, h_0, f_0). By induction, since a successful trace exists for (S_1, SK_1, h_1, f_1) of length $n - 1$, then I' exists such that $I'; S_1$ is successful from (S_1, SK_1, h_1, f_1), with

- if $h_0 \neq f_0$ then the stack's element to be duplicated is present in SK_0, thus: SK_1 will be equal to SK_0 with on top the pushed duplicate of the head entry of SK_0, $h_1 = h_0 + 1$ and $f_1 = f_0$. It follows that $I'; \text{DUP}; S_1$ is successful from S_0 assuming that Γ_0 is satisfiable.
- if $h_0 = f_0$ then the stack's element to be duplicated is not present in SK_0 (i.e. $SK_0 = \epsilon$), in which case a constraint in Γ_0 will require x_{f_0} to be provided before I', thus: SK_1 will be $[x_{f_0}, x_{f_0}]$, $h_1 = h_0 + 1$ and $f_1 = f_0 - 1$. It follows that $\text{PUSH } x_{f_0}; I'; \text{DUP}; S_1$ is successful from S_0 assuming that Γ_0 is satisfiable.

Other cases can be solved analogously.   □

5.3 Implementation

The presented symbolic verification framework has informed the implementation of SCRIPT ANALYSER, an open source application implemented in Haskell, available at https://github.com/RKlompUU/SCRIPTAnalyser.

Given an *output script S*, the current version of the tool returns all the existing satisfiable Γ for each successful computation of S. Such Γs are specifications of (all the possible) *input scripts I* which can be used to redeem the associated transaction. SCRIPT ANALYSER works by an exhaustive traversal of the space of successful traces, as soon as an error or inconsistency in Γ is detected, the trace is abandoned.

Satisfiability of Γ is done by application of well-known Finite Domain Constraint Solvers. The current version of the tool uses the solver embedded in *swi-prolog* [4]. Other solvers, e.g. *GNU Prolog* [2], will be experimented with.

An extensive experimentation over the non-standard transactions that have appeared in the blockchain is being carried out.

6   Two Non-standard Transactions

We present the analysis of two relatively complex output scripts from the blockchain. These scripts have been chosen as complex enough examples to make non-trivial the precise understanding of their intended meaning and the full conditions for redeemability. As such, any introduced bugs during development of SCRIPT programs like these would arguably be difficult to notice without formal verification. Figure 5a shows the output script of a transaction[8] that was inserted into the Blockchain's 269,760th block. Following the symbolic rules, there are two different Γs derivable:

```
 1 DUP;
 2 SIZE;
 3 PUSH (int: 64);
 4 PUSH (int: 67);                      1 IF;
 5 WITHIN;                              2    OP_2;
 6 SWAP;                                3    PUSH <bs length: 65>;
 7 HASH256;                            4    PUSH <bs length: 33>;
 8 PUSH <bs length: 32>;              5    OP_2;
 9 EQUAL;                              6    CHKMSIG;
10 AND;                                7 ELSE;
11 IF;                                 8    OP_2;
12    POP;                             9    PUSH <bs length: 65>;
13 ELSE;                              10        % bs differs from bs at line 3
14    PUSH <bs length: 65>;          11    PUSH <bs length: 33>;
15    CHKSIG_VERIFY;                 12        % bs differs from bs at line 4
16 ENDIF;                             13    OP_2;
17 PUSH <bs length: 65>;             14    CHKMSIG;
18 CHKSIG                             15 ENDIF
```

(a) Example A   (b) Example B

Fig. 5. Two output script examples.

---

[8] With ID: 75bb6417afc7500a6389201a67bfc2428a1241170a214bbf6833a389191036fe.

$\Gamma_0 := \text{Sig } x_{-1} \, bs_{\text{line: 17}} \, \wedge$

$($

  $\text{Hash } x_0 == bs_{\text{line: 8}} \, \wedge$

  $\text{Size } x_0 < 67 \, \wedge$

  $\text{Size } x_0 >= 64$

$) \, \wedge$

...omitted type constraints...

$\Gamma_1 := \text{Sig } x_{-1} \, bs_{\text{line: 17}} \, \wedge$

  $\text{Sig } x_0 \, bs_{\text{line: 14}} \, \wedge$

  $\neg($

    $\text{Hash } x_0 == bs_{\text{line: 8}} \, \wedge$

    $\text{Size } x_0 < 67 \, \wedge$

    $\text{Size } x_0 >= 64$

  $) \, \wedge$

...omitted type constraints...

Solving for the former (Γ_0) implies that the *true*-branch of the IF instruction is taken, and the latter (Γ_1) implies that the *false*-branch is taken. For both Γs the input script must instantiate variables $\{x_0, x_{-1}\}$ and x_{-1} must be a valid signature. If the transaction is redeemed following Γ_0's constraints, x_0 must be a valid hash input such that the result is equal to some constant byte string and its type is constrained by the Size constraints to $[64, 67)$. Whereas, if the transaction is redeemed following Γ_1's constraints, x_0 must be a valid signature.

Figure 5b shows the output script of a transaction[9] that was inserted into the Bitcoin's 290,456th block. Again, since both branches of the IF instruction produce valid constraint sets, the tool finds two solutions for Γ:

$\Gamma_0 := x_{-4} = true \, \wedge$

  $\text{MultiSig } [x_{-2}, x_{-1}][bs_{\text{line: 3}}, bs_{\text{line: 4}}] \, \wedge$

  $x_0 = true \, \wedge$

  $(x_{-3}, \top) \, \wedge$

  ...omitted type constraints...

$\Gamma_1 := x_{-4} = true \, \wedge$

  $\text{MultiSig } [x_{-2}, x_{-1}][bs_{\text{line: 9}}, bs_{\text{line: 11}}] \, \wedge$

  $x_0 = false \, \wedge$

  $(x_{-3}, \top) \, \wedge$

  ...omitted type constraints...

For both Γ_0 and Γ_1 variables $x_{-4}, .., x_0$ must be instantiated by the input script. Depending on the value of x_0, the *true*-branch is taken (Γ_0, when $x_0 = true$) or the *false*-branch is taken (Γ_1, when $x_0 = false$). x_{-1} and x_{-2} must be valid signatures for both Γs. However, note that the public keys these variables must match with are different depending on which Γ is solved by the input script. This shows that there exist *two* identity pairs that may redeem the transaction. x_{-3} is in both Γs popped from the stack due to the bug in CHKMSIG, and must only be present but is not further used and hence constrained. Additionally, in both Γs, x_{-4} must be some value equal to *true*. It can be argued that the inclusion of this constraint on variable x_{-4} is a minor bug of this output script that is caused by the _VERIFY variant of CHKMSIG that is applied as the final operation (following both the *true*-, as well as the *false*-branch). We consider this

---

[9] With ID: cd2dacbd05389580cb569985b3a8b1db67ea6cc84371223590e241a5026d0a8a.

a bug since it necessarily increases the redeeming transaction's fee, as it imposes the presence of an additional PUSH operation in the input script, increasing the transaction's size. Though the trained eye should have no trouble spotting this bug in the code, it is clear that the constraints generated by our prototype tool better highlight the bug's presence.

7 Future Work

By setting up multiple linked transactions (partially) via offchain communication, parties can establish smart contracts that are automatically enforced by the Bitcoin ledger. Consider for example the following communication pattern that establishes a smart contract wherein party A provides a deposit for a pre-specified duration to party B[10]. Messages sent to BC represent transmissions to the Blockchain.

$$A \rightarrow B : P_k A$$
$$B \rightarrow A : P_k B$$
$$A \rightarrow B : \text{hashed } tx_1$$
$$B \rightarrow A : tx_2$$
$$A \rightarrow BC : tx_1$$
$$A \rightarrow BC : tx_2'$$

With $P_k A$ and $P_k B$ public keys belonging to A and B respectively, tx_1 a transaction with A placing bitcoins inside a fresh address and locking these until provided correct signatures by A and B, tx_2 a transaction that partially signs tx_1 with B's signature and unlocks the locked bitcoins after the specified duration (enabling A to reclaim the deposit), and tx_2' fully signing tx_1. Through application of this contract, B is guaranteed that A indeed deposited currency, and A is guaranteed that the deposit will be reclaimable after the prespecified duration.

Ultimately, we are interested in deriving, from the communication sequence in conjuction with the output scripts, all possible behaviors (i.e. the range of effects) of the smart contract that the participants can trigger with the knowledge they each have after each communication step. This information can then be used to verify that the designed smart contract will indeed behave as expected.

8 Conclusions

We introduced a symbolic analysis of *open* script. An *open* script is an incomplete program, i.e. the *output scripts* in Bitcoin's transactions. These can be *closed* by prepending a set of instructions, i.e. the *input scripts* in Bitcoin's transactions. Through application of the symbolic evaluation rules, the constraints expressed

---

[10] Source: https://en.bitcoin.it/wiki/Contract.

by an *output script*, which are the ones that must be met by the *input script*, can be derived automatically, and be further analysed, either manually or (partially) automatically. We have shown that these constraints can, for example, show the non existence of a redeeming *input script*, e.g. due to type error(s) in the *output script*, or contradiction(s) in the constraints imposed by the *output script*. Results have been presented of analyses on two relatively complex non-standard *output scripts*. Such results have been obtained automatically by means of an open source application that we developed. Such results, beyond confirming that the two *output scripts* are redeemable, clarify by means of the generated constraints the required encrypted knowledge.

Currently, the evaluation rules and the prototype tool cover a relevant portion of SCRIPT's language. Interesting research for future work involves extending both, e.g. starting by the inclusion of locktime operations. On a longer term, we are planning to extend the symbolic evaluation to the analysis of smart contracts that are defined with multiple linked transactions in conjunction with off-chain communication, à la cryptographic protocol analysis.

References

1. Github - bitcoin/bitcoin: Bitcoin core integration/staging tree. https://github.com/bitcoin/bitcoin/. Accessed 12 June 2018
2. The gnu prolog web site. http://gprolog.org/. Accessed 18 June 2018
3. Script - bitcoin wiki. https://en.bitcoin.it/wiki/Script
4. Swi-prolog. http://www.swi-prolog.org/. Accessed 18 June 2018
5. Andrychowicz, M., Dziembowski, S., Malinowski, D., Mazurek, Ł.: Modeling bitcoin contracts by timed automata. In: Legay, A., Bozga, M. (eds.) FORMATS 2014. LNCS, vol. 8711, pp. 7–22. Springer, Cham (2014). https://doi.org/10.1007/978-3-319-10512-3_2
6. Andrychowicz, M., Dziembowski, S., Malinowski, D., Mazurek, Ł.: Secure multiparty computations on bitcoin. In: 2014 IEEE Symposium on Security and Privacy (SP), pp. 443–458. IEEE (2014)
7. Bartoletti, M., Pompianu, L.: An empirical analysis of smart contracts: platforms, applications, and design patterns. In: Brenner, M., et al. (eds.) FC 2017. LNCS, vol. 10323, pp. 494–509. Springer, Cham (2017). https://doi.org/10.1007/978-3-319-70278-0_31
8. Bartoletti, M., Zunino, R.: Bitml: a calculus for bitcoin smart contracts. Technical report, Cryptology ePrint Archive, Report 2018/122 (2018)
9. Bhargavan, K., et al.: Formal verification of smart contracts: short paper. In: Proceedings of the 2016 ACM Workshop on Programming Languages and Analysis for Security, pp. 91–96. ACM (2016)
10. Bonneau, J., Miller, A., Clark, J., Narayanan, A., Kroll, J.A., Felten, E.W.: Sok: Research perspectives and challenges for bitcoin and cryptocurrencies. In: 2015 IEEE Symposium on Security and Privacy (SP), pp. 104–121. IEEE (2015)
11. Delgado-Segura, S., Pérez-Sola, C., Navarro-Arribas, G., Herrera-Joancomartı, J.: Analysis of the bitcoin utxo set. In: The 5th Workshop on Bitcoin and Blockchain Research (2018)

12. Delmolino, K., Arnett, M., Kosba, A., Miller, A., Shi, E.: Step by step towards creating a safe smart contract: lessons and insights from a cryptocurrency lab. In: Clark, J., Meiklejohn, S., Ryan, P.Y.A., Wallach, D., Brenner, M., Rohloff, K. (eds.) FC 2016. LNCS, vol. 9604, pp. 79–94. Springer, Heidelberg (2016). https://doi.org/10.1007/978-3-662-53357-4_6

13. Gerard, D.: Smart contracts, stupid humans: new major ethereum erc-20 token bugs batchoverflow and proxyoverflow (2018). https://davidgerard.co.uk/blockchain/2018/04/26/smart-contracts-stupid-humans-new-major-erc-20-token-bugs-batchoverflow-and-proxyoverflow/

14. Atzei, N., Bartoletti, M., Cimoli, T., Lande, S., Zunino, R.: SoK: unraveling bitcoin smart contracts. In: Bauer, L., Küsters, R. (eds.) POST 2018. LNCS, vol. 10804, pp. 217–242. Springer, Cham (2018). https://doi.org/10.1007/978-3-319-89722-6_9

15. Nakamoto, S.: Bitcoin: a peer-to-peer electronic cash system. Bitcoin project white paper (2009)

16. Szabo, N.: Formalizing and securing relationships on public networks. First Monday 2(9) (1997)

17. Wood, G.: Ethereum: a secure decentralised generalised transaction ledger. Ethereum Proj. Yellow Paper 151, 1–32 (2014)

Self-reproducing Coins as Universal Turing Machine

Alexander Chepurnoy[1,2]([✉]), Vasily Kharin[3], and Dmitry Meshkov[1]

[1] Ergo Platform, Moscow, Russia
catena@protonmail.com
[2] IOHK Research, Hong Kong, China
alex.chepurnoy@iohk.io
[3] Research Institute, Moscow R&D Lab, Moscow, Russia
v.kharin@protonmail.com

Abstract. Turing-completeness of smart contract languages in blockchain systems is often associated with a variety of language features (such as loops). On the contrary, we show that Turing-completeness of a blockchain system can be achieved through unwinding the recursive calls between multiple transactions and blocks instead of using a single one. We prove it by constructing a simple universal Turing machine using a small set of language features in the unspent transaction output (UTXO) model, with explicitly given relations between input and output transaction states. Neither unbounded loops nor possibly infinite validation time are needed in this approach.

Keywords: Smart contracts · Turing-completeness
Blockchain · Cellular automata

1 Introduction

Blockchain technology has become widely adopted after the introduction of Bitcoin by Nakamoto [10]. This peer-to-peer electronic cash ledger drew the enormous attention from the public, which resulted in rapid development of the technology and appearance of hundreds of alternative cryptocurrency projects. It also turned out that the blockchain applications expand quite far beyond the simple ledger niche. The rules of transaction validation can incorporate complicated logic, which is the essence of so-called smart contracts. In the case of Bitcoin the logic is implemented in the special-purpose Script language, which is believed not to be Turing complete. This belief stimulated the development of other smart contract platforms with the emphasis on the language universality. Particularly, in Ethereum [5] the *jump* opcode was introduced in a virtual machine assembly language in order to incorporate unlimited loops. In practice this resulted in various vulnerabilities and DoS attacks [3] since transaction computation cost (so-called *gas*) can only be calculated in runtime. Moreover, Turing-completeness of Ethereum is still a subject of debates mostly due to

© Springer Nature Switzerland AG 2018
J. Garcia-Alfaro et al. (Eds.): DPM 2018/CBT 2018, LNCS 11025, pp. 57–64, 2018.
https://doi.org/10.1007/978-3-030-00305-0_4

the undecidability of the halting problem in combination with a bounded block validation time. The gas limit is often viewed as a fundamental component preventing Turing-completeness [9].

A Turing-complete programming language is a language which allows description of a universal Turing machine. A universal Turing machine is the Turing machine which can simulate any other Turing machine; its existence is one of the main results of the Turing theory [12]. The study of Turing machines is strongly motivated by the Church—Turing thesis, which states that any computation in the intuitive sense can be performed on a Turing machine. The thesis is often viewed as a definition of computation and computability [13]. The set of known computation devices and models was rapidly growing during the twentieth century, and the methods of their analysis were improved as well. The usual way of proving the Turing-completeness of a system, a device or a language is by using it to emulate a system that is already proven to be Turing complete. A system which we are using in this work is one-dimensional cellular automaton Rule 110. It was conjectured to be Turing complete by Wolfram [16]. The conjecture was proven by Cook [7] based on previous works by Post [11].

The utter simplicity of Rule 110 makes it an appealing basis for proving Turing-completeness. In the present work we construct Rule 110 automaton algorithm for UTXO blockchain and implement it in ErgoScript smart contract language [6]. We require neither loops, nor jump operator, nor recursive calls inside a transaction. Instead, we treat the computation as if it is occurring between the transactions (or maybe blocks). In this context transaction chaining and replication furnishes us with potentially infinite loops and recursion, while a combination of outputs for multiple transactions yields analog of a potentially infinite tape. The underlying idea of complexity growth is similar to the one expressed in [14, 15].

This paper is structured as follows: in Sect. 2, we first describe a naive implementation of Rule 110 using a simple Bitcoin-like scripting language. Then we discuss the pitfalls arising from compliance with blockchain properties, and show a way to overcome them. Section 3 describes an implementation for the real-world blockchains, and also sketches a discussion on the nature of computation in the framework of blockchain scripting and validation rules. In Appendix A we describe a structure of a general-purpose guarding script for an output which can be transformed into an actual algorithm along with a transformation procedure.

2   Rule 110 Implementation

In this section we describe an implementation of Rule 110 cellular automaton. The automaton is transforming one-dimensional string of zeros and ones by applying evolution rules. One step of evolution for one bit is defined by its value c together with the values of the two neighboring bits—the left one ℓ and the right one r, along with a transition rule defined in Algorithm 1 ("$\oplus$" stands for XOR operation).

Algorithm 1. Transition function of the Rule 110 automaton

```
1: function CALCBIT(ℓ, c, r)
2:     return (ℓ ∧ c ∧ r) ⊕ (c ∧ r) ⊕ c ⊕ r
3: end function
```

For automaton implementation in a blockchain we use Bitcoin-like trans-actions consisting of inputs and outputs. Every output consists of a guarding *script* and a *payload*, while an input is a reference to an output from a previous transaction. We assume that the current state of the automaton is stored in the transaction output's *payload*. The general idea is to use the next transaction as a single step of the system evolution. In order to achieve this, two main condi-tions must be satisfied. First, the *payload* of at least one newly generated output should contain the updated state of the automaton. Second, this output must contain exactly the same script. These conditions require the transaction input to have access to the output's *scripts* and *payloads*. It is implicitly present in the vast amount of existing blockchains, since in most cases scripts verify the signature of the spending transaction, which is constructed over the byte array containing the new outputs. However, this way of accessing output's data may be hardly exploitable. In the paper we assume that the guarding script of an input has direct access to the spending transaction outputs.

Keeping all these in mind, we come to the following validation script:

Algorithm 2. Script, that ensures that the transaction performs correct rule 110 transformation keeping the same rules for further iterations

```
 1: function VALIDATE(in, out)
 2:     function ISRULE110(inLayer, outLayer)
 3:         function PROCCELL(i)
 4:             ℓ ← inLayer[i − 1 mod inLayer.size]
 5:             c ← inLayer[i]
 6:             r ← inLayer[i + 1 mod inLayer.size]
 7:             return CALCBIT(ℓ, c, r)
 8:         end function
 9:         return outLayer = inLayer.indices.map(PROCCELL)
10:     end function
11:     return ISRULE110(self.payload, out[0].payload) ∧ (self.script = out[0].script)
12: end function
```

The script performs two checks. First, it takes the payload of a current input and ensures, that the result of Rule 110 application equals to the payload of the first output. Second, it checks that the guarding script of the first output is the same as a script of the input. The full implementation of this script in the smart contract language of an existing UTXO blockchain Ergo is provided at [2].

With this script, the cellular automaton evolution may be started by chaining transactions in a blockchain. Figure 1 shows three transactions (on the left), each one representing the iteration of the automaton (on the right).

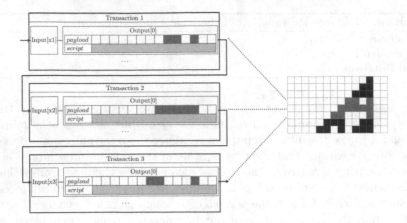

Fig. 1. Transaction chain following Rule 110. See Algorithm 2 for the *script* field description.

Potentially infinite evolution of a cellular automaton, which is required for Turing-completeness, can be modeled by chaining potentially infinite number of transactions in the blockchain. However, there is a pitfall left. Size of the data stored in output must have an upper-bound, and validation time for a transaction must be bounded as well, otherwise blockchain is losing its security properties[1].

The natural workaround is to split the automaton state between transactions once it becomes too large. As an extreme case one can make a transaction output play a role of a single bit of the automaton. While being inefficient, this implementation keeps the logic simple and complies with the requirements of

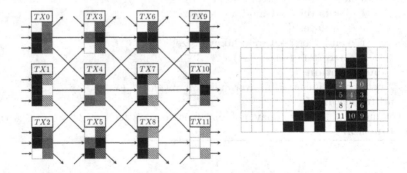

Fig. 2. Evolution of the cellular automaton described in Algorithm 3. Every non-boundary transaction spends three outputs, and generates three new ones with identical bit values. Hatching indicates "mid" flag being unset. Numbers in the cells on the right pane correspond to the transaction numbers on the left.

---

[1] For example, in the Bitcoin backbone protocol model from [8], block validation should happen within finite and a-priori known round duration.

the blockchain and of potentially infinite evolution in space and time. The pseudocode of the corresponding script is provided in the Algorithm 3 and its implementation in ErgoScript contract language is provided at [1]. Figure 2 schematically shows the sequence of transactions (on the left), that corresponds to some area evaluation (on the right) of the automaton run.

The script works as follows. Every output's payload contains its bit value val, the column index x, and the minimal x index at the current step n. As the grid expands by one at every step, $-n$ also serves as the row number. By default, the transaction spends three inputs (corresponding to the three neighboring bits

---

Algorithm 3. Validation script for the output representing the single bit, and the unbound grid

---

```
 1: function VERIFY(in, out)              ▷ "in" and "out" are lists of inputs and outputs
 2:     function OUTCORRECT(out, script)                          ▷ output structure check
 3:         scriptCorrect ← out[0].script = script
 4:         isCopy1 ← out[1] = out[0].copy(mid← true)
 5:         isCopy2 ← out[2] = out[0].copy(mid← false)
 6:         return (¬out[0].mid) ∧ scriptCorrect ∧ isCopy1 ∧ isCopy2
 7:     end function
 8:     function CORRECTPAYLOAD(in, out)                          ▷ output payload check
 9:         ▷ mid flag is only set for the middle input
10:         inMidCorrect ← in[1].mid ∧ ¬(in[0].mid ∨ in[2].mid)
11:         ▷ input positions are correct; n is the index of leftmost column
12:         inYCorrect ← (in[1].n = in[0].n) ∧ (in[2].n = in[0].n)
13:         inXCorrect ← (in[1].x = in[0].x+1) ∧ (in[2].x = in[1].x+1)
14:         ▷ bits satisfy Rule 110
15:         inValCorrect ← out[0].val=CALCBIT(in[0].val, in[1].val, in[2].val)
16:         ▷ output position matches the input one
17:         outPosCorrect ← out[0].x = in[1].x ∧ (out[0].n = in[0].n−1)
18:         return inValCorrect ∧ inXCorrect ∧ inYCorrect ∧
                    inMidCorrect ∧ outPosCorrect ∧ in.size=out.size=3
19:     end function
20:     if in[0].x=in[0].n ∧ in.size=1 then          ▷ leftmost — add 2 zeros to the left
21:         middle ← in[0].copy(x←in[0].n−1, val←0, mid← true)
22:         left ← in[0].copy(x←in[0].n−2, val←0, mid← false)
23:         realIn ← left ++ middle ++ in
24:     else if in[0].x=in[0].n ∧ in.size=2 then ▷ next to leftmost — add 0 to the left
25:         left ← in[0].copy(x←in[0].n−1, val←0, mid← false)
26:         realIn ← left ++ in
27:     else if in[0].x=−1 ∧ in.size=2 then          ▷ rightmost — add 0 to the right
28:         right ← in[0].copy(x← 1, val←0, mid← false)
29:         realIn ← in ++ right
30:     else                                                             ▷ normal cell
31:         realIn ← in
32:     end if
33:     return CORRECTPAYLOAD(realIn, out) ∧ OUTCORRECT(out, in[0].script)
34: end function
```

---

from the previous row), and creates three outputs with the same bit value by the automaton rule. One output flagged by *mid* is supposed to be spent for new value with the column number x, and another two—for the columns $x \pm 1$ (see Fig. 2). In case the transaction creates the boundary cells, either one or two inputs are emulated to have zero bit values (lines 20–32). The overall validation script checks the correctness of the positions of inputs (lines 12 and 13) and outputs (line 17), correspondence of the bit values (line 15), the correctness of the *mid* flag assignment for inputs (line 10) and the fact that all outputs are identical except the *mid* flag, which is set only once (lines 2–7).

Since the Turing-completeness of Rule 110 was proven in [7], we conclude that even though the scripting language itself does not allow loops, Turing-completeness of the system can be achieved by combining multiple transactions together. Note that our language requirements are not very demanding, just about bit operations, comparisons, assignments, and by-index access.

3 Discussion

The crucial move in our work is unwinding recursive calls by means of transaction chaining, although the language we use contains neither cycles nor recursion. By doing this we let a program to be executed over a sequence of transactions and blocks. This approach allows us to run programs in potentially infinite time on top of the blockchain while there is a strict upper-bound for block validation time.

A single transaction in the blockchain approximately corresponds to a single step of a computing machine. The step may be as complex as language built-ins allow; however, for security reasons it should be possible to estimate its running time before the actual evaluation.

One can wonder how evolving data structures (a blockchain and a corresponding UTXO set) along with programmable validation rules constitute a Turing machine. Obviously, we do need to include clients, forming transactions, and honest majority of miners, including transactions into blocks, as a component of the machine as well—their efforts are making the input tape of the machine. The same is true for Ethereum and other blockchains with smart contracts: the blockchain as a data structure does not endorse any computations—they should be initialized by a client.

Our approach can be used for Turing-completeness proofs of various smart contract languages in general. For example, it might be possible to prove that smart contracts of Waves platform [4] are actually Turing complete, although the authors claimed the opposite. Rule 110 implementation is not required for practical cases, it just guarantees that any algorithm can be potentially implemented. Despite existence of this guarantee, efficient usage of self-reproducing coins in practice may require new machinery, including development environments and high-level smart contract languages for the multiple-transactions computations.

Acknowledgments. Authors thank Manuel Chakravarty, Oksana Klimenko, and Georgy Meshkov for the discussions and helpful comments on early drafts of this paper.

A   Appendix

This section addresses a question of guarding script conversion into the procedure being executed by a client or a miner. Note that the guarding script itself does not explicitly prescribe the course of computational actions needed to produce a valid transaction. It rather describes the algorithm of telling whether the result of the actions is correct or not. As an example, one could set a guarding script in the form $5^{out[0].x} \bmod 23 = 13$. This script structure is admissible, but it is hard to say that it describes an actual program of discrete logarithm calculation. In our particular case the solution is simple. If the guarding script is of the form $(out[0].x = f(in)) \wedge (something)$ with f being some function, then in order to satisfy the condition one can replace the equality check with a variable assignment. Hence if we require the script to be conjunction of equality checks containing the fields of the outputs solely on the left hand sides, and functions of the inputs on the right hand sides, then it actually defines the program (assuming that the inputs are fixed). It is fully present in the Algorithm 2. Another problem is collecting the right set of inputs for the transaction. Suppose one wants to spend $in[0]$. If the condition for $in[1]$ is conjunction of the expressions of type $in[1].x = f(in[0])$, then finding the suitable $in[1]$ is the lookup over the possible inputs with field x being the key. Therefore, if the guarding script can be represented in the form

$$\left(\bigwedge_i \bigwedge_j (out[i].x_j = f_{ij}(in)) \right) \wedge$$
$$(\bigwedge_i in[1].x_i = g_{1i}(in[0])) \wedge (\bigwedge_i in[2].x_i = g_{2i}(in[0], in[1])) \wedge \ldots, \quad (1)$$

it can be efficiently converted to the transaction generation algorithm:

Here the last if-statement is the consistency check. Note that both Algorithms 2 and 3 can be represented as the desired form (1) with the length checks.

Algorithm 4. Transaction creation algorithm

1: **for** in[0] ← UTXO **do**
2:     i ← 0
3:     **while** *scripts of in[0]...in[i] have rule g() for in[i + 1]* **do**
4:         in[i+1] ← UTXO(g(in[0]...in[i]))
5:         i ← i+1
6:     **end while**
7:     j ← 0
8:     **while** *scripts of in[0]...in[i] have rule f() for out[j]* **do**
9:         out[j] ← f(in[0]...in[i])
10:         j ← j+1
11:     **end while**
12:     **if** tx(in,out).isValid **then return** tx
13:     **end if**
14: **end for**

References

1. One bit per output rule 110 implementation in ergoscript smart contract language. https://git.io/vj6rX
2. One layer per output rule 110 implementation in ergoscript smart contract language. https://git.io/vj6sw
3. Atzei, N., Bartoletti, M., Cimoli, T.: A survey of attacks on ethereum smart contracts (SoK). In: Maffei, M., Ryan, M. (eds.) POST 2017. LNCS, vol. 10204, pp. 164–186. Springer, Heidelberg (2017). https://doi.org/10.1007/978-3-662-54455-6_8
4. Begicheva, A., Smagin, I.: RIDE: a smart contract language for waves. Apograf.io, v1.1 (2018). https://apograf.io/articles/14027
5. Buterin, V., et al.: A next-generation smart contract and decentralized application platform. white paper (2014). https://git.io/vj6X9
6. Chepurnoy, A.: σ-state authentication language, an alternative to bitcoin script. In: International Conference on Financial Cryptography and Data Security. pp. 644–645. Springer (2017)
7. Cook, M.: Universality in elementary cellular automata. Complex Syst. $\mathbf{15}(1)$, 1–40 (2004)
8. Garay, J., Kiayias, A., Leonardos, N.: The bitcoin backbone protocol: analysis and applications. In: Oswald, E., Fischlin, M. (eds.) EUROCRYPT 2015, Part II. LNCS, vol. 9057, pp. 281–310. Springer, Heidelberg (2015). https://doi.org/10.1007/978-3-662-46803-6_10
9. Miller, A.: Ethereum isn't turing complete and it doesn't matter anyway. IC3 NYC Blockchain Meetup, talk (2016). https://www.youtube.com/watch?v=cGFOKTm_8zk
10. Nakamoto, S.: Bitcoin: A peer-to-peer electronic cash system (2008)
11. Post, E.L.: Formal reductions of the general combinatorial decision problem. Am. J. Math. $\mathbf{65}(2)$, 197–215 (1943)
12. Turing, A.M.: On computable numbers, with an application to the entscheidungs problem. Proc. Lond. Math. Soc. $\mathbf{2}(1)$, 230–265 (1937)
13. Turing, A.M.: Systems of logic based on ordinals. Proc. Lond. Math. Soc. $\mathbf{2}(1)$, 161–228 (1939)
14. Von Neumann, J.: The general and logical theory of automata. Cereb. Mech. Behav. $\mathbf{1}(41)$, 1–2 (1951)
15. Von Neumann, J., Burks, A.W.: Theory of self-reproducing automata. IEEE Trans. Neural Netw. $\mathbf{5}(1)$, 3–14 (1966)
16. Wolfram, S.: Theory and Applications of Cellular Automata: Including Selected Papers 1983–1986. World scientific, River Edge (1986)

CBT Workshop: Second Layer, Off-chain Transactions and Transparency

Split Payments in Payment Networks

Dmytro Piatkivskyi$^{(\boxtimes)}$ and Mariusz Nowostawski

NTNU, Trondheim, Norway
{dmytro.piatkivskyi,mariusz.nowostawski}@ntnu.no

Abstract. Traditional blockchain systems, such as Bitcoin, focus on transactions in which entire amount is transferred from one owner to the other, in a single, atomic operation. This model has been re-used in the context of payment networks such as Lightning network. In this work, we propose and investigate new payment model, called *split payments*, in which the total amount to be transferred is split into unit-amounts and is transferred independently through the same or different routes. By splitting the payments this way, we achieve an improved total liquidity of the payment network, simplify the route advertising, reduce the amount of funds needed to be locked in the channels, and improve the privacy properties.

1 Introduction

The scalability problem of Bitcoin has received considerable attention by the community. Various solutions have been proposed [1–3] and one of the most promising is the utilization of off-chain transactions, for example through the Lightning network [4]. Off-chain payment network is based on the concept of state channels that can operate offline, consulting the blockchain only when opening or closing a channel. The state channels form a payment network which allows for peer-to-peer instantaneous transactions.

The payment networks ultimately solve the inherent blockchain scalability limitation, however, the payment networks themselves are limited in many ways. They require careful consideration and appropriate balancing of multiple, often competing, trade offs. Many properties of the network will depend on the way the network organizes itself. Implementation choices will make a great difference. In this paper we demonstrate how to better organize the network. In particular, we suggest to abandon the idea of single atomic payments and to embrace the concept of money flows, and the use of split payments. We show that splitting payments into a number of unit payments improves a number of important properties, such as liquidity, funds lock-in, and privacy.

2 Background and Past Work

The Lightning network is a payment protocol built on top of the Bitcoin protocol. It allows for transaction throughput scaling by keeping and updating Bitcoin transactions off-chain. A Lightning network transaction is processed within

J. Garcia-Alfaro et al. (Eds.): DPM 2018/CBT 2018, LNCS 11025, pp. 67–75, 2018.
https://doi.org/10.1007/978-3-030-00305-0_5

Lightning channels which are actually Bitcoin transactions. The idea is that two users mutually fund a Bitcoin transaction, the *Funding* transaction, and spend it returning the invested funds with the *Commitment* transaction. They both sign the commitment transactions, but only publish the funding transactions on the blockchain. Once a channel is established, i.e. the funding transaction reaches the blockchain, funds can be moved within the channel (up to the channel capacity) by simply updating the commitment transaction. When any participant wants to spend funds outside the payment network, the channel is closed by publishing the current state of the commitment transaction to the blockchain.

One can route a payment through intermediate nodes. For example, if there is a channel between Alice and Bob and a channel between Bob and Charlie, Alice can send funds to Charlie through Bob. The technique that makes payment routing possible is called *Hashed Timelock Contract* (HTLC). For more details on its implementation the reader should refer the original paper [4].

Payment networks are not a new concept. They are studied under different variations of the notion – trust networks [5–7], credit networks [8], path-based transaction (PBT) networks [9] and Payment-Channel Networks (PCN) [10].

There were efforts undertaken to improve the Lightning network. Flare [11] suggests maintaining routing tables to be able to discover paths in the network. Roos et al. [9] proposed an alternative routing scheme that is privacy preserving. Grunspan and Pérez-Marco [12] put forward an idea of ant routing where path lookup requests are passed from node to node in the network. Decker et al. [13] suggested an improvement over the Lightning transaction update mechanism. Malavolta et al. [14] studied the mechanism which binds transactions together, so they can be routed. Another paper from this research group [10] demonstrated a rather surprising trade off between privacy and concurrency in PCNs, and impossibility to achieve both simultaneously. In the later parts of this article, we will show that our proposed mechanism addresses and mitigates the problem. Piatkivskyi et al. [15] brought attention to the problem of colluding nodes and discussed how it influences forensics of the Lightning network. Herrera-Joancomarti et al. [16] gave an overview on the state of the art in privacy issues of payment networks.

3   Split Payments

3.1   Payment Splitting Proposal

The core idea of our proposal is to split payments into a number of smaller sub-payments of equal amounts, i.e. a number of payments of unit amounts, and send them independently, not preserving the atomicity property. There are various ways to split payments up. One way of doing so is amounts of the orders of 10. If a user wants to pay 23 k satoshi, she splits the payment into 2 sub-payments of 10 k satoshi and 3 sub-payments of 1 k satoshi.

Split payments are to be sent independently. At the moment of payment initiation, the sender calculates the cheapest path and begins establishing HTLCs by that path starting with the larger sub-payments. If at any point of time an

HTLC establishment fails, or the sender receives a fee update, she suspends the sub-payments for which HTLCs have not yet been established and re-calculates the cheapest path again. Then the suspended sub-payments are resumed to be sent by the new cheapest path. It may happen that for some larger sub-payment there is no path of needed capacity. In such a case the sub-payment has to be further split. If there is no capacity to route any payments in the needed direction, the whole sub-payment queue is suspended for a timeout. After the timeout is elapsed, an attempt to send the sub-payment is repeated. This process could continue indefinitely until the payment is complete. The user sets a time frame within which the payment is expected to execute. We call such parameter time to live (TTL). Obviously, some payments have to be carried out instantly, while other can wait. It will make a trade off between the time it takes to complete a payment and the fee paid for that payment. A payment is considered successful if all sub-payments are successfully delivered within the set TTL. If a payment has not been delivered within the set TTL, it is marked as failed, even though it could have been partially sent. Such payments are not sent back, consequentially failed payments change the balances of the nodes en route. Partial transitions are further discussed in the following sections.

3.2   Atomic Multi-path Payments

Atomic multi-path payments (AMP) [17] are the implementation of the concept of flows in a flow network. There are number of principal differences that sets AMP and split payments apart. The main difference is that the whole AMP flow executes atomically, that is either all of the sub-payments are sent at once or none. For that, each extended sub-payment remains pending until all sub-payment flows are extended. That increases the duration of funds being locked.

The superiority of split payments success rate comes from the fact that an AMP fails if maximum flow between two nodes is less than the payment amount. Split payments still attempt to execute. As sub-payments are timely spread, there is a chance that within the execution window some payments will pass in the opposite direction increasing the maximum amount that can be sent. A substantial disadvantage is that a payment can be only partially executed. Notwithstanding the transaction acknowledgement complications, we deem partial payments harmless as the rest of the payment can be sent on-chain using splicing [18], if to be sent from a Lightning channel. We stress that partially executed payments do not introduce additional inconvenience. If a payment cannot be executed, it has to be sent in any other way anyway. The non-executed part of a payment can be sent the very same way the whole failed payment would have to be sent.

3.3   Network Analysis

Privacy. The privacy benefits of the proposed strategy are many. First of all, there is no need for routing nodes to disclose current channel capacities. Instead, the paying node, knowing the static topology, can simply request unit payments. The probability that a particular path is able to route a payment is relatively high, given the small unit payment amount. Besides, the fact that all the payments could only be of a certain unit amount makes the payment correlation analysis difficult. Timing analysis will be significantly complicated as there expected to be a large number of such unit payments in the network.

Security. In our proposal the collateral risk is relatively low with split payments because all the actual payments are of unit amount only. If a sub-payment gets stuck, the sender stops using the routing node that failed. Moreover, as there exists a threat of losing money to colluded receiver and a node en route [15], the maximum loss is limited by the amount of the largest sub-payment. If the sender loses money to the colluding nodes, it can simply stop casting the flow.

Concurrency. Split payments transform the problem of possible occurrence of a deadlock into a performance bottleneck. While deadlocks are still theoretically possible, for it to happen a number of sub-payments totaling to the channel capacity have to conglomerate simultaneously at two nodes. We consider the chance of such a deadlock negligible, resolving the trade-off between privacy and concurrency in payment networks described in [10].

Lower fees. The described use of network will presumably yield lower fees for transactions. First of all, it may happen that the cheapest path is not able to process the whole payment due to capacity limitation. Secondly, since payments are sent sequentially, it may happen that a cheaper path will appear some time after the payment has been issued. Most importantly, the more efficient network will naturally drive the transaction cost down.

4   Simulation

A massive effort have been invested into developing a Lightning network simulator called Blyskavka (a Ukrainian word for Lightning). The simulator is meant to be open source, yet making it public requires certain preparations which hinders the release. Blyskavka is a multi-agent simulator that was built for general purpose payment network simulations. It is written in java and uses MASON [19] as a simulation engine. Blyskavka simulates the Lightning network operation rather than the Lightning network itself, meaning it does not simulate the actual transactions being signed and the blockchain communication. It does open and close channels that are modelled as graph edges. It also simulates HTLC's by blocking and then releasing amounts on the path.

The simulation works with the *Newman-Watts–Strogatz* model of the small-world network family, the *uniform random* graph model and a custom model that we call *peripheral*. The *peripheral* graph model differentiates between the core network that consists of routing nodes and the wallet nodes that connect to the core network — the peripheral network. The core network is generated following any other model. Having generated the core network, the wallet nodes are added, choosing randomly K routing nodes to connect to.

The simulation is discrete event based. Each simulation step a node decides what to do—whether to send a payment or not. In all the experiments the payment frequency for each node is once every 25 simulation steps. If a node decides to transfer money, it randomly with uniform distribution selects the destination node and the payment amount within the set range—between 0.1 and 20. As a result, nodes create uniform and symmetric traffic in the network. As payments can be delayed, they are scheduled as well. Each step a payment makes an attempt to execute itself – atomic payments at once, split payments a unit amount sub-payment at a time. If a payment cannot be executed, it is scheduled for the next step until it is out of time to live (TTL). The simulation is flexible on what metrics it can take measurements of. For the purpose of the described research, only success rate was of interest.

For this research we generate both, hub-and-spoke and organic topologies. Hub-and-spoke topology correspond to the *peripheral* graph model, organic topology is described by either the *Newman-Watts–Strogatz* model or by the *uniform random* graph model.

In our experiments we study networks of 1000 and 10000 nodes with different level of connectivity, defined by the parameter K. The small network size is dictated by the poor scalability of the simulator. Hub-and-spoke network has the core network consisting of 20 nodes for the network size of 1000 nodes and 50 nodes for the network size of 10000 nodes. The numbers are chosen deliberately so that the success rate starts low enough to show its increase with *TTL* value. Each node, regardless if it is a routing or wallet node, has K channels with initial capacity of 5 on each side. For this research channel cost is disregarded.

Intuitively, and then proven experimentally, the organic topology efficiency grows with the number of channels in the network. Organic topology with $K = 2$ is very inefficient, hence we set $K = 4$. To match the total funds invested into the hub-and-spoke network under scrutiny, the initial channel capacities should remain 5. We also generate higher connectivity networks with $K = 4$ for hub-and-spoke network and $K = 8$ for organic network.

5   Experiments

It is hard to study the effects a change of a variable causes in the various network properties. For that, all variables that could also affect the success rate of the network have to be fixed, while still conserving the adequate liveliness and soundness of the network. To reduce the number of confounding variables, we randomly generate an instance of a particular network topology, with a given fixed properties. Any comparison is done then for exactly the same network configuration.

In the experiments described in this article TTL is an independent variable, i.e. we study the dependency of success rate on the TTL value. For that, TTL is being varied from 50 simulation steps (where slight TTL increase brings a considerable difference in success rate) to 2000 simulation steps (where there is no longer any substantial increase in success rate with growing value of TTL). That demonstrates how the network improves with longer TTL.

The experiments were performed within a strictly defined framework. Each run lasts at least $N = 3 * TTL$ simulation steps and repeated multiple times to investigate the variance across runs. Furthermore, network topologies were generated randomly and for the same configuration there were generated multiple instances of the same topology, to compensate for a particular instance favouring one or the other model, just out of pure chance of the connectivity of a given instance.

The ultimate benchmark for the network we deem the success rate. To adequately measure it, we run the simulation for a number of steps N, but stop accounting transactions into statistics TTL steps before it finishes. This leaves each transaction enough time to either complete or fail. The transactions in the network, however, are continuously generated and they continue creating traffic (Fig. 1).

5.1 Split payments vs. AMP

The core of the experiments was focused on the comparison of split payments and AMPs. The first thing to notice is the striking difference the splitting makes across all charts, particularly in case of the organic topology. With $TTL > 1000$,

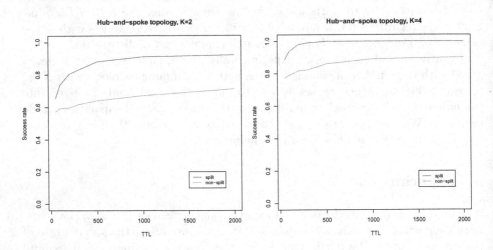

Fig. 1. A 20-1k hub-and-spoke network.

the difference is above 35%. The hub-and-spoke network also shows a significant improvement which is more constant and makes up over 10% improvement, reaching 20% difference for $TTL > 1000$. Those experimental results demonstrate the superiority of split payments when it comes to liquidity. Apart from proving the better performance of split payments these graphs provide hints about what network configurations are more efficient. Even though promising, those hints are not to be considered facts and need to be verified in a more rigorous manner.

Better connectivity networks. In all of the experiments we keep the amount invested in the network at the same level to make the comparisons meaningful. Therefore, when increasing the number of channels K twofold, we divide the average channel capacity by 2. All the figures suggest that it is better to invest less in a single channel and have more channels established. In other words, the more interconnected the network the greater its performance.

Hub-and-spoke topology efficiency. Hub-and-spoke topology is by far outperforming the organic topology, even when the latter has twice as many channels (of half capacity, so the total investment in the network remains constant). Important to note that wallet nodes in the hub-and-spoke topology are not considered when routing. If they take part relaying payments, the efficiency, hence the liquidity, grows considerably. This suggests that in spite of all the shortcomings, some form of centralization will be present as it constitutes a major factor to the network efficiency.

High intensity traffic. Having the same core network, but increased number of wallet nodes increases the success rate in the hub-and-spoke network. The organic network, on the other hand, suffers from the growing number of nodes. On the other hand, the splitting strategy shows the best efficiency for larger organic topologies making the difference of about up to 65%, taking up 34%

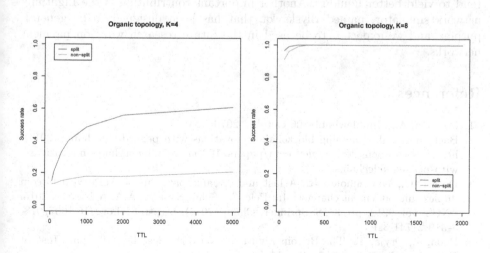

Fig. 2. An organic topology of 1000 nodes.

success rate of atomic multi-path payments to 99% of split payments. This is a rather considerable improvement over the atomic baseline.

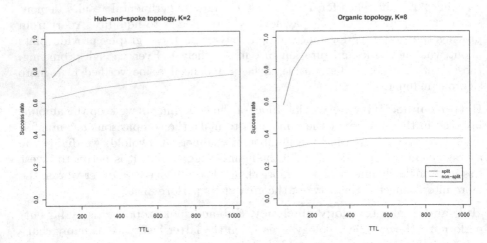

Fig. 3. Networks of 10000 nodes.

6   Conclusions

We have introduced the area of research focusing on payment networks and money flows. We have investigated an improvement in the design of the payment network, based on the split payment model. The new strategy has been experimentally demonstrated to substantially increase the liquidity of payment network. We have investigated what payment network topological characteristics tend to yield better liquidity. Another important contribution is the Lightning network simulator, named Blyskavka, that has been designed to be general-purpose and we expect it to be used in the future research work on payment networks.

References

1. Poelstra, A.: Mimblewimble, 06 October 2016
2. Back, A., et al.: Enabling blockchain innovations with pegged sidechains (2014). http://www.opensciencereview.com/papers/123/enablingblockchain-innovations-with-pegged-sidechains
3. Decker, C., Wattenhofer, R.: A fast and scalable payment network with bitcoin duplex micropayment channels. In: Pelc, A., Schwarzmann, A.A. (eds.) SSS 2015. LNCS, vol. 9212, pp. 3–18. Springer, Cham (2015). https://doi.org/10.1007/978-3-319-21741-3_1
4. Poon, J., Dryja, T.: The Bitcoin Lightning Network: Scalable Off-Chain Instant Payments. Draft version 0.5.9.2, 14 January 2016

5. Ghosh, A., Mahdian, M., Reeves, D.M., Pennock, D.M., Fugger, R.: Mechanism design on trust networks. In: Deng, X., Graham, F.C. (eds.) WINE 2007. LNCS, vol. 4858, pp. 257–268. Springer, Heidelberg (2007). https://doi.org/10.1007/978-3-540-77105-0_25
6. Karlan, D., Mobius, M., Rosenblat, T., Szeidl, A.: Trust and social collateral*. Q. J. Econ. **124**(3), 1307–1361 (2009)
7. Resnick, P., Sami, R.: Sybilproof transitive trust protocols. In: Proceedings of the 10th ACM Conference on Electronic Commerce, EC 2009, pp. 345–354. ACM, New York (2009)
8. Dandekar, P., Goel, A., Govindan, R., Post, I.: Liquidity in credit networks: a little trust goes a long way. In: Proceedings of the 12th ACM Conference on Electronic Commerce, EC 2011, pp. 147–156. ACM, New York (2011)
9. Roos, S., Moreno-Sanchez, P., Kate, A., Goldberg, I.: Settling payments fast and private: efficient decentralized routing for path-based transactions. CoRR, arXiv:abs/1709.05748 (2017)
10. Malavolta, G., Moreno-Sanchez, P., Kate, A., Maffei, M., Ravi, S.: Concurrency and privacy with payment-channel networks. In: Proceedings of the 2017 ACM SIGSAC Conference on Computer and Communications Security, CCS 2017, pp. 455–471. ACM, New York (2017)
11. Prihodko, P., Zhigulin, S., Sahno, M., Ostrovskiy, A., Osuntokun, O.: Flare: An approach to routing in lightning network (2016)
12. Grunspan, C., Pérez-Marco, R.: Ant routing algorithm for the Lightning Network. ArXiv e-prints, June 2018
13. Decker, C., Russell, R., Osuntokun, O.: eltoo: A Simple Layer2 Protocol for Bitcoin. https://blockstream.com/eltoo.pdf (2018)
14. Malavolta, G., Moreno-Sanchez, P., Schneidewind, C., Kate, A., Maffei, M.: Multi-hop locks for secure, privacy-preserving and interoperable payment-channel networks. IACR Cryptology ePrint Archive, 2018:472 (2018)
15. Piatkivskyi, D., Axelsson, S., Nowostawski, M.: A Collusion Attack on the Lightning Network – Implications for Forensics (2017)
16. Herrera-Joancomartí, J., Pérez-Solà, C.: Privacy in bitcoin transactions: new challenges from blockchain scalability solutions. In: Torra, V., Narukawa, Y., Navarro-Arribas, G., Yañez, C. (eds.) MDAI 2016. LNCS (LNAI), vol. 9880, pp. 26–44. Springer, Cham (2016). https://doi.org/10.1007/978-3-319-45656-0_3
17. Osuntokun, O.: AMP: Atomic Multi-Path Payments over Lightning, 06 February 2018
18. Reducing the number of blockchain transactions used by the LN, and the fees paid to confirm them, 21 December 2017
19. Luke, S., Cioffi-Revilla, C., Panait, L., Sullivan, K., Balan, G.: MASON: a multi-agent simulation environment. Simulation **81**(7), 517–527 (2005)

Payment Network Design with Fees

Georgia Avarikioti, Gerrit Janssen, Yuyi Wang$^{(\boxtimes)}$, and Roger Wattenhofer

ETH Zurich, Zurich, Switzerland
{zetavar,gjanssen,yuwang,wattenhofer}@ethz.ch

Abstract. Payment channels are the most prominent solution to the blockchain scalability problem. We introduce the problem of network design with fees for payment channels from the perspective of a Payment Service Provider (PSP). Given a set of transactions, we examine the optimal graph structure and fee assignment to maximize the PSP's profit. A customer prefers to route transactions through the PSP's network if the cheapest path from sender to receiver is financially interesting, i.e., if the path costs less than the blockchain fee. When the graph structure is a tree, and the PSP facilitates all transactions, the problem can be formulated as a linear program. For a path graph, we present a polynomial time algorithm to assign optimal fees. We also show that the star network, where the center is an additional node acting as an intermediary, is a near-optimal solution to the network design problem.

Keywords: Blockchain · Layer 2 · Channels · Lightning protocol

1 Introduction

Scaling the transaction throughput on blockchain systems, such as Bitcoin [12] and Ethereum [1], is a fundamental problem and an active research direction [4]. Many solutions have been proposed, in particular sharding [8,10], sidechains [3] and channels [2,5,9,13]. Channels seem to be the most promising solution since they allow transactions to occur securely off-chain, and use the blockchain only for resolving disputes.

We study the problem from the viewpoint of a Payment Service Provider (PSP). The PSP wants to establish an alternative payment network for customers to execute transactions. We assume a PSP can open a channel between two parties without acting as an intermediate node; this can be done using three-party channels. The two parties and the PSP join a three-party channel funded only by the PSP who then loans money to the other parties. We assume that the PSP will eventually get his money back in fiat currency as he provides a service similar to credit cards (the risk lies to the PSP). Furthermore, the PSP signs each new state if and only if the fees have the correct value. This way he enforces the fee assignment on the channels.

Initially, a PSP will compete with the blockchain: customers only prefer the alternative network if the total fees cost less than the blockchain. We introduce

© Springer Nature Switzerland AG 2018
J. Garcia-Alfaro et al. (Eds.): DPM 2018/CBT 2018, LNCS 11025, pp. 76–84, 2018.
https://doi.org/10.1007/978-3-030-00305-0_6

the network design problem for the PSP, whose goal is to decide the graph structure and the fee assignments in order to maximize its profit.

Our contributions are as follows. First, we provide a linear program formulation for the problem on trees when the PSP wants to facilitate all transactions, proving that this problem variation is in the complexity class P. Then, we show that the optimal fee assignment for any path has only $0/1$ values on the fees, assuming 1 is the cost of posting a transaction on the blockchain, and we present an efficient dynamic programming algorithm to compute the optimal fees. In addition, we prove that the star network is a near-optimal solution of the general network design problem, when we allow an additional node to be added as a payment hub and assume the optimal network is connected. This implies that a PSP can achieve almost maximum profit by creating a payment hub, the construction of which has already been studied in [6,7].

2   Preliminaries and Notation

In this section, we define the *Channels Network Design with Fees (CNDF)* problem. We assume the PSP can renew the channels and change the network structure in specific epochs to avoid timing attacks; hence, we only consider a limited set of transactions corresponding to an epoch. Now, given a set of transactions between a fixed number of participants, we wish to create a payment network and assign fees to its channels to maximize the profit for the PSP. To formally define the problem, we introduce the following notation.

We define a channel network as a graph $G = (V, E)$ with a set of vertices V and a set of edges E. Each node $v \in V$ denotes one of n participants wishing to use our network, hence $|V| = n$. An edge $e \in E$ between two nodes i and j represents an open channel C_{ij}, with $|E| = m$. Thus, the set of edges E represents the open channels of our network. For simplicity, we assume that all edges of the graph are undirected, as we assume the capacity of every channel to be infinite, in other words, the PSP has deep pockets and is able to fund channels with a significant amount of capital. Further, we define the cost of each edge in the network to be 1. This represents the cost of opening a channel by submitting a funding transaction to the blockchain as described in [5,13].

Given a sequence of transactions for n participants, we can define a transaction matrix $T \in \mathbb{N}^{n \times n}$. An entry $T[i, j]$ denotes the number of transactions from i to j and back. Note that matrix T is symmetric since the transactions' direction do not matter. If there are no transactions for a pair (i, j) of nodes, then the corresponding matrix entry is 0. Transactions where sender and receiver are identical are meaningless, thus the diagonal entries of the matrix are 0.

For each edge $e \in E$ we can assign a fee $f_e \in \mathbb{R}$. We require every fee to be non-negative. Moreover, we require the fees to be at most 1, which is the cost of any transaction on the blockchain. Allowing the fee on an edge to be more than 1 is equivalent to deleting this edge from the network, since the customers will always prefer to use the blockchain where the transaction fee is 1. We denote by f_E a fee assignment for the set of edges E.

To measure the value of a network we introduce a profit function. The profit of a payment network depends on the structure of the underlying graph, the fee assignments and the transactions carried out between participants in the network. Given a transaction matrix T, we define the profit of a graph $G = (V, E)$ as follows:

$$p(G, T, f_E) = -m + \sum_{i,j \in V} \sum_{e \in path(i,j)} f_e \cdot X_{ij} \cdot T[i,j],$$

$$\text{where } X_{ij} = \begin{cases} 1, & \text{if the participant chooses to use the network,} \\ & \text{i.e. } \sum_{e \in path(i,j)} f_e \leq 1 \\ 0, & \text{otherwise} \end{cases}$$

where $path(i, j)$ denotes the set of edges of the shortest path (cheapest sum of fees on edges) from sender i to receiver j in the graph G.

We include a pair of nodes (i, j) in the profit calculation only if this sum of fees on the shortest path is at most 1. Finally, we subtract from the profit the number of edges m, since each transaction that opens a channel costs 1 in the blockchain.

Now, we formally define the problem as follows.

Definition 1 *(CNDF). Given a transaction matrix $T \in \mathbb{N}^{n \times n}$, return a graph $G = (V, E)$ with $|V| = n$, and fee assignments on edges f_E, such that the profit function $p(G, T, f_E)$ is maximized.*

In the following two sections we study a relaxed version of the problem, where the network structure is given. Our goal is to calculate the optimal fee assignments. Specifically, in Sect. 3 we examine trees; trees are very natural as they connect a set of nodes with a minimal number of edges, and opening each edge costs a blockchain transaction. In addition we want all customers to prefer the PSP network, thus all paths in a given tree must cost less than 1.

3   A Linear Program for Trees

In this section, we find a solution to CNDF restricted to trees. We assume that every transaction makes sense in the tree, i.e., the sum of the fees on the path of every transaction is at most 1. Therefore, by the model stated above, every user of the payment network will always use the network, and no transaction goes directly on the blockchain. It turns out this problem can be solved efficiently, as stated by the following result.

Theorem 1. *Given any tree and any transaction matrix, there exists a polynomial time algorithm to optimize the profit if every transaction can connect using the payment network.*

Proof. To solve this variation of the problem, we can use linear programming to find the optimal profit along with an optimal assignment of fees. In order to do so for some given tree $G = (V, E)$ and a given transaction matrix T, we need to first determine the objective function that we want to maximize. Moreover, we need to specify suitable inequality constraints.

We compute the objective function by analyzing how many times each transaction uses each edge in the network. This gives us an objective function

$$f(x) = \sum_{i=0}^{m-1} c_i \cdot x_i.$$

The argument of the objective function, a vector $x = (x_0, \cdots, x_{m-1})$ with $m = |E|$ components represents the fees of the edges that we wish to maximize, and c_i denotes the number of times the edge i is used by transactions. Then, to determine the inequality constraints which are imposed by the constraint that each transaction must have a total fee of at most 1, we define one inequality for every transaction t:

$$\sum_{i=0}^{m-1} e_i \cdot x_i \le 1,$$

where $e_i = 1$ if edge i was used for transaction t, and 0 otherwise. Solving this linear program (in polynomial time) finds the optimal vector x of fees.   □

In the following section, we remove the additional assumption that all the transactions should be facilitated by the PSP's network. The problem, now, is more complicated since the selection of transactions cannot be expressed as a linear program (but only as an ILP). Thus, we study the problem in more restricted graph structure: paths.

4   Dynamic Program for Paths

In this section we present Algorithm 1, a polynomial-time dynamic program that achieves optimal profit in chain networks. We prove that the optimal solution has only fees that are either 0 or 1. First we compute tensor M, where $M[i, j, k]$ is the profit from all transactions in the interval $[i, k]$ when the fee of edge j is 1 and every other fee is 0. Then, we compute matrix P, the maximum entry of which is the optimal profit. $P[lastX, x - 1]$ denotes the maximum profit when setting the fee of the edge with index $lastX$ to 1 (it is possible that more edges have a fee of 1 before that, but $lastX$ is the last edge where this is the case) and only using the edges up to $x - 1$. $M[lastX + 1, x, y]$ denotes the profit from edges in the interval $[lastX + 1, y]$ while the x-th edge's fee is 1. For some fixed x, y we iterate over all possible profits of the preceding part of the graph, add it to the profit of the corresponding current interval and only consider the maximal profit (if larger that setting the x-th edge's fee to 1).

To retrieve a fee assignment that has optimal profit, we can do the following: We define an additional matrix E, where the entries of each row are initialized

---

Algorithm 1. Dynamic Program for Paths

Initialization ....

n = number of nodes, m = number of edges, i.e., $n - 1$
Set all entries of $M[m, m, m]$ to 0
Set all entries of $P[m, m]$ to 0

Compute tensor M ....
1 **for** *every* $1 \leq i \leq j \leq k \leq m$:
2      $p = 0$
3   **for** *every entry* $T[u,v]$ *in* T:
4   **if** $u \leq j < v$:
5              $p = p + T[u, v]$
6      $M[i, j, k] = p$

Compute the dynamic programming table ....
7 **for** *every* $1 \leq x \leq y \leq m$:
8      $P[x, y] = M[1, x, y]$
9   **for** $lastX = 1$ **to** $x - 1$:
10   **if** $P[lastX, x-1] + M[lastX+1, x, y] > P[x, y]$:
11              $P[x, y] = P[lastX, x - 1] + M[lastX + 1, x, y]$
12   Store edges with a fee of 1, i.e., x and edges that have a fee of
                1 for $P[lastX, x - 1]$
13 profit = maximum entry in P
14 fee assignment = edges with a fee of 1 stored for the maximum table entry

---

with the number of the row. Now, every time we update an entry $P[x, y]$, we
set $E[x, y] = [x, E[lastX, x - 1]]$. These denote the edges that are assigned a fee
of 1 to attain the calculated profit. When the algorithm has ended, we read the
entry $E[x', y']$, where x', y' are the indices of the maximum value in P, and set
the fee of the edge contained in $E[x', y']$ to 1 in the optimal fee assignment.

Correctness and Runtime. We prove the correctness of Algorithm 1 and analyze
its time complexity. In Algorithm 1, an edge is either assigned a fee of 1 or 0.
The following lemma states that these are indeed the only two values we need
to consider.

Lemma 1. *For every given path and for every set of transactions, the optimal
profit can always be achieved by assigning edges a fee 0 or 1.*

Proof. Assume that we are given some optimal fee assignment $f = (f_1, f_2, \ldots, f_m)$ on the path of length m, and but this assignment may use other values, not only 0 or 1. We show that only using 0 and 1 one also can reach the same (or even more) profit.

Based on the given fee assignment f, we compute the set S of all maximal intervals (i.e., there does not exist a pair of intervals (i, j) and (i', j') such that $i \leq i'$ and $j \geq j'$) where the sum of the fees on the edges in that interval is less or equal to 1. That is, an interval (i, j) is in S if and only if it satisfies that $\sum_{k=i}^{j} f_k \leq 1$ and $\sum_{k=i-1}^{j} f_k > 1$ (or $i = 1$) and $\sum_{k=i}^{j+1} f_k > 1$ (or $j = m$). The optimal profit can be obtained by solving a linear program. It is well known that every linear program reaches its optimal at the vertex of the feasible region. Hence, we only need to show that every entry of every vertex of the feasible region defined above is either 0 or 1. Equivalently, we show that every feasible solution is a convex combination of vectors with only 0 and 1.

We prove this by induction on the length of the path. For the base case, when the length is 1, i.e., a single edge, it is trivial. Now assume that this result holds for paths of length smaller than m, and we prove that it also holds for length equals to m. The key observation is that, for any path, there always exists an assignment f' with only 0 and 1 such that $\sum_{k=i}^{j} f'_k = 1$ for every $(i, j) \in S$, as follows:

1. Let $f'_k = 0$ for all k.
2. For k from 1 to m, consider all intervals (i, j) in S such that $i \leq k \leq j$. If all such intervals (i, j) satisfy $\sum_{t=i}^{j} f'_t = 0$, then let $f'_k = 1$.

We define $K := \{k : f'_k = 1\}$ and let $\theta := \min\{f_k : k \in K\}$. Now we write f as a convex combination $f = \theta \cdot f' + (1 - \theta) \cdot f''$. Since $\sum_{k=i}^{j} f'_k = 1$ for every $(i, j) \in S$, it follows that $\sum_{k=i}^{j} f''_k \leq 1$ for every $(i, j) \in S$. By the definition of θ, we know that there exists at least one index t such that $f''_t = 0$ ($f_t = \theta$). According to these two facts, f'' can be considered as a feasible solution for the path of length $n - 1$, which by the induction hypothesis is also a convex combination of vectors with only 0 and 1. The lemma is proved. □

The above lemma is useful in pruning search space, but it is still exponential (2^m) if we do a brute force search. Our dynamic programming method makes the search space polynomial in m, which is shown in the following theorem.

Theorem 2. *Algorithm 1 returns the optimal solution and the time complexity of the algorithm is $\mathcal{O}(n^5)$.*

Proof. Let $OPT(x, y)$ denote the profit of the sub-path from edge 1 up to and including edge y where we set the fee of edge x ($x \leq y$) to 1. We claim that $OPT(x, y)$ fulfills the following recurrence:

$$OPT(x, y) = \max \begin{cases} M[1, x, y] & \text{(Case 1)} \\ P[lastX, x-1] + M[lastX+1, x, y] & \text{(Case 2)} \end{cases}$$

If $OPT(x, y)$ is equal to *(Case 1)*, this means that we reach the maximum profit in the subgraph from edge 1 to y by only setting the fee of edge x to 1 in the entire subgraph. Consequently, every transaction, that only uses edges from this subgraph, can generate profit.

Otherwise, if $OPT(x, y)$ happens to be *(Case 2)*, we know that there are at least two edges with a fee of 1 in the subgraph from edge 1 to y, namely on edge x and on edge $lastX$. Therefore, profit is generated by transactions in the first part of the subgraph, i.e. from edge 1 to $x - 1$, and at the same time in the second part, that is from $lastX + 1$ to y. However, no transactions, which use edges in both parts of the subgraph, can generate profit, as such a transaction would then cross both edges with a fee of 1.

Because of this, we can iterate over every possible sum of the profits of $P[lastX, x - 1]$ and $M[lastX + 1, x, y]$ and choose the maximum thereof. Note, that we do not necessarily choose the maximum for both terms, but instead pick the maximal sum or otherwise we might only obtain a locally optimal solution. This method can be used, since we were able to split the subgraph from 1 to y in two parts as explained above. Moreover, we have already precomputed both terms: $M[lastX + 1, x, y]$ was computed at the very beginning of the algorithm and $P[lastX, x - 1]$ is always an entry of the table that was the result of a prior computation with exactly the same recurrence.

The tensor M can be computed in time $\mathcal{O}(n^5)$. The computation of the table P can be accomplished in time $\mathcal{O}(n^3)$, since we have 3 loops that iterate over parts of the edge indices. Therefore, the complete algorithm can be implemented with runtime $\mathcal{O}(n^5)$.   □

5   Payment Hub: A Near-Optimal Solution

In this section, we present a near-optimal solution to the *CNDF problem*. Please note that the optimal solution is not always a tree. For example, if we consider three nodes with many transactions between every pair, the optimal payment network is the triangle with a fee of 1 on each edge. A tree will connect the three nodes with a two-edge path, hence none of the trees achieve maximum profit. We show that if the optimal network is connected, then the star graph, where the center is an additional node acting as a payment hub, is a near optimal solution.

We denote $opt(T)$ the profit, G_{opt} the graph and $f_{E_{opt}}$ the fee assignment of the optimal solution for a given transaction matrix T. Moreover, we denote $S = (V_S, E_S)$ the star graph that includes all nodes V and an additional one, c, as the center of the star. We assign uniform fees to all the edges, $f_e = 0.5, \forall e \in E_S$.

Theorem 3. *If G_{opt} is connected, then $p(S, T, f_{E_S}) \geq opt(G_{opt}, T, f_{E_{opt}}) - 1$.*

Proof. If G_{opt} is one connected component, then $|E_{opt}| \geq n - 1$. For the star graph S, we have $V_S = V + c$ and $|E_S| = n \leq E_{opt} + 1$. Furthermore, the sum of fees on all shortest path is equal to 1 due to the uniform fees equal to 0.5 and the star structure. The profit function maximizes its value when all transactions go through the graph G_{opt} with total fee equal to 1, hence

$$opt(G_{opt}, T, f_{E_{opt}}) \le \sum_{i,j \in V} T[i,j] - |E_{opt}| \le \sum_{i,j \in V} T[i,j] - |E_S| + 1 = p(S, T, f_{E_S}) + 1$$

The last equality holds since the sum on every shortest path equals to 1.   □

Discussion on network connectivity. In a monetary system we expect some nodes to be highly connected, representing big companies that transact with many nodes on the network. These highly connected nodes assist in connecting the entire network in one big connected component, as we initially assumed.

6   Related Work

The Lightning Network [13] for Bitcoin [12] and the Raiden Network [2] for Ethereum [1] are the most prominent implemented decentralized path-based transaction networks for payment channels, even though similar proposals existed earlier [5].

Recent work has mainly focused on designing routing algorithms for these networks. The goal of these algorithms is to efficiently find a route in the network that has enough capital to facilitate the current transaction. Prihodko et al. introduced Flare [14], a routing algorithm for the Lightning network. Flare can quickly discover routes but nodes need to collect information on the Lightning network topology. The IOU credit network SilentWhispers [11] utitizes landmark routing to discover multiple paths and then performs multiparty computation to decide how many funds to send along each path. A more recent work by Roos et al. [15] introduces SpeedyMurmurs, which uses embedding-based path discovery to find routes from sender to receiver. In all these algorithms, the task is to find a route to facilitate a customer's transaction through the payment network. Routing very much is orthogonal to our goal of finding the right fees.

Heilman et al. [7] propose a Bitcoin-compatible construction of a payment hub for fast and anonymous off-chain transactions through an untrusted intermediary. Green et al. present Bolt [6] (Blind Off-chain Lightweight Transactions) for constructing privacy-preserving unlinkable and fast payment channels. Both protocols focus on constructing anonymous and private systems that can act as payment hubs. We show that constructing a payment hub is a near optimal strategy with respect to a PSP's profit.

7   Conclusion

To the best of our knowledge, we are the first to introduce a framework for network design with fees on payment channels. We present algorithms that calculate the optimal fee assignments given a path or a tree as a graph structure. Furthermore, we prove the star is a near-optimal solution when we allow adding an extra node to act as an intermediary for the customers. This implies that the construction of payment hubs is an almost optimal strategy for a PSP.

References

1. Ethereum white paper. https://github.com/ethereum/wiki/wiki/White-Paper
2. Raiden network (2017). http://raiden.network/
3. Back, A., et al.: Enabling blockchain innovations with pegged sidechains (2014). https://www.blockstream.com/sidechains.pdf
4. Croman, K., et al.: On scaling decentralized blockchains. In: Clark, J., Meiklejohn, S., Ryan, P.Y.A., Wallach, D., Brenner, M., Rohloff, K. (eds.) FC 2016. LNCS, vol. 9604, pp. 106–125. Springer, Heidelberg (2016). https://doi.org/10.1007/978-3-662-53357-4_8
5. Decker, C., Wattenhofer, R.: A fast and scalable payment network with bitcoin duplex micropayment channels. In: Pelc, A., Schwarzmann, A.A. (eds.) SSS 2015. LNCS, vol. 9212, pp. 3–18. Springer, Cham (2015). https://doi.org/10.1007/978-3-319-21741-3_1
6. Green, M., Miers, I.: Bolt: anonymous payment channels for decentralized currencies. In: Proceedings of the 2017 ACM SIGSAC Conference on Computer and Communications Security, CCS 2017, pp. 473–489 (2017)
7. Heilman, E., Alshenibr, L., Baldimtsi, F., Scafuro, A., Goldberg, S.: TumbleBit: an untrusted bitcoin-compatible anonymous payment hub. In: Network and Distributed Systems Security Symposium 2017 (NDSS), February 2017
8. Kokoris-Kogias, E., Jovanovic, P., Gasser, L., Gailly, N., Syta, E., Ford, B.: OmniLedger: a secure, scale-out, decentralized ledger via sharding (2017)
9. Lind, J., Eyal, I., Pietzuch, P., Sirer, E.G.: Teechan: payment channels using trusted execution environments. arXiv preprint arXiv:1612.07766 (2016)
10. Luu, L., Narayanan, V., Zheng, C., Baweja, K., Gilbert, S., Saxena, P.: A secure sharding protocol for open blockchains. In: Proceedings of the 2016 ACM SIGSAC Conference on Computer and Communications Security, pp. 17–30. ACM (2016)
11. Malavolta, G., Moreno-Sanchez, P., Kate, A., Maffei, M.: SilentWhispers: Enforcing security and privacy in decentralized credit networks. In: Network and Distributed Systems Security Symposium 2017 (NDSS)
12. Nakamoto, S.: Bitcoin: a peer-to-peer electronic cash system (2008)
13. Poon, J., Dryja, T.: The bitcoin lightning network: Scalable off-chain instant payments (2015). https://lightning.network
14. Prihodko, P., Zhigulin, S., Sahno, M., Ostrovskiy, A., Osuntokun, O.: Flare: an approach to routing in lightning network (2016). https://bitfury.com/content/downloads/whitepaper_flare_an_approach_to_routing_in_lightning_network_7_7_2016.pdf
15. Roos, S., Moreno-Sanchez, P., Kate, A., Goldberg, I.: Settling payments fast and private: Efficient decentralized routing for path-based transactions. In: Network and Distributed Systems Security Symposium (NDSS) (2018)

Atomic Information Disclosure of Off-Chained Computations Using Threshold Encryption

Oliver Stengele[(✉)] and Hannes Hartenstein

Institute of Telematics, Karlsruhe Institute of Technology, Karlsruhe, Germany
{oliver.stengele,hannes.hartenstein}@kit.edu

Abstract. Public Blockchains on their own are, by definition, incapable of keeping data private and disclosing it at a later time. Control over the eventual disclosure of private data must be maintained outside a Blockchain by withholding and later publishing encryption keys, for example. We propose the Atomic Information Disclosure (AID) pattern based on threshold encryption that allows a set of key holders to govern the release of data without having access to it. We motivate this pattern with problems that require independently reproduced solutions. By keeping submissions private until a deadline expires, participants are unable to plagiarise and must therefore generate their own solutions which can then be aggregated and analysed to determine a final answer. We outline the importance of a game-theoretically sound incentive scheme, possible attacks, and other future work.

Keywords: Consensus · Off-chain construction · Atomic disclosure

1 Introduction

Decentralised consensus systems like Bitcoin and Ethereum brought with them the prospect of widespread disintermediation. However, it was soon realised that not every interaction could feasibly be recorded on a Blockchain. By using off-chain constructions, a Blockchain can still serve as coordinator and final arbiter, thus maintaining all the security guarantees, while minimising the space and effort required for permanent records.

Recently, off-chain mechanisms have been used to execute tasks that are too complex for the Blockchain, or rather the Smart Contract execution environment [11]. A prominent example of this concept is TrueBit [15]. However, there is a class of problems that are not well suited for systems like TrueBit. These problems follow the concept of a seminal paper by Ken Thompson on trust [16], namely that they are best approached through independent reproduction and verification [17] rather than individual and sequential challenges.

To facilitate independence in producing and reproducing solutions to a given task, the disclosure of said solutions is crucial. After all, if a solution is known,

© Springer Nature Switzerland AG 2018
J. Garcia-Alfaro et al. (Eds.): DPM 2018/CBT 2018, LNCS 11025, pp. 85–93, 2018.
https://doi.org/10.1007/978-3-030-00305-0_7

then actually performing work to reproduce the same result or just copying it without performing any work is indistinguishable for an outside observer. To preempt this problem, we propose the use of threshold encryption to allow an arbitrary number of submissions to be disclosed atomically. By that we mean that participants can publicly commit to a solution, without revealing it to anyone, in such a way that all submissions will be disclosed simultaneously.

The remainder of this position paper is structured as follows. The subsequent Sect. 2 opens with motivating examples for the application for the proposed pattern and follows with related work from various fields of research. In Sect. 3, we outline the Atomic Information Disclosure (AID) pattern and discuss it in Sect. 4, in which we also enumerate future work and conclude the paper.

2   Problem Motivation and Related Work

In this section, we describe three examples for the application of the AID pattern and outline how previous works relate to our approach.

Compilation of Software. As mentioned previously, Ken Thompson famously described how compilers could be compromised to embed flaws into binaries compiled with them, without leaving any indications for said compromise in the source code of the compiler [16]. As a countermeasure, Wheeler presents the concept of *Diverse Double-Compiling* [17], where the outputs of a potentially compromised and a trustworthy compiler are compared against each other to determine a correct build. In lieu of a single trusted compiler, we can use the AID pattern to generalise the concept by Wheeler to an arbitrary number of compilers in the hopes that the majority of them are not compromised. An interesting pitfall specific to this example stems from the fact that benign and malicious versions of the same binary can be very hard to distinguish. Making use of similarity metrics when analysing the results of multiple independent compilations could therefore cause more harm than good. We address this further in Sect. 4.

Verification of Software. Similar to the first example, we can also look towards the verification of software that has already been compiled for a possible application of the AID pattern. Asking a single company to check a given piece of software for certain (security) properties leaves one open to the possibility of fraud. The company could simply certify that every property is fulfilled, without actually performing any work. The AID pattern can be used to pit several companies against each other, forcing them to perform their duties faithfully.

Experimental Science. Lastly, we also note similarities between the functionality of the AID pattern and the scientific process regarding experiments. Reproducibility of results is one of the hallmarks of science. Contrary to the current model of publishing results and expecting others to either reproduce or refute them, which is open to plagiarism, a lack of reproduction, and other issues, a methodology based on atomic disclosure would preempt these problems by enabling independent groups of scientists to perform experiments in parallel and disclose their results simultaneously.

There are some similarities between these use cases that deserve explicit mention. In all cases, the effort necessary to produce and reproduce results is significant and comparable to each other. There is also an entire set of possible results from which a final answer is to be selected. And lastly, the trustworthiness or reliability of results grows with independent reproduction. As mentioned previously, it is the independence of reproduced solutions that we aim to achieve through the AID pattern.

Now, we will go over previous works from rather different areas of research that our approach is related to.

With Bitcoin [12], the feasibility of a Blockchain-based consensus system was first demonstrated. Ethereum [5] later generalised this concept to build a global state machine complete with a programmatic method for interacting with it, namely *Smart Contracts* [14].

Both in Bitcoin and in Ethereum, *miners* compete against each other to verify transactions submitted by users and publish them in newly mined blocks that are appended to the Blockchain. The miner that finds a new block is rewarded by the system for providing an integral service[1]. The remaining miners are then expected to check the newly published block for validity and to decide whether to build upon this new block, thereby proclaiming their accordance with it, or fork the Blockchain by building on top of the previous block in the event that they disagree with the new block. This verification of published blocks is not rewarded in any way, but is nevertheless a critical requirement to ensure the security properties of the Blockchain.

In the case of Bitcoin, the verification of new blocks is negligible compared to the process of mining. In Ethereum, however, this is not necessarily the case considering that arbitrarily complex Smart Contracts have to be executed in order to check the validity of any given block. Luu et al. [11] demonstrated that honest miners can be presented with a *verifier's dilemma* if the verification of published blocks requires non-negligible effort: If the miners choose to perform the verification, they put themselves at a disadvantage with regard to finding new blocks; if they forgo the verification, they risk mining on an invalid branch of the Blockchain. To combat this, Ethereum limits the amount of computation that can be executed and that must be verified within a block.

In general, it would seem that Blockchain-based consensus systems with mutual verification inevitably place an upper bound on the complexity of computations that can be executed and on whose results the system provides consensus. To circumvent these limitations, several mechanisms have been proposed in the past that allow processes to run *off-chain* while still relying on the Blockchain as the coordinator and final arbiter in case of dispute. Eberhardt and Tai [9] present an overview of common off-chain patterns. While their list was compiled

---

[1] Note that this reward requires the agreement of other miners. If they fork the Blockchain and the block in question becomes *stale*, then the miner in question will not receive any reward.

from past experiences, we look towards a new set of problems with our approach that has not been tackled yet.

Similar to off-chain patterns, in the sense that they enable the circumvention of the previously mentioned complexity bound, but vastly larger in terms of scale, are entire platforms like TrueBit [15]. In order to ensure the validity of outsourced computations, TrueBit employs a *verification game*, where a solver and a verifier narrow down the point of contention in the outsourced computation until it can be executed by Ethereum miners who subsequently resolve the dispute. While TrueBit would appear quite suitable for the problems at hand, we note that problems with a set of valid solutions could be challenged ad infinitum. Concurrently and independently generated solutions appear to be a valid approach to overcome this problem.

As previously mentioned, we propose to use a threshold encryption scheme to facilitate the submission of solutions in such a way that they become public simultaneously, thus allowing each solver to work independently. Threshold encryption was first introduced by Desmedt [7, 8] and later improved by Pedersen [13] and Boneh [4]. Broadly speaking, threshold encryption enables the sharing of decryption capabilities among a group of parties such that t of them, called a *threshold*, have to cooperate in order to perform the decryption. The contribution by Pedersen [13] is especially noteworthy for demonstrating that a threshold encryption scheme can be constructed without a trusted dealer who would generate and distribute the individual key shares. Boneh [4] then improved the efficiency of threshold encryption schemes without trusted dealers to the point where an Ethereum Smart Contract could potentially verify the correctness of the setup and later perform decryption operations if enough parties publish their respective key share. The necessary operations fall within integer arithmetic that should be practical within Smart Contracts.

Very recently, Kokoris-Kogias et al. [10] have also employed threshold encryption to achieve distributed access control on a public ledger. While their construction of *One-Time Secrets* appears functionally similar to the AID pattern, their architecture requires the sender of a secret to be the trusted dealer in the threshold encryption setup. Our approach, by contrast, requires a dealerless threshold encryption scheme so that multiple senders can encrypt their secrets into one atomically disclosable pile. Our more open use-case also necessitates an incentive scheme and other security mechanisms.

In a way, the AID pattern could be classified as a form of pseudonymous voting on a correct solution to a given task. Voting on Blockchains is a comparatively young but quite fruitful area of research [1,2,18]. In a similar vein, but related to a very different area of computer science, one could also draw parallels between our pattern and *MapReduce* [6], with the *Map* phase being the off-chained computation and the *Reduce* step as the election of a final solution by a Blockchain.

3   Atomic Information Disclosure Pattern

In this section, we describe an off-chain pattern to solve a resource-intensive problem that requires parallel, independent reproduction of solutions through the use of threshold encryption. An overview of this pattern is presented in Fig. 1. The general idea of our pattern is to have an arbitrary number of participants generate solutions to a given task which are then published to a Blockchain where a final solution is elected from the candidates based on the number of times it was reproduced independently. Threshold encryption keeps the submissions private until the submission phase is over.

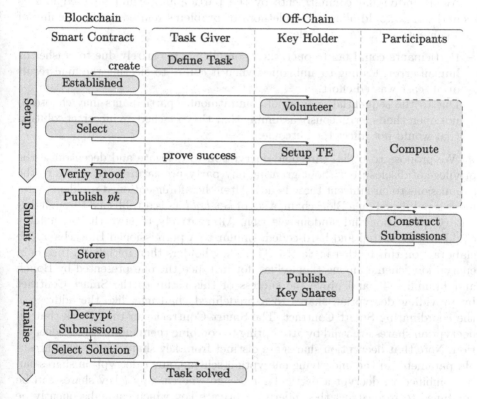

Fig. 1. Sequence diagram of our off-chain pattern. Threshold encryption is abbreviated as TE.

It is at this point important to note that we only discuss the general approach in this position paper. Crucial components such as the incentive scheme or implementation details are left as future work, see Sect. 4.

Setup Phase. Initially, a task giver defines a Smart Contract that includes:

- The problem to be solved,
- A schedule for the subsequent phases,
- The logic for selecting a final solution from the submitted candidates.

This initial problem statement also includes integrity preserving references to any required data. In order to facilitate the independent generation of solutions, submissions need to be kept private until the stated submission deadline is expired. Since a public Blockchain is, by definition, incapable of executing this task, the privilege of revealing submissions has to be kept outside the respective Blockchain system.

While individual commitments by the participants could be used in this scenario, this would allow for a plethora of problems related to the opening of said commitments. For example:

- Participants could fail to open their commitments entirely due to crashes or human error, leading to ambiguity when it comes to electing the final result or at least wasted effort.
- Due to the sequential opening of commitments, participants may choose to not open theirs, erroneously assuming that they reached an incorrect solution that would not affect the outcome.

We propose to utilise threshold encryption to delegate and decentralise the privilege of disclosure without granting any party premature read access to the submissions to circumvent these issues. After the aforementioned problem statement is published on a Blockchain, a set of *key holders* is established through voluntary application and random selection. Alternatively, trustworthy key holders could also be vetted and hard-coded, similar to a permissioned Blockchain. We elaborate on this further in Sect. 4. These key holders then initialise a threshold encryption scheme among themselves, for instance the one presented by Boneh and Franklin [4], and prove the success of this setup to the Smart Contract by providing decryption shares to a predefined challenge, like the address of the coordinating Smart Contract. The Smart Contract can then check that all decryption shares are valid by attempting to combine them into a correct decryption. Note that decryption shares are distinct from key shares. If t is the threshold parameter of the underlying encryption scheme, any t decryption shares can be combined to decrypt a particular message whereas any t key shares can be combined to reconstruct the underlying private key which can subsequently be used to decrypt any message encrypted with this scheme, both past and future. We will employ the latter in the last phase of our pattern. Once the setup is complete, the key holders generate and publish a public key on the Blockchain that can be used to encrypt submissions. Note at this point that a threshold encryption scheme without a trusted dealer is essential for this application, as the dealer would otherwise be able to read all submissions and could therefore subvert the entire process.

Submission Phase. Once the key holders have successfully initialised the threshold encryption scheme, participants can construct submissions by using the corresponding public key to encrypt their individual results. Depending on the expected number of submissions, they can either be recorded on the Blockchain itself or directed to off-chain storage like Ethereum Swarm or IPFS [3]. Keep in mind that participants could have started the necessary computation immediately after the task was published, parallel to the setup of the threshold encryption scheme. The submission phase lasts as long as the task giver specified in the beginning.

Finalisation Phase. To begin the finalisation phase, the key holders are expected to publish their respective key share. This also serves as an irrevocable termination of the submission phase. If at least t key holders do this, all submissions will become readable to the public simultaneously. It is worth pointing out that once $t - 1$ key holders publish their key shares, the remaining key holders gain read access to the submissions. While this is certainly an advantageous position, it is very fleeting, since only one more key share suffices to extend read access to the public, and it is not very exploitable, as no new submissions by the key holders would be accepted at this point. The now public submissions can then be analysed and a final result can be elected based on the logic defined in the initial Smart Contract.

4   Discussion and Future Work

The purpose of this position paper is mainly to propose the use of threshold encryption in conjunction with Blockchains, especially those supporting Smart Contracts, to facilitate the concurrent and independent solving by multiple parties of certain problems that benefit from it. This benefit lies mainly in the increased certainty about the correctness of the solution. As such, several key aspects are left for future work. In this section, we elaborate on these and highlight possible pitfalls.

Probably the most crucial component after the functionally necessary primitives is the incentive scheme. Without a reason to both participate and to produce correct solutions, the whole scheme is futile. This issue becomes somewhat circular, given that we attempt to determine a correct solution through the process we try to incentivise based on the correctness of submitted solutions. Furthermore, the incentive scheme has to deal with possible collusions and bribery of task givers, participants, and key holders. This is doubly relevant since we do not enforce these roles to be disjoint. A task giver may also be a key holder and may also provide a solution. We intend to construct and game-theoretically analyse an incentive scheme in a future work.

Related to the incentive scheme but best viewed separate are possible attacks against the AID pattern. In general terms, we expect attacks that pursue any combination of these three goals:

- Influence the selection of the accepted solution
- Gain rewards disproportionate to the exerted effort
- Prevent the pattern from working entirely (*Denial of Service*)

Established off-chain mechanisms, like the Challenge-Response pattern mentioned by Eberhardt [9], may prove useful in stifling some of these attacks. One technique that deserves special mention at this point is sybil attacks. Without a widely adopted identity scheme, it is up to the incentive scheme to discourage participants from submitting the same solution multiple times though sybil accounts to either sway the final election or reap greater rewards compared to only submitting once. Similarly, a sybil attack on the threshold encryption scheme could enable the attacker to gain premature read access on the submissions. A collusion between sufficiently many key holders can accomplish the same goal without producing evidence on-chain. Here, a mechanism for rewarding the betrayal of such a collusion on-chain could be used as a countermeasure. The parametrisation of the encryption scheme and the selection of key holders is therefore a crucial line of defence. When deciding the parameters of the encryption scheme, availability and collusion resistance have to be weighed against each other carefully since they can be seen as opposing goals. The easier it is for the key holders to complete the protocol (availability), the lower might be the resistance to collusion, and vice versa.

The system used to store submissions is also a crucial component to mention at this point. During the entire process, it has to be available in addition to ensuring the integrity of submitted solutions. It would also be useful if the system could employ size and rate limits to impede denial of service attacks.

Lastly, we plan to put our pattern into practice with a functional prototype. Of primary interest in this regard are the costs for its execution and the strain we put on the selected Blockchain system relative to the number of participants.

One interesting pitfall we have already identified is the use and abuse of similarity metrics when electing final solutions. If the concrete application allows for such a metric to be defined in the initial Smart Contract, one might be inclined to use it to cluster submissions together in order to not require exact replication. This way, a more robust and reliable selection process might be possible compared to just looking for the number of reproductions. However, we must remark that the opposite is also possible. Since the metric is part of the initial Smart Contract, and therefore public, an attacker might construct malicious submissions that are similar, in terms of the metric, to the likely majority solution but functionally nefarious. The aforementioned clustering mechanism could then lend credence to such a malicious solution and increase the chances of its election as the final answer. This example serves to demonstrate how crucial the selection logic in the coordinating Smart Contract is.

In conclusion, we believe that the combination of threshold encryption and Blockchain-based consensus systems holds great potential for various applications that have not been feasible before. The ability to delegate the disclosure of data not to a singular third party but to a collective of key holders without granting premature read access promises to find application in various contexts. The off-chain pattern we outlined here is hopefully only a first step.

Acknowledgements. This work was supported by the German Federal Ministry of Education and Research within the framework of the project KASTEL_ISE in the Competence Center for Applied Security Technology (KASTEL).

We would like to thank the anonymous reviewers for their feedback, especially for bringing the work by Kokoris-Kogias et al. [10] to our attention.

References

1. Bartoletti, M., Pompianu, L.: An empirical analysis of smart contracts: platforms, applications, and design patterns. In: Brenner, M., et al. (eds.) FC 2017. LNCS, vol. 10323, pp. 494–509. Springer, Cham (2017). https://doi.org/10.1007/978-3-319-70278-0_31
2. Bartolucci, S., Bernat, P., Joseph, D.: SHARVOT: secret SHARe-based VOTing on the blockchain. arXiv.org, March 2018
3. Benet, J.: IPFS - Content Addressed, Versioned, P2P File System. arXiv.org, July 2014
4. Boneh, D., Franklin, M.: Efficient generation of shared RSA keys. In: Kaliski, B.S. (ed.) CRYPTO 1997. LNCS, vol. 1294, pp. 425–439. Springer, Heidelberg (1997). https://doi.org/10.1007/BFb0052253
5. Buterin, V.: A next-generation smart contract and decentralized application platform. White paper (2014)
6. Dean, J., Ghemawat, S.: MapReduce - simplified data processing on large clusters. Commun. ACM **51**(1), 107 (2008)
7. Desmedt, Y.: Society and group oriented cryptography: a new concept. In: Pomerance, C. (ed.) CRYPTO 1987. LNCS, vol. 293, pp. 120–127. Springer, Heidelberg (1988). https://doi.org/10.1007/3-540-48184-2_8
8. Desmedt, Y.: Threshold cryptosystems (1993)
9. Eberhardt, J., Tai, S.: On or off the blockchain? Insights on off-chaining computation and data. In: De Paoli, F., Schulte, S., Broch Johnsen, E. (eds.) ESOCC 2017. LNCS, vol. 10465, pp. 3–15. Springer, Cham (2017). https://doi.org/10.1007/978-3-319-67262-5_1
10. Kokoris-Kogias, E., et al.: Hidden in plain sight - storing and managing secrets on a public ledger. IACR Cryptology ePrint Archive (2018)
11. Luu, L., Teutsch, J., Kulkarni, R., Saxena, P.: Demystifying incentives in the consensus computer. In: The 22nd ACM SIGSAC Conference, pp. 706–719. ACM Press, New York (2015)
12. Nakamoto, S.: Bitcoin: a peer-to-peer electronic cash system. bitcoin.org (2008)
13. Pedersen, T.P.: A threshold cryptosystem without a trusted party. In: Davies, D.W. (ed.) EUROCRYPT 1991. LNCS, vol. 547, pp. 522–526. Springer, Heidelberg (1991). https://doi.org/10.1007/3-540-46416-6_47
14. Szabo, N.: Formalizing and securing relationships on public networks. First Monday **2**(9) (1997)
15. Teutsch, J., Reitweißner, C.: A scalable verification solution for blockchains. people.cs.uchicago.edu, March 2017
16. Thompson, K.: Reflections on trusting trust. Commun. ACM **27**(8), 761–763 (1984)
17. Wheeler, D.: Countering trusting trust through diverse double-compiling. In: 21st Annual Computer Security Applications Conference (ACSAC 2005), pp. 33–48. IEEE (2005)
18. Zīle, K., Strazdiņa, R.: Blockchain use cases and their feasibility. Appl. Comput. Syst. **23**(1), 12–20 (2018)

Contour: A Practical System for Binary Transparency

Mustafa Al-Bassam$^{(\boxtimes)}$ and Sarah Meiklejohn

University College London, London, UK
{mustafa.al-bassam.16,s.meiklejohn}@ucl.ac.uk

Abstract. Transparency is crucial in security-critical applications that rely on authoritative information, as it provides a robust mechanism for holding these authorities accountable for their actions. A number of solutions have emerged in recent years that provide transparency in the setting of certificate issuance, and Bitcoin provides an example of how to enforce transparency in a financial setting. In this work we shift to a new setting, the distribution of software package binaries, and present a system for so-called "binary transparency." Our solution, Contour, uses proactive methods for providing transparency, privacy, and availability, even in the face of persistent man-in-the-middle attacks. We also demonstrate, via benchmarks and a test deployment for the Debian software repository, that Contour is the only system for binary transparency that satisfies the efficiency and coordination requirements that would make it possible to deploy today.

1 Introduction

Systems that require a large degree of trust from participants can be made accountable through transparency, where information about the decisions within the system are made globally visible, thus enabling any participant to check for themselves whether or not the decisions comply with what they perceive to be the rules.

One of the technical settings in which the idea of transparency has been most thoroughly—and successfully—deployed is the issuance of X.509 certificates. This is partially due to the many publicized failures of major certificate authorities (CAs) [14,19]. A long line of recent research [3,7,16,18,20,21,25,28] has provided and analyzed solutions that bring transparency to the issuance of both X.509 certificates ("certificate transparency") and to the assignment of public keys to end users ("key transparency").

Many of these systems share a fundamentally similar architecture [5]: after being signed by CAs, certificates are stored by *log servers* in a globally visible append-only log; i.e., in a log in which entries cannot be deleted without detection. Clients are told to not accept certificates unless they have been included in such a log, and to determine this they rely on *auditors*, who are responsible for checking inclusion of the specific certificates seen by clients. Because auditors

© Springer Nature Switzerland AG 2018
J. Garcia-Alfaro et al. (Eds.): DPM 2018/CBT 2018, LNCS 11025, pp. 94–110, 2018.
https://doi.org/10.1007/978-3-030-00305-0_8

are often thought of software running on the client (e.g., a browser extension), they must be able to operate efficiently. Finally, in order to expose misbehavior, *monitors* (inefficiently) inspect the certificates stored in a given log to see if they satisfy the rules of the system.

To detect log equivocation, these systems use *gossiping* protocols [6,24], where the auditor and monitor periodically exchange information on their current and previous views of the log, which allows them to detect whether or not their views are *consistent*, and thus whether or not the log server is misbehaving by presenting "split" views of the log. If such attacks are possible, then the accountability of the system is destroyed, as a log server can present one log containing all certificates to auditors (thus convincing it that its certificates are in the log), and one log containing only "good" certificates to monitors (thus convincing them that all participants in the system are obeying the rules).

While gossiping can detect this misbehavior, it is ultimately a retroactive mechanism—i.e., it detects this behavior after an auditor has already accepted a certificate as valid and it is too late—and is thus most effective in settings where (1) no persistent man-in-the-middle (MitM) attack can occur, so the line of communication between an auditor and monitors remains open, and (2) some form of external punishment is possible, to sufficiently disincentivize misbehavior on the basis of detection. Specifically for (1), if an auditor has no means of communication that is not under an adversary's control for the foreseeable future (a scenario we refer to as a persistent MitM attack), then the adversary may block all gossip being sent to and from the auditor, and thus monitors may never see evidence of log servers misbehaving.

Various systems have been proposed recently that use proactive transparency mechanisms designed to operate in settings where these assumptions cannot be made, such as Collective Signing [27] (CoSi), but perhaps the most prominent example of such a system is Bitcoin (and all cryptocurrencies based on the idea of a *blockchain*). In Bitcoin, all participants have historically played the simultaneous role of log servers (in storing all Bitcoin transactions), auditors, and monitors (in checking that no double-spending takes place). The high level of integrity achieved by this comes at great expense to the participants, in terms of computational resources (the Bitcoin blockchain is currently over 100 GB). CoSi [27] achieves this property by allowing a group of witnesses to collectively sign statements to indicate that they have been "seen," but assumes the setup and maintenance of a Sybil-free set of witnesses, which introduces a large coordination effort.

Because of the effectiveness of these approaches, there has been interest in repurposing them to provide not only transparency for certificates or monetary transfers, but for more general classes of objects ("general transparency" [8]). One specific area that thus far has been relatively unexplored is the setting of software distribution ("binary transparency"). Bringing transparency to this setting is increasingly important, as there are an increasing number of cases in which actors target devices with malicious software signed by the authoritative keys of update servers. For example, the Flame malware, discovered in 2012, was signed by a rogue Microsoft certificate and masqueraded as a routine Microsoft software update [14]. In 2016, a US court compelled Apple to produce and sign custom firmware in order to disable security measures on a phone that the FBI wanted to unlock [11].

Challenges of Binary Transparency. Aside from its growing relevance, binary transparency is particularly in need of exploration because the techniques described above for both certificate transparency and Bitcoin cannot be directly translated to this setting. Whereas certificates and Bitcoin transactions are small (on the order of kilobytes), software binaries can be arbitrarily large (often on the order of gigabytes), so cannot be easily stored and replicated in a log or ledger.

Most importantly, by their very nature software packages have the ability to execute arbitrary code on a system, so malicious software packages can easily disable gossiping mechanisms, and we cannot assume that the auditor always has a means of communication that is not under an adversary's control. Specifically, as discussed earlier a malicious adversary may perform a MitM attack to prevent gossip while presenting an auditor a malicious view of the log, and the log may itself contain a malicious software update that executes code to disable gossiping. This makes retroactive methods for detecting misbehavior uniquely poorly suited to this setting, in which clients need to know that a software package has been inspected by independent parties *before* installing it, not after. Binary transparency systems relying on such retroactive methods, based on Certificate Transparency, are currently being proposed for Firefox [1].

Our Contributions. We present Contour, a solution for binary transparency that utilizes the Bitcoin blockchain to proactively prevent clients from installing malicious software, even in the face of long-term MitM attacks. Concretely, we contribute a realistic threat model for this setting and demonstrate that Contour is able to meet it; we also show, via comparison with previous solutions, that Contour is currently the only solution able to satisfy these security properties while still maintaining efficiency and a minimal level of coordination among the various participants in the system. We also provide a prototype implementation that further demonstrates the efficiency of Contour, and finally provide an argument for its practicality via a test deployment for the Debian software repository. Putting everything together, we view Contour as a solution for binary transparency that is ready to be deployed today.

2   Related Work

There is a significant volume of work on the idea of transparency, particularly in the settings of certificates and keys. While Contour uses similar techniques to previous solutions within these other contexts, to the best of our knowledge it is the first full deployable solution in the context of binary transparency.

In terms of certificate transparency, AKI [16] and ARPKI [3] provide a distributed infrastructure for the issuance of certificates, thus providing a way to prevent rather than just detect misbehavior. Certificate Transparency (CT) [18] focuses on the storage of certificates rather than their issuance, Ryan [25] demonstrated how to handle revocation within CT, and Dowling et al. [7] provided a proof of security for it. Eskandarian et al. [9] propose how to make some aspects of gossiping in CT more privacy-friendly using zero-knowledge proofs. CONIKS [21] focuses instead on key transparency, and thus pays more attention to privacy and does not require the use of monitors (but rather has users monitor their own public keys).

In terms of solutions that avoid gossip, Fromknecht et al. [12] propose a decentralized PKI based on Bitcoin and Namecoin, and IKP [20] provides a way to issue certificates based on Ethereum. EthIKS [4] provides an Ethereum-based solution for key transparency and concurrently with our work, Catena [28] provides one based on Bitcoin. While both Catena and Contour utilize similar recent features of Bitcoin to achieve efficiency, they differ in their focus (key vs. binary transparency), and thus in the proposed threat model; e.g., they dismiss eclipse attacks [26] on the Bitcoin network, whereas we consider them well within the scope of a MitM attacker. Chainiac [23] is a system for proactive software update transparency based on a verifiable data structure called a skipchain. Chainiac uses a consensus mechanism based on Collective Signing (CoSi) [27], leading to the need for an authority to maintain a Sybil-free set of nodes. CoSi [17,27] is a general consensus mechanism that shares our goal of providing transparency even in the face of MitM attacks and thus avoids gossiping, but requires setting up a distributed set of "witnesses" that is free of Sybils. This is a deployment overhead that we avoid.

3   Background

3.1   Software Distribution

Software distribution on modern desktop and mobile operating systems is managed through centralized software repositories such as the Apple App Store, the Android Play Store, or the Microsoft Store. Most Linux distributions such as Debian also have their own software repositories from which administrators can install and update software packages using command-line programs.

To reduce the trust required in these repositories, efforts such as *deterministic builds* allow users to verify that a compiled binary corresponds to the published source code of open-source software. While this prevents developers from inserting malicious code into the compiled binaries, it does not address the targeted malware threat that Contour aims to solve, in which the source code (or binary) for one targeted set of users is different from the copy received by everyone else.

3.2   Distributed Ledgers

Briefly, the Bitcoin [22] blockchain is (literally) a chain of blocks. Each block contains two components: a *header* and a list of transactions. In addition to other metadata, the header stores the hash of the block (which, in compliance with the proof-of-work consensus mechanism, must be below some threshold in order to show that a certain amount of so-called "hashing power" has been expended to form the block), the hash of the previous block (thus enabling the chain property), and the root of the Merkle tree that consists of all transactions in the block.

On the constructive side, Bitcoin transactions can store small amounts of arbitrary data. One mechanism to do this is the script opcode OP_RETURN, which can be used to embed up to 80 bytes of arbitrary data.

Another aspect of Bitcoin that enables additional development is the idea of an Simple Payment Verification (SPV) client. Rather than perform the expensive verification of every Bitcoin transaction, these clients check only that a given transaction has made it into some block in the blockchain. As this can be achieved using only the root hashes stored in the block headers, such clients can store only these headers (which are small) and verify only Merkle proofs of inclusion obtained from "full" nodes (which is fast), and are thus significantly more efficient than their full node counterparts.

On the destructive side, various attacks have been demonstrated that undermine the security guarantees of Bitcoin. In *eclipse* attacks [2,13,15], an adversary exploits the topology of the Bitcoin network to interrupt, or at least delay, the delivery of announcements of new transactions and blocks to a victim node. More expensive "51%" attacks, in which the adversary controls more than half of the collective hashing power of the network, allow the adversary to fork the blockchain, and it has been demonstrated [10] that such attacks can in fact be carried out with far less than 51% of the hashing power.

4   Threat Model and Setting

We consider a system with five types of actors, described below.

Service: The service is responsible for producing actions, such as the issuance of a software update. In order to have these binaries authorized, they must be sent to the authority.

Authority: The authority is responsible for publishing *statements* that declare it has received a given software binary from a service. These statements also claim that the authority has published these binaries in a way that allows them to be inspected by the monitor. The authority is also responsible for placing its statements into a public *audit log*, where they can be efficiently verified by the auditor.

Monitor: The monitor is responsible for inspecting the binaries published by the authority and performing out-of-band tests to determine their validity (e.g., to ensure that software updates do not contain malware).

Auditor: The auditor is responsible for checking specific binaries against the statements made by the authority that claim they are published.

Client: The client receives software updates from either the authority or the service, along with a statement that claims the update has been published for inspection. It outsources all responsibility to the auditor, so in practice the auditor can be thought of as software that sits on the client (thus making the client and auditor the same actor, which we assume for the rest of the paper).

As discussed in the introduction, it is especially crucial in the setting of binary transparency to consider adversaries that can perform persistent man-in-the-middle attacks, as it is realistic that they would be able to compromise the client's machine. We do not need to make the contents of the audit log private, as binaries are assumed to be public information, but we do need to guarantee privacy for the specific binaries that a client downloads, as this could reveal that a client has a software version susceptible to malware. Finally, even though binaries are typically large, we need to nevertheless provide a solution efficient enough to be deployed in practice.

Keeping these requirements in mind, we aim in all our security goals to defend against the specified attacks in the face of malicious authorities that, in addition to performing all the usual actions of the authority, can also perform man-in-the-middle attacks on the auditor's network communications. If additional adversaries are considered we state them explicitly.

S1: No split views. We should prevent split-view attacks, in which the information contained in the audit log convinces the auditor that the authority published a binary, and thus it is able to be inspected by monitors, whereas in fact it is not and only appears that way in the auditor's "split" view of the log.

S2: Availability. We should prevent attacks on availability, in which the information contained in the audit log convinces the auditor that a binary is available to be inspected by monitors, when in fact the authority has not published it or has, after the initial publication, lost it or intentionally taken it down.

S3: Auditor privacy. We should ensure that the specific binaries in which the auditor is interested are not revealed to any other parties. We thus consider how to achieve this not only in the face of malicious authorities, but in the case in which all parties aside from the auditor are malicious.

5 Design of Contour

Contour and its security properties make use of a blockchain, whose primary purpose—as we see in Sect. 6—is to provide an immutable ledger that prevents split-view attacks. Because the Bitcoin blockchain is currently the most expensive to attack, we use it here and in our security analysis in Sect. 6, but observe that any blockchain could be used in its place. An authority must initially establish a known Bitcoin address that Contour commitments are published with. As knowledge of the private key associated with the Bitcoin address is required to

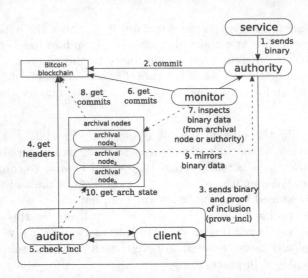

Fig. 1. The overall structure of Contour. Dashed lines represent steps that are required only if archival nodes are used.

sign transactions to spend transaction outputs sent to the address, this acts as the root-of-trust for the authority. This address can be an embedded value in the auditor software. An initial amount of coins must be sent to the Bitcoin address to enable it to start making transactions from the address.

5.1   Logging and Publishing Statements

To start, the authority receives information from services; i.e., software binaries from the developers of the relevant packages (Step 1 of Fig. 1). As it receives such a binary, it incorporates its hash as a leaf in a Merkle tree with root h_T. The root, coupled with the path down to the leaf representing the binary, thus proves that the authority has seen the binary, so we view the root as a batched statement attesting to the fact that the authority has seen all the binaries represented in the tree. Once the Merkle tree reaches some (dynamically chosen) threshold n in size, the authority runs the commit algorithm (Step 2 of Fig. 1) as follows:

commit(h_T): Form a Bitcoin transaction in which one of the outputs embeds h_T by using OP_RETURN. One of the inputs must be a previous transaction output that can only be spent by the authority's Bitcoin address (i.e. a standard Bitcoin transaction to the authority's address). The other outputs are optional and may simply send the coins back to the authority's address, according to the miner's fees it wants to pay. (See Sect. 7 for some concrete choices.) Sign the transaction with the address's private key and publish to the Bitcoin blockchain and return the raw transaction data, denoted tx.

Crucially, the commit algorithm stores only the root hash in the transaction, meaning its size is independent of the number of statements it represents. Furthermore, if the blockchain is append-only—i.e., if double spending is prevented—then the log represented by the commitments in the blockchain is append-only as well.

5.2 Proving Inclusion

After committing a batch of binaries to the blockchain, the authority can now make these binaries accessible to clients. When a client requests a software update, the authority sends not only the relevant binary, but also an accompanying proof of inclusion, which asserts that the binary has been placed in the log and is thus accessible to monitors (Step 3 of Fig. 1).

To generate this proof, the authority must first wait for its transaction to be included in the blockchain (or, for improved security, for it to be embedded k blocks into the chain). We denote the header of the block in which it was included as head_B. The proof then needs to convince anyone checking it of two things: (1) that the relevant binary is included in a Merkle tree produced by the authority and (2) that the transaction representing this Merkle tree is in the blockchain. This means providing a path of hashes leading from the values retrieved from the blockchain to a hash of the statement itself.

For a given binary bin, the algorithm prove_incl thus runs as follows:

> prove_incl(tx, head_B, bin): First, form a Merkle proof for the inclusion of tx in the block represented by head_B. This means forming a path from the root hash stored in head_B to the leaf representing tx; denote these intermediate hashes by π_{tx}. Second, form a Merkle proof for the inclusion of bin in the Merkle tree represented by tx (using the hash h_T stored in the OP_RETURN output) by forming a path from h_T to the leaf representing bin; denote these intermediate hashes by π_{bin}. Return (head_B, tx, π_{tx}, π_{bin}).

5.3 Verifying Inclusion

To verify this proof, the auditor must check the Merkle proofs, and must also check the authority's version of the block header against its own knowledge of the Bitcoin blockchain. This means that the auditor must first keep up-to-date on the headers in the blockchain, which it obtains by running an SPV client (Step 4 in Fig. 1). By running this client, the auditor builds up a set $S = \{\text{head}_{B_i}\}_i$ of block headers, which it can check against the values in the proof of inclusion. This means that, for a binary bin, check_incl (Step 5 in Fig. 1) runs as follows:

> check_incl(S, bin, (head_B, tx, π_{tx}, π_{bin})): First, check that $\text{head}_B \in S$; output 0 if not. Next, extract h_T from tx (using the hash stored in the OP_RETURN output), form $h_{\text{bin}} \leftarrow H(\text{bin})$, and check that π_{bin} forms a path from the leaf h_{bin} to the root h_T. Finally, form $h_{\text{tx}} \leftarrow H(\text{tx})$, and check that π_{tx} forms a path from the leaf h_{tx} to the root hash in head_B. If both these checks pass then output 1; otherwise output 0.

As well as verifying the inclusion proof, the auditor must also check that the address that the proof's transaction was sent from matches the authority's address (i.e. one of the transaction inputs must be a previous transaction output that can only be spent by the authority's address).

5.4   Ensuring Availability

Independently of auditors, monitors must retrieve all commitments associated with the authority from the blockchain and mirror their binaries (Steps 6 and 7 of Fig. 1). This means `get_commits` runs as follows:

`get_commits`(): Retrieve all transactions in the blockchain sent with the authority's address, and return the hashes stored in the `OP_RETURN` outputs.

After checking the binaries against their commitments, the monitors then inspect them—to, e.g., ensure they are not malware—in ways we consider outside of the scope of this paper.

While the system we have described thus far functions correctly and allows monitors to detect if an authority has committed to a binary but not published it, in order to make the binaries themselves available for inspection, we assume the monitors can mirror the authority's logs. It therefore fails to satisfy our goal of availability in the event that the authority goes down at some point in time.

We thus consider the case where the authority commits binaries to the blockchain, but—either intentionally or because it loses the data sometime in the future—does not supply the data to monitors. While this is detectable, as monitors can see that there are commitments in the blockchain with no data behind them, to disincentive this behavior requires some retroactive real-world method of punishment. More importantly, it prevents the monitor from pinpointing specific bad actions, such as malicious binaries, and thus from identifying potential victims of the authority's misbehavior.

Because of this, it is thus desirable to not only enable the detection of this form of misbehavior, but in fact to prevent it from happening in the first place. One way to achieve this is to have auditors mirror the binary themselves and send it to monitors before accepting it, to ensure that they have seen it and believe it to be benign. While this would be effective, and is arguably practical in a setting such as Certificate Transparency (modulo concerns about privacy) where the objects being sent are relatively small, in the setting of software distribution—where the objects being sent are large binaries—it is too inefficient to be considered.

Instead, we propose a new actor in the ecosystem presented in Sect. 4: archival nodes, or *archivists*, that are responsible for mirroring all data from the authority (Steps 8 and 9 in Fig. 1). To gain the extra guarantee that the data is available to monitors, auditors may thus use any archival nodes of which they are aware to check their state (i.e., the most recent block header for which they have data from the authority) and ensure that they cover the block headers relevant to the proofs they are checking (Step 10 in Fig. 1). This means adding the following interaction:

`get_arch_state`(a): The auditor (optionally) runs this function to obtain the state of an archivist a of which it is aware. This is simply the latest block header for which the archival node has mirrored the data behind the commitments held within.

Using archival nodes makes it possible to continue to pinpoint specific bad actions in the past (e.g., the publication of malware), even if the authority loses or stops providing this data, but we stress that their usage is optional and affects only availability. Essentially, archival nodes allow for a more granular detection of the misbehavior of an authority, but do come at the cost of requiring additional nodes to store a potentially large amount of data. If such granularity is not necessary, or if the system has no natural candidates with the necessary storage requirements, then archival nodes do not need to be used and the system still remains secure. In Sect. 8 we explore the role of the archival nodes in the Debian ecosystem and discover that, while the storage costs are indeed expensive, there is already at least one entity playing this role.

6 Evaluation

No Split Views (S1). In order to prevent split views, we rely on the security of the Bitcoin blockchain and its associated proof-of-work-based consensus mechanism. If every party has the same view of the blockchain, then split views of the log are impossible, as there is a unique commitment to the state of the log at any given point in time. The ability to prevent split views therefore reduces to the ability to carry out attacks on the Bitcoin blockchain.

If the adversary cannot carry out an eclipse attack, then it can perform a split-view attack only if it can fork the Bitcoin blockchain. This naïvely requires it to control 51% of the network's mining power, which, using the formula for the probability of finding a block based on the network target[1], has an estimated cost of roughly 120K USD per hour in electricity and 2043M USD in hardware costs as of December 2017's mining difficulty level[2], assuming the cost of electricity is 0.10 USD per kilowatt hour, and the mining hardware used is the Antminer S9 (14 TH/s), which retails at 2400 USD[3]. Regardless of the exact number, it is generally agreed that carrying out such an attack is prohibitively expensive.

If an eclipse attack is possible, due to the adversary's MitM capability, the adversary can "pause" the auditor at a block height representing some previous state of the log, and can prevent the auditor from hearing about new blocks past this height. It is then free to mine blocks at its own pace, and so performing a split-view attack would be significantly cheaper. As a key distinguishing property of Contour's threat model is that split-view attacks should be prevented even in the face of an adversary that can carry out such attacks, it is important to

---

[1] https://en.bitcoin.it/wiki/Generation_Calculator.
[2] blockchain.info/charts/hash-rate.
[3] www.amazon.com/Antminer-S9-0-10W-Bitcoin-Miner/dp/B01GFEOV0O.

consider the nuances and costs of this attack, especially as we are not aware of any previous literature considering the costs of eclipse attacks on Bitcoin nodes.

The cost of performing an eclipse attack depends on how much time the adversary has to perform a split-view attack, as the hash rate depends on the number of mining rigs available. As an estimate, if auditors consider a Bitcoin transaction to be confirmed after 6 blocks (the standard for most Bitcoin wallets), then as of December 2017 the attack would cost 95K USD in electricity and 8.3M USD in hardware costs if the adversary wants to perform the attack within a week, using the same electricity and hardware cost assumptions as before. This would mean, however, that the auditor would receive a new block only every 1.4 days, which would be detectable as an eclipse attack. If auditors conservatively require that new blocks arrive in intervals of up to three hours before assuming that they are the victim of an eclipse attack, then as of December 2017 an attack would cost roughly 91.8M USD in hardware costs (the electricity cost remains at 95K USD, as the number of average hashing attempts needed remains the same).

Availability (S2). While the decentralized (and thus fully replicated) nature of the blockchain can guarantee availability, it guarantees these properties only with respect to the commitments to statements made by the authority, rather than with respect to the statements—and thus the binaries—themselves. As discussed in Sect. 5.4, the use of the blockchain thus does not guarantee that binaries are actually available for inspection, or will be in the future.

Even just using monitors, Contour can already detect that an authority committed a statement without making the statement data (i.e., the actual binaries) available. Using the archival nodes introduced in Sect. 5.4, we can achieve a stronger notion of availability—in which as long as the binaries have been published at some point they can be retrieved indefinitely into the future—as long as these nodes are honest about whether or not they have mirrored the data.

In binary transparency, many ISPs and hosting providers already provide their customers local mirrors of Debian repositories. We therefore envision that ISPs can act as archival nodes on behalf of their hosting clients, which creates a decentralized network of archival nodes. We elaborate on the overheads required to do so in Sects. 7 and 8.

Auditor Privacy (S3). As the auditor receives pre-formed proofs of inclusion from the authority (as opposed to having to request them for specific binaries, as they would in all certificate and key transparency systems), retrieves commitments directly from the blockchain, auditors do not engage in any form of gossip with monitors, and receives the latest block hash from archival nodes without providing any input of its own. We thus achieve privacy by design, as at no point does the auditor reveal the statements in which it is interested to any other party.

One particular point to highlight is that Contour achieves auditor privacy despite the fact that auditors run SPV clients, which are known to potentially introduce privacy issues due to the use of Bloom filtering and the reliance on full nodes. This is because the proofs of inclusion contain both the raw transaction data and the block header, so the auditor does not need query a full node for the inclusion of the transaction and can instead verify it itself (and, as a bonus, saves the bandwidth costs of doing so).

7   Implementation and Performance

To test Contour and analyze its performance, we have implemented and provided benchmarks for a prototype Python module and toolset that developers can use. We have released the implementation as an open-source project.

Set of developer APIs and corresponding command-line tools. We used SHA-256 as the hashing algorithm to build Merkle trees, and a Python-based Bitcoin library `pycoinnet` (https://github.com/richardkiss/pycoinnet/) in order to develop the SPV client.

To evaluate the performance of our implementation, we tested all the operations listed above on a laptop with an Intel Core i5 2.60 GHz CPU and 12 GB of RAM, that was connected to a WiFi network with a connection of 5 Mbit/s. We also assume that a batch to be committed contains 1 million statements.

Number of Transactions Per Block. The overhead of both generating and verifying a proof of inclusion is dependent on the number of transactions in a Bitcoin block. To capture the worst-case scenario, we consider the maximum number of transactions that can fit into a block. Currently, the Bitcoin block size limit is 1 MB, up to 97 bytes of which is non-transaction data. The minimum transaction size is 166 bytes, so the upper bound on the number of transactions in a given block is 6,023. While this is higher than the number of transactions that Bitcoin blocks currently contain,[4] we use it as a worst-case cost and an acknowledgment that Bitcoin is evolving and blocks may grow in the future.

Authority Overheads. To run `commit` and `prove_incl`, an authority must have access to the full blocks in the Bitcoin blockchain, as well as the ability to broadcast transactions to the network. Rather than achieve these by running the authority as a full node, our implementation uses external blockchain APIs supplied by blockchain.info and blockcypher.com. This decision was based on the improved efficiency and ease of development for prototyping, but it does not affect the security of the system: authorities do not need to validate the blockchain, as invalid blocks from a dishonest external API simply result in invalid inclusion proofs that are rejected by the auditor.

To run `commit`, an authority must first build the Merkle tree containing its statements. Sampled over 20 runs, the average time to build a Merkle tree for 1M statements was $5.9\,\text{s}$ ($\sigma = 0.29\,\text{s}$). After building the tree, an authority next embeds its root hash (which is 32 bytes) into an `OP_RETURN` Bitcoin transaction to broadcast to the network. Sampled over 1,000 runs, the average time to generate this transaction—in the standard case of one input and two outputs, one for `OP_RETURN` and one for the authority's change—was $0.03\,\text{s}$ ($\sigma = 0.007\,\text{s}$).

---

[4] https://blockchain.info/charts/n-transactions-per-block.

The average total time to run `commit` was thus 5.93 s, and it resulted in 235 bytes (the size of the transaction) being broadcast to the network.

Next, to run `prove_incl`, the authority proceeds in two phases: first constructing the Merkle proof for its transaction within the block where it eventually appears, and next constructing the Merkle proof for each statement represented in a transaction. The time for the first phase, averaged over 1M runs and for a block with 6,023 transactions (our upper bound from Sect. 7), was 8.5 μs. This only needs to be done once per batch. The time for the second phase, averaged over 1M runs, was 12 μs for each individual statement Generating inclusion proofs for all the statements in the batch would thus take around 12 s. In terms of bandwidth and storage, a block up to 1 MB in size needs to be downloaded in order to generate the inclusion proof from the block's transaction Merkle tree. In terms of the memory costs, the size of the Merkle tree for 1M leaves in memory is 649 MB.

Additionally, in order to ensure that its transaction makes it into a block quickly, the authority may want to pay a fee. The recommended rate as of December 5 2017 is 154 satoshis/byte (https://bitcoinfees.info), so for a 235-byte transaction the authority can expect to pay 36,190 satoshis. As of December 5 2017, this is roughly 4.21 USD. We stress, however, that the Bitcoin price is notoriously volatile (for example, the same transaction would have cost only 0.28 USD at the beginning of 2017), so this and all other costs stated in fiat currency should be taken with a grain of salt.

Auditor Overheads. For the auditor, we considered two costs: the initial cost to retrieve the necessary header data (`sync`), and the cost to verify an inclusion proof (`check_incl`). We do not provide benchmarks for the `Auditor.get_arch_state` call, as this is a simple web request that returns a single 32-byte hash.

To run `sync`, auditors use the Bitcoin SPV protocol to download and verify the headers of each block, which are 80 bytes each. As of December 5 2017, there are 497,723 valid mined blocks, which equates to 39.8 MB of block headers. Once downloaded, however, the auditor needs to keep only the 32-byte block hash, so only 15.9 MB of data needs to be stored on disk. Going forward, the Bitcoin network generates approximately 144 blocks per day, so the amount of downloaded data will be 11.5 kB daily, and the amount of stored data will increase by 4.6 kB daily.

To verify the validity of the block headers in the chain, the client must perform one SHA-256 hash per block header; averaged over five runs, it took us 116 seconds for the Python SPV client to download and verify all the block headers. This process needs to be performed only once per auditor.

To run `check_incl`, we again use our upper bound from Sect. 7 and assume every block contains 6,023 transactions. This means the inclusion proof contains: (1) an 80-byte block header; (2) the raw transaction data, which is 235 bytes; (3) a Merkle proof for the transaction, which consists of $\log(6023) - 1$ 32-byte hashes (the root hash is already provided in the block header); and (4) a Merkle proof for the statement, which consists of $\log(1000000) - 2$ 32-byte hashes (the root hash is already provided in the transaction data, and the auditor computes the statement hash itself). The total bandwidth cost is therefore around 1275 bytes. Averaged over 1M runs, the time for the auditor to verify the inclusion proof was $224\,\mu s\,(\sigma = 62.14\,\mu s)$.

Monitor Overheads. Monitors must run a Bitcoin full node in order to get a complete uncensored view of the blockchain. As of December 2017, running a full node requires 145 GB of free disk space, increasing by up to 144 MB daily. It took us around three days to fully bootstrap a full node and verify all the blocks, although this operation needs to be performed only once per monitor.

Archival Nodes Overheads. Like monitors, archival nodes need to run a Bitcoin full node. Additionally, archival nodes must download and store all the data from the authority. The costs here are entirely dependent on the number and size of the statements; we examine the costs for Debian in Sect. 8.

In order for archival nodes to know which statement data to download from authorities to independently rebuild the Merkle tree roots committed in Bitcoin transactions and check that they match with the data provided, authorities must point the archival nodes to the location of the data. Again, this is dependent on the mechanism that the authority uses to make the data available.

As in Debian, however, archives use statements that represent files. We may therefore expect that, in addition to a Merkle tree, authorities would use meta-data files to link each leaf in the tree to a file on the server that archival nodes then mirror; this would be particularly useful in a setting—like Debian—where it would be undesirable to reorganize files that are already stored. The meta-data file would consist of a mapping of 32-byte hashes to filenames. The average Debian package filename is 60 bytes, so including such a metadata file would introduce an average storage overhead, for both authorities and archival nodes, of 92 bytes per statement.

8   Use Case: Debian

To go beyond basic benchmarks and analyze the operation of Contour on a real system, we used it to audit software binaries in the Debian repository. Our results show that, as desired, Contour provides a way to add transparency to this repository without major changes to the existing infrastructure and with minimal overheads.

We extracted the software package metadata for all processor architectures and releases of Debian from the Debian FTP archive over a one-week period from January 20–27 2017. The archive is updated four times a day. At the beginning of this period there were 976,214 unique software binaries available for download from the Debian software repositories, constituting 1.7 TB of data, and by the end there were 980,469.

To initiate the system, we first committed to all the existing 976,214 software packages. The Debian package metadata already contains the SHA-256 hashes for these packages, so we only needed to build a Merkle tree from these hashes (rather than compute them ourselves first). This took approximately 6 seconds (which is in line with the benchmarks in 7).

As the archive was updated, we kept track of the package hashes being added and created a new batch for each update. The average batch size was 1,040, and the average time to build a Merkle tree for the batch was 0.0052 seconds. Recall from Sect. 7 that committing one transaction to the blockchain costs roughly 0.28 USD in fees, so this would cost 1.12 USD per day.

In terms of overhead for archival nodes, to fully satisfy availability they must store all the data from the authority, as well as deleted packages (which should be monitored as well). This means storing 1.7 TB, and an additional average of 11 GB per day, or 4 TB per year. There are already 269 Debian mirrors hosting the full 1.7 TB data set,[5] and at least one mirror hosting all the deleted packages too, effectively acting as an archival node.[6] This is by far the highest overhead incurred by our system, and we expect that only a small number of mirrors would have the storage capacity to run an archival node.

As discussed in Sect. 7, we can also enable archival nodes to rebuild Merkle trees with minimal changes to the existing Debian archive infrastructure. This requires storing only an additional 84 kB metadata file per batch (containing the mapping from hashes to filenames), and an initial 79 MB metadata file. These metadata files consist of a mapping of hashes of software packages to their filenames in the Debian archives.

Finally, the proof of inclusion of each software package would need to be added to the software package (.deb) files as metadata when downloaded by a Debian device using a command such as apt install. At 980 K software packages, this would require a maximum of 1.3 kB of extra storage and bandwidth for end-user devices per package downloaded. Given that the average package size is 1337 kB, this is only a 0.1% overhead. 1.3 GB of extra storage is required for Debian repository mirrors to store the proofs of inclusion, which is only a 0.07% overhead.

9   Conclusion

We have proposed a system that provides proactive transparency and does not require the initial coordination of forming a Sybil-free set of nodes. We have demonstrated that, even for attackers that are capable of performing persistent man-in-the-middle attacks, compromising the integrity of the system requires millions of dollars in energy and hardware costs. We also saw that Contour could be applied today to the Debian software repository with relatively low overhead to existing infrastructure, and with no changes or coordination required for any participant who does not wish to opt in.

Acknowledgements. Mustafa Al-Bassam is supported by a scholarship from the Alan Turing Institute, and Sarah Meiklejohn is supported by EPSRC grant EP/N028104/1.

---

[5] www.debian.org/mirror/list.
[6] snapshot.debian.org/.

References

1. Security/binary transparency - mozillawiki (2017). https://wiki.mozilla.org/Security/Binary_Transparency
2. Apostolaki, M., Zohar, A., Vanbever, L.: Hijacking Bitcoin: Large-scale Network Attacks on Cryptocurrencies (2016). arXiv:abs/1605.07524
3. Basin, D., Cremers, C., Kim, T.H.-J., Perrig, A., Sasse, R., Szalachowski, P.: ARPKI: attack resilient public-key infrastructure. In: ACM CCS 2014, pp. 382–393 (2014)
4. Bonneau, J.: EthIKS: using ethereum to audit a CONIKS key transparency log. In: Clark, J., Meiklejohn, S., Ryan, P.Y.A., Wallach, D., Brenner, M., Rohloff, K. (eds.) FC 2016. LNCS, vol. 9604, pp. 95–105. Springer, Heidelberg (2016). https://doi.org/10.1007/978-3-662-53357-4_7
5. Chase, M., Meiklejohn, S.: Transparency overlays and applications. In: ACM SIGSAC Conference on Computer and Communications Security (2016)
6. Chuat, L., Szalachowski, P., Perrig, A., Laurie, B., Messeri, E.: Efficient gossip protocols for verifying the consistency of certificate logs. In: IEEE Conference on Communications and Network Security (2015)
7. Dowling, B., Günther, F., Herath, U., Stebila, D.: Secure logging schemes and certificate transparency. In: Askoxylakis, I., Ioannidis, S., Katsikas, S., Meadows, C. (eds.) ESORICS 2016. LNCS, vol. 9879, pp. 140–158. Springer, Cham (2016). https://doi.org/10.1007/978-3-319-45741-3_8
8. Eijdenberg, A., Laurie, B., Cutter, A.: Verifiable Data Structures (2015). github.com/google/trillian/blob/master/docs/VerifiableDataStructures.pdf
9. Eskandarian, S., Messeri, E., Bonneau, J., Boneh, D.: Certificate transparency with privacy. CoRR, abs/1703.02209 (2017)
10. Eyal, I., Sirer, E.G.: Majority is not enough: bitcoin mining is vulnerable. In: Financial Cryptography and Data Security (2014)
11. Farivar, C.: Judge: Apple must help FBI unlock San Bernardino shooter's iPhone (2016). arstechnica.com/tech-policy/2016/02/judge-apple-must-help-fbi-unlock-san-bernardino-shooters-iphone/
12. Fromknecht, C., Velicanu, D., Yakoubov, S.: A decentralized public key infrastructure with identity retention. IACR Cryptology ePrint Archive, Report 2014/803 (2014). eprint.iacr.org/2014/803.pdf
13. Gervais, A., Ritzdorf, H., Karame, G., Capkun, S.: Tampering with the delivery of blocks and transactions in bitcoin. In: ACM CCS 2015 (2015)
14. Goodin, D.: "Flame" malware was signed by rogue Microsoft certificate (2012). arstechnica.com/security/2012/06/flame-malware-was-signed-by-rogue-microsoft-certificate/
15. Heilman, E., Kendler, A., Zohar, A., Goldberg, S.: Eclipse attacks on bitcoin's peer-to-peer network. In: USENIX Security 2015 (2015)
16. Kim, T.H.-J., Huang, L.-S., Perrig, A., Jackson, C., Gligor, V.: Accountable key infrastructure (AKI): a proposal for a public-key validation infrastructure. In: WWW 2013, pp. 679–690 (2013)
17. Kogias, E.K., Jovanovic, P., Gailly, N., Khoffi, I., Gasser, L., Ford, B.: Enhancing bitcoin security and performance with strong consistency via collective signing. In: USENIX Security 2016 (2016)
18. Laurie, B., Langley, A., Kasper, E.: Certificate Transparency (2013)
19. Leyden, J.: Inside 'Operation Black Tulip': DigiNotar hack analysed (2011). www.theregister.co.uk/2011/09/06/diginotar_audit_damning_fail/

20. Matsumoto, S., Reischuk, R.M.: IKP: Turning a PKI Around with Blockchains. IACR Cryptology ePrint Archive, Report 2016/1018 (2016). eprint.iacr.org/2016/1018
21. Melara, M.S., Blankstein, A., Bonneau, J., Felten, E.W., Freedman, M.J.: CONIKS: bringing key transparency to end users. In: USENIX Security 2015 (2015)
22. Nakamoto, S.: Bitcoin: a peer-to-peer electronic cash system (2008). bitcoin.org/bitcoin.pdf
23. Nikitin, K., et al.: CHAINIAC: Proactive software-update transparency via collectively signed skipchains and verified builds. In: 26th USENIX Security Symposium (USENIX Security 17), pp. 1271–1287 (2017). USENIX Association, Vancouver
24. Nordberg, L., Gillmor, D., Ritter, T.: Gossiping in CT (2016). tools.ietf.org/html/draft-ietf-trans-gossip-03
25. Ryan, M.D.: Enhanced certificate transparency and end-to-end encrypted mail. In: NDSS 2014 (2014)
26. Singh, A., Ngan, T.-W.J., Druschel, P., Wallach, D.S.: Eclipse attacks on overlay networks: threats and defenses. In: IEEE Conference on Computer Communications (2006)
27. Syta, E., et al.: Keeping authorities "honest or bust" with decentralized witness cosigning. In: IEEE Symposium on Security and Privacy ("Oakland") (2016)
28. Tomescu, A., Devadas, S.: Catena: Efficient Non-equivocation via Bitcoin. In: IEEE Symposium on Security and Privacy ("Oakland") (2017)

CBT Workshop: Consensus, Mining Pools and Performance

What Blockchain Alternative
Do You Need?

Tommy Koens[✉] and Erik Poll

Radboud University, Nijmegen, The Netherlands
{tkoens,E.Poll}@cs.ru.nl

Abstract. With billions of dollars spent on blockchain, there clearly is
a need to determine if this technology should be used, as demonstrated
by the many proposals for decision schemes. In this work we rigorously
analyze 30 existing schemes. Our analysis demonstrates contradictions
between these schemes – so clearly they cannot all be right – and also
highlights what we feel is a more structural flaw of most of them, namely
that they ignore alternatives to blockchain-based solutions. To remedy
this, we propose an improved scheme that does take alternatives into
account, which we argue is more useful in practice to decide an optimal
solution for a particular use case.

1 Introduction

Ever since the invention of blockchain in 2008 [46], this technology has piqued
the interest of industry, and many blockchain initiatives have arisen. Over a
1000 patents [1] in this technology were filed, and it is estimated that blockchain
global spending reaches 2 billion US dollar in 2018 [15].

Following the blockchain hype [48], many initiatives discovered that
blockchain as it is used in for example Bitcoin and Ethereum is not a panacea.
Instead, alternative blockchain technologies have been proposed that fit better.
To be able to determine if, and if so which blockchain is needed in a particular
scenario, various decision models have been proposed. However, there are significant differences between such schemes. In fact, some schemes provide different
answers for the same scenario. This raises the question: Which decision scheme
should you use? This paper addresses that question and makes the following
contributions:

- We perform a critical analysis of decision schemes in Sect. 3. Our analysis
  demonstrates some contradictions between schemes and suggests that none
  of the schemes is complete, in that they do not take current limitations of
  blockchain technology into account and ignore what alternative database technologies besides blockchain there are.

© Springer Nature Switzerland AG 2018
J. Garcia-Alfaro et al. (Eds.): DPM 2018/CBT 2018, LNCS 11025, pp. 113–129, 2018.
https://doi.org/10.1007/978-3-030-00305-0_9

– To repair this omission, we propose a new scheme in Sect. 4, which does take these alternatives into account. With our scheme the need for blockchain of for alternative technologies can be determined. We discuss our scheme in Sect. 5. Given the global interest and financial resources spend on blockchain, our scheme can be used as a sanity check for blockchain initiatives.

Section 6 discusses future work and we summarize our conclusions in Sect. 7.

2   Background

Blockchain technology underlying cryptocurrencies such as Bitcoin and Ethereum offers a unique property. Namely, it allows for reaching agreement on a single state of a shared ledger by a consortium of unknown participants [50]. Transaction sets, called blocks, are proposed at frequent time intervals, where each block includes the cryptographic hash of its predecessor block. This creates a chain of blocks, which explains the term blockchain. Two important characteristics of this technology, as it is originally used in e.g. Bitcoin, are that the blockchain is *permissionless* and *public*. Permissionless means that anyone may join or leave the network at will. Public means that anyone, in principle, may propose a new state of the ledger.

However, there currently are several issues with this technology. First, it performs poorly regarding transaction scalability. For example, Ripple, a technology that is not blockchain-based [9,28], claims to be able to scale to 50.000 transactions per second (tps) [27], whereas Bitcoin can handle 7 tps and Ethereum 14 tps. Second, although a blockchain is a form of database, it is currently not suited to store large amounts of transaction data.

Furthermore, some authors [51,52,55] claim that blockchain is an immutable ledger. However, this is a misconception, as blockchains are mutable. First of all, an important purpose of this technology is that state changes are made possible. Therefore, state stored on the blockchain is by default mutable. Mutability may also refer to the stored transactions on the ledger. Again, these transactions are also mutable, although they are much harder to change than state. For example, anyone with over half of Bitcoin's network resources can rewrite the ledger's history [35], which is also called mutable-by-hashing-power [38]. Recent work suggests that even a quarter of the resources is sufficient to ultimately achieve the same goal [39]. Another example that further illustrates the mutability of blockchains is the hard fork of Ethereum after the DAO hack, where 50 million dollars worth of Ether was stolen through a bug in a smart contract. The current ledger called Ethereum Classic left the funds stolen. However, a new ledger (called Ethereum) was created, returning the stolen funds, thus undoing the hack and rewriting history. Although blockchains are mutable, in most cases it is hard to rewrite history. However, there are scenarios where easy mutability is a requirement, for example, because of the need to correct accidental mistakes.

To overcome these blockchain issues (scalability, performance, hard to alter history), alternative database technologies may be more useful. For example, permissioned and public database technology can be found in Ripple [27], which uses a distributed ledger [28]. Here, anyone may join the network and read from the ledger, but only a limited set of participants may propose new ledger states. Also, permissioned and private database technologies have been proposed, for example in R3 Corda [25]. Here, participation in the network is by invitation only, and also a limited number of the participants may propose new states.

Following these types of database technologies, initiatives have to decide which technology is appropriate for a particular scenario. To support this decision making process, decision schemes for database technologies, and in particular blockchain, have been proposed. However, the decision schemes are not always clear in what is meant with blockchain.

2.1 Blockchain Terminology

We observed that the term blockchain is used arbitrarily in the schemes. Indeed, Birch et al. [34] and Maull [45] also state that many authors use the term blockchain in different ways. Interestingly, in the original work by Nakamoto [46] the term blockchain is not used, but the term distributed time-stamp server is used. Pahl [47], Birch et al. [34] and Lin [43] state that blockchain is a distributed ledger. Pahl [47] also calls blockchain is a distributed database, while Birch et al. [34] use the term 'shared ledger'. Wüst and Gervais distinguish permissionless and permissioned blockchains, and provide examples for each type. Their Corda example, however, can be considered a decentralized database [22]. Although Corda is heavily inspired by blockchain systems [26], Corda does not use a chain of blocks. These examples show that, indeed, various terms are used interchangeably and are not always correctly.

The terminology for the different solutions we use in this paper is illustrated in Fig. 1 and explained below. We distinguish two types of databases: central databases (DBs) and distributed databases. In a central database, data is centrally stored. Following this, a central ledger is a central database with the inclusion of transaction interaction. Transaction interaction [12] refers to the interdependency of transactions of different participants. For example, a Bitcoin account with a balance of 0 can only create a valid transaction after it receives a transaction that increases its current balance. Additionally, a shared central ledger can be used when multiple writers are present.

A distributed database stores data across multiple locations, and provides read and write access to participants. Following this, a distributed ledger is a distributed database with the inclusion of transaction interaction. We consider blockchain (BC) to be particular form of distributed ledger technology (DLT), as here *unknown* participants can read from and write to the ledger, and reach consensus on the state of the ledger.

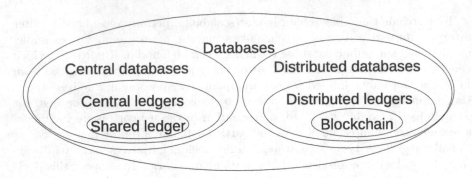

Fig. 1. Our classification of database technologies

3   Evaluation of Decision Schemes

In this section we analyze 30 blockchain decision schemes, listed in Table 1. We classify the schemes by type, based on the question(s) they answer. We also classify the choices that the schemes involve, listed in Table 2, and we investigate contradictions between some of the schemes.

3.1   An Overview of Schemes

We found 30 decision schemes in the literature and on the web, and included all schemes found; see Table 1. Five schemes are represented as a questionnaire, indicated by a 'Q' in Table 1. The remaining 25 schemes are represented by a flow diagram, indicated by an 'F' in Table 1, where a sequence of binary choices lead to an end state that provides the optimal solution for a given scenario.

We observe that all schemes can be classified in (a combination of) three models, where each model addresses a primary question:

- **Model 1: Determine if blockchain should be used.** Schemes that aim to determine if you should use a distributed ledger or, more specific, blockchain.
- **Model 2: Determine blockchain type.** These schemes aim to determine which type of blockchain fits best to a particular problem.
- **Model 3: Determine alternative technologies.** The third model suggests alternative technologies such as traditional databases.

A classification of each scheme towards these three models can be found in Table 1 (column: Model). Additionally, we counted the number of end states (column: #ES) for each decision scheme. This already shows that there exists a difference between similar scheme types and number of end states. Furthermore, we grouped the various end state descriptions (column: End states), according to our terminology definition in Sect. 2, in the columns below. Typically, in the literature blockchains are classified in three categories:

- Permissionless (anyone may write to the ledger) and public (anyone may read from the ledger).

- Permissioned and private (only a limited set of participants may read from the ledger).
- Permissioned and public.

From these columns we also note various levels of granularity of end state descriptions. For example, it is not clear if end state B.1.a (public BC) is permissionless (similar to B.1.c) or permissioned (similar to B.3.b). Also, Birch et al. [34]

Table 1. An overview of decision schemes

No.	DS name	Ref.	F/Q	Model	#ES	End states
1	CapGemini	[7]	Q	1	2	A.1.a; A.2.a
2	Cooke	[19]	F	1	2	A.1.a; A.2.a
3	Gardner	[16]	F	1	2	A.1.a; A.2.a
4	Lixar	[20]	F	1	2	A.1.a; A.2.a
5	Meunier	[29]	Q	1	2	A.1.a; A.2.a
6	Nandwani	[18]	F	1	1	A.1.b
7	PWC	[24]	Q	1	2	A.1.a; A.2.a
8	Verslype	[17]	F	1	2	A.1.b; A.2.a
9	Birch	[34]	F	2	4	B.1; B.2; B.3; B.4
10	Saiko	[8]	F	2	3	B.1.a; B.3.c; B.4.a
11	Bico	[5]	F	1,2	4	A.2.a; B.4.a; B.3.c; B.1.a
12	Chand	[21]	F	1,2	3	A.2.a; B.4.a; B.1.a
13	Hyperledger	[13]	F	1,2	3	A.2.a; B.1.a; B.3.a
14	Ico	[32]	F	1,2	3	A.2.a; B.3.a; B.1.a
15	Lin	[43]	F	1,2	4	A.2.a; B.4.a; B.3.c; B.1.a
16	Meuller	[31]	F	1,2	3	A.2.a; B.1.a; B.3.a
17	Pahl	[47]	F	1,2	5	A.1.a; A.2.a; B.1.c; B.3.b; B.4.b
18	Peck	[49]	F	1,2	3	A.2.a; B.3.a; B.1.a
19	Suichies	[4]	F	1,2	4	A.2.a; B.1.a; B.3.c; B.4.a
20	WEF	[33]	F	1,2	5	A.2.a; A.3 (x2); A.1.a (x2)
21	Wüst	[56]	F	1,2	4	A.2.a; B.1.b; B.3.b; B.4.b;
22	DHS	[29]	F	1,3	7	C.1.d; C.1.a (x3); C.1.b; C.1.c; A.1.a
23	Greenspan	[12]	Q	1,3	3	A.1.a; A.2.a; C.1.a
24	IBM	[14]	F	1,3	2	A.1.b; C.1
25	Lewis	[2]	F	1,3	3	A.2.b; A.1.a; C.1.a
26	Xu	[57]	F	1,3	2	C.1; A.1.a
27	Deloitte	[10]	Q	1,2,3	4	A.1.a; C.1; B.1.b; B.3.a
28	Henkel	[6]	F	1,2,3	5	A.1.a; A.2.a; B.1.a; B.3.a; B.4.a
29	Maull	[45]	F	1,2,3	4	A.2; B.1; B.3; B.4
30	Quindazzi	[23]	F	1,2,3	5	A.2.a; C.1; B.1; B.3; B.4

introduce new terminology, such as the public double permissionless DLT (B.2). This includes the reward mechanism of writing to the ledger which, when intrinsic to the consensus process, is called double permissionless. An extrinsic mechanism where a writer receives a physical reward (e.g. cash) is called permissionless [34].

A. Model 1 end states

1. DLT is a good fit.
   (a) Use BC.
   (b) Let's talk.
2. DLT is not a good fit.
   (a) Don't use BC.
   (b) Problem of standards.
3. BC may be a good solution.

C. Model 3 end states

1. Consider alternative approaches.
   (a) Central database. suitable
   (b) Encrypted DB.
   (c) Managed DB.
   (d) Consider email/spreadsheets.

B. Model 2 end states

1. Public permissionless DLT.
   (a) Public BC.
   (b) Permissionless BC.
   (c) Public permissionless BC.
2. Public double permissionless DLT.
3. Public permissioned DLT.
   (a) Permissioned BC.
   (b) Public permissioned BC.
   (c) Hybrid BC.
4. Private permissioned DLT.
   (a) Private BC.
   (b) Private permissioned BC.
5. Private double permissioned DLT.

3.2   Model 1 Scheme End States

Model 1 schemes aim to determine if you should use a blockchain. Several schemes, for example Pahl, Gardner, and Greenspan, give a clear yes-or-no answer whether a blockchain should used or not. Other schemes are more conservative. For example Peck, Meuller, and DHS, only say that blockchain may be an option. Typically, these schemes do not elaborate what further conditions have to be met to determine if blockchain should (or should not) be used.

3.3   Model 2 Scheme End States

Model 2 schemes aim to determine which type of blockchain is needed. Typically, these schemes also answer the question whether you should you a blockchain or not, so they are also model 1 schemes.

Both Saiko and Birch et al. propose a type 2 scheme only. Interestingly, Saiko considers three types of blockchains, although uses the terms blockchain and ledger interchangeably. In contrast, Birch et al. consider four distributed ledger types, although in their work they do provide examples that include blockchain. The main difference between the two schemes is that Birch et al. suggest two types of public ledgers and two types of private ledgers, whereas Saiko suggests a single public ledger and two types of private ledgers. Here, again, we observe a difference in schemes, similar to model 1 schemes.

However, we consider blockchain variants not a viable option, as better, alternative technologies are available. We will discuss this further in Sect. 5.

3.4 Model 3 Scheme End States

Model 3 schemes also consider alternative technologies other than blockchain. One of the outcomes of IBM's scheme is 'consider alternative approaches', but it does not say what these alternatives might be. The scheme by DHS does suggest some concrete alternatives, such as a database or a managed database. Quindazzi refers to the traditional ledger (as in the current banking system) as an alternative to other types of ledgers. However, these suggestions are generic and do not point out which type of database should be used. Clearly, the end states of which type of database to use can be refined in these models.

3.5 Scheme Questions

In this section we analyze all schemes, and group and classify the questions that are used to determine an end state; see Table 2. To be able to reach any of the three model end states (as discussed in the previous section), each question should lead to an answer which holds a (database) technology property. In particular, we are interested in questions that differentiate between technologies [41], which we label 'T'. For our scheme we currently consider the remaining questions as not relevant. We classified the questions as follows:

1. Our first question type refers to determining which database type is needed. We label these as 'T'.
2. Also, there exist questions that address the current limitations of blockchain, which we label as 'L'.
3. A particular set of questions focus on the system design, instead of technological properties. For example '(do you need) censorship resistance' and 'where is consensus determined' are design questions. These scheme questions consider this to be a prerequisite for the use of a technology. We do not consider these questions for our scheme, as they do not distinguish between technologies from a technical perspective. We label these questions as 'E'.
4. We label our fourth question type as process questions, 'P'. The answers to these questions also do not in particular differentiate between technologies. Therefore, these questions types in the schemes are irrelevant for determining if, and if so, which database technology can be used. For example, the questions 'aiming to remove third parties?', 'looking to reduce costs?', and 'can participants adopt?' are process related questions. We do not include these questions in our scheme, see Sect. 4.

   Also, some schemes (e.g. Cooke, Suichies, WEF) include the question 'Are writers interests unified?' to determine the appropriateness of blockchain, and consider that if this is indeed true, no blockchain is needed. However, the interests of the honest participants may be aligned, but not the interests of a malicious participant. The point here being that when choosing a particular technology, the basic issues (such as the double spend attack in blockchain) should be considered as part of the system. Therefore, the interests of participants by default are not aligned, which is why we consider this question not to be relevant for our scheme.

5. Two questions stand out because these are the questions that we aim to answer, namely if, and if so which blockchain is needed in a particular scenario. These two questions, which we label 'D', are 'Traditional approach results in consistency loss?', and 'Can other technologies offer a solution?'. Again, we exclude these particular questions from our scheme, as they do not differentiate between technologies.

Including the Questionnaires. The questionnaires consist of a list of questions that must be answered affirmatively to determine if blockchain may be a suitable solution However, only the schemes by Greenspan and Deloitte state that all questions must be answered affirmatively for this technology to be useful. Therefore, because of the schemes boolean end states, these can be considered a flow diagram, too. The questionnaires by Capgemini, PWC and Meunier provide an approximation of the number of questions that must be answered affirmative, making it unclear when exactly blockchain is useful.

From all questionnaires we can conclude that there are two end states, similar to scheme model 1. Although the questionnaires do not follow a particular flow, their questions can be classified, similar to the questions made in the flow diagrams. Therefore, we include their questions in Table 2, too.

Summary. From Table 2 we observe that most questions are process questions. Moreover 25 out of the 30 schemes contain questions that do not contribute to the overall question the scheme aims to answer. Furthermore, none of the schemes address all tech type questions. This suggests the need for a new scheme.

3.6   Inconsistency Between Schemes

There are clear contradictions between some of the schemes: these schemes come to different conclusions based on identical answers to the questions used in the schemes. Below we give some examples of contradictions we observed.

Comparison 1: Cooke vs. Gardner. We present our results in Table 3. From this table we observe that making similar decisions in the schemes may lead to different answers. The difference can be explained by the additional question by Cooke, namely 'are writers interests unified?'. Cooke considers this a relevant question, whereas Gardner's scheme omits this question. As discussed in the previous paragraph, we consider this question not to be relevant for deciding which scheme to use as one must assume that writers interest always are misaligned.

Comparison 2: Wüst vs. Hyperledger. In Table 4 we compare the two schemes of Hyperledger and Wüst in deciding which type of blockchain could be used. In this comparison a difference in terminology appears, as the scheme by Wüst is more fine-grained. Whereas Wüst uses a combination of two axis (permissionless/permissioned, and, public/private) to describe blockchain, Hyperledger uses only two terms (either permissioned, or public). Here, the Hyperledger scheme could be improved by using similar end states as Wüst.

Table 2. Scheme questions classification

No.	Question	Class.
1	Traditional approach is insufficient? [6,10,17,21]	D
2	Can other technologies offer a solution? [2,6,31,49]	D
3	Aiming to remove third parties? [24,33,57]	P
4	Are you working with digital assets? [7,33]	P
5	Where is consensus determined? [4,5,8,19,23,24,29,43,45]	P
6	Do you need censorship resistance? [49]	E
7	How is the incentive structure determined? [34]	E
8	Are there contractual relations? [6,14,31,33,45]	P
9	Rules of tx do not change frequently? [13]	P
10	Sensitive identifiers stored? [2,11,14,21]	P
11	Requires a market approach? [14]	P
12	Looking to reduce costs? [14]	P
13	Looking to improve discoverability? [14]	P
14	Is there a real (business) problem? [2,6,31]	P
15	Can participants adapt? [2,6,29]	P
16	Do the benefits justify the cost of adoption? [2]	P
17	Is this a 'blockchains are free' play? [2]	P
18	Need an immutable log? [11,13,29,32]	E
19	Are there relative simple business rules? [14,17,29]	P
20	Many participants transacting? [29,31]	P
21	Is data integrity required? [7]	P
22	Do you need to share operational data? [7]	P
23	Are there transaction rules set? [12]	P
24	Who stands behind the assets? [12]	P
25	Can the project be open sourced? [21]	P
26	Participants trust each other? [4,5,7,8,12,16,20,23,29,33,45,49,56]	P
27	Participants interests aligned? [4,5,8,13,18,23,31–33,43]	P
28	Need a database? [4,5,7,8,10–13,16,18,20,23,24,32,33,43,45,47,56]	T
29	Can you use a TTP? [2,4,5,8,10–12,16,17,20,21,23,29,31,33,34,43,45,56,57]	T
30	Shared write access? [4,5,8,10–14,16–18,24,33,34,43,47,49,56]	T
31	Participants known? [4–6,8,12,18,23,31,33,34,45,47,56]	T
32	Need to control functionality? [4,8,19,23,33,43,45,49]	T
33	Public transactions? [2,4,5,7,8,14,17–19,21,29,32,33,43,45,47,49]	T
34	Is there transaction interaction? [10,12,21,24]	T
35	Do you need high transaction throughput? [14,17,21,24,29,31,33,45]	L
36	Do you need to store large transactional data? [21,33]	L

Table 3. Comparing scheme choices of Cooke, and Gardner

	Cooke	Gardner
Question	Answer	
Do you need a database?	Yes	Yes
Are there multiple writers?	Yes	Yes
Are writers trusted?	Yes	Yes
Conclusion	Undetermined	You don't need a blockchain

Table 4. Scheme end state comparison between Wüst and Hyperledger

	Wüst	Hyperledger
Transaction visibility:	Yes	Yes
Leads to:	Public permissioned blockchain	Public blockchain
Transaction visibility:	No	No
Leads to:	Private permissioned blockchain	Permissioned blockchain

Comparison 3: IBM vs. Verslype. The IBM scheme suggests that working with complex business logic may be an argument for using a blockchain. In contrast, Verslype suggests that simple business rules may be an argument for using a blockchain. Clearly, these two schemes contradict each other. It is not clear which scheme is correct, as there is a lack of description of what this specific question means. A possible explanation for the apparent contradiction is that the two schemes consider different types of blockchain. Complex business rules can be, to some extent, captured by smart contracts. Therefore, the IBM scheme is probably considering a blockchain similar to Ethereum that supports smart contracts. However, not all blockchains can deal with complex smart contracts; for instance, Bitcoin does not. Therefore, the scheme by Verslype is probably considering a blockchain as used in Bitcoin.

Summary. These comparisons show that inconsistencies between schemes may be explained by several factors. First, the comparison between the schemes of Cooke and Gardner show clear contradictions. Second, the comparison between Wüst and Hyperledger shows that there is a difference in granularity of the end state description. Finally, some inconsistencies between schemes may explained by the schemes considering different types of blockchain solutions, as we assume is the case in the contradiction between IBM and Verslype.

4   A New Scheme

In this section we propose a new scheme that is based on the three scheme models identified in Sect. 3. Our scheme aims to answer three questions:

1. Should you use a blockchain? (scheme model 1).
2. If so, which type of blockchain is best? (scheme model 2).
3. If not, which alternative database technology is best? (scheme model 3).

We include alternative technologies in our scheme, and we focus only on the questions that differentiate between technologies. Because of this, our scheme aims to replace all 30 schemes.

4.1   Scheme Questions and End States

In explaining our scheme, we use our terminology from Sect. 2. Our new scheme starts with the need for storing state (1, see Fig. 2). If indeed a database is needed and there exists only a single writer (2) that performs state updates, a central database (end state II, see Fig. 2) can be used.

If, however, there are multiple writers (2) and there exists the need to control functionality (3) by a specific party a shared central database (III) should be used. Here we assume that there exists such a specific party, and that the writers trust this party. Controlling database functionality may include setting the rules on how database permissions are set (such as create, store, delete), how the data is stored in the database (a relational database or an object oriented database), or how the database can be queried (e.g. ServerSQL, or MySQL). Similarly, if all participants agree that a third party (4) provides states updates, also a shared central database should be used. Note that we omit the question 'Is public verifiability required?', in contrast to, for example, Wüst and Gervais [56], as we consider this to be a design question. In particular for blockchain, this question is inherent to the technology. For all other technologies some form of public verifiability could be present, example by giving auditors access to the ledger.

Thus, so far we consider that there is a need to store state and multiple participants are present that do not wish to use a single party for state updates.

The next question is about transaction interaction. If no transaction interaction (5) is required, a distributed database could be used, for example the cloud storage network Storj (IV) [30].

If transaction interaction is required, participants are known (e.g. through a certificate authority) (6), and anyone can join the network (7), again a distributed ledger could be used, for example Ripple (V). When a form of access control (7) is in place, still, a distributed ledger can be used, for example Corda (VI). Note that, in principle, a blockchain *could* be used in these cases (IV, V, VI). However, other technologies are present that do not lack the current drawbacks of blockchain. As one of the anonymous reviewers pointed out: "Blockchains are often sufficient but not often necessary".

If participants are unknown, then blockchain may provide a solution. Here, our scheme is in line with Perlman [50] who states that a blockchain can achieve consensus amongst a consortium of unknown participants. Our scheme also takes some of the current limitations of blockchain into account. Currently, blockchain is limited in processing a large number (a ball park figure is greater than 2000 transactions per second) of transactions (8). and is not fit for storing large amounts (e.g. Tera-bytes) of transactional data (9). Although current research in scalability has shown significant improvements, for example Omniledger [42], there are currently no real life implementations on a global scale. Then, according to our scheme, there is currently no solution available (VII). However, if these two properties do not matter, then a public permissionless blockchain (VIII) should be used.

5   Discussion

Following our scheme, blockchain is only needed where there exists a group of unknown participants that wish to reach consensus. Blockchain *could* be used in any case where there exists a need for a database. This may give rise to the notion of public permissioned blockchains and private permissioned blockchains, which are in essence a shared database [3, 45]. However, using blockchain in those cases where alternative technologies are suggested in our scheme may not be the best choice, considering the issues blockchain currently has, as discussed in Sect. 2. This is why our scheme includes only one type of blockchain, namely the 'classic' public and permissionless blockchain.

Schemes closely related to our work, for example Wüst and Gervais, Peck, Pahl, and Lin et al., address the question 'do you need a blockchain?'. Their schemes suggest either to use a type of blockchain, or not to use a blockchain. This, however, is misleading as the scheme suggests that blockchain is needed, whereas other technologies are available. Such technologies do not have the current limitations of blockchain. In fact, these technologies have been tested over time and have proven to provide a functionality that is desired. We argue that the end states of decision schemes should at least include technologies that provide the desired functionality, and where possible without the limitations of blockchain. Therefore, we argue that the schemes that do not include alternative technologies are incomplete and hence wrong.

Also, in our analyses we labeled a large number of scheme questions as 'process', as these questions do not contribute to the overall question the scheme aims to answer, as discussed in Sect. 3. The questions labeled 'process', therefore, should not be included in these decision making schemes. Additionally, we labeled 9 questions as 'tech' meaning that these in fact do contribute to any of the scheme goals. We used these 9 questions and created a new scheme, together with the end states of alternative technologies, see Fig. 2. As our scheme includes all relevant questions of the identified schemes and questionnaires, includes end states that suggest alternative technologies, and our scheme determines if blockchain should be used, we argue that our scheme can replace the identified 30 schemes.

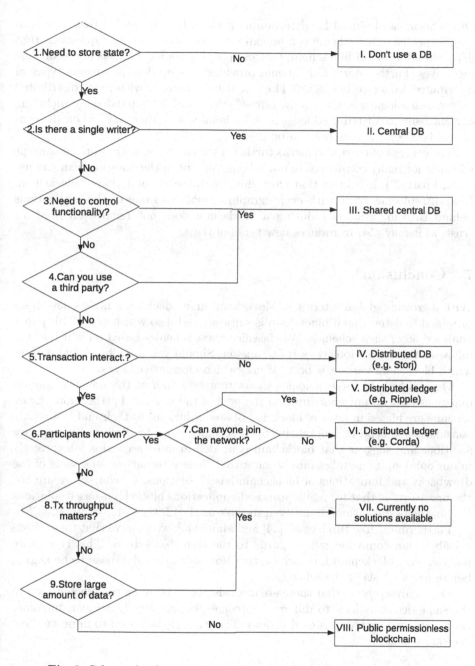

Fig. 2. Scheme for determining which type of database is appropriate

6 Future Work

Our scheme can be used for determining if blockchain is needed from a technical perspective. Our scheme can be extended with non-technical questions that drive the adoption of blockchain, for example philosophical beliefs and economic incentives. Furthermore, our scheme provides an overview of various types of distributed ledger technologies. This could be expanded with more distributed ledger technologies. Additionally, our scheme could be expanded by including current issues of distributed ledgers. Additionally, a further analysis on the consensus between the schemes can be made.

The concept of trust also merits further research. Trust is a important concept which is not really considered in our scheme (except in the question 'can you use a third party?'). It is clear that trust shifts with the introduction of blockchain. Indeed, replacing trust with cryptographic proofs was one of the motivations behind Bitcoin. Still, introducing a blockchain does not remove all need for trust, as it may also introduces new types of trust.

7 Conclusion

With a growing global interest in blockchain, many decision schemes have been proposed to determine if blockchain is suitable, and if so which type. This paper analyzed 30 of such schemes. We classified these schemes based on which of the following three questions they try to answer: Should you use a blockchain? If so, which blockchain variant is best? If not, which alternative is best?

Our analysis of these schemes shows that over half of the schemes contain questions that do not contribute to the goal of the scheme. Furthermore, many schemes are biased in favor of blockchain-based solutions, as their end states only consider some type of blockchain. Such schemes seem to disregard alternative solutions and suggest that blockchain is needed in most scenarios – incorrectly in our opinion, if one takes into account that these alternatives lack some of the drawbacks and limitations of blockchain-based solutions. Of course, we are not the first to argue that for many proposed applications blockchain-based solutions are not the best solution, or not even suitable at all [12,36,37,40,44,49,50,53,54].

Furthermore, like Birch et al. [34] and Maull [45], we observe that there exists a Babylonian confusion with regards to the term blockchain. This is why we put the term blockchain into perspective alongside other database technologies, before our analysis of the schemes.

Our analysis shows that there are inconsistencies between the schemes, where the same decisions lead to different outcomes, or, conversely, similar outcomes can be reached with opposing decisions. There clearly is a need to improve these decision schemes.

We argued that if one uses a blockchain-based solution, only a public permissionless blockchain really makes sense. Although other blockchain types *could* be used in some scenarios, alternative technological solutions are then always a better choice as they lack some of the downsides and limitations of blockchain. Finally, our scheme is a practical guide for blockchain initiatives that need to determine which technology is suitable for a particular scenario.

Acknowledgements. We would like to thank the anonymous reviewers for their constructive feedback.

References

1. Lee, A.: Blockchain patent filings dominated by financial services industry. http://patentvue.com/2018/01/12/blockchain-patent-filings-dominated-by-financial-services-industry/
2. Lewis, A.: Blockchain cheat sheet v0.1. https://bitsonblocks.files.wordpress.com/2016/01/2016-01-26-fintech-finals-hk.pdf?lipi=urn%3Ali%3Apage%3Ad_flagship3_pulse_read%3BQH2LGbmzRKy9rZY9N4nfsA%3D%3D
3. Narayanan, A.: "Private blockchain" is just a confusing name for a shared database. https://freedom-to-tinker.com/2015/09/18/private-blockchain-is-just-a-confusing-name-for-a-shared-database/
4. Suichies, B.: Why blockchain must die in 2016. https://medium.com/@bsuichies/why-blockchain-must-die-in-2016-e992774c03b4
5. Best of ICOs: The blockchain test. https://hackernoon.com/should-we-ico-51964dccadbe
6. Henkel, B.: Beginning blockchain: key questions to getting started. https://www.ca.com/en/blog-mainframeai/beginning-blockchain-key-questions-to-getting-started.html
7. Cap Gemini - SAI trends. https://sai.be/UserContent/FPAX7KUQ45F7B9C4KPZQ_SAI%20trends%20-%20December%202017%20-%20handout.pdf
8. Saiko, D.: Blockchain technology. http://www.cambridgefx.com/blog/blockchain-technology/
9. Schwartz, D.: The Ripple protocol consensus algorithm. https://ripple.com/files/ripple_consensus_whitepaper.pdf
10. Deloitte: I. Blockchain - a new model for health information exchanges. www.semanticscholar.org/paper/I.-Blockchain%E2%80%94A-New-Model-for-Health-Information-I./b99277c3eecfe6d3dd784fe572a45780ffd040e2
11. DHS: Most companies don't need blockchain. https://medium.com/@sbmeunier/when-do-you-need-blockchain-decision-models-a5c40e7c9ba1
12. Greenspan, G.: Avoiding the pointless blockchain project. https://www.multichain.com/blog/2015/11/avoiding-pointless-blockchain-project/
13. Hyperledger: Blockchain decision path. https://steemit.com/ethereum/@whd/fast-method-to-rate-ico-basing-on-hyperledger-course-at-edx
14. IBM: How to decide when to use blockchain. https://www.ibm.com/developerworks/community/blogs/gcuomo/resource/BLOGS_UPLOADED_IMAGES/HowToDecideWhenToUseBlockchain.jpg
15. IDC: New IDC spending guide sees worldwide blockchain spending growing to $9.7 billion in 2021. https://www.idc.com/getdoc.jsp?containerId=prUS43526618

16. Gardner, J.: Do you need a blockchain? https://twitter.com/Disruptepreneur/status/755857596423077888/photo/1?ref_src=twsrc%5Etfw
17. Verslype, K.: Beslissingsmodel: Wanneer blockchain gebruiken? https://www.smalsresearch.be/beslissingsmodel-wanneer-blockchain-gebruiken/
18. Nandwani, K.: Do you really need to use blockchain for your application? https://www.linkedin.com/pulse/when-use-b-word-can-blockchain-actually-help-kunal-nandwani/
19. Cooke, L.: Blockchain technology. http://www.cambridgefx.com/blog/blockchain-technology/
20. Lixar: Blockchain part 2. https://lixar.com/lixar-blog/tech/blockchain-part-2/
21. Chand, M.: Do you need a blockchain. https://www.c-sharpcorner.com/article/do-you-need-a-blockchain2/
22. Hearn, M.: Corda: a distributed ledger. https://docs.corda.net/_static/corda-technical-whitepaper.pdf
23. Quindazzi, M.: Do you really need a blockchain? https://twitter.com/mikequindazzi/status/787760892783894528
24. PWC: Blockchain: the $5 billion opportunity for reinsurers. https://www.pwc.com/gx/en/financial-services/publications/assets/blockchain-for-reinsurers.pdf
25. R3: Corda. https://docs.corda.net/
26. Brown, R.G., Carlyle, J., Grigg, I., Hearn, M.: Corda: an introduction. https://docs.corda.net/_static/corda-introductory-whitepaper.pdf
27. Ripple: One frictionless experience to send money globally. https://ripple.com/
28. Ripple: Reaching consensus in the XRP ledger. https://ripple.com/build/reaching-consensus-xrp-ledger/
29. Meunier, S.: When do you need blockchain? Decision models. https://medium.com/@sbmeunier/when-do-you-need-blockchain-decision-models-a5c40e7c9ba1
30. Wilkinson, S., et al.: Storj. A peer-to-peer cloud storage network. https://storj.io/storj.pdf
31. Mueller, T.: Will blockchain solve my business problem? https://medium.com/contractus/do-i-need-a-blockchain-for-my-business-project-8f8cada7f3ac
32. Verified ICOs: Is a blockchain really required? https://medium.com/@VerifiedICOs/is-a-blockchain-really-required-1a68c7791fa1
33. World Economic Forum: Blockchain beyond the hype. http://www3.weforum.org/docs/48423_Whether_Blockchain_WP.pdf
34. Birch, D., Brown, R.G., Parulava, S.: Towards ambient accountability in financial services: shared ledgers, translucent transactions and the technological legacy of the great financial crisis. J. Paym. Strat. Syst. **10**(2), 118–131 (2016)
35. Bonneau, J., Miller, A., Clark, J., Narayanan, A., Kroll, J.A., Felten, E.W.: SoK: research perspectives and challenges for bitcoin and cryptocurrencies. In: 2015 IEEE Symposium on Security and Privacy (SP), pp. 104–121. IEEE (2015)
36. Buitenhek, M.: Understanding and applying blockchain technology in banking: evolution or revolution? J. Digit. Bank. **1**(2), 111–119 (2016)
37. Carter, L., Ubacht, J.: Blockchain applications in government. In: Proceedings of the 19th Annual International Conference on Digital Government Research: Governance in the Data Age, p. 126. ACM (2018)
38. de Leon, D.C., Stalick, A.Q., Jillepalli, A.A., Haney, M.A., Sheldon, F.T.: Blockchain: properties and misconceptions. Asia Pac. J. Innov. Entrep. **11**(3), 286–300 (2017)
39. Eyal, I., Sirer, E.G.: Majority is not enough: bitcoin mining is vulnerable. In: Christin, N., Safavi-Naini, R. (eds.) FC 2014. LNCS, vol. 8437, pp. 436–454. Springer, Heidelberg (2014). https://doi.org/10.1007/978-3-662-45472-5_28

40. Gerard, D.: Attack of the 50 Foot Blockchain: Bitcoin, Blockchain, Ethereum & Smart Contracts. CreateSpace Independent Publishing Platform (2017)
41. Koens, T., Poll, E.: The Drivers behind Blockchain Adoption: The Rationality of Irrational Choices, Workshop on Large Scale Distributed Virtual Environments (LSDVE) at EuroPar (2018). To appear
42. Kokoris-Kogias, E., Jovanovic, P., Gasser, L., Gailly, N., Ford, B.: Omniledger: a secure, scale-out, decentralized ledger. IACR Cryptology ePrint Archive, 2017:406 (2017)
43. Lin, Y.-P., et al.: Blockchain: the evolutionary next step for ICT E-agriculture. Environments 4(3), 50 (2017)
44. Mattila, J., Seppälä, T., Holmström, J.: Product-centric information management: a case study of a shared platform with blockchain technology (2016)
45. Maull, R., Godsiff, P., Mulligan, C., Brown, A., Kewell, B.: Distributed ledger technology: applications and implications. Strat. Change 26(5), 481–489 (2017)
46. Nakamoto, S.: Bitcoin: A Peer-to-Peer Electronic Cash System (2008). https://bitcoin.org/bitcoin.pdf
47. Pahl, C., El Ioini, N., Helmer, S.: A decision framework for blockchain platforms for IoT and edge computing. In: International Conference on Internet of Things, Big Data and Security (2018)
48. Panetta, K.: Top trends in the gartner hype cycle for emerging technologies (2017). https://www.gartner.com/smarterwithgartner/top-trends-in-the-gartner-hype-cycle-for-emerging-technologies-2017/
49. Peck, M.E.: Blockchain world. Do you need a blockchain? This chart will tell you if the technology can solve your problem. IEEE Spectr. 54(10), 38–60 (2017)
50. Perlman, R.: Blockchain: hype or hope? Login USENIX Mag. 42(2), 68–72 (2017)
51. Peters, G.W., Panayi, E.: Understanding modern banking ledgers through blockchain technologies: future of transaction processing and smart contracts on the internet of money. In: Tasca, P., Aste, T., Pelizzon, L., Perony, N. (eds.) Banking Beyond Banks and Money, pp. 239–278. Springer, Cham (2016). https://doi.org/10.1007/978-3-319-42448-4_13
52. Pilkington, M.: 11 blockchain technology: principles and applications. In: Research Handbook on Digital Transformations, p. 225 (2016)
53. Pisa, M., Juden, M.: Blockchain and economic development: Hype vs. reality. Center for Global Development Policy Paper, 107 (2017)
54. Puthal, D., Malik, N., Mohanty, S.P., Kougianos, E., Yang, C.: The blockchain as a decentralized security framework. IEEE Consum. Electron. Mag. 7(2), 18–21 (2018)
55. Tapscott, D., Tapscott, A.: Blockchain Revolution: How the Technology Behind Bitcoin is Changing Money, Business, and the World. Penguin, London (2016)
56. Wüst, K., Gervais, A.: Do you need a blockchain? IACR Cryptology ePrint Archive, 2017:375 (2017)
57. Xu, X., et al.: A taxonomy of blockchain-based systems for architecture design. In: 2017 IEEE International Conference on Software Architecture (ICSA), pp. 243–252. IEEE (2017)

Valuable Puzzles for Proofs-of-Work

Colin Boyd[✉] and Christopher Carr

Norwegian University of Science and Technology, Trondheim, Norway
{colin.boyd,chris.carr}@ntnu.no

Abstract. Proof-of-work (PoW) is used as the consensus mechanism in most cryptocurrencies. PoW-based puzzles play an important part in the operation and security of a cryptocurrency, but come at a considerable energy cost. One approach to the problem of energy wastage is to find ways to build PoW schemes from valuable computational problems. This work proposes calibration of public key cryptographic systems as a suitable source of PoW puzzles. We describe the properties needed to adapt public key cryptosystems as PoW functions suitable for decentralised cryptocurrencies and provide a candidate example.

Keywords: Proof-of-work · Useful computation · Blockchain

1 Introduction

Proof-of-work (PoW) mechanisms are an integral part of modern cryptocurrencies, such as Bitcoin and the numerous altcoin variants [20], where they are used to maintain consensus. Despite their successful employment for this task, a source of contention for proofs-of-work is the energy wastage associated with their use [14,16]. On the other hand, the developers of Bitcoin claim that the waste of energy is analogous to the energy expenditure of other financial institutions, such as banks and credit card companies [20]. Even so, the high energy consumption of PoW systems is a concern, and one that is not easily avoided. A main purpose of PoW is to manage the Sybil vulnerability problem [7]. Devising an authority-free decentralised cryptocurrency, that does not suffer from Sybil vulnerabilities and does not use PoW, remains an open problem.

The approach of this work is to design a PoW mechanism that is useful outside of the cryptocurrency it is intended to support. While the energy expenditure would still continue, there would at least be some other value in the execution of the PoW function. The intention is to provide insight into the construction of PoW functions from arbitrary computational puzzles. To illustrate the applicability of this idea, a particular focus is placed on public-key schemes.

Adapting public-key schemes for use as PoW has potential advantages:

1. It can incentivise calibration techniques in software and hardware through the reward structure.

J. Garcia-Alfaro et al. (Eds.): DPM 2018/CBT 2018, LNCS 11025, pp. 130–139, 2018.
https://doi.org/10.1007/978-3-030-00305-0_10

2. It can provide data points to more accurately set safe parameter choices for public key schemes.
3. It can be used for specific public-key schemes to encourage their analysis.

While some public key schemes have undergone considerable practical analysis in the past, this is not true in general. The level of scrutiny applied to any specific scheme is sometimes unclear, especially when the underlying problem has been recently introduced, as in the case of the ring learning with errors problem [5]. Public, large-scale analysis of cryptosystems is not without precedent. RSA Laboratories famously offered cash prizes for factoring large composite numbers [17]. The approach was relatively successful, as many of the challenges remain un-factored, and general understanding of factoring algorithms increased.

Building PoW puzzles from public key schemes has the potential to increase the awareness and level of scrutiny applied to them, and to encourage analysis – both valuable to the cryptographic community. In fact, using a market-driven approach, inherent in competitive proof-of-work schemes, can have the effect of incentivising clever cryptanalytic techniques as well as smart specific hardware designs that target weaknesses in a given scheme. If public key based puzzles stand up to scrutiny for a period of time, without major speedups or breakthroughs, the level of confidence in the scheme's security will grow.

RELATED WORK. The idea of utilising the computational work carried out in PoW schemes for some useful purpose has been around for a while and was first proposed by Dwork and Naor [8]. Despite useful puzzles being addressed early on, there are still relatively few candidates. It seems that a significant problem lies in finding candidate puzzles that can be moulded into a PoW puzzle.

The cryptocurrency Primecoin [11] uses the search for Cunningham Prime Chains as the PoW function. This example demonstrates the possibility to find puzzles that satisfy some of the conditions for adaptability into a proof-of-work mechanism. Gridcoin [22] rewards users for their attempts to solve @home puzzles, for example folding@home [21]. But Gridcoin does not offer decentralisation, equating to simply handing out tokens for the effort of solving certain puzzles. Ball et al. [1] demonstrate the adaptability of specific problems, known as the Orthogonal Vectors and 3SUM problems, into a PoW framework. They rely on a distributed problem board, where specified delegated parties issue problems that can be used to create challenges. We aim to devise authority free, decentralised, proofs-of-work, and so no delegated party or problem board is required.

There are other works that examine the energy expenditure problem in PoW systems. Most solutions rely on removing the competitive computational aspect of proof-of-work, replacing it with some different method, such as proof-of-stake [10], proof-of-activity [2] or proof-of-commitment [6]. Tschorsch and Scheuermann [19] give a concise overview of these alternatives.

CONTRIBUTIONS. The primary goal is to give some insight into the possibility of adapting generic computational puzzles into a PoW framework. This is achieved by stating and explaining the reasoning behind the requirements for this adaptation, and providing definitions and formalism where necessary. Using the

Schnorr signature scheme as an example, a transformation into a PoW scheme is described.

2   Puzzles and Their Properties

Most decentralised cryptocurrencies use a consensus mechanism which relies on the partial pre-image resistance of a chosen hash function.

A notable gain in understanding from the use of the SHA-256 hash function in Bitcoin is that, despite the speedups and development of efficient hardware, there is no evidence of a solution finding method that is any better than brute force search. Another useful insight gained is the ability to quantify the time it would take to find a full preimage of a message digest. This ability is crucial when selecting the difficulty parameter for cryptocurrencies that use PoW.

In order to derive such benefits for more general problems, we need to fit them into a cryptocurrency PoW framework. Puzzles used for Bitcoin-like consensus have certain characteristics which are fundamental to the smooth operation of the cryptocurrency. In order to use alternative puzzles for the PoW mechanism, it is necessary to construct them with these characteristics in mind. We would like to retain the Bitcoin structures, such as blocks and transactions, and identify the abstract interface to the PoW puzzle. We start by defining a puzzle set.

Definition 1 (Puzzle Set). *A puzzle set PS is a tuple of three efficient algorithms* Setup, GenPuz, FindSol *and a deterministic algorithm* VerSol. *Let* λ *be the setup parameter,* $\mathcal{D}$ *the difficulty space,* Str *the message space,* $\mathcal{P}$ *the puzzle space and* Sol *be the solution space.*

1. Setup(1^λ) : *Select* $\mathcal{D}, Str, \mathcal{P}, Sol$ *and return* $(\mathcal{D}, Str, \mathcal{P}, Sol)$.
2. GenPuz($d \in \mathcal{D}, m \in Str$) : *Return* $p \in \mathcal{P}$ *or* $\perp$.
3. FindSol($m \in Str, p \in \mathcal{P}, t \in \mathbb{N}$) : *Return* $s \in Sol$ *after at most t steps.*
4. VerSol($m \in Str, p \in \mathcal{P}, s \in Sol$) : *Return* true *or* false.

A puzzle set may be defined without a solution finding algorithm. It is included here only for completeness. From now on the FindSol algorithm is purposefully omitted. If a solution finding algorithm is included, then there is a correctness requirement as follows: Let $params \leftarrow$ Setup(1^λ) and $p \leftarrow$ GenPuz(d, m), where $d \in \mathcal{D}$ and $m \in Str$, then there exists $t \in \mathbb{N}$ where

$$\Pr[\text{VerSol}(m, p, s) = \text{true} \mid s \leftarrow \text{FindSol}(m, p, t)] = 1.$$

The Bitcoin puzzle fits the structure of Definition 1 where: $\mathcal{D}$ is the set of valid difficulty levels; Str is the combination of hash of the previous block header and the set of valid user inputs (nonce, transactions and other parameters); $\mathcal{P}$ is just the concatenation of the difficulty and valid input strings; and Sol is the set of hash inputs that hash below the current target.

A new puzzle must have the interfaces of Definition 1, but must also satisfy some properties to ensure that the incentive properties of Bitcoin are retained. We call these *fairness requirements* (FRs). It is not possible to prove what are the correct fairness requirements without extensive real-world trials, because they depend on human behaviour. Thus we define properties based on the perceived critical properties of the Bitcoin puzzle. We can also take guidance from previous efforts to define puzzle properties, including those of Miller et al. [12,13], Narayanan et al. [14], and Biryukov and Khovratovich [3].

FR.1 *Creator Free:* Finding a solution to one puzzle must not give any advantage in solving of any other.

Once a Bitcoin puzzle is solved, the solution is distributed to all participants and used to form a new puzzle. Specifically, the header information from a previous block is used as input to the next block. The header data is unpredictable until a solution is found, so even the solver will have no extra information to help make a start on finding the next puzzle solution.

In essence, this requirement aims to ensures that no party has an advantage in finding the solution to the new puzzle, even if they have solved the previous one. We note however, that this is not satisfied in existing implementations. It has been shown that it is possible to perform *selfish mining* [9,18], where the solver of the previous block does not distribute the solution immediately in order to gain some time advantage on solving the next one.

To formally define FR.1 we first describe two security experiments in Fig. 1. In both experiments the goal of the adversary $\mathcal{A}$ is to solve any one of the set of puzzles defined using the inputs $m_i = (m_{1,i}, m_{2,i})$. The difference between the two experiments is that in the first $\mathcal{A}$ selects both $m_{1,i}$ and $m_{2,i}$ for input into the GenPuz algorithm, and in the second $m_{1,i}$ is selected at random from the $\mathcal{S}tr$ set. This reflects the Bitcoin puzzle set where the input string consists of two parts: one coming from the previous block and one which can be influenced by the miner. The ability to influence the first part should not help an adversary.

$\mathbf{Exp}^{\mathsf{PzSol}}_{\mathcal{A},d,n,t}$:

$\quad m_{1,1}, m_{1,2}, \ldots, m_{1,n} \leftarrow \mathcal{A}$

$\quad m_{2,1}, m_{2,2}, \ldots, m_{2,n} \leftarrow \mathcal{A}$

$\quad \{m_i = (m_{1,i}, m_{2,i}) | \forall i \in \{1, 2, \ldots, n\}\}$

$\quad p_1 \leftarrow \mathsf{GenPuz}(d, m_1), p_2 \leftarrow \mathsf{GenPuz}(d, m_2), \ldots, p_n \leftarrow \mathsf{GenPuz}(d, m_n)$

$\quad s \leftarrow \mathcal{A}$

$\quad \textbf{return } (m_i, p_i, s) \text{ for some } i \in \{1, 2, \ldots, n\}$

$\mathbf{Exp}^{\mathsf{PzSolR}}_{\mathcal{A},d,n,t}$:

$\quad m_{1,1}, m_{1,2}, \ldots, m_{1,n} \xleftarrow{\$} \mathcal{S}tr$

$\quad m_{2,1}, m_{2,2}, \ldots, m_{2,n} \leftarrow \mathcal{A}$

$\quad \{m_i = (m_{1,i}, m_{2,i}) | \forall i \in \{1, 2, \ldots, n\}\}$

$\quad p_1 \leftarrow \mathsf{GenPuz}(d, m_1), p_2 \leftarrow \mathsf{GenPuz}(d, m_2), \ldots, p_n \leftarrow \mathsf{GenPuz}(d, m_n)$

$\quad s \leftarrow \mathcal{A}$

$\quad \textbf{return } (m_i, p_i, s) \text{ for some } i \in \{1, 2, \ldots, n\}$

Fig. 1. Creator free experiments

For the experiments in Fig. 1 we define the game G to **win**, for some diffi-culty d, fixed n, for some efficient $\mathcal{A}$ returning (m_i, p_i, s), $i \in \{1, 2, \ldots, n\}$ and running in at most time t, if $\texttt{VerSol}(m_i, p_i, s)$ returns true. Succinctly we write $\mathbf{Exp}^{G}_{\mathcal{A},d,n,t} = 1$, else we write $\mathbf{Exp}^{G}_{\mathcal{A},d,n,t} = 0$.

Definition 2 (Creator Free). *Let PS be a puzzle set with setup parameter λ. We say that PS is creator free if for any d, n and any efficient $\mathcal{A}$ running in time t we can define an efficient $\mathcal{B}$ running in approximately the same time $t' \approx t$, such that*

$$\Pr[\mathbf{Exp}^{\mathsf{PzSol}}_{\mathcal{A},d,n,t} = 1] - \Pr[\mathbf{Exp}^{\mathsf{PzSolR}}_{\mathcal{B},d,n,t'} = 1] \leq \mathsf{negl}(\lambda).$$

FR.2 *Puzzle independence:* It should not be possible to use the effort expended to solve one puzzle, to solve another.

Puzzle independence requires that even if you can create multiple puzzles, all the effort expended towards solving any specific one of them will not give any advantage in solving another distinct puzzle. In Bitcoin, puzzles are indepen-dent as one cannot use the work directed towards solving one block, to help with the solution to another. This is because each new puzzle is formed by an unpredictable pseudo-random string each time, for each block.

$\mathbf{Exp}^{\mathsf{PzIndR}}_{\mathcal{A},d,n,t}$:

> $m_{1,1}, m_{1,2}, \ldots, m_{1,n} \xleftarrow{\$} \mathcal{S}tr$
> $m_{2,1}, m_{2,2}, \ldots, m_{2,n} \leftarrow \mathcal{A}$
> $\{m_i = (m_{1,i}, m_{2,i}) | \forall i \in \{1, 2, \ldots, n\}\}$
> $p_1 \leftarrow \mathsf{GenPuz}(d, m_1), p_2 \leftarrow \mathsf{GenPuz}(d, m_2), \ldots, p_n \leftarrow \mathsf{GenPuz}(d, m_n)$
> **return** $(m_i, p_i, s_i) \forall i \in \{1, 2, \ldots, n\}$

Fig. 2. Puzzle independence experiment

For Fig. 2, as in Fig. 1, we define the game G to **win**, for some difficulty d, fixed n, for some algorithm $\mathcal{A}$ returning (m_i, p_i, s_i), $\forall i \in \{1, 2, \ldots, n\}$ and running in at most time t, if $\texttt{VerSol}(m_i, p_i, s_i)$ returns true for every i.

Definition 3 (Puzzle Independence). *Let PS be a puzzle set with setup parameter λ. We say that PS has puzzle independence if for any d, n and any efficient $\mathcal{A}$ running in time t we can define an efficient $\mathcal{B}$ running in at most time t'/n, where $t' \approx t$ such that*

$$| \Pr[\mathbf{Exp}^{\mathsf{PzIndR}}_{\mathcal{A},d,n,t} = 1] - (\Pr[\mathbf{Exp}^{\mathsf{PzIndR}}_{\mathcal{B},d,1,t/n} = 1])^n | \leq \mathsf{negl}(\lambda).$$

FR.3 *Chance to win:* Every participant should have some non-negligible chance of solving a puzzle before any other.

In Bitcoin, the probability of being the first to solve the puzzle is directly proportional to one's share of the computational power directed towards the puzzle at a given time. Note that FR.3 only asks for some non-negligible chance that a participant can win, it does not require any specific probability distribution. Previous authors [3, 14] have proposed a related property called *progress-free* which states that solving a puzzle should be a Poisson process. Such a definition may be too strict; it excludes some useful examples, while the concrete parameters used will determine what is sufficient incentive for a small user to participate.

In addition to the fairness requirements, there are practical requirements (PRs) that can be identified to ensure that any new puzzle is useable in a real system. We mostly give these informally, since usability is not easy to quantify.

PR.1 *Linkable puzzles:* A previous puzzle solution can be used to form a new puzzle.

The security of transactions within a PoW based distributed ledger relies on encoding the transactional data along with the puzzle. For this data to persist, the solution of each puzzle is used to form a new puzzle, so the puzzle solution acts as a pointer to the previous transactions. This forms the ledger. Specifically in Bitcoin, each new block contains information relating to the previous block.

Definition 4 (Linkable). *Let PS be a puzzle set with setup parameter λ, then we say that a PS is linkable if $Sol \subseteq Str$.*

PR.2 *Efficiently Verifiable:* The solution must be efficient and quick to verify by all parties.

PR.3 *Tunable:* The difficulty, or expected number of computational steps, of finding a puzzle solution must be adjustable in order to increase and decrease the difficulty of finding a solution to a puzzle.

PR.4 *Valuable:* Puzzles should provide some useful function in the finding of their solution, other than their purpose within the PoW scheme.

3   Generic Bitcoin-Like Construction

We can now describe a generic construction for a Bitcoin-like puzzle in Definition 5. This is an abstract version of the Bitcoin puzzle construction, where each puzzle instance is generated by a hash output where the input has two parts, in addition to a difficulty parameter.

Definition 5 (Bitcoin-like puzzle). *A Bitcoin-like puzzle generation algorithm is a puzzle set, described by three algorithms:*

- $\mathsf{Setup}(1^\lambda) : \mathcal{D} = \mathbb{Z}, Str = \{0,1\}^*, \mathcal{P} = \{0,1\}^{n_1}, Sol = \{0,1\}^{n_2}$ *for some $n_1, n_2 \in \mathbb{N}$.*
- $\mathsf{GenPuz}(d, m = (m_1, m_2))$ *computes $\tilde{p} \leftarrow H(m_1 \| m_2) \| d$ for $H : \{0,1\}^* \rightarrow \{0,1\}^{n_3}$, where H is a pseudo-random function with $n_3 \in \mathbb{N}$, and returns $p \leftarrow \mathsf{CreatePuz}(\tilde{p}) \| \tilde{p}$, where $\mathsf{CreatePuz}$ is a deterministic algorithm, with running time parameterised by λ.*

- VerSol(m, p, s) *returns* true *if* $p = p' \leftarrow$ GenPuz(d, m) *and* CheckSol(p, s) *returns* true, *else it returns* false, *where* CheckSol *is a deterministic boolean algorithm.*

The next result shows that any Bitcoin-like puzzle satisfies FR.1 and FR.2. The proof is omitted due to space constraints.

Theorem 1. *Let PS be a Bitcoin-like puzzle generation algorithm with setup parameter* λ. *If H is a random oracle, then for a fixed* $d \in \mathcal{D}$, *a fast and efficient* GenPuz *algorithm, PS is creator free and is linkable.*

Moreover, *PS* is efficiently verifiable if both H and CheckSol combined terminate in time significantly less than the time required to find a solution. The puzzle set *PS* is tunable if when d is increased, it takes on average more computational steps to find a corresponding puzzle and solution p, s that satisfies VerSol, and vice-versa.

Figure 3 further describes the puzzle chaining process. This process explicitly defines the solution to a previous puzzle as part of the message, which is used to generate the next puzzle. This links the puzzles and the solutions together. Figure 3 is in practice how one would expect a PoW mechanism to operate, though there may be different variations.

Bitcoin-like Chained Puzzle:

Let *PS* be a Bitcoin-like puzzle generation algorithm as in Defn. 5. For any $i > 0, i \in \mathbb{N}$, with predefined constant $s_0 \in \mathcal{Sol}$, the Bitcoin-like chained puzzle is defined by:

1: $s = s_{i-1}$.
2: $a_i =$ input(). \\collect auxiliary inputs
3: $m = (s, a_i)$.
4: $p_i =$ GenPuz(d, m).
5: $s_i =$ input(). \\attempts to find the puzzle solution
6: **-If:** VerSol(m, p_i, s_i) returns true, $s = s_i$, **goto** 2.
7: **Else: goto** 5.

Fig. 3. Bitcoin-like chained puzzle

4   Schnorr Signature Puzzles

The Schnorr signature scheme public key generation procedure, as described by Boneh [4], selects random primes p and q such that $q|p - 1$, an element $g \in \mathbb{Z}_p^*$ of order q, an element $a \in \mathbb{Z}_q$ and computes $y = g^a \in \mathbb{Z}_p^*$. The scheme also uses some public hash function $H : \{0, 1\}^* \rightarrow \mathbb{Z}_q$. The public parameters are (p, q, g, y, H), with a as the private key.

The goal is to create Bitcoin-like puzzles by describing a method for generating random public keys, without corresponding private keys. The puzzle is then to find a corresponding private key, or otherwise form a signature on the input

Setup(1^λ) :
      1: **Return:** $\mathcal{D} = \mathbb{N}, Str = \{0,1\}^*, \mathcal{P} = (\mathbb{Z}^4, H : Str \to \mathbb{Z}), Sol = \mathbb{Z}^2$,
      for some pseudo-random function H.

GenPuz($d \in \mathcal{D}, m \in Str$) :
      1: **Select:** $\hat{m}$.
      2: **Return:** $p = \hat{m}\|d$.

VerSol($m \in Str, p \in \mathcal{P}, s \in Sol$) :
    1: **Input:** $(m, F(p)), s = (\sigma, \gamma)$.
    2: **–If:** $p = p' \leftarrow$ GenPuz(d, m), continue, else return false.
    3: **Run:** $v = g^\sigma y^{-\gamma} \mod \mathbb{Z}_p$.
    4: **–If:** $H(m|v) = \gamma, \pi = $ true, else $\pi = $ false.
    5: **Return:** π.

Fig. 4. Schnorr signature puzzle algorithms

message. A puzzle set for the Schnorr signature forgery puzzle is described in Fig. 4.

To complete the puzzle definition, we need to define the function F used in the VerSol algorithm of Fig. 4. Due to space constraints we omit the details, but the general idea is to use a deterministic version of the parameter generation process from the FIPS digital signature standard [15, Appendix A]. Using the value $\hat{m}$ as the parameter seed, first q, then p, then g and finally the public verification key y, are all generated. This method generates the public key without a corresponding secret key. Finding the secret key, or otherwise signing the message m becomes the PoW challenge. By relying on the randomness provided by the hash function H, this puzzle set is linkable and creator free by Theorem 1.

We are not able to prove that puzzle independence (FR.2) holds for the Schnorr puzzle due to the nature of the puzzle generation algorithm. If two distinct puzzles are generated with the same initial primes p and q, then this could give an advantage to a potential solver who has retained some computation for the number field sieve algorithm. We conjecture that in practical cases the puzzles will have the FR.2 property, since selecting a p and q that have been used before is very unlikely.

5 Conclusion

An abstract puzzle construction has been demonstrated as well as describing how the Schnorr signature scheme can be used for a stand-in PoW scheme. Moreover, the parameter generation is applicable to DSA and ElGamal signatures with only minor alterations. The clear route for future work is to adapt different types of public-key schemes, or puzzles in general, for use in PoW systems using the requirements here. A wider variety of puzzles may not only prove to be more valuable in terms of the actual puzzle, but could also potentially help with resistance to the design of ASICs for specific fixed puzzles.

References

1. Ball, M., Rosen, A., Sabin, M., Vasudevan, P.N.: Average-case fine-grained hardness. Cryptology ePrint Archive, Report 2017/202 (2017). http://eprint.iacr.org/2017/202
2. Bentov, I., Lee, C., Mizrahi, A., Rosenfeld, M.: Proof of activity: extending Bitcoin's proof of work via proof of stake [extended abstract]. SIGMETRICS Perform. Eval. Rev. **42**(3), 34–37 (2014)
3. Biryukov, A., Khovratovich, D.: Equihash: asymmetric proof-of-work based on the generalized birthday problem. In: NDSS 2016. The Internet Society, February 2016
4. Boneh, D.: Schnorr digital signature scheme. In: van Tilborg, H.C.A., Jajodia, S. (eds.) Encyclopedia of Cryptography and Security, 2nd edn., pp. 1082–1083. Springer, Heidelberg (2011)
5. Bos, J.W., Costello, C., Ducas, L., Mironov, I., Naehrig, M., Nikolaenko, V., Raghunathan, A., Stebila, D.: Frodo: take off the ring! Practical, quantum-secure key exchange from LWE. In: Weippl, E.R., Katzenbeisser, S., Kruegel, C., Myers, A.C., Halevi, S. (eds.) ACM CCS 2016, pp. 1006–1018. ACM Press, October 2016
6. Clark, J., Essex, A.: CommitCoin: carbon dating commitments with bitcoin. In: Keromytis, A.D. (ed.) FC 2012. LNCS, vol. 7397, pp. 390–398. Springer, Heidelberg (2012). https://doi.org/10.1007/978-3-642-32946-3_28
7. Douceur, J.R.: The Sybil attack. In: Druschel, P., Kaashoek, M.F., Rowstron, A.I.T. (eds.) Peer-to-Peer Systems, First International Workshop, IPTPS (2002)
8. Dwork, C., Naor, M.: Pricing via processing or combatting junk mail. In: Brickell, E.F. (ed.) CRYPTO 1992. LNCS, vol. 740, pp. 139–147. Springer, Heidelberg (1993). https://doi.org/10.1007/3-540-48071-4_10
9. Eyal, I., Sirer, E.G.: Majority is not enough: bitcoin mining is vulnerable. In: Christin, N., Safavi-Naini, R. (eds.) FC 2014. LNCS, vol. 8437, pp. 436–454. Springer, Heidelberg (2014). https://doi.org/10.1007/978-3-662-45472-5_28
10. Kiayias, A., Konstantinou, I., Russell, A., David, B., Oliynykov, R.: A provably secure proof-of-stake blockchain protocol. Cryptology ePrint Archive, Report 2016/889 (2016). http://eprint.iacr.org/2016/889
11. King, S.: Primecoin: a cryptocurrency using the search for Cunningham prime chains as the proof-of-work mechanism (2013). http://primecoin.io/. Accessed Jan 2018
12. Miller, A., Juels, A., Shi, E., Parno, B., Katz, J.: Permacoin: repurposing bitcoin work for data preservation. In: 2014 IEEE Symposium on Security and Privacy, pp. 475–490. IEEE Computer Society Press, May 2014. https://doi.org/10.1109/SP.2014.37
13. Miller, A., Kosba, A.E., Katz, J., Shi, E.: Nonoutsourceable scratch-off puzzles to discourage bitcoin mining coalitions. In: Ray, I., Li, N., Kruegel, C. (eds.) ACM CCS 2015, pp. 680–691. ACM Press, October 2015
14. Narayanan, A., Bonneau, J., Felten, E.W., Miller, A., Goldfeder, S.: Bitcoin and Cryptocurrency Technologies - A Comprehensive Introduction. Princeton University Press (2016). ISBN: 978-0-691-17169-2
15. National Institute of Standards and Technology: Digital Signature Standard (DSS), July 2013. http://dx.doi.org/10.6028/NIST.FIPS.186-4

16. O'Dwyer, K.J., Malone, D.: Bitcoin mining and its energy footprint. In: Irish Signals and Systems Conference 2014 and 2014 China-Ireland International Conference on Information and Communications Technologies (ISSC 2014/CIICT 2014). IET (2014)
17. RSA-Laboratories: RSA factoring challenges. http://www.isiloniq.com/emc-plus/rsa-labs/historical/the-rsa-challenge-numbers.htm. Accessed Jan 2017
18. Sapirshtein, A., Sompolinsky, Y., Zohar, A.: Optimal selfish mining strategies in bitcoin. In: Grossklags, J., Preneel, B. (eds.) FC 2016. LNCS, vol. 9603, pp. 515–532. Springer, Heidelberg (2017). https://doi.org/10.1007/978-3-662-54970-4_30
19. Tschorsch, F., Scheuermann, B.: Bitcoin and beyond: a technical survey on decentralized digital currencies. IEEE Commun. Surv. Tutorials **18**(3), 2084–2123 (2016)
20. Web: Bitcoin Wiki. https://en.bitcoin.it/wiki/Main_Page. Accessed Jan 2018
21. Web: Folding@home. http://folding.stanford.edu/. Accessed Feb 2018
22. Web: Gridcoin. https://gridcoin.us (2017). Accessed June 2018

A Poisoning Attack Against Cryptocurrency Mining Pools

Mohiuddin Ahmed, Jinpeng Wei$^{(\boxtimes)}$, Yongge Wang, and Ehab Al-Shaer

University of North Caroline at Charlotte, Charlotte, NC 28223, USA
{mahmed27,jwei8,yonwang,ealshaer}@uncc.edu

Abstract. This paper discusses a potentially serious attack against public crypto-currency mining pools. By deliberately introducing errors under benign miners' names, this attack can fool the mining pool administrator into punishing any innocent miner; when the top miners are punished, this attack can significantly slow down the overall production of the mining pool. We show that an attacker needs only a small fraction (e.g., one millionth) of the resources of a victim mining pool, which makes this attack scheme very affordable by a less powerful competing mining pool. We experimentally confirm the effectiveness of this attack scheme against a few well-known mining pools such as Minergate and Slush Pool.

Keywords: Crypto currency · Mining pool · Invalid share
DoS attack · Stratum protocol

1 Introduction

The emergence of bitcoin in 2009 [24] paves the way for many other crypto-currencies like monero, litecoin, and etherium. Crypto-currency is the cryptographically protected digital currency that is built upon the blockchain platform. Blockchain is like a public ledger that keeps track of all transactions in each crypto-currency. Blockchain is shared across all users of a specific crypto-currency. Before adding any transaction to the blockchain, the transaction needs to be verified, which is called *mining*. The person or group of people who is verifying the transaction is called miner. For the verification of a transaction, the miner receives a reward in the form of crypto-currency where the mining is performed.

In order to verify a transaction, miners have to solve a cryptographic puzzle. Since the task of solving the cryptographic puzzle is computation-intensive, the more computation power a miner has, the more likely he/she can solve the puzzle. If miners follow mining protocol honestly, they can increase their mining power in two ways: (1) *solo mining*, in which a miner can buy new resources and deploy those to mine transactions, and (2) *pool mining*, in which miners form a pool and share their resources to solve the cryptographic puzzle. In pool mining, the reward is distributed among the pool members based on their contributions. Solo

© Springer Nature Switzerland AG 2018
J. Garcia-Alfaro et al. (Eds.): DPM 2018/CBT 2018, LNCS 11025, pp. 140–154, 2018.
https://doi.org/10.1007/978-3-030-00305-0_11

mining is almost obsolete now due to the increasing difficulty of crypto-currency mining and the emergence of task specific hardware like ASICs. Instead, pool mining has become a more promising way of mining due to the trade-off between revenue gain and power usage by resources.

One important design issue of pool mining is the accurate measurement of member contributions. To achieve this, two methods have been proposed: Proof of Work (PoW) and Proof of Stake (PoS). PoW has been used in bitcoin system to reach consensus on the blockchain status and to defend against double-spending attacks: each worker's computational power is calculated based on the *shares* he submits to the pool. Under PoS, each pool member's capability of creating the next block is proportional to the amount of *coin ages* he has, and the coin age is defined as currency amount times holding period [11,20].

The reward provided by the crypto-currency network encourages miners to increase their mining power through illegal means, represented in multiple kinds of attacks. One such way is hijacking benign users' machines and using them to mine on behalf of the attacker, e.g., botnet mining [17] and drive-by-cryptocurrency mining [4]. A second major type of attack is DDoS [16]. There are two incentives to perform those DDoS attacks. Firstly, slowing down the mining task of a pool through DDoS attack might give an unfair decisive advantage to other pools to win the race for the next bundle of crypto-currency rewarded for verifying a transaction. Secondly, delayed operation of a pool may discourage future users to join victim pool and current users might leave the pool for a better one.

We propose a way of indirect DDoS attack on the mining or crypto-currency protocol or implementation. Although there have been some attacks [27] using implementation or protocol vulnerability of mining and crypto-currency, no previous work used indirect DDoS on the user and pool at the same time. Our attack is mainly focused on PoW (Proof of Work) based pool mining.

More specifically, we propose to degrade the productivity of a target mining pool by poisoning its members' mining results, which causes the pool server to penalize its benign miners. This attack is enabled by two factors: (1) a lack of miner authentication and (2) the invalid share policy of the mining pools. The first factor allows an attacker to submit invalid shares on behalf of a benign miner, and when the number of invalid shares reaches certain threshold, they trigger penalty or ban of benign members of the mining pool based on the second factor. Since the ban or penalty to benign pool members are imposed inadvertently by the pool manager, we consider our attack technique indirect and subtle. This attack can be employed by one mining pool to lower the expected success outlook of a competing mining pool. The essence of our attack is to turn the invalid shares policy of mining pools against themselves.

We make the following contributions:

- We propose a novel attack scheme that can fool the mining pools into punishing their productive members.
- We implement a prototype of attack tool that can submit a large number of invalid shares using the Stratum protocol.

– We evaluate the effectiveness of our attack against Slush Pool and Minergate.

The rest of this paper is organized as follows. Section 2 gives technical background information about pool-based crypo-currency mining and invalid share policy adopted by mining pools. Section 3 describes the details of our attack method. Section 4 presents both theoretical and empirical evaluation of our attack scheme against Minergate and Slush Pool. Section 5 discusses possible remediation of the attack. Related work is mentioned in Sect. 6, and Sect. 7 concludes the paper.

2 Technical Background

Most of the crypto-currencies currently available on the market are distributed and decentralized in nature. Those crypto-currency ecosystems consist of users, miners, blockchain, and mining pools. Users use crypto-currency in the form of transaction. Miners verify the transaction and append the verified transaction to the publicly shared ledger called blockchain. Miners are rewarded by the crypto-currency network for verifying each transaction, which gives them incentives.

2.1 Blockchain and Mining Pool

Blockchain is a public ledger that records all of the verified transactions. Miners add new transactions to the blockchain after verification. Verification of transaction is called mining, which is to solve a cryptographic puzzle. The cryptographic puzzle to solve is generating a hash that is smaller than a set value provided by the network. The set value is called *difficulty* of the network. For bitcoins, this difficulty value is adjusted dynamically such that blocks are generated at an average rate of one every ten minutes [1]. Different cryto-currency use different hashing algorithms. For example, bitcoin and bitcoincash uses SHA-256 hashing algorithm, Litecoin and Dogecoin uses Scrypt hashing algorithm, Dash (DASH) and CannabisCoin (CANN) uses X11 hashing algorithm, Monero and Bytecoin uses Cryptonight algorithm and, ethereum and ethereum classic use Ethash algorithm.

Since solving the cryptographic puzzle is a computation intensive task, it became increasingly difficult task for solo miners to solve the puzzle. To solve this problem mining pool has emerged. In a mining pool, all members work together to mine each block and share their revenues when one of them mines a block. Although joining a pool does not change a miner's expected revenue, it decreases the variance and makes the monthly revenues more predictable.

Popular mining pools consist of thousands of miners. For example, btc.com mining pool has around 56k workers for bitcoin and around 31k workers for bitcoin cash crypto-currency. The hashrate of this pool is 8.7 EH/s for bitcoin and 401.9 PH/s for bitcoin cash. Here, pool hashrate is the aggregation of all workers' hashrate. Each worker's hashrate is calculated based on the valid shares that he submits. For example, if a worker submits one share of difficulty one, it means that this worker checks $2^{number\ of\ trailing\ zeros\ in\ target\ value}$ hash values to generate the valid share. Again, submitting one share of difficulty two is like submitting two shares of difficulty one.

Moreover, mining pools often offer variable share difficulty, in which the pool assigns share targets to miners adaptively based on their computational ability. The purpose of adaptive share difficulty is to make sure that the task is neither too difficult, thus enabling miners to prove work is done, nor too easy, thus reducing the overhead on the pool to verify submitted shares.

2.2 Cryptographic Puzzle

The cryptographic puzzle to solve is to find a hash using data from assigned job that is less than a provided *target value*. For bitcoin, the puzzle consists of a target value and a tuple, *F = (block version number || hash of previous block || root of merkle tree || timestamp || Nbits)*, here || denotes concatenation. *target* and all fields of tuple *F* will be proved in the assigned job. *Nbits* is the encoded share difficulty. *Extranonce2* is changed by the miners by incrementing it in addition to incrementing nonce, so that there are more possible hashes that can be tried with a given set of transactions. Given the target and tuple *F*, the miners will try to find a pair iterating over *Extranonce2* and *nonce* such that it satisfies the following equation

$$H^2(nonce||F) < target \tag{1}$$

Here, H^2 means double SHA-256 hashing operation for bitcoin.

2.3 Stratum-Mining Pool Communication Protocol

Stratum is a clear text communication protocol built over TCP/IP using JSON-RPC format [6]. Although there is no official documentation for this protocol, biticoinwiki [2] provides details about the protocol. In this section we provide an overview of Stratum protocol implemented by Slushpool [6] as observed in captured packets of mining in slushpool.

Subscription of Miner. In order to register in a mining pool that supports Stratum protocol, the miner first subscribes through a subscription connection message *[Mining.subscribe, params]*, which describes the miner's capability through *params*. The mining pool server will respond with a subscription response message in the following format *[subscription, extranonce1, extranonce2_size]*. Here, *subscription* is an array of 2-item tuples, each with name of subscribed notification and subscription ID. *extranonce1* is a hex-encoded, per-connection unique string that will be used for creating generation transactions later, and *extranonce2_size* is the number of bytes that the miner uses for its *Extranonce2* counter.

Authorization of Miner. After each connection subscription request, the miner authenticates with the pool through a miner authorization request message in the following format: *[Mining.authorize, username, password]*

Here, the *username* has two parts: miner's username and worker id to authorize multiple workers. The *password* field is provided in clear text, and it is optional for most mining pools.

Share Difficulty Notification. Following a successful authorization of miner, the pool server sends a share difficulty notification with the minimum share difficulty the pool server is willing to accept using *Mining.set_difficulty*.

Assignment of Job. Since the Stratum mining protocol works in publish-subscribe manner, all of the subscribed and authorized miners will be notified when a new job is available in the pool and will be assigned using different parameters in the following format: *[Mining.notify, job_id, params, clean_jobs]*. Here, the *params* field contains all of the puzzle parameters such as the fields of tuple F mentioned in Sect. 2.2. *clean_jobs* is a Boolean which indicates whether a miner should drop all previous jobs and work exclusively on the current one.

Submission of Shares. Once a miner finds a solution that satisfies the requirement provided in *Mining.set_difficulty* method using all of *params* from *Mining.notify* job assignment response and miner's calculated *nonce* and *extranonce2*, it will send the solution to the pool for verification and credit in the following format *[Mining.submit, user_id, job_id, time, nonce, extranonce2]*.

Here, *user_id* is obtained from the response of *Mining.authorize* request, *job_id* is obtained from the *Mining.notify* response. *nonce* and *extranonce2* is the puzzle solution which meets the difficulty provided in *Mining.set_difficulty*. The pool server will use these values to reconstruct the F value mentioned in Sect. 2.2 and verify that Relation 1 is satisfied. The pool server will respond with a status message denoting *accepted* or *rejected*. A share can be rejected for two reasons: *stale share* which is submitted too late, and *bad share* which does not satisfy the difficulty requirement.

In summary, as shown in Fig. 1, after the subscription and authorization of miner by pool server through *mining.subscribe* and *mining.authorize* API, the pool server will send the share difficulty and multiple new jobs to solve through *mining.set_difficulty* and *mining.notify* API. Now, the miner has to find a *nonce* and *extranonce2* for every job it wants to solve that will satisfy the share difficulty set by the pool server and submit it to the pool server through *mining.submit* API.

2.4 Invalid Share Policy

From our study, crypto-currency mining pools have to face the issue of cheating by pool members (i.e., those who do not do the job but just submit invalid

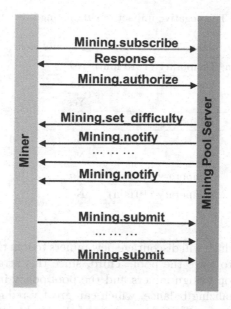

Fig. 1. Interaction between miner and mining pool server

shares). Therefore, they establish various penalty policies for such participants. For example, the Minergate policy [23] mentions: "Open source pools by default ban users if the percentage of invalid shares is bigger than 25%. However, MinerGate does not allow hackers to cheat the pool and follow certain policies for invalid share. For sending invalid share user gets penalty and his unconfirmed balance decreases, sending multiple invalid shares will lead to negative unconfirmed balance. This will prevent cheaters from having funds in confirmed balance." In Table 1, we summarize the negative impact of submitting invalid shares to several public mining pools. We can see that misbehaving users are often banned to some extent and their wallets can even be locked.

As we mention in Sect. 2.3, password is not required at most mining pools when authorizing miners, which means that anyone can impersonate other miners during crypto-currency mining. Therefore, an adversary can leverage this fundamental "vulnerability" of the mining pool protocol for an effective attack, in which the attacker's goal is to cause the mining pool administrator to mistakenly penalize innocent miners.

3   Attack Method

In this paper, we propose a way to attack mining pools using the publicly available information about the mining pool, miners and mining APIs. This attack will decrease the hashrate of a mining pool in two ways. First, since the pool server will have to validate invalid shares submitted by the attacker, it will add workload to the pool server. Second, decreasing pool hashrate will decrease the

Table 1. The negative impact of submitting invalid shares

Mining site	Banned	Payouts locked	Balance reduced
moneroocean.stream	Temporary (1–10 min)	No	No
xmrpool.net	Yes	No	No
supportxmr.com	Yes	Yes	No
www.viaxmr.com	Temporary	No	No
minergate.com	No	No	Yes
slushpool.com	Yes	No	No
moriaxmr.com	Temporary (10 min)	No	No
ratchetmining.com	Temporary (10 min)	No	No

earning of the pool, which will discourage new miners to join the pool and encourage affected miners to leave the pool. Third, since this attack submits invalid shares on behalf of top benign miners and the pool policy imposes penalty like ban of miners or penalizing balance, which can greatly reduce the productivity of the pool and encourage affected members of the pool to leave.

In this section, we outline steps to perform an attack on mining pools. Each step will be elaborated in subsequent subsections. The steps as shown in Fig. 2 are given below:

1. Collect mining pool and miner information
2. Collect mining API information
3. Submit invalid shares to attack miner reputation
4. Check attack results
   (a) if the pool marks the submitted shares as invalid we are successful and exit
   (b) otherwise restart from step 1 by collecting new information about pool, miner and API

In the following, we describe the details of how an attacker can collect miner account information in Sect. 3.1 and mining API information in Sect. 3.2. Then we discuss the actual attack scheme in Sect. 3.3.

3.1   Collecting Mining Pool and Miner Information

Collecting the mining pool and miner information is the first step of our attack. Based on the available resources to perform the attack, we can select the appropriate pool. In the case of bitcoin, BTC.com provides a list of pools and their hash rate distribution (Fig. 3 and [3]). Using this list, we can decide which pool(s) can be attacked successfully with the available resources. Since all of the mining pools publicly share their server addresses for each supported crypto-currency, mining pool server addresses can be collected from the targeted pool's website. Miner's username and contribution to a specific pool can be collected in two

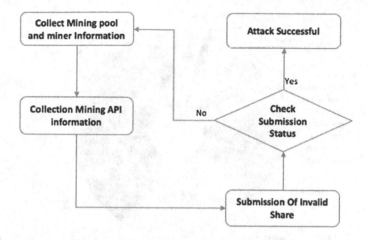

Fig. 2. The flowchart of proposed approach

ways. First, some pools like sluspool.com and minergate.com share information about the top contributors [7, 25] of the pool and the corresponding user names of the miners. Second, since the communication between the mining pool and miners happens through the Stratum protocol, a clear-text JSON format, we can figure out the mining pool's top contributors by traffic analysis if we know the miner or mining pool's address as described in [27]. For slushpool [25], the top 100 miners contribute more than 90% hashrate of the pool. Therefore, submitting invalid shares on behalf of these top contributors will trigger the pool policy to penalize the miners, which will encourage the top miners to leave the pool. Additionally, departure of attacked miners will drastically decrease the hashrate of the pool. For our analysis, we used publicly available information about miners and mining pools.

3.2 Collecting Mining API Information

Most of the mining pools follow standard API name provided by Stratum protocol [2, 6]. However, some of the mining pools like Minergate [5] do not follow the standard API name. These pools use customized API name instead. Thus, lack of standard Stratum protocol API name calls for network traffic analysis to discover API name used by the corresponding mining pool. To get the API name used by a specific mining pool, we can mine in the pool using their mining application (e.g., [8–10]) as a benign user and capture the network traffic of the mining application. Since Stratum is a clear text JSON format protocol, the captured traffic will reveal the API name used by the mining pool.

In our analysis, Minergate [5] mining pool does not follow the Stratum protocol standard [6]. However, mining as a benign user using Minergate's mining application [10] and capturing the mining traffic from the application reveal the API name used by the Minergate pool server. For the subscription and authorization of miner, Minergate's API name is "login" wheres the standard Stratum

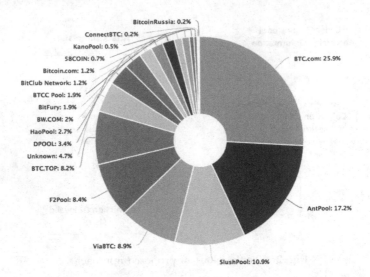

Fig. 3. Hash rate distribution of mining pools

API name is "subscribe" and "authorize". Captured traffic of Minergate application for miner authorization is given below:

```
{"id":"1","jsonrpc":"2.0","method":"login","params":{"agent":
"MinerGateMac/6.9","login":"iden1930@gmail.com", "pass":""}}
```

Similarly, traffic analysis of Minergate application also tells us the structure of the JSON-RPC method to submit shares:

```
{"id":"2","jsonrpc":"2.0","method":"submit","params":{"id":"id
corresponding to username returned in login response", "job_id":
"Job id corresponding to job returned in login response", "nonce":
"Random value", "result":"Random value"}}
```

3.3   Attacking Miners' Reputation

After getting a victim miner's username by the approach described in Sect. 3.1, our next step is to mine badly on behalf of this miner. We cannot use the official mining software because it is designed to mine honestly. Therefore, we have to create a special tool that speaks the mining pool language in order to interact with the pool server but actually does not do any real mining.

We build a tool to carry out our scheme. First we need to know the protocol to login to the pool server, get new jobs, and submit results, including method names and the parameters.

We obtain the above necessary information by analyzing the official mining software (e.g., [8–10]). From the documentation provided by mining pools, we learn the command line arguments needed to run the mining executable, such as the username, mining pool address, and port number. Next, we apply the traffic analysis discussed in Sect. 3.2 to learn the mining API.

Using what we learned from software analysis and traffic analysis, we can now form the login request and submit it to the pool server using a TCP connection. In response to the login request, the pool server returns data containing *job data, job_id, target, time_to_live* and *user_id* corresponding to the username. At that point, the task of a legitimate miner is to find a nonce and extranonce2 that will generate a hash of job data concatenated with a nonce and extranonce2 that is less than the provided target. As our goal is not to help the legitimate miner, we will not generate the hash, instead we randomly generate a nonce, extranonce2, and the result. It is less likely to get a valid share from random selection as getting a good share is a difficult task. Now, we submit the random nonce, random extranonce2, and result to the pool server which will most likely recognize it as an invalid share. We have developed a tool that can send a large number of invalid shares to the pool server in a short period of time.

4 Evaluation

4.1 Feasibility of the Attack in Terms of Required Resources: Theoretical Analysis

We will show that an attacker needs only *a small fraction of* the resources of a top miner in order to successfully attack the top miner, i.e., to cause the mining pool administrator to mistakenly penalize the top miner.

Since a top miner submits valid shares at a very high rate, the attacker also has to submit invalid shares at a very high rate in order to make the percentage of invalid shares of the top miner reach the threshold to be punished. This seems to imply that the attacker would also need significant amount of resources, which increases the cost of the attack and if the cost is too high, the attack would not be worth it. However, our analysis below shows that the attacker can reach the required submission rate of invalid shares at a much lower cost (e.g., 1 millionth of) than the top minor. This is due to the fact that the top miner has to perform a large number of (e.g., 2^{32}) hashing operations between share submissions, while the attacker does not have to.

Specifically, the same amount of resource can be used to submit invalid shares at a much higher rate than to mine and then submit valid shares. As an illustration, let's consider a concrete case. Based on empirical data provided in [27], the average time for a miner with hashrate 4096 GH/s to find a share with difficulty 1024 is

$$\frac{1024 * 2^{32}}{4096 * 2^{30}} = 1 \tag{2}$$

seconds. In other words, such a miner can submit one (1) valid share per second.

On the other hand, suppose the network bandwidth between the miner and the pool server is 640 Mbps or 80M bytes per second, since the average size of network packets containing the shares is 80 bytes, a bad miner can send up to

$$80M/80 = 2^{20} = 1,048,576 \tag{3}$$

invalid shares per second. Here we assume that the bad miner can utilize the entire network bandwidth in the ideal case.

Based on the above two equations, the share submission rate difference (invalid vs valid) is 1,048,576 times. In other words, to reach the same share submission rate, an attacker requires one millionth of resources that a benign miner would need.

The above analysis of attack cost is still an over-estimation because the attacker does not need to submit the same number of invalid shares as the top miner in order to succeed. This is because the percentage threshold of invalid shares to punish a miner is much lower than 50%. Formally, suppose the attacker and the top miner use the same kinds of mining nodes, the share submission rate difference between malicious nodes (MNs) and honest nodes (HNs) is n times, the percentage threshold to punish a miner is r, and one MN can beat x HNs, we can compute x as follows. In one time unit, the MN can produce n invalid shares, while the x HNs produce x valid shares, so the invalid share percentage is $\frac{n}{x+n}$; when the threshold is reached, i.e., $\frac{n}{x+n} = r$, we have $x = \frac{n}{r} - n = \frac{1-r}{r} * n$. For example, if $n = 1,000,000$ and $r = 0.2$, one MN can beat $\frac{1-0.2}{0.2} * 1,000,000 = 4,000,000$ HNs. This means that an attacker can use much less resource to get a benign miner punished.

4.2   Experimental Evaluation

We have experimentally confirmed the feasibility of getting a victim miner penalized by mining badly on his behalf.

To validate our approach, we create a user account at Minergate. Now, our tool uses this account username to submit invalid shares to Minergate pool server following the procedure described in Sect. 3.3. After submitting around 40,000 invalid shares, the account balance decreases from 0.00002398 to 0.00001973, which follows the invalid share policy of Minergate pool. Figures 4 and 5 show the change in our account state before and after we ran our tool.

We also perform the same actions using one existing miner's username at Minergate, and the response from the mining pool server indicates that it detects the submitted shares as invalid. Although we are not able to check whether the pool administrator penalizes the victim miner (because we do not know that miner's password), the Minergate invalid share policy mentions that the pool administrator should penalize the miner for every invalid share. As the pool administrator penalizes our account for submitting invalid shares, it should penalize the victim miner as well for submitting invalid shares. For ethical consideration, we did not carry out a large-scale and sustained attack against the victim miner's account. In reality, it is quite likely that a determined attacker would launch a serious attack in order to bring down the productivity of a victim mining pool.

Fig. 4. Account status before mining for Aeon Coin

Fig. 5. Account status after submission of 40,000 invalid shares for Aeon Coin

4.3   Responsible Disclosure

Due to the potential serious damage that our attack scheme can inflict to public mining pools and the pool-based mining ecosystem in general, we have initiated the process to notify affected mining pools. We have contacted Slush Pool through their Twitter account (@slush_pool) and the Twitter account of the CEO and co-founder Jan Capek. Jan has expressed great interest in our proposed attack, and the discussion between Slush Pool and us is still going on. We also contacted Minergate through its customer service email.

5   Possible Remediation of the Attack

The poisoning attack described in this paper would be defeated if the mining pool server enforces miner authentication. Since the attacker would not know the password of the innocent miner, she will not be able to authenticate and then mine on behalf of the victim miner. The Stratum protocol, which is used by many popular mining pools, already supports user authentication (see Sect. 2.3).

Unfortunately, this feature is often not used at those mining pools, perhaps to minimize the performance overhead. Therefore, we highly recommend that mining pools enforce miner authentication.

We also recommend that pool mining protocols adopt encryption (e.g., HTTPS). Currently, mining protocols such as Stratum is clear text based, which is susceptible to Man-in-the-Middle (MITM) attacks. Basically, an MITM attacker can eavesdrop on the communication between an innocent miner and a mining pool server to steal security credentials and session tokens, and then use them to inject bogus messages that translate to submissions of invalid shares on behalf of innocent miners. Adding encryption would raise the bar for the MITM attackers.

6   Related Work

As [13] points out, a mining pool might be able to increase its revenue by attacking other pools. Eyal et al. propose Selfish Mining [14], an attack against the Bitcoin mining protocol that allows colluding miners to obtain a revenue larger than their fair share.

Mining pools have been constant targets of DDoS attacks. According to empirical studies [16], mining pools are the second-most targeted Bitcoin service after currency exchanges. Among 49 mining pools, 12 encountered DDoS attacks, and at least one mining pool (Altcoin.pw) had to shut down because of DDoS attacks. However, most of these DDoS attacks are performed actively by isolating targeted pool from other parts of the network or making it unavailable to the pool members. Most of those DDoS attacks can be detected using current DDoS detection tools like cloudFire since the attackers are using the network, not the mining or crypto-currency protocol or implementation to perform those attacks. Moreover, [18] presents a game-theoretic analysis of DDoS attacks against bitcoin mining pools.

Most of the existing attacks [15,19,21,22,26] against mining pools are at the network level, not at the protocol level. In [15,19,26], the authors discuss an eclipse attack on bitcoin network that is at the network level. [21] proposes the fork after withholding attack in which miner's dilemma [13] does not hold. [12] discusses the block withholding attack and the corresponding attacker's strategies based on the mining consensus protocol. In [13], Eyal presents a 51% attack using 51% resources of the network, which can be achieved using our proposed attack scheme.

7   Conclusion

The increasing popularity of crypto-currency has encouraged the formation of large and collaborative mining pools. Unfortunately, the huge economic impact of crypto-currency mining has also brought forth various attacks against mining pools. In this paper, we identify a serious attack scheme that can significantly slow down the production rate of a mining pool. The attacker can cause innocent and productive miners of a pool to be punished by submitting invalid mining results on behalf of the victim miners. This attack essentially takes advantage of a combination of the lack of miner authentication and the penalty policy established by mining pools with respect to invalid shares. We present a theoretical analysis to show that an attacker needs only a small fraction (e.g., millionth) of the resources of a victim miner to succeed, making the attack very affordable. We also experimentally confirm the feasibility of our attack against Slush Pool and Minergate. Our study strongly suggests that we should rethink the design of pool mining protocols.

Acknowledgement. This work is partially supported by the US National Security Agency (NSA) under grant number H98230-17-1-0354, and the US DoD Army Research Office (ARO) under grant number W911NF-17-1-0437. The views and conclusions contained in this paper are those of the authors and should not be interpreted as necessarily representing the official policies, either expressed or implied, of the United States National Security Agency or Army Research Office. We also thank the anonymous reviewers for their insightful comments.

References

1. Hash Rate Proof. https://slushpool.com/help/manual/hashrate-proof
2. bitcoinwiki Stratum-protocol (2018). https://en.bitcoin.it/wiki/Stratum_mining_protocol. Accessed 28 May 2018
3. btc.com (2018). https://pool.btc.com/pool-stats. Accessed 28 May 2018
4. Drive by cryptocurrency mining (2018). https://www.malwarebytes.com/pdf/white-papers/Drive-By-Cryptocurrency-Mining-Malwarebytes-Labs-Report.pdf. Accessed 28 May 2018
5. minergate (2018). https://minergate.com/. Accessed 28 May 2018
6. Slushpool Stratum-protocol (2018). https://slushpool.com/help/manual/stratum-protocol. Accessed 28 May 2018
7. slushpool top contributor (2018). https://slushpool.com/stats/hall-of-fame/. Accessed 28 May 2018
8. ASIC and FPGA miner in C for bitcoin (2018). https://github.com/ckolivas/cgminer. Accessed 16 June 2018
9. BFGMiner a modular ASIC/FPGA Bitcoin miner (2018). http://bfgminer.org/. Accessed 16 June 2018
10. Cryptocurrency GUI miner 8.1 & Mining Pool (2018). https://minergate.com/download/win (2018). Accessed 16 June 2018
11. Buterin, V., Griffith, V.: Casper the friendly finality gadget. In: arXiv preprint arXiv:1710.09437 (2017)
12. Courtois, N.T., Bahack, L.: On subversive miner strategies and block withholding attack in bitcoin digital currency. CoRR abs/1402.1718 (2014). http://arxiv.org/abs/1402.1718
13. Eyal, I.: The miner's dilemma. In: 2015 IEEE Symposium on Security and Privacy, pp. 89–103, May 2015. https://doi.org/10.1109/SP.2015.13
14. Eyal, I., Sirer, E.G.: Majority is not enough: Bitcoin mining is vulnerable. In: Proceedings of the Eighteenth International Conference on Financial Cryptography and Data Security (FC 2014) (2014)

15. Heilman, E., Kendler, A., Zohar, A., Goldberg, S.: Eclipse attacks on bitcoin's peer-to-peer network. In: Proceedings of the 24th USENIX Conference on Security Symposium, SEC 2015, pp. 129–144. USENIX Association, Berkeley (2015). http://dl.acm.org/citation.cfm?id=2831143.2831152

16. Huang, D.Y., Dharmdasani, H., Meiklejohn, S., Dave, V., Grier, C., Mccoy, D., Savage, S., Weaver, N., Snoeren, A.C., Levchenko, K.: Botcoin: monetizing stolen cycles (2014)

17. Huang DY, Dharmdasani H, M.S.: Empirical analysis of denial-of-service attacks in the bitcoin ecosystem. In: Proceedings of the Network and Distributed System Security Symposium. Reston, Virginia: Internet Society (2014)

18. Johnson, B., Laszka, A., Grossklags, J., Vasek, M., Moore, T.: Game-theoretic analysis of DDoS attacks against bitcoin mining pools. In: Böhme, R., Brenner, M., Moore, T., Smith, M. (eds.) FC 2014. LNCS, vol. 8438, pp. 72–86. Springer, Heidelberg (2014). https://doi.org/10.1007/978-3-662-44774-1_6

19. Karame, G.O., Androulaki, E., Capkun, S.: Double-spending fast payments in bitcoin. In: Proceedings of the 2012 ACM Conference on Computer and Communications Security, CCS 2012, pp. 906–917. ACM, New York (2012). https://doi.org/10.1145/2382196.2382292, https://doi.acm.org/10.1145/2382196.2382292

20. King, S., Nadal, S.: PPCoin: peer-to-peer crypto-currency with proof-of-stake. In: self-published paper, August 2012

21. Kwon, Y., Kim, D., Son, Y., Vasserman, E., Kim, Y.: Be selfish and avoid dilemmas: fork after withholding (FAW) attacks on bitcoin. In: Proceedings of the 2017 ACM SIGSAC Conference on Computer and Communications Security, CCS 2017, pp. 195–209 ACM, New York (2017). https://doi.acm.org/10.1145/3133956.3134019, https://doi.org/10.1145/3133956.3134019

22. Luu, L., Saha, R., Parameshwaran, I., Saxena, P., Hobor, A.: On power splitting games in distributed computation: the case of bitcoin pooled mining. In: 2015 IEEE 28th Computer Security Foundations Symposium, pp. 397–411, July 2015. https://doi.org/10.1109/CSF.2015.34

23. MinerGate: Invalid shares policy. https://minergate.com/faq/invalid-shares-policy. Accessed 05 Feb 2018

24. Nakamoto, S.: Bitcoin: a peer-to-peer electronic cash system (2008). http://bitcoin.org/bitcoin.pdf. Accessed 28 May 2018

25. Nakamoto, S.: Slushpool hashrate (2018). https://slushpool.com/stats/?c=btc. Accessed 28 May 2018

26. Nayak, K., Kumar, S., Miller, A., Shi, E.: Stubborn mining: generalizing selfish mining and combining with an eclipse attack. In: 2016 IEEE European Symposium on Security and Privacy (EuroS P), pp. 305–320, March 2016. https://doi.org/10.1109/EuroSP.2016.32

27. Ruben Recabarren, B.C.: Hardening stratum, the bitcoin pool mining protocol. In: 1st Workshop on Bitcoin Research

Using Economic Risk to Model Miner Hash Rate Allocation in Cryptocurrencies

George Bissias[1]([⊠]), Brian N. Levine[1], and David Thibodeau[2]

[1] College of Information and Computer Sciences, UMass Amherst, Amherst, USA
gbiss@cs.umass.edu, levine@cs.umass.edu
[2] Florida Department of Corrections, Tallahassee, USA
davidpthibodeau@gmail.com

Abstract. Abrupt changes in the miner hash rate applied to a proof-of-work (PoW) blockchain can adversely affect user experience and security. Because different PoW blockchains often share hashing algorithms, miners face a complex choice in deciding how to allocate their hash power among chains. We present an economic model that leverages Modern Portfolio Theory to predict a miner's allocation over time using price data and inferred risk tolerance. The model matches actual allocations with mean absolute error within 20% for four out of the top five miners active on both Bitcoin (BTC) and Bitcoin Cash (BCH) blockchains. A model of aggregate allocation across those four miners shows excellent agreement in magnitude with the actual aggregate as well a correlation coefficient of 0.649. The accuracy of the aggregate allocation model is also sufficient to explain major historical changes in inter-block time (IBT) for BCH. Because estimates of miner risk are not time-dependent and our model is otherwise price-driven, we are able to use it to anticipate the effect of a major price shock on hash allocation and IBT in the BCH blockchain. Using a Monte Carlo simulation, we show that, despite mitigation by the new difficulty adjustment algorithm, a price drop of 50% could increase the IBT by 50% for at least a day, with a peak delay of 100%.

Keywords: Economic modeling · Performance · Cryptocurrencies

1 Introduction

Understanding how and why miners apply their hash rate to a given proof-of-work (PoW) blockchain is critical to understanding both the security and user experience of that chain. *In this paper, we show that miner hash rate allocations among blockchains can be largely explained by miner risk tolerance and fiat trade price movements in the coins minted by those chains.* Our aim is not to establish causation, but we find that abrupt changes in the price of one coin relative to the others is correlated with an abrupt change in miner hash rate allocations. Such rapid drops in hash rate on a given blockchain present a security risk in

© Springer Nature Switzerland AG 2018
J. Garcia-Alfaro et al. (Eds.): DPM 2018/CBT 2018, LNCS 11025, pp. 155–172, 2018.
https://doi.org/10.1007/978-3-030-00305-0_12

that the probability of a double-spend attack increases inversely proportional to the work applied to the chain [15]. A sudden drop in hash rate can also result in a temporary increase in inter-block time, which constitutes a lapse in user experience. Such a direct link between trade price and service quality is without precedent among conventional financial services. It is analogous to credit card transactions being processed more slowly whenever the stock price of Visa Inc. drops.

Miners typically invest in ASICs, which are hardware implementations of a particular PoW algorithm. Therefore, they can easily shift or *reallocate* their hash rate between blockchains that share the same PoW algorithm. Currently, the two largest blockchains, by market cap, that share the same algorithm are Bitcoin (BTC) and Bitcoin Cash (BCH). It is broadly acknowledged that the price of BCH relative to BTC is a strong determinant of miner allocation [3–5]. But direct comparison of prices is problematic. For example, the *difficulty adjusted reward index* (DARI) is a popular measure of the relative profitability of mining on BTC versus BCH [6]. However, according to the DARI, one coin is always more profitable than the other— so why does each miner typically divide its hash rate allocation between chains? In the present work, we show how the allocation can be explained by miners' tolerance to variance in coin prices.

Contributions. Our primary contribution is an economic model for miner hash rate allocation, which we develop as an application of the Modern Portfolio Theory of Markowitz [13]. We show that the model is capable of accurately explaining the hash rate allocations of four out of the top five mining pools mining both BTC and BCH over a six and a half month period[1]. During that timespan, the model's mean absolute error is at or less than 20% for those four miners, and the predicted aggregate allocation demonstrates a Pearson correlation coefficient of 0.649 when compared to actual. In contrast, estimates of allocations based only on short-term price changes or the DARI result in correlation coefficients of just 0.298 and 0.165, respectively. Our second contribution is demonstrating that the hash rate allocation resulting from the economic model is capable of accurately predicting major changes in the inter-block time (IBT) for BCH. Over the same time interval, the IBT predicted by our economic model shows a Pearson correlation coefficient of 0.849 with the actual IBT. Because our predictions are based primarily on the volatility of historical prices, the implication of this strong agreement is that deviation in IBT can be largely explained by the risk associated with fluctuations in coin prices. Finally, we use synthetic price data and hash rate allocations from our economic model in simulation to shows how the IBT would be affected by large fluctuations in the price of BCH. We find that even with the new difficulty adjustment algorithm employed by BCH, a price drop of 50% could increase the IBT by 50% for at least a day, with a peak delay of 100%.

---

[1] Data is available from http://traces.cs.umass.edu.

2   Background

Mining Markets. Nearly every blockchain project uses a proof-of-work (PoW) algorithm that is common to other projects. For example, of the top 50 cryptocurrencies by market capitalization[2], eight use SHA256 [15] including Bitcoin Cash and Bitcoin, seven use Ethash [2] including Ethereum and Ethereum Classic, and 11 use Scrypt [16] including Litecoin and Dogecoin. For PoW algorithms common to multiple currencies, miners are able to apportion their hardware among them, and can also rapidly change this allocation. Miners began manufacturing ASICs for SHA256 in 2013 [7], and ASICs for the Scrypt algorithm became available in 2014 [1]. ASICs for the Ethash algorithm were also introduced recently [20]. Mining with ASICs requires a large capital expenditure to purchase the hardware, and that investment has the effect of locking miners into a specific PoW algorithm in the medium-term. As a result, blockchain projects that share the same PoW algorithm form *multi-chain mining markets* comprised of miners who possess ASICs suitable for that algorithm.

Profitability of Mining. Although mining markets have existed for several years, a miner's choice of hash rate distribution among blockchains, which we term *allocation*, remains somewhat mysterious [8]. A complicating factor is that most miners participate via a *mining pool*, which aggregates the hash power of its constituents and distributes mining rewards according to their hash rate. The allocation represented by a mining pool depends on that pool's policy. Most allow individual miners to either choose the blockchain on which they wish to mine, or follow the pool's choice of the most profitable chain [4,5]. However, it's not always obvious how to determine profitability [3]. What seems clear is that the choice of allocation is related to short-term profitability [6]. But long-term financial and idealogical concerns likely also play an important role.

Ignoring idealogical and long-term financial determinants, there are several factors that contribute to the relative profitability of mining between blockchains in the same mining market, including: *(i)* the relative fiat trade value of each coin; *(ii)* any hinderances to converting mining profits into fiat currency (e.g., poor coin liquidity); and *(iii)* the relative difficulty in mining the coins. The question of relative difficulty is particularly interesting from a technical standpoint because generally each blockchain in a mining market implements a different difficulty adjustment algorithm (DAA). The update frequency and accuracy of each DAA, relative the others, plays a critical role in how profitability changes over time.

Difficulty Adjustment Algorithms. In this paper, we present an in-depth analysis of mining profitability in the SHA256 mining market where Bitcoin (BTC) and Bitcoin Cash (BCH) together comprise 99% of the market cap; together these two comprise 67% of the market cap of all cryptocurrencies. In BTC, the difficulty is recalibrated every 2016 blocks by adjusting it either up or down inversely proportional to the deviation in mean inter-block time from optimal[3]. Since the hard fork on November 13, 2017, BCH performs a similar

---

[2] https://minethecoin.com.
[3] http://github.com/bitcoin/bitcoin/blob/master/src/pow.cpp#L49.

adjustment except that it occurs every block and covers a window of 144 prior blocks[4]. Prior to the November 13 hard fork, BCH used the same DAA as BTC except that it also implemented an Emergency Difficulty Adjustment algorithm (EDA) [18]. The EDA simply cut the difficulty by 20% any time that it took more than 12 h to mine the last six blocks.

3   Related Work

There are several past works related to our contributions. To the best of our knowledge, we are the first work to evaluate, in a multi-blockchain market, the link between prices, hash rate allocation, and system performance. Most past work related to mining efficiency has focused on mining on a single blockchain. Rosenfeld [17] was one of the first authors to explore financial incentives in mining pools. He detailed several payout schemes and showed how they fare against several types of miner behavior. One particularly interesting behavior is called *pool hopping*, which involves a miner switching between pools mining the same coin in order to gain higher profits. This behavior is the *single-blockchain* analog to the *multi-blockchain* mining we analyze in this paper. Fisch et al. [12] conducted an analysis of pool payout strategies for mining on a single blockchain using discounted utility theory. They found that the geometric pay pool—in which rewards are concentrated at the winning block and decay exponentially over the preceding shares—achieves the optimal equilibrium utility for miners. Our focus is not on payout strategies for pools.

Meshkov et al. [14] considered miners switching between multiple blockchains. They argued that it is profitable for a miner to *hop* between blockchains with the same PoW algorithm, causing oscillations in difficulty that the miner can use to boost profit. The paper calculates the expected additional reward for the miner and shows that under this scheme the expected average inter-block time (IBT) on both chains exceeds the target time. The work is similar to ours in that it considers the profitability of moving hash rate between blockchains—however, it stops short of developing an economic model of hash rate allocation. In particular, the authors do not account for the influence of coin price on allocation; nor do they attempt to determine an equilibrium allocation. Moreover, it is not clear that chain hopping is currently pervasive in blockchains. For example, if miners do commonly engage in chain hopping on BCH, then the results from the paper predict that IBT should substantially exceed the target of 600 seconds, but we find the mean IBT to be 604 seconds since the November 13, 2017 hard fork.

Several authors have formulated economic models of the mining ecosystem in an effort to predict or explain coin price. In contrast, we are not attempting to discover what drives price, but rather how price drives system performance. For example, Cocco and Marchesi [10] used an agent-based model of the mining process to show its relationship to Bitcoin price. The model had some success in

---

[4] http://github.com/bitcoincashorg/bitcoincash.org/blob/master/spec/nov-13-hard-fork-spec.md.

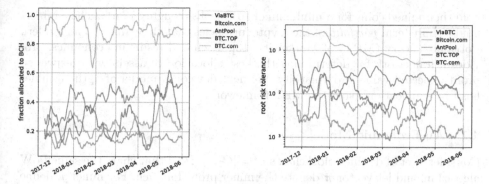

Fig. 1. Fraction of miner hash rate allocated to the BCH blockchain instead of the BTC blockchain (left) and square root of risk tolerance (right). Shown here are only the top five miners that historically mine on both chains. In the right plot, risk tolerance is in units of the USD price of BTC + BCH at the given time.

predicting large price peaks as well as some statistical properties of the Bitcoin ecosystem. Chiu et al. [9] developed a general equilibrium monetary model for Bitcoin and similar cryptocurrencies. A major consequence of the model is that cryptocurrencies must trade off between immediacy and finality of settlements.

4 Miner Hash Allocation

In this section, we develop a theory of how and why, in economic terms, miners distribute their hash power among competing blockchains. The recent split of Bitcoin Cash (BCH) from Bitcoin (BTC) provides an important case study for us: each currency is highly valued and both rely on the same PoW algorithm. As a result, it is trivial for miners to distribute their hash power among the two blockchains as they see fit. This presents a conundrum for us: at any given time, it is almost always more profitable to mine exclusively on one chain or the other; yet, among miners that participate in mining on both chains, hash rate allocation is typically divided between the two. Figure 1 (left) plots the history of several mining pools' allocation of hash rates to BCH as a fraction of their respective total resources. Thus, it appears that miners are not actually acting in purely greedy fashion, and we require a model that accounts for this nuance.

We hypothesize that miners are acting in a manner so as to maximize their profit subject to a particular risk tolerance. That is to say, miners seek greater profits, but they are also sensitive to the high volatility of holding cryptocurrencies. The exposure to this volatility is quantifiable: most blockchains impose a multi-block *cooldown period* during which miners are not allowed to spend their newly minted coins. For example, in both BTC and BCH, miners are required to hold their mined coins for a minimum of 101 blocks (roughly $17\,\text{h}$)[5]. Thus, miners hold a short-term *portfolio* of the cryptocurrencies that they mine[6]. The Modern Portfolio Theory (MPT) of Markowitz [13], a seminal result in economics, provides a framework for determining the best allocation of assets with respect to profit expected value and volatility. We next develop a model of optimal miner hash rate allocation using the MPT framework.

4.1 An Economic Model

Consider a set of distinct blockchains $C = [C_1, \ldots, C_n]$ that share the same PoW algorithm, and let vector $\boldsymbol{\pi}$ denote the miner profit for each. For miner j, define $\boldsymbol{w}_j = [w_{1j}, \ldots, w_{nj}]$ to be the *allocation* of this hash rate to the blockchains C. And let vector $\boldsymbol{h} = [h_1, \ldots, h_m]$ denote the total hash rate for each miner across all blockchains. The *aggregate allocation* among all miners is given by

$$w = \sum_j w_j \frac{h_j}{e^T h}, \tag{1}$$

where e is the vector of all ones. Aggregate allocation captures the overall distribution of mining power among all blocks chains C.

We pause here to illustrate the definitions above. Suppose that miner M_1 produces $5E$ total hashes per second (where "E" denotes Exahash) and allocates 30% of his hash rate to BTC and 70% to BCH. Meanwhile miner M_2 produces $3E$ hashes per second and allocates 10% and 90% of her hash rate to BTC and BCH, respectively. In terms of the notation above, we let C_1 and C_2, respectively, denote the BTC and BCH blockchains. Vectors $\boldsymbol{w_1} = [0.3, 0.7]$ and $\boldsymbol{w_2} = [0.1, 0.9]$ are the allocations for miners M_1 and M_2, respectively. And the total hash rate vector is $\boldsymbol{h} = [5E, 3E]$. Finally, the aggregate allocation is given by $\boldsymbol{w} = [0.3\frac{5}{8} + 0.1\frac{3}{8}, 0.7\frac{5}{8} + 0.9\frac{3}{8}] = [0.225, 0.775]$.

Next, define $\Sigma = Cov(\boldsymbol{\pi})$, or the covariance of $\boldsymbol{\pi}$, which we call the *volatility matrix*. For a miner's allocation $\boldsymbol{w}_j$, the *risk* is given by $\boldsymbol{w}_j^T \Sigma \boldsymbol{w}_j$. And the *risk tolerance* of miner j, given by ρ_j, is defined as his maximum allowable risk. MPT predicts that a rational miner j seeking to maximize expected profits will solve the following problem (although perhaps not explicitly):

PROBLEM MaxProfit(j):

Maximize: $E[\boldsymbol{w}_j^T \boldsymbol{\pi}]$
Subject to: $\boldsymbol{w}_j^T \Sigma \boldsymbol{w}_j = \rho_j$, $\boldsymbol{w}_j^T e = 1$,
and $e = [1, \ldots, 1]$

---

[5] http://github.com/bitcoin/bitcoin/blob/master/src/consensus/consensus.h#L19, http://github.com/BitcoinUnlimited/BitcoinUnlimited/blob/release/src/consensus/consensus.h#L31.
[6] Note that miners can conceivably sell their coins to another party before the end of the cooldown period, but because the purchasing party must assume the associated risk, we expect that the transaction price must also take into account the volatility of the coin.

We solve `MaxProfit` using Lagrange multipliers in similar fashion to Dhrymes [11]. However, in our formulation we do not allow for a portion of the portfolio to be allocated at the risk-free rate of return because we assume that miners are locked into their investment in mining hardware. Thus, we solve the system of equations associated with the critical points of the following Lagrangian:

$$L_j = w_j{}^T E[\pi]+$$
$$\lambda_{j1}(\rho_j - w_j{}^T \Sigma w_j)+ \qquad\qquad (2)$$
$$\lambda_{j2}(1 - w_j{}^T e),$$

which yields the following solution.

$$w_j = \Sigma^{-1}\frac{E[\pi]-\lambda_{j2}e}{2\lambda_{j1}} \qquad\qquad a = e^T \Sigma^{-1} e$$

$$\lambda_{j1} = \tfrac{1}{2}(b - a\lambda_{j2}) \qquad\qquad b = e^T \Sigma^{-1} E[\pi] \qquad (3)$$

$$\lambda_{j2} = \frac{b}{a} \pm \frac{\sqrt{(b^2-ac)(1-a\rho_j)}}{a(1-a\rho_j)} \qquad\qquad c = E[\pi]^T \Sigma^{-1} E[\pi].$$

4.2   Profit and Volatility in Multi-chain Mining

In a typical portfolio optimization problem [13], the profit for an asset, π, is defined as the change in asset value over a given period of time Δt. However, miners are *creating* assets as opposed to merely acquiring them, so their profit should nominally account for the full fiat trade value of each coin that they mine. Still, miners contribute hash power to each blockchain, which amounts to an associated cost. Therefore, the ideal measure of profit is one that normalizes the fiat price of cumulative coinbase rewards by the relative difficulty.

Another complication is that miners can change their allocation at any time and for little-to-no cost. Thus, we hypothesize that they will re-evaluate Problem `MaxProfit` at every instant t. Hence, we seek parameterized representations of the profit vector and volatility matrix: $\pi(t)$ and $\Sigma(t)$. To that end, let $R = [R_1(t), \ldots, R_n(t)]$ be a vector representing the fiat value of coinbase reward for each blockchain at time t (fees are ignored in this model). And define $D = [D_1(t), \ldots, D_n(t)]$ to be the associated difficulties for those chains at the same time. We define the profit at time t by

$$\pi(t) = R(t)/D(t)\frac{e^T D(t)}{e^T R(t)}, \qquad\qquad (4)$$

where "/" denotes component-wise division and e is the vector of all ones. Note that our definition for $\pi(t)$ is equivalent to the *Difficulty Adjusted Reward Index* (DARI), a popular mining profitability metric [6], except that we ignore fees and normalize by the aggregate fiat value of all chains, $e^T R(t)$, and total difficulty, $e^T D(t)$. Normalizing by $e^T R(t)$ is necessary because cryptocurrency prices can fluctuate significantly over short periods, and normalization allows us to more directly compare profits at different times. Similarly, normalizing by $e^T D(t)$ allows us to ignore the effect of fluctuations in total hash rate on miner profit.

Given our definition for $\boldsymbol{\pi}(t)$, the expected profit vector, $E[\boldsymbol{\pi}(t)]$, can be approximated by the sample mean over all $\boldsymbol{\pi}$ from time $(t - \Delta t)$ until t. For volatility, we hypothesize that miners are concerned about price changes only over the short cooldown period Δc that extends from the time a coin is mined until the time it can be traded for fiat currency. Thus, we seek to capture relative changes in profit between all blockchains during Δc. For simplicity, we assume that Δc is the same for all chains. Finally, we define the volatility matrix by $\Sigma(t) = Cov(\boldsymbol{\pi}(t) - \boldsymbol{\pi}(t - \Delta c))$. $\Sigma(t)$ can be approximated by the sample covariance over the set of vectors: $\{\boldsymbol{\pi}(x) - \boldsymbol{\pi}(x - \Delta c) \mid t - \Delta t \leq x \leq t\}$.

5   Model Validation and Parameter Fitting

In general, a miner's choice in hash rate allocation results from a complex combination of economically rational profit seeking and more subtle ideological considerations. As such, we do not expect that the solution to Problem MaxProfit can fully predict miner allocations; however, in this section we seek to demonstrate that it is capable of explaining much of their behavior. To do so, we analyzed approximately 6.5 months of price and blockchain data from BCH and BTC between November 14, 2017 and June 1, 2018. We intentionally omit data prior to the BCH hard fork on November 13, 2017, which introduced a new DAA. Prior to the fork, both BCH block times and prices were exceptionally irregular due to high price volatility as well as rampant manipulation of the EDA [19]. As a result, it is very difficult to accurately estimate actual miner allocations or infer their risk tolerance during the EDA time period.

For each blockchain, we calculated the time-parameterized profit vector and volatility matrix as described in Sect. 4.2 using hourly price data from the Bitfinex exchange. We chose unique but fixed values for lookback Δt and risk tolerance ρ for each miner using the techniques described in Sects. 5.1 and 5.2. For both BTC and BCH chains, we set $\Delta c = \lfloor 101/6 \rfloor$ hours to match their 101-block cooldown period. We analyzed each of the top five mining pools on BCH that are also active on BTC, excluding the mining by pools that do not claim blocks. We determined the actual allocations for each miner, $\boldsymbol{w}_j(t)$, by first calculating the average fraction of blocks produced per hour on each blockchain using an exponentially weighted moving average with a half-life of 10 h. Estimating hash allocation from mined blocks is very noisy, and using a weighted average of recent blocks allowed us to arrive at a more smooth estimate. These average block rates were translated into allocations after normalizing by the relative difficulty of each chain.

5.1   Inferred Miner Risk

Our economic model predicts that each miner allocates her hash rate based on the historical profit for each coin as well as her personal risk tolerance. A miner's risk can be inferred from her current allocation and volatility matrix $\Sigma(t)$. According to the model, we assume that any given miner will exhibit a consistent risk tolerance. Furthermore, for a given risk tolerance, we anticipate that the actual allocation chosen by miners will match the economic allocation produced by the model.

Risk ρ_j is measured in units of squared deviation in profit. And because profit is normalized by the sum of fiat prices of each chain in C (see Sect. 4.2), the square root of risk, or *root risk*, also has units of BTC + BCH (which we write as BTC+, for short). Therefore, the root risk can be interpreted as the maximum deviation in profit, in units of BTC+, that is tolerated by the miner during the cooldown period Δc. For example, when 1 BTC trades for 10 BCH (BCH/BTC = 0.1), a miner with root risk 0.043, who is allocated entirely to BCH, will tolerate a decrease to BCH/BTC = 0.05 during Δc.

Figure 1 (right) shows the root risk for each of the top five mining pools that mine both BTC and BCH. The relative risk tolerance among miners remains very consistent over time. The Bitcoin.com mining pool exhibits the highest risk tolerance, while BTC.com shows the lowest. ViaBTC maintains root risk roughly between 0.01 and 0.1 BTC+, while AntPool and BTC.TOP typically range from 0.003 to 0.03 BTC+, and BTC.com fluctuates between 0.001 and 0.01 BTC+. In absolute terms, Bitcoin.com also demonstrates the largest variation in risk tolerance, showing a high of 0.3 BTC+ at the end of November and recent low near 0.06 BTC+. From Fig. 1 (left) we can see that differences in risk tolerances are roughly reflected by the choice in miner allocations. For example, Bitcoin.com is mostly allocated to mining BCH, while BTC.com mines BTC almost exclusively.

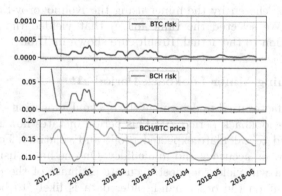

Fig. 2. Risk and price juxtaposed. The top two facets show the risk for BTC and BCH associated with allocating all hash rate to either the BTC or BCH blockchain, respectively. The bottom facet shows the price ratio of BCH to BTC; the price for each was drawn from the Bitfinex exchange where it was quoted in terms of USD.

Figure 2 juxtaposes the risk associated with mining exclusively on the BTC or BCH blockchains with the BCH/BTC trade price ratio taken from USD quotes on the Bitfinex exchange. The risks for each blockchain were calculated using a lookback of $\Delta t = 48$. Problem `MaxProfit` utilizes information from all three facets to derive the economic allocation. There are several notable features in these curves. First, from Fig. 1 (right), we can see that risk rose sharply for miners allocated to BCH near the end of 2017. The top two facets of Fig. 2 indicate that this was a period where risk in mining BCH rose far faster than for BTC, while the bottom facet shows that BCH simultaneously made major gains on BTC in terms of price. We hypothesize that this indicates that miners are willing to relax their risk tolerance at times when they anticipate major gains for one coin over another (in this case BCH over BTC). Second, not all major price movements will result in increased risk for the current allocation. Because it was gradual, the increase in the price of BCH relative to BTC at the end of April is not accompanied by a large rise in risk for either blockchain. Nevertheless, we do see from Fig. 1 (left) that mining pools BTC.TOP and AntPool substantially increased their BCH allocation during this time. As a result, their risk rose accordingly.

Despite the tendency for risk tolerance to fluctuate during abrupt price movements, Fig. 1 (right) still reflects overall consistency in inferred root risk for most miners except Bitcoin.com. For the remaining miners, we believe that a single risk tolerance ρ_j chosen for each miner j is sufficient to describe much of that miner's behavior, and therefore our economic model may provide a reliable prediction of their allocation of hash power. In order to choose ρ_j for a given miner, we tested 8 equally spaced risk values falling between the 25th and 75th percentiles of the historical inferred risk values for that miner. For each risk value, and each possible lookback chosen from the set described in Sect. 5.2, we calculated the economic allocations using our model and compared them to the actual allocations chosen by the miner using the Kolmogorov-Smirnov test for goodness-of-fit. We selected the value for ρ_j that yielded the best fit of the economic allocation to the actual. Results are shown in Table 1.

5.2   Determining Miner Lookback Period Δt

Risk is only one factor used to determine the optimal allocation. Another important factor is the lookback period Δt. This period dictates how much historical data will be used to calculate expected profit and volatility. For miners there is a tradeoff between accuracy and immediacy. On one hand, using the entirety of historical data will yield the most accurate estimate of the overall value of the statistics. But on the other hand, older data is likely to be less relevant, particularly when market characteristics can change abruptly.

We determined the optimal Δt_j for miner j by testing the following values.

$$S = \{4\text{-}22 \text{ in increments of } 6\} + \{24\text{-}144 \text{ in increments of } 24\}$$
$$+\{168\text{-}1344 \text{ in increments of } 168\} \tag{5}$$

For each $\Delta t_j \in S$ and each potential risk value ρ_j (chosen according to the procedure described in Sect. 5.1), we determined the optimal economic allocation by solving MaxProfit using statistics $E[\pi(t)]$ and $\Sigma(t)$, which were formed as described in Sect. 4.2. We then chose the values for Δt_j and ρ_j for miner j

Table 1. Optimal lookback (hours) and risk parameters and mean absolute error for the top 5 miners who mine both BTC and BCH based on observable data.

Mining Pool	Lookback	Risk	Mean error
ViaBTC	144	6.42 e-04	20.0%
BTC.TOP	16	8.54 e-05	20.7%
Bitcoin.com	1,008	2.40 e−03	36.0%
AntPool	10	3.33 e-05	17.0%
BTC.com	4	3.81 e−06	14.4%

corresponding to the economic allocation that yielded the best fit relative to the actual allocation according to the Kolmogorov-Smirnov test. Table 1 shows the chosen values for Δt_j and ρ_j for the top five miners. We use these values in the remainder of our analysis.

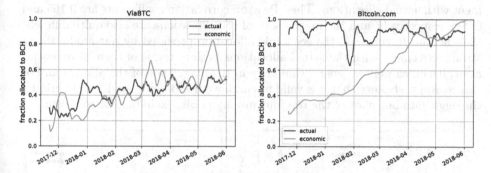

Fig. 3. Actual and economic hash rate allocations for the two largest pools that mine both BTC and BCH: ViaBTC (left) and Bitcoin.com (right). In each figure, the actual allocation (blue) is compared to the optimal economic allocation (orange), the latter of which is formed using parameters chosen from Table 1 for each miner.

5.3   Comparing Actual to Optimal Allocations

Figure 3 compares actual allocations to allocations from our risk and price-driven economic model for the two largest pools participating in both BTC and BCH mining: ViaBTC and Bitcoin.com. We determined the optimal economic allocations by selecting the parameters from Table 1 and solving Problem MaxProfit. Figure 3 shows strong agreement between economic and actual allocations for ViaBTC. On the other hand, the economic allocation for Bitcoin.com shows very poor agreement with actual during the months prior to April, 2018. As a result, we hypothesize that there do not exist any single values for risk tolerance and lookback that can describe the hash rate allocation of Bitcoin.com over the entire time period. This hypothesis is corroborated by Fig. 1 (right), which shows that inferred root risk has been decreasing rapidly since late November 2017. For this reason, we omit the Bitcoin.com mining pool from the remainder of our analysis, as its allocations are not described well by our economic model.

Figure 4 shows the absolute error and aggregate allocation for the top four pools (excluding Bitcoin.com) that participate in mining on both BTC and BCH. Together, these pools constitute approximately 48% of the total hash rate for BCH. From the plot of absolute error, we can see that economic and actual allocations are typically quite close for the four mining pools; Table 1 shows that their mean error is at or below 20%. The low error results in strong agreement between the actual and economic aggregate allocations, shown in Fig. 4 (right). We used Eq. 1 for aggregating both actual and economic allocations.

For comparison, we also plot two other price-driven allocations: $D(BCH)$ / $(D(BCH) + D(BTC))$ and $P(BCH)$ / $(P(BCH) + P(BTC))$. The function D denotes the DARI, which is the value of the given chain's coinbase in USD divided by the current difficulty (we ignore fees). And the function P denotes the USD trade price. Neither the relative DARI nor relative price show strong agreement with actual allocations. Their Pearson correlation coefficients are 0.165 and 0.298, respectively, and the magnitudes of the allocations are also quite different than actual. In contrast, the economic allocation provided by our model shows strong agreement with the actual allocations both in terms of correlation coefficient, 0.649, as well as general similarity in the magnitude of the allocation. For this reason we believe that it is valid to employ our economic model in describing the aggregate behavior of the top four mining pools, excluding Bitcoin.com.

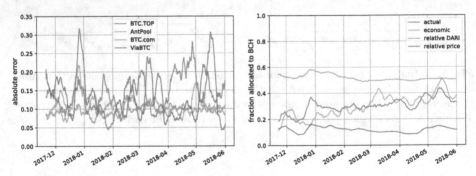

Fig. 4. Absolute error between economic and actual allocations (left) and aggregate allocation (right) for the top four pools (excluding Bitcoin.com) mining both BTC and BCH.

6   Using Risk to Explain Change in Inter-Block Time

Based on the economic model introduced in Sect. 4.1, we hypothesize a direct relationship between short-term price fluctuations and deviation in inter-block time (IBT). In particular, we hypothesize that a large change in the expected profit $E[\pi(t)]$ will lead to a large change in a miner's hash rate allocation $w_j(t)$, which will propagate to the aggregate allocation $w(t)$ defined by Eq. 1, and ultimately impact IBT until the difficulty is adjusted.

Let $T = [T_1, \ldots, T_n]$ denote the target IBT for each blockchain. If we assume that the elapsed time δt was short enough that no blockchain has yet substantially updated its difficulty, then the expected IBT will have changed by

$$\delta T = w(t)/w(t + \delta t) \circ T, \tag{6}$$

where "$\circ$" and "$/$" denote element-wise vector multiplication and division.

Prediction of Change in IBT. Equation 6 provides a means of using our economic model to predict the change in IBT from only historical price data and miner risk tolerances. We analyzed historical data from November 14, 2017, until June 1, 2018 using the aggregate economic allocation (with parameters chosen from Table 1) to estimate the change in IBT for the BCH blockchain from one 6 h period to the next (non-overlapping) 6 h period. The experiment used the top four mining pools, excluding Bitcoin.com, which constitute approximately 48% of the total hash rate on BCH during that time. Figure 5 shows the result of these predictions compared to actual change in IBT using a 7-day rolling average for both curves.

Despite being quite noisy, the figure shows a strong correlation between predicted and actual IBT change throughout the six and a half month timeframe. The Pearson correlation coefficient between predicted and actual IBT is 0.849. In addition to correlation, the predicted change in IBT also echoes the magnitude of changes in actual IBT. However, the predicted result does appear to consistently under-estimate the extent of change by as much as 0.05. There are two possible reasons for this inaccuracy. First, our price data is accurate only to the nearest hour, so it is possible that the full extent of large price shocks is not reflected in the economic allocation. And second, ignoring the effects of the DAA introduces a subtle bias. The DAA is much better at compensating for an IBT that is too short as opposed to too long. When the IBT is short, more blocks are arriving, so the algorithm has more opportunities to adjust the difficulty. In contrast, when the IBT is very long, few adjustments are made since the difficulty cannot be changed between blocks. Thus, IBT change less than 1 tends to be minimal while change greater than 1 tends to be exaggerated. Indeed changes below 1 are small enough that the 7 day rolling average of the actual IBT eliminates them entirely. But because the predicted IBT does not model the effects of the DAA, it treats drops in allocation identically to spikes.

7   DAA Susceptibility to Price Shocks

In this section, we use our economic model to quantify how specific price changes affect inter-block times (IBTs) via changes in hash rate allocation. We show that even with a proactive controller that adjusts the difficulty every block, like the DAA currently implemented for BCH, large enough price shocks can still lead to long delays in IBT with affects being felt for a day or more. In reality, prices and

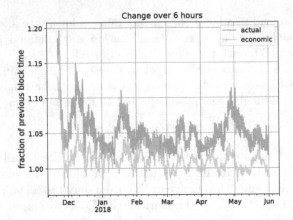

Fig. 5. Predicted (blue) and actual (pink) change in BCH inter-block time during one 6 h period compared to the next (non-overlapping) 6 h period. Predicted change in block time is calculated using Eq. 1 and solving Problem `MaxProfit` with parameters chosen from Table 1. (Color figure online)

their volatility are not the only determinants of miner behavior, but in Sects. 5 and 6 we presented evidence that these economic factors are often sufficient for accurately explaining real world miner allocations and ultimately IBT.

Blockchains compensate for changes in hash rate with an algorithmic change in *difficulty*. Ideally, the difficulty is changed so that IBT remains at a desired mean, which is 600 seconds per block for BCH. Below, we quantify how a *price shock*—a single, sudden rise or drop in price of BCH compared to BTC—can change IBT given the current BCH difficulty adjustment algorithm (DAA). We begin by characterizing typical price changes in BCH relative to BTC using price data from November 2017 through May 2018. We then quantify how various changes in BCH price can affect allocation and IBT under a simplifying assumption that all miners are applying the economic model.

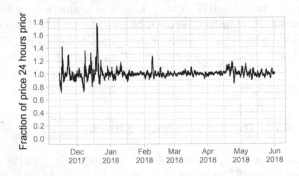

Fig. 6. The fraction of a given hour's price to the price 24 h earlier, where price is defined as BCH/(BTC+BCH). 98% of the time, the fraction is between 0.8 and 1.2.

Figure 6 shows, for each hour, the fraction change in price from the previous 24-h period to the next (non-overlapping) 24-h period. Price is defined as BCH/(BTC+BCH). As the plot shows, 98% of the time, daily price changes are no greater than 20%. However, eight times the price changed approximately 30% or more and once it changed by 80%. Thus, there exists historical precedence for a *maximum* 24-h change of nearly 100%.

Section 6 argued that the aggregate allocation given by solving Problem MaxProfit and applying Eq. 1 can be used to roughly predict actual IBT changes even without taking into account the effect of the DAA on block time regularization. We speculated that our failure to take the effect of the DAA into account was a major cause of the downward bias in the prediction. Regardless of the reason for the bias, Fig. 5 shows that the aggregate economic allocation can accurately predict major changes in IBT, and if anything, might tend to underestimate the extent of increases in IBT. Thus, we believe that our economic allocation provides a sufficiently accurate estimate of actual miner allocations to be used to predict the effect of a price shock on IBT.

Price Shock Experiment. To quantify the effects of various price shocks, we ran a block-generation simulator that updated the synthetic coin price every block. All prices for BCH were initially set to p, the mean USD value for BCH between November 2017 through May 2018. Each experiment introduced exactly one shock $x \in (0, 4]$, which set all prices subsequent to this *shock block* to px. Thus, the BCH prices for each experiment formed a step function with a step up in price after the shock block when $x > 1$ and a step down when $x < 1$. To establish baseline volatility, we also added uniform random noise in the range $[-0.1p, 0.1p]$ to all prices. Prices for BTC were generated similarly except that no shock was introduced and the base price p was set to BTC's mean USD price over the same time period. For each experiment, corresponding to a separate shock, we ran at least 180 trials of the following Monte Carlo (MC) simulation. *(i)* We formed the aggregate economic allocation for the top four miners (excluding Bitcoin.com) by solving Problem MaxProfit using the synthetic prices for the given experiment and parameters from Table 1 and substituting the result into Eq. 1. *(ii)* The difficulty was initially set to an arbitrary value and allowed to reach equilibrium at the pre-shock price. *(iii)* We stepped through the generation of each block, adjusting the allocation every block according to the economic allocations to determine the hash rate for the mining process. *(iv)* After each block, we ran the DAA to adjust the difficulty according to the IBT of the mined blocks.

Figure 7 (Top) shows the median change in economic allocation over all simulation trials that results from a single price shock x given by the value shown in the legend. Figure 7 (Bottom) shows the corresponding changes in mean IBT. Overall, we see that, even with compensation from the DAA, a drop in price of as little as 50% can increase mean IBT by more than 50% for an entire day, while a drop to 10% of the original value can double the mean IBT for at least a day. Similarly, a rapid price increase by 50% is expected to raise the mean IBT

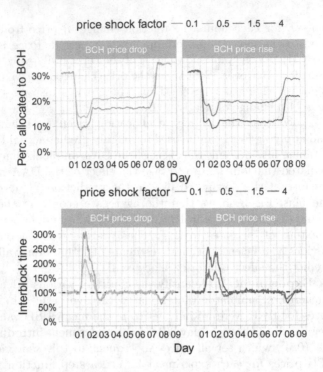

Fig. 7. The change in allocations (Top) and therefore inter-block time (Bottom) that results from a single price shock that is larger than typical. The price shock is determined by a multiplier, shown in the legend. Allocations decrease as volatility increases, which causes inter-block time to rise. For example a shock of 1.5 increases the price by 50% on day 1 and from there the price does not change. (From Monte Carlo simulation, risk and lookback parameters from the top four BCH miners excluding Bitcoin.com.)

by 50% for at least a day, and an 800% price increase could more than double the mean IBT for a day or more.

It is somewhat counterintuitive that both price drops (left plots) and increases (right plots) result in lower economic allocations initially, and in the long run, allocations actually stabilize to higher values after a price drop and lower values after a spike. Allocations drop immediately after the shock date because volatility has risen for BCH relative to BTC, regardless of the direction of the shock. Essentially the economic allocation follows the maxim, "what goes up must come down". However, it is reasonable to question how realistic this aspect of the economic model is during a price spike for BCH. Indeed, Figs. 1 (left) and 2 indicate that all of the top five miners except Bitcoin.com increased their allocation in BCH after it massively gained in price on BTC at the end of 2017, despite the commensurate rise in risk. On the other hand, both ViaBTC and Bitcoin.com reduced their allocation after the price (and risk) increase at the end of May. The long-term rise in allocation after a price drop is simply due to the fact that the baseline volatility relative to BTC becomes slightly lower after prices have stabilized and cleared every miner's lookback period. The opposite is true for the relative volatility after a price spike.

Another feature of the price shock simulation is the delayed after-shock observed approximately seven days later. Mathematically, this is the result of the expiration of the longest lookback period, corresponding to ViaBTC (see Table 1). Prior to the date in question, there exist prices in the lookback from both before and after the shock. Thus, the volatility remains high relative to the baseline. However, once the last pre-shock price has cleared the lookback period, volatility abruptly returns to baseline, causing a substantial increase in allocation to BCH and a corresponding decrease in IBT. Over the course of approximately one day, the DAA returns the IBT to normal. Although we do believe that it is plausible that miners use price data from the recent past to determine their current allocation, it is perhaps unlikely that they implement such a hard cutoff as to produce a sudden shift in allocation. For that reason we regard the aftershock as a modeling idiosyncrasy.

8   Conclusions

We have presented an economic model of miner hash rate allocation inspired by Modern Portfolio Theory. The model is sufficient to explain, with low error, the individual allocations of four of the top five mining pools active on both BTC and BCH blockchains. Taken together, they form a very accurate model of aggregate miner allocation between BTC and BCH using only historical price data, a single risk value, and a single lookback period for each miner. Using this aggregate allocation alone, it is possible to correctly predict major changes in actual inter-block time (IBT). Our model is also capable of analyzing theoretical price scenarios. It predicts that either a 50% drop or increase in the price of BCH relative to BTC can increase BCH inter-block times by 50% for a day or more.

References

1. ZeusMiner Announces The First Scrypt ASIC Miners To Ship Worldwide, April 2014. https://finance.yahoo.com/news/zeusminer-announces-first-scrypt-asic-070800384.html
2. Ethash, Aug 3 2017. https://github.com/ethereum/wiki/wiki/Ethash
3. Hash Rate Tug-Of-War, November 2017. https://blog.slushpool.com/hash-rate-tug-of-war-96d20d482af4
4. ViaBTC Mining Pool Will Automatically Switch Between BTC and BCH Mining, April 2017. http://nulltx.com/viabtc-mining-pool-will-automatically-switch-between-btc-and-bch-mining
5. Auto-Profit Switch, June 2018. https://pool.enchanthq.com/article/75/autoprofit-switch
6. fork.lol, June 2018. http://fork.lol
7. Mining, February 2018. http://en.bitcoin.it/wiki/Mining
8. Why aren't miners switching to BCH? April 2018. http://www.reddit.com/88h8ji

9. Chiu, J., Koeppl, T.: The Economics of Cryptocurrencies – Bitcoin and Beyond, April 2017. https://www.chapman.edu/research/institutes-and-centers/economic-science-institute/_files/ifree-papers-and-photos/koeppel-april2017.pdf
10. Cocco, L., Marchesi, M.: Modeling and simulation of the economics of mining in the bitcoin market. PLoS ONE **11**(10), e0164603 (2016)
11. Dhrymes, Phoebus J.: Portfolio theory: origins, Markowitz and CAPM based selection. In: Guerard, John B. (ed.) Portfolio Construction, Measurement, and Efficiency, pp. 39–48. Springer, Cham (2017). https://doi.org/10.1007/978-3-319-33976-4_2
12. Fisch, B., Pass, R., Shelat, A.: Socially optimal mining pools. In: Devanur, N.R., Lu, P. (eds.) Web and Internet Economics, pp. 205–218 (2017)
13. Markowitz, H.: Portfolio selection. J. Finance **7**(1), 77–91 (1952)
14. Meshkov, D., Chepurnoy, A., Jansen, M.: Revisiting difficulty control for blockchain systems. In Cryptocurrencies and Blockchain Tech., pp. 429–436 (2017)
15. Nakamoto, S.: Bitcoin: A Peer-to-Peer Electronic Cash System, May 2009
16. Percival, C.: Stronger key derivation via sequential memory-hard functions. In: The BSD Conference (BSDCan), May 2009
17. Rosenfeld, M.: Analysis of bitcoin pooled mining reward systems, June 2011
18. Song, J.: Bitcoin Cash Difficulty Adjustments, August 2017. http://medium.com/@jimmysong/bitcoin-cash-difficulty-adjustments-2ec589099a8e
19. Wilmoth, J.: Bitcoin ABC proposes november hard fork to stabilize bitcoin cash mining difficulty, October 2017. https://www.ccn.com/bitcoin-abc-proposes-hard-fork-to-stabilize-bitcoin-cash-mining-difficulty
20. Wood, A.: Bitmain Releases Ethash ASIC Miners, April 2018. http://cointelegraph.com/news/bitmain-releases-ethash-asic-miners

CBT Workshop: Deadlocks, Attacks and Privacy

Avoiding Deadlocks in Payment Channel Networks

Shira Werman[(✉)] and Aviv Zohar

The Hebrew University of Jersualem, Jerusalem, Israel
shira.werman@mail.huji.ac.il, avivz@cs.huji.ac.il

Abstract. Payment transaction channels are one of the main proposed approaches to scaling cryptocurrency payment systems. Recent work by Malavolta *et al.* [7] has shown that the privacy of the protocol may conflict with its concurrent nature and may lead to deadlocks. In this paper we ask the natural question: can payments in routing networks be routed so as to avoid deadlocks altogether? Our results show that it is in general NP-complete to determine whether a deadlock-free routing exists in a given payment graph. On the other hand, Given some fixed routing, we propose another way to resolve the problem of deadlocks. We offer a modification of the protocols in lightning network and in Fulgor [7] that pre-locks edges in an order that guarantees progress, while still maintaining the protocol's privacy requirements.

1 Introduction

Bitcoin is a digital cryptocurrency network and a worldwide payment system. Bitcoin transactions are maintained in a public ledger known as the blockchain, a database replicated among mutually distrusted users, who update it by means of a global consensus algorithm based on proof-of-work [9].

The nature of the Bitcoin protocol limits the scalability of the network to only tens of transactions per second. To overcome this issue, a system of off-chain payment channels have been proposed [11]. In that system a pair of users adds a single opening transaction to the blockchain where they lock their bitcoins in a deposit secured by a Bitcoin script. Then they can perform mutual off-chain payments by agreeing on the distribution of the deposit balance. To close the channel, the users can broadcast a new transaction of the final balances to the blockchain. This approach can be expanded to open channel paths between users, thus creating a payment-channel network that enables a higher number of payments with only few interactions with the underlying blockchain.

Any payment network must offer solutions to many issues, among these, the privacy of transacting participants, and concurrency problems. In a recent paper Malavolta *et al.* [7] formalize the privacy standards and analyze the trade-off between privacy and concurrency in payment channel networks. They demonstrate that payment networks that enforce non-blocking progress inevitably reduce the anonymity set for sender and receiver of a payment, thereby weakening privacy guarantees.

© Springer Nature Switzerland AG 2018
J. Garcia-Alfaro et al. (Eds.): DPM 2018/CBT 2018, LNCS 11025, pp. 175–187, 2018.
https://doi.org/10.1007/978-3-030-00305-0_13

In this work we further explore issues related to the concurrency problem in off-chain payment networks. First, we describe the network model and define a deadlock in this model. We then show that finding a deadlock free routing for several flows in a payment network is NP-hard. Lastly, we propose a modification to the payment protocol in payment networks which enables both privacy and concurrency.

1.1 Related Work

Blockchain scalability is a major issue today with many different approaches to scaling. Payment channels constitute one of the main approaches, and come in several versions and with various extensions [2]. The Lightning network is the prominent proposition for Bitcoin [11] and Raiden [3] for Ethereum. Other solutions have been proposed such as Plasma offering a scalable framework of smart contracts that will work as a second layer for Ethereum [10]. Miller *et al.* [8] propose payment channels that reduce the time coins are locked in intermediate channels along a payment path.

'Teechan' has been proposed by Lind *et al.* [6] offering a full-duplex payment channel framework that can be deployed without having to modify existing blockchain protocols, but relying strongly on secure hardware.

Payment channels networks face many challenges such as routing, liquidity, privacy, concurrency and many more. Prihodko *et al.* [12] Offer an algorithm for routing in the lightning network. Dandekar *et al.* [4] study the question of liquidity in payment networks showing the similarity to general flow networks.

Rohrer *et al.* [13] offer an algorithm to find multiple payment routes in a payment channel network, based on general flow-networks algorithms which elevates concurrency. Roos *et al.* [14] propose a new algorithm for routing in the network which ensure privacy, efficiency and scalability. In these algorithms the route is found based on a general algorithm, unlike in our setting in which the sender decides on the route according to his criterion.

2   Background

2.1   Payment Channels

A payment channel is a framework that allows two users: u_1, u_2, to execute many small transfers without committing them all to the Bitcoin blockchain. The users add an opening transaction to the blockchain where they deposit bitcoins into a multi-signature address controlled by both users. They can then update the balance of the deposit using smart contracts that ensure that both users agree on a re-distribution of the payments. Each individual is able to commit the aggregate of all transfers to the blockchain in case the other party stops cooperating or leaves [5, 11].

The channel's capacity is limited in each direction as the amount of funds in the joint channel is finite. More specifically, the amount of money u_1 can pay u_2 is limited to the amount of money that is ascribed to u_1 in the multi-signature address.

When the channel is no longer needed, or when it has reached its capacity's limit, a closing transaction is included in the blockchain in which each user receives the amount of bitcoins according to the most recent distribution.

2.2 Payment Channel Networks

The single-channel framework can be leveraged to create a more connected network of payment channels: A sender s can send money to a receiver t even if they do not have an open channel between them. This is done by finding a path of open channels from sender to receiver $p = (s = u_0, u_1, ..., u_n = t)$, such that the capacity in each channel is larger or equal to the amount of money that is being transferred. Once a path if found, s can send b bitcoins to u_1, u_1 sends it to u_2 and so on, until finally t receives his money.

To ensure that an intermediate user u_i in the path does not lose bitcoins in the process a hashed timelock contract [1] is used. With a HTLC, the receiver can claim the payment only if he can provide a pre-image of a cryptographic hash, that he obtains if money was taken by the next node in the path. Such evidence that the node can retrieve funds from the channel must be provided within a certain deadline. Otherwise, the money returns to the sender.

In a payment path in the classic payment-channel set up, t creates a random key R and computes its hash value $h = H(R)$. He then sends h to s, and now s can set up a HTLC with u_2 which is dependent on R and expires after time T. A HTLC is then set at each payment channel in the path to t such that the expiration time is decreasing. When a HTLC is set between u_{n-1} and t, t can reveal R to claim his money. Every user in the path from t back to the source of the payment can then fulfill the contract and receive his bitcoins. Since the timeout of the HTLC between u_i and u_{i+1} is smaller than the timeout of the HTLC between u_{i-1} and u_i, u_i will have time to pull his bitcoins after R is revealed to him and his money has been transferred to u_{i+1} [11]. In bidirectional payment channels, additional mechanisms must be combined with these described here to ensure that no node replays an old message that represents an outdated allocation of the funds within the channel (an allocation that may award this node a higher payment).

3 Network Model

In our model the payment channel network is represented as a directed weighted graph $G = (V, E)$, where the set V of vertices represents the users in the network and the set E of edges are the open channels between users. The weight of each edge $c(u, v)$ denotes the channel's capacity limit, that is the amount of coins user u can pay user v.

In this model, a bi-directional channel is represented by two directed edges, one in each direction. This is sufficient for our discussion, since the amount of money that can be transferred in one direction may be different than the amount that can be transfered in the opposite direction. If a transfer of b bitcoins along an edge from u to v is executed, the capacity of the edge is updated: $c(u,v) = c(u,v) - b$. The capacity of the edge in the opposite direction is similarly increased.

A valid transfer of b bitcoins from a sender s to a receiver t is a path $P = (s = u_0, u_1, ..., u_n = t)$ from s to t, such that $\forall 1 \le i \le n-1$, $c(u_i, u_{i+1}) \ge b$. We will assume that the network utilizes *source routing*, i.e., that the source node s chooses the path through which payments are routed to the target t. Since a user's objective is to minimize the cost of the fees in a transfer, we can assume there are no cycles in transfer routes.

Finally, we define the individual payment routing problem, which is the problem of selecting a route between a single source and target (this is the problem faced by the individual payer in the network):

Definition 1 (Individual Payment Routing Problem). *The individual payment routing problem is a tuple (G, c, s, t, b) where $G = (V, E)$ is a directed graph representing the nodes and payment channels, $c : E \to \mathbf{R}_+$ is a function assigning capacities to the channels, $s, t \in V$ are a source and target destination respectively, and b is the amount of bitcoins to send from s to t.*

The solution to this problem is a path P in the graph.

Definition 2 (Individually Feasible Solution). *In the context of an individual payment routing problem, We say that a certain path P is an* individually feasible solution *to the routing problem if P is a simple path, from s to t, and the capacity $c(e)$ of every edge $e = (u_i, u_{i+1})$ between users in the path is larger or equal to b.*

Furthermore we define the fully clearing payment set as follows:

Definition 3 (Fully Clearing Payment Set). *The fully clearing payment set is a set of individually feasible payments in a network that have an order of execution that ensures that they can all be carried out.*

4   Routing and Deadlocks in Payment Channel Networks

4.1   Opening a Payment Route

Intuitively, the basic construction of a payment route is based on setting up a sequence of channels, and revealing a secret to the last node in the path. The secret allows the last node to retrieve money from the last payment channel in the path, but would also reveal the secret to the preceding node, which will enable it too to pull money from the channel leading to it. Hence, each node that loses money, can ensure that it regains it by pulling money from the previous node in the path. The payment thus propagates back to the initial node which is the source of the payment.

To be more precise, We describe a path set up as proposed in [7] using multi-hop HTLC. First of all, the sender s creates a key for each pair of users in the path by sampling n strings x_i and for each pair (u_i, u_{i+1}) defining the hash value of $y_i = H(\bigoplus_{j=i}^{n} x_j)$ Where H is an arbitrary hash function. He also generates a proof π_i to guarantee that each y_i is well-formed, without having to reveal all of the x_j. He then sends (x_i, y_i, π_i, z_i), where z_i is a timeout parameter, to each user u_i in the path through a direct communication channel. We refer the reader to [7] for more details.

After verifying that all the values are correct, each pair of users (u_i, u_{i+1}) starting from the sender, establish a HTLC as described in Sect. 2.2. Once the HTLC between (u_{n-1}, t) is established, the receiver can release x_n, and pull his money. Then in reverse order each intermediate user can produce the key $\bigoplus_{j=i}^{n} x_j$ and is able to pull his money.

Notice, that once a HTLC has been established between u_i and u_{i+1} as part of a payment path the money is locked. If u_i wants to cancel the HTLC's distribution he needs u_{i+1}'s consent for creating a new commitment transaction. This might result in money loss for u_{i+1}, since he has an open HTLC with u_{i+2}, making it problematic for him to forgo the old contract.

4.2 Deadlocks in Payment Channel Networks

A deadlock in a payment network is a situation in which several simultaneous payments share edges in their paths in such a manner that none of the payments can go through. That is, while each payment is individually feasible, together they may not be able to send money through edges that lack capacity. Further more, each payment is holding up an edge that does not have enough capacity for all transfers and each payment is waiting for an edge that is being held up by another payment request.

Indeed, in payment networks the channel capacity is limited, so if two payment routes contain the same edge, they may not be able to pass through at the same time. Furthermore, paths are composed of several edges that are acquired (via the HTLC setup) one after the other. A payment can then block an edge with an established HTLC and wait for another edge that is being held up by another transfer etc. This can happen only if there is a cycle in the network's graph. Such situations can in fact result in a deadlock.

In our model we assume that when several payments are executed concurrently, the edges between the users in the paths are being taken up one edge at a time, in a certain order which respects the inner ordering of each path. For example, let us suppose two payments occur concurrently: payment 1 composed of edges $p_1 = (e_1, .., e_n)$ and payment 2 composed of edges $p_2 = (e'_1, .., e'_m)$. Then the edges are being taken up by each path in a certain order: $(r_1, ..., r_{n+m})$, where for each edge $e_i \in p_1$ there is j such that $r_j = e_i$ and is associated only with it and similarly for each edge $e'_i \in p_2$ there is k such that $r_k = e'_i$ and is associated only with it. Furthermore if for $i < j$, r_i, r_j are both associated with edges from path p_1 or are both associated with edges from path p_2, then r_i is before r_j in p_1 or in p_2 respectively. A concrete example of a deadlock in a payment network is depicted in Fig. 1.

Proposition 1. *Every deadlock problem between a set of individually feasible payments has an equivalent deadlock problem between a fully clearing payment set.*

Proof. Given a set of individually feasible payments through paths $p_1, ..., p_n$: $\{(p_1, b_1), ..., (p_n, b_n)\}$, we extend the set with flows $\{(\bar{p}_1, b_1), ..., (\bar{p}_n, b_n)\}$. Where $\bar{p}_i$ is a flow along the reverse of the path p_i.

Notice that if the flow along p_i is executed, and then the reverse flow along $\bar{p}_i$ follows, then the network capacities are effectively reset. As all flows are originally individually feasible, other flows can proceed.

We additionally extend each path p_i and its inverse, with a single edge of capacity b_i exactly that can be used initially only in the direction of p_i. This ensures that $\bar{p}_i$ can be executed only after p_i, hence, if all original flows are deadlocked, none of the inverse flows can proceed, and the new setting is deadlocked as well. □

From now on, when we refer to a deadlock between an arbitrary set of individually feasible payments, we will assume that the set is the equivalent fully clearing set without specifying so.

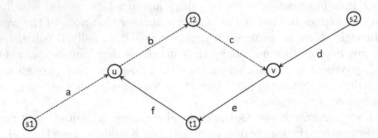

Fig. 1. Illustration of two blocking payments: payment 1 from s_1 to t_1 and payment 2 from s_2 to t_2. Each payment is of 1 bitcoin and the capacity of each edge is 1. The capacity of the edge in the opposite direction is 0. The order of the execution is: $(a_1, d_2, b_1, e_2, c_1, f_2, e_1, b_2)$, where for each $x \in \{a, ..., f\}$, x_1 is associated with edge x in path 1, and similarly x_2 is associated with edge x in path 2. The inverse payments' edges come after that. Each edge is labeled with the label of the payment that has reached it first (payment 1 in a dashed line, payment 2 in a solid line). Payment 1 is unable to acquire edge e, and payment 2 is unable to acquire edge b, thus they are deadlocked. Notice that if the ordering was different, such that payment 1 was carried out fully, then its inverse and then payment 2 and its inverse, all payments would have been able to go through.

A well established method for detecting possible deadlocks is to use the resource allocation graph. Here we define a similar notion: the *edge allocation graph* for payment networks, which is a graph that keeps track of which resources (edges) are needed for each payment.

Definition 4 (Edge Allocation Graph). *Given a set $\mathcal{P} = \{p_i\}_{i=1}^{m}$ of individually feasible solutions to a set of payment routing problems $\{(G, c, p_i)\}_{i=1}^{m}$, we can derive the edge allocation graph $G' = (V', E')$ as follows:*

There are two types of vertices in V': $v_1, ..., v_m$ represent the payment paths in $\mathcal{P}$. For each i, $v_i = p_i$. $v_{m+1}, ..., v_n$ represent the edges E, between the users that are part of each payment path. For each j, $v_j = e_j$.

The graph has an associated vertex weight function $w : V' \to \mathbb{R}_+$. For the path vertices $v_1, ..., v_m$, $w(v_i)$ denotes the transfer amount b_i, and for edge vertices $v_{m+1}, ..., v_n$, $w(v_j)$ denotes the capacity of that edge $c(e_j)$.

Proposition 2. *A deadlock in a payment channel network can occur (under some ordering) iff its associated allocation graph contains a simple cycle and for each edge vertex e_j in the cycle, $w(e_j) < w(p_{i-1}) + w(p_i)$, where p_{i-1} and pi are e_j's neighbors in G' that are in the cycle.*

Proof. If there is a deadlock in the graph in a certain ordering then there is a path p_1 which is holding up edge e_1 and waiting for edge e_n, p_2 is holding up e_2 and waiting for e_1 etc. In the associated allocation graph there will be an edge between vertex p_1 and e_1, between e_1 and p_2 etc. Finally there will be an edge between e_n and p_1. So the graph contains a cycle: $(p_1, e_1, p_2, e_2, ..., p_n, e_n, p_1)$. Also notice that in the original graph, each edge e_i in the deadlock does not have enough capacity for both paths' p_{i-1} and p_i transfer amounts, which means that in G, $c(e_i) < b_{i-1} + b_i$. So in G', $w(e_i) < w(p_{i-1}) + w(p_i)$.

If there is a cycle in the allocation graph, denote it by $(e_1, p_1, e_n, p_n, e_{n-1}, p_{n-1}, ..., p_2, e_1)$ and for each i, $w(e_i) < w(p_{i-1}) + w(p_i)$. Then we can set the following ordering: $(e_{1-p1}, e_{2-p2}, ..., e_{n-pn}, e_{1-pn}, ..., e_{n-p1})$. Notice that in this ordering, path p_1 held up edge e_1 before path p_2 and there was not enough capacity for both and so on. So under this ordering there is a deadlock between paths $p_1, ..., p_n$ in G. □

4.3   The Safe Routing Problem

While in routing networks each individual sender picks their own route, it is possible to wonder if there is a way to prescribe a route for each sender such that deadlocks are avoided and progress is guaranteed. A trivial example, is a complete graph (a clique) where we can assign any payment from u to v a direct route on the edge u, v. In this case there would be no deadlocks. Can we do so for other graphs?

In this section we show that even a centralized coordinating node will in general need to solve a hard computational problem in order to find individually feasible routes. We begin by defining the Safe Routing Decision Problem.

Definition 5 ((G,c,K) Safe Routing Decision Problem). *The (G,c,K) safe routing problem is the problem of deciding whether there exist individually feasible paths connecting the k given pairs of vertices $K = \{(s_1,t_1,b_1),...,(s_k,t_k,b_k)\}$ such that the routing solution is deadlock-safe, and feasible with edge capacities c.*

Proposition 3. (G,c,K) *Safe Routing Problem* $\in NP$.

Proof. There is a polynomial verifier for (G,c,K). Given a graph, routing and its associated ordering we will create its resource allocation graph in polynomial time:

First we will create vertices for all edges and payment paths and assign them the applicable weights. Then we will go over each path and stretch an edge from the path vertex to all of it's edges' associated edge vertices.

At the end of this process we will search for a cycle in G' such that the edge vertices e_j in the cycle satisfy: $w(e_j) < w(p_{i-1}) + w(p_i)$, where p_{i-1} and p_i are e_j's neighbors in the cycle. If such a cycle is found the verifier will return false, otherwise it will return true. As we have shown, the allocation graph contains a cycle in which all edge vertices' weights satisfy the above inequality iff there is a deadlock in the network.   □

Proposition 4. (G,c,K) *Safe Routing Problem* $\in NP$ *Complete.*

Proof. We show a polynomial reduction from 3-SAT to the (G,c,k) safe routing problem.

Given a 3CNF boolean expression, composed of variables $x_1,...,x_n$ and clauses $c_1,...,c_m$, we construct an instance of the (G,c,K) safe routing problem such that each payment is of 1 bitcoin, and the capacity of each edge is 1. It will consist of a directed graph G, and m terminal pairs, $(s_{c1},t_{c1}),...,(s_{c_m},t_{c_m})$. We shall prove that there is a individually feasible deadlock free routing in G if and only if the boolean expression is satisfiable.

To describe our construction, we need a gadget X_j defined for each variable x_j as follows: X_j consists of two incoming vertices x_j^{in}, $\bar{x}_j^{in}$, two outgoing vertices x_j^{out}, $\bar{x}_j^{out}$ and 4 additional vertices. The vertices are connected as a cycle as depicted in Fig. 2.

Now the graph G is constructed as follows: for each clause c_i we add a terminal pair (s_{ci},t_{ci}). Then we connect the terminal pair to each variable gadget c_i is composed of. If c_i consists of a variable x_j we will stretch an edge from s_{ci} to x_j^{in} and from x_j^{out} to t_{ci}. If it consists of its negation we will stretch an edge from s_{ci} to $\bar{x}_j^{in}$ and from $\bar{x}_j^{out}$ to t_{ci}. See Fig. 2 for more details.

This completes the construction of G. All together G contains $2m+8n$ vertices, $6m+8n$ edges and m terminal pairs, thus it can be constructed in polynomial time from a boolean expression, composed of n variables and m clauses.

Now suppose that there is an assignment to the variables that will make the entire given expression true. Then we can find a deadlock free routing of G as follows:

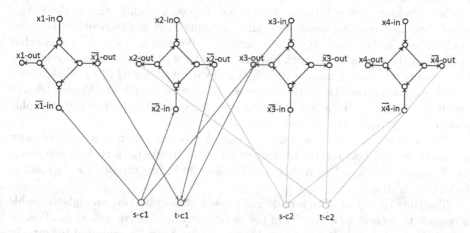

Fig. 2. Example of reduction graph for $3 - SAT = c_1 \wedge c_2$ where $c_1 = (\bar{x}_1 \vee \bar{x}_2 \vee x_3)$ and $c_2 = (x_2 \vee \bar{x}_3 \vee \bar{x}_4)$. Each clause has two associated vertices: s_{c1} and t_{c1} for c_1 which are connected to gadgets x_1, x_2, x_3 and s_{c2} and t_{c2} for c_2 which are connected to gadgets x_2, x_3, x_4.

For each clause c_i, at least one of the literals is true, so for a path from s_{ci} to t_{ci} we will choose the corresponding edge from s_{ci} to that variable's gadget, pass through 3/4 of the cycle, and go through the gadget's outgoing edge to t_{ci}. Notice that the only edges in terminals' paths that can be shared, are the edges that are in a variable's gadget. Since the assignment can not give the same variable true and false, if two clause terminals paths share a gadget, they will both enter and exit through the same vertices according to the assignment and thus no deadlock can occur.

Conversely, suppose that G has a non-deadlock routing. Each path from a source vertex s_{ci} has to pass through a gadget X_j in order to get to t_{ci}. So we will assign the corresponding variable x_j true if s_{ci} is connected to x_j^{in} and false otherwise. If there are gadgets with no routes passing through, we will assign the corresponding variable true. Notice that if two paths share a gadget then they both have to enter through the same vertex, otherwise the routing will cause a deadlock. Thus each variable in the boolean expression will be assigned only true or false, and so the described assignment is legal. Clearly, for each clause at least one literal is true, so the entire boolean expression it true.   □

5   A Deadlock-Free Payment Network Protocol

In [7] two algorithms have been proposed: Rayo, which provides non-blocking progress but reduces the privacy guarantees, and Fulgor, which maintains privacy but is a blocking protocol. In this section we propose a modification of the Fulgor algorithm that resolves deadlocks, thus showing that a protocol maintaining both privacy and concurrency can be achieved. We assume for our protocol that vertices in the payment network have IDs. We thus propose that each edge e in the network will have a unique ID associated with it, denoted $id(e)$. This ID can be set, e.g., using the IDs or IP addresses of the edge's vertices. When s tries to create a payment path he will lock edges in order dictated by the lexicographic ordering of the identifiers of the edges.

We propose that when s wants to send b bitcoins through a path of open channels, he will first send a request to all edges in the path to lock b bitcoins for T amount of time. The requests will be sent in lexicographic order according to the edges' IDs.

The time span T sent to a node in the path should be long enough to enable a request to be sent to all nodes in the path, but not long enough as to allow an attack on the network. A time span that is too long can be exploited for attacks by allowing a malicious user to lock edges for a long time thus delaying transfers and preventing payments to go through. This is a challenge that all time based protocols such as HTLC face.

If an edge receives a locking request and does not have enough capacity, it should abort the payment by sending an abort message to the sender (through the open communication channel). If it can accept the request, it should send an accepting message to the sender and lock b bitcoins. If an edge receives a new request within the time range of a previous request and it does not have enough capacity for both, it should abort the new request.

If all edges accepted the request, s should proceed as described before: he sets up a HTLC with u_1, u_2 then sets a HTLC with u_3 and so on. That is, he creates the HTLC, but this time ordering edges according to their order in the path (this is required so that money is not stolen from one of the intermediate nodes).

5.1   Protocol Description

In the following we will describe in detail the set-up operations. We assume that each edge has an internal state $e.lockedCoins$ which stores the amount of locked coins in the edge and the timeout for each value. This information can be maintained in a list of tuples.

initialize_path(P,b,T): The sender sorts the list P of edges in the path to t according to the lexicographic order of their IDs. Then he sends a request to the tail node of the edge with the minimal ID to set aside b bitcoins for T time. See Algorithm 1 for more detail.

Algorithm 1. initialize_path(P, b, T)

1: $P \leftarrow sort(P)$ ▷ sort P by id's of edges in P
2: $u \leftarrow$ tail of edge $P[1] = (u, v)$
3: $v \leftarrow$ head of edge $P[1] = (u, v)$
4: lock_request(u, v, b, T) ▷ Send u a request to lock b bitcoins in the channel to v for T time.

---

receive_lock_request(m): Upon receiving a request message m to lock b bitcoins, the intermediate node u checks if it has enough capacity in the edge to v. If it doesn't it sends 0 to abort the payment. Then u checks the edge (u, v)'s internal mode to verify that the sum of the new payment with the amount of locked coins which timeout has not passed does not exceed the capacity. If it does, u aborts the payment. If it decides to proceed with the payment it sends 1 through the communication channel and adds (b, T) to $u.lockedCoins$. See Algorithm 2 for more detail.

Algorithm 2. receive_lock_request(m)

1: **if** c(u,v) $< b$ **then**
2:     $Send(m\_sender, 0)$
3:     **return**
4: locked_sum $\leftarrow 0$
5: **for** (b', T') in $(u, v).lockedCoins$ **do**
6:     **if** T' has not passed **then**
7:        locked_sum $\leftarrow$ locked_sum $+ b'$
8:     **else**
9:        delete (b', T')
10: **if** c(u,v) $< b +$ locked_sum **then**
11:     $Send(m\_sender, 0)$
12:     **return**
13: $(u, v).lockedCoins$.append(b, T)
14: $Send(m\_sender, 1)$
15: **return**

Algorithm 3. *receive_lock_resp.* (m, P)

1: **if** m *is* 0 **then**
2:     **return**
3: find i such that $P[i]$ tail $= u$
4: **if** P[i+1] != null **then**
5:     $u' \leftarrow$ tail of edge $P[i + 1]$
6:     $v' \leftarrow$ head of edge $P[i + 1]$
7:     lock_request(u', v', b, T)
8: **else**
9:     call Fulgor

---

receive_lock_response(m, P): Upon receiving a response m from an intermediate user u, s checks its value. If it's 0, s does not continue to build the path and the coins in the path that have already been locked will be released after the timeout has passed. If it's 1, s finds the edge with the following ID and sends its tail node a request. If u was the last hop in the path, s proceeds to execute the Fulgor algorithm. See Algorithm 3 for more detail.

5.2   Protocol Properties

We will now show that the protocol maintains the following properties:

Lemma 1. *Balance security is maintained. An intermediated node can not lose money.*

Proof. Notice that no money is actually set aside before the HTLC is established. As explained above, hash time locked contracts (HTLC) ensure balance security [1]. □

Lemma 2. *Privacy is maintained. The set-up maintains the anonymity set for sender and receiver of a payment.*

Proof (sketch). As shown in the algorithm descriptions in Sect. 5.1 the protocol can be executed using the Fulgor algorithm described in [7], with a slight addition of locking bitcoins before the actual setup. This addition does not affect the privacy guarantees since it only requires another message from the sender to an intermediate user and an acceptance message from the intermediate user to the sender. These messages can be sent through the communication channels which are used for sending the HTLC set-up and they do not require additional exposure. As proven in [7] Fulgor maintains the privacy requirements. □

Lemma 3. *Progress is maintained. This set-up enables non-blocking progress.*

Proof. Assume by way of contradiction that there is a routing of transfers which contains a circular wait. Namely there is a sequence of paths $p_1, ..., p_n$ with senders $s_1, ..., s_n$, such that p_1 is holding edge $e_1 = (u_1, v_1)$ which is part of p_2's route, p_2 is holding edge $e_2 = (u_2, v_2)$ which is part of p_3's route, etc., and lastly p_n is holding edge $e_n = (u_n, v_n)$ which is part of p_1's route.

As described in Algorithm 1, when initializing a path the sender sorts the edges in the path according to the lexicographic order of their IDs and sends the request for locking coins one by one by that order. Notice that if s_n did not succeed in locking edge e_{n-1} he would have received a negative response from u_{n-1} and would not continue to build the path, as shown in Algorithm 3. Since he is holding up edge e_n that means that s_n sent a request to lock coins to u_n by sending *lock_request* and received a positive response. So we can deduce that s_n sent the request for edge e_n before edge e_{n-1} which means that $id(e_n) > id(e_{n-1})$. Through that same logic $id(e_{n-1}) > id(e_{n-2}), ..., id(e_2) > id(e_1)$, $id(e_1) > id(e_n)$. Contradiction!

⇒ A circular wait can not occur in this setup. □

6   Conclusions

Off-chain payment channels networks have to deal with many challenges such as liquidity, concurrency, privacy and many more. In [7] it has been proposed that there is no routing algorithm offering non-blocking progress and full privacy.

In this work we have shown that assigning routes for a group of payments in the current network protocol such that there is no deadlock in the system is an NP-complete problem. We further proposed a new protocol that ensures deadlock free routings while preserving the desired privacy properties.

References

1. Bitcoin wiki: Hashed timelock contracts. https://en.bitcoin.it/wiki/Hashed_Timelock_Contracts
2. Bitcoin wiki: Payment channels. https://en.bitcoin.it/wiki/Payment_channels
3. Raiden network. Project's website: https://raiden.network/
4. Dandekar, P., Goel, A., Govindan, R., Post, I.: Liquidity in credit networks: a little trust goes a long way. In: Proceedings of the 12th ACM Conference on Electronic Commerce, pp. 147–156. ACM (2011)
5. Decker, C., Wattenhofer, R.: A fast and scalable payment network with bitcoin duplex micropayment channels. In: Pelc, A., Schwarzmann, A.A. (eds.) SSS 2015. LNCS, vol. 9212, pp. 3–18. Springer, Cham (2015). https://doi.org/10.1007/978-3-319-21741-3_1
6. Lind, J., Eyal, I., Pietzuch, P., Sirer, E.: Teechan: Payment channels using trusted execution environments. arXiv preprint arXiv:1612.07766 (2016)
7. Malavolta, G., Moreno-Sanchez, P., Kate, A., Maffei, M., Ravi, S.: Concurrency and privacy with payment-channel networks, pp. 455–471 (2017)
8. Miller, A., Bentov, I., Kumaresan, R., McCorry, P.: Sprites: payment channels that go faster than lightning. arXiv preprint arXiv:1702.05812 (2017)
9. Nakamoto, S.: Bitcoin: a peer-to-peer electronic cash system (2009). http://www.bitcoin.org/bitcoin.pdf
10. Poon, J., Buterin, V.: Plasma: Scalable autonomous smart contracts. White paper (2017)
11. Poon, J., Dryja, T.: The bitcoin lightning network: Scalable Off-Chain instant payments. https://lightning.network/lightning-network-paper.pdf
12. Prihodko, P., Zhigulin, S., Sahno, M., Ostrovskiy, A., Osuntokun, O.: Flare: an approach to routing in lightning network. White Paper (2016). (bitfury.com/content/5-white-papers-research/whitepaper_flare_an_approach_to_routing_in_lightning_network_7_7_2016.pdf)
13. Rohrer, E., Laß, J.-F., Tschorsch, F.: Towards a concurrent and distributed route selection for payment channel networks. In: Garcia-Alfaro, J., Navarro-Arribas, G., Hartenstein, H., Herrera-Joancomartí, J. (eds.) ESORICS/DPM/CBT - 2017. LNCS, vol. 10436, pp. 411–419. Springer, Cham (2017). https://doi.org/10.1007/978-3-319-67816-0_23
14. Roos, S., Moreno-Sanchez, P., Kate, A., Goldberg, I.: Settling payments fast and private: Efficient decentralized routing for path-based transactions. arXiv preprint arXiv:1709.05748 (2017)

Coloured Ring Confidential Transactions

Felix Engelmann[✉], Frank Kargl, and Christoph Bösch

Institute for Distributed Systems, Ulm University, Ulm, Germany
{felix.engelmann,frank.kargl,christoph.boesch}@uni-ulm.de

Abstract. Privacy in block-chains is considered second to functionality, but a vital requirement for many new applications, e.g., in the industrial environment. We propose a novel transaction type, which enables privacy preserving trading of independent assets on a common block-chain. This is achieved by extending the ring confidential transaction with an additional commitment to a colour and a publicly verifiable proof of conservation. With our coloured confidential ring signatures, new token types can be introduced and transferred by any participant using the same sized anonymity set as single-token privacy aware block-chains. Thereby, our system facilitates tracking assets on an immutable ledger without compromising the confidentiality of transactions.

Keywords: Coloured coins · Privacy · Confidential ring signature
Commitments

1 Introduction

Trading is a basic human trait that extends to the digital world. Individual trading without the need of intermediaries is enabled by block-chain technology. Participants of a block-chain reach a global consensus on which trades are valid and in which order. To achieve this, all transactions must be validated by peers and checked for violations of conservation rules, e.g., creating an asset out of thin air. The basic approach is to use plain-text transaction receipts, visible for everyone which makes validation of the transactions straightforward.

The issue with these plain-text receipts is, that trades often include valuable information for other parties, using the knowledge for their leverage. Independent research [6,9] realised, that privacy in block-chain systems is important to support the same features as analogue trades. Monero therefore introduced ring confidential transactions to hide the sender identity (using ring signatures), the recipient identity (using one-time payment addresses), and the amount transferred (using commitments) from the public, while maintaining the possibility to verify the conservation. The real sender is indistinguishably concealed within a set of decoys. To prove ownership of an asset, which is attached to a public key,

This work was partially funded by the Federal Ministry of Economic Affairs and Energy on the basis of a decision by the German Bundestag. The authors thank Henning Kopp for the technical discussions during the sketching phase.

© Springer Nature Switzerland AG 2018
J. Garcia-Alfaro et al. (Eds.): DPM 2018/CBT 2018, LNCS 11025, pp. 188–196, 2018.
https://doi.org/10.1007/978-3-030-00305-0_14

a ring signature is used instead of a regular digital signature. The verifier of a ring signature can check that the signer knows at least one of the corresponding private keys, but not which one. To prevent double spending of the same asset, the ring signature has to include a specific tag, which stores the identity of the signer in an encrypted form. If two signatures have the same tag, they can be linked and the second signature is invalid. Thus, no two assets can belong to the same public key. This requirement demands for one-time recipient addresses, which, in addition, serve the purpose of hiding the recipient from the public. Therefore, a one-time key is derived from the long-term recipient public key, for which only the recipient can derive the correct one-time private key. These one-time addresses prevent multiple transaction outputs to be linked to a common owner. This works well, if all transaction inputs are of equal value. However, transaction inputs with different values, still allow for deducing the real sender by comparing the transaction in- and outputs. In order to prevent this kind of sender derivation and to add privacy, the transaction value is hidden inside a commitment. Additively homomorphic Pedersen commitments [7] allow the sender to prove that the input minus the output of a transaction is zero, thereby proving the conservation without disclosing the amount. A detailed description of the techniques used is summarised by Alonso et al. [1].

The added privacy compared to fully visible transaction receipts restricts features, such as Turing complete smart contracts, which are common on non-privacy aware block-chains. Smart contracts are recipients, whose behaviour is governed by code. A prominent use-case of smart contracts is the management of tokens. These tokens can be sub-currencies or used to track assets independent of the block-chain's native currency.

In this paper, we introduce an extension to the ring confidential transaction to support sub-currencies with the benefit of privacy aware trading. Our construction features multiple coexisting asset types, also known as colours. A transaction can transfer exactly one colour, but the decoy inputs can be from any colour, having the same anonymity set as single-colour privacy aware block-chains. The colour of the transaction is only known to the interacting parties (sender and recipient of the current transaction), but not to anyone else, achieving a fully privacy aware verification of colour conservation from inputs to outputs.

With the help of our new transaction type, all participants of the block-chain can introduce new token types for their own purposes. The consensus verifies that a new colour does not yet exist to prevent unauthorised issuance of existing tokens. All the new tokens will benefit from the privacy aware transactions without the barrier of creating an independent chain per colour. A new block-chain per colour reduces the opportunities for decoys in a transaction which negatively impacts the privacy of the whole system. On top, multiple colours on a single block-chain facilitate future on-chain atomic swap operations between colours.

2   Preliminaries

Our contribution extends the ring confidential transaction (ringCT), which is prominently used in Monero for the `RCTTypeFull`, to support a colour attribute for in- and outputs of a transaction. In this section, we describe the required building blocks, an additively homomorphic commitment scheme and a linkable ring signature, which are the same as for the ringCT. In addition to this, a full ringCT requires range proofs, but as our extension does not require an adaptation thereof, we refer the reader to the work of Noether et al. [6] for the full construction.

We use elliptic curve cryptography for our commitments and signatures. An elliptic curve is a group with the possibility to add an element, also called point, to another or itself resulting in a new point on the curve. This allows for the multiplication of a scalar x to a point. A curve standardises a base point G, which is the generator of a preferably large subgroup. Elliptic curves are suited for cryptography, as calculating x given $P = xG$ is hard, known as the discrete logarithm problem. This property can be used to generate private-public key pairs $(\mathrm{sk} = x, \mathrm{pk} = xG)$.

2.1   Pedersen Commitments

To hide a value a in an Elliptic Curve Pedersen commitment [7] requires two points, where one can be the base point G and the second point $H = \psi G$ must be created, such that ψ is unknown to anyone. A *nothing up my sleeve* generation of H can be generated by hashing the base point with a hash function $\mathcal{H}$ mapping from a point to another point with $H = \mathcal{H}(G)$. G and H are the public parameters of the given system. To build a commitment to a value a, a secret, random blinding factor x is generated and then combined to

$$C(a, x) = xG + aH.$$

Pedersen commitments are perfectly hiding and computationally binding under the discrete logarithm assumption. A commitment $C(0, x) = xG$ is binding but not hiding. By publishing the point $C(a, x)$, the sender commits to the value a, and can only change the choice by brute-force searching for a different pair x', a' satisfying $C(a, x) = xG + aH = x'G + a'H$ which has a negligible chance of success.

The Pederson commitment has the desirable property, that finding the value y with $C(a, x) = yG$ for $a \neq 0$ and $x \neq 0$ is difficult according to the discrete logarithm problem. However, given that $a = 0$, the commitment is reduced to $C(0, x) = xG + 0H = xG$. Then the private key to the committed point is x which is used to sign the commitment and thus proving knowledge of x.

An additional feature of the commitments are their homomorphicity in regard to addition. Three commitments $C_1(5, x_1), C_2(3, x_2), C_3(2, x_3)$ can be summed together like $C_1 - (C_2 + C_3) = x_1G + 5H - (x_2G + 3H + x_3G + 2H) = (x_1 - x_2 - x_3)G$ resulting in a commitment to zero C_0 with secret key $x_1 - x_2 - x_3$. Whoever can sign the sum of the commitments proves knowledge of all the components and proves that the sum of values is 0. For values which should be in plain-text, but which are needed to perform calculations, a commitment can be opened, by immediately disclosing a and x.

2.2   Multilayered Linkable Spontaneous Ad-Hoc Group Signature

The second building block we require for our colour extension is the Multilayered Linkable Spontaneous Ad-Hoc Group Signature (MLSAG). This is a modification of the Fujisaki-Suzuki (FS) [3] and the Liu-Wei-Wong (LWW) [4] signatures to increase their space efficiency. It provides a signature where the signer can prove knowledge of a set of private keys which are embedded in a larger set of decoys. The verifier can not deduce for which subset the signer knows the private keys. If any one of the private keys is reused, the two resulting signatures can be linked together, preventing double spending of a single output. The keygen, sign, verify and link algorithms are described according to Noether et al. [6].

$(P^j, x_j) \leftarrow$ **ML.Keygen**(1^λ): Generate a vector of m private keys x_i for $i = 1, \ldots, m$ with the corresponding public keys $P^i = x_i G$.

$(P_i^j, I_j) \leftarrow$ **ML.Keyselect**(P^j): Select a set of $n - 1$ vectors, each containing m public keys $\{P_i^j\}_{i=1,\ldots,n}^{j=1,\ldots,m}$ from other users. For a secret index π, corresponding to the signer, all the secret keys x_j must be known, such that $x_j G = P_\pi^j$ and let $I_j = x_j \mathcal{H}(P_\pi^j)$ for $j = 1, \ldots, m$.

$\sigma \leftarrow$ **ML.Sign**$(\mathfrak{m}, P_i^j, x_j, I_j)$: Let $\mathfrak{m}$ be the message to sign. For $j = 1, \ldots, m$ and $i = 1, \ldots, \pi - 1, \pi + 1, \ldots, n$ draw s_i^j and α_j as secure, random scalars. With a hash function $\mathfrak{h} : \{0,1\}^* \rightarrow \mathbb{Z}_q$, compute $L_\pi^j = \alpha_j G$ and $R_\pi^j = \alpha_j \mathcal{H}(P_\pi^j)$ for $j = 1, \ldots, m$. Continue with the vector $i = \pi + 1$ as

$$c_{\pi+1} = \mathfrak{h}(\mathfrak{m}, L_\pi^1, R_\pi^1, \ldots, L_\pi^m, R_\pi^m)$$
$$L_{\pi+1}^j = s_{\pi+1}^j G + c_{\pi+1} P_{\pi+1}^j \text{ and } R_{\pi+1}^j = s_{\pi+1}^j \mathcal{H}(P_{\pi+1}^j) + c_{\pi+1} I_j$$

and calculate L and R for each increment of i mod n until $i = \pi - 1$ like

$$c_{\pi-1} = \mathfrak{h}(\mathfrak{m}, L_{\pi-2}^1, R_{\pi-2}^1, \ldots, L_{\pi-2}^m, R_{\pi-2}^m)$$
$$L_{\pi-1}^j = s_{\pi-1}^j G + c_{\pi-1} P_{\pi-1}^j \text{ and } R_{\pi-1}^j = s_{\pi-1}^j \mathcal{H}(P_{\pi-1}^j) + c_{\pi-1} I_j.$$

Given $c_\pi = \mathfrak{h}(\mathfrak{m}, L_{\pi-1}^1, R_{\pi-1}^1, \ldots, L_{\pi-1}^m, R_{\pi-1}^m)$, we calculate s_π^j with $\alpha_j = s_\pi^j + c_\pi x_j$ mod l (modulus curve order l) and the output consists of

$$\sigma = (c_1, s_1^1, \ldots, s_1^m, s_2^1, \ldots, s_2^m, \ldots, s_n^1, \ldots, s_n^m, I_1, \ldots, I_m). \tag{1}$$

$0/1 \leftarrow$ **ML.Verify**$(\mathfrak{m}, \sigma, P_i^j)$: Starting with $i = 1$ and c_1, calculate L_i^j and R_i^j for all i and j. If $c_{n+1} = c_1$, the signature is valid and 1 is returned, 0 otherwise.

$0/1 \leftarrow$ **ML.Link**(σ, σ'): If the signatures σ and σ' share an I_j, they used the same private key x_j in the signing process and 1 is returned, 0 otherwise.

The MLSAG signature scheme must satisfy the the following correctness conditions: For every $\lambda, m \in \mathbb{N}$, every $n \in \mathbb{N}\backslash\{1\}$, every $(P^j, x_j) \leftarrow$ **ML.Keygen**(1^λ), and every $\mathfrak{m}$, it holds with high probability that

ML.Verify$(\mathfrak{m}, \sigma \leftarrow$ **ML.Sign**$(\mathfrak{m}, P_i^j \leftarrow$ **ML.Keyselect**$(P^j), x_j, I_j), P_i^j) = 1.$

The MLSAG satisfies the following security properties which are proven in the original LWW signature description [4] and the construction by Noether et al. [6]:

- *Unforgeability:* negligible probability of producing a valid signature without knowledge of all private keys in one vector.
- *Linkability:* negligible probability of being able to produce two different signatures using the same private key in both.
- *Signer Ambiguity:* negligible additional probability of guessing the secret index, even by knowing private keys of decoy inputs.

3   Our Coloured Ring Confidential Transaction

Having explained the necessary building blocks, we proceed with a detailed description of the RCTTypeFull ringCT and highlighted the additional elements required for our extension in red.

In- and Outputs. Our transaction requires inputs, which are outputs of previous transactions. The sender selects m inputs to be used. Depending on how many decoys per input $(n-1)$ the sender wants to include in the transaction, additional $m \cdot (n-1)$ inputs are selected. Each input contains a public key P_i^j, which was generated as a one-time payment address. The amount a each input holds is stored in a Pedersen commitment $C_i^j(a, b)$ with blinding factors b. The sender only knows $a_{j,in}$ and $b_{j,in}$ and x_j for the inputs $(P_\pi^j = x_j G, C_\pi^j(a_{j,in}, b_{j,in}))$ under its control. All real inputs make up one vector

$$\{(P_\pi^1, C_\pi^1(a_{1,in}, b_{1,in})), \ldots, (P_\pi^m, C_\pi^m(a_{m,in}, b_{m,in})\}$$

at the secret index π. The decoy vectors at $i = 1, \ldots, \pi - 1, \pi + 1, \ldots, n$ are assembled equally, with neither knowledge of the private keys for P_i^j nor of the blinding factors and amounts of the commitments C_i^j.

We introduce the colour property as an additional commitment in each input. Colours are defined as scalars f_i. Each input gets an additional commitment F_i^j to a colour. For the sender owned inputs, the colours $f_{j,in}$ and blinding factors $u_{j,in}$ of the commitments $F_\pi^j(f_{j,in}, u_{j,in})$ are known. An input $(P_\pi^j, C_\pi^j(a_{j,in}, b_{j,in}), F_\pi^j(f_{j,in}, u_{j,in}))$ is now composed of the recipient one-time key and two commitments. The q outputs of a transaction are also represented as a tuple of three elements $(P_k, C_k(a_{k,out}, b_{k,out}), F_k(f_{out}, u_{k,out}))$ for $k = 1, \ldots, q$ with the blinding factors $b_{k,out}$ and $u_{k,out}$ randomly drawn and secret.

Conservation. The sum of amounts of all inputs into a transaction must always be greater or equal to the sum of all output amounts, so the plain-text equation $\sum_{j=1}^m a_{j,in} - \sum_{k=1}^q a_{k,out} = 0$ translates to a commitment equation

$$\sum_{j=1}^m C_i^j - \sum_{k=1}^q C_k = C_0^i \tag{2}$$

resulting in a commitment C_0^i to zero. For $i = \pi$ in Eq. (2), the signer knows all amounts $a_{j,in}$ and blinding factors $b_{j,in}$, which make up the private key to C_0^π. This conservation ensures, that no asset is created in a transaction.

To ensure, that the real inputs are all from the same colour, the colour commitments F_i^j are checked in pairs to the colour commitment of the first output F_1. Again we can use a commitment to zero $F_i^j - F_1 = F_0^{i,j}$, which does not disclose the colour. Unlike the summation of the amounts, comparing aggregate commitments utilising the homomorphic property is not secure and could lead to the following attack. An attacker creates a transaction with two input colours $f_{in} - \epsilon$ and $f_{in} + \epsilon$ and an output f_{out}. If we only verify that $f_{in} - \epsilon + f_{in} + \epsilon = 2 f_{out}$ the inputs are not necessarily from the same colour. This conservation rule only supports one colour per transaction. Transactions with multiple colours involved, maintaining the signer ambiguity is supported by an extended version of our scheme currently in development.

Signature. The n commitments from the amounts and $n \cdot m$ commitments from the colour checks can now be signed by an MLSAG from Sect. 2.2. To bind a zero commitment to the originating spend key, and to have independent link tags, the public key is added to the commitment. As the sender knows the private key x_j to the spend key P_π^j and the components of the commitments to colour and value, it can still sign the sum of commitment and P_π^j with $x_{m+1+j} = x_j + f_{j,in} - f_{1,out}$. The following set of vectors is used as key input P_i^j into the **ML.sign**$(\mathrm{m}, P_i^j, x_j, I_j)$ algorithm with I_j from the **ML.Keyselect** algorithm:

$$
P := \left[\left\{ P_1^1, \ldots, P_1^m, \sum_{j=1}^m (P_1^j + C_1^j) - \sum_k C_k, P_1^1 + F_1^1 - F_1, \ldots, P_1^m + F_1^m - F_1 \right\}, \right.
$$

$$
\ldots, \left\{ P_\pi^1, \ldots, P_\pi^m, \sum_{j=1}^m (P_\pi^j + C_\pi^j) - \sum_k C_k, P_\pi^1 + F_\pi^1 - F_1, \ldots, P_\pi^m + F_\pi^m - F_1 \right\},
$$

$$
\left. \ldots, \left\{ P_n^1, \ldots, P_n^m, \sum_{j=1}^m (P_n^j + C_n^j) - \sum_k C_k, P_n^1 + F_n^1 - F_1, \ldots, P_n^m + F_n^m - F_1 \right\} \right].
$$

Output Proofs. The amounts are values modulus the curve order l, so overflows can be used to create new assets in a transaction. To counter this, the ringCT uses range proofs [2,5] to confine the output amounts to the interval $[0, 2^{64}]$. Our extension has to make sure, that all outputs are commitments to the same colour. We achieve this by appending $q - 1$ signatures for the zero commitments $F_1 - F_k = F_0^k$ for $k = 2, \ldots, q$.

Public Verification. The complete transaction with the references of the inputs and outputs and the ring signature σ is broadcast and anyone is able to verify the transaction and the conservation of assets. Therefore the vectors of public keys P_i^j are read from the referenced inputs together with the amount and colour commitments. The points for checking the conservation are calculated. The transaction is accepted if $\mathbf{ML.Verify}(\sigma, \mathtt{m}, P_i^j) = 1$ and $\mathbf{ML.Link}(\sigma, \sigma') = 0$ for all other transactions σ'.

4   Discussion

In this section we evaluate the theoretical impact of our extension and discuss its implications on the privacy of the whole system.

Correctness. The correctness of the proposed scheme, is satisfied by the availability of a rightful owner of an output and it's corresponding key to transfer the funds of one colour to another address. This is given under the correctness of the non-colour aware ringCT. The restriction of real in- and outputs being of the same colour only separates the transactions into different asset types, but within each of them, funds can be transferred.

Size and Performance Overhead. The MLSAG signature size increases significantly compared to a RCTTypeFull transaction. The current MLSAG signature (Eq. (1)) requires $(n(m + 1) + 1 + m)32 + \epsilon$ Bytes, with ϵ being the size of variable length encoded positions of the ring members. In addition to this, the q outputs require $q(1 + 64 \cdot 2 + 64)32$ Bytes for the Borromean range proofs [5] including signatures and commitments proving a range of 64 bit.

Our extension depends on longer vectors because of the colour equivalency proofs. The signature size then increases by $n \cdot m$ additional random values $s_{1,m+2}, \dots, s_{1,m+1+m}, \dots, s_{n,m+2}, \dots, s_{n,m+1+m}$ to $(n(m + 1 + m) + 1 + m)32 + \epsilon$ Bytes. The range proofs for the amount stay exactly the same. To prove that the colours of the outputs are all the same, we need additional $q - 1$ signatures for pairwise commitments to zero.

The range proofs use most of the space of the current transactions, so that our increase in signature size is quite negligible. Only for a high number of inputs, the impact is significant. Comparing only the signature sizes, our new approach requires approximately twice the space. With the introduction of bullet proofs [2] the range proof size will no longer increase linearly, but logarithmically leading to a greater influence of the colour overhead.

Security Analysis. Our construction uses the MLSAG and Pedersen commitments in a unmodified version as black-boxes and can therefore rely on the guarantees provided by these primitives.

The addition of a token colour provides a second attribute with which transactions can be related. In a transaction with multiple inputs, an attacker who knows that referenced inputs have different colours can discard these from the anonymity set. Assuming a worst-case uniform distribution over colours of transactions the probability of selecting a complete decoy vector with the same colour is $\frac{1}{\chi^m}$ and vanishing with the number of inputs m and a total of χ colours.

For a more likely distribution of transaction frequencies modelled by a power law, with most outputs in the native colour, the probability to find a one-colour decoy is higher. A Zipf distribution results in a probability of approximately one in each 20 decoy vectors having 2 equal colours for a transaction with two inputs and a reasonable 200 colours in total.

Initial Colour Creation. The ability to transfer privacy aware coloured tokens requires a token issuing protocol to begin with. A simple way is to allow an additional output in a transaction granting the output address a defined number of tokens in a new colour. With an open colour commitment, the transaction is only valid, if the colour is new with respect to all previous colour initiation transactions. Depending on the usage of the new token type, the amount can be an open commitment, to publicly announce the total supply of the token, or, if not needed, be confidential.

5   Related Work

Confidential Assets. Poelstra et al. [8] created a protocol to hide transaction values and allow the transaction of multiple assets on the same block-chain. They use Pedersen commitments to store the amount of each UTXO and because of it's homomorphic properties, can publicly verify the conservation. To mark different assets, a *asset tag* in the form of a commitment to a curve point is added to each output. These asset tags must be generated, such that no factor in any pair of assets is known to anyone. By the discrete logarithm assumption it is hard to verify that no such factors exist for newly introduced assets. While this is no limitation of block-chains with a predefined number of different assets, the dynamic addition of new asset types by untrusted participants can introduce asset which might have a nontrivial factor to an existing one. Moreover their scheme does not support sender set anonymity.

Hidden in Plain Sight: Transacting Privately on a Blockchain. Oleg Andreev at Chain Inc. also proposed a multi asset transaction[1] with the same fundamental techniques as the confidential assets. They also represent different assets as orthogonal curve points and need to verify that the factors between assets are not known to anyone. As the work before, sender anonymity can not be satisfied by hiding the real transaction input in an anonymity set.

6   Conclusion

We introduced an extension to the ring confidential transaction to support multiple colours of tokens to coexist on one block-chain. The transaction is publicly

---

[1] https://blog.chain.com/hidden-in-plain-sight-transacting-privately-on-a-blockchain-835ab75c01cb.

verifiable to transfer only assets in a single colour, without disclosing it. To achieve a high grade of anonymity, the decoy inputs can be of any token colour. Thereby, we allow for an easy issuance of privacy preserving tokens which benefit from each other by disguising themselves with each other. On top, our approach can use all the existing privacy preserving mechanisms in place, such as an anonymous peer to peer network, to maintain the privacy of the participants. Compared to contending solutions, we only require a small adaptation of an existing protocol.

References

1. Alonso, K.M., Joancomartì, J.H.: Monero-privacy in the blockchain (2018). https://urldefense.proofpoint.com/v2/url?u=https-3A__ eprint.iacr.org_2018_535&d=DwICAg&c=vh6FgFnduejNhPPD0fl_ yRaSfZy8CWbWnIf4XJhSqx8&r=8pdeajTECkGg7liCE2coz4KdRwElEr3FQX_ jYRdcVprH4Ev8v5ZWCYnpPJWwDKNa&m=02zPfAFc2LLmq8CEh5Rp9WWgx7_ hdZiLtoX1FNI_gG8&s=CZn8ZZRRRD_abxthfDUHPIjCZLzx6aPb8EUoNY3RuVw& e=
2. Bünz, B., Bootle, J., Boneh, D., Poelstra, A., Wuille, P., Maxwell, G.: Bulletproofs: efficient range proofs for confidential transactions. Technical report, Cryptology ePrint Archive, Report 2017/1066 (2017). https://eprint.iacr.org/2017/1066
3. Fujisaki, E., Suzuki, K.: Traceable ring signature. In: Okamoto, T., Wang, X. (eds.) PKC 2007. LNCS, vol. 4450, pp. 181–200. Springer, Heidelberg (2007). https://doi. org/10.1007/978-3-540-71677-8_13
4. Liu, J.K., Wei, V.K., Wong, D.S.: Linkable spontaneous anonymous group signature for ad hoc groups. In: Wang, H., Pieprzyk, J., Varadharajan, V. (eds.) ACISP 2004. LNCS, vol. 3108, pp. 325–335. Springer, Heidelberg (2004). https://doi.org/10.1007/ 978-3-540-27800-9_28
5. Maxwell, G., Poelstra, A.: Borromean ring signatures (2015)
6. Noether, S., Mackenzie, A.: Ring confidential transactions. Ledger 1, 1–18 (2016)
7. Pedersen, T.P.: Non-interactive and information-theoretic secure verifiable secret sharing. In: Feigenbaum, J. (ed.) CRYPTO 1991. LNCS, vol. 576, pp. 129–140. Springer, Heidelberg (1992). https://doi.org/10.1007/3-540-46766-1_9
8. Poelstra, A., Back, A., Friedenbach, M., Maxwell, G., Wuille, P.: Confidential assets. In: Financial Cryptography Bitcoin Workshop (2017). https://blockstream.com/ bitcoin17-final41.pdf
9. Sasson, E.B., et al.: Zerocash: decentralized anonymous payments from bitcoin. In: 2014 IEEE Symposium on Security and Privacy (SP), pp. 459–474. IEEE (2014)

Pitchforks in Cryptocurrencies:

Enforcing Rule Changes Through Offensive Forking- and Consensus Techniques (Short Paper)

Aljosha Judmayer[1(✉)], Nicholas Stifter[1,2], Philipp Schindler[1],
and Edgar Weippl[1,2]

[1] SBA Research, Vienna, Austria
{a.judmayer,n.stifter,p.schindler,e.weippl}@sba-research.org
[2] Christian Doppler Laboratory for Security and Quality Improvement
in the Production System Lifecycle (CDL-SQI),
Institute of Information Systems Engineering, TU Wien, Wien, Austria

Abstract. The increasing number of cryptocurrencies, as well as the rising number of actors within each single cryptocurrency, inevitably leads to tensions between the respective communities. As with open source projects, (protocol) forks are often the result of broad disagreement. Usually, after a permanent fork both communities "mine" their own business and the conflict is resolved. But what if this is not the case? In this paper, we outline the possibility of malicious forking and consensus techniques that aim at destroying the other branch of a protocol fork. Thereby, we illustrate how merged mining can be used as an attack method against a permissionless PoW cryptocurrency, which itself involuntarily serves as the parent chain for an attacking merge mined branch of a hard fork.

1 Introduction

Merged mining is already known for posing a potential issue to the child cryptocurrencies, as for example demonstrated in the case of CoiledCoin[1], however so far no concrete example that merged mining can also pose a risk to the parent chain has been given. Since, (parent) cryptocurrencies can not easily prevent being merge mined[2], an attack strategy using this approach would be applicable against a variety of permissionless PoW cryptocurrencies. In this paper, we describe a scenario where merged mining is used as a form of attack against a parent chain in the context of a hostile protocol fork.

1.1 System Model and Attack Goals

For our attack scenario, we assume a permissionless PoW based cryptocurrency B, whose miners cannot agree whether or not to change the consensus rules.

---

[1] cf. https://bitcointalk.org/index.php?topic=56675.msg678006#msg678006.
[2] The inclusion of a hash value within a block to provably attributed it to the creator of the proof-of-work (PoW) is enough to support merged mining [7].

© Springer Nature Switzerland AG 2018
J. Garcia-Alfaro et al. (Eds.): DPM 2018/CBT 2018, LNCS 11025, pp. 197–206, 2018.
https://doi.org/10.1007/978-3-030-00305-0_15

Some of the miners want to adapt the consensus rules in a way such that newly mined blocks may not be valid under the old rules, i.e., perform a hard fork. Thereby, we differentiate between the following actors:

- **Backward compatible miners ($\mathcal{B}$):** The fraction of miners (with hash rate β) in a currently active cryptocurrency B which does not want to change the consensus rules of B.
- **Change enforcing miners ($\mathcal{C}$):** The fraction of miners (with hash rate α) in a currently active cryptocurrency B which wants to change the consensus rules, i.e., perform a hard fork. Moreover, they want to make sure, that only their branch of the fork survives.
- **Neutral miners ($\mathcal{N}$):** The set of miners (with hash rate ω) that has no hard opinion on whether or not to change the consensus rules. They want to maximize their profits and act rationally to achieve this goal, with the limitation that they want to avoid changes as far as possible. If there is no immanent need which justifies the implementation costs for adapting to changes, they will not react[3].

For our example, we assume that $\mathcal{C}$ wants to increase the block size, while $\mathcal{B}$ does not want to implement any rule change. The goal of the attackers in $\mathcal{C}$ is twofold: (1) *Enforce* a change of the consensus rules in the respective cryptocurrency. (2) *Destroy* the other branch of a fork which uses the same PoW and does not follow the new consensus rules.

1.2   Background

For this paper, we are only interested in forking scenarios that are *not bilateral*. In a bilateral fork, conflicting changes are intentionally introduced to ensure that two separate cryptocurrencies emerge [16]. An example for such a scenario would be the changed chain ID between Ethereum and Ethereum Classic. It is commonly believed that in a non-bilateral forking event, the only reliable possibility to enforce a change requires that the majority of the mining power supports the change. Thereby, two main cases can be distinguished according to [16]:

If the introduced change *reduces* the number of blocks that are considered valid under the new consensus rules, all new blocks are still considered valid under the old rules, but some old blocks are no longer considered valid under the new rules. An example for such a scenario would be a *block size decrease*. In this case the first goal (*enforce*) of our attack is easy to achieve if $\alpha > \beta + \omega$ holds, since any fork introduced by α will eventually become the longest chain and be adopted by β and ω because of the heaviest chain rule. If $\mathcal{B}$ decides to continue a minority branch, they have to declare themselves as a new currency B' and change their consensus rules to permanently fork off the main chain in B such that larger blocks are again possible. Therefore, the goal to *enforce* is clearly

---

[3] This should capture the observation that not all miners immediately perform merged mining if it is possible, even though it would be rational to do so [7].

reached in such a case. However, the *destroy* goal cannot be reached directly if B forks to a new cryptocurrency B'.

If the introduced change *expands* the set of blocks that are considered valid under the new consensus rules, then some blocks following the new rules will not be considered valid under the old rules. Therefore, any mined block that is only valid under the new rules will cause a fork. An example for such a scenario would be a *block size increase*[4]. In this case a permanent hard fork will only occur if the chain containing blocks following the new rules grows faster, i.e., $\alpha > \beta + \omega$ holds. The result would be that the forking event creates two different currencies: Cryptocurrency C, which includes big blocks, and cryptocurrency B, which forked from the main chain after the first big block. Therefore, again the *destroy* goal cannot be reached directly. To reach the goal *destroy*, some miners in C could be required to switch to the new currency B and disrupt its regular operation, e.g., by mining empty blocks. This of course has the drawback that the respective attacking miners that switched from C to B do not gain any profits in C, and their rewards in B will be worthless if they succeed in destroying the B fork.

The *pitchfork* attack method proposed in this paper aims to achieve both attack goals simultaneously, even in cases where $\alpha < \beta + \omega$ holds.

2   Pitchfork Attack Description

The basic idea of a pitchfork attack is to use merged mining as a form of attack against the other branch of a fork, in a permissionless PoW Cryptocurreny, that is the result of a disputed consensus rule change. The pitchfork should reduce the utility of the attacked branch to such an extent, that the miners abandon the attacked branch and switch to the branch of the fork which performs merged mining and follows the new consensus rules. We call the cryptocurrency up to the point of the fork *ancestor* cryptocurrency $\bar{B}$. After the forking event, the *backward compatible* cryptocurrency, which still follows the same rules, is denoted as B, whereas the *change enforcing* cryptocurrency branch that uses merged mining and the new consensus rules is denoted as C.

To execute the attack, the new merge mined branch C accepts valid *empty blocks* of B as a PoW for C. In the nomenclature of merged mining the chain B, which should be attacked, is called the *parent chain* and chain C is called the *child chain*. For a valid parent block b of B, the following additional requirements need to be satisfied: (i) The block b has to be empty. Therefore, the contained Merkle tree root in the header of the respective block must only include the hash of the (mandatory) coinbase transaction. Given the corresponding coinbase transaction, it can then be verified that b is indeed empty. (ii) The coinbase transaction of b must include the hash of a valid block c for C. The header of block c contains a Merkle tree root with the actual transactions performed in C.

---

[4] Our example, in which C wants to increase the block size and B does not want to implement any rule change, would resemble such an *expanding* protocol change.

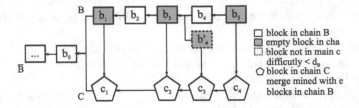

Fig. 1. Example of blocks mined in the two chains B and C after the forking event.

Figure 1 shows the two cryptocurrencies after the fork. The last block in the ancestor cryptocurrency $\bar{B}$ before the forking event is b_0. The first empty block that is merge mined is b_1 in this example. This block (b_1) is valid under the old rules and fulfills the difficulty target in B. Moreover, the block b_1 was mined by a miner in C, which happens with probability α, and contains the hash of block c_1 in its coinbase. Therefore b_1 serves as a valid PoW for C as well. Block b_2 was not mined by a miner in C, which happens with probability $1 - \alpha$, and therefore it is not empty and does not contain a hash for a valid block for C in its coinbase. This shows that the two chains are not necessarily synchronized regarding their number of blocks. The block interval in C depends on the difficulty target of C. Since we assume that the attacker does not control the majority of the hash rate ($\alpha < \beta + \omega$), the difficulty d in C should be lower than in B at the beginning of the attack, i.e., $d_C < d_B$ holds. If the difficulty has been adjusted in C, then the overall number of blocks should be approximately the same for both chains. In such a case, there might be empty blocks such as b'_4, which do fulfill the difficulty target for C, but not for B. Still, if $d_C < d_B$ holds, then over time a fraction of all blocks in B, corresponding to α, will be mined by a miner in C. If we assume that $\alpha \approx 0.34$ then approximately every third block in B should be empty.

Side Note Regarding Difficulty: Theoretically it would be possible that chain C requires the same, or an even a higher difficulty than chain B. If $d_C \geq d_B$, then chain C would contain less blocks than chain B, this of course would have a negative effect on the latency in chain C, i.e., the time it takes till a transaction is confirmed. However any merge mined blocks that meet the difficulty requirement d_C will be considered valid in B. For example, when $d_C = d_B$, the number of blocks in C relative to B would only correspond to the fraction of the hash rate (α) that performs merged mining. Nevertheless, since chain C increased the block size, the throughput could theoretically remain the same or even be higher than in chain B (depending on the actual implementation). Some examples regarding an increased block size are discussed in [3,6]. Alternatively, Bitcoin-NG [4] could also be applicable. The latter approach would have the added benefit that the negative impact on latency and confirmation times is mitigated. To illustrate our attack, it is not of particular relevance which adaptation is used to increase the throughput in C.

2.1   Effects of the Attack

In the simplest case, if no counter measures are taken by the chain under attack, a pitchfork reduces the utility of the target chain B by the number of empty blocks, corresponding to the hash rate of the attackers (α). Considering the limited block size in B and past events in Bitcoin[5], where the number of unconfirmed transactions in the mempool peaked at around $175,000$ in December 2017, a hash rate of $\alpha \approx 0.34$ would likely have a non negligible impact on the duration of such periods, and hence transaction fees and confirmation times. This could sway both users and miners in $\mathcal{N}$ to switch to the attacking chain C, which further reinforces the attack. Two other advantages of the attack are, that it is *pseudonymous* and that the risk in terms of currency units in B is *parameterizable*.

Pseudonymous: Since the pitchfork attack is executed by miners through producing new blocks that are, in addition, merge mined with the attacking chain, it is in theory possible to hide the identities of the attackers because no unspent transaction outputs need to be involved in the attack that could have a traceable history. However, additional care needs to be taken by these miners to ensure that their identity is not inadvertently revealed through their behavior [7].

Parameterizable: The attack is not an all-in-move and its costs, in terms of currency units in B, can be parameterized. The goal of the attack is to destroy the original chain B, but if this fails the attackers may not lose much. Due to merged mining the main costs of a failed attack result from the forgone profits from transaction fees that are not collected in chain B. Additional costs created by merged mining, i.e., running and additional full node for chain B, can be negligible compared to the overall costs related to mining [12]. Moreover, even a failed attack on B can still be profitable for the attacking miners, since the attackers in C are early adopters of C. If the value of the newly created cryptocurrency C increases enough, the additional income may not only compensate the reduced income from mining empty blocks in B, but could even create a surplus for the miners in C. In addition, the attack can be made compatible with other available cryptocurrencies that can be merge mined with B. Therefore, additional revenue channels from existing merge mined cryptocurrencies are not affected by the pitchfork and can even help to subsidize the attack.

As a further parameterization for the attack, it is also possible to execute it in stages. To test whether there is enough support for chain C, it is possible to first start with relatively low risk to the attackers by not requiring them to mine empty blocks and instead only demand the creation of smaller blocks which can still include high fee transactions. From there, the attackers can reduce the number of permissible transactions step by step. At a final stage, all coins earned through mining empty blocks in B can also be used to fund additional attacks, such as triggering additional spam transactions in B as soon as the 100 blocks cooldown period has passed. For instance, splitting the coinbase rewards into many individual outputs of a high enough value with different lock times and

---

[5] https://blockchain.info/charts/mempool-count?timespan=1year.

rendering the output scripts as *anyone can spend* can lead to a large influx of additional transactions, as users (and miners) compete to scoop up these free currency units. This is easy to verify as an additional rule in C, however more complex attack scenarios such as those outlined in [1, 10, 14] may also be included as additional consensus rules.

3   Countermeasures

In this section we outline some countermeasures that can be taken by B.

Fork away empty blocks in B: The miners in B can decide to fork off empty blocks and just build on top of blocks containing transactions. This requires the coordinated action of all miners in B. If $\beta > \alpha + \omega$ this approach will work in general. A possible counter reaction by the attackers in C would be to introduce dummy transactions to themselves in their blocks in B. Therefore, it has to be ensured that those transactions are indeed dummies. For example: All used output addresses of every transaction belong to the same entity, but this must not be correlated given just the block b_n in B. One way to achieve this, is to require that all output addresses in a block have been derived from the miner's public key of the respective block, like in an Hierarchically Deterministic (HD) Wallet[6] construction. The *master public key property* of such a construction allows that future ECDSA public keys can be derived from current ones. This is done by adding a multiplication of the base point with a scalar value to the current public key. The corresponding secret key is derived in the same manner, but can only be computed by its owner. If it is not possible to perform a transaction to an address for which the miner does not have the corresponding private key, the utility of every transaction in the block is very limited. To check this condition on an arbitrary block b_n, the public key of the miner as well as the scalar value for the multiplication is required. These values can be added to the coinbase transaction of the corresponding block c_n in C.

If such dummy transactions are used, the miners of B would be required to monitor the chain C to deduce which block in B has been merge mined with C and includes only dummy transactions. If B finds such a block they then can still cause a fork in B to ignore it. Besides being more complex, this also poses a potential risk for all transactions in B. Since the block b_n could be released before c_n, there is no way to tell whether or not b_n was indeed merged mined and hence includes a hash to c_n before c_n has been published in C. With this knowledge, miners in C can intentionally create forks in B when releasing c_n. By slightly relaxing the rules for dummy transaction and allowing, for example, one transaction output address that is not required to be derivable by the HD construction, double spends can be executed more easily in B. In this particular case miners of merged mined blocks can include a regular transaction that they want to double spend in their block, being assured that this block will

---

[6] cf. BIP32 https://github.com/bitcoin/bips/blob/master/bip-0032.mediawiki.

get excluded in retrospect by all miners β in B if c_n is released. Therefore, more fine grained exclusion rules on transaction level would be necessary.

These examples illustrate, that it is non-trivial to change the consensus rules in B such that the effects of a pitchfork attack are mitigated. Every change of the defender leads to an arms race with the attacker. Moreover, excluding all merge mined blocks in B requires active monitoring of C to detect them. Therefore, at least the miners in $\mathcal{B}$ have to change their individual consensus rules – which they wanted to avoid in the first place.

Use mining power to launch a counter-attack on C: Miners in $\mathcal{B}$ can use their mining power to stall the attacking chain C. However, this has several limitations: Since every block in C requires an empty parent block in B as part of its PoW, miners cannot create empty merge mined blocks in C while at the same time creating full blocks in B. To stall chain C, at least a fraction of β, e.g., $\beta_a \leq \beta$ has to mine empty blocks in B to create empty merge mined blocks for C. Thereby, the counter-attackers would actually help the pitchfork attack. For our analysis, we assume that the difficulty target in C is indeed lower than in B, i.e., $d_C < d_B$ holds. To clearly overtake the pitchfork chain C, the counter-attacking miners need to have more than 50% of the hash rate in C. If not, the lost throughput, caused by empty blocks in C, might be compensated by the increased block size. This introduces the first constraint for the counter-attackers that the hash rate β_a they dedicate to the counter-attack must follow $\beta_a \geq \alpha$. However, the counter-attackers must also take care not to push the total hash rate dedicated towards attacking B to over 50% in B, otherwise more destructive attack rules than mining empty blocks, such as requiring non-empty blocks to be ignored, may be rendered effective. If the defenders are able to reliably identify all attackers' blocks they can try to fork them away in B. However the disadvantages of any (additional) attack rules, such as anyone-can-spend transactions or fork-away-non-empty blocks, still apply and can cause damage to B through their own blocks mined by β_a. The second constraint hence requires that for a counter attack, the bound $\alpha + \beta_a < 0.5$ for the share of blocks in the heaviest chain of B holds.

Depending on the exact implementation of merged mining in C, the counter-attackers have some options to avoid that their empty blocks in B, which they are required to provide as PoW, further reduce the utility of B. For example, in a naïve approach they could only submit PoW solutions to C that fulfill the difficulty target for C but not for B. This has the marked disadvantage that any blocks meeting the difficulty target of B also cannot be submitted as solutions in C, effectively reducing the counter-attackers' hash rate β_a in C by a factor dependent on the particular difference in difficulty between C and B. A better counter-attack can be achieved if the defenders intentionally construct blocks for the parent chain B that are unlikely to end up in the main chain, yet are still accepted as a valid proof-of-work in C. For instance, stale branches in B could be created and extended, however this is only effective if the freshness requirements for parent blocks in C are not too tight. In both cases, since β_a is no longer contributing toward the effective hash rate of B, its remaining honest miners

$\omega + \beta - \beta_a$ must still retain a hash rate that exceeds that of the adversary to ensure that honest blocks constitute a majority of the heaviest chain. Therefore, the original attacker gains an advantage from merged mining since he can use his full hash rate in both chains at the same time. Moreover, the counter-attacking fraction of the miners would forgo their rewards in B for the duration of the counter-attack.

Figure 2 shows the hash rates achievable by the defender/counter-attacker on the respective chains B and C for different values for the hash rate α of the pitchfork attacker. In this figure the simplified assumption is made that the total hash rate of neutral miners ω is zero and hence the total hash rate of the defender/counter-attacker ($\beta = 1 - \alpha$) can be split between the two chains B and C arbitrarily. In this case, an attacker with $\alpha > \frac{1}{3}$ total hash rate cannot be countered on both chains simultaneously without losing the majority $\beta < 0.5$ on one of the chains.

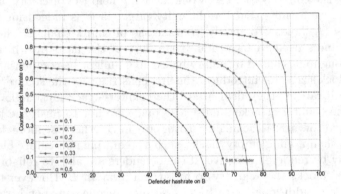

Fig. 2. Calculation for the hash rates of the defender/counter-attacker in the respective chains B and C for different values of pitchfork attacker hash rate α

4 Related Work

In [7] it is argued that merged mining could also be used as an attack vector against the parent chain, however no concrete examples are given. Different forking techniques in the context of cryptocurrencies are described in [16]. The focus is placed on a non-malicious forking technique called *velvet fork*, initially proposed in [8]. Different methods that can be used in hostile blockchain takeovers are described in [2], placing the focus on attacks where the attacker has an extrinsic motivation to disrupt the consensus process, i.e., Goldfinger attacks [9]. The example given in the paper at hand is a concrete instance of such a situation. Therefore, most of the described methods can be used in conjunction with our proposed attack. The same holds true for the large body of work on bribing [1,11] and incentive attacks that distract the hash rate of participants [14,15]. Furthermore, selfish mining and its variants [5,13] may be used in combination with pitchfork attacks.

5   Discussion and Future Work

In this paper, we outline that merged mining can be used as an attack method against a PoW cryptocurrency in the context of a hostile protocol fork. The general idea of such an *offensive consensus attack* is, that the participants of the offensive system are required to provably attack a different system as part of the consensus rules. We show that such attacks are theoretically possible and can lead to an arms race in which defenders are forced to adapt their consensus rules. Still, the consequences as well as the economic and game theoretic incentives of such attacks have yet to be analyzed in greater detail to better understand if they are practicable, and if so, how to protect against them.

Acknowledgments. We thank Georg Merzdovnik and Alexei Zamyatin as well as the participants of Dagstuhl Seminar 18152 "Blockchains, Smart Contracts and Future Applications" for valuable discussions and insights. This research was funded by Bridge Early Stage 846573 A2Bit, Bridge 1 858561 SESC, Bridge 1 864738 PR4DLT (all FFG), CDL-SQI at the Institute of Information Systems Engineering TU Wien, and the competence center SBA-K1 funded by COMET.

References

1. Bonneau, J.: Why buy when you can rent? bribery attacks on bitcoin consensus. In: BITCOIN 2016: Proceedings of the 3rd Workshop on Bitcoin and Blockchain Research, February 2016
2. Bonneau, J.: Hostile blockchain takeovers (short paper). In: 5th Workshop on Bitcoin and Blockchain Research, Financial Cryptography and Data Security 2018 (FC). Springer (2018)
3. Croman, K., et al.: On scaling decentralized blockchains. In: Clark, J., Meiklejohn, S., Ryan, P.Y.A., Wallach, D., Brenner, M., Rohloff, K. (eds.) FC 2016. LNCS, vol. 9604, pp. 106–125. Springer, Heidelberg (2016). https://doi.org/10.1007/978-3-662-53357-4_8
4. Eyal, I., Gencer, A.E., Sirer, E.G., van Renesse, R.: Bitcoin-NG: a scalable blockchain protocol. In: 13th USENIX Security Symposium on Networked Systems Design and Implementation (NSDI 2016). USENIX Association, March 2016
5. Eyal, I., Sirer, E.G.: Majority is not enough: bitcoin mining is vulnerable. In: Christin, N., Safavi-Naini, R. (eds.) FC 2014. LNCS, vol. 8437, pp. 436–454. Springer, Heidelberg (2014). https://doi.org/10.1007/978-3-662-45472-5_28
6. Gervais, A., Karame, G.O., Wüst, K., Glykantzis, V., Ritzdorf, H., Capkun, S.: On the security and performance of proof of work blockchains. In: Proceedings of the 2016 ACM SIGSAC, pp. 3–16. ACM (2016)
7. Judmayer, A., Zamyatin, A., Stifter, N., Voyiatzis, A.G., Weippl, E.: Merged mining: curse or cure? In: CBT 2017: Proceedings of the International Workshop on Cryptocurrencies and Blockchain Technology, September 2017
8. Kiayias, A., Miller, A., Zindros, D.: Non-interactive proofs of proof-of-work. Cryptology ePrint Archive, Report 2017/963 (2017). Accessed 03 October 2017
9. Kroll, J.A., Davey, I.C., Felten, E.W.: The economics of bitcoin mining, or bitcoin in the presence of adversaries. In: Proceedings of WEIS, vol. 2013, p. 11 (2013)

10. Liao, K., Katz, J.: Incentivizing blockchain forks via whale transactions. In: Brenner, M., Rohloff, K., Bonneau, J., Miller, A., Ryan, P.Y.A., Teague, V., Bracciali, A., Sala, M., Pintore, F., Jakobsson, M. (eds.) FC 2017. LNCS, vol. 10323, pp. 264–279. Springer, Cham (2017). https://doi.org/10.1007/978-3-319-70278-0_17
11. McCorry, P., Hicks, A., Meiklejohn, S.: Smart contracts for bribing miners. In: 5th Workshop on Bitcoin and Blockchain Research, Financial Cryptography and Data Security 2018 (FC). Springer (2018)
12. Narayanan, A., Bonneau, J., Felten, E., Miller, A., Goldfeder, S.: Bitcoin and cryptocurrency technologies (2016). http://bitcoinbook.cs.princeton.edu/. Accessed 29 Mar 2016
13. Nayak, K., Kumar, S., Miller, A., Shi, E.: Stubborn mining: generalizing selfish mining and combining with an eclipse attack. In: 1st IEEE European Symposium on Security and Privacy. IEEE (2016)
14. Teutsch, J., Jain, S., Saxena, P.: When cryptocurrencies mine their own business. In: Financial Cryptography and Data Security (FC 2016), February 2016
15. Velner, Y., Teutsch, J., Luu, L.: Smart contracts make bitcoin mining pools vulnerable. In: Brenner, M., et al. (eds.) FC 2017. LNCS, vol. 10323, pp. 298–316. Springer, Cham (2017). https://doi.org/10.1007/978-3-319-70278-0_19
16. Zamyatin, A., Stifter, N., Judmayer, A., Schindler, P., Weippl, E., Knottebelt, W.J.: (Short Paper) A wild velvet fork appears! Inclusive blockchain protocol changes in practice. In: 5th Workshop on Bitcoin and Blockchain Research, Financial Cryptography and Data Security 2018 (FC). Springer (2018)

DPM Workshop: Privacy Assessment and Trust

Towards an Effective Privacy Impact and Risk Assessment Methodology: Risk Analysis

Majed Alshammari$^{(\boxtimes)}$ and Andrew Simpson

Department of Computer Science, University of Oxford,
Wolfson Building, Parks Road, Oxford OX1 3QD, UK
{majed.alshammari,andrew.simpson}@cs.ox.ac.uk

Abstract. Privacy Impact Assessments (PIAs) play a crucial role in providing privacy protection for data subjects and supporting risk management. From an engineering perspective, the core of a PIA is a risk assessment, which typically follows a step-by-step process of risk identification and risk mitigation. In order for a PIA to be holistic and effective, it needs to be complemented by an appropriate privacy risk model that considers legal, organisational, societal and technical aspects. We propose a data-centric approach for identifying and analysing potential privacy risks in a comprehensive manner.

1 Introduction

It is widely recognised that the potential impacts of data-processing activities need to be proactively assessed in the early stages of the design process [12]. This has led to the emergence of the concept of a *Privacy Impact Assessment* (PIA)—a process that identifies and mitigates the impact of an initiative on privacy with stakeholders' participation [19]. In order for a PIA to be holistic and effective, it is necessary for it to be complemented by an appropriate privacy risk model that considers legal, organisational, societal and technical aspects.

Privacy is a multifaceted concept that requires multidisciplinary considerations [8]. Privacy engineering, therefore, requires a sufficiently robust privacy risk model to identify potential privacy risks. The identified risks can then be addressed through risk management approaches, which include the selection and application of risk controls. We extend prior work by referring to fundamentals from the broader literature to underpin the main concepts of PIAs along with their meanings and properties. We present a data-centric approach that illustrates the main steps of identifying and analysing potential privacy risks in a meaningful manner. Through a realistic case study, we demonstrated the usefulness and applicability of this approach in a specific context. We argue that this contribution lays the foundation for systematic and rigorous PIA methodologies.

© Springer Nature Switzerland AG 2018
J. Garcia-Alfaro et al. (Eds.): DPM 2018/CBT 2018, LNCS 11025, pp. 209–224, 2018.
https://doi.org/10.1007/978-3-030-00305-0_16

2 Background and Motivation

Ensuring that the processing of personal data is conducted fairly and lawfully is one of the main challenges in the context of data protection. This challenge has raised concerns over data-processing activities that may lead to privacy violations or harms. *Privacy by Design (PbD)* [7] has been advocated as a response [8].

To realise the concept of PbD in the system development lifecycle (SDLC), potential privacy risks need to be proactively analysed and their potential harms need to be appropriately assessed [15]. In some jurisdictions, 'legal compliance checks' [15] or 'prior checking' [9] are the most commonly used privacy assessment procedures. These procedures are often not conducted by engineers; rather, auditors, lawyers or data protection authorities utilise a check-list to check compliance with legal frameworks [15]. With the advent of information and communication technologies, holistic and effective impact assessments are considered as complements to, or replacements for, these assessment procedures [15]. This has contributed to the emergence and wide use of the concept of PIAs.

A PIA is an ongoing process that begins at the earliest possible stages [20]. As such, PIAs are considered as a key means to address one of the main concerns of embedding privacy into the early stages of the design process, which is the manifestation of PbD [11]. Existing PIA processes strive to achieve the aim of PbD by applying its foundational principles [15].

The core of a PIA is a risk assessment, which typically follows a step-by-step process of risk identification and risk mitigation [15]. While PIAs are expected to follow the same philosophy, existing PIA processes largely fall short in this regard [15]. These limitations leave a number of open questions: *(1) How can we develop a privacy risk model that defines and/or refines key concepts and assessable risk factors, as well as the relationships among the factors?; (2) How can we identify potential privacy risks in a contextual and comprehensive manner to ensure the provision of end-to-end privacy protection?;* and *(3) What is the appropriate level of detail for such a model?*

3 An Analysis of PIA Processes

To identify data-processing activities that may lead to privacy violations or harms, it is essential to represent these activities in a way that is amenable to risk analysis and compliance checking. Rigorous data models need to be adopted to support the management and traceability of the processing and flow of personal data, as well as to help support identifying the planned, actual and potential data flows and processing. Such data models are expected to represent data-processing activities in a comprehensive manner and at an appropriate level of abstraction. This includes: personal data items, data-processing activities, involved actors, and their roles and responsibilities. Such information helps establish the context in which personal data is processed and identify system boundaries.

Some PIA processes, such as the BSI IT-Grundschutz [5], apply security risk analysis to privacy principles, which are typically given at a high level of abstraction, instead of relying upon a set of concrete protection goals. This, in turn, reduces privacy protection to the concepts of anonymity, pseudonymity, unobservability and unlinkability [4,15]. Thus, targets of evaluation—i.e. personal data and data-processing activities—need to comply with legal frameworks and standards, and ensure that they will not lead to potential privacy violations and harms. These targets define the scope of PIAs. As privacy principles are semantically different from concrete data-processing activities, it is difficult to use them for assessing these activities and describing design decisions at an architectural level. Accordingly, privacy principles need to be translated into concrete and auditable protection goals to aid engineers in specifying design strategies.

In order to conduct an appropriate privacy risk analysis that goes beyond a traditional security analysis, it is essential to develop a risk model that defines the key risk factors that have an impact on privacy risks, and to establish a conceptual relationship among these factors [12]. Existing PIA guidance documents, however, are not accompanied with proper guidelines or conceptual models that describe key risk factors to sufficiently support privacy risk assessment [15].

PIAs need to be complemented by an appropriate privacy risk model that goes beyond traditional security risk models. Such a model needs to consider not only legal and organisational aspects, but also societal and technical aspects. The model needs to refer to fundamentals from the legal privacy literature to underpin the main concepts, the key risk factors and the conceptual relationship between these factors. This addresses the first question of Sect. 2 ("How can we develop a privacy risk model that defines and/or refines key concepts and assessable risk factors, as well as the relationships among the factors?").

Importantly, a privacy risk model needs to adopt a sufficiently robust model that facilitates end-to-end privacy protection and serves as the basis for the identification, analysis and assessment of potential privacy risks in a proactive, comprehensive and concrete manner. Such a robust model needs to sufficiently and contextually represent data-processing activities in a way that is amenable to risk analysis and compliance checking. This addresses the second question of Sect. 2 ("How can we identify potential privacy risks in a contextual and comprehensive manner to ensure the provision of end-to-end privacy protection?").

In addition, an appropriate analysis approach needs to be adopted to systematically describe how combinations of risk factors are identified to be analysed. Such an approach needs to consider the appropriateness of the starting points of risk assessment and the level of abstraction in the context of privacy and data protection. This addresses the third question of Sect. 2 ("What is the appropriate level of detail for such a model?").

4   A Privacy Risk Model

We review two privacy risk analysis methodologies [10,12] upon which we build by refining the concepts, risk factors and relationships among these factors. We have chosen these models as they define and distinguish the key notions, risk factors and relationships among these factors in the context of privacy and data protection. To compare, we refer to fundamentals from the legal privacy literature to underpin the key concepts and risk factors along with their meanings, properties and relationships. In particular, we refer to the boundaries of privacy harm [6] to understand the specific characteristics and categories of privacy harms. In addition, we refer to Solove's taxonomy [16] to understand the specific characteristics of adverse privacy events and associated categories. Finally, we leverage the concept of contextual integrity [13] to understand the main characteristics of appropriate flow of personal data with reference to context-relative informational norms, from which vulnerabilities can be derived.

We define and/or refine the basic concepts used in conducting risk assessments to be appropriately applied in the context of privacy and data protection.

A *threat* is an event or action with the potential for privacy violation, or which might adversely impact the privacy of data subjects through the processing of personal data via inappropriate collection, retention, access, usage, disclosure or destruction. In our risk model, the threat concept can be decomposed into a threat source and a threat event.

A *threat source* is an entity with the capability to process (lawfully or unlawfully, fairly or unfairly) data belonging to a data subject and whose actions may instantly and/or eventually, accidentally or deliberately manifest threats, which may lead to privacy violations or harms. Each type of a threat source can be characterised by: type (insider or outsider; individual, institution or government; human or non-human), motives (stemming from the value of personal data), resources (including skills and background knowledge that helps re-identify data subjects), role (the way in which a concerned entity participates in processing operations), and responsibility. The specified attributes of a threat source are used to assess the capability of exploiting vulnerabilities. As such, a threat source is more relevant to vulnerability analysis than impact assessment. We use the concept of a threat source to ensure that it can be used appropriately for modelling actors with malicious and benign purposes. Joyee De and Le Métayer [12] use the concept of risk source to refer both to unauthorised entities processing personal data and to entities with legitimate processing capabilities. In [10], risk sources are those who act, accidentally or deliberately, on the supporting assets, on which the primary assets rely. Accordingly, threat sources who act, accidentally or deliberately, on the primary assets are not modelled. As such, we refine these concepts to be used appropriately at an appropriate level of abstraction. With regards to threat sources who act on the supporting assets, we refine the standard definition of threat action. A *threat action* is an intentional act (actively or passively) through which a threat source exploits the vulnerabilities of the supporting assets. It is important to separate the concept of the threat action to engage with the supporting asset and the threat event when a threat source acts against the primary asset.

A *threat event* is a technical event that may happen at specific points in time which has an effect, consequence or impact, especially a negative one, on the privacy of data subjects. Such events involve adverse actions justified by reference to personal data. A threat event is a possible source of privacy violations or harms: it occurs as a result of a successful exploitation of one or more vulnerabilities by one or more sources. Each type of threat event can be characterised by: nature (continuous or discrete; excessive or necessary; anticipated or unanticipated), scope (an individual, a specific group of individuals or whole society), and category (according to the taxonomy of privacy). Joyee De and Le Métayer [12] and the CNIL methodology [10] use the concept of 'feared events'. By referring to them as feared events, we may limit those to internal and unpleasant emotions and perceptions caused by the threat. As such, we use the notion of 'threat events' to describe harmful or unwanted events that may not be anticipated by data subjects. Since these events not only describe the data subject's perceptions, we prefer to use threat events to describe unwanted, unwarranted or excessive processing activities that will lead to actual adverse consequences. They refer to a non-exhaustive list of common categories of feared events that an analyst should consider. However, we prefer to consider a well-known classification of such events. For the purpose of this paper, we consider only technical threats that are processing-related. In particular, we focus on data-processing activities, which are composed of adverse actions that are justified by reference to personal data, and events that cause the performance of these actions, which can and do constitute privacy violations or create privacy harms.

A *privacy vulnerability* is a weakness or deficiency in personal data modelling, the specification or implementation of processing operations, or privacy controls, which makes an exploitation of an asset more likely to succeed by one or more threat sources. Successful exploitations lead to threat events that can result in privacy violations or harms. In our context, assets can be classified into *primary assets* and *supporting assets* [10]. The former refers to personal data that is directly concerned with processing operations, as well as processes required by legal frameworks and standards. The latter refers to system components on which the primary assets rely. For the purpose of this paper, we focus on the primary assets and associated vulnerabilities. Each type of vulnerability can be characterised by exploitability and severity. These are used to estimate the seriousness of a vulnerability.

The CNIL methodology [10] uses the concept of vulnerability, which refers to a characteristic of a supporting asset that can be used by risk sources and allowing threats to occur. In contrast, Joyee De and Le Métayer [12] use the concept of 'privacy weakness' to refer to a weakness in the data protection mechanisms. By using this concept, they aim to include weaknesses that may not be considered by using the concept of vulnerability, such as inappropriate functionality from which privacy harms may stem. As such, we use the concept of vulnerability with a broader view to not identify them only within data protection mechanisms. Privacy vulnerabilities can be found in the implemented privacy controls and the specified processing operations along with required personal. In addition, we use the classification of assets of [10].

A *privacy violation* is an unfair and/or unlawful action that accidentally or deliberately breaches privacy-related laws, regulations, unilateral policies, contracts, cultural norms or principles. Such actions are triggered by occurrences of threat events that result from the successful exploitation of one or more vulnerabilities. In reality, inappropriate processing of personal data may lead to privacy violations, which may involve a variety of types of activities that may lead to privacy harms [16]. Importantly, the presence of a privacy violation does not mean that it will necessarily create an actual privacy harm. Further, privacy harms can occur without privacy violations [6]. Each type of privacy violation can be characterised by: type (unlawful or unfair), degree (excessive or limited), and scope (an individual, a group of individuals or whole society).

Joyee De and Le Métayer [12] and the CNIL methodology [10] do not distinguish between privacy violations and harms.

A *privacy harm* is the adverse impact (incorporeal, financial or physical) of the processing of personal data on the privacy of a data subject, a specific group of data subjects or society as a whole, resulting from one or more threat events. A widely held view conceptualises a privacy harm as the negative consequence of a privacy violation [6]. However, privacy harms are related to, but distinct from, privacy violations. This implies that it is not necessary for an actor to commit a privacy violation for a privacy harm to occur and vice versa. Each privacy harm can be characterised by: type (subjective or objective), category (incorporeal, financial or physical), adverse consequences (last for a short time, last for a certain length of time or last for a long time), and affected data subjects (a data subject, a specific group of data subjects, or whole society). Subjective privacy harm represents the perception of inappropriate processing of personal data that results in unwelcome mental states, such as anxiety, embarrassment or fear, whereas objective privacy harm represents the actual adverse consequence, such as identity theft that stems from the potential or actual inappropriate processing of personal data [6].

The CNIL methodology [10] uses the concept of prejudicial effect to assess how much damage would be caused by all the potential impacts. As such, feared events are ranked by estimating their severity based on the level of identification of personal data and the prejudicial effect of these potential impacts. To identify potential impacts of feared events, consequences on the identity and privacy of data subjects and human rights or civil liberties need to be identified. This means that it does not characterise privacy harms to facilitate their identification and analysis. In contrast, Joyee De and Le Métayer [12] use the concept of privacy harms with specific attributes and categories. In our approach, we use the same concept with more details to identify privacy harms at a detailed level of abstraction according to the properties and boundaries identified in [6].

5   An Analysis Approach

Risk analysis approaches differ with respect to the starting points of risk assessments and levels of abstraction. In order for risk assessments to be effective, they need to synthesise multiple analysis approaches to identify the key factors of risk. Potential privacy risks need to be identified, analysed and assessed in a systematic manner. As such, our approach consists of four steps.

Step 1: Context Establishment. Establishing the context in which personal data is processed plays a crucial role in understanding the scope under consideration by identifying all the useful information for privacy risk analysis. This includes the types of personal data to be processed (primary assets that need to be protected), along with its sources; the purposes for, and the manner in which, this data is processed; involved actors and their assigned roles and responsibilities; relevant legal frameworks and standards; and domain-specific constraints.

As discussed in Sect. 4, primary assets are classified into *personal data* and *processes*. As such, personal data, associated processes and involved actors need to be represented in a way that is amenable to analysis. While describing systems in multiple views is important [15], we emphasise the importance of data-management models that represent data and associated processing activities at a detailed level of abstraction. We believe that data lifecycles are better at describing processing activities in a detailed level of abstraction.

The Abstract Personal Data Lifecycle (APDL) Model [2] was developed to represent data-processing activities in a way that is amenable to analysis and compliance checking. It represents the personal data lifecycle in terms of lifecycle stages, along with associated activities and involved actors. It can be used to complement a PIA for describing the planned, actual and potential processing of personal data, which, in turn, helps facilitate the management and traceability of the flow of personal data from collection to destruction [2].

Accordingly, we adopt the APDL model to represent the primary assets, along with involved actors. Personal data is represented in the *DataModelling* stage. This stage represents the relevant objects, associated properties, relationships and constraints for the purpose of specifying the minimum amount of required personal data. Processes are abstractly represented in eight stages: *Initiation, Collection, Retention, Access, Review, Usage, Disclosure* and *Destruction*. In each stage, data-processing activities and those required by legal frameworks and standards are concretely represented in *StageActivity, StageEvent* and *Stage-Action*. In addition, involved actors and the way in which they participate in processing activities are represented in *LifecycleRole* and *LifecycleActor*. We use the UML [14] profile for the APDL model proposed in [1] to represent personal data, associated processes and involved actors.

Step 2: Vulnerability Analysis. We assume that identifying and analysing vulnerabilities of the *supporting assets* is part of security risk analysis to ensure availability, integrity or confidentiality of the primary assets. We focus only on vulnerabilities of the *primary assets* to protect the privacy of data subjects and ensure the contextual integrity.

The first step is to define a baseline model of processing that describes the targets of evaluation (primary assets) at an appropriate level of abstraction. To this end, we adopt the concept of contextual integrity [13], which was developed to bring the social layer into view by identifying four main elements: contexts, attributes, actors and transmission principles. These elements constitute *context-relative informational norms*, which govern the flow of information in a particular context to ensure its appropriateness. From a technical perspective, these norms can be adapted by including processing activities as an element to consider both the flow of personal data and the processing of this data (we refer to the adapted norms as context-relative processing norms). In so doing, contextual integrity is about the appropriate flow and processing of personal data.

In order to comprehensively identify and analyse all possible vulnerabilities of the primary assets, a baseline model, which describes personal data, associated processes and involved actors, needs to be represented in a way that is amenable to analysis. As such, the baseline model of processing can be described in terms of context-relative processing norms. We adopt the APDL model as a source to capture and represent personal data, associated processing activities, involved actors and their assigned roles in each stage of the lifecycle. In addition, processing principles—which can be derived from legal frameworks, standards or domain-specific constraints—are represented as constraints for each data-processing activity in each stage of the data lifecycle. We use the UML profile for the APDL model to describe the context-relative processing norms in a widely-used modelling notation.

Once the context-relative processing norms, which constitute a complete baseline model, are established, vulnerabilities can be derived from how these norms would be breached or disrupted to violate contextual integrity. Crucially, each element of each processing norm (data attributes, data-processing activities, actors and processing principles) need to be considered separately to ensure that: the data attributes are sufficient to fulfil the data-processing activity; the data-processing activity is assigned to authorised actors according to their roles and responsibilities; and the constraints (pre and post-conditions) are modelled in a way that ensures the data-processing activity is specified in conformity with the processing principles. Improper data model and a lack of data minimisation are examples of weaknesses for the elements of *attributes* and *processing principles* respectively. These vulnerabilities may be exploited by a threat source and lead to the identification of a data subject as a threat event. For each vulnerability, its exploitability and severity need to be identified and estimated in relation to the attributes of Sect. 4.

Step 3: Threat Analysis. In order to identify all possible *threat sources*, it is necessary to establish the context in which personal data is collected and processed (as per Step 1). The context helps support engineers in understanding the scope of analysis, multiple stakeholders, the nature and sensitivity of the processed data. Once the context is established, a list of actors involved in the processing of personal data can be identified, along with assigned roles and responsibilities. In particular, the Initiation stage can be used to concretely identify the types of personal data to be collected and processed, and to abstractly identify involved actors and their roles and responsibilities. In order to identify involved actors at a detailed level of abstraction, we use the basic types of lifecycle roles (data modeller, data subjects, data controllers, data processors and third parties) in each stage of the lifecycle as a source of such details. A lifecycle role is a set of logically related activities that are expected to be conducted together and assigned to different actors as responsibilities according to their capabilities. In addition, a list of entities with interests or concerns in the value of these types of personal data can be identified. All such entities are potential threat sources. For each threat source, its type, motives, resources, role and responsibilities need to be identified in relation to its attributes.

Once the context is established, and vulnerabilities and threat sources are identified, a list of *threat events* with the potential to adversely impact the privacy of data subjects can be identified. We adopt the taxonomy of privacy [16] as a means for characterising adverse privacy events. The taxonomy helps facilitate the identification of these events in a comprehensive and concrete manner. It classifies the most common adverse events into four basic groups: information collection, information processing, information dissemination and invasions. Adverse events are arranged with respect to a model that begins with the data subject, from which various entities collect personal data. Data holders process the collected data. They may also disseminate or release the processed data to other entities. The progression from collection through processing to dissemination is indicative of the personal data moving further away from the control of the data subject. In the last group of adverse events (invasions) the progression is toward the data subject and does not necessarily involve personal data [16].

The taxonomy was developed to serve as a framework for the future development of the field of privacy law. In our approach, however, we focus only on data-driven adverse events that are more related to primary assets than supporting assets. From a technical perspective, these adverse events need to be arranged around a widely used model in the field of systems engineering for describing the processing of data. The taxonomy classifies the most common adverse events into four basic groups that to a certain extent are arranged around a well-known processing model: the input-process-output (IPO) model. The first three groups (information collection, information processing and information dissemination) represent the input, process and output stages of the model respectively. The fourth group (invasions) is not related to that model as invasions are not only caused by technology and invasive adverse events do not always involve personal data; rather they directly affect data subjects. As such, we consider only some aspects of these events that involve personal data throughout the collection and disclosure stages of the lifecycle. We use the IPO model as a starting point towards describing these events at a detailed level of abstraction. As such, we adopt the APDL as a model around which we arrange these events. We map the basic groups of adverse events onto the stages of the data lifecycle. Additional detail about the conceptual relationship between the categories of the taxonomy of privacy and the stages of the APDL model is illustrated in [3]. Each type of an adverse threat event can be characterised by a set of attributes according to the nature of a processing operation in each stage of the lifecycle that reflects the manner in which personal data is collected, processed and disseminated.

Step 4: Privacy Harm Analysis. Once privacy vulnerabilities, threat sources and threat events are identified, *privacy violations* can be identified as illegitimate or unanticipated data-processing activities that may result from the occurrence of threat events without negative consequences on data subjects. In particular, for each possible exploitation, privacy violations are activities that can be conducted without adverse actions taken against data subjects, as well as without their knowledge. For each type of privacy violation, its degree and scope need to be identified in relation to its attributes.

Once privacy vulnerabilities, threat sources and threat events are identified, *privacy harms* can be derived from these events as potential adverse consequences on the privacy of data subjects. We use the categories of privacy harms of [12] that have been identified in previous attempts from a legal perspective [13,16]. In particular, privacy harms are classified into: physical; economic or financial harms; mental or psychological harms; harms to dignity or reputation; and societal or architectural harms [12]. We arrange these categories of harms around the APDL model according to its lifecycle stages, associated data-processing activities and their corresponding threat events. Additional detail about mapping these categorises onto the stages of the APDL model is illustrated in [3]. For each type of privacy harm, its type, adverse consequences and affected data subjects need to be identified in relation to its attributes.

6   A Case Study

6.1   Overview

The European Electronic Toll Service (EETS) aims to support interoperability between electronic road toll systems at a European level to calculate and collect road-usage tolls. The main actors involved in the EETS are service providers, toll chargers and users. EETS providers are legal entities that grant access to EETS to road users [18]. Toll chargers are public or private organisations that are responsible for levying tolls for the circulation of vehicles in an EETS domain [18]. A user is an individual who subscribes to an EETS provider in order to get access to EETS [18]. By signing a contract, a user is required to provide a set of personal data specified by a responsible toll charger, as well as to be informed about the processing of their personal data in relation to applicable law and regulations. Accordingly, the EETS provider provides the user with an On-Board Unit (OBU) to be installed on-board a vehicle to collect, store, and remotely receive and transmit time, distance and location data over time. This data, together with the user's and vehicle's parameters, are specified to declare the toll of circulating a vehicle in a specific toll domain [17].

Due to space limitations, we do not provide an exhaustive list of vulnerabilities, etc. Rather, we give examples to illustrate the usability and applicability of our approach in this particular context.

6.2   Context Establishment

All useful information that helps establish the context has been already captured by the APDL model in [1]. The establishment of the context in which personal data is collected and processed consists of three steps. The first step is to specify the types of personal data along with their attributes (captured by classes stereotyped by «PersonalData») and the main purpose for which this data is collected and processed (captured by a class stereotyped by «Purpose» along with its lawfulness, fairness and proportionality). With reference to the APDL model, the main purpose is to 'electronically calculate and collect road-usage tolls' and the types of personal are:

- Identification and contact data—*EETS User:* user ID, name, billing address (collected from the EETS user, whether the user is the driver, owner, lesser or fleet operator of the vehicle)
- Vehicle classification parameters—*Vehicle:* licence plate, classification code (collected from the EETS user)
- Location data—*LocationData:* time, distance, place (collected by OBUs)

The second step is to specify or model both actual data-processing activities and privacy-related processes required by legal frameworks and standards in each stage of the APDL model. These processes are abstractly captured from classes stereotyped by «Initiation», «Collection», etc. With a focus on location data, we illustrate a data-processing activity in the collection stage of the APDL model: it is abstractly captured from the *CollectingUsageData* class, which is stereotyped by «Collection». The stereotyped class also captures other important details: location data sources (OBUs), available choices (the user is entitled to subscribe to EETS with the EETS providers of their choice among other choices: the national or local manual, automatic or electronic toll services), collection method (OBUs using satellite positioning systems), consent type (implicit by signing a contract) and relevant GPS principles (Collection Limitation). In addition, processes are concretely captured from classes stereotyped by «StageActivity», «StageAction» and «StageEvent». Each stage activity contains a set of actions that represent its executable steps and a set of events that cause the execution of these actions. The data-processing activity is concretely captured from the *CollectingLocationData* class, which is stereotyped by «StageActivity». At this level of detail, it aims to collect road-usage data to be used for tolls declaration and calculation. The stereotyped class also captures other important details in terms of constraints: pre-conditions (the privacy notice is communicated to EETS users at or before the collection time in a clear and concise manner; their implicit consent is obtained at or before the collection time in an informed manner by subscribing to the service; and the minimum necessary amount of location data is modelled to fulfil the stated purpose); and post-conditions (the road-usage data has been successfully collected). This activity is decomposed into two classes: *CollectLocationData* and *Collect*, which are stereotyped by «StageAction» and «StageEvent» respectively. CollectLocationData class captures the time of usage, the covered distance and the place on which the vehicle is circulating on a particular toll domain for tolls declaration and calculation. The Collect class captures the occurrence of circulating a vehicle on a particular toll domain to collect location data.

The third step is to specify or model involved actors (captured by classes stereotyped by «LifecycleRole» and «LifecycleActor»). Each lifecycle stage includes a number of lifecycle roles, each of which is played by different actors according to their capabilities and responsibilities. With reference to the APDL model, *CollectionAgent* is a type of data processor role that consists of logically related activities for collecting road usage data, and *ServiceProvider* is a type of involved actors who are capable of, and responsible for, performing the activities of the collection agent as a role to which are assigned. Responsibilities are captured from stage activities in which a lifecycle actor participates and to which a lifecycle role is associated.

Establishing the context in which personal data is collected and processed requires specifying or modelling 'personal data', 'data-processing activities' and 'involved actors' along with their roles and responsibilities. The APDL model has served as a preliminary acquisition step to capture all required data that support privacy risk analysis and compliance checking.

6.3 Vulnerability Analysis

In our approach the focus is on vulnerabilities of *primary assets* to protect the privacy of data subjects and ensure contextual integrity. The first step of vulnerability analysis is to develop a baseline model of the processing of personal data. The baseline model captures all appropriate data-processing activities in all stages of the APDL model. In order to develop a baseline model, we need to establish a context-relative processing norm for each data-processing activity. The main elements that constitute these norms are captured from stage activities in the established context. Due to space limitations, we identify only a context-relative processing norm for the *CollectingLocationData* activity:

> In the context of EETS, the collection of a certain type of personal data (location data: time, distance, place) about an EETS user (acting as a data subject) by an EETS provider (acting as a data processor on behalf of a toll charger) is governed by processing principles derived from applicable legal frameworks... and standards...

In this case, legal framework principles—for example, DIRECTIVE 95/46/EC— are as follows. Personal data must be: processed fairly and lawfully; collected for specified, explicit and legitimate purposes; adequate, relevant and not excessive; and accurate and up to date. In addition, the relevant GPS principle is *Collection Limitation*. Importantly, principles of legal frameworks and standards are modelled as pre- and post-conditions for each stage activity.

Once all context-relevant processing norms are defined in relation to the APDL model, a complete baseline model can be developed to serve as the basis for deriving privacy vulnerabilities. The second step of vulnerability analysis is to derive all possible vulnerabilities of the primary assets from the identified context-relevant processing norms. They can be derived by examining all the main elements that constitute each processing norm—i.e. any possible breach of a processing norm can be derived as a vulnerability. With reference to the above processing norm, a possible vulnerability with regards to *attributes*, as an element, is 'an improper data model' (PV.1) that directly or indirectly links location data to users' IDs. Another possible vulnerability with regards to *processing principles*, as an element, is 'a lack of data minimisation' (PV.2) that facilitates inadequate, irrelevant and excessive collection of location data in an interval basis, which is not necessary for the main purpose. Additional examples of privacy vulnerabilities are listed in [3].

6.4   Threat Analysis

Threat Sources. In reference to the established context, EETS providers (TS.1) are involved in the processing of 'identification and contact data' and 'location data' by playing the role of data processors who grant access to EETS to EETS users. They may act accidentally or deliberately as threat sources while they process personal data lawfully to calculate and communicate personalised fees (road-usage tolls) for each EETS user by the end of the tax period—or unlawfully for further processing with the motivation of profiling EETS users, discriminatory social sorting or providing better services. The utility of 'location data' and 'identification and contact data' in this context makes such data highly valuable to EETS providers. The value of this data stimulates the motives of EETS providers to exploit vulnerabilities of the primary assets. In particular, it has a market value when it is exploited by EETS providers for administrative and commercial purposes—for example, it gives an EETS provider a competitive advantage with respect to their competitors. According to the attributes of a threat source, EETS providers are insiders and institutions. EETS providers have technical skills and detailed background knowledge about conceptual, logical and physical data models, as well as about the processing operations. It also implies that they have legitimate privileges to collect and process location-related data according to their roles and responsibilities. Based on these, they have access rights to both the 'fine-grained location data' and 'identification and contact data'. They also have reasonable resources (both technical and financial) to get benefit from the values of the collected data by creating comprehensive and identifiable profiles. Additional examples of threat sources are listed in [3].

Threat Events. In a straightforward implementation of the EETS architecture, the calculation of road-usage tolls is performed remotely at EETS providers' back-office systems. The OBU collects, stores, and remotely receives and transmits time, distance and place over time to the EETS provider's back-office systems. These systems are in charge of processing location data to calculate personalised road-usage tolls and communicate the final premium to EETS user at the end of the tax period. As mentioned, a threat event occurs as a result of a successful exploitation of one or more vulnerabilities by one or more threat sources. With reference to the identified vulnerabilities and threat sources, we identify the most significant threat events with the potential to adversely impact the privacy of EETS users that may happen at specific points in time. The identification of these events needs to be conducted according to the stages of the data lifecycle.

In the collection stage, for example, threat events that may lead to privacy violations or harms are related to the manner in which personal data is collected.

By exploiting PV.2, TS.1 may use OBUs to excessively collect irrelevant location data (TE.1) in a fine-grained manner about EETS users. With reference to the adapted taxonomy of adverse privacy events, this threat event is a type of 'surveillance'. It is characterised as continuous, overt and extensive: continuous via the collection of location data over time; overt via informing the EETS user about the manner in which location data will be collected when signing the contract; and extensive via the excessive collection of location data in a fine-grained manner throughout national and international toll domains. Surveillance outside toll domains compromises reasonable expectations of privacy as it may reveal hidden details that would not ordinarily be observed by others. Additional examples of threat events, along with the corresponding threat sources and privacy vulnerabilities, are listed in [3].

6.5   Harm Analysis

Privacy Violations. In the collection stage, for example, 'passive collection of location data outside toll domains' is a privacy violation that may result from the occurrence of the threat event 'excessive collection of location data', which results from the successful exploitation of 'a lack of data minimisation' by EETS providers. Its degree is excessive as it collects fine-grained location data outside toll domains, whether they are national or international. Its scope is individuals who are subscribed to EETS. This privacy violation is considered as an illegitimate and unanticipated data-processing activity without adverse consequences. In particular, fine-grained location data is collected in ways EETS users would not reasonably expect; also, this data is collected passively without the knowledge and consent of EETS users. In addition, the collection of location data outside toll domains does not have legitimate grounds as they are irrelevant and inadequate for the purposes for which location data is collected. Most importantly, this privacy violation is assumed to be without adverse actions against EETS users.

Privacy Harms. Privacy harm analysis is the most important step of any privacy risk-analysis approach. Harms are derived from the undesirable consequences of threat events as potential adverse actions taken against data subjects. In this paper, we consider only the objective category of privacy harms as the subjective category is mainly about the perception of unwanted observation.

For each stage of the data lifecycle, the potential undesirable consequences of each threat event need to be identified. Then, these consequences need to be analysed to determine whether they can partially contribute to, or completely lead to a negative action that uses personal data against the data subject in an unanticipated or coerced manner. Most broadly, a privacy harm may result from a series of adverse consequences of multiple threat events. In the collection stage, for example, the main undesirable consequence of TE.1 is gathering a large amount of fine-grained location data that has been collected over time as comprehensive driving records (UC.1), which may include complete driving history or driving history for a specific period for EETS users. Additional examples of undesirable consequences are listed in [3].

By analysing the identified undesirable consequences, together with the relevant privacy vulnerabilities and threat sources, we can derive a reasonable set of privacy harms. For example, the privacy harm 'increased car insurance premium' (PH.1) occurs as EETS providers can make excessive inference to derive EETS users' driving patterns and share anonymised patterns with car insurance providers (TS.7). Insurance providers may make inference to re-identify current and potential customers with the aim of calculating car insurance premium based on the types of vehicle use and health conditions, which are derived from their driving patterns. Additional examples of privacy harms, along with associated threat sources, privacy vulnerabilities, threat events and undesirable consequences of these events, are listed in [3].

7   Conclusion

We have presented an approach that helps support engineers in identifying and analysing potential privacy risks in a comprehensive and contextual manner. It refers to fundamentals from the legal privacy literature to refine key concepts and assessable risk factors, as well as the conceptual relationships among these factors. Such fundamentals help support the distinction between privacy harms and violations and their main sources by providing boundaries and properties of privacy harms. In addition, fundamentals bring the legal and social layers into consideration by defining context-relative processing norms. They also facilitate the identification of adverse events in a systematic manner by providing a taxonomy of harmful activities and their corresponding harms. They also support the taxonomy by providing two main principles: (1) the limiting principle to help protect against reduction of the concept of privacy, and (2) the rule of recognition to support the identification of novel privacy harms as they emerge.

We limit our approach to a risk model and analysis approach that describes how combinations of risk factors are identified and analysed at a consistent level of detail. In order to propose a complete risk-assessment methodology, an assessment approach that associates values with the risk factors needs to be developed to functionally combine the values of those factors and estimate the levels of the identified risks.

Acknowledgments. The authors would like to thank the reviewers for their constructive comments.

References

1. Alshammari, M., Simpson, A.: A UML profile for privacy-aware data lifecycle models. In: Katsikas, S.K., et al. (eds.) CyberICPS/SECPRE -2017. LNCS, vol. 10683, pp. 189–209. Springer, Cham (2018). https://doi.org/10.1007/978-3-319-72817-9_13
2. Alshammari, M., Simpson, A.: Personal data management: an abstract personal data lifecycle model. In: Teniente, E., Weidlich, M. (eds.) BPM 2017. LNBIP, vol. 308, pp. 685–697. Springer, Cham (2018). https://doi.org/10.1007/978-3-319-74030-0_55

3. Alshammari, M., Simpson, A.C.: Towards an effective PIA-based risk analysis: an approach for analysing potential privacy risks (2017). http://www.cs.ox.ac.uk/publications/publication11663-abstract.html
4. BSI (Bundesamt für Sicherheit in der Informationstechnik): Risk analysis on the basis of IT-Grundschutz, BSI Standard 100-3 (2008). https://www.bsi.bund.de/EN/TheBSI/thebsi_node.html
5. BSI (Bundesamt für Sicherheit in der Informationstechnik): IT-Grundschutz-Kataloge (2011). https://www.bsi.bund.de/DE/Themen/ITGrundschutz/ITGrundschutzKataloge/itgrundschutzkataloge_node.html
6. Calo, R.: The boundaries of privacy harm. Indiana Law J. **86**, 1131–1162 (2011)
7. Cavoukian, A.: Privacy by design (2009). https://www.privacybydesign.ca/content/uploads/2009/01/privacybydesign.pdf
8. Cavoukian, A., Shapiro, S., Cronk, R.J.: Privacy engineering: proactively embedding privacy, by design (2014). https://www.privacybydesign.ca/content/uploads/2014/01/pbd-priv-engineering.pdf
9. Clarke, R.: Privacy impact assessment: its origins and development. Comput. Law Secur. Rev. Int. J. Technol. Pract. **25**(2), 123–135 (2009)
10. Commission Nationale de l'Informatique et des Libertés (CNIL): Methodology for privacy risk management (2016). https://www.cnil.fr/sites/default/files/typo/document/CNIL-ManagingPrivacyRisks-Methodology.pdf
11. Fineberg, A., Jeselon, P.: A foundational framework for a privacy by design – privacy impact assessment (2011). http://privacybydesign.ca/content/uploads/2011/11/PbD-PIA-Foundational-Framework.pdf
12. De, S.J., Le Métayer, D.: PRIAM: a privacy risk analysis methodology. In: Livraga, G., Torra, V., Aldini, A., Martinelli, F., Suri, N. (eds.) DPM/QASA -2016. LNCS, vol. 9963, pp. 221–229. Springer, Cham (2016). https://doi.org/10.1007/978-3-319-47072-6_15
13. Nissenbaum, H.F.: Privacy in Context: Technology, Policy, and the Integrity of Social Life. Stanford University Press, Stanford (2009)
14. Object Management Group: OMG Unified Modeling Language (OMG UML) (2015). http://www.omg.org/spec/UML/
15. Oetzel, M.C., Spiekermann, S.: A systematic methodology for privacy impact assessments: a design science approach. Eur. J. Inf. Syst. **23**(2), 126–150 (2014)
16. Solove, D.J.: A taxonomy of privacy. Univ. Pennsylvania Law Rev. **154**(3), 477–564 (2006)
17. The European Commission: The European Electronic Toll Service (EETS): 2011 Guide for the Application of the Directive on the Interoperability of Electronic Road Toll Systems (2011). http://ec.europa.eu/transport/themes/its/road/application_areas/electronic_pricing_and_payment_en
18. The European Union: Official Journal of the European Communities: Commission Decision 2009/750/EC of 6 October 2009 on the definition of the European Electronic Toll Service and its technical elements (2009). http://eur-lex.europa.eu/legal-content/EN/TXT/HTML/?uri=CELEX:32009D0750&from=EN
19. Wright, D.: The state of the art in privacy impact assessment. Comput. Law Secur. Rev. **28**(1), 54–61 (2012)
20. Wright, D., Wadhwa, K., De Hert, P., Kloza, D.: A Privacy Impact Assessment Framework for data protection and privacy rights (2011). http://www.piafproject.eu/Deliverables.html

Privacy Risk Assessment: From Art to Science, by Metrics

Isabel Wagner[✉] and Eerke Boiten

Cyber Technology Institute, De Montfort University, Leicester, UK
{isabel.wagner,eerke.boiten}@dmu.ac.uk

Abstract. Privacy risk assessments aim to analyze and quantify the privacy risks associated with new systems. As such, they are critically important in ensuring that adequate privacy protections are built in. However, current methods to quantify privacy risk rely heavily on experienced analysts picking the "correct" risk level on e.g. a five-point scale. In this paper, we argue that a more scientific quantification of privacy risk increases accuracy and reliability and can thus make it easier to build privacy-friendly systems. We discuss how the impact and likelihood of privacy violations can be decomposed and quantified, and stress the importance of meaningful metrics and units of measurement. We suggest a method of quantifying and representing privacy risk that considers a collection of factors as well as a variety of contexts and attacker models. We conclude by identifying some of the major research questions to take this approach further in a variety of application scenarios.

Keywords: Privacy risk metrics · Privacy impact assessment

1 Introduction

A privacy impact assessment (PIA) is the process of identifying and mitigating privacy risks in an existing or planned system. During a privacy impact assessment, organizations identify possible privacy risks, then quantify and rank these risks, and finally take decisions on whether and how to reduce, remove, transfer, or accept the risks. "PIA" also refers to the document produced in this process, and it is generally seen as a *living* document in systems development. This is because privacy risks can change over time: as a result of choices made during design and implementation; as a result of evolution of the system and its data governance; and as a result of developments in processing technology and availability of related information in the system's environment.

PIAs are an essential component of Privacy by Design [5], an approach to dealing with privacy in a proactive rather than reactive way. They have been recommended by national data protection authorities for more than 5 years already [6,13]. In the new European data protection regulation GDPR (General Data Protection Regulation) [11], PIAs (called "data protection impact assessments")

© Springer Nature Switzerland AG 2018
J. Garcia-Alfaro et al. (Eds.): DPM 2018/CBT 2018, LNCS 11025, pp. 225–241, 2018.
https://doi.org/10.1007/978-3-030-00305-0_17

are mandated for some cases, including surveillance, data sharing, and new technologies. This is relevant worldwide because of the GDPR's global reach. As PIAs include consultation with stakeholders, they are also a useful mechanism for obtaining their buy-in in what might otherwise be seen as "creepy" data processing processes.

However, the wider application and impact of PIAs may be limited because privacy risk assessments currently rely heavily on experience, analogy and imagination, that is, risk assessment more closely resembles an *art* than a science. We argue that a more scientific approach to risk assessment can improve the outcomes of privacy impact assessments by making them more consistent and systematic. Beyond the use to measure and communicate an individual privacy risk, we envision uses of these privacy risk metrics for at least five more purposes: to quantify the effect of privacy controls, to compare the effects of different controls, to analyze trends in privacy risk over time, to compute a system's aggregate privacy risk from its components, and to rank privacy risks.

Contributions. In this paper, we investigate how to quantify privacy risk systematically with the aim of moving privacy risk assessment from being an art closer to being a science. We focus on *data* driven privacy (i.e. the impact of data decisions, possibly outside the data sphere) because this is the scope of the GDPR, currently the strongest driver of PIAs. In line with the common decomposition of risk into impact and likelihood, we discuss quantification of impact and likelihood separately and suggest possible metrics for each (Sects. 4 and 5). We then discuss how metrics for impact and likelihood can be combined to form privacy risk metrics that can be used directly in privacy impact assessments and privacy requirements engineering (Sect. 6). We illustrate an initial approach to measuring and representing privacy risk in a case study with two typical known privacy risks (Sect. 7). Finally, we highlight open issues in the area of privacy risk quantification and set out an agenda for further research.

2   State of the Art

Before we discuss the benefits and building blocks of a more scientific method for quantifying privacy risk, we briefly describe the state of the art in risk assessment, privacy risk assessment, and privacy measurement.

Risk Assessment. Risk is commonly calculated as some function of likelihood and impact. Several proposals exist to determine the risk of *security* threats, for example the NIST guidelines [18] or the OWASP Risk Rating Methodology [20]. These are often cited in the privacy literature because security risks can be quite close to privacy risks. An important difference between security and privacy risk, however, is that harm to individuals is a primary consideration for privacy risk (even if organizations may translate that into reputational and regulatory risks), whereas it is of secondary importance for security risk.

Both NIST and OWASP rate impact and likelihood on Likert scales, e.g. from "very low" to "very high", with no clear guidelines on how to determine the position on this scale. For example, the NIST guidelines [18] list examples of adverse impacts, such as harm to operations, assets, or individuals, and explain how the expected extent of each impact should be mapped to the Likert scale: "significant" financial loss, for example, is a moderate impact, while "major" financial loss is high impact. Likelihood is split into the likelihood that a threat event occurs, and the likelihood that an adverse impact results from the threat event. The ratings for likelihood and impact are then combined according to a table that indicates the resulting risk rating for each combination of the separate Likert scale ratings. For example, "low" impact and "very high" likelihood result in a "low" overall risk. These impact and likelihood ratings are subjective, i.e., they may be rated differently by different people, and the resulting risk ratings may not be accurate or reliable. In addition, while these tables allow to distinguish between the lowest and highest risks, they only give a partial ordering of risks. For example, it may not be possible to decide the ordering of one risk with low impact and high likelihood and another with high impact and low likelihood.

Privacy Risk Assessment. The OWASP top-10 list of privacy risks in web applications [24] ranks privacy risks by their ratings for impact and likelihood. Likelihood is measured as the frequency with which the risk occurs in existing websites (determined via a survey of web developers and privacy/security experts), with a score of 0 indicating under 25%, and 3 indicating 75% or above. Impact is measured in five dimensions as limited (1), considerable (2), or devastating (3): two dimensions for organizational impact (reputation, finance) and three dimensions for impact on individuals (reputation, finance, freedoms). The final impact score is the average of the five scores.

Recently superseded guidance on privacy risk management by the French data protection regulator CNIL [7] assesses risk *severity*, which is based on the possible *prejudicial effects* – similar to impact – and on the level of *identifiability* of data. The latter includes aspects of impact, i.e., the loss of highly identifiable data is more impactful, as well as aspects of likelihood, i.e., the ease of exploiting a data loss as a privacy attack depends on the level of identifiability of the targets in the data set. Albakri et al. [1] employ this notion to abstract from attackers' motivation and capacity, by assessing both privacy and security risks on the basis of exploitability rather than likelihood.

Several bodies have published lists of known privacy risks, for example data protection authorities [8], researchers [9], and regulators. Although these lists can serve as starting points for privacy impact assessments, they typically do not include a quantification or ranking of specific privacy risks.

Privacy Measurement. Most privacy metrics that have been proposed in the literature [28] focus on measuring the amount of privacy that a privacy enhancing technology can provide against some adversary, for example expressed as the adversary's error, uncertainty, or information gain. Some privacy metrics focus on the adversary's success rate and may thus be suitable to quantify the likelihood of a privacy violation (see Sect. 5). Very few privacy metrics measure risk directly, for example, the privacy score in social networks [16] is computed as the sensitivity of profile items multiplied by their visibility. However, this metric has limited applicability because of its focus on social networks, and because it does not consider harm to individuals.

3   Benefits and Building Blocks for Privacy Risk Metrics

We see four important benefits that can be achieved through the increased accuracy and reliability of a more scientific and systematic way of measuring privacy risk. First, when building new systems, risk metrics could allow to compare the risks associated with different ways of building the system. In particular, for systems that are composed of smaller building blocks, risk could be measured on the level of building blocks, and composition rules would allow to compute the overall risk. In effect, such risk metrics allow to rationalize and substantiate decisions about how systems that affect privacy are built and evaluated.

Second, risk metrics are also needed in privacy requirements engineering [9], which is a similar process to privacy impact assessment (PIA), but with the goal of deriving formal privacy requirements and identifying suitable protections in the form of privacy-enhancing technologies. The privacy requirements engineering process can identify many risks and thus needs a way to prioritize risks. For example, the LINDDUN method [9] uses risk scores, but does not state specifically how these scores should be determined.

Third, risk metrics can also allow to set thresholds for when the regulator needs to be consulted (e.g., as per GDPR guidance by the UK's Information Commissioner's Office [14]), and thresholds for when privacy risks are too high to permit data collection or processing. Thresholds can also play an important role in organizations' decisions to *accept* certain risks – for example, in large organizations often risks need to associated with million dollars' damages before they warrant the board's attention. Even vaguely defined metrics can support a *triage* process on an identified collection of risks to determine the risks' priorities based on their severities.

Fourth, companies that offer cyber insurance benefit from accurate risk metrics to correctly determine insurance premiums. With their past experiences of incidents that they have already paid given amounts out on, there is no doubt that they already hold the largest vault of monetary valuations of privacy risks, but are unlikely to share this, for commercial reasons.

Building Blocks for a More Scientific Risk Quantification. An important foundation of a more scientific approach is the ability to measure and predict the relevant quantities, i.e. the likelihood (Sect. 5) and impact (Sect. 4) of privacy violations.

To make the measurement of privacy risk more systematic, we decompose the impact and likelihood of privacy risk into more fine-grained components. As Fig. 1 shows, we decompose impact into the four components scale, sensitivity, expectation, and harm, and decompose likelihood into the likelihoods of attack, of adverse effect, and exploitability. Because these components are more specific than the high-level concepts of impact and likelihood, it should be easier to find meaningful metrics for them.

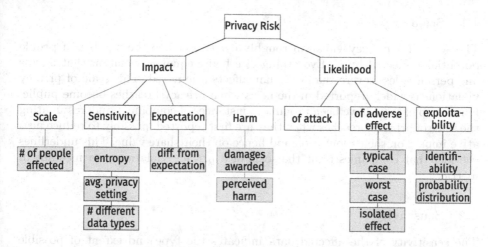

Fig. 1. Components of privacy risk.

However, measuring these quantities is complicated by the fact that the measurement necessarily relies on information known in the present. Future data sharing or future technologies available to adversaries, such as advanced re-identification algorithms, can significantly increase the privacy risk (but typically do not decrease the risk). Function creep – the repurposing of collected data with the intent of realizing new functions – is also associated with an increase of privacy risk. Any present-day measurement of privacy risk should therefore be treated as a lower boundary on the real privacy risk.

Units of measurement are important to make risk metrics more understandable and manageable. Risks measured using the same unit can be meaningfully aggregated, for example when computing the total privacy risk from contributing risk factors, and directly compared, for example when considering different technical alternatives or when triaging and prioritizing risks. When units differ, or when there is no unit at all (e.g., in Likert scales), such operations become more difficult or fundamentally dubious.

In business, financial value may be acceptable as the ultimate unit which is used to quantify direct costs – even reputation and human lives. However, certainly the public sector does not operate on a competitive or financial basis, and may prefer units that more closely relate to the concept of privacy risk.

4   Impact Quantification

To make the measurement of privacy impact more systematic, privacy impact metrics should be based on four key components (see Fig. 1): scale, sensitivity, user expectations, and harm. Because of the intangible nature of some of these components, we expect that their quantification will have to use proxy measures instead of measuring the component directly.

4.1 Scale

The scale of a privacy violation roughly corresponds to the number of people potentially affected by it. Everything else being equal, a violation that affects one person is less severe than one that affects a hundred. This scale of privacy violations is widely reported in the news when privacy breaches become public. For example, there have been prominent instances of companies underestimating the scale of privacy breaches when they are first reported, possibly to reduce negative impact on their reputation and hence on their share value. This underlines the fact that companies treat the scale of a privacy violation as a meaningful metric.

4.2 Sensitivity

The sensitivity of the affected data indicates the type and extent of possible harm to individuals. The sensitivity of data is not necessarily fully aligned with the GDPR's categories of *personal data* and *special category data* – credit card data are classified as personal data, but can cause direct financial harm, whereas trade union membership is classified as special category data, but its exposure would not be seen as harmful in many countries.

Importantly, if the privacy of more than one type of data is breached, then the overall sensitivity may be higher than a linear combination of individual sensitivities. For example, the information that a given person was at a location (e.g. a celebrity at a nightclub) may not be that sensitive, but the combination of that information with another person being at the same location at the same time may produce sensitive evidence of a meeting between the two.

The sensitivity of data is thus difficult to quantify. Metrics from information theory could be used to measure the amount of information (in bits) revealed by a privacy breach; this will often be indicative of the level of identifiability, but *amount* does not fully coincide with *sensitivity*. Another approach that is useful when users can choose their individual privacy settings is to compute sensitivity statistically from the privacy settings of a large number of users [16].

4.3 Expectation

The expectation individuals have of how their data will be treated, and how much a privacy violation deviates from this expectation, indicates as how "creepy" a privacy violation will be perceived. For example, users usually expect that their data will be handled according to their personal privacy settings. Users may also have expectations where their data is stored, for example, the leak of electronic health records from a third party server located in a foreign country would be unexpected because people may not expect that the storage of health records is outsourced abroad. Depending on social norms, there may also be a reasonable expectation of privacy in public places [19]. The GDPR makes it explicit that the legality of data processing may depend on user expectations[1]. An approach to quantify this deviation from expectation may be to first state the expectation in terms of Solove's taxonomy of privacy [23], i.e. to state which aspects of information collection, information processing, information dissemination, or invasion are expected by individuals. Then, a specific privacy violation can be analyzed with respect to the number of aspects that differ from the stated expectation.

4.4 Harm

The harm to affected individuals can be financial, but can also be harm to their reputation, harm caused by discrimination, distress, or anxiety, and harm due to breaches of the individual's rights and freedoms. These privacy harms are all covered by (European) data protection legislation[2] and it was established before the GDPR came in that individuals can sue for damages even where harms are not material [12].

An important contributing factor in this is what has actually happened to the data: has it been exposed, modified, processed non-transparently, or used to make a decision affecting individuals? If exposed, to whom and what harms could and would they cause, given existing and potential future information available to the receivers of the data?

Similarly to sensitivity, harm may be cumulative. For example, a single data disclosure may not be very harmful on its own, but a series of disclosures over a period of time may finally allow an adversary to link data and cause serious harm. This also means that it can be hard to attribute privacy harm to a single privacy breach, which may lead to a dissolution of corporate responsibility, especially when privacy breaches occur along the supply chain.

Harm can also encompass organizational harm, for example reputation damage after the discovery of a privacy breach, or financial damage through loss of customers or regulatory fines.

Finally, individuals may have different perceptions of the harm itself, especially non-financial harm. As a result, harm is difficult to quantify. A useful proxy measure may be to estimate the amount of damages a court would be likely to grant. However, not everything can be measured in money, and expressing harm in monetary terms may not do justice to the extent of the harm caused. In this

---

[1] For example, Recital 47 on the legal basis of "legitimate interest" requires "taking into consideration the reasonable expectations of data subjects based on their relationship with the controller."

[2] See GDPR Recital 75: "The risk to the rights and freedoms of natural persons, of varying likelihood and severity, may result from data processing which could lead to physical, material or non-material damage, in particular: where the processing may give rise to discrimination, identity theft or fraud, financial loss, damage to the reputation, loss of confidentiality of personal data protected by professional secrecy, unauthorized reversal of pseudonymization, or any other significant economic or social disadvantage; where data subjects might be deprived of their rights and freedoms or prevented from exercising control over their personal data" [11].

case, a Likert scale could be used to estimate the extent of each type of harm affected by a privacy breach.

5   Likelihood Quantification

Quantifying the likelihood of a privacy violation is somewhat more tangible than quantifying the impact. Quantifying likelihood is particularly important because most privacy controls affect the likelihood of a privacy violation instead of its impact. The NIST guide on privacy engineering [3] focuses on the likelihood of "problematic data actions." However, we believe that a thorough quantification of likelihood needs to take into account three aspects of likelihood: the likelihood of an attack, the likelihood of an adverse effect, and exploitability.

5.1   Likelihood of Attack

The likelihood of an attack focuses on the adversary's motivation to cause a privacy violation. This is very difficult to quantify because it may depend on specific circumstances. For example, an adversary may be more motivated to breach medical data privacy when a celebrity has recently been admitted to a specific hospital. The arrival of the celebrity may even cause a perfectly innocent staff member at the hospital to turn into an adversary who misuses their access to patient records.

Instead of attempting to estimate this likelihood directly, we believe that it is reasonable to assume that a motivated attacker is present (i.e., assume a likelihood of 1), and to focus on quantifying the other aspects of likelihood.

5.2   Likelihood of Adverse Effect

The likelihood that an adverse effect actually materializes can similarly depend on specific circumstances, and adverse effects may be very rare or not easily attributable to a single privacy violation. The focus on harm to the individual that is required to assess privacy risk means that it is not sufficient to assess the typical case, but that the worst case also needs to be considered. Therefore, instead of estimating the exact probability distribution for the occurrence of adverse effects, we believe that it is more beneficial to assess privacy impact for three distinct points on this distribution: the impact on the typical user, the impact on the individual who would be affected worst, and the impact that would be caused if the adversary didn't have any additional information, i.e., the impact caused if this was a single, isolated privacy violation.

5.3   Exploitability

Exploitability focuses on the adversary's ability to cause a privacy violation. Specifically, a systematic quantification should focus on the probability that a specific privacy violation occurs against an adversary with specific aims, capabilities and additional knowledge that corresponds with a realistic attack model. Considering possible adversaries explicitly is necessary to make the likelihood quantification meaningful and highlights the assumptions made during the privacy risk assessment.

An adversary is any party that is interested in private data, whether within the organization that holds the data, a connected organization such as a service provider, or an external third party [10]. Privacy risks can exist even in the absence of attacks, for example through human error and accident. Both can be modeled as attacks by non-malicious insider adversaries. Privacy risks can occur as a collateral effect even if the adversary is not primarily driven by a privacy-related motivation. For example, an adversary targeting critical national infrastructure may gather information for a spear-phishing attack, and in the process cause privacy harms, even though this is not the primary goal.

There is a wide variety of adversary models considered in the literature (see [28] for an overview). For adversaries that aim to breach privacy it is especially important to consider inference algorithms that allow the adversary to learn private information from public observations as well as the adversary's prior knowledge because combining data types can increase both likelihood and impact of a privacy breach.

An important factor in exploitability is identifiability: many privacy attacks are based on knowledge of sensitive information about an identified person. A re-identification attack, in itself an abstract privacy attack, can be the essential stepping stone in this, for example starting from "anonymized information or "big data". Quantification of re-identification risk is difficult [2], not least because there may be large differences between the possibilities of re-identifying a specific individual (such as Governor Weld by Latanya Sweeney [26]), any individual of choice, or all individuals in a given data set. The GDPR [11, Recital 26] nevertheless requires an explicit assessment of what an adversary may "reasonably likely" use in attempting to re-identify information.

The result of modeling possible adversaries is a set of probability distributions that indicate how likely it is for each adversary to succeed in breaching privacy.

6   Privacy Risk Metrics

Similarly to security risk metrics, a privacy risk metric could be defined as a combination of metrics for impact and likelihood of privacy violations. However, our discussion in the previous sections has shown that both the impact and the likelihood of privacy risk are composed of several components that are not easily integrated. For impact, using our suggested metrics above, we would need to combine the number of people affected, the differences in user expectations, bits of information revealed, and the (monetary equivalent of) harm to individuals. Ideally, this combination should result in a metric with a meaningful unit, and not just an arbitrary number. For likelihood, we need to consider both the likelihood of adverse effects and the exploitability for different kinds of adversaries.

As a result, the typical method of adding or multiplying Likert scores does not appear suitable for privacy risk.

In the Introduction, we argued that privacy risk metrics are needed for five purposes: to quantify the effect of privacy controls, to compare the effects of different controls, to analyze trends in privacy risk over time, to compute a system's aggregate privacy risk from its components, and to rank privacy risks. Each of these purposes has a minimal requirement for the scale of measurement [25] used by the privacy risk metric. For example, we need at least an ordinal scale to rank privacy risks, and a ratio scale to analyze aggregate privacy risk in complex systems. To analyze trends in privacy risk and to compare different privacy controls, an ordinal scale is strictly speaking sufficient, but may not be fine-grained enough to give meaningful or informative results. We show which scale of measure is required to support each of the five purposes in Table 1.

Table 1. Measurement scales required for different purposes of privacy risk metrics

Purpose	Scale of measure
Effectiveness of privacy controls	Ordinal
Comparison of privacy controls	Ordinal
Trends in privacy risk	Ordinal
Calculation of system risk from components	Ratio
Ranking of privacy risks	Ordinal

We can see that Likert scores (ordinal, but coarse-grained) can be sufficient for some purposes. However, they are not suitable to analyze the aggregate privacy risk in a complex system, and they are not desirable because, as we have argued, they depend on subjective judgment and may therefore differ depending on who is performing the risk assessment. In some cases, however, it seems unavoidable to use an ordinal scale, for example to express that an individual's freedoms have been infringed, or the level of distress experienced by an individual.

In these cases, it is unclear how two or more ordinal measures, e.g., for different types of harm, should be combined because the commonly used operations – addition and multiplication – are not defined for ordinal scales [25]. The usual method of adding or multiplying impact and likelihood scores assigns numerical scores to the levels on the ordinal scale, thus creating a false sense of an interval or ratio scale, for which addition or multiplication would be permitted.

To achieve a clean combination of impact and likelihood metrics, we suggest to measure the individual components separately and combine them visually. For example, as shown in the case studies in Sect. 7 (Figs. 2 and 3), the impact metrics can be combined in a radar plot, and the likelihoods for each adversary type can be indicated with probability density functions or summarized in box plots. This approach respects the essential multidimensionality of privacy risk and allows to choose appropriate scales for each type of impact. For example, employment-related harms could be assessed using a 5-point Likert scale ranging from "annoying day" to "off with stress" to "fired/end of career," whereas the scale of the privacy violation could be assessed using the number of individuals affected.

7 Case Study: Privacy Risks in a Flashlight App

To illustrate how a privacy risk assessment can analyze and visualize the components of privacy risk that we have presented so far, we analyze an example application for a mobile device, focusing on two privacy threats from the OWASP top-10 list of privacy risks in web applications [24].

We consider a mobile application that allows users to use their phone as a flashlight. During installation, the app has requested permission to geolocate the user [22], and during usage the app displays advertisements [17].

7.1 Collection of Data Not Required for Primary Purpose

The threat that an application collects data that is not required for its primary purpose is rated on the OWASP list as the sixth-highest risk, with high impact and very high frequency.

Assuming that the app stores phone identifiers and user locations in a database, a privacy violation can be expected to affect all users of the app. Correspondingly, the radar plot in Fig. 2 shows that the scale is 100% in all cases.

The sensitivity of the data can be classified as very high because geolocation data can allow inferences about behaviors, employment, health, and beliefs. This is especially the case if the app can run in the background and continue to record location data even when not in use.

The expectation of users is that a flashlight app does not collect, process, or share geolocation information [15]. However, because the example app does collect and process location data, the expectation differs from reality in two aspects.

The app can cause harm to individual users in terms of reputation damage, financial harm, distress, and a threat to life.

Reputational harm could be caused if, for example, it became public knowledge that an individual regularly located in the red light district. In the worst case, this could have severe consequences for employment or personal relationships. The typical user may not have visited particularly sensitive locations, and therefore the typical reputational harm would be much less severe.

Financial harm could be caused if an insurance company obtained the data, determined that some customers were regularly located at a fast-food restaurant, and decided that these customers should be paying higher insurance premiums. In the worst case, the financial harm could therefore equal the additional yearly cost of insurance to these users, whereas the typical user might not suffer any financial harm.

Harm in terms of distress could be caused if the data revealed a user's home location and patterns of their absence from home. As a result, users might become afraid of burglaries. In the worst case, a user might happen to be a stalking victim and may now have to relocate to avoid the stalker.

Harm as a threat to life could be caused if the app was used in a critical environment such as a warzone. In the worst case, a soldier using the flashlight app – maybe because the traditional flashlight has failed – might be targeted by an enemy drone or hand grenade because the app has leaked the soldier's location [21].

We can estimate the likelihood of a privacy violation in terms of exploitability for three cases. First, if the data has been collected but never used, an external adversary would be limited to sniffing network traffic, which would be a relatively difficult attack. Second, if the data has been leaked to the public, or if an insider adversary has misused their access privileges, then re-identification attacks are much easier to perform. Third, the data is most easily exploited if an adversary has additional information that allows to link phone identifiers to real user identities.

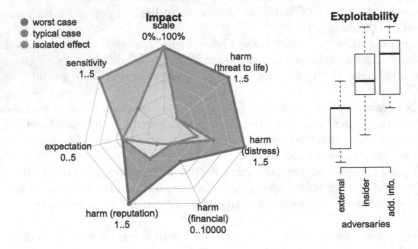

Fig. 2. Privacy risk caused by collection of data not required for primary purpose.

7.2 Sharing of Data with Third Party

The threat that an application shares data with a third party is the seventh-highest risk on the OWASP list, with high impact and high frequency. We assume that the flashlight app shares data with an advertising network, and that the ad network also uses device fingerprinting to track user activity across all of their applications. Figure 3 visualizes the impact and exploitability for this risk.

Similarly to the first example, the privacy violation can affect all users. However, in some cases, users may have fewer or less interesting interactions with their phones, or may be using ad blockers. In these cases, the scale in terms of the number of affected users would be reduced.

The sensitivity of the data can vary depending on the type of activities that a user performs. In the worst case, these can allow far-reaching inferences about the user's behaviors, purchases, and social life, but we expect that possible inferences in the typical case will be somewhat more limited.

The expectation of users is that a flashlight app does not collect, process, or share device fingerprints, all of which happen in this example. The reality therefore differs from expectation in three aspects.

The primary harms caused by sharing of data with a third party are two abstract types of harm: the violation of basic rights, and the loss of control over data. The violation of rights is relatively limited, with the exception of children, who are afforded more protection and whose rights are thus affected to a higher degree. In contrast, the loss of control is fairly severe because the user not only loses control over their data, but is also not informed of the data sharing.

The secondary harms caused by data sharing concern how the third party uses the data, and can be grouped in distress, financial harm, and reputational harm. Harm in terms of distress can be caused by targeted advertising, which is typically a rather low-level annoyance. However, device fingerprinting increases an individual's identifiability, which, in the worst case, might lead to the identification of specific individuals as criminals.

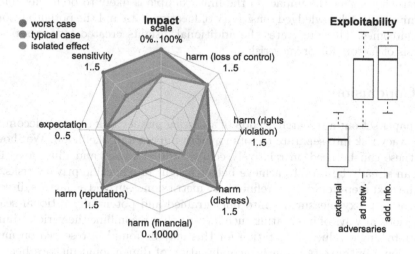

Fig. 3. Privacy risk caused by sharing of data with third party.

Financial harm can be caused by differential pricing, that is, the case when users are offered higher prices for products or services based on their profile.

Harm in terms of reputation damage can be caused, for example, if ads targeted to one user appeared on other users' devices that were falsely attributed to the targeted user, for example the spouse's phone. In a typical case, this may only ruin birthday surprises, but in the worst case could lead to more severe consequences for relationships or employment.

We can estimate the exploitability of this privacy risk for three types of adversaries. First, the ad network itself is similar to the insider adversary in the first example, but may be more easily able to exploit the risk because it already has additional data from tracking the user across applications. Second, an external adversary who can only sniff network traffic would be somewhat more limited than the external adversary in the first example because behavioral profiling data is less easily recognizable than geolocation data. Finally, an adversary with the ad network's knowledge plus additional information that can be linked to specific users is similarly powerful as in the first example.

7.3   Discussion

We have considered two significant and well-known abstract privacy risks in a concrete scenario, with significant differences on the outcomes in several dimensions of privacy risk as well as in the adversary profiles. Considering the separate factors and adversaries has led to a deeper understanding and more detailed representation of the risks. Quantitative information mostly remained on Likert scales, which means that not all questions we might ask of these scenarios, such as "which risk is worse", have received precise answers.

The OWASP list puts these risks at the same impact level. However, our analysis shows that the impact in the first example is likely to be higher due to the universally acknowledged sensitivity of location data and the potential worst-case outcomes. This illustrates the additional insights created by our separate analysis of factors for privacy risk.

8   Conclusion

This paper set out a research agenda of assessing privacy risk through decomposing privacy risk into separate factors for both impact and likelihood. We showed how these can be used on relatively coarse ordinal scales, and illustrated how this can already be used to achieve better insight into specific privacy risks.

The next step would be to refine these metrics, measuring the factors directly, or through proxy measures – into finer-grained and potentially rational scales; and to look at ways of integrating such metrics that recombine the various dimensions into single values. Inspiration for this may be found in research on multi-dimensional optimization. Such recombination of dimensional metrics becomes essential for several of the potential uses of privacy risk measurement that we indicated above.

The spectrum of metrics that may arise from such refinements and combinations of elementary measurements is likely to be rich. This means that *validation* of the alternatives becomes essential, in the first place through considering multiple extensive scenarios with rich collections of privacy risks, for example in the contexts of smart cities or educational data analytics. It has been shown that the strength of privacy metrics can differ between scenarios, and that many metrics have weaknesses at least in some scenarios [27].

There are also mathematical criteria for evaluating privacy metrics. One of these is monotonicity, i.e. that metrics should indicate lower privacy for stronger adversaries [27]. In addition, it may be helpful to calibrate new privacy risk metrics against a database of cases with known privacy risk, for example past cases where the impact is not speculative anymore, in particular with regard to privacy expectation and non-financial harm.

Finally, as with all rigorous methods supporting systems development, we should also take an economical aspect into account. In privacy risk measurement, we should avoid the false economy of accuracy, noting that "the time cost of accuracy quite often outweighs the benefits for the organization" [4]. The GDPR should increase the uptake of privacy impact assessment in general, but it should not lead to a perception of the process as so complex that it becomes a compliance tool for which cutting corners is desirable.

Acknowledgment. This work was supported by the UK Engineering and Physical Sciences Research Council (EPSRC) grant EP/P006752/1. We thank Lee Hadlington, Richard Snape, and the expert participants of our workshop on "Privacy risk: harm, impact, assessment, metrics" in January 2018 for their thoughts and discussions.

References

1. Albakri, A., Boiten, E., de Lemos, R.: Risks of sharing cyber incident information. In: 1st International Workshop on Cyber Threat Intelligence Management (CyberTIM) (2018, to appear)
2. Boiten, E.: What is the unit of security? (2016). FOSAD Summer School 2016. http://www.sti.uniurb.it/events/fosad16/Programme.html
3. Brooks, S., Garcia, M., Lefkovitz, N., Lightman, S., Nadeau, E.: An introduction to privacy engineering and risk management in federal systems. Technical report NIST IR 8062, National Institute of Standards and Technology, Gaithersburg, MD, January 2017. https://doi.org/10.6028/NIST.IR.8062
4. Calder, A., Watkins, S.: IT Governance: An International Guide to Data Security and ISO27001/ISO27002. Kogan Page, London (2015)
5. Cavoukian, A.: Privacy by design: the 7 foundational principles (2011). https://www.ipc.on.ca/wp-content/uploads/Resources/7foundationalprinciples.pdf
6. Commission Nationale de l'Informatique et des Libertés: Methodology for privacy risk management: How to implement the data protection act (2012). https://www.goo.gl/o3aN85
7. Commission Nationale de l'Informatique et des Libertés: Privacy impact assessment (PIA) 1: Methodology (2018). https://www.cnil.fr/sites/default/files/atoms/files/cnil-pia-1-en-methodology.pdf
8. Commission Nationale de l'Informatique et des Libertés: Privacy impact assessment (PIA) 3: Knowledge bases (2018). https://www.cnil.fr/sites/default/files/atoms/files/cnil-pia-3-en-knowledgebases.pdf

9. Deng, M., Wuyts, K., Scandariato, R., Preneel, B., Joosen, W.: A privacy threat analysis framework: supporting the elicitation and fulfillment of privacy requirements. Requirements Eng. **16**(1), 3–32 (2011). https://doi.org/10.1007/s00766-010-0115-7

10. Eckhoff, D., Wagner, I.: Privacy in the smart city - applications, technologies, challenges and solutions. IEEE Commun. Surv. Tutorials **20**(1), 489–516 (2018). https://doi.org/10.1109/COMST.2017.2748998

11. European Parliament and Council of the European Union: Regulation (EU) 2016/679 of the European Parliament and of the Council of 27 April 2016 on the protection of natural persons with regard to the processing of personal data and on the free movement of such data (General Data Protection Regulation). https://eur-lex.europa.eu/legal-content/EN/TXT/?uri=uriserv: OJ.L_.2016.119.01.0001.01.ENG&toc=OJ:L:2016:119:TOC

12. Evans, K.: Vidal-hall and risk management for privacy breaches. IEEE Secur. Priv. **13**(5), 80–84 (2015). https://doi.org/10.1109/MSP.2015.94

13. Information Commissioner's Office: Data Protection Impact Assessments (DPIAs) (2018). https://ico.org.uk/for-organisations/guide-to-the-general-data-protection-regulation-gdpr/data-protection-impact-assessments-dpias/

14. Information Commissioner's Office (ICO): Guide to the General Data Protection Regulation (GDPR), May 2018. https://ico.org.uk/for-organisations/guide-to-the-general-data-protection-regulation-gdpr/

15. Lin, J., Amini, S., Hong, J.I., Sadeh, N., Lindqvist, J., Zhang, J.: Expectation and purpose: understanding users' mental models of mobile app privacy through crowd-sourcing. In: Proceedings of the 2012 ACM Conference on Ubiquitous Computing, pp. 501–510. ACM, Pittsburgh (2012)

16. Liu, K., Terzi, E.: A framework for computing the privacy scores of users in online social networks. ACM Trans. Knowl. Discov. Data **5**(1), 6:1–6:30 (2010). https://doi.org/10.1145/1870096.1870102

17. Meng, W., Ding, R., Chung, S.P., Han, S., Lee, W.: The price of free: privacy leakage in personalized mobile in-app ads. In: NDSS. Internet Society (2016). https://doi.org/10.14722/ndss.2016.23353

18. National Institute of Standards and Technology (NIST): Guide for Conducting Risk Assessments. NIST Special Publication 800-30 r1, September 2012. https://doi.org/10.6028/NIST.SP.800-30r1

19. Nissenbaum, H.: Privacy as contextual integrity. Wash. L. Rev. **79**, 119 (2004)

20. Open Web Application Security Project: OWASP Risk Rating Methodology (2018). https://www.owasp.org/index.php/OWASP_Risk_Rating_Methodology

21. Pérez-Peña, R., Rosenberg, M.: Strava Fitness App Can Reveal Military Sites, Analysts Say. https://www.nytimes.com/2018/01/29/world/middleeast/strava-heat-map.html

22. SnoopWall: Flashlight apps threat assessment report (2014). https://lintvwish.files.wordpress.com/2014/10/flashlight-spyware-appendix-2014.pdf

23. Solove, D.J.: A taxonomy of privacy. Univ. Pennsylvania Law Rev. **154**(3), 477–564 (2006). https://doi.org/10.2307/40041279

24. Stahl, F., Burgmair, S.: OWASP Top 10 Privacy Risks Project (2017). https://www.owasp.org/index.php/OWASP_Top_10_Privacy_Risks_Project

25. Stevens, S.S.: On the theory of scales of measurement. Science **103**(2684), 677–680 (1946)

26. Sweeney, L.: k-anonymity: a model for protecting privacy. Int. J. Uncertainty Fuzziness Knowl. Based Syst. **10**(05), 557–570 (2002)

27. Wagner, I.: Evaluating the strength of genomic privacy metrics. ACM Trans. Priv. Secur. **20**(1), 2:1–2:34 (2017). https://doi.org/10.1145/3020003
28. Wagner, I., Eckhoff, D.: Technical privacy metrics: a systematic survey. ACM Comput. Surv. (CSUR) **51**(3) (2018)

Bootstrapping Online Trust: Timeline Activity Proofs

Constantin Cătălin Drăgan$^{(\boxtimes)}$ and Mark Manulis

Surrey Centre for Cyber Security, University of Surrey, Guildford, UK
c.dragan@surrey.ac.uk, mark@manulis.eu

Abstract. Establishing initial trust between a new user and an online service, is being generally facilitated by centralized social media platforms, i.e., Facebook, Google, by allowing users to use their social profiles to prove "trustworthiness" to a new service which has some verification policy with regard to the information that it retrieves from the profiles. Typically, only static information, e.g., name, age, contact details, number of friends, are being used to establish the initial trust. However, such information provides only weak trust guarantees, as (malicious) users can trivially create new profiles and populate them with static data fast to convince the new service.

We argue that the way the profiles are used over (longer) periods of time should play a more prominent role in the initial trust establishment. Intuitively, verification policies, in addition to static data, could check whether profiles are being used on a regular basis and have a convincing footprint of activities over various periods of time to be perceived as more trustworthy.

In this paper, we introduce *Timeline Activity Proofs* (TAP) as a new trust factor. TAP allows online users to manage their timeline activities in a privacy-preserving way and use them to bootstrap online trust, e.g., as part of registration to a new service. In our model we do not rely on any centralized social media platform. Instead, users are given full control over the activities that they wish to use as part of TAP proofs. A distributed public ledger is used to provide the crucial integrity guarantees, i.e., that activities cannot be tampered with retrospectively. Our TAP construction adopts standard cryptographic techniques to enable authorized access to encrypted activities of a user for the purpose of policy verification and is proven to provide *data confidentiality* protecting the privacy of user's activities and *authenticated policy compliance* protecting verifiers from users who cannot show the required footprint of past activities.

1 Introduction

Social interactions have always been guided by the trust between the parties involved. The problem with setting initial trust arises when there exists no pre-established relationship between the entities. In this case they need to trust some third party to facilitate the initial communication.

© Springer Nature Switzerland AG 2018
J. Garcia-Alfaro et al. (Eds.): DPM 2018/CBT 2018, LNCS 11025, pp. 242–259, 2018.
https://doi.org/10.1007/978-3-030-00305-0_18

In the online environment, many existing social media platforms, e.g., Facebook, Google, LinkedIn, act as identity providers for their users and offer what is called a *social login* service. This service, often realised based on the Open ID Connect framework [14], is widely used as a trust anchor upon the initial registration of a new user to an online service, and can also be used for subsequent authentication procedures. As part of the social login, a user can authorize other parties, e.g., mobile applications, online services, to access data kept in the user's social profile such as contact information, number of connections, posts, comments, photographs, etc.

At the moment, upon registration, many applications and online services are using only static data such as the user's name, age, contact details, total number of connections/friends, etc. The initial trust is thus established through a limited snapshot of the profile. This, however, offers only weak trust guarantees. Due to the ease of setting up social profiles, only little time would be needed to setup a "fake" profile and populate it with snapshot data to satisfy the checks that an online service performs on new users. The main reason is that such snapshots lack the historic perspective and cannot be used to decide whether a profile has been used frequently over a longer period of time.

One way to reduce the possibility of creating fake profiles fast is to consider the longevity and frequency of the profile's online interaction. This can be done by looking into the user's *timeline activities* such as posts, comments, photographs, and other interactions, and using them as an additional trust factor. There are, however, a number of privacy challenges associated with timeline activities in existing centralized social networks. First, users typically do not have full control over which activities can be accessed by authorised third parties. The access is defined by the settings of the social login provider and is often based on the "all-or-nothing" sharing approach. Users would be forced to directly modify their timeline, e.g., remove some of their activities, to be able to restrict what type of information they wish to release to third parties. More importantly, users are not aware of the amount of information that is stored or shared by the social service provider. After the Cambridge Analytica scandal [11], Facebook offered a better understanding about the data they collect [17], i.e., the received and declined friend requests, entire conversations or files exchanged via the Facebook messenger, and history of calls and messages on mobile phones. There is also the lack of transparency over the information which third parties acquire from the social service provider [16].

The above shows a more general problem with centralized social services for using timeline activities to facilitate online trust establishment, namely the need to trust the social service provider to protect the privacy of user's activities. The lack of trust naturally leads to the following question: *Can timeline activities be fully controlled by the users (without reliance on any centralized service provider) and used as an additional trust factor in online interactions?*

The main challenge behind putting users in full control of their activities is the integrity. Note that in order to be used as a trust factor that reduces the risk of fast creation of fake profiles it is important to guarantee that activities cannot be tampered with. In case of centralized social services, the integrity of the timeline activities is guaranteed by the social service provider and in most cases users are not allowed to introduce new activities retrospectively, but can still remove them if needed. A decentralized system where timeline activities are fully controlled by the users would need to achieve similar guarantees with respect to their integrity.

Distributed public ledgers can be a solution, such that users can keep footprints of their timeline activities, and authorize third parties to access them. The integrity of activities would be ensured by the properties of the ledger that acts as an append-only list, and where previous activities can be updated by introducing new activities that would be linked to them. The ability of users to remove an activity depends on how the data is stored and how it is linked with the ledger. We anticipate a hybrid approach, where sensitive data will be encrypted and stored in an external database, such that hashes to this encrypted data are committed to the public ledger.

Such a system would enable users to authorize third parties to access their activities at any level of granularity and over different periods of time, thus offering higher flexibility to define verification policies.

Our Contribution. In this paper we propose *Timeline Activity Proofs* (TAP) allowing users to establish trust with online parties based on user's activities and without relying on any centralized service provider. TAP can be used as a building block that adds a new trust factor—timeline activities—to an online trust establishment process. TAP keeps the user's timeline activities by storing pairs of (time, entry) in a distributed public ledger, with the user computing the entry from the activity, and the ledger appending a timestamp prior to recording it. A stored entry can contain public descriptors of the activity, i.e., name and additional keywords (tags), and a ciphertext of the actual activity data. Furthermore, the entry is linked to the user who owns the activity via a digital signature. TAP uses symmetric encryption to preserve privacy of the activity data. A dedicated key management ensures that independent symmetric keys are pseudo-randomly derived for each activity record. Such key derivation approach also enables granular disclosure of activities to verifiers as part of the proof protocol that is performed between the user and the verifier on input of a public activity-based verification policy. For the proofs in TAP we define two security properties: *data confidentiality*, an indistinguishability property protecting privacy of the activity data from unauthorised access, and *authenticated policy compliance*, a soundness property ensuring that only legitimate owners of activities can use them for proofs and that verification policies can be passed only if the user has committed suitable activities that can satisfy them into the public ledger.

Related Work. Prior works have also focused on ensuring privacy in social networks, by following two main directions in eliminating the need for a central service provider. The first by distributing the functionalities of the social network, e.g., Safebook [5] that provides a distributed privacy-preserving social media platform. The second by realizing diverse functionalities of the centralized social network in a distributed manner using cryptographic techniques [1,9]. Both of these approaches (and specifically their realization) are focused on achieving privacy for the user and his data, and less on the user's behavior. This has integrity implication for ensuring trust, as users can alter at any time their activity and make any claim they wish, i.e., in Safebook [5] integrity means protection against unauthorized tampering, with the user being authorized at any time to change his data.

A concept for establishing initial trust based on activities is the approach used by China's Social Credit System, called Sesame Credit [13]. There, the social activities of an individual are used to compute a "social score" that is used as a trust factor in the online environment. However, this is done without any privacy and under the control of a central authority where the user has no control of which social activities are stored.

2 Modeling Timeline Activity Proofs

2.1 Entities and Their Roles

Users. Each *user* owns a digital identity, that we model by using a secret-public key pair $(\mathsf{sk}, \mathsf{pk})$. The public key pk is used as the public identifier in our system, and any statement made by a user will be accompanied by this public key. They can create multiple digital identities by generating multiple secret-public key pairs.

Users are in charge of submitting their online activities, and can do so with any of the digital identities they posses. Furthermore, they have full control over which activities would be submitted, and what information should they include.

Users create activities that are stored in a ledger. Later, they would be used to prove statements about the users that submitted them. These activities are bound to users via public keys and appropriate authenticators. When an activity is added to the ledger, a timestamp with the time of the submission is appended to it; the user has no control over this time. Later, this time can be used as historic evidence of users performing these actions at a particular time.

In practice, users can be ordinary people, businesses (online shops, services, etc.), or any other organizations with an online presence.

Public Ledger. We use a distributed public ledger to maintain a list of activities. The ledger is assumed trusted, and offers protection for the integrity of the data. This core functionality of the ledger is modeled by considering an *append-only list*. Moreover, the types of entries that can be introduced are restricted to a clear entry format that has to be respected, via a validation mechanism for the data in the entry.

The ledger is tasked with maintaining the timeline for the data. More precisely, the ledger will have a *tamper-proof time mechanism*, and add timestamps to each entry. The method for registering time to each entry is simplified by assuming there exists no delay between the time an entry is received and the time it gets added.

In its essence a public ledger is just a secure append-only database. This narrow view of the storage format, allows for more complex search queries. One can define a search mechanism that considers the certain constraints on the information from the entry and the time it was added. Then, apply this search to all entries in an efficient manner, and extract only those that satisfy the search condition.

Formally, the public ledger $\mathsf{PL}(\mathsf{data}, \mathsf{val}, \mathsf{clock})$ = $(\mathsf{Setup}, (\mathsf{GetTime}, \mathsf{GetInterval}), \mathsf{Append}, \mathsf{Search})$ consists of an information type data, an evaluation mechanism val for the validity of the information, an internal clock, and the following algorithms:

- $\mathsf{Setup}(\lambda)$: pp. Given as input the security parameter λ, it generates a list of public parameters pp that contains *an empty append-only list* for storing entries. In addition, it initializes the clock.
- $(\mathsf{GetTime}, \mathsf{GetInterval})$: (time, i). $\mathsf{GetTime}()$ outputs the current time value of clock. $\mathsf{GetInterval}(\mathsf{time})$ returns the interval i for a given time.
- $\mathsf{Append}(\mathsf{data})$: $(\mathsf{time}, \mathsf{data}) \cup \{\bot\}$. Given some data as input, it returns either an entry $(\mathsf{time}, \mathsf{data})$ that has been registered in the append-only list, or an error symbol $\bot$. First, it evaluates data based on the val mechanism, and aborts with $\bot$ if it fails. Then, it calls $\mathsf{time} \leftarrow \mathsf{GetTime}()$, creates an entry $(\mathsf{time}, \mathsf{data})$ and appends it to the append-only list. If this last operation succeeds, it returns the entry, otherwise it returns the same error symbol $\bot$.
- $\mathsf{Search}(Q)$: L. Given a search query Q, it returns a (possibly empty) list of valid entries L from the ledger that satisfy the search conditions. The search query Q can depend on the information in data and its time.

Remark 1 (Instantiations). There are a number of existing implementations for distributed public ledgers with the most notable being *Bitcoin* [12] and *Ethereum* [18]. Both offer a secure timestamping system that records the time when each entry was processed. The search functionality is not native to these systems, but recent results, i.e., smartbit [15], do offer a method for searching. However, these two solutions impose a limitation on the size of the data that can be stored.

Public Ledger with External Database. In general, a public ledger offers an idealized approach for the integrity of data, with no method of data removal, even for the user who submitted that data. In practice, one would like to consider scenarios where users would want to remove their activity data. In light of this, it is natural to apply a hybrid approach with the data being stored in a separate (distributed) database, and use periodic commitments, similar to the approach in [7] suggested for decentralized anonymous credentials. The link between the records in the database and the entries in the ledger can be maintained by a unique id $\mathsf{rec_{id}}$ of an activity record. We can extend the definition of public ledgers to consider an external (distributed) database with records of the form $(\mathsf{rec_{id}}, \mathsf{data})$, and adapt the format for the entries in the ledger to consider commitments to that record: $(\mathsf{time}, \mathsf{rec_{id}}, \mathsf{H}(\mathsf{data}, \mathsf{rec_{id}}))$, where H is a cryptographic hash function. The following changes to the algorithms defined for the public ledger would account for the use of the database: Setup, in addition to initialization of the ledger, would also initialize the database; Append would record the data in the database, prior to adding its commitment to the ledger; and Search would first look in the database, and then filter invalid records based on the commitments in the ledger. The following algorithm would then allow users to remove their activity data from the database:

- Remove(data) : $rec_{id} \cup \{\perp\}$. If the record $(rec_{id}, data)$ has been removed from the database it returns rec_{id}; otherwise it returns the error symbol $\perp$.

Remark 2 (Time Delays). The time a data entry is recorded in the ledger, can be used to construct a correct timeline that later can be used to evaluate statements about the user. Due to how current ledgers are implemented there exists a delay between the time a transaction is sent and the time it is added to the ledger, even more so in the case of hybrid approaches. This time difference may lead to situations where statements that should hold (based on the time they were submitted) would not.

One can deal with this situation by first defining a fixed bound on the delay that one may expect when submitting entries to the ledger. Then, either relax the verification policy to consider time intervals for activities (that may depend on this delay) instead of a fixed time, or consider two timestamps with one provided by the user and an other introduced by the ledger. For the latter solution, we can include verification over the difference between these two timestamps w.r.t the expected delay.

Verifiers. *Verifiers* can define policies over timeline activities. Through interaction with a user a verifier can check whether this user satisfies their policy based on the user's activities submitted to the ledger. First, the verifier extracts from the ledger records that they deem relevant for their verification, i.e., based on the type of activity, the time it was submitted, and user's public key. Then, they request authorization from the user to open these entries and assert if they satisfy the verifier's policy.

2.2   Modeling Timeline Activities

Timed Activities. Activities model online actions performed by a user. They serve as historic evidence of trust, and are defined based on the following template:

$$\langle pk, atime, aname, count, adata, [tags] \rangle$$

- pk is the public identity of the user who created this activity;
- atime is the time the activity was submitted;
- aname describes the type of activity created, e.g. *photo, address, email*. They are predefined and each user can select only one type for each activity.

- count identifies an activity among other activities of the same type submitted within the same time interval;
- adata is the actual activity data. This information is never added directly to the ledger, only an encrypted version, denoted cdata, is added;
- [tags] is an optional field that introduces additional information not captured by the name of activity. It is a set of name-value pairs (tname, tvalue), e.g., a photo may contain the tags $\{(people, \text{John}), (location, \text{New York}), (date, 2017\text{-}01\text{-}01)\}$.

Remark 3. In our TAP construction the tags remain in clear. This feature allows verifiers to search more efficiently and identify which entries in the ledger could be used for verification. Further extensions may include symmetric searchable encryption techniques, e.g., [4], to additionally protect the privacy of the tags.

The activities must follow a predefined public format that contains the set of allowed activity names aname $\in$ ANames, and the set of optional permitted tag names tname $\in$ TNames. Such format is needed for independent formulation of verification policies.

Each activity can uniquely be identified by a tuple (pk, atime, aname, count), with count being a unique counter value assigned to activities of the name type aname in the time interval GetInterval(atime), for the user pk.

Activities can be separated based on the number of occurrences of the same type that the user can create:

- *static.* This type of activity should appear once, e.g., date of birth, name at birth, unique social security number, etc.
- *dynamic.* There is no restriction on the number of activities of this type, e.g., posting pictures on Facebook, change of email or post address, etc.

Policies and Verification of Timeline Activities. Activities are submitted with the purpose of building some historic evidence that would later be used to prove certain statements about their owners. This verification is modeled using a *policy* Ψ over a set of activities A, and outputs whether they satisfy Ψ, i.e., $\Psi(A) = 1$. The policy Ψ is not specific to any particular user, and doesn't use the pk component of the activity.

We consider two categories of policies based on the information required from the input activities:

- *meta-data policy*, where only information from the public components of the activities, i.e., the name, time, counter, and tags, used to evaluate the policy; and
- *data-dependent policy*, where information from the actual data of the activities is required, in addition to some of the meta-data.

The former type of policy can be easily evaluated by verifiers regardless the information contained in the data. While the latter can only be evaluated with an evaluation mechanism over that activity data, i.e., directly checking whether a photograph contains certain elements/keywords. We assume the policy includes such mechanism.

Example 1. Consider an online method that verifies the documents needed for opening a bank account, before setting an in-person interview. Some of the requirements include a valid identification document, i.e., passport or id card, and the address with a proof of living there for the past 3 months. The user pk_U that applies to this verification on May 2017, has the following activities stored in the ledger that could be used.

$$< pk_U, 2017\text{-}01\text{-}01T01\text{:}01\text{:}01, \text{id card}, \ldots >$$
$$< pk_U, 2017\text{-}01\text{-}02T03\text{:}04\text{:}05, \text{utility bill}, \ldots >$$
$$< pk_U, 2017\text{-}02\text{-}03T04\text{:}05\text{:}06, \text{utility bill}, \ldots >$$
$$< pk_U, 2017\text{-}03\text{-}04T05\text{:}06\text{:}07, \text{utility bill}, \ldots >$$

The verifier extracts these entries form the ledger by looking at the public key of the user, and the activity name and time. Then, interacts with the user to obtain the authorization needed to see the information from the id card and bills. If he can confirm the bills are under the user's real name (obtained from the id card), and that the address on those bills is the same as the one the user has provided, the verification succeeds (returns true) and the verifiers makes an appointment for this user.

2.3 Linking Timeline Activities with the Public Ledger

We map the abstract ledger to the type of information required to store user activities, and specify the condition that define validity of data. Entries in the ledger contain plain information like user, activity type, counter, the optional tags, and a ciphertext of the activity data. Every entry is also accompanied by an authenticator to certify that the entry has been submitted by the user pk. In our construction we use digital signatures as authenticators. The validity check ensures that the authenticator can be verified with the public key.

- data = (pk, aname, count, cdata, [tags], σ) with pk the user public key, aname the type of activity, count the counter for the same type of activity, cdata the encrypted version of adata, [tags] the optional tags, and σ the authenticator that this submitted activity belongs to user pk.
- val(pk, aname, count, cdata, [tags], σ) returns true if the authenticator σ verifies for the statement (aname, count, cdata, [tags]) using pk; otherwise it returns false.

To make the entries in the ledger consistent with the format of activities, described in Sect. 2.2, we view the components (time, data) of an entry as

$$(pk, time, aname, count, cdata, [tags], \sigma).$$

Typically, verifiers that evaluate a policy for users are assumed to already have the relevant inputs through some prior interaction with the user. Due to the outsourcing of data by the user to the ledger, we have a search mechanism allowing the policy verifier to extract needed information. We model the ledger as a database and use queries to search for entries that satisfy conditions used in the policy. These queries are generated based on the conditions the policy imposes over the activities. The conditions in the query can only look at the following components of an activity: public key, name, time, counter, and tags. The output of this type of search is more general than the one described by the conditions in the policy. The user is then tasked with providing a proof that a subset of those entries (that the verifier has found in the ledger) contain activities that satisfy the policy. We detail in the next section how our model of TAP realizes this.

Example 2. Consider the policy Ψ used in Example 1, and a public ledger that contains entries $(\mathsf{pk}, \mathsf{atime}, \mathsf{aname}, \mathsf{count}, \mathsf{cdata}, [\mathsf{tags}])$. We define our search query as a *select* command that looks for the latest entries that have the user's public key, an activity name in {id card, passport}, and 3 activities that point to a fixed address in the last 3 months. As the address can be realized by a number of different activities, we need to look for entries that contain { phone bill, utility bill, tax ...}.

2.4   Timeline Activity Proofs: Definition

Definition 1 (Timeline Activity Proofs). TAP = (Setup, KGenU, SubmitU, IProofU, IProofV) *with access to* PL(data, val) *defined in Sect. 2.3, consists of the following algorithms:*

- Setup(λ) : pp. *This algorithm is run by a trusted third-party and generates all public parameters required by the system. This includes the predefined activity names* ANames, *and tag names* TNames. *Furthermore, it calls* PL.Setup *to initialize the ledger and create an empty append-only list, and start the clock.*
- KGenU(pp) *is a user run algorithm that returns either a valid secret-public key pair* (sk, pk), *or an error symbol* $\perp$ *to symbolize that it failed. It creates locally a secret-public key pair* (sk, pk). *The term secret key is used generically to contain all secret information that the user would require in the system, i.e. signing keys and the seed for activity based encryption key derivation. Moreover, it is possible for users to call this algorithm multiple times and register multiple public identities/pks that can be used in the system.*
- SubmitU(pp, sk, (aname, adata, [tags])) *is an algorithm run by user* (sk, pk) *that wants to submit the activity* (aname, adata, [tags]), *to the public ledger* PL. *It returns either an entry* (pk, atime, aname, count, cdata, [tags], σ) *that has been successfully added to* PL, *or an error symbol* $\perp$ *if the submission failed. If required, there may exist some prior interaction with the ledger* PL, *where the user could for instance synchronize the time or authenticate to the system. The user performs the following steps. First, he computes the counter* count *based on the activity name and time, an encryption* cdata *of* adata, *and the authenticator* σ. *Then, following an successful interaction with* PL *by calling* Append(pk, aname, count, cdata, [tags], σ) *at time* atime, *an entry is added to the ledger. Without loss of generality we can trivially extend this algorithm*

to take as input a list of activities, each generating individual entries in the ledger.

- IProof *is an interactive protocol between a user* (sk, pk) *and a verifier to check whether the user satisfies the policy* Ψ. *Both parties have access to* PL, *and can easily search and extract information from the public ledger.*
    - IProofU(pp, sk, Ψ) *is an algorithm run by the user that interacts with* IProofV *to authenticate the user and prove its compliance with the policy* Ψ. *The algorithm completes successfully with* succ *or aborts with* abort.
    - IProofV(pp, pk, Ψ) *is an algorithm run by a verifier to assess if the user with* pk *satisfies* Ψ. *It searches through the ledger, by calling* PL.Search(Q), *for a search query Q built from Ψ for user* pk. *Using the obtained list of valid entries, it interacts with* IProofU *to ensure the user proves that he satisfies the policy Ψ. The output of this algorithm is a boolean value that is set to true if the user can be authenticated and he satisfies the policy; and false otherwise.*

The system satisfies the following correctness property:

$$\langle \text{succ}, \text{true} \rangle \leftarrow \langle \text{IProofU}(\text{pp}, (\text{pk}, \text{sk}), \Psi), \text{IProofV}(\text{pp}, \text{pk}, \Psi) \rangle ,$$

that holds for any policy Ψ, any pp $\leftarrow$ Setup(λ), and any user (sk, pk) $\leftarrow$ KGenU(pp), if there exists A such that $\Psi(A) = 1$ and :

$$A = \left\{ \begin{array}{l|l} \text{(atime, aname, count,} & \text{user (sk, pk) has added entry} \\ \text{adata, [tags])} & \text{(pk, atime, aname, count, cdata, [tags], } \sigma) \\ & \text{to PL by making the call} \\ & \text{SubmitU(pp, sk, (aname, adata, [tags]))} \end{array} \right\} .$$

Remark 4 (TAP with external database). We can extend Definition 1 to account for the removal of the activity data by the user. For this we can introduce the algorithm Remove that calls PL.Remove(pk, aname, count, cdata, [tags], σ) defined in Sect. 2.1. Since the commitments to all records remain in the public ledger, users can also temporary remove their activity records from the external database if they do not want to delete them completely.

2.5   Security Properties

In this section we introduce the security properties TAP schemes should satisfy. They are centered around the confidentiality of activity data, and the policy verification of authenticated users.

Oracles for $\mathcal{A}$. The adversary $\mathcal{A}$ has access to the list of entries in the public ledger PL and can interact with it to add or search for entries. Furthermore, he has access to the functionalities of TAP and can submit activities in the name of some honest user, for which he does not know the secret key, and play the role of any of the participants in the interactive proof protocol. All oracles are based on the algorithms in PL and TAP:

- Append($\cdot$): It calls PL.Append($\cdot$), and returns its output;
- Search(Q): It calls PL.Search(Q), and returns its output;
- Cor(pk): It returns the sk correspond to the pk used in the two experiments;
- Submit($\cdot, \cdot, [\cdot]$): It returns the output of TAP.SubmitU(pp, sk, ($\cdot, \cdot, [\cdot]$)), for the user (sk, pk) generated in the main body of the two experiments;
- IProofU($\cdot$): The adversary plays the role of a malicious verifier in the interactive IProof protocol with an honest user - that calls TAP.IProofU(pp, sk, $\cdot$);
- IProofV($\cdot$): The adversary plays the role of a malicious prover in the interactive IProof protocol with an honest verifier - that calls algorithm TAP.IProofV(pp, pk, $\cdot$).

$Exp_{\mathcal{A},\text{TAP}}^{\text{dc},\beta}(\lambda)$

1:    pp $\leftarrow$ Setup(λ)

2:    (sk, pk) $\leftarrow$ KGenU(pp)

3:    (aname, adata$_1$, adata$_2$, [tags]) $\leftarrow \mathcal{A}_1^{\text{Append}(\cdot),\text{Search}(\cdot),\text{Submit}(\cdot),\text{IProofU}(\cdot)}$(pp, pk)

4:    (pk, atime, aname, count, cdata$_\beta$, [tags], σ_β) $\leftarrow$

       SubmitU(pp, sk, (aname, adata$_\beta$, [tags]))

5:    $\beta' \leftarrow \mathcal{A}_2^{\text{Append}(\cdot),\text{Search}(\cdot),\text{Submit}(\cdot),\text{IProofU}(\cdot)}$(atime, count, cdata$_\beta$, σ_β)

6:    **return** $\beta' \wedge \mathcal{A}$ did not call IProofU(pp, sk, Ψ) with

       (pk, atime, aname, count, cdata$_\beta$, σ_β, [tags]) $\in$ Search(Q)

       for Q - search query based on Ψ and pk

Fig. 1. Data confidentiality experiment

Data Confidentiality. A fundamental property of TAP is the *privacy of data* that ensures no information concerning the data of an activity is leaked by the entry in the ledger for that activity, except the information provided from the name, counter and tags assigned to it. This is formalized in Fig. 1, where we consider a PPT adversary $\mathcal{A}$ that is required to distinguish between two private data values by seeing an entry in the ledger of one of them. The activity data that is transformed in an entry, is independent of the adversary and we parametrize the experiment with a random bit β to mark this. Moreover, this entry is attributed to a user for which the adversary doesn't know the secret key. The adversary can use oracle access to submit activities in the name of this user, or ask for proofs for policies that do not contain the entry he is challenge on. This restriction is needed to remove trivial attacks where the adversary can win the game by asking for a policy that checks if there exists an entry that contains one of the private data. In addition to entries made for this user pk, the adversary can introduce in the ledger entries for other users which he controls (knows their secret key).

Definition 2 (Data Confidentiality). *A* TAP *scheme satisfies data confidentiality, if no PPT adversary $\mathcal{A}$ can distinguish between $Exp_{\mathcal{A},\mathsf{TAP}}^{dc,0}$ and $Exp_{\mathcal{A},\mathsf{TAP}}^{dc,1}$ defined in Fig. 1, i.e., the following advantage is negligible in λ:*

$$\mathsf{Adv}_{\mathcal{A},\mathsf{TAP}}^{dc} = \left| \Pr\left[Exp_{\mathcal{A},\mathsf{TAP}}^{dc,0}(\lambda) = 1\right] - \Pr\left[Exp_{\mathcal{A},\mathsf{TAP}}^{dc,1}(\lambda) = 1\right] \right|.$$

Authenticated Policy Compliance. This property ensures only authorized users can prove to an honest verifier they satisfy the verifier's policy. It requires the adversary $\mathcal{A}$ to "forge" this authorization by either *impersonating a user* that may satisfy the policy and for which the adversary doesn't know the secret key, or by *faking the evidence* for activities he did not put into the ledger (even if he knows the secret key). To evaluate if the adversary is capable of providing fake evidence when he does not satisfy the policy, we need to apply the policy over all activities that have been submitted for a single user. As the activity data is relevant in establishing if a policy is satisfied, we restrict the adversary to provide evidence only for policies that consider activities added by Submit. Furthermore, the policy that is verified must be valid, $\neg\Psi(\emptyset)$, that is it must not return true independent of the input. We formalize these conditions in Fig. 2, where we consider a PPT adversary that submits entries to the ledger and wins if he can convince an honest verifier to return true. Because of the interactive nature of the algorithm in IProof we restrict the adversary to not call the verification oracle IProofV in the same time an instance of IProofU is opened.

Definition 3 (Authenticated Policy Compliance). *A* TAP *scheme ensures authenticated policy compliance, if no PPT adversary $\mathcal{A}$ can win the experiment $Exp_{\mathcal{A},\mathsf{TAP}}^{apc}$ defined in Fig. 2, i.e., the following advantage is negligible in λ:*

$$\mathsf{Adv}_{\mathcal{A},\mathsf{TAP}}^{apc} = \Pr\left[Exp_{\mathcal{A},\mathsf{TAP}}^{apc}(\lambda) = 1\right].$$

3   Our TAP Construction

In this section we describe our general construction and analyze its security properties. We start with standard cryptographic primitives [10] that are used as building blocks, and the method to compute encryption keys that hide the activity data.

3.1   Building Blocks

Our construction relies on a *pseudo-random function* PRF : $\{0,1\}^\lambda \times \{0,1\}^* \to \{0,1\}^{poly(\lambda)}$ [8], and an *existentially unforgeable digital signature scheme* DS = (KGen, Sign, Verify) [6]. We rely further on a *symmetric encryption scheme* SE = (KGen, Enc, Dec) with two security requirements: *indistinguishability under chosen plaintext attack (IND-CPA)*, and *wrong-key detection (WKD)* [2]. The WKD property is not standard and has been introduced to bound the winning

$Exp^{apc}_{\mathcal{A},\text{TAP}}(\lambda)$

1 : $\text{pp} \leftarrow \text{Setup}(\lambda)$

2 : $(\text{sk}, \text{pk}) \leftarrow \text{KGenU}(\text{pp})$

3 : $\mathcal{A}^{\text{Append}(\cdot),\text{Search}(\cdot),\text{Cor}(\cdot),\text{Submit}(\cdot),\text{IProofU}(\cdot),\text{IProofV}(\cdot)}(\text{pp}, \text{pk})$

4 :   **return** $\mathcal{A}$ made a call to $\text{IProofV}(\cdot)$ with

      $\text{true} \leftarrow \text{IProofV}(\text{pp}, \text{pk}, \Psi) \wedge \neg\Psi(\emptyset) \wedge \mathcal{A}$ not running $\text{IProofU}(\cdot) \wedge$

$$\begin{pmatrix} \mathcal{A} \text{ did not call Cor(pk)} \vee \\ \forall\, e = (\text{pk}, \cdot, \cdot, \cdot, \cdot, [\cdot]) \in \text{Search}(Q), \text{ for } Q \text{ based on } \Psi \text{ and pk}, \\ \mathcal{A} \text{ did not not add } e \text{ using Append}(\cdot) \wedge \\ \neg\Psi(A) \text{ for } A = \{(\text{pk}, \text{atime}, \text{aname}, \text{count}, \text{adata}, [\text{tags}]) |\text{ for} \\ \text{entries added by Submit}(\cdot) \text{ to the ledger PL}\} \end{pmatrix}$$

Fig. 2. Authenticated policy compliance experiment

probability of an adversary in successfully decrypting a ciphertext with two different keys. More precisely, any efficient adversary has a negligible probability to win the game where he computes different keys $k \neq k'$ s.t. the expression $\text{Dec}(k', \text{Enc}(k, m)) \neq \bot$ holds, for all messages m. The WKD property is used in Lemma 2, see also Remark 6.

3.2 Key Management

Activities are submitted directly by users who control the type of information they add to the ledger. For each activity $(\text{pk}, \text{atime}, \text{aname}, \text{count}, \text{adata}, [\text{tags}])$, the activity data adata is private, and is never stored in plain. This component in the activity is encrypted with a symmetric encryption scheme SE before being appended to the ledger. The encryption keys are an important part of the policy verification proof, and as such the user is required to store them securely.

Our solution for key management is to use the PRF to derive the encryption keys on demand, and reduce the amount of storage space on the user's side. For each user, a random seed $s \in \{0,1\}^\lambda$ is chosen, and *time interval keys* $tk_i = \text{PRF}_s(\text{pk}, i)$ are derived for the time interval i first. These are then used to derive *activity type keys* $ak_j = \text{PRF}_s(tk_i, j)$ for some activity name aname_j in time interval i. Finally, the *activity record keys* $rk_k = \text{PRF}_s(ak_j, \text{count}_k)$ are derived and used by the user to encrypt the activity data. During the submission process of an activity (algorithm SubmitU in Fig. 3), first the time interval is defined by $i \leftarrow \text{PL.GetInterval}(\text{atime}_i)$, followed by the computation for the record key

$$rk_k = \text{PRF}_s(\text{PRF}_s(\text{PRF}_s(\text{pk}, i), \text{aname}_j), \text{count}_k),$$

given the activity $(\text{pk}, \text{atime}_i, \text{aname}_j, \text{count}_k, \text{adata}, [\text{tags}])$.

An interesting and useful feature of this key management approach is that all activity record keys are overwhelmingly unique. This is ensured by the pseudo-randomness of the PRF, and the uniqueness of the inputs.

3.3   Generic Construction

In the following we provide a high-level intuition behind our construction, which is specified in Figs. 3 and 4. A trusted third-party initializes the public ledger PL and creates public parameters which includes the initialization of the append-only list, and the clock. Moreover, he defines the set of allowed activity names and tags.

Users generate their own signing/verification key pair (sigk, pk) for the digital signature scheme DS. Additionally, they generate a seed s that is used to derive a time-dependent key hierarchy for submitting activities. The pk is used as public identifier for the user in the system, while sk = (sigk, s) should be stored securely. The user may have multiple identities in our system, by generating new signing keys and a new seed.

Activities (aname, adata, tags) are submitted directly by users who control what type of information is added to the ledger. Each data adata is stored encrypted with a unique key that follows the procedure described in the Sect. 3.2. To authenticate the activity, the user provides a signature before appending it to the ledger.

The verification of historic evidence is performed interactively between a user (sk, pk) with sk = (sigk, s) and a verifier w.r.t the policy Ψ. We formalize this interaction in Fig. 4, where both parties communicate over an authenticated and confidential channel. Both the user and the verifier have access to the public ledger PL. The verifier searches PL for entries that match the descriptors from the policy for this user, and returns false if any of them are invalid. Then, it sends to the user the list L obtained from the search with a fresh nonce c. The user checks if the list of entries he received is identical to what he has retrieved from the ledger, and aborts if they do not match. The user re-computes the activity record keys for the records in L, and gives them as part of the key set K to the verifier together with a signature over the nonce received. The verifier returns true, if upon successful decryption using the received keys the activities satisfy Ψ, and the signature verifies.

Remark 5 (Correctness). The correctness of TAP is ensured by the method in which activity record keys are computed. The keys derived upon submission of activity data in Line 6 of SubmitU, in Fig. 3, are identical with the activity record keys computed by the user in Fig. 4. Because the PL.Append in Line 9 of SubmitU in Fig. 3 calls internally atime' ← GetTime(), it is important that atime and atime' map to the same interval i.

3.4   Security Analysis

Lemma 1. *The* TAP *construction in Figs. 3 and 4 offers data confidentiality if* SE *is IND-CPA and* PRF *is pseudo-random.*

Setup(λ)	SubmitU(pp, (sigk, s), (aname, adata, [tags]))
1 : $D \leftarrow$ define ANames	1 : atime $\leftarrow$ PL.GetTime()
and TNames	2 : $i \leftarrow$ PL.GetInterval(atime)
2 : pp $\leftarrow$ PL.Setup(λ)	3 : $L \leftarrow$ PL.Search("all (pk, atime, aname, $\cdot$, $\cdot$, [$\cdot$])
3 : **return** (pp, D)	with $i \leftarrow$ PL.GetInterval(atime)")
	4 : **if** ($L = \emptyset$) **then** count $\leftarrow$ 0
KGenU(pp)	5 : **else** count $\leftarrow$ last counter from $L + 1$
1 : $s \leftarrow_\$ \{0,1\}^\lambda$	6 : $rk \leftarrow$ PRF$_s$(PRF$_s$(PRF$_s$(pk, i), aname), count)
2 : (sigk, pk) $\leftarrow$ DS.KGen(λ)	7 : cdata $\leftarrow$ SE.Enc(rk, adata)
3 : **return** ((sigk, s), pk)	8 : $\sigma \leftarrow$ DS.Sign(sigk, (aname, count, cdata, [tags]))
	9 : PL.Append(pk, aname, count, cdata, [tags], σ)

Fig. 3. The setup, user key generation, and submission of activities for TAP.

Proof. All ciphertexts in the ledger are encrypted with unique keys derived via PRF using unique public key-seed (pk, s) pair and a unique triple composed of the activity name, time frame, and counter. Using the pseudo-random property of PRF and the fact that s is kept secret from the adversary, we can be sure the adversary obtains only a negligible advantage, by just looking at entries in the ledger for this user pk.

Our construction provides this unique key per activity as proof in the interactive IProof protocol, when the adversary plays the role of a verifier and calls the oracle IProofU(pp, sk, $\cdot$, $\cdot$, [$\cdot$]). First, we show that the adversary has negligible advantage to obtain the key used for the challenge ciphertext - that encrypts adata$_\beta$.

Before the challenge, the adversary may call the IProofU oracle and ask for keys of (valid) entries in the ledger. Even if the adversary can predict what input the PRF will take, i.e., name, time and counter for an activity, $\mathcal{A}_1$ obtains only negligible information due to the pseudo-randomness property of PRF. The component $\mathcal{A}_2$ is restricted to not ask this exact key from the IProofU queries. Moreover, all subsequent proofs - keys, that may be linked to the key used to encrypt the challenge also produce a negligible advantage via the pseudo-randomness property of PRF. Therefore, the adversary only obtains a negligible advantage w.r.t the encryption key for the challenge.

We conclude this proof by using the IND-CPA security of the symmetric encryption scheme SE that encrypted the challenge, as the adversary doesn't have access to the encryption/decryption key.

Lemma 2. *The* TAP *construction in Figs. 3 and 4 ensures authenticated policy compliance, if* DS *is existentially unforgeable,* SE *is WKD, and* PRF *is pseudorandom.*

Proof. We upper bound the advantage of the adversary in winning this game by the following two probabilities, with all of them restricting the adversary

IProofU(pp, sk, Ψ) with sk = (sigk, s)	IProofV(pp, pk, Ψ)
$Q \leftarrow$ construct from Ψ and pk	$Q \leftarrow$ construct from Ψ and pk
	$L \leftarrow$ PL.Search(Q)
	$c \leftarrow_{\$} \{0,1\}^{poly(\lambda)}$
	for (pk, atime, aname, count, cdata, [tags], σ) $\in L$
	if $\neg$DS.Verify(pk, (aname, count, cdata, [tags]), σ)
	then return false
	$\xleftarrow{\quad c, L \quad}$
if ($L \neq$ PL.Search(Q)) then return abort	
$K \leftarrow \emptyset$	$A \leftarrow \emptyset$
for (atime, aname, count, cdata, [tags]) $\in L$ do	
$i \leftarrow$ PL.GetInterval(atime)	
$rk \leftarrow$ PRF$_s$(PRF$_s$(PRF$_s$(pk, i), aname), count)	
$K \leftarrow K \cup \{rk\}$	
$\sigma_P \leftarrow$ DS.Sign(sigk, (c, K)) $\xrightarrow{\quad S, \sigma_P \quad}$	
	for $0 \leq i \leq |L|$ do
	data $\leftarrow$ SE.Dec($K[i], L[i]$)
	$A \leftarrow A \cup \{atime, aname, data, [tags]\}$
return succ	return $\Psi(A) \wedge$ DS.Verify(pk, (c, K), σ_P)

Fig. 4. The interactive protocol IProof for TAP. It is assumed that the user and verifier are communicating over an authenticated and confidential channel.

not to run IProofU when running the particular instance of IProofV used in the experiment outcome:

- Exp_1: the adversary *convinces a honest verifier to return true when he doesn't ask for the secret key*. This is defined exactly as experiment in Fig. 2 where we remove the second part of the disjunction in the return.
- Exp_2: the adversary *convinces a honest verifier to return true when he doesn't satisfy the policy*. This is defined exactly as experiment in Fig. 2 where we remove the first part of the disjunction in the return.

Bound on Exp_1. The secret key of a user contains a signing key sigk and a seed s. We use the fact the adversary does not know sigk, and can not provide real signed messages with this key when impersonating the user. To convince the verifier to return true (on any adversarial policy) the adversary needs to sign the message that gives the encryption keys. This message is a new message in the system for which there should exists no signature, as it contains a fresh commitment given by IProofV. Therefore, the adversary must forge a signature and break the existential unforgeability of DS. To complete that reduction to the security of DS we are using the fact the adversary can not run a man-in-the-middle attack where he uses IProofU to create proofs for this verifier.

Bound on Exp_2. The adversary to "show" he satisfies a policy when in fact he doesn't, must claim that an entry corresponds to an activity different than the one he has actually submitted. This claim is with respect to the data in the activity, otherwise he would have directly satisfied the policy if the data was not required. More precisely, the adversary needs to provide a decryption key such that he obtains a valid decryption different from the one submitted. The WKD property of SE ensures that if the adversary uses a decryption key different from the one used to encrypt, then the ciphertext would not decrypt to anything valid. As such the adversary would need to compute a decryption key that coincides with the encryption key, and this is deemed improbable by the pseudo-randomness property of PRF.

Remark 6. While the wrong-key detection property is required for the proof of Lemma 2, we observe that in practice this requirement can be lifted. This is because, for current practical symmetric encryption schemes, e.g. AES based, if a different key is used, then the message would look random, and make it unlikely to obtain *something meaningful.* Therefore, the policy would not succeed given such random-looking messages.

4   Conclusion and Future Directions

Timeline Activity Proofs (TAP) proposed in this work allow users to store their online interactions and build a timeline of their activities. These can later be used by users to prove statements that consider past activities and by this increase the trustworthiness of their online identities (e.g. profiles). Additionally, we propose a construction that gives access to plain data to verifiers capturing today's method for social login. As a future research direction it would be interesting to see if TAP can be extended with functionalities that allow for certain statements to be proven without disclosing the decryption keys. This brings us closer to the zero-knowledge techniques used in *(decentralized) anonymous credentials* [3,7].

Another possible research direction is to consider a feedback mechanism. Currently, users self-issue activities and trust is ensured by the amount of information the user is providing. Using a feedback mechanism to rate these activities, e.g., the one used by Amazon, eBay to rate sellers, could increase the trust guarantees further.

Acknowledgements. Constantin Cătălin Drăgan and Mark Manulis were supported by the EPSRC project TAPESTRY (EP/N02799X).

References

1. Barth, A., Boneh, D., Waters, B.: Privacy in encrypted content distribution using private broadcast encryption. In: Di Crescenzo, G., Rubin, A. (eds.) FC 2006. LNCS, vol. 4107, pp. 52–64. Springer, Heidelberg (2006). https://doi.org/10.1007/11889663_4
2. Canetti, R., Tauman Kalai, Y., Varia, M., Wichs, D.: On symmetric encryption and point obfuscation. In: Micciancio, D. (ed.) TCC 2010. LNCS, vol. 5978, pp. 52–71. Springer, Heidelberg (2010). https://doi.org/10.1007/978-3-642-11799-2_4

3. Chaum, D.: Security without identification: transaction systems to make big brother obsolete. Commun. ACM **28**(10), 1030–1044 (1985)
4. Curtmola, R., Garay, J.A., Kamara, S., Ostrovsky, R.: Searchable symmetric encryption: improved definitions and efficient constructions. In: ACMCCS, pp. 79–88 (2006)
5. Cutillo, L.A., Molva, R., Strufe, T.: Safebook: a privacy-preserving online social network leveraging on real-life trust. IEEE Commun. Mag. **47**(12), 94–101 (2009)
6. Diffie, W., Hellman, M.E.: New directions in cryptography. IEEE Trans. Inf. Theory **22**(6), 644–654 (1976)
7. Garman, C., Green, M., Miers, I.: Decentralized anonymous credentials. In: NDSS (2014)
8. Goldreich, O., Goldwasser, S., Micali, S.: How to construct random functions. J. ACM **33**(4), 792–807 (1986)
9. Günther, F., Manulis, M., Strufe, T.: Cryptographic treatment of private user profiles. In: Danezis, G., Dietrich, S., Sako, K. (eds.) FC 2011. LNCS, vol. 7126, pp. 40–54. Springer, Heidelberg (2012). https://doi.org/10.1007/978-3-642-29889-9_5
10. Katz, J., Lindell, Y.: Introduction to Modern Cryptography, 2nd edn. CRC Press, Boca Raton (2014)
11. Matthew Rosenberg, N.C., Cadwalladr, C.: How Trump Consultants Exploited the Facebook Data of Millions, 17 March 2018. https://www.nytimes.com/2018/03/17/us/politics/cambridge-analytica-trump-campaign.html
12. Nakamoto, S.: Bitcoin: a peer-to-peer electronic cash system (2008)
13. Nguyen, C.: China might use data to create a score for each citizen based on how trustworthy they are, 26 October 2016. http://uk.businessinsider.com/china-social-credit-score-like-black-mirror-2016-10
14. OpenID Connect Framework. https://openid.net. Accessed 16 June 2018
15. Smartbit. https://www.smartbit.com.au. Accessed 18 June 2018
16. Symeonidis, I., Tsormpatzoudi, P., Preneel, B.: Collateral damage of Facebook Apps: an enhanced privacy scoring model. IACR Cryptology ePrint Archive, Report 2015/456
17. Tiku, N.: Facebook will make it easier for you to control your personal data, 28 March 2018. https://www.wired.com/story/new-facebook-privacy-settings
18. Wood, G.: Ethereum yellow paper (2014)

DPM Workshop: Private Data and Searches

Post-processing Methods for High Quality Privacy-Preserving Record Linkage

Martin Franke[✉], Ziad Sehili, Marcel Gladbach, and Erhard Rahm

Database Group, University of Leipzig, Leipzig, Germany
{franke,sehili,gladbach,rahm}@informatik.uni-leipzig.de

Abstract. Privacy-preserving record linkage (PPRL) supports the integration of person-related data from different sources while protecting the privacy of individuals by encoding sensitive information needed for linkage. The use of encoded data makes it challenging to achieve high linkage quality in particular for dirty data containing errors or inconsistencies. Moreover, person-related data is often dense, e.g., due to frequent names or addresses, leading to high similarities for non-matches. Both effects are hard to deal with in common PPRL approaches that rely on a simple threshold-based classification to decide whether a record pair is considered to match. In particular, dirty or dense data likely lead to many multi-links where persons are wrongly linked to more than one other person. Therefore, we propose the use of post-processing methods for resolving multi-links and outline three possible approaches. In our evaluation using large synthetic and real datasets we compare these approaches with each other and show that applying post-processing is highly beneficial and can significantly increase linkage quality in terms of both precision and F-measure.

Keywords: Record linkage · Post-processing · Privacy
Linkage quality

1 Introduction

Privacy-preserving record linkage (PPRL) is the task of identifying records across different data sources referring to the same real-world entity, without revealing sensitive or personal information [47]. In contrast to traditional record linkage (RL), PPRL has to protect sensitive data to ensure the privacy and confidentiality of the entities, usually representing persons [43]. PPRL techniques are required in many areas, for instance in medical and health care applications. A typical use case is the integration of patient-related data from different sources, i.e., hospitals, registries and insurance companies, to allow comprehensive analysis and research about certain diseases or treatments [13,23,25,29]. Other use cases for PPRL techniques include epidemiological or demographical studies as well as marketing analysis [47].

© Springer Nature Switzerland AG 2018
J. Garcia-Alfaro et al. (Eds.): DPM 2018/CBT 2018, LNCS 11025, pp. 263–278, 2018.
https://doi.org/10.1007/978-3-030-00305-0_19

To preserve the privacy of represented entities, PPRL techniques have to ensure that no personal identifiers or other sensitive information is revealed during or after the linkage process. For an adversary it should be impossible to identify a person or to infer any sensitive information, like a person's state of health. Therefore, the data needed for analysis, e.g., medical data, is separated from the data required for linkage. Record linkage is conducted by comparing commonly available attributes, called quasi-identifiers (QIDs), like first and last name or date of birth. Since such QIDs also contain private information, these attributes are encoded (masked) for PPRL to preserve privacy. Consequently, such data encodings have to be highly secure while still allowing linkage, i.e., they still have to enable efficient similarity calculations between records. Real-world data often contains errors or inconsistencies [15, 36]. Hence, encoding techniques for PPRL have to support approximate matching to achieve high linkage accuracy.

A high linkage quality is essential for practical applicability of PPRL, especially in the medical domain. Ideally, a PPRL approach should find all matches, despite possible data quality problems in the source databases. On the other hand, false matches should be strictly avoided, as otherwise (medical) conclusions based on incorrect assumptions could be made.

Classification models are used to decide whether a record pair represents a match or a non-match. For traditional RL sophisticated classification models based on supervised machine learning approaches, e.g., support vector machines or decision trees, can be used to achieve highly accurate linkage results [4]. Moreover, linkage results could be manually reviewed to increase final quality or to adjust parameter configurations. In contrast, currently most PPRL approaches only apply threshold-based classification based on a single threshold, as training data is usually not available in a privacy-preserving context [43]. In general, it is also not feasible to manually inspect actual QID values of records because this would give up part of the privacy. Finally, recent encoding techniques often aggregate all attribute values into a single binary encoding making it hard to deploy attribute-wise or rule-based classification [43, 47]. All these effects likely reduce linkage quality of PPRL, indicating the demand for refined classification techniques [8].

In this paper, we study post-processing methods for improving linkage quality of PPRL in terms of precision. By using simple threshold-based classification approaches, only low linkage accuracy is likely achieved in PPRL scenarios dealing with *dirty* or *dense* data. Dirty data such as missing or erroneous attribute values can lead to a low similarity between matching records that are thus easily missed with a higher similarity threshold. Another problem case are dense data where many non-matching records can have a high similarity. For example, members of a family often share the same last name and address leading to a high similarity for different persons. Datasets focusing on a specific city or region also tend to have many persons with similar addresses. For such dense data there can be many non-matching record pairs with a similarity above a fixed threshold.

A key drawback of classification approaches based on a single threshold is that they often produce multi-links, i.e., one record is linked (matched) to many records of another source, and moreover, each record pair exceeds the similarity threshold. But, assuming deduplicated source databases, each record can at most match to one record of another source. Hence, the linkage result should exclusively contain one-to-one links as otherwise precision is deteriorated. Therefore, we analyze methods that can be executed after any (threshold-based) classification to clean multi-links, i.e., to transform the linkage result such that only one-to-one links occur in the final result. In particular, we make the following contributions:

- We study three post-processing strategies for the cleaning of multi-links, or selection of match candidates respectively, to increase the overall linkage quality of PPRL, especially when dealing with dense or dirty data.
- We evaluate the different post-processing approaches using large synthetic and real datasets showing different data characteristics and difficulty levels.
- In our evaluation, we consider both linkage quality in terms of recall, precision and F-measure, as well as efficiency in terms of runtime.

In Sect. 2, we outline the basic PPRL process and discuss related work in the field of PPRL. Then, we formalize the multi-link cleaning problem that we want to address with post-processing (Sect. 3) and describe approaches for solving it (Sect. 4). In Sect. 5, we evaluate selected approaches in terms of quality and efficiency. Finally, we conclude.

2 Background and Related Work

In this section we describe the overall PPRL process and discuss related work.

2.1 PPRL Process

A PPRL pipeline contains multiple steps which are shown in Fig. 1. Following previous work, we assume a three-party protocol, where a (trusted) third party, called linkage unit (LU), is required [43]. The LU conducts the actual linkage of encoded records from two or more database owners (DBOs). While we focus on only two DBOs with their respective databases D_A and D_B the PPRL process can be extended to multiple DBOs. In the following, each step of the PPRL process is described and relevant techniques are discussed. It is assumed that general information and parameters are exchange in advance between the DBOs.

Data Pre-processing: At first, the source databases to be linked need to be pre-processed by the DBOs. Pre-processing includes deduplication, data cleaning and standardization. In each individual database, duplicate records may occur due to inconsistent or repetitive recording processes. Therefore, the DBOs have to internally link and deduplicate their databases to ensure that a record from one data source can only be linked to at maximum one record from another data

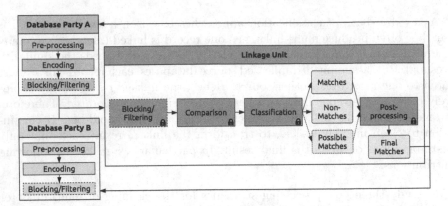

Fig. 1. Outline of the basic PPRL process under a three-party protocol. Steps in dotted boxes are optional. Steps with a lock symbol process encoded data.

source. Furthermore, data cleaning and standardization is required since real-world data often contain erroneous, missing, incomplete, inconsistent or outdated data [15]. Data cleaning techniques aim at curating or weakening such errors, e.g., by filling in missing data or removing unwanted values [4]. Moreover, different data sources often use different formats and structures to represent data. Hence, standardization techniques are used to overcome heterogeneity by transforming data into well-defined and consistent forms [36]. Ideally, all DBOs conduct the same pre-processing steps to reduce heterogeneity thereby facilitating high linkage quality. However, even extensive pre-processing may not resolve all quality issues, as inconsistencies, like contradicting or outdated values, are hard to detect.

Encoding: We focus on RL with the additional challenge to preserve the privacy of referenced entities. Consequently, each record needs to be encoded to protect sensitive data. A widely-used approach is to encode each record into a Bloom filter (BF) [43,47]. A BF [1,39,40] is a bit array of fixed size m where initially all bits are set to zero. k independent cryptographic hash functions are used to map a set of record features into the BF. Each hash function takes as input every feature from the feature set and produces a value in $[0, m-1]$. Then, the bits at the resulting k positions are set to one for every feature. The set of features can be extracted in several ways from the record attributes. In general, for each record attribute a function is defined, which takes as input the attribute value and outputs a set of feature values. Typically, all QID values of a record are represented as string and then split into a set of **q**-grams (substrings of length q), where q is equal for each attribute. Several BF variants have been proposed for PPRL to either improve quality [20,44,45] or privacy properties [8,35,38,40,41]. Multiple studies have analyzed attacks on BF variants and respective hardening techniques [5,24,26,27,35].

Blocking/Filtering: The trivial approach to link two databases is to compare every possible record pair of the two data sources. To overcome this quadratic complexity blocking or filtering techniques are used to reduce the number of record comparisons [4]. This is achieved by pruning record pairs not fulfilling defined blocking or filter criteria and are hence unlikely considered to be a match. The output of this step are candidate record pairs that need to be further compared. Blocking and filtering can be executed on encoded or uncoded data. Most privacy-preserving approaches perform blocking or filtering at the LU side on encoded data (bit vectors) [47]. State-of-the-art blocking techniques can significantly reduce the search space by applying blocking based on locality-sensitive hashing (LSH) [8, 21, 22] or performing filtering based on multibit-trees [3, 38] or pivot-based filtering for metric distance functions [42].

Comparison: Each candidate pair is compared in detail by using (binary) similarity measures, mainly the Jaccard or Dice similarity [43]. The output of this step are candidate pairs with their respective similarity score. The similarity score is a numerical value in $[0, 1]$ determining how similar two records are.

Classification: Most PPRL approaches use a single similarity threshold which is used to classify candidate record pairs into matches, i.e., records representing the same real-world entity, and non-matches [43]. A second threshold can be used to add a third class consisting of possible matches where no clear decision is possible. Another common approach is the probabilistic method developed by Fellegi and Sunter [4, 10].

Finally, the match result, e.g., the IDs of matching record pairs, is returned to the DBOs. However, by using simple threshold-based classification approaches, multi-links occur in the final match result. Since commonly deduplicated databases are assumed, the desired outcome should be a linkage result consisting of only one-to-one links between records. We address this problem by introducing a post-processing step after classification to clean multi-links in the linkage result. The main problem in the post-processing step is to decide which candidates should be selected leading to only one-to-one links and high linkage quality.

2.2 Related Work

PPRL and RL have been addressed by numerous research studies and approaches as summarized in several surveys and books [4, 9, 43, 47]. The key challenge of PPRL is to achieve high linkage quality and scalability to potentially large datasets while preserving the privacy of represented entities by using secure encodings and protocols. In order to achieve a high linkage quality previous work mostly focuses on developing or optimizing encoding techniques to support approximate matching, attribute weighting or different data types [19, 43, 45, 46]. Besides, efficient blocking and filtering techniques have been proposed that do not compromise linkage quality outcome [47].

The problem of post-processing corresponds to *weighted bipartite graph matching problems* [48]. In fact, applying a one-to-one matching restriction, i.e., to clean multi-links, is highly related to problems in graph theory like the *assignment problem* (AP) or the *stable marriage problem* (SMP). Various algorithms have been developed to solve such kind of problems [17,48]. The most prominent approaches are variants of the *Hungarian algorithm* (*Kuhn-Munkres algorithm*) [34] for solving AP as well as variants of the *Gale-Shapley algorithm* [12,14,16,31] for solving SMP.

For PPRL, post-processing methods have only been studied to a limited extent so far: Though several approaches were considered for RL, they were not comparatively evaluated in a PPRL context [2,4,8,9,28]. As a consequence, it is unknown to which degree post-processing is useful and which method is suited best for PPRL. Note that privacy restrictions only allow simple approaches for match classification so that the need for post-processing is increased for PPRL.

A similar post-processing problem, namely selecting the most probable correspondences from a mapping, has been studied in the field of schema [7,30,33] and ontology matching [32]. In [7,33] best match selection strategies, called *MaxN* or *Perfectionist Egalitarian Polygamy*, are used to enforce a one-to-one cardinality constraint by selecting only candidates offering the best similarity scores. Additionally, algorithms for solving the *maximum weighted bipartite graph matching problem* and the SMP have been considered as selection strategies [30,32].

3   Problem Definition

After the classification step (see Sect. 2) all candidate record pairs $\mathbf{C}$ are classified into matches $\mathbf{C_{Match}}$ and non-matches $\mathbf{C_{Non-Match}}$. We assume, that a simple threshold-based approach is used for classification. Thus, the class of matches $\mathbf{C_{Match}}$ contain all candidate record pairs with a similarity score $sim(\cdot, \cdot)$ above a single predefined similarity threshold $\mathbf{t}$, i.e., $\mathbf{C_{Match}} = \{(a,b)|a \in D_A, b \in D_B, sim(a,b) \geq t\}$. We also assume that the databases to be linked are deduplicated before linkage.

The set of matches $\mathbf{C_{Match}}$ constitutes a *weighted bipartite* linkage or similarity graph $\mathbf{G} = (\mathbf{V_A}, \mathbf{V_B}, \mathbf{L})$. Let $\mathbf{V_A}$ and $\mathbf{V_B}$ be two partitions consisting of vertices representing records (entities) from database D_A or database D_B respectively, which occur in the linkage result, i.e., are part of a record pair classified as match. Thus, $\mathbf{V_A} = \{a \in D_A \mid \exists b \in D_B : (a,b) \in C_{Match}\}$ and $\mathbf{V_B} = \{b \in D_B \mid \exists a \in D_A : (a,b) \in C_{Match}\}$. $\mathbf{L}$ denotes the set of edges representing links between two records classified as match. Each edge (link) has a property for the similarity score of the record pair. Between records of the same database no direct link exists. An example linkage graph is depicted in Fig. 2.

After classification it is still possible that the linkage graph contains multi-links, i.e., one-to-many, many-to-one or many-to-many links. Since deduplicated databases are assumed, only one-to-one links should be present in the final linkage result. Hence, the aim of post-processing is to find a *matching* (match mapping) over $\mathbf{G}$. A matching $\mathbf{M} \subseteq \mathbf{L}$ is a subset of links such that each record in $\mathbf{V} = \mathbf{V_A} \cup \mathbf{V_B}$ appears in at most one link, i.e., contributes to at most one matching record pair. As a consequence, post-processing applies a one-to-one link (cardinality) restriction on the set of classified matches $\mathbf{C_{Match}}$.

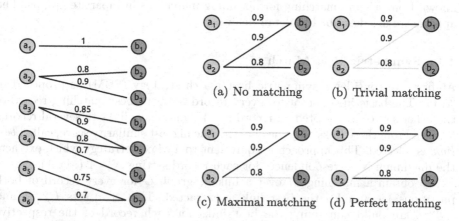

Fig. 2. Example linkage graph containing several multi-links.

Fig. 3. Types of matchings.

In general, several matchings over $\mathbf{G}$ can be found. Thus, the challenge of post-processing is to select the matching yielding the best linkage quality in terms of either recall, precision or F-measure. Ideally, no true-match should be pruned (no loss of recall) while resolving all multi-links to improve precision. Links providing high similarity scores should be favored over those with a low similarity, e.g., near t, as very high similarities typically indicate definite matches. Also other link features, like link degree, can be used for link prioritization [37].

A matching can be selected in such a way that it fulfills certain properties. Basic types of matchings are **trivial**, **maximal**, **maximum** and **perfect** matchings [48]. A matching $\mathbf{M}$ is called *maximal*, if any link not in $\mathbf{M}$ is added to $\mathbf{M}$, then $\mathbf{M}$ would be no longer a matching. If a matching is not maximal then it is a *trivial matching*. Furthermore, if a matching contains the largest possible number of edges (links) then it is a *maximum matching*. Each maximum matching is also maximal but not vice versa. Finally, a *perfect matching* is defined as a matching where every vertex of the graph is incident to exactly one edge of the matching. Every perfect matching is maximum and hence maximal. However, not for every linkage graph a perfect matching exists. The different types of matchings are illustrated in Fig. 3.

Since PPRL is confronted with potentially large datasets containing millions of records [47], post-processing approaches need to be scalable and efficient.

4   Post-processing Strategies for PPRL

We now present post-processing strategies for PPRL to enable a one-to-one link restriction on the linkage result. We chose three frequently used approaches known from schema matching for obtaining matchings in bipartite graphs. The approaches are described in detail below.

4.1   Symmetric Best Match

At first, we consider a symmetric best match strategy (SBM) as proposed in [7,33]. The basic idea is that for every record only the best matching record of the other source is accepted. A record $a \in V_A$ may have links to several records $b \in V_B$. From these links only the one with the highest similarity score, called *best link*, is selected. This approach is equivalent to a MaxN strategy which extracts the maximum N correspondences for each record setting $N = 1$ (Max1).

To obtain a matching M over a linkage graph G for every record of both partitions V_A and V_B the best link is extracted. Thus, two sets L_A^{Max1} and L_B^{Max1} are build containing the best links for each record of the respective partition, e.g., $L_A^{Max1} = \{(a,b) \in L \mid \forall b' \in V_B : (b \neq b' \wedge (a,b') \in L) \rightarrow (sim(a,b') \leq sim(a,b))\}$. Then, the final matching is obtained by building the intersection of these two sets, i.e., $M_{SMB} = M_{Max1\text{-}both} = L_A^{Max1} \cap L_B^{Max1}$. Since the best links from both partitions are considered this strategy is also called *Max1-both*.

In Fig. 4(a) Max1-both is applied on the linkage graph from Fig. 2. It is important to note that the obtained matching is not maximal. Since only record pairs with a common best link are accepted, other record pairs are excluded from the matching even if they do not violate the one-to-one link restriction and have a relative high similarity.

4.2   Stable Marriage and Stable Matchings

The stable marriage problem (SMP) [12] is the problem of finding a *stable matching* (SM) between two sets of elements given an (strictly) ordered preference list for each element. A matching is defined as *stable*, if there are no two records of the different partitions who both have a higher similarity to each other than to their current matching record. Used as post-processing method for PPRL several extensions to the classic SMP need to be considered [17,31]:

Unequal Sets: Usually, an SMP instance consists of two sets of elements having the same cardinality. The partitions of the linkage graph are in general of different size, i.e., $|V_A| \neq |V_B|$, as not every record may have a duplicate in the other source.

Incomplete Preference Lists with Ties: In traditional SMP each element has a preference list that *strictly* orders *all* members of the other set. Since blocking or filtering techniques are used for PPRL not every record $a \in V_A$ has a link to a record $b \in V_B$ and vice versa. Moreover, a record may have two

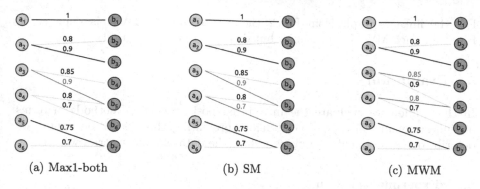

(a) Max1-both   (b) SM   (c) MWM

Fig. 4. Illustration of the resulting linkage graph from Fig. 2 after applying different post-processing methods. For Max1-both (a) the link a_4–b_6 is removed since the best link for a_4 is to b_5. In contrast, for SM (b) the link a_4–b_6 is included as it does not violate the one-to-one-link restriction nor the stable property. For the MWM (c), the links a_3–b_4 and a_4–b_5 are included in the matching as the sum of their similarities is higher than for a_3–b_5 and a_4–b_6. However, the MWM is not stable due to the links a_3–b_4 and a_4–b_5, as a_3 and b_5 prefer each other over their current matching records.

links with the same similarity score to two different records of the other source, called *tie* or *indifference* [16], e.g., $sim(a, b_1) = 0.9$ and $sim(a, b_2) = 0.9$ where $a \in V_A$ and $b_1, b_2 \in V_B$. The simplest way to handle indifference is to break ties arbitrary [16]. Also secondary link features can be used for resolving ties [37].

Symmetry: For SMP it is not required that two elements prefer each other the same (asymmetric preference). In our case, the SMP instance is symmetric since the similarity of a record pair is symmetric.

To obtain a SM the Gale-Shapley algorithm [12] or one of its variants taking the described extensions into account [16,17,31] can be used. A simple approach is to order all links (or candidate pairs) based on their similarity score to process them iteratively in descending order. The current link is added to the final matching if it does not violate the one-to-one-link restriction. The algorithm stops if all links have been processed [30]. In Fig. 4(b) a SM for the linkage graph from Fig. 2 is depicted. In contrast to matchings obtained by the SBM strategy, SMs are maximal. In general, multiple SMs may exists for a linkage graph.

4.3   Maximum Weight Matchings

As third method we consider to find a *maximum weight matching* (MWM). A MWM is a matching that has maximum weight, i.e., that maximizes the sum of the overall similarities between records in the final linkage result. This problem corresponds to the assignment problem (AP) which consists of finding a MWM in a weighted bipartite graph. To solve the AP on bipartite graphs in polynomial time the Hungarian algorithm (Kuhn-Munkres algorithm) can be used [34].

For the linkage graph from Fig. 2 the corresponding MWM is depicted in Fig. 4(c). Each MWM is maximal, but does not have to be stable.

5 Evaluation

In this section we evaluate the introduced post-processing methods in terms of linkage quality and efficiency. Before presenting the evaluation results we describe our experimental setup as well as the datasets and metrics we use.

5.1 Experimental Setup

All experiments are conducted on a desktop machine equipped with an Intel Core i7-6700 CPU with $8 \times 3.40\,\text{GHz}$, 32 GB main memory and running Ubuntu 16.04.4. and Java 1.8.0_171.

5.2 PPRL Setup

Following previous work, we implemented the PPRL process as three-party protocol utilizing BFs as privacy technique as proposed by Schnell [40]. To overcome the quadratic complexity we make use of LSH-based blocking utilizing the family of hash functions which is sensitive to the Hamming distance (HLSH) [8]. The respective hash functions are used to build overlapping blocks in which similar records are grouped. For HLSH-based blocking mainly the two parameters Ψ, determining the number of hash functions used for building a blocking key, and Λ, defining the number of blocking keys, are important for high efficiency and linkage quality outcome [11]. Based on [11] we empirically set Ψ and Λ individual for each dataset as outlined in Table 1 leading to high efficiency and effectiveness. Finally, we apply the Jaccard similarity to determine the similarity of candidate record pairs [18].

5.3 Datasets

For evaluation we use synthetic and real datasets containing one million records with person-related data. An overview about all relevant dataset characteristics and parameters is given in Table 1. The synthetic datasets $\mathbf{G_1}$ and $\mathbf{G_2}$ are generated using the data generator and corruption tool GeCo [6]. We customized the tool by using lookup files containing German names and addresses with realistic frequency values drawn from German census data[1]. Moreover, we extended GeCo by a *family* and *move rate* used for G_2. The family rate determines how many records of a dataset belong to a family. All records of the same family agree on their last name and address attributes. The size of each family is chosen randomly between two and five. To simulate moves we added a move rate that defines in how many records the address attributes are altered. The move

---

[1] https://www.destatis.de/DE/Methoden/Zensus_/Zensus.html.

rate does not introduce data errors like typos, instead it simulates inconsistencies between data sources. A generated dataset D consists of two subsets, D_A and D_B, to be linked with each other. While the original tool requires all records of D_B to be duplicates to records of D_A we changed the tool to support arbitrary degrees of overlaps between D_A and D_B. As a consequence, records in both D_A and D_B may have no duplicate which is more realistic. We also use a refined model to corrupt records by allowing a different number of errors per record instead of a fixed maximum number of errors for all records. We may thus generate duplicates such that 50% of the duplicates contain no error, 20% one error and 10% two errors while the remaining 20% have an address change (move rate). For the real dataset **N**, we use subsets of two snapshots of the North Carolina voter registration database (NCVR) at different points in time.[2]

Table 1. Dataset characteristics and used parameters.

Characteristic	G_1	G_2	N
Type	Synthetic (GeCo)		Real (NCVR)
$|D_A|$	800 000	700 000	500 000
$|D_B|$	200 000	300 000	500 000
$|D_A \cap D_B|$	200 000 (100 %)	150 000 (50 %)	250 000 (50 %)
Attributes	First name, last name, city, zip, date of birth		First Name, middle name, last name, city, year of birth
q-grams	$q = 2$ (bigrams), no character padding		
g	28		25
$|Errors|/record$	2	0 - 2 : 0 (40 %) 1 (30 %) 2 (10 %)	
$|Errors|/attr$	0 - 1	0 - 2	
Moves		20 %	
Families		25 %	
m	1024		
k	26		29
BF type	CLK with random hashing [40,41]		
HLSH key length Ψ	16		
HLSH keys Λ	20		30

5.4 Evaluation Metrics

To asses the linkage quality we measure *recall*, *precision* and *F-measure*. Recall measures the proportion of true-matches that have been correctly classified as matches after the linkage process. Precision is defined as the fraction of classified matches that are true-matches. Finally, F-measure is the harmonic mean of recall and precision. To evaluate efficiency we measure the *execution times* of the post-processing methods in seconds.

---

[2] http://www.ncsbe.gov/.

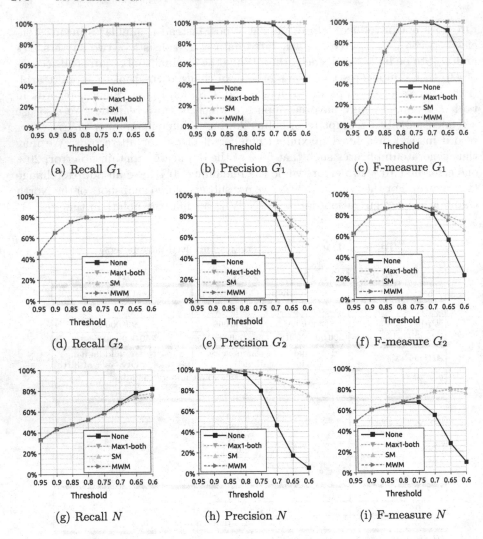

Fig. 5. Quality results for the datasets G_1, G_2 and N.

5.5   Evaluation Results

In order to analyze the impact of post-processing on the linkage quality we compare the three strategies described in Sect. 4 to the standard PPRL without post-processing. The aim of post-processing is to optimize precision while recall is ideally preserved. The results in Fig. 5 show the obtained linkage quality for datasets G_1, G_2 and N.

Dataset G_1 is based on settings of the original GeCo tool with 100% overlap and a fixed error rate. We observe that a high linkage quality is achieved even if post-processing is disabled with near-perfect recall for $t \leq 0.8$ and near-perfect precision for $t \geq 0.7$. The three post-processing methods achieve very similar results for G_1: While recall remains stable, precision and consequently F-measure can be significantly improved to almost 100% even for low thresholds $t \leq 0.7$. This is due to the high overlap of the two subsets making false-matches after post-processing only possible if a record has a higher similarity to a record having no duplicate than to its actual true-match. Despite this best-case situation simulated with G_1, only low precision is achieved for low threshold values without post-processing.

For datasets G_2 and N overall a lower linkage quality is obtained since the data is more dense making it harder to separate matches and non-matches. Similar to G_1, precision significantly decreases for G_2 using lower threshold values. All post-processing strategies can again improve precision for lower threshold values. The best results are achieved for Max1-both outperforming both SM and MWM. SM yields slightly better results than MWM. For the synthetic datasets G_1 and G_2, post-processing does not increase the top F-measure but the best linkage quality is reached with a wider range of threshold settings thereby simplifying the choice of a suitable threshold.

The post-processing methods are most effective for the real dataset N. Here a higher recall can only be achieved for lower threshold values $t \leq 0.7$ but precision drops dramatically in this range without post-processing due to a high number of multi-links. As a result, the best possible F-measure is limited to only 67%. By contrast, the use of post-processing can maintain a high precision even for lower thresholds at only small decrease in recall compared to disabled post-processing. As a result, the top F-measure is substantially increased to around 80% underlining the high effectiveness and significance of the proposed post-processing. Again, the use of Max1-both is most effective followed by SM.

Additionally, we comparatively evaluated the post-processing strategies in terms of runtime. The results depicted in Fig. 6 show that Max1-both achieves the lowest execution times even for low thresholds. The extended Gale-Shapley algorithm we used for SM shows a significant performance decrease for lower similarity thresholds, most notably for dataset N and $t \leq 0.7$. For higher thresholds $t > 0.7$ the runtimes are very similar to those of Max1-both. The computation of the MWM by using the Hungarian algorithm incurs a high computational complexity and massive memory consumption. As a consequence, we were not able to obtain a MWM for low threshold values (compare Fig. 5). Hence, we consider the MWM approach as not scalable enough for large datasets with millions of records.

In conclusion, both Max1-both and SM are able to significantly improve the linkage quality of PPRL, especially for low thresholds, while showing good performance. In our setup, the execution of the entire PPRL process takes only a few minutes. Hence, introducing post-processing taking a few seconds for execution does not affect the overall performance. In general, Max1-both can achieve the best linkage quality in terms of precision and F-measure. For applications favoring recall over precision, a SM should be applied.

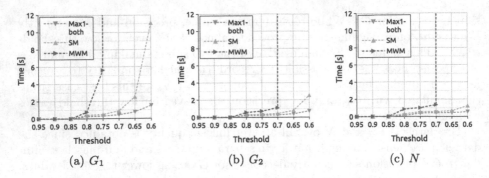

(a) G_1 (b) G_2 (c) N

Fig. 6. Runtime results for the datasets G_1, G_2 and N.

6   Conclusion

We evaluated different post-processing methods for PPRL to restrict the linkage result to only one-to-one links. Our evaluation for large synthetic and real datasets containing one million records showed that without post-processing only low linkage quality is achieved, especially when dealing with dense or dirty data. In contrast, using a symmetric best match strategy for post-processing is a lightweight approach to raise the overall linkage quality. As a side effect, by using post-processing the similarity threshold used for classification can be selected lower without compromising linkage quality. Since in practical applications a appropriate threshold is hard to define, this fact becomes highly beneficial.

In future, we plan to investigate further post-processing strategies using further link features and other heuristics. We also plan to analyze post-processing methods for multi-party PPRL where more than two databases need to be linked.

References

1. Bloom, B.: Space/time trade-offs in hash coding with allowable errors. CACM **13**(7), 422–426 (1970)
2. Böhm, C., de Melo, G., Naumann, F., Weikum, G.: LINDA: distributed web-of-data-scale entity matching. In: ACM CIKM, pp. 2104–2108 (2012)
3. Brown, A.P., Borgs, C., Randall, S.M., Schnell, R.: Evaluating privacy-preserving record linkage using cryptographic long-term keys and multibit trees on large medical datasets. BMC Med. Inf. Decis. Making **17**(1), 83 (2017)
4. Christen, P.: Data Matching: Concepts and Techniques for Record Linkage, Entity Resolution, and Duplicate Detection. Springer, Heidelberg (2012). https://doi.org/10.1007/978-3-642-31164-2
5. Christen, P., Schnell, R., Vatsalan, D., Ranbaduge, T.: Efficient cryptanalysis of bloom filters for privacy-preserving record linkage. In: Kim, J., Shim, K., Cao, L., Lee, J.-G., Lin, X., Moon, Y.-S. (eds.) PAKDD 2017. LNCS (LNAI), vol. 10234, pp. 628–640. Springer, Cham (2017). https://doi.org/10.1007/978-3-319-57454-7_49
6. Christen, P., Vatsalan, D.: Flexible and extensible generation and corruption of personal data. In: ACM CIKM, pp. 1165–1168 (2013)

7. Do, H.H., Rahm, E.: COMA - a system for flexible combination of schema matching approaches. In: VLDB, pp. 610–621 (2002)
8. Durham, E.A.: A framework for accurate, efficient private record linkage. Ph.D. thesis, Vanderbilt University (2012)
9. Elmagarmid, A.K., Ipeirotis, P.G., Verykios, V.S.: Duplicate record detection: a survey. IEEE TKDE 19(1), 1–16 (2007)
10. Fellegi, I.P., Sunter, A.B.: A theory for record linkage. JASA 64(328), 1183–1210 (1969)
11. Franke, M., Sehili, Z., Rahm, E.: Parallel privacy preserving record linkage using LSH-based blocking. In: IoTBDS, pp. 195–203 (2018)
12. Gale, D., Shapley, L.S.: College admissions and the stability of marriage. Am. Math. Mon. 69(1), 9–15 (1962)
13. Gibberd, A., Supramaniam, R., Dillon, A., Armstrong, B.K., OConnell, D.L.: Lung cancer treatment and mortality for Aboriginal people in New South Wales, Australia: results from a population-based record linkage study and medical record audit. BMC Cancer 16(1), 289 (2016)
14. Gusfield, D., Irving, R.W.: The Stable Marriage Problem: Structure and Algorithms. MIT Press, Cambridge (1989)
15. Hernández, M.A., Stolfo, S.J.: Real-world data is dirty: data cleansing and the merge/purge problem. Data Min. Knowl. Discovery 2(1), 9–37 (1998)
16. Irving, R.W.: Stable marriage and indifference. Discrete Appl. Math. 48(3), 261–272 (1994)
17. Iwama, K., Miyazaki, S.: A survey of the stable marriage problem and its variants. In: IEEE ICKS, pp. 131–136 (2008)
18. Jaccard, P.: The distribution of the flora in the alpine zone. New Phytol. 11(2), 37–50 (1912)
19. Karapiperis, D., Gkoulalas-Divanis, A., Verykios, V.S.: Distance-aware encoding of numerical values for privacy-preserving record linkage. In: IEEE ICDE, pp. 135–138 (2017)
20. Karapiperis, D., Gkoulalas-Divanis, A., Verykios, V.S.: FEDERAL: a framework for distance-aware privacy-preserving record linkage. IEEE TKDE 30(2), 292–304 (2018)
21. Karapiperis, D., Verykios, V.S.: A distributed framework for scaling up LSH-based computations in privacy preserving record linkage. In: Proceedings of the BCI (2013)
22. Karapiperis, D., Verykios, V.S.: A fast and efficient hamming LSH-based scheme for accurate linkage. KAIS 49(3), 861–884 (2016)
23. Kho, A.N., Cashy, J.P., Jackson, K.L., Pah, A.R., Goel, S., Boehnke, J., Humphries, J.E., Kominers, S.D., Hota, B.N., Sims, S.A., et al.: Design and implementation of a privacy preserving electronic health record linkage tool in Chicago. JAMIA 22(5), 1072–1080 (2015)
24. Kroll, M., Steinmetzer, S.: Automated cryptanalysis of bloom filter encryptions of health records. In: ICHI (2014)
25. Kuehni, C.E., et al.: Cohort profile: the Swiss childhood cancer survivor study. Int. J. Epidemiol. 41(6), 1553–1564 (2012)
26. Kuzu, M., Kantarcioglu, M., Durham, E., Malin, B.: A constraint satisfaction cryptanalysis of bloom filters in private record linkage. In: Fischer-Hübner, S., Hopper, N. (eds.) PETS 2011. LNCS, vol. 6794, pp. 226–245. Springer, Heidelberg (2011). https://doi.org/10.1007/978-3-642-22263-4_13

27. Kuzu, M., Kantarcioglu, M., Durham, E.A., Toth, C., Malin, B.: A practical approach to achieve private medical record linkage in light of public resources. JAMIA **20**(2), 285–292 (2013)
28. Lenz, R.: Measuring the disclosure protection of micro aggregated business microdata: an analysis taking as an example the German structure of costs survey. J. Official Stat. **22**(4), 681 (2006)
29. Luo, Q., et al.: Cancer-related hospitalisations and unknownstage prostate cancer: a population-based record linkage study. BMJ Open **7**(1), e014259 (2017)
30. Marie, A., Gal, A.: On the Stable Marriage of Maximum Weight Royal Couples. In: AAAI Workshop on Information Integration on the Web (2007)
31. McVitie, D.G., Wilson, L.B.: Stable marriage assignment for unequal sets. BIT Numer. Math. **10**(3), 295–309 (1970)
32. Meilicke, C., Stuckenschmidt, H.: Analyzing mapping extraction approaches. In: OM, pp. 25–36 (2007)
33. Melnik, S., Garcia-Molina, H., Rahm, E.: Similarity flooding: a versatile graph matching algorithm and its application to schema matching. In: IEEE ICDE, pp. 117–128 (2002)
34. Munkres, J.: Algorithms for the assignment and transportation problems. SIAM J. **5**(1), 32–38 (1957)
35. Niedermeyer, F., Steinmetzer, S., Kroll, M., Schnell, R.: Cryptanalysis of basic bloom filters used for privacy preserving record linkage. JPC **6**(2), 59–79 (2014)
36. Rahm, E., Do, H.H.: Data cleaning: problems and current approaches. IEEE Data Eng. Bull. **23**(4), 3–13 (2000)
37. Saeedi, A., Peukert, E., Rahm, E.: Using link features for entity clustering in knowledge graphs. In: Gangemi, A., et al. (eds.) ESWC 2018. LNCS, vol. 10843, pp. 576–592. Springer, Cham (2018). https://doi.org/10.1007/978-3-319-93417-4_37
38. Schnell, R.: Privacy-preserving record linkage. In: Methodological Developments in Data Linkage, pp. 201–225 (2015)
39. Schnell, R., Bachteler, T., Reiher, J.: Privacy-preserving record linkage using Bloom filters. BMC Med. Inf. Decis. Making **9**(1), 41 (2009)
40. Schnell, R., Bachteler, T., Reiher, J.: A novel error-tolerant anonymous linking code. GRLC, No. WP-GRLC-2011-02 (2011)
41. Schnell, R., Borgs, C.: Randomized response and balanced bloom filters for privacy preserving record linkage. In: IEEE ICDMW (2016)
42. Sehili, Z., Rahm, E.: Speeding up privacy preserving record linkage for metric space similarity measures. Datenbank-Spektrum **16**(3), 227–236 (2016)
43. Vatsalan, D., Christen, P., Verykios, V.S.: A taxonomy of privacy-preserving record linkage techniques. Inf. Syst. **38**(6), 946–969 (2013)
44. Vatsalan, D., Christen, P.: scalable privacy-preserving record linkage for multiple databases. In: ACM CIKM, pp. 1795–1798 (2014)
45. Vatsalan, D., Christen, P.: Privacy-preserving matching of similar patients. J. Biomed. Inf. **59**, 285–298 (2016)
46. Vatsalan, D., Christen, P., O'Keefe, C.M., Verykios, V.S.: An evaluation framework for privacy-preserving record linkage. JPC **6**(1), 3 (2014)
47. Vatsalan, D., Sehili, Z., Christen, P., Rahm, E.: Privacy-preserving record linkage for big data: current approaches and research challenges. In: Zomaya, A.Y., Sakr, S. (eds.) Handbook of Big Data Technologies, pp. 851–895. Springer, Cham (2017). https://doi.org/10.1007/978-3-319-49340-4_25
48. West, D.B., et al.: Introduction to Graph Theory, vol. 2. Prentice Hall, Upper Saddle River (2001)

δ-DOCA: Achieving Privacy in Data Streams

Bruno C. Leal[1], Israel C. Vidal[1], Felipe T. Brito[1], Juvêncio S. Nobre[2], and Javam C. Machado[1(✉)]

[1] Laboratório de Sistemas e Banco de Dados, Computer Science Department, Universidade Federal do Ceará, Fortaleza, CE, Brazil
{bruno.leal,israel.vidal,felipe.timbo,javam.machado}@lsbd.ufc.br
[2] Department of Statistics, Universidade Federal do Ceará, Fortaleza, CE, Brazil
juvencio@ufc.br

Abstract. Numerous real world applications continuously publish data streams to benefit people in their daily activities. However, these applications may collect and release sensitive information about individuals and lead to serious risks of privacy breach. Differential Privacy (DP) has emerged as a mathematical model to release sensitive information of users while hindering the process of distinguishing individuals' records on databases. Although DP has been widely used for protecting the privacy of individual users' data, it was not designed, in essence, to provide its guarantees for data streams, since these data are potentially unbounded sequences and continuously generated at rapid rates. Consequently, the noise required to mask the effect of sequences of objects in data streams tend to be higher. In this paper, we design a new technique, named δ-DOCA, to publish data streams under differential privacy. Our approach provides a strategy to determine the sensitivity value of DP and reduces the necessary noise. Our experiments show that the application of δ-DOCA to anonymize data streams not only reduced significantly the necessary noise to apply differential privacy, but also allowed for the output data to preserve the original data distribution.

Keywords: Data privacy · Data stream · Differential privacy

1 Introduction

Data streams are unbounded sequences of data objects, continuously generated at rapid rates. In general, due to the physical limitations of the computational resources in streaming data processing, there is no control over the order in which data is received and, furthermore, data elements must be discarded or archived after processing. These characteristics force stream algorithms to be incremental and to maintain fast processing with low complexity, to deal with memory and time limitations [14]. Data collected and published by applications like sensor networks, financial applications and moving object tracking can be used to benefit individuals. For instance, moving object tracking allows optimal route

J. Garcia-Alfaro et al. (Eds.): DPM 2018/CBT 2018, LNCS 11025, pp. 279–295, 2018.
https://doi.org/10.1007/978-3-030-00305-0_20

computation since the number of cars per area is released in real-time. However, these applications may collect sensitive information about these individuals and lead to severe risks of privacy breach.

Differential privacy (DP) [5] has emerged in the last decade as a new paradigm to release sensitive information while giving a statistical guarantee for privacy. It has received considerable attention from the privacy community due to its inherent characteristic of being independent of background knowledge or even computational power. DP ensures that the addition or removal of an individual will not substantially affect the outcome of any statistical analysis performed in the dataset. Differential privacy is a definition satisfied by a randomized algorithm, usually called a mechanism. It provides privacy introducing randomness to prevent the identification of an individual. The Laplace mechanism is the most common and simple method to achieve differential privacy. A mechanism which achieves differential privacy is associated with a sensitivity, which measures how much difference an individual will make in a dataset. As the value of sensitivity grows, the addition of noise required to mask the effect of all the individuals of the datasets tends to be higher [7].

Although differential privacy has been widely used as a strong model for protecting the privacy of individual users' data, it was not designed, in essence, to provide its guarantees for streaming data. There are some challenges in publishing data streams under differential privacy, especially when dealing with the publishing of a dataset in its original format, with full records, in a non-interactive context. In this context, the data holder publishes an anonymized version of the data [5]. Since data streams are unbounded sequences of data objects, it is not possible to determine the exact value of sensitivity, which depends on the data domain, because such characteristic is not known at first in streaming data. Also, even if the sensitivity value could be calculated in a specific domain, it would tend to be higher in a non-interactive context, demanding thus a high volume of noise to protect the data.

Applying differential privacy to protect the privacy of individuals' information, in the context of streaming data, is a valuable issue that needs to be addressed. Hence, in this paper we address the problem of publishing data streams under differential privacy while maintaining higher data utility. In particular, the main contributions of this paper are:

1. We define a restrictive domain of a data streaming adjusted to a specific parameter δ, allowing for determining the sensitivity value of differential privacy.
2. We develop a solution for enhancing data utility when applying differential privacy considering a known domain in streaming data.
3. We conduct an extensive empirical evaluation of three different real datasets showing that our approach is suitable and effective for streaming data.

The remainder of this paper is organized as follows. Section 2 presents a brief discussion of related work in different publishing contexts. After that, Sect. 3 introduces δ-DOCA, an approach that takes place in two stages for publishing a data stream protected by differential privacy. Section 4 reports the results obtained in the experimental evaluation with three real datasets. Finally, Sect. 5 presents conclusions and indicates future research directions.

2   Related Work

In the literature, solutions for privacy are mainly divided into two contexts [5]: (i) the interactive context, in which it is provided an interface, whereby queries can be submitted on the dataset and the answers are anonymized; (ii) the non-interactive context, where an anonymized version of the data is published.

Differential Privacy was initially designed with the purpose of protecting the results of interactive queries [5]. However, non-interactive publishing allows for more flexibility for data analysis since it does not assume any premises of how the data will be used after the release. In non-interactive publishing, items are generated from the original dataset applying a differentially private mechanism to form a new dataset, on which the queries are run.

Studies related to non-interactive publishing generally present useful solutions for statistic analyses and works often focus on counting queries. For instance, the work in [2] generates an anonymized dataset capable of answering questions such as "which data fraction satisfies a given predicate?", where no restrictions upon the predicate are made. In [18] there is a solution for private publishing of histograms and [9] proposes an algorithm to release a dataset for specific statistic queries. This dataset is created based on a distribution, which is privately generated to represent the original dataset, being continuously adjusted for new queries. Nonetheless, they present specific restrictions to the publishing format, which limits other types of data usage.

In more recent works, there are solutions for publishing private datasets that present the same format of the original data. A method called PrivBayes was proposed in [19] to deal with the issue of high-dimensional data publishing, which may demand a high volume of noise to protect data. PrivBayes consists in constructing a model based on Bayesian networks to generate samples from this model. [1] also offers a solution that generates samples from a model, but, in this case, publishing is based on the concept of plausible deniability, which, in order to publish a record generated from a model, verifies if it could have been generated from, at the most, k original records.

Closer solutions to δ-DOCA can be found in [15,16], in which data publishing follows a process of perturbation added with the DP noise on a microaggregated version of the original data. [16] combines k-anonymity syntactic model [17] with the more robust privacy guarantees offered by DP. The approach generates microaggregation clusters to satisfy the k-anonymity model, in which its cluster centroid represents each individual. The authors argue that this reduces the distortion caused when adding DP noise. The noise is computed by the Laplace mechanism with sensitivity $\Delta f = \frac{n}{k} * \frac{\Delta(X)}{k}$, where X is the original dataset and n is the number of individuals records, so $\frac{n}{k}$ represents the number of clusters.

Considering such formula, one can notice that sensitivity depends upon the size n and the knowledge on the X domain.

The authors in [15] follow the same line of thought of [16], i.e., it performs a stage of microaggregation before adding noise. However, the restriction of minimum size for clusters is moderated with the aim of reducing the impact of an individual on the group, and, consequently, on the sensitivity value. The sensitivity for publishing a group in this work is $\Delta c = \Delta D/|C|$, where D is the original dataset and ΔD is the greatest possible variation of a record in D. Notice that, in this work, the sensitivity depends on the knowledge of the domain D and the cluster size, but not on the dataset size. The noise for each group is obtained through the Laplace mechanism with scale $\Delta c/\epsilon$.

The works mentioned so far only deal with the publishing of static datasets, and their solutions do not apply directly to the context of data streaming. Some attention has, however, been devoted to the protection of data published out of data streaming [4,6]. The solution applied in [4], for instance, protects results from persistent counting queries in the context of IoT for an individual's state in a given logic time. From this results, it is possible to derive other persistent queries, for example, the number of connected users at each monitored access point. It is also possible to monitor if a given temporal event occurs, e.g., verify if the number of connections in an access point is greater than a threshold. However, to the best of our knowledge, no work in the context of data streaming performs publishing of the full record type.

The δ-DOCA approach designed in this paper works in the full records publishing context of works [15,16], but also attacking the context of the continuous release of data streaming.

3 δ-DOCA

δ-DOCA (**D**ifferential Privacy **O**nline **C**lustering and **A**nonymization with Domain Bounded by δ) is a data stream publishing approach differentially private for numerical and univariate data. Given a proportion of publishing δ, differential privacy is applied to a non-interactive context. Thus, an anonymized version of the data in the original format (full record) is obtained, as it occurs with the microaggregated publishing of syntactic models, e.g., k-anonymity [17]. This type of publishing is generally more suitable for analysis [15], since it does not assume any premise of data use, whereas the interactive scenario of differential privacy allows for only a limited number of queries [16]. Additionally, the δ-DOCA approach provides a strategy to decrease the sensitivity in noise addition, maintaining data utility without compromising individual privacy.

In this context, there are two main problems to be addressed: (i) due to the unpredictability of data values and their continuous flow, it is not possible to specify a domain a priori and, therefore, a sensitivity value for differencial privacy application; (ii) even with a established domain, the sensitivity to publish data in a non-interactive manner must be high to protect them entirely, i.e., the necessary noise level to protect individuals' privacy is very high and, consequently, published data do not reflect original data, having no utility for analytical purposes.

To tackle the aforementioned problems, we have designed δ-DOCA, which acts in two different stages. The first stage, so-called Domain Bounding by δ, defines the domain of a data streaming with low information loss or suppression, regulated by a parameter δ. The greater the delta, the fewer the data items to be suppressed. δ-DOCA applies the streaming data domain to calculate the value of the sensitivity for differential privacy. Considering the high volume issue in the context of non-interactive publishing, the second stage, called DOCA, presents a solution to enhance utility, which is based upon an online microaggregation prior to adding noise to data. The improvement of utility relies on the assumption that the necessary noise to protect the microaggregated value of the group is reduced to an extent that compensates the information loss caused by the microaggregation per se [15,16].

3.1 Domain Bounding by δ

The primary purpose of this stage is to define a restrictive domain of a data streaming $\mathcal{S}$, allowing for determining the differential privacy sensitivity (Δf) for a specific δ. Without such restriction, this domain would be immeasurable, considering the features of unpredictability and continuous flow of potentially unlimited data streaming. The parameter δ establishes the proportion of data to be published and falls within the interval $[0,1]$, where 1 indicates that all records should be published, and 0 the opposite, i.e., no record should be published. Hence, complement $1 - δ$ points out the suppression level.

In order to calculate both limit inferior and limit superior of the domain $\mathcal{D} = [v_{low}, v_{sup}]$ capable of reaching the publishing level specified by δ, we apply an online quantile [8] updated continuously with each new item originated from $\mathcal{S}$. The values v_{low} and v_{sup} are defined as follows: $v_{low} = ((1-δ)/2)$-quantile and $v_{sup} = ((δ+1)/2)$-quantile. They are calculated every time a new item is generated from $\mathcal{S}$ until reaching the stability $\mathcal{D}$. Figure 1 presents an overview of our strategy. Once this condition is met, this stage stops being executed, generating the domain $\mathcal{D}$, with limit inferior v_{low} and superior v_{sup}, at the moment the stability validation of the domain is reached.

The idea behind this stage is that $\mathcal{D}$ eventually becomes stable, that is, the variation in v_{low} and v_{sup} is non-significant. Notice that, in the definition of the sensitivity of DP [5,7], the sensitivity is given by the maximum possible variation of a single individual. Considering the stable domain $\mathcal{D}$, the greatest possible difference is then given by the absolute difference between the superior and inferior values of the interval. Thus, it is possible to calculate the differential privacy sensitivity $\Delta f = |v_{low} - v_{sup}|$.

In order to stabilize the range $\mathcal{D}$, we advocate the use of a symmetrical asymptotic two-sided confidence interval distribution-free conservative with $100(δ)\%$ confidence, $δ \in (0,1)$, which is given by $[X_{\lfloor n((1-δ)/2)\rfloor}; X_{\lfloor n((δ+1)/2)\rfloor}]$, where $X_{(1)} \leq X_{(2)} \leq \cdots \leq X_{(n)}$ denoting the order statistics of the sample. For details, see for example [10]. Notice that as an asymptotic confidence interval

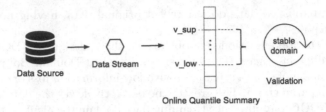

Online Quantile Summary

Fig. 1. An overview of stage 1 – domain bounding by δ.

guarantees the stabilization, the greater the sample, the better is the defined domain $\mathcal{D}$, which should not be a problem, since this paper works in the context of data streams, which are potentially infinite. However, in cases where the sample is small or moderate in size, a resampling strategy, e.g., Bootstrap, can be used to assure that the calculated domain $\mathcal{D}$ represents the stream's actual domain.

For the stability validation of $\mathcal{D}$, the following definition is provided:

Definition 1. *(Stable domain) Given the tolerance parameter λ and n as the total number of records that arrived in the stream so far. Let l_i be the i-th value of $((1-\delta)/2) - quantile$ and s_i the i-th value of $((\delta+1)/2) - quantile$. Let $X_{low} = (l_{n-m+1}, ..., l_n)$ and $X_{sup} = (s_{n-m+1}, ..., s_n)$ where m is the given number of consecutive quantile values to be verified for the stabilization. Also let c_v be the coefficient of variation function (Eq. 1). If $|X_{low}| = m$ and $c_v(X_{low}) \leq \lambda$ and the same conditions hold for X_{sup}, the domain $\mathcal{D} = [l_n, s_n]$ is considered stable.*

$$c_v(X) = \frac{\sigma(X)}{\mu(X)}, \text{ where } \sigma \text{ is the standard deviation and } \mu \text{ is the mean.} \quad (1)$$

Given the stable domain $\mathcal{D} = [v_{\text{low}}, v_{\text{sup}}]$, this stage generates as output for the next step all new items $r_i \in \mathcal{S}$ such that $v_{\text{low}} \leq r_i \leq v_{\text{sup}}$, i.e., if $r_i \in \mathcal{D}$, then r_i will be anonymized and published in the following stages, otherwise r_i is suppressed.

Discussion. The domain bounding phase leads to the stability validation of $\mathcal{D}$ in order to separate the tuples to be suppressed and the ones to be anonymized and published. For the items to be suppressed, it is possible to apply anonymization by naively using differential privacy, i.e., generating noise for each item with the Laplace mechanism with the scale $\Delta f/\epsilon$, where $\Delta f = |v_{\text{low}} - v_{\text{sup}}|$. However, even for small values of δ (high suppression), the sensitivity value to protect publishing in a non-interactive context is still very high and, therefore, the amount of noise required to protect data also becomes elevated. Consequently, it is necessary an additional solution for enhancing utility.

3.2   Online Clustering and Anonymization

This stage, so-called DOCA, presents a strategy for enhancing data utility when applying differential privacy in the context of non-interactive publishing, considering the data streaming of a known domain. To this intent, our approach adapts the process of anonymization established in [15], which presents a solution for differentially private publishing in context of static datasets. This process performs a microaggregation before noise is added from the Laplace mechanism. The noise starts, therefore, to be generated for a cluster centroid after microaggregation, instead of being obtained for the original value of each element.

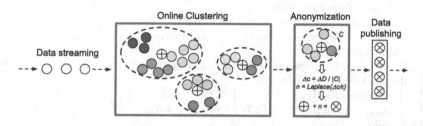

Fig. 2. DOCA overview – online clustering and anonymization.

The contribution of DOCA is divided into two sub-phases according to the overview presented in Fig. 2: (i) Online Clustering and (ii) Anonymization with microaggregation and noise addition. To adapt the solution of [15], the first sub-phase acts creating clusters for microaggregation in an online context, continuously generating groups that supply the next anonymization sub-phase. The solution presented in Algorithm 1 (DOCA) meets the execution of these two sub-phases and satisfies the execution restrictions in the context of data streaming.

Online Clustering. The strategy of anonymization with utility improvement, offered in [15], consists in performing microaggregation before adding noise to data. In this strategy, the volume of noise depends on two factors other than privacy budget ϵ: sensitivity and group size. The key to adapt this strategy to the context of data streaming is thence the continuous formation of groups for online microaggregation.

For the process of online microaggregation and anonymization, it is necessary to take into account the data streaming characteristics that strongly impact this process [14]: (1) data is potentially unlimited, which hinders its representation in the memory as a whole; (2) the microaggregation algorithm must take linear time, at the most, to allow for online execution; (3) each item of the data streaming is subject to a delay constraint between its input and output, which, in DOCA is the maximum time from the input until its anonymized publishing. For simplicity's sake, the arrival of a new item in the data streaming was adopted as the unit of time.

Algorithm 1. DOCA

Input: S, Δf, β, m, ϵ, *delay_constraint*
Output: Updates online clusters C
```
/* S: the continuously updated data stream                        */
/* Δf: the domain sensitivity, ε: privacy budget                  */
/* β: maximum number of clusters in memory                        */
/* m: maximum number of clusters used to calculate τ             */
/* τ: info loss avg of the last m published clusters             */
/* delay_constraint: maximum number of interactions from the record
   input until its output                                         */
```
1   $C = [\,]$, $I = [\,]$, $\tau = 0$, $min_t = +\infty$, $max_t = -\infty$;
2   **foreach** *new Record* $r \in S$ **do**
3       $min_t = \min(r, min_t)$; $max_t = \max(r, max_t)$;
4   Cluster c = BestSelection(r, C, τ, min_t, max_t);
5   add r in c;
6   Record r_e = GetExpiringRecord(*delay_constraint*);
7   **if** r_e *is not Null* **then**
8   Cluster $c_e = \{c_i \in C | r_e \in c_i\}$;
9           $i_{loss} = (\max(c_e) - \min(c_e)) / (max_t - min_t)$;
10   add i_{loss} in I;
11   τ = mean of the last m values $\in I$;
            /* Anonymization and publishing of cluster c_e */
12          $\Delta c = \Delta f / size(c_e)$;
13   η = ramdom sample from Laplace(0, $\Delta c/\epsilon$);
14   χ = centroid value of c_e;
15   **foreach** $r_i \in c_e$ **do**
16              $r_i = \chi + \eta$;
17   publish c_e;
18   remove c_e from C;

The anonymization made by DOCA adds, besides the information loss generated by the microaggregation, the noise from the Laplace mechanism [7] to guarantee Differential Privacy. This noise is directly proportional to sensitivity (Δf) and inversely proportional to the group size to which it is applied. In order to minimize noise, it is important that the solution adopted for online grouping seeks the optimization of the following features simultaneously:

1. not to restrict group size, that is, the bigger the group, the lower the volume of noise;
2. to guarantee representativity of centroids so that the volume of noise compensates the information loss of the microaggregation.

To obtain groups that better suit the aforementioned characteristics, we devise a new online clustering algorithm as a variation of the solution offered by [3]. The online clustering is described in lines 3, 4 and 5, where the choice of the best cluster for an item (line 4) is separated in Algorithm 2 for better understanding. The clustering aims to minimize the information loss of a group

---

Algorithm 2. BestSelection

    Input: r, C, τ, min_t, max_t
    Output: Cluster c_{best}

1   $C_{min} = [\,]$, $C_{best} = [\,]$, $e_{min} = +\infty$;
2   **foreach** $c \in C$ **do**
3      $e_i = $ GetEnlargment(r, c);
4      $e_{min} = \min(e_{min}, e_i)$;
5   **foreach** $c \in C$ **do**
6      $e_j = $ GetEnlargment(r, c);
7   **if** $e_j == e_{min}$ **then**
8   add c in C_{min};
9         $c_{test} = $ copy of c;
10   add r in c_{test};
11        $i_{lossTest} = (\max(c_{test}) - \min(c_{test}))\, /\, (max_t - min_t)$;
12   **if** $i_{lossTest} < \tau$ **then**
13   add c in C_{best};
14 **if** C_{best} *is* $\emptyset$ **then**
15   **if** *size of* $C < \beta$ **then**
16      $c_{new} = $ new Cluster;
17   add c_{new} in C;
18   **return** c_{new};
19   **else**
20   **return** a cluster from C_{min} with smallest size;
21 **else**
22   **return** a cluster from C_{best} with smallest size;

---

based on a threshold τ, continuously updated (Algorithm 1 line 11) as the average of information loss from the last m published groups. The updating process of τ is performed this way to be automatic and based on the information loss from the latest published clusters. Thus, the information loss of each published group is computed in line 9 of Algorithm 1. Such information loss (i_{loss}) seeks to measure the cluster generalization in relation to the total generalization. The total generalization, in its turn, consists of the maximum difference between the items of greatest and smallest value until the current interaction. It is observed that this value will equal to Δf in the worst scenario. As a result, the algorithm aims to minimize the information loss of each cluster with the goal of generating clusters with well-represented centroids. Besides that, a cluster will grow as long as it keeps good representativity, or until a tuple within the cluster reaches the delay constraint.

Anonymization. This sub-phase consists in verifying if there exists a tuple that reached the delay constraint and, for this reason, must be published (Algorithm 1 line 6). To this intent, the group to which this tuple belongs to is published, i.e., the tuple together with the other tuples from the same group. The anonymization steps of this group occur from lines 12 to 17 of Algorithm 1. To publish the group, its centroid value χ is calculated as the average of the elements of the group. After that, the noise value η to be inserted in the group is computed, given by a random sample obtained from the Laplace distribution with mean zero and scale $\Delta c/\epsilon$ (line 12), as defined in [15]. Next, the value of all tuples in the group is replaced by $\chi + \eta$ and the anonymized group is published. Finally, the group with all its elements is removed from memory.

Notice that Δc does not depend upon the size of the dataset so that the anonymization strategy can be directly applied to the context of microaggregation in data streaming. Furthermore, as argued in [15], a unique Laplace noise sample must be generated for the whole group. Otherwise, if a different noise were generated for each tuple, the amount of noise generated would be greater than in the traditional approach, considering that in this manner, besides the noise of the traditional approach, there would be information loss resulting from the microaggregation step.

As δ-DOCA acts in the online context, it is important to mention that it satisfies the memory limitation constraint, as well as the restriction of time processing to the output. Given that DOCA treats the arrival of a new tuple as a unit of time, consequently, there will never be more tuples in processing than the value established for the delay constraint. Also, the complexity constraint for online processing is satisfied, since the number of iterations for the clustering of a new item (Algorithm 2) is limited by the input parameter β (maximum number of clusters). The cost of calculating the centroid of the cluster and generating the required Laplace noise takes constant time. The cost of anonymizing and publishing a cluster (Algorithm 1 lines 12 to 18), in its turn, is linear on the cluster size that in the worst case[3] is limited by the delay constraint.

4 Experimental Evaluation

The two stages that compose δ-DOCA, i.e., Domain Bounding by δ and DOCA, can be used independently. However, in the experiments, δ-DOCA is evaluated as a whole, that is, the output from stage 1 is used as input for stage 2. In our experiments, we show that in stage 1 the domain $\mathcal{D}$ became stable in an acceptable number of interactions for datasets with different levels of skew. We also demonstrate that the number of items outputted from stage 1 satisfies the proportion specified by δ. As expected, the value of sensitivity, resulted from $\mathcal{D}$, is still very high and the naive anonymization gets no utility for analysis. After performing Stage 2, we obtained a high utility improvement when compared to the previous strategy.

In order to evaluate δ-DOCA, three real world datasets were used to simulate data streaming: CC [13], LOANS [12] and BACKBLAZE [11]. The main characteristics of these datasets are detailed in Table 1. From CC, the attribute *Amount* was used. The attribute *loan_amount* was collected from LOANS. From BACKBLAZE, it is used the attribute *smart_9_raw* from data collected in January 2017. The skew presented is measured by the asymmetry coefficient given

---

[3] All elements in the same cluster.

Table 1. Data sets characteristics.

Dataset	CC	LOANS	BACKBLAZE
Data size	284,807	671,205	1,989,462
Unique values	32,767	479	42,762
min	0.0	25.0	1.0
max	25691.16	100000.0	66413.0
skew	16.9776	9.7954	0.7365

by $\frac{1}{n*s^3} \sum_{i=1}^{n}(X_i - \bar{X})^3$, where n stands for the dataset size, s for the standard deviation and $\bar{X}$ for the mean.

Five executions of δ-DOCA were performed for each combination of parameters for each dataset. For each execution, the data were randomly shuffled to simulate a data streaming. This strategy is used because, given the online nature of δ-DOCA, the order in which data arrives can be relevant to the final result. The result is presented as the average of the five executions. The number of executions cannot be high to avoid biased results, because, when using the Laplace mechanism, the average of results tend to approximate to the real answer.

4.1   Domain Bounding by δ Evaluation

Step 1 is evaluated with different proportions of publishing (δ) and also with different levels of tolerance (λ) as detailed in Definition 1 with all combinations between $\delta = \{0.95, 0.9, 0.85, 0.8, 0.75, 0.70\}$ and $\lambda = \{0.02, 0.01, 0.001\}$. These λ values were chosen considering the metric adopted for stabilization (coefficient of variation) that returns values in the range $[0, 1]$, and as closest of zero, less variation is accepted (see Eq. 1 for variation). To compute the stabilization from Definition 1, we set $m = 10,000$ for all the experiments. This value of m is shown to be suitable for the different magnitudes and distributions skew of the three datasets and cannot be considered high, as δ-DOCA is designed to work with potentially unlimited data. The column *begin of pub* from Tables 2, 3 and 4 presents the moment when the data start to be published. Notice that, in most cases, the values do not exceed m by more than three times.

Even for a high degree of publishing with δ equals to 0.95 (95% of the data), in the less skewed dataset (BB) the domain was reduced by 33.7% in the smallest reduction case. In the most skewed dataset (CC) the domain was reduced by 99.45%. Notice that, the lower the domain, the lower the sensitivity and, consequently, the better the utility is. The reason why δ-DOCA is capable of reducing the domain so significantly is that few extreme values push the domain to a high range, even though almost all data can be represented in a very smaller range.

Tables 2, 3 and 4 show for the three datasets that the bounded domain of the first stage of our contribution holds for almost all combination of parameters δ and λ. We believe that the cases where the condition did not hold were due to the limited size of the datasets; if the data streaming was long enough, the condition would eventually hold, especially for datasets very skewed, like CC.

Table 2. Stage 1 experimental results from CC [13].

Delta	Lambda	Begin of pub.	Published	Published %	dom. reduc. %
0,95	0,02	21799,2	197567,8	75.1178	99.3580
	0,01	16534,6	255858,2	95.3731	97.5749
	0,005	22072,8	186689,2	71.0551	99.4536
0,9	0,02	11074,2	193831,2	70.8102	99.4617
	0,01	13480,6	246092,6	90.7008	98.5732
	0,005	29356,6	229708,2	89.9258	98.5828
0,85	0,02	14813,4	227114,6	84.1181	99.2128
	0,01	12713,6	235644,4	86.6048	98.9762
	0,005	17137,4	201337,6	75.2212	99.3588
0,8	0,02	33772	239106,8	95.2632	97.6473
	0,01	17230,6	231569,6	86.5438	98.9823
	0,005	31187,8	219492,4	86.5418	98.9820
0,75	0,02	17833,4	240934,2	90.2382	98.5928
	0,01	11125,4	230379	84.1775	99.2081
	0,005	17283,8	254200,8	95.0197	97.6565
0,7	0,02	16869,6	190175	70.9778	99.4559
	0,01	40277,6	183363,2	74.9824	99.3623
	0,005	24814	218439,8	84.0237	99.2162

4.2 δ-DOCA Evaluation

The stage 2 of our approach is evaluated regarding utility. In this step, there is utility loss coming from two different sources: (i) microaggregation and (ii) Laplace noise, added to achieve differential privacy. It is proportional to $\Delta c = \Delta f/|C|$, where Δf is computed based on the output $\mathcal{D}$ from stage 1. δ-DOCA is compared with the naive strategy of publishing the differential privacy data without an online microaggregation step, just adding the Laplace noise with mean zero and scale $\Delta f/\epsilon$ to each item. This Δf is also computed based on the output $\mathcal{D}$ from step 1. From now on, this strategy will be called *baseline*. For the experiments, we adopted the following parameters for Algorithm 1: *delay constraint* = 1000, *beta* = 50, $m = 100$ and *epsilon* = 1.0. This comparison was chosen because, to the best of our knowledge, there has been hitherto no work published that considers the differential privacy publishing of a data streaming in non-interactive scenarios.

Figure 3 shows the Mean Squared Errors (MSE) for δ-DOCA and *baseline*. The horizontal axis shows each combination of δ and λ and the vertical axis exhibits the MSE value. The results for each dataset are presented by pairs of subplots. Figure 3a and b show the results for *baseline* and δ-DOCA, respectively, for CC. Figure 3c and d are the results for LOANS as Fig. 3e and f presents the results for BACKBLAZE. For all experiments, the MSE decreases around 99%

Table 3. Stage 1 experimental results from LOANS [12]

Delta	Lambda	Begin of pub.	Published	Published %	dom. reduc. %
0,95	0,02	12907,8	633694,2	96.2625	95.8090
	0,01	20077	625925,4	96.1293	95.9290
	0,005	30524,2	616722,4	96.2600	95.8090
0,9	0,02	11102,6	607629,6	92.0506	97.2343
	0,01	19058	600012,4	92.0062	97.2243
	0,005	26534,4	592551,8	91.9166	97.2593
0,85	0,02	12447,8	566115	85.9371	98.0095
	0,01	16384	561783,6	85.7919	98.0445
	0,005	30473,2	549678,4	85.7883	98.0445
0,8	0,02	11272,6	536792	81.3403	98.4146
	0,01	16790,2	531772,4	81.2588	98.4296
	0,005	31922,8	518465,8	81.1012	98.4546
0,75	0,02	12046	505711,4	76.7207	98.6997
	0,01	10954,8	506528,6	76.7177	98.6997
	0,005	11435,8	506152	76.7165	98.6997
0,7	0,02	16353,4	481473,4	73.5237	98.8447
	0,01	15873,8	481508,8	73.4754	98.8497
	0,005	27846,2	473205	73.5535	98.8447

when using δ-DOCA. As mentioned before, the *baseline* strategy has resulted in almost no utility. It evidences that a utility improvement step is in fact necessary. Notice that, since the differences of MSE are so high when comparing *baseline* and δ-DOCA, the graphics in Fig. 3 are exhibited in the logarithmic scale. Still, from Fig. 3, we can infer that the MSE error increases exponentially with the linear increase of δ. It is also possible to see that λ has no substantial impact on the noise volume.

So far, we have shown that the microaggregation step in δ-DOCA had a significant decrease in the noise volume added when compared to *baseline*. However, it is also essential to show that the data anonymized by δ-DOCA can represent well the original data distribution. To compare the two distributions, we evaluated the histogram intersection between the original and anonymized data, which is given by Eq. 2, where O is the histogram of original data, A is is the histogram of anonymized data and n is the number of bins.

$$\frac{\sum_{i=1}^{n} min(O_i, A_i)}{\sum_{i=1}^{n} A_i} \tag{2}$$

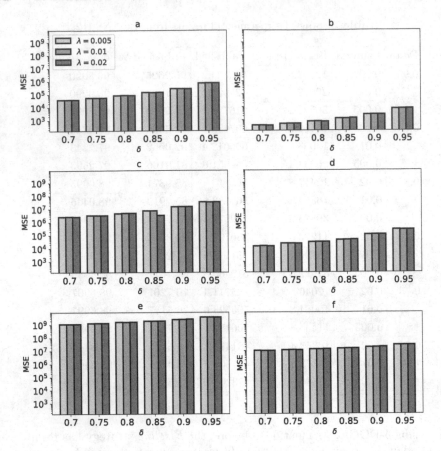

Fig. 3. *baseline* x δ-DOCA MSE.

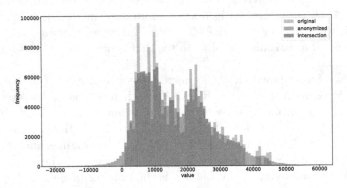

Fig. 4. Comparison between original data and anonymized data for BACKBLAZE with δ = 0.95, λ = 0.02, 100 bins and 96.59% intersection area.

Table 5 displays the average intersection of all experiments for each dataset, as well as the worst and best case obtained. In that case, 100 bins were adopted. For all datasets, the anonymized data can represent the original data with high accuracy. The histogram intersection is also good to show visually the similarity between the two distributions, as presented in Fig. 4 for one execution of δ-DOCA to BACKBLAZE using $\delta = 0.95$ and $\lambda = 0.02$.

Table 4. Stage 1 experimental results from BACKBLAZE [11].

Delta	Lambda	Begin of pub.	Published	Published %	dom. reduc. %
0,95	0,02	16319,6	1873740,8	94.9624	33.8162
	0,01	18855,4	1870190,8	94.9045	33.9267
	0,005	25578,4	1866033,6	95.0174	33.7084
0,9	0,02	12240	1778105,4	89.9294	44.7085
	0,01	24136	1768642,2	89.9922	46.2474
	0,005	37828,4	1757087,6	90.0317	46.5320
0,85	0,02	11007,2	1682444,8	85.0384	53.0064
	0,01	13980,2	1679558,8	85.0203	52.8570
	0,005	16232,8	1674137,6	84.8426	53.2332
0,8	0,02	10631,2	1587354	80.2167	56.5741
	0,01	13039,4	1581434,2	80.0149	57.0785
	0,005	19703,2	1574487	79.9329	57.0689
0,75	0,02	10040,4	1484931	75.0184	61.0230
	0,01	11494,2	1491345	75.3978	60.6981
	0,005	14937	1475130,8	74.7082	61.1868
0,7	0,02	10365	1389293,6	70.1984	64.0360
	0,01	11012,4	1386616,6	70.0860	64.2363
	0,005	14495,4	1381876,6	69.9698	64.1113

Table 5. Histogram intersection: original data x δ-DOCA anonymized data.

Dataset	Avg intersection %	Intersection min %	Intesection max %
CC	0.9492	0.9296	0.9616
LOANS	0.9419	0.9145	0.9688
BACKBLAZE	0.9616	0.9558	0.9682

5 Conclusion

This paper presented δ-DOCA, a strategy to anonymize data streams in a non-interactive context, with the addition of noise directly on the data. To this intent, at first, the data domain is defined and adjusted by a δ, obtaining the sensitivity value of the differential privacy. Then, the stage of utility improvement is performed, which makes use of the Laplacian noise addition to online-defined groups. The results of the experiments showed a significant reduction of the noise added, while maintaining a high level of privacy, preserving the characteristics of the original dataset.

Many future work opportunities arise from our results. They include: (i) adapting δ-DOCA to support data streaming with multiple attributes; (ii) defining a model to adjust the parameters of the online microaggregation; and, (iii) supporting multiple records from the same individual.

References

1. Bindschaedler, V., Shokri, R., Gunter, C.A.: Plausible deniability for privacy-preserving data synthesis. Proc. VLDB Endow. **10**(5), 481–492 (2017)
2. Blum, A., Ligett, K., Roth, A.: A learning theory approach to non-interactive database privacy. In: Proceedings of the Fortieth Annual ACM Symposium on Theory of Computing, STOC 2008, pp. 609–618. ACM, New York (2008)
3. Cao, J., Carminati, B., Ferrari, E., Tan, K.L.: Castle: continuously anonymizing data streams. IEEE Trans. Dependable Secure Comput. **8**(3), 337–352 (2011)
4. Chen, Y., Machanavajjhala, A., Hay, M., Miklau, G.: Pegasus: data-adaptive differentially private stream processing. In: Proceedings of the 2017 ACM SIGSAC Conference on Computer and Communications Security, CCS 2017, pp. 1375–1388. ACM, New York (2017)
5. Dwork, C.: Differential privacy. In: Bugliesi, M., Preneel, B., Sassone, V., Wegener, I. (eds.) ICALP 2006. LNCS, vol. 4052, pp. 1–12. Springer, Heidelberg (2006). https://doi.org/10.1007/11787006_1
6. Dwork, C., Naor, M., Pitassi, T., Rothblum, G.N.: Differential privacy under continual observation. In: Proceedings of the Forty-second ACM Symposium on Theory of Computing, STOC 2010, pp. 715–724. ACM, New York, (2010)
7. Dwork, C., Roth, A.: The algorithmic foundations of differential privacy. Found. Trends Theor. Comput. Sci. **9**(3–4), 211–407 (2014)
8. Greenwald, M., Khanna, S.: Space-efficient online computation of quantile summaries. SIGMOD Rec. **30**(2), 58–66 (2001)
9. Hardt, M., Ligett, K., McSherry, F.: A simple and practical algorithm for differentially private data release. In: Proceedings of the 25th International Conference on Neural Information Processing Systems, NIPS 2012, vol. 2, pp. 2339–2347. Curran Associates Inc., USA (2012)
10. Meeker, W.Q., Hahn, G.J., Escobar, L.A.: Statistical Intervals: A Guide for Practitioners and Researchers. Wiley Series in Probability and Statistics, 2nd edn. Wiley, New York (2017)
11. Backblaze: The raw hard drive test data. https://www.backblaze.com/b2/hard-drive-test-data.html. Accessed 22 Apr 2018
12. Data Science for Good: Kiva Crowdfunding: Kiva loans. https://www.kaggle.com/kiva/data-science-for-good-kiva-crowdfunding/data. Accessed 16 Apr 2018
13. Worldline and Machine Learning Group (ULB): Credit card fraud detection. https://www.kaggle.com/mlg-ulb/creditcardfraud. Accessed 11 Apr 2018
14. Silva, J.A., ER, F., RC, B., ER, H., ACPLFD, C., JA, G.: Data stream clustering: a survey. ACM Comput. Surv. **46**(1), 13:1–13:31 (2013)

15. Soria-Comas, J., Domingo-Ferrer, J.: Differentially private data sets based on microaggregation and record perturbation. In: Torra, V., Narukawa, Y., Honda, A., Inoue, S. (eds.) MDAI 2017. LNCS (LNAI), vol. 10571, pp. 119–131. Springer, Cham (2017). https://doi.org/10.1007/978-3-319-67422-3_11
16. Soria-Comas, J., Domingo-Ferrer, J., Sánchez, D., Martínez, S.: Enhancing data utility in differential privacy via microaggregation-based k-anonymity. VLDB J. **23**(5), 771–794 (2014)
17. Sweeney, L.: k-anonymity: a model for protecting privacy. Int. J. Uncertain. Fuzziness Knowl. Based Syst. **10**(5), 557–570 (2002)
18. Xu, J., Zhang, Z., Xiao, X., Yang, Y., Yu, G., Winslett, M.: Differentially private histogram publication. VLDB J. **22**(6), 797–822 (2013)
19. Zhang, J., Cormode, G., Procopiuc, C.M., Srivastava, D., Xiao, X.: Privbayes: private data release via bayesian networks. ACM Trans. Database Syst. **42**(4), 25:1–25:41 (2017)

Data Oblivious Genome Variants Search
on Intel SGX

Avradip Mandal[1($\boxtimes$)], John C. Mitchell[2], Hart Montgomery[1], and Arnab Roy[1]

[1] Fujitsu Laboratories of America, Sunnyvale, CA, USA
[2] Stanford University, Stanford, CA, USA
avradip@gmail.com

Abstract. We show how to build a practical, private data oblivious genome variants search using Intel SGX. More precisely, we consider the problem posed in Track 2 of the iDash Privacy and Security Workshop 2017 competition, which was to search for variants with high χ^2 statistic among certain genetic data over two populations. The winning solution of this iDash competition (developed by Carpov and Tortech) is extremely efficient, but not memory oblivious, which potentially made it vulnerable to a whole host of memory- and cache-based side channel attacks on SGX. In this paper, we adapt a framework in which we can exactly quantify this leakage. We provide a memory oblivious implementation with reasonable information leakage at the cost of some efficiency. Our solution is roughly an order of magnitude slower than the non-memory oblivious implementation, but still practical and much more efficient than naive memory-oblivious solutions–it solves the iDash problem in approximately 5 min. In order to do this, we develop novel definitions and models for oblivious dictionary merging, which may be of independent theoretical interest.

1 Introduction

A *trusted execution environment* (TEE) is a secure area of a main processor. In particular, a TEE attempts to simulate a 'black box' environment: users (even with physical access) of the main processor may only see the inputs to and outputs from the TEE, and learn nothing about the data or processes inside the TEE. This 'black box' premise potentially allows for private, secure distributed or cloud-based computations on data that previously were only known to be possible from very heavyweight, impractical cryptography (or even not known to be possible!).

Examples of TEEs available today include Intel's SGX (Software Guard Extensions), ARM's TrustZone, AMD's Secure Execution Environment, and Apple's Secure Enclave. There are many different types of TEE in existence today, but in this work we will focus on SGX, which is currently the most studied TEE.

TEEs are particularly exciting for applications where we want third parties to perform computations on secret data. For instance, if we assume a secure

J. Garcia-Alfaro et al. (Eds.): DPM 2018/CBT 2018, LNCS 11025, pp. 296–310, 2018.
https://doi.org/10.1007/978-3-030-00305-0_21

TEE, it is known how to build many powerful cryptographic primitives that run with very small overhead when compared to native computations: fully homomorphic encryption [SCF+15], functional encryption [FVBG17], and even obfuscation [NFR+17] are all known to be practical with trusted hardware. Coupled with other cryptographic techniques, these primitives implicitly allow a vast range of functionality for TEEs: things like secure linux containers [ATG+16], oblivious multi-party machine learning [OSF+16], and blockchain smart contract messaging techniques [ZCC+16] are possible and efficient when TEEs are used.

iDash Competition. To further illustrate the power of TEEs, consider the following scenario: suppose a medical research institution wants to outsource aggregation and statistical computation on genome data to a TEE based cloud server. Individuals would send their encrypted genome to the cloud server. TEE would decrypt the encrypted data, perform statistical computation and send back the end result to the research institute. With traditional cryptography, to achieve comparable security we would require functional encryption for very complicated functions, which is only known from indistinguishability obfuscation (and is extremely inefficient). This scenario almost exactly describes the 'track 2' problem given in this past year's iDash competition [iDa17], which is a privacy and security workshop devoted to using cryptographic techniques to help solve problems in computational biology and genetics. In Sect. 3 we will describe the problem in details. Among proposed solution, the best solution was due to Carpov and Tortech [CT18], which performed the computation on 27.4 GB of data in only 65 s of client-side preprocessing time and 7 s of enclave time.

Side Channels. Unfortunately, it is easy to see that there are many ways a potential adversary can learn about computations in the TEE–even if the TEE is 'perfectly' secure, as long as it has finite computational power, finite memory, and connections to other outside systems, there are ways for an adversary to learn things about secret information. For instance, an adversary could measure the time that a particular computation takes and use that to infer things about secret information involved in the computation. Often, the TEE does not have enough internal memory to store all of the data needed for a particular computation. In this case, it must store (encrypted) data in outside locations, like regular memory or hard disks. When this happens, an adversary can observe the memory access patterns of the program running inside the TEE and also potentially learn secret information.

These kinds of attacks are called *side channel* attacks and have been widely known in the cryptographic community since Paul Kocher's famous paper [Koc96] which long predates modern trusted hardware. The history of side channel attacks include things like observing how long a computation takes [Koc96], tracking the memory access patterns of a particular program [KSWH98, Pag02], and measuring power consumption at given times when the program is run [MDS99].

Side channel attacks on SGX and other TEEs have been proposed for almost as long as the TEEs themselves have existed. Most of the side channel attacks on

SGX have focused on the cache [GESM17,BMD+17]–in other words, the lack of 'memory obliviousness' of programs–but there have been other side channel attacks, including attacks based on timing [WKPK16]. In addition, there has been a lot of research done with the goal of mitigating these side channel attacks. Many techniques, like oblivious RAM (ORAM) [Gol87] or path ORAM [SvDS+13b] are very general and can do a lot to mitigate these side channel attacks. In fact, there has been quite a bit of research lately on preventing certain classes of side channel attacks in SGX [SLKP17,SCNS16,SLK+17]. Unfortunately, the generality of many of these techniques typically implies a large overhead, and thus the resulting TEE-based schemes are not very efficient. Oblivious B+ tree implementations using shuffle index are also well known [VFP+15]. However, as described in Sect. 3.1, in our context the optimal data structure is dictionary or hash table.

Our Contributions. Like many other SGX-based protocols, all of the submissions in 'Track 2' of the past year's iDash competition were potentially vulnerable to side channel attacks. In this paper, we show how to build a provably side channel resistant variant of the fastest (and winning) submission [CT18]. We employ a number of techniques, including oblivious shuffles and dictionary merging, as well as clever cache management, in order to provide provable resistance to side channel attacks.

While our side channel resistant construction massively outperforms what generic solutions like ORAM would give, it is still not quite as efficient as the native solution in [CT18]. While the solution of [CT18] takes 65 s of preprocessing time and 7 s of enclave computation time, our memory oblivious solution which only leaks aggregate intersection sizes among input data (see Sect. 6 for details) takes 28 s preprocessing time and about 5 min of enclave computation time– significantly less efficient than the non-memory oblivious solution, but certainly practical.

In order to achieve memory obliviousness, we construct new definitions and models for oblivious dictionary merging. These models help us to formally state properties about memory obliviousness and may be of independent theoretical interest.

Outline. The rest of the paper is as follows: in Sect. 2, we discuss the security model we use around SGX. We next define the genomic search problem from the iDash Track 2 that we have alluded to earlier in Sect. 3. We also explain the (non-side channel resistant) winning solution in this section. In Sect. 4, we discuss how to make the previously discussed solution memory oblivious (and thus, side channel resistant). Then, in Sect. 5, we discuss how to merge dictionaries in a memory-oblivious way, which is a critical component for our overall solution. We discuss our experimental results in Sect. 6.

2   Security Model of SGX

A program is called data oblivious if its memory access trace can be simulated by a simulator with access to only some observable information. In theory, one can use Oblivious RAM implementations to make a program data oblivious. However, generic application of ORAM [SVDS+13a] techniques with small amount of trusted memory has a large overhead, compared to native running time. But what is trusted memory inside an SGX enclave? A conservative approach might be to consider only the CPU registers as trusted memory. On the other end of the spectrum, an optimistic approach can assume all available enclave memory (about 96 MB) as trusted memory. Taking this optimistic approach authors in [EZ17, ZDB+17] showed many SQL like database operations can be performed in an data oblivious manner with very little performance overhead.

A reasonable model of trusted memory lies somewhere in between. All data in the Last Level Cache (LLC) remain unencrypted. So it's quite natural to assume the LLC is part of the trusted memory. However, the size of the LLC available to the enclave program is controlled by the adversary with a 4KB (cache line) granularity.

To be reasonably conservative, in this paper we assume that all memory accesses are visible to the adversary. In particular, we follow the model of Chan et al. [CGLS18], who introduced the notion of adaptive strongly oblivious simulation security for arbitrary stateless functionalities and Oblivious Random Access Machines (ORAM). Given a stateless functionality f, some leakage function $\texttt{leakage}_f$, $\texttt{Alg}_f$ obliviously implements f with leakage $\texttt{leakage}_f$ if

- $\texttt{Alg}_f$ correctly computes the same function f except with negligible probability for all inputs,
- the sequence of addresses requested (and whether each request is read or write) by $\texttt{Alg}_f$ do not reveal more information than the allowed leakage.

Formally,

Definition 1. $\texttt{Alg}_f$, *obliviously implements the functionality f with leakage function* $\texttt{leakage}_f$, *iff there exists a p.p.t. simulator Sim, such that for any non-uniform p.p.t. adversary $\mathcal{A}$, $\mathcal{A}$'s view in the following two experiments are indistinguishable or equivalently* $\| \Pr[b_{real} = 1] - \Pr[b_{sim} = 1] \|$ *is negligible in terms of security parameter λ.*

Algorithm 1. Real Experiment	**Algorithm 2.** Simulated Experiment
procedure $\text{EXPT}_{\mathcal{A}}^{\text{REAL,ALG}_f}(1^\lambda)$	**procedure** $\text{EXPT}_{\mathcal{A}}^{\text{SIM,ALG}_f}(1^\lambda)$
$\quad \mathcal{A} \to I$	$\quad \mathcal{A} \to I$
$\quad \text{out}, \text{addresses} \leftarrow \texttt{Alg}_f(I)$	$\quad \text{out} \leftarrow f(I)$
$\quad \mathcal{A}(\text{out}, \text{addresses}) \to b_{\text{real}} \in$	$\quad \text{addresses} \leftarrow \text{Sim}(\texttt{leakage}_f(I))$
$\{0,1\}$	$\quad \mathcal{A}(\text{out}, \text{addresses}) \to b_{\text{sim}} \in \{0,1\}$
end procedure	**end procedure**

Here *addresses* in the real experiment denotes the sequence of addresses requested by $\texttt{Alg}_f$ along with the information whether each access is read or write.

Case Study: Oblivious Sort. Traditional implementations of sort typically proceed by repetitively comparing two values and swapping them or doing nothing depending on the result of the comparison. This induces them to produce different access patterns based on the data values themselves, and as such they are not oblivious. However, some algorithms such as bitonic sorting [Bat68] are data independent, and hence oblivious. In addition, "swap or not"-based sorting algorithms can be made oblivious by accessing the same memory locations regardless of the comparison outcome. In Sect. 4, we will use oblivious sort primitives for oblivious implementation of genome variants search.

Case Study: Oblivious Shuffle. Oblivious shuffle is a simple but important stateless oblivious primitive. As the name suggests, the shuffle algorithm takes a sequence of n elements as input and outputs a uniformly random permutation of the sequence. Consequently, an oblivious shuffle is an algorithm whose memory accesses can be simulated irrespective of the input and the output, and hence also the actual permutation that was employed. A natural way to do an oblivious shuffle is to pair each entry with a uniformly random number and then oblivious sort the pairs with respect to the random numbers. Other efficient algorithms which are not based on sorting also exist [OGTU14]. In Sect. 5, we will use oblivious shuffle primitives for realizing oblivious dictionary merging.

3   Whole Genome Variants Search

In this section we provide a very short introduction to genomics and describe the Genome Variants Search algorithm which identifies genes responsible for certain hereditary diseases.

DNA (Deoxyribonucleic acid) is a chain of nucleotides with the shape of a double helix. It carries genetic information in all living organisms. The complete genetic material of an organism is called its genome, and DNA is identical in every cell of our body. A very long DNA chain forms what is called a chromosome. Humans have 23 pairs of chromosomes, and each pair has one chromosome from the person's father and one from the mother. Any two humans share about 99.9% of their DNA. The remaining 0.1% DNA tracks the difference between two individuals. Most of these differences occur in the form of what is called a Single Nucleotide Polymorphism (SNP). A SNP is a variation in a single nucleotide that occurs at a specific position in the genome (compared to a reference genome). Moreover, a SNP can be either heterozygous or homozygous, depending on whether a set of homologous chromosomes (pairs of choromosomes with one coming from the father, another from mother) differ or are identical on that particular position, respectively.

One important aspect of modern day genomics is identifying genes or SNPs responsible for certain diseases. Given SNPs from two groups of users–case (individuals showing traits of the disease) and control (individuals representing healthy population)–one can perform Pearson's χ^2 test of association to determine whether presence of certain SNP is associated to disease susceptibility or not. SNPs with high χ^2 statistic are thought to be responsible for the disease.

3.1   Track 2 of the iDASH 2017 Challenge: χ^2 Test for Whole Genome Variants Search

The goal of Track 2 of the iDASH Privacy & Security Workshop 2017 competition [iDa17] was to develop a scalable and secure solution using SGX technology for whole genome variants search among multiple individuals. The input data is Variant Call Format (VCF) files containing sensitive SNP information from case and control groups of users. Logically, a single VCF file corresponds to a single individual and is a collection of SNPs, along with the information whether the SNPs are homozygous or heterozygous. Suppose we have n_1 case users and n_2 control users. To evaluate χ^2 statistic for a particular SNP s, one needs to find out how many times it is present among case and control users by single counting heterozygous occurrences and double counting homozygous occurrences. Suppose a_s is the count of SNP s among case users and a_s' among control users. Note, $(2n_1 - a_s)$ and $(2n_2 - a_s')$ are the absence counts of SNP s among case and control users. Now, for the SNP s observed frequencies O_s, and expected frequencies (assuming no association) E_s can be stated as

$$O_s = [a_s, a_s', 2n_1 - a_s, 2n_2 - a_s']$$
$$E_s = [r(a_s + a_s'), (1 - r)(a_s + a_s'), 2n_1 - r(a_s + a_s'), 2n_2 - (1 - r)(a_s + a_s')],$$

where the ratio $r = \frac{n_1}{n_1 + n_2}$. From the observed and expected frequencies the χ^2 test statistic for SNP s can be calculated as

$$\sum_{j=0}^{3} \frac{(O_s[j] - E_s[j])^2}{E_s[j]}. \tag{1}$$

The p-value for the SNP s is the probability that a random variable following a χ^2 distribution with degree of freedom one[3] attains a value larger than the computed test statistic. To find the top k most significant SNPs, one needs to compute p-values for all SNPs present in the genome data set and output k SNPs with least p-values or equivalently output k SNPs with highest χ^2 test statistic.

In the iDash competition pre-processing and compression of individual VCF files were allowed, with the constraint that any operation involving multiple VCF files cannot be performed at the pre-processing stage. It must be done inside the SGX enclave. This constraint correctly depicts the real life use case, where each VCF file is owned by the corresponding human individual. They can pre-process and compress their own information and send it to remote SGX enclave running on a possibly adversarial computational server. Honest individuals following the protocol are not expected to communicate among them, they are only supposed to send their information to the SGX enclave running in the computational server.

The computationally expensive step in the above calculation is finding out 'count' of every SNP among case and control users. The natural way to evaluate these count values is as follows.

---

[3] χ^2 distribution with degree of freedom d is defined as sum of square of d independent standard normal variables.

- represent individual VCF files as dictionaries (collection of (key, value) pairs) as follows:
  - For an user u belonging to the Case group, for all SNPs s present in its VCF file we have

$$\text{Dict}_u[s].\text{Case} = \begin{cases} 1, & \text{if } s \text{ is heterozygous for user } u \\ 2, & \text{if } s \text{ is homozygous for user } u \end{cases}$$

$$\text{Dict}_u[s].\text{Cont} = 0$$

  - For user v in the Control group it is exactly the opposite. That is for all SNP s present in user v's VCF file $\text{Dict}_v[s].\text{Case} = 0$ and $\text{Dict}_v[s].\text{Cont}$ is either one or two depending whether s is heterozygous or homozygous for user u.

  If we query the dictionary Dict_u with any SNP not present in user u's VCF file, it returns zero in both case and control counters. In other words $s' \notin \text{Dict}_u.\text{Keys}$, we have $\text{Dict}_u[s'].\text{Case} = \text{Dict}_u[s'].\text{Cont} = 0$.

- Merge all user dictionaries. Where the dictionary merging operation is defined as follows. For all $s \in \text{Dict}_A.\text{Keys} \cup \text{Dict}_B.\text{Keys}$,

$$(\text{Dict}_A \cup \text{Dict}_B)[s].\text{Case} = \text{Dict}_A[s].\text{Case} + \text{Dict}_B[s].\text{Case}$$

$$(\text{Dict}_A \cup \text{Dict}_B)[s].\text{Cont} = \text{Dict}_A[s].\text{Cont} + \text{Dict}_B[s].\text{Cont}$$

After merging we have the merged dictionary

$$\text{Dict}_{\text{Merge}} = \cup_{u \in \text{case users} \cup \text{control users}} \text{Dict}_u$$

$\text{Dict}_{\text{Merge}}$ contains count of SNPs among case and control users. After building the dictionary rest of the calculation is relatively straight–forward. The whole process is described in Algorithm 3, where Merge is the functionality that takes dictionaries (containing SNPs as keys and corresponding counter as value) as input, and the merged dictionary as output. In other words

$$\text{Merge}(\text{Dict}_1, \cdots, \text{Dict}_n) \rightarrow \text{Dict}_1 \cup \cdots \cup, \text{Dict}_n.$$

CalcChiSquare is a function that takes

$$(\text{number of case users}, \text{number of control users}, (snp, (\text{Case}, \text{Cont})))$$

as input and outputs $(snp, \chi^2\text{-statistic})$ where χ^2-statistic is calculated according to Eq. (1). $\text{ForEach}^f(\mathcal{V})$ is a functionality which outputs the list $\{f(v) : v \in \mathcal{V}\}$.

3.2   The Winning Solution of the iDash Track 2 Challenge [CT18]

The main challenge in the above computation is memory access optimization. The input data size is in the order of tens of gigabytes, whereas SGX enclaves are limited to about 96 MegaBytes of usable memory without paging. Moreover, inside SGX enclaves, the last level cache (LLC) miss penalty is considerably

---

Algorithm 3. Genome variants search to find top k SNPs

INPUT: : User set $\mathcal{U} = \mathcal{U}_{\text{Case}} \cup \mathcal{U}_{\text{Cont}}$ and SNP dictionaries Dict_u for all $u \in \mathcal{U}$, size of case and control user groups.

OUTPUT: : Top k SNPs $(snp_1, \cdots, snp_k)$

1: **procedure** GVS($\{\text{Dict}_u : \forall u \in \mathcal{U}\}, n_1 = \|\mathcal{U}_{\text{Case}}\|, n_2 = \|\mathcal{U}_{\text{Cont}}\|$)

2:      $\text{Dict}_{\text{Merge}} \leftarrow \text{Merge}(\{\text{Dict}_u : u \in \mathcal{U}\})$

3:      $\text{List}_{SNP} \leftarrow \textbf{ForEach}^{\text{CALCCHISQUARE}(n_1, n_2, \cdot)}(\text{Dict}_{\text{Merge}})$

4:      $\text{List}_{SNP}.\text{SORT}()$ ▷ Sorts the list in a decreasing order based on *chisquare* value

5:      **return** $\text{List}_{SNP}[1:k].snp$ ▷ Output top k SNPs

6: **end procedure**

---

higher compared to native execution because this requires an extra round of encryption/decryption. This extra cost is by design, because in SGX architecture the main random access memory (RAM) always remains encrypted.

In Algorithm 3 the size of the $\text{Dict}_{\text{case}}$ and $\text{Dict}_{\text{cont}}$ dictionaries become the bottleneck. Even if we compress the SNPs and keep a single dictionary with separate case and control counters, we need at least 4 bytes to encode a SNP and $2 + 2 = 4$ bytes to store the two counters. However, in the sample data set provided in the competition there were about 5.5 Million unique SNPs. This means a trivial lower bound for the total size of the merged dictionaries is $(4 + 4) * 5.5 = 44$ MB. Even though, this lower bound is well short of the 96 MB limit to avoid page faults, this is far bigger than typical LLC size which is 6 or 8 MB. A typical memory efficient dictionary or hash-map implementation usually involves a random memory access for each key access. This leads to an almost mandatory cache fault for every dictionary access if we cannot fit the dictionary inside the LLC. As a result, any SGX implementation of the Sect. 3.1 algorithm typically incurs about a factor of two slowdown compared to native execution. To address this issue Carpov and Tortech [CT18] adopted an ingenious

---

Algorithm 4. Cache friendly Genome variants search to find top k SNPs

---

INPUT: : User set $\mathcal{U} = \mathcal{U}_{\text{Case}} \cup \mathcal{U}_{\text{Cont}}$ and SNP dictionaries $\text{Dict}_{u,i}$ for all $u \in \mathcal{U}$ and $i \in [1, n]$, size of case and control user groups.

OUTPUT: : Top k SNPs $(snp_1, \cdots, snp_k)$

1: **procedure** GVS($\{\text{Dict}_{u,i} : \forall u \in \mathcal{U}, i \in [1, n]\}, n_1 = \|\mathcal{U}_{\text{Case}}\|, n_2 = \|\mathcal{U}_{\text{Cont}}\|$)

2:      $\text{List}_{SNP} \leftarrow \varPhi$

3:      **for all** $i \in [1, n]$ **do**

4:            $\text{Dict}_{\text{Merge},i} \leftarrow \text{Merge}(\{\text{Dict}_{u,i} : u \in \mathcal{U}\})$

5:            $\text{List}_{Temp} \leftarrow \textbf{ForEach}^{\text{CALCCHISQUARE}(n_1, n_2, \cdot)}(\text{Dict}_{\text{Merge},i})$

6:            $\text{List}_{SNP}.\text{INSERT}(\text{List}_{Temp})$

7:            $\text{List}_{SNP}.\text{SORT}()$ ▷ Sorts the list in a decreasing order based on *chisquare* value

8:            $\text{List}_{SNP} \leftarrow \text{List}_{SNP}[1:k]$ ▷ Only keep top k elements of the list

9:      **end for**

10:     **return** List_{SNP} ▷ Output top k SNPs

11: **end procedure**

---

yet simple horizontal partitioning technique to reduce the memory requirement so that everything could be done within the LLC. The key observation is instead of building the large dictionary containing all SNPs and then finding the top k SNPs among them, we can partition the SNPs in various batches and process each batch independently while updating a global list of the top k SNPs.

We can divide the key space $\mathcal{K}$ (all possible values of SNPs) of the dictionaries into n disjoint parts $\mathcal{K}_1, \cdots, \mathcal{K}_n$. This in turn divides each user dictionary Dict_u into n disjoint smaller dictionaries $\text{Dict}_{u,1}, \cdots, \text{Dict}_{u,n}$ such that

$$\text{Dict}_u = \text{Dict}_{u,1} \cup \cdots \cup \text{Dict}_{u,n}.$$

4   Oblivious Genome Variants Search

Algorithms described in the previous section are not memory oblivious in general. In this section, we show under certain conditions the algorithms can be implemented in a memory oblivious way. Non memory oblivious SGX implementations might leak some non trivial information such as number of common SNPs among any two persons. Moreover, if some of the individuals are malicious and they collude with the server they can figure out exactly which SNPs are present in other individual's VCF files. $\mathcal{U}_{\text{Case}}$ be the set of users belonging to the case group and $\mathcal{U}_{\text{Cont}}$ be the set of users belonging to the control group. Every user $u \in \mathcal{U}_{\text{Case}} \cup \mathcal{U}_{\text{Cont}}$ sends their input I_u to a centralized server $\mathcal{S}$, which runs a Genome Variants Search algorithm inside its SGX enclave. It's worth mentioning that every user u must

- perform a remote attestation with S, to ensure it is running the appropriate executable inside SGX enclave and
- perform a key exchange with the enclave and send I_u by encrypting and authenticating with the exchanged key,

to ensure the data can only be accessed by the enclave. I_u is some encoding of the VCF data corresponding to user u. In Algorithm 3 we have $I_u = \text{Dict}_u$, where as in Algorithm 4 we have $I_u = \{\text{Dict}_{u,i} : i \in [1, n]\}$. GVS be the function which takes I_u's as input and outputs top k SNPs.

From a high level perspective the Genome Variant Search algorithms described in previous section have three distinct steps:

1. Merge input dictionaries to form a merged dictionary.
2. Calculate chi-Square statistic for each entry.
3. Sort the dictionary entries based on the chi-square statistic.

Chi-square statistic calculation is trivially memory oblivious (can be implemented by an arithmetic circuit). There are many well known perfectly memory oblivious sorting [AKS83, CGLS18, Bat68, Goo14] techniques which do not leak any side information. In Sect. 5 we discuss how to obliviously implement the dictionary Merge routine under various reasonable leakage functions. Once we have oblivious implementations of the dictionary merge routine and sort routine, next theorems show we can quantify the leakage in Algorithms 3 and 4.

Theorem 1. *If the* Merge *routine in Algorithm 3 is implemented obliviously with leakage function* $leakage_{Merge}$ *and the* Sort *routine in line 3 is implemented by some perfect oblivious sort implementation, then Algorithm 3 becomes an oblivious implementation of GVS with leakage function* $leakage_{GVS}$, *where*

$$leakage_{GVS}(\{Dict_u : \forall u \in \mathcal{U}\})$$
$$= leakage_{Merge}(\{Dict_u : \forall u \in \mathcal{U}\}) \cup \{\|Dict_{Merge}\|, \|\mathcal{U}_{Case}\|, \|\mathcal{U}_{Cont}\|\}.$$

Proof Sketch. We construct a simulator for GVS, given a simulator for Merge, given as Algorithm 5. We can show that the real algorithm is indistinguishable from the simulator by hopping over a single hybrid. In the hybrid, we replace the merging step with the corresponding simulator, which just takes the leakage due to the merge as input. In the next hop, which is to the final simulator, we sample $Dict_u$ from random, instead of using the real input $Dict_u$. The sampling is done as follows: first $\|Dict_{Merge}\|$ number of unique keys are sampled from the domain of keys. Then the values of $Dict_u$ at those keys are assigned arbitrarily. We recall that the in construction of the merged list the input array is scanned linearly and the number of positions scanned only depends on the number of entries, *i.e.*, $\|Dict_u\|$, and not their values. Hence the addresses utilized in this part of the simulator would be indistinguishable from the hybrid.

Algorithm 5. Simulator for GVS

INPUT: $leakage_{Merge}(\{Dict_u : \forall u \in \mathcal{U}\}) \cup (\|Dict_{Merge}\|, n_1 = \|\mathcal{U}_{Case}\|, n_2 = \|\mathcal{U}_{Cont}\|)$.

OUTPUT: addresses.

1: **procedure** SIM-GVS($leakage_{Merge}(\{Dict_u : \forall u \in \mathcal{U}\}) \cup (\|Dict_{Merge}\|, n_1, n_2)$)
2:   List$_{SNP} \leftarrow \emptyset$.
3:   addresses-dict-merge $\leftarrow$ SIM-MERGE($leakage_{Merge}(\{Dict_u : \forall u \in \mathcal{U}\})$)
4:   Sample $Dict_{Merge}$ randomly, constrained by $\|Dict_{Merge}\|$.
5:   List$_{SNP} \leftarrow$ **ForEach**$^{CALCCHISQUARE(n_1, n_2, \cdot)}(Dict_{Merge})$
6:   List$_{SNP}$.SORT()   ▷ Sorts the list in a decreasing order based on *chisquare* value
7:   addresses-extra $\leftarrow$ Addresses used in Steps 5-6.
8:   **return** addresses-dict-merge, addresses-extra   ▷ Output all addresses
9: **end procedure**

Theorem 2. *If the* Merge *routine in Algorithm 4 is implemented obliviously with leakage function* $leakage_{Merge}$ *and the* Sort *routine in line 6 is implemented by some perfect oblivious sort implementation, then Algorithm 4 becomes an oblivious implementation of GVS with leakage function* $leakage_{GVS}$, *where*

$$leakage_{GVS}(\{Dict_{u,i} : \forall u \in \mathcal{U}, i \in [1, n]\},)$$
$$= \left(leakage_{Merge}(\{Dict_{u,1} : \forall u \in \mathcal{U}\}), \cdots, leakage_{Merge}(\{Dict_{u,n} : \forall u \in \mathcal{U}\}) \right)$$
$$\cup \{\|Dict_{Merge,1}\|, \cdots, \|Dict_{Merge,n}\|, \|\mathcal{U}_{Case}\|, \|\mathcal{U}_{Cont}\|\}$$

The proof of this theorem is fairly similar to the last one: instead of simulating the merge monolithically, the simulation is done partition by partition. The arguments for the rest of the algorithm carry over straightforwardly.

5   Oblivious Dictionary Merging

In the previous section, we showed that given a procedure to obliviously merge multiple dictionaries we can obliviously implement the Genome Variants Search algorithms. In this section show how oblivious dictionary merging can be done.

In Sect. 3.1, we defined the notion of dictionary merging in the context of genome variants search. However, the algorithms described in this section work for generic dictionary merging operations. A dictionary or associative array Dict is a dynamic collection of (key, value) pairs, such that each possible *key* appears only once in the collection. It usually supports insert, delete, update and lookup operations based on the key. The operator [ ] is used as an access operator. That is if (key, value) ∈ Dict, then Dict[key] returns a reference to value. Let Dict.Keys denote the set of all keys in the dictionary. For any key ∉ Dict.Keys,

- as rvalue Dict[key] returns Null. In other words value = Dict[key] sets the variable value to Null.
- as lvalue Dict[key] inserts a pair (key, value) to the dictionary and returns a reference to the variable value. In other words Dict[key] = value inserts (key, value) into the dictionary Dict.

Let $\mathcal{V}$ be the set of all possible values excluding Null. $\oplus$ be a binary operator over $\mathcal{V}$. It can be naturally extended to $\mathcal{V} \cup \{\texttt{Null}\}$ as follows. For any value $\in \mathcal{V}$,

$$\text{value} \oplus \texttt{Null} = \text{value}, \qquad \texttt{Null} \oplus \text{value} = \text{value}, \qquad \texttt{Null} \oplus \texttt{Null} = \texttt{Null}.$$

For the Genome Variants Search application described in Sect. 3.1, $\oplus$ operator over (Case, Cont) pairs is defined as $a \oplus b = (a.\text{Case} + b.\text{Case}, a.\text{Cont} + b.\text{Cont})$. For any two dictionaries Dict_1 and Dict_2, the Merge operation (also represented by the operator $\cup$) is defined as follows. First $(\text{Dict}_1 \cup \text{Dict}_2).\text{Keys} = \text{Dict}_1.\text{Keys} \cup \text{Dict}_2.\text{Keys}$. Second for all key $\in (\text{Dict}_1 \cup \text{Dict}_2).\text{Keys}$, we have $(\text{Dict}_1 \cup \text{Dict}_2)[key] = \text{Dict}_1[key] \oplus \text{Dict}_2[key]$.

For more than two dictionaries the Merge operation is defined inductively. For $n \geq 2$, we have

$$\text{Dict}_1 \cup \cdots \cup \text{Dict}_n = (\text{Dict}_1 \cup \cdots \cup \text{Dict}_{n-1}) \cup \text{Dict}_n.$$

Dictionaries or hash tables are usually implemented either by chaining or by open addressing. [Che17] is a short summary and comparison of various hash table implementations. It suggests open address based hash table implementation Robin Hood [CLM85] is probably the fastest memory efficient implementation. For the purpose of this paper, we will assume the hash table memory is contiguous, which is the case for all open addressing based hash tables.

This means we can sequentially access all elements of the hash table by a linear sweep. The memory addresses accessed in this operation are independent of the hash table content.

The location of any (key, value) pair in the contiguous memory is determined by hash(key). We will assume the function hash is a random oracle [BR93], to ensure that the pair (key, value) gets stored in a random location independent of the variable key. The idea behind an almost ideal (in terms of leakage) dictionary merging is pretty simple and can be described in three high level steps:

1. Sequentially access all (key, value) pairs of all input dictionaries Dict_1, $\cdots$, Dict_n and store them in a large array Array of size $\|\text{Dict}_1\| + \cdots + \|\text{Dict}_n\|$.
2. Obliviously shuffle Array and generate Array'.
3. Build the new dictionary $\text{Dict}_{\text{Merge}}$ by sequentially traversing Array'.

The memory access pattern in first two steps are completely independent of the input data. However, the last step leaks some non trivial information. A resourceful adversary can track how the memory locations within the contiguous storage are being accessed. The location of a dictionary entry corresponding to key gets determined by hash(key). By the random oracle property of the hash function, the location does not reveal anything about the content of key. Also, because of the oblivious shuffle this address does not reveal from which input dictionary Dict_i the key is coming from. But the adversary can observe how many times each address location is getting accessed. This in turn leaks the collision distribution of the input dictionaries, which is essentially the following information.

$$\sum_{i=1}^{n} \|\text{Dict}_i\|, \quad \sum_{1 \le i < j \le n} \|\text{Dict}_i \cap \text{Dict}_j\|, \quad \sum_{1 \le i < j < k \le n} \|\text{Dict}_i \cap \text{Dict}_j \cap \text{Dict}_k\|,$$
$$\cdots, \|\text{Dict}_1 \cap \text{Dict}_2 \cap \cdots \cap \text{Dict}_n\|.$$

6 Experimental Results

For our experimental results, we use the public dataset available as part of the iDash 2017 competition [iDa17]. The dataset consists of VCF files from two groups of individuals, case group Case whose members show symptoms of some particular disease and control group Cont consisting of healthy individuals. The total size of the two thousand VCF files is about 27.4 GB. We ran our experiments on an Intel NUC6i7KYK, which has 6 MB of LLC. In comparison, the platform used in [CT18] had 8 MB LLC size. Our baseline implementation takes 28 s for pre-processing (or total time for client side computation). In the baseline non oblivious implementation of Algorithm 4, the computation time inside the SGX enclave is 16 s. On the other hand, the winning candidate from [CT18] reports about 65 s of pre-processing time and 7 s of enclave running time. The pre-processing is mainly bounded by the SSD read write speed. Our pre-processing is faster because we used a larger block size (every VCF file is divided only in

15 parts). On the other hand, [CT18]'s enclave running time is almost half that of ours for two main reasons: first, our enclave is single threaded, as opposed to 8 threads in [CT18]. In fact, our dictionary implementation is not thread safe. Second, we have only 6 MB of cache memory. [CT18] had 8 MB.

The oblivious dictionary merging algorithm described in Sect. 5 has a crucial drawback. It requires oblivious shuffling of a very large array containing all the input data. After compression the total size of input data is about 4.5 GB. In the baseline implementation we partitioned the data in 15 parts, to fit individual dictionaries inside the LLC. After this partitioning, the output of each Merge call in Algorithm 4 fits well within the LLC, but the input is still large: about 4.5 GB /15 = 300 MB. For an efficient memory oblivious shuffle we needed to fit the input data within LLC. To address this we can further partition the input data and shuffle each partition independently. This partitioning actually leaks more information, such as the collision patterns among different partitions. In our implementation in every partition we take 256 SNPs each from 16 users and shuffle them together. We used Batcher's bitonic merge sort algorithm [Bat68] for oblivious shuffling. We also used SipHash [AB12] as our choice of random oracle. To our knowledge, this is the fastest known pseudorandom function for short input sizes. In this parameter setting the enclave running time is about 5 minutes. This shows even though memory oblivious implementation is practical if we are willing to leak some amount of collision distributions, it is still considerably slower than the non oblivious implementation. One thing to note is that the performance of the scheme is dependent upon the choice of data partitioning and hence information leakage. Finding a better data partitioning technique which would allow minimal leakage and the fastest possible performance remains an open problem.

References

[AB12]   Aumasson, J.-P., Bernstein, D.J.: SipHash: a fast short-input PRF. In: Galbraith, S., Nandi, M. (eds.) INDOCRYPT 2012. LNCS, vol. 7668, pp. 489–508. Springer, Heidelberg (2012). https://doi.org/10.1007/978-3-642-34931-7_28

[AKS83] Ajtai, M., Komlós, J., Szemerédi, E.: An $O(n \log n)$ sorting network. In: 15th Annual ACM Symposium on Theory of Computing, pp. 1–9, Boston, MA, USA, 25–27 April 1983. ACM Press (1983)

[ATG+16] Arnautov, S., et al.: SCONE: secure Linux containers with Intel SGX. OSDI **16**, 689–703 (2016)

[Bat68] Batcher, K.E.: Sorting networks and their applications. In: Proceedings of the April 30-May 2, 1968, Spring Joint Computer Conference, pp. 307–314. ACM (1968)

[BMD+17] Brasser, F., Müller, U., Dmitrienko, A., Kostiainen, K., Capkun, S., Sadeghi, A.-R.: Software grand exposure: SGX cache attacks are practical. arXiv preprint arXiv:1702.07521, p. 33 (2017)

[BR93]   Bellare, M., Rogaway, P.: Random oracles are practical: a paradigm for designing efficient protocols. In: Ashby, V. (ed.) ACM CCS 93: 1st Conference on Computer and Communications Security, pp. 62–73, Fairfax, Virginia, USA, 3–5 November 1993. ACM Press (1993)

[CGLS18] Chan, T.H.H., Guo, Y., Lin, W.-K., Shi, E.: Cache-oblivious and data-oblivious sorting and applications. In: Proceedings of the Twenty-Ninth Annual ACM-SIAM Symposium on Discrete Algorithms, pp. 2201–2220. SIAM (2018)

[Che17] Chern, F.: Writing a damn fast hash table with tiny memory footprints (2017). http://www.idryman.org/blog/2017/05/03/writing-a-damn-fast-hash-table-with-tiny-memory-footprints. Accessed 7 June 2018

[CLM85] Celis, P., Larson, P., Munro, J.I.: Robin Hood hashing (preliminary report). In: 26th Annual Symposium on Foundations of Computer Science, pp. 281–288, Portland, Oregon, 21–23 October 1985. IEEE Computer Society Press (1985)

[CT18] Carpov, S., Tortech, T.: Secure top most significant genome variants search: iDASH 2017 competition. Cryptology ePrint Archive, Report 2018/314 (2018). https://eprint.iacr.org/2018/314

[EZ17] Eskandarian, S., Zaharia, M.: An oblivious general-purpose SQL database for the cloud. arXiv preprint arXiv:1710.00458 (2017)

[FVBG17] Fisch, B., Vinayagamurthy, D., Boneh, D., Gorbunov, S.: IRON: functional encryption using intel SGX. In: Thuraisingham, B.M., Evans, D., Malkin, T., Xu, D. (eds.) ACM CCS 17: 24th Conference on Computer and Communications Security, pp. 765–782, Dallas, TX, USA, 31 October–2 November 2017. ACM Press (2017)

[GESM17] Götzfried, J., Eckert, M., Schinzel, S., Müller, T.: Cache attacks on Intel SGX. In: Proceedings of the 10th European Workshop on Systems Security, EuroSec 2017, pp. 2:1–2:6. ACM, New York (2017)

[Gol87] Goldreich, O.: Towards a theory of software protection and simulation by oblivious RAMs. In: Aho, A. (ed.) 19th Annual ACM Symposium on Theory of Computing, pp. 182–194, 25–27 May 1987. ACM Press, New York City (1987)

[Goo14] Goodrich, M.T.: Zig-zag sort: a simple deterministic data-oblivious sorting algorithm running in $O(n \log n)$ time. In: Shmoys, D.B. (ed.) 46th Annual ACM Symposium on Theory of Computing, pp. 684–693, 31 May–3 June 2014. ACM Press, New York (2014)

[iDa17] IDASH privacy & security workshop (2017). http://www.humangenomeprivacy.org/2017/competition-tasks.html. Accessed 7 June 2018

[Koc96] Kocher, P.C.: Timing attacks on implementations of Diffie-Hellman, RSA, DSS, and other systems. In: Koblitz, N. (ed.) CRYPTO 1996. LNCS, vol. 1109, pp. 104–113. Springer, Heidelberg (1996). https://doi.org/10.1007/3-540-68697-5_9

[KSWH98] Kelsey, J., Schneier, B., Wagner, D., Hall, C.: Side channel cryptanalysis of product ciphers. In: Quisquater, J.-J., Deswarte, Y., Meadows, C., Gollmann, D. (eds.) ESORICS 1998. LNCS, vol. 1485, pp. 97–110. Springer, Heidelberg (1998). https://doi.org/10.1007/BFb0055858

[MDS99] Messerges, T.S., Dabbish, E.A., Sloan, R.H.: Investigations of power analysis attacks on smartcards. Smartcard 99, 151–161 (1999)

[NFR+17] Nayak, K., et al.: HOP: hardware makes obfuscation practical. In: ISOC Network and Distributed System Security Symposium - NDSS 2017, San Diego, CA, USA. The Internet Society (2017)

[OGTU14] Ohrimenko, O., Goodrich, M.T., Tamassia, R., Upfal, E.: The Melbourne Shuffle: improving oblivious storage in the cloud. In: Esparza, J., Fraigniaud, P., Husfeldt, T., Koutsoupias, E. (eds.) ICALP 2014. LNCS, vol. 8573, pp. 556–567. Springer, Heidelberg (2014). https://doi.org/10.1007/978-3-662-43951-7_47

[OSF+16] Ohrimenko, O., et al.: Oblivious multi-party machine learning on trusted processors. In: USENIX Security Symposium, pp. 619–636 (2016)

[Pag02] Page, D.: Theoretical use of cache memory as a cryptanalytic side-channel. Cryptology ePrint Archive, Report 2002/169 (2002). http://eprint.iacr.org/2002/169

[SCF+15] Schuster, F., et al.: VC3: trustworthy data analytics in the cloud using SGX. In: 2015 IEEE Symposium on Security and Privacy, pp. 38–54, San Jose, CA, USA, 17–21 May 2015. IEEE Computer Society Press (2015)

[SCNS16] Shinde, S., Chua, Z.L., Narayanan, V., Saxena, P.: Preventing page faults from telling your secrets. In: Chen, X., Wang, X., Huang, X. (eds.) ASIACCS 16: 11th ACM Symposium on Information, Computer and Communications Security, pp. 317–328, Xi'an, China, 20 May–3 June 2016. ACM Press (2016)

[SLK+17] Seo, J., et al.: SGX-shield: enabling address space layout randomization for SGX programs. In: ISOC Network and Distributed System Security Symposium - NDSS 2017, San Diego, CA, USA. The Internet Society (2017)

[SLKP17] Shih, M.-W., Lee, S., Kim, T., Peinado, M.: T-SGX: eradicating controlled-channel attacks against enclave programs. In: ISOC Network and Distributed System Security Symposium - NDSS 2017, San Diego, CA, USA. The Internet Society (2017)

[SVDS+13a] Stefanov, E., et al.: Path ORAM: an extremely simple oblivious RAM protocol. In: Proceedings of the 2013 ACM SIGSAC Conference on Computer & Communications Security, pp. 299–310. ACM (2013)

[SvDS+13b] Stefanov, E., et al.: Path ORAM: an extremely simple oblivious RAM protocol. In: Sadeghi, A.-R., Gligor, V.D., Yung, M. (eds.) ACM CCS 13: 20th Conference on Computer and Communications Security, pp. 299–310, Berlin, Germany, 4–8 November 2013. ACM Press (2013)

[VFP+15] De Capitani, S., Vimercati, D., Foresti, S., Paraboschi, S., Pelosi, G., Samarati, P.: Shuffle index: efficient and private access to outsourced data. ACM Trans. Storage (TOS) 11(4), 19 (2015)

[WKPK16] Weichbrodt, N., Kurmus, A., Pietzuch, P., Kapitza, R.: AsyncShock: exploiting synchronisation bugs in Intel SGX enclaves. In: Askoxylakis, I., Ioannidis, S., Katsikas, S., Meadows, C. (eds.) ESORICS 2016. LNCS, vol. 9878, pp. 440–457. Springer, Cham (2016). https://doi.org/10.1007/978-3-319-45744-4_22

[ZCC+16] Zhang, F., Cecchetti, E., Croman, K., Juels, A., Shi, E.: Town crier: an authenticated data feed for smart contracts. In: Weippl, E.R., Katzenbeisser, S., Kruegel, C., Myers, A.C., Halevi, S. (eds.) ACM CCS 16: 23rd Conference on Computer and Communications Security, pp. 270–282, Vienna, Austria, 24–28 October 2016. ACM Press (2016)

[ZDB+17] Zheng, W., Dave, A., Beekman, J.G., Popa, R.A., Gonzalez, J.E., Stoica, I.: Opaque: an oblivious and encrypted distributed analytics platform. In: NSDI, pp. 283–298 (2017)

DPM Workshop: Internet of Things

Developing GDPR Compliant
Apps for the Edge

Tom Lodge[1]([✉]) [iD], Andy Crabtree[1] [iD], and Anthony Brown[2] [iD]

[1] School of Computer Science, University of Nottingham, Nottingham, UK
{thomas.lodge,andrew.crabtree}@nottingham.ac.uk
[2] Horizon Digital Economy Research, University of Nottingham, Nottingham, UK
anthony.brown@nottingham.ac.uk

Abstract. We present an *overview* of the Databox application development environment or SDK as a means of enabling trusted IoT app development at the network edge. The Databox platform is a dedicated domestic platform that stores IoT, mobile and cloud data and executes local data processing by third party apps to provide end-user control over data flow. Key challenges for building apps in edge environments concern *(i)* the complexity of IoT devices and user requirements, and *(ii)* supporting privacy preserving features that meet new data protection regulations. We examine how the Databox SDK can ease the burden of regulatory compliance and be used to sensitize developers to privacy related issues in the very course of building apps.

Keywords: Internet of Things · Edge computing · Databox
Data protection · GDPR · Trusted application development · SDK

1 Introduction

The predominant paradigm for computing is centred in the cloud. However, as the Internet of Things (IoT) emerges, the requirement to push increasing volumes of data to the network for centralized storage and processing will impact system resilience, network traffic, latency and privacy. An alternative approach is to "extend the cloud to where things are" [1] and shift data storage and processing to the edge of the network. In this model, nodes at the edge perform the bulk of storage and processing, keeping data off the core network, reducing latency and improving the potential for data privacy. The model has gained significant traction in recent years, and the IDC [2] predicts investment in edge infrastructure will reach up to 18% of total spend by 2020.

This work was supported by the Engineering and Physical Sciences Research Council (Grant Numbers EP/M001636/1, EP/N028260/1, EP/M02315X/1).

The domestic space is seeing a growth in dedicated hardware that brings more data storage and processing to the edge [3–7]. Many of these products unify access to connected home devices and provide facilities (voice, web UIs, apps) for automation and control. With new General Data Protection Regulation (GDPR) in Europe [8], and growing concern amongst ordinary people about the (ab)use of personal data, we anticipate this space will grow to include new domestic platforms that take a more principled approach to exploiting personal data generated by IoT devices, mobile and cloud services. The Databox platform [9] provides one of several [10–12] instantiations of domestic 'privacy-preserving' edge-based solutions, running data processors (apps) within a sandboxed environment where access to and use of data is constrained by user-negotiated contracts.

The distinguishing feature of such platforms is that processing moves to the data, rather than data to the processing, and data distribution is limited to the results of local queries enabling the 'data minimisation' that is required under GDPR. Developing apps that run on these platforms is challenging. There are challenges that are already familiar to IoT developers: *(i)* processing data from an increasingly heterogeneous range of data sources, *(ii)* across a wide variability of domestic environments and *(iii)* competing systems with inconsistent patterns of behaviour [13], plus *(iv)* the need to support multiple users with diverse requirements. There are also new challenges that come from the need to meet new data protection regulation and (thereby) gain user trust. This requires that developers demonstrably respond to the requirements of data protection regulation in the apps they produce [14]. Moreover 'developers' is a broad category including makers, hobbyists, and enthusiasts. Development environments must therefore enable data protection across a broad cohort while providing developers and end-users alike with the tools they need to build the (often niche) functionality that they require.

Our end-user development environment (SDK) has been designed to build apps for the Databox platform and to: *(i)* simplify IoT app development for domestic environments, in particular data processing across multiple devices and sensors; *(ii)* open up development to a broad cohort of developers and *(iii)* enable compliance with key features of GDPR. Though our SDK addresses all of these challenges, this paper focuses exclusively upon *(iii)*, i.e. how developers can be supported when creating domestic IoT privacy preserving apps that are compliant with the letter and spirit of GDPR.

This paper has two main contributions: *(i)* an assessment of the implications of GDPR upon the creation of edge-based personal data processing systems *(ii)* design and implementation of a development environment for building GDPR compliant domestic apps. This latter contribution has relevance beyond a description of design and implementation choices; it points to a new set of general features we expect will be of value to any development environment geared towards writing code that operates upon personal data.

2   Related Work

We briefly consider 3 interconnected areas of work: *(i)* domestic smart hubs, *(ii)* privacy preserving environments and *(iii)* developer support.

2.1   Domestic Smart Hubs

The multitude of different standards, network and data protocols employed within the domestic IoT space has resulted in the emergence of IoT ecosystems aimed at providing *(i)* interoperability across devices *(ii)* control interfaces for device management, and *(iii)* support for home automation. Within the open source community, many IoT systems have also been designed to run on local hardware, whether ARM, x86 or embedded system such as Arduino and Raspberry Pi [15–18]. These systems are aimed at technically competent users and are underpinned by programming frameworks to support further extension.

There is also a highly competitive startup scene, with a range of products on the market aimed at the general consumer [19–21], typically offering easy integration with IoT devices and polished control interfaces. The most significant inroads have been made by the large Internet companies. Amazon's 'Echo' [3] is installed in tens of millions of households, for example, and Google's 'Home' [5] is gaining market share as is Apple's HomePod [4]. These systems perform some local storage and processing as a means of reducing latency and reliance on an upstream network, but still use companion cloud-based systems when needed. However, the mechanisms and processes utilised by these cloud systems remain opaque to the end user. Not only is there a lack of transparency around the flow and use of data, there are notably few features enabling users to restrict data flow or exploit it for individual purposes.

2.2   Privacy Preserving Environments

Personal Data Management Services, whether cloud-based [22] or at the edge [23] store consumer data and provide explicit contracts to underpin data exchange.

The Databox platform is a privacy preserving domestic smart hub that permits controlled access to a data subject's personal data, set out in explicit user-agreed contracts called Service Level Agreements (SLAs).

The system provides abstractions for data sources (IoT devices or cloud-based services such as Twitter), drivers (privileged code that communicates with datasources), datastores (local repositories of user data) and apps (code that processes data). Apps are untrusted code, and can only ever communicate with datastores (to read data or actuate a device) with explicit consent from a user. All components (including apps) run in isolated Docker[1] containers. Restrictions are enforced through an arbiter. Figure 1 *(1,2 and 3)* shows the token exchange. At app install time the SLA is parsed, and permissions granted (the arbiter is informed app X can do action Y). Tokens are not minted until the app requests

---

[1]   https://www.docker.com.

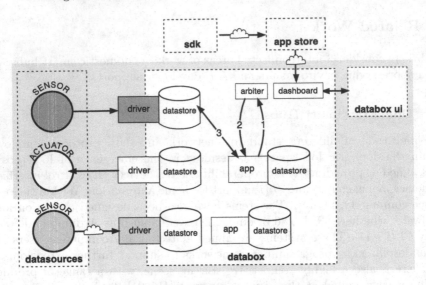

Fig. 1. Databox platform architecture

one (usually just before it performs an action). Tokens have expiry dates and can be cached and reused until expiry, after which a new one must be requested. The wider Databox ecology consists of an app store; a repository of databox apps that can be downloaded to an individual Databox, and an SDK; a web-based development environment for constructing apps. Users interact with the Databox through a web frontend, which provides a set of interfaces for installing new apps (part of which will require users to review the app contract) and to view/monitor/remove running apps. The platform is responsible for auditing all accesses to datastores and enforcing SLAs.

2.3   Developer Support

The matter of developer support for IoT hubs is not straightforward. Commercial and open source ecosystems provide development environments that support the creation of new product integrations or bespoke functionality oriented around a product's features [6,24–26] and are typically targeted at competent and/or professional programmers. However, Newman [27] has noted that the burgeoning array of connected domestic devices makes it intractable for developers to build applications to keep pace with the needs of users. He thus argues for the need to support end-user programming to allow a diverse cohort of people to *"compose the functionality that they need"*. Perhaps as a result of these observations, we have seen a proliferation of graphical end-user programing environments [28–31] aimed at masking device/service/protocol heterogeneity and helping connect IoT and webservices in new and interesting ways. The most popular, IFTTT, enjoys a considerable user base [32]. However, given the focus upon technical simplicity, privacy preserving features are given scant regard. Indeed [33] found that 50% of the nearly 20,000 IFTTT 'recipes' they examined contained secrecy or integrity violations that could lead to harm.

3   GDPR Compliance and Its Influence on Developers

In GDPR a data controller *"determines the purposes and means of process-ing personal data"*. When developing applications that run upon IoT hubs, if app developers receive personal data, they are controllers. Similarly, if develop-ers create the app on behalf of a third party they must demonstrate 'privacy by design' principles. Development environments, therefore, must take this into account. Article *5(2)* states: *"the controller shall be responsible for, and be able to demonstrate, compliance with the principles [of GDPR]"*.

In working through the regulation we posit that IoT app developers are impli-cated in two broad areas: *(i)* transparency and *(ii)* articulating and appropriately reducing risk. GDPR explicitly mentions a requirement for risk assessment in Article *35* (data protection impact assessments), though the mention of risk and mechanisms for its reduction are sprinkled throughout various clauses. Article *25 (1)* explicitly requires risk assessment and reduction is performed *"at the time of the determination of the means for processing"*, i.e. at app development time.

GDPR's risk concerns are oriented around data disclosure and automated profiling. Other risks such as physical risk (e.g. switching on an empty ket-tle, closing an automatic garage door), fall outside its scope, though clearly must be given due consideration by developers. Automated profiling relates to harms from unfair, inaccurate algorithmic decisions (whether deliberate or unintentional) that have socially consequential outcomes (e.g. denial of credit/employment/healthcare). This is a burgeoning area of research [34–36] and we have begun early exploration with two new features in our SDK (see our special purpose profiling node and runtime inspection interface in Sect. 4).

Transparency relates to adequate provision of information relating to the col-lection, processing and use of personal data in order that users have information to *(i)* provide informed consent and *(ii)* control (restrict, extend, halt) its use. Transparency is in itself advocated in GDPR as a tool to reduce risk, and many of the basic "rights" enshrined by the regulation are predicated upon it, i.e. the right to object, the right to be informed and the right to restrict processing.

When considering the impact of GDPR upon developers, we assume the platform (i.e. IoT hub, such as Databox) will take most responsibility for data security, notification of breaches, ongoing data storage and access (Articles *5, 16, 17, 20, 25, 30, 32–34*). That is not to disregard their importance or to suggest that the developer can be disconnected from these concerns, only that they sit outside the scope of this work.

Given this scope, Table 1 distils the 99 key parts of the Articles (*5, 7, 12, 13, 21, 22, 25, 35*) that implicate developers with regard to data disclosure risk and/or transparency requirements. The 3rd column *(R/T)* marks each clause as

Table 1. GDPR clauses relevant to developers

Art	Relevant clauses	R/T
5	(a) processed lawfully, fairly and in a transparent manner in relation to the data subject ('lawfulness, fairness and transparency');	T
	(b) collected for specified, explicit and legitimate purposes and not further processed in a manner that is incompatible with those purposes;	T
	(c) adequate,relevant and limited to what is necessary in relation to the purposes for which they are processed ('data minimisation')	R
7	4. Where processing is based on consent, the controller shall be able to demonstrate that the data subject has consented to processing of his or her personal data	T
	8. The data subject shall have the right to withdraw his or her consent at any time. [...] It shall be as easy to withdraw consent as to give it	T
12	1. provide any information [...] relating to processing to the data subject in a concise, transparent, intelligible and easily accessible form, using clear and plain language	T
	7. The information to be provided [..] may be provided in combination with standardised icons in order to give in an easily visible, intelligible and clearly legible manner a meaningful overview of the intended processing	T
13	2 (f) the existence of automated decision-making, including profiling, referred to in Article 22(1) and (4) and, at least in those cases, meaningful information about the logic involved, as well as the significance and the envisaged consequences of such processing for the data subject	T
21	1. The data subject shall have the right to object, on grounds relating to his or her particular situation, at any time to processing of personal data concerning him or her which is based on points (e) or (f) of Article 6(1), including profiling based on those provisions	T
22	1. The data subject shall have the right not to be subject to a decision based solely on automated processing, including profiling, which produces legal effects concerning him or her or similarly significantly affects him or her	R
	2. Paragraph 1 shall not apply if the decision is: (c) based on the data subject's explicit consent	T
25	1. [..] the controller shall, both at the time of the determination of the means for processing and at the time of the processing itself, implement appropriate technical and organisational measures, such as pseudonymisation, [..] such as data minimisation	R
	2. The controller shall implement appropriate technical and organisational measures for ensuring that, by default, only personal data which are necessary for each specific purpose of the processing are processed	R
35	1. Where a type of processing in particular using new technologies, and taking into account the nature, scope, context and purposes of the processing, is likely to result in a high risk to the rights and freedoms of natural persons, the controller shall, prior to the processing, carry out an assessment of the impact of the envisaged processing operations on the protection of personal data	R

either relating to risk (R) or transparency (T). Note that for the sake of brevity we do not include Article *13's* list of information to be provided; interested readers are directed to Article *13(1)* in the full text [8]. A few clauses remain open to interpretation and have garnered considerable debate in the legal and academic communities. Nevertheless, it is our view that the spirit of GDPR is clear and developer tools have a necessary role in helping meet requirements.

4   The Databox SDK

The SDK is a fully featured web-based environment for building Databox apps. It provides facilities for testing, tools for data visualisation, context-sensitive help, skeleton code generation, basic static type checking and code management (Fig. 2).

The SDK models apps as information flows (inspired by the flow-based programming paradigm [37]) and abstracts the Databox platform architecture into four 'node' types: *datastores, processors, profilers and outputs. Datastores* represent all devices (or services) that generate data. Datastores are device independent, i.e. a smart plug datastore will present a consistent data schema in the SDK, independent of the specific device or manufacturer it maps to at runtime. *Processor* nodes operate on data; it is here custom behaviours and logic are encoded. Processor nodes typically consume one or more inputs and send results to one or more outputs. *Profiler* nodes are a special category of processing node that *infer new information* about a data subject. In treating profilers differently from processing nodes, we aim (in subsequent iterations of the SDK) to sensitise developers to GDPR's more restrictive covenants around "automated profiling" by providing facilities to assess the fairness of profiling on target users [34]. *Output* nodes perform an action, such as actuation, visualization, or data export.

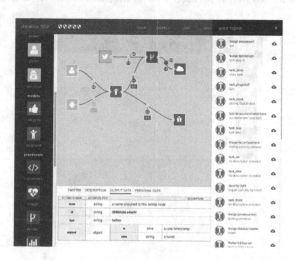

Fig. 2. Inputs, processors, profilers and outputs

When developers publish an app from the SDK, they are prompted for information needed to construct the SLA (user-negotiated contract). Once deployed, the app's datasource nodes interact with the Databox platform API to request permissions to access data according to the terms of the SLA. This functionality is transparently provided by the SDK, insulating developers from the detail.

4.1 Features Enabling GDPR Compliance

In Sect. 3 we presented the set of GDPR clauses that will implicate developers building apps for domestic IoT hubs. We scoped the problem into (i) assessing and reducing disclosure risk and (ii) transparency on what/how/why personal data is being processed.

Our SDK sensitizes developers to data disclosure risk by (i) providing ongoing risk breakdowns as developers build apps (ii) tracking personal data as it moves through an app. Our SDK addresses GDPRs requirements for transparency by (i) creating GDPR compliant contracts that embed the information required for data-subjects to provide informed consent, (ii) automatically providing facilities for runtime data flow inspection. We expand on each of these in turn.

Provision of Ongoing Risk Breakdown. Our development environment generates an overall risk rating for apps, based on the aggregate risk of the nodes from which it is composed.

Our environment also reflects risks that fall outside the remit of GDPR (such as physical risks mentioned earlier). Each node in the development environment has an in-built schema (provided by the environment, not the developer) that provides, amongst other things, a risk score and breakdown based upon current configuration (e.g., the hardware it works with, the proposed data rate, the particular actuation to be performed). As configuration options are modified and

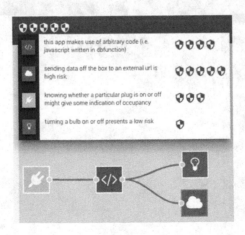

Fig. 3. SDK risk overview

nodes are introduced or removed, the score and breakdown will update to reflect the changes (Fig. 3). Those characteristics of a node that will most influence the global risk score are currently *(i)* whether it exports any data off the box, *(ii)* it triggers physical actuation, *(iii)* it utilizes insecure/leaky/non-compliant hardware, *(iv)* it uses unverified code or libraries.

It may be reasonably argued that "risk" is a subjective concept that covers an indeterminate number of possibilities, and will be influenced by more than just an app's construction and configuration (e.g., the deployment environment can profoundly influence risk likelihood and harms). However we would counter that in conceptualising even a crude notion of risk, the environment will sensitize developers to important concerns *in the course of building apps*, i.e. at the point where they are likely to enact change. We view our risk overview as a "placeholder" and expect that further research and subsequent iterations will lead to improved risk calculations.

Our final risk rating and breakdown is also made available to app store users to further motivate and drive the development of low risk and even 'no risk' apps.

Tracking Personal Data. To help developers assess the risks of personal data disclosure, at a minimum, we require they are able to *(i)* differentiate between data that is personal, sensitive or neither and *(ii)* track the flow of personal data, so that processing risk (e.g. inference attacks made possible by combining data) and exposure risk (e.g. location data being exported off the box) can be identified. Our goal is to help developers assess disclosure vulnerabilities prior to deployment (i.e. statically) rather than at run-time; Databox has its own mechanisms for managing dataflows at runtime.

All data that is output from a node has a corresponding personal data schema. The schema allows developers not only to view the flow of personal data through an app, but to reveal points within an app where further personal inference is possible (e.g. when multiple items of personal data or profiling could be combined to infer a new item of personal data). Take, for example, an algorithm that processes a user's gender, postcode and age. These three items may

Table 2. 6 personal data types

Label	Type	Ordinal	Description	Example
i1	Identifier	Primary	Data that directly identifies a data subject	Full name, picture
i2	Identifier	Secondary	Data that indirectly identifies a data subject	Mac address, username, (age, postcode, birthplace)
p1	Personal	Primary	Data that is evidently personal	Friends, mortgage, salary
p2	Personal	Secondary	Inferred personal data	Gender, age, income (from browsing data)
s1	Sensitive	Primary	GDPR special categories of data	Criminal convictions, health record
s2	Sensitive	Secondary	Inferred sensitive data	Race (from postcode), sexuality (from image)

be enough, with minor effort, to infer a user's identity (perhaps using an auxiliary public dataset). Less obviously, perhaps: an algorithm that utilises mobile phone accelerometer data may be able, assuming a high enough sampling frequency, to infer a user's height, weight and gender [38] or smart metering data may reveal personal habits [39] or occupancy [40]. As a start, inspired by GDPR, our schema specifies six top-level personal data types (Table 2). In our schema (Table 3), the *(type, ordinal)* attributes establish the top-level type and the *category, subtype and description* attributes (originated by us) provide further context. The schema has a *required* attribute to denote which attributes must be present for a schema to apply. For example, if an IoT camera provides a timestamp, bitmap and light reading, only the bitmap attribute is required for the data to be treated as personal.

Table 3. Personal data schema

Attribute	Description
Type	*identifier* | *sensitive* | *personal*
Ordinal	*primary* | *secondary*
Category	*physical* | *education* | *professional* | *state* | *contact* | *consumption...*
Subtype	Sensitive will include biometric, health, sexual, criminal. Personal includes education, profession, consumption.
Description	Details of this particular item of personal data (and method of inference if secondary)
Required	List of attributes of this data that must be present in order for this to constitute as personal data

The schema is extended for secondary (i.e. inferred) types, to specify the conditions that must be satisfied to make an inference possible (Table 4). We currently support two types of condition: *(i)* attributes – the additional set of items of personal data items that, when combined could lead to a new inference; *(ii)* granularity – the threshold sampling frequency required to make an inference. When multiple attribute and/or granularity conditions are combined, all must hold for an inference to be satisfied. Finally our status attribute distinguishes

Table 4. personal data schema

Attribute	Description
Confidence	An accuracy score for this particular inference, ranging from 0 to 1
Conditions	List of *granularity* | *attribute*
Evidence	Where possible, a set of links to any evidence that details a particular inference method
Status	*Inferred* | *inferrable*

between personal data where *(i)* an inference has been made, and *(ii)* the data is available to make inference possible. For example, browsing data and gender may be enough to infer whether an individual is pregnant (i.e. these two items combined make pregnancy inferable) but if a node makes an actual determination on pregnancy, then the resulting data is inferred. We also make two additional assumptions:

- When building a flow, the SDK assumes all data sources belong to the same user. Our next version will formalize this.
- The schema permits data to be tagged as personal even if it is not associated (directly or indirectly) with an individual. Although GDPR specifies that any data that cannot be related to a "natural person" is not personal, we take the view that any items of personal data may still, given the necessary context, be used to identify an individual.

When making use of the schema in the SDK, datasources will define the personal data that they generate, whereas processing and profiling nodes will generate schemas based on the transforms they run on their input data. For example, the combine processing node whose job is to merge attributes from its inputs, auto-generates an output schema by combining the schemas of all input attributes to be merged. Thus it is the SDK's role and not the developer's, to calculate how schemas propagate through an app.

To illustrate a basic example in the SDK, consider Table 5 which outlines the relevant parts of the accelerometer schema for the flows in Fig. 4.

Table 5. Part of the accelerometer datastore personal schema

Attribute	Description
Type	Personal
Subtype	Gender
Ordinal	Secondary
Required	[x,y,z]
Conditions	Type: granularity, threshold: 15, unit: Hz

In the left-hand flow, *p2* is output from the accelerometer to show that personal data (i.e. a user's gender) is *inferable* from the *x, y, z* components of its data (it is semi-transparent to denote it is *inferable* rather than *inferred*). Similarly, with the profile node, i1 is output to show *fullname* is a primary identifier. When these are merged in the combine processor, the output schema will contain the accelerometer's *p2*, and the profile's *i1*. In the right-hand flow, the combine node is configured to only combine the *x* and *y* components of the accelerometer data with the profile data. Since *x, y* and *z* are all marked as required (Table 5) for a gender inference to be possible, the combine node's output schema will only contain *i1* (and not *p2*).

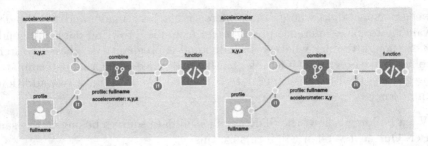

Fig. 4. Combining personal data in the SDK

The SDK will automatically recalculate and re-represent the flow of personal data whenever a node or edge is removed, added or reconfigured. As flows get more complex this becomes invaluable; it helps developers to quickly determine how changes in configuration will alter the flow of personal data.

In tracking personal data the SDK also flags points in an app that may require further attention. When downstream nodes use inferred data with a low confidence score (provided by the schema), developers are warned that processing is based on potentially incorrect data. When any personal data is being exported off the box (i.e. connected to the export node), developers are reminded to ensure data minimisation applies.

Creating GDPR Compliant Contracts. When a user installs an app on the Databox they are presented with an SLA. The goal of the SLA is to provide transparency and to fulfil the information to be provided to users when personal data are collected (Articles *12–18*). The SLA is a multi-layered notice that furnishes the information in an easily readable format (see [41] for further details). Where appropriate, SLAs enable end-users to exercise granular choice over data sampling and the elements of an app's processing they consent to. SLAs are not static notices then, but dynamic, user-configurable consent mechanisms that surface and articulate who wants to access which connected devices and what they want to process personal data for. They are constructed from a *manifest* file that sets out all possible configurations, and which is submitted alongside an app when it is published. The SDK streamlines this process; given its knowledge of an app's construction it already knows the data sources being accessed (and at which granularity), the processing taking place and the outputs, all of which are automatically embedded in the manifest. At app publication time, when an app uses multiple data sources, the developer is invited to mark each flow from each source as compulsory or optional, which translates to a set of granular consent options at install time. All that remains is for the developer to provide a description of the app and its benefits, and the remaining statutory information required by GDPR.

Runtime Inspection. Though the development environment ensures that the sources of data that an app operates on and what it outputs to are made transparent, the way in which the app operates, i.e., how a decision is arrived at, or how a data flows through an app remains opaque to a user at app runtime.

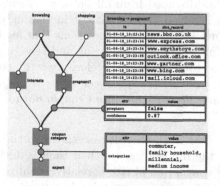

Fig. 5. App inspection interface

This becomes an important matter to surface under Article *13* of GDPR, which requires that meaningful information about the logic involved in automated processing is provided to the data subject. All apps built in the SDK record the path and state of all data as it moves through a flow. SDK apps are all bundled with an interface that uses this path information to make apps 'inspectable' at runtime. By way of example, Fig. 5 shows part of an inspection interface on the Databox UI for an app that processes browsing and shopping data to send coupon requests to a third party. The top of the interface shows of the app's datastores, in this case, browsing and shopping. A user can select any node in the path to get a real-time feed of the data entering and exiting it. This is a nascent first step towards satisfying Article *13*. More important at this stage, is that data flow capture is built into apps to support user-inspection interfaces. We are already seeing alternative representations in research [42]; one interesting approach uses 'comic strip' visualisation techniques to communicate the logic of automated processing to end users [43].

4.2 Future Research for the SDK

A number of interesting challenges have emerged which we are keen to explore in greater detail and which are, we think, of broad relevance.

Algorithmic Intelligibility for Developers. Our work on making the operation and intent of apps intelligible to end-users is at an early stage and touches on a rapidly expanding area of research. However research into how an app's processing can be made intelligible to app creators (i.e. developers) is underrepresented in the literature. End-user oriented development environments reduce the competencies necessary for creating apps and expand the cohort of potential app developers. In addition, access to machine learning toolkits such as Google's TensorFlow enable developers to utilise complex machine learning algorithms whilst remaining divorced from all but a rudimentary understanding of the models and logic involved. This makes it increasingly easy for developers to make naïve use of machine-learning algorithms that lead to unfair, incorrect, and ultimately harmful outcomes. Educating and sensitising developers to the implications of the code they create is therefore a worthy goal. As [44] succinctly state: *"in many cases what the data subject wants is not an explanation – but rather for the disclosure, decision or action simply not to have occurred"*.

Articulating Risk. Our work on risk assessment in the SDK argues for sensitising developers to the implications of their choices during app construction. Yet, as discussed, our conception of risk is relatively simple. We aim to improve upon this by representing risk as two metrics: likelihood (what is the probability of occurrence?) and harm (what bad things will happen if it does occur?). To make this tractable, the SDK will need to take into account the app's intended deployment context in addition to the personal data it operates on. For example, an app that visualises a user's browsing history on a screen at home will carry different risks from one that exposes the same data to an employer.

5   Conclusion

The emergence of the IoT is driving a shift in data storage and processing to the edge of the network to reduce traffic and latency and to improve resilience and the potential for data privacy. We have argued that GDPR raises an unmet challenge in supporting IoT app development that requires: *(i)* a broad cohort of developers be provided with clear information on the risks that attach to the use of personal data and *(ii)* that all necessary features and information are embedded in apps in order that end-users are provided with the information they need to provide informed consent and the facility to examine an app's operation at runtime. We have presented the design and implementation of a set of developer features (risk breakdown, personal data tracking, compliant contracts and runtime inspection) aimed at meeting these requirements. In doing so, we have taken a step towards identifying how we can improve support for developers who write code to process personal data.

References

1. Fog Computing and the Internet of Things: Extend the Cloud to Where the Things Are. https://www.cisco.com/c/dam/en_us/solutions/trends/iot/docs/computing-overview.pdf. Accessed 26 June 2018
2. IDC FutureScape: Worldwide IoT 2018 Predictions. https://www.idc.com/getdoc.jsp?containerId=US43171317. Accessed 26 June 2018
3. Amazon Echo. https://en.wikipedia.org/wiki/Amazon_Echo. Accessed 26 June 2018
4. Apple HomePod. https://www.apple.com/uk/homepod. Accessed 26 June 2018
5. Google Home. https://store.google.com/product/google_home. Accessed 26 June 2018
6. Home Assistant. https://www.home-assistant.io. Accessed 26 June 2018
7. nCube. https://ncubehome.co.uk. Accessed 26 June 2018
8. Regulation (EU) 2016/679 of the European Parliament and of the Council of 27 April 2016 on the protection of natural persons with regard to the processing of personal data and on the free movement of such data, and repealing Directive 95/46/EC (General Data Protection Regulation). Official J. Eur. Union, L119, 1–88, April 2016
9. Chaudhry, A., Crowcroft, J., Howard, H., Madhavapeddy, A., Mortier, R., Haddadi, H., McAuley, D. : Personal data: thinking inside the box. In Proceedings of the Fifth De-cennial Aarhus Conference on Critical Alternatives, pp. 29–32. Aarhus University Press (2015)
10. Lee, S., Wong, E. L., Goel, D., Dahlin, M., Shmatikov, V.: PiBox: a platform for privacy-preserving apps. In: Proceedings of NSDI, pp. 501–514 (2013)
11. Giffin, D.B., Levy, A., Stefan, D., Terei, D., Mazières, D., Mitchell, J.C., Russo, A.: Hails: protecting data privacy in untrusted web applications. In: Proceedings of OSDI, pp. 47–60 (2012)
12. Willis, D., Dasgupta, A., Banerjee, S.: ParaDrop: a multi-tenant platform to dynamically install third party services on wireless gateways. In: Proceedings of the 9th ACM Workshop on Mobility in the Evolving Internet Architecture, pp. 43–48. ACM (2014)
13. Youngblood, G.M., Cook, D.J., Holder, L.B.: A learning architecture for automating the intelligent environment. In: Proceedings of the Conference on Innovative Applications of Artificial Intelligence, pp. 1576–1583. MIT Press, Cambridge (2005)
14. How GDPR Will Change the Way You Develop. https://www.smashingmagazine.com/2018/02/gdpr-for-web-developers. Accessed 26 June 2018
15. Domoticz. https://domoticz.com. Accessed 26 June 2018
16. OpenHAB. https://www.openhab.org. Accessed 26 June 2018
17. OpenRemote. http://www.openremote.com. Accessed 26 June 2018
18. Project Things. https://iot.mozilla.org. Accessed 26 June 2018
19. Cozify. https://en.cozify.fi. Accessed 26 June 2018
20. Fibaro. https://www.fibaro.com. Accessed 26 June 2018
21. Vera. http://getvera.com. Accessed 26 June 2018
22. Mydex. https://mydex.org. Accessed 26 June 2018
23. Hub of All Things. https://hubofallthings.com. Accessed 26 June 2018
24. Android Things. https://developer.android.com/things/index.html. Accessed 26 June 2018
25. Apple HomeKit. https://www.apple.com/uk/ios/home. Accessed 26 June 2018

26. Samsung SmartThings. http://www.samsung.com/uk/smartthings. Accessed 26 June 2018
27. Newman, M.W.: Now we're cooking: recipes for end-user service composition in the digital home. Position Paper- CHI 2006 Workshop IT@Home (2006)
28. IFTTT. https://ifttt.com. Accessed 26 June 2018
29. Stringify. https://www.stringify.com. Accessed 26 June 2018
30. Yeti. https://getyeti.co. Accessed 26 June 2018
31. Zapier. https://zapier.com. Accessed 26 June 2018
32. Mi, X., Feng Q., Ying, Z., XiaoFeng, W.: An empirical characterization of IFTTT: eco-system, usage, and performance. In: Proceedings of the 2017 Internet Measurement Conference, pp. 398–404. ACM, New York (2017)
33. Surbatovich, M., Jassim, A., Lujo B., Anupam D., Limin, J.: Some recipes can do more than spoil your appetite: analyzing the security and privacy risks of IFTTT recipes. In: Proceedings of the 26th International Conference on World Wide Web, International World Wide Web Conferences Steering Committee, pp. 1501–1510 (2017)
34. Attacking Discrimination in ML. https://research.google.com/bigpicture/attacking-discrimination-in-ml. Accessed 26 June 2018
35. Eslami, M., Krishna Kumaran, S.R., Sandvig, C., Karahalios, K.: Communicating algorithmic process in online behavioral advertising. In: Proceedings of the 2018 CHI Conference on Human Factors in Computing Systems, p. 432. ACM (2018)
36. Ribeiro, M.T., Singh, S., Guestrin, C.: Why should I trust you?: explaining the predictions of any classifier. In: Proceedings of the 22nd ACM SIGKDD International Conference on Knowledge Discovery and Data Mining, pp. 1135–1144. ACM (2016)
37. Morrison, J.P.: Flow-based programming. In: Proceedings of the 1st International Workshop on Software Engineering for Parallel and Distributed Systems, pp. 25–29 (1994)
38. Weiss, G.M., Lockhart, J.W.: Identifying user traits by mining smart phone accelerometer data. In: Proceedings of the Fifth International Workshop on Knowledge Discovery from Sensor Data, pp. 61–69. ACM (2011)
39. Smart meters review TV viewing habits. http://www.h-online.com/security/news/item/Smart-meters-reveal-TV-viewing-habits-1346385.html. Accessed 26 June 2018
40. Kim, Y., Schmid, T., Srivastava, M.B., Wang, Y.: Challenges in resource monitoring for residential spaces. In: Proceedings of the First ACM Workshop on Embedded Sensing Systems for Energy-Efficiency in Buildings, pp. 1–6. ACM (2009)
41. Crabtree, A., Lodge, T., Colley, J., Greenhalgh, C., Mortier, M.: Building accountability into the Internet of Things: the IoT Databox Model. J. Reliable Intell. Environ. SSRN (2018)
42. Wang, Q., Hassan, W.U., Bates, A., Gunter, C.: Fear and logging in the Internet of Things. In: Network and Distributed Systems Symposium (2018)
43. Schreiber, A., Struminski, R.: Tracing personal data using comics. In: International Conference on Universal Access in Human-Computer Interaction, pp. 444–455 (2017)
44. Edwards, L., Veale, M.: Slave to the algorithm: why a right to an explanation is probably not the remedy you are looking for. Duke L. Tech. Rev. **16**, 18 (2017)

YaPPL - A Lightweight Privacy Preference Language for Legally Sufficient and Automated Consent Provision in IoT Scenarios

Max-R. Ulbricht(✉)⊙ and Frank Pallas⊙

TU Berlin, Information Systems Engineering,
Einsteinufer 17, 10587 Berlin, Germany
{mu,fp}@ise.tu-berlin.de
http://www.ise.tu-berlin.de

Abstract. In this paper, we present YaPPL—a Privacy Preference Language explicitly designed to fulfill consent-related requirements of the GDPR as well as to address technical givens of IoT scenarios. We analyze what criteria consent must meet in order to be legally sufficient and translate these into a formal representation of consent as well as into functional requirements that YaPPL must fulfill. Taking into account further nonfunctional requirements particularly relevant in the IoT context, we then derive a specification of YaPPL, which we prototypically implemented in a reusable software library and successfully instantiated in a proof of concept scenario, paving the way for viable technical implementations of legally sufficient consent mechanisms in the IoT.

Keywords: Privacy preference language · Internet of Things · Consent

1 Introduction

In a world pervaded by connected things, where mobile phones, wearables, environmental sensors and smart home components constantly communicate with backend infrastructures and, through these, are dynamically interconnected with further services, it becomes increasingly challenging for device owners to keep track and control of respective data transfers. Due to the foreseeably growing complexity of such IoT environments, technical mechanisms and tools will become virtually indispensable for effectively exerting individual control over ones data.

At the same time, the collection and provision of legally sufficient consent—which is foundational for many realistic IoT applications—becomes increasingly

This work is part of a project supported by funds of the Federal Ministry of Justice and Consumer Protection (BMJV) based on a decision of the Parliament of the Federal Republic of Germany via the Federal Office for Agriculture and Food (BLE) under the innovation support programme.

J. Garcia-Alfaro et al. (Eds.): DPM 2018/CBT 2018, LNCS 11025, pp. 329–344, 2018.
https://doi.org/10.1007/978-3-030-00305-0_23

difficult, given the strict requirements of the GDPR (General Data Protection Regulation) on the one and the technical characteristics and constraints of IoT environments on the other hand. Without proper ways for obtaining and actually implementing legally sufficient consent, however, many practical IoT applications and services would lack the necessary basis of lawfulness and could thus not be implemented in a legally compliant way.

In this context, two core problems can be identified: First, individual consent must be adequately specific with regard to utilizers and purposes in order to provide a legally sufficient basis for the collection and processing of personal data. Current practices and technical approaches for consent provision—especially in the IoT context with dynamically changing interconnections of devices and multiple services—do typically not meet this requirement but rather follow an approach of overly "broad consent" instead. Second, consent must also fulfill form-related obligations such as informedness or explicitness. Meeting these obligations requires appropriate interfaces, which IoT devices typically lack.

To solve these challenges and pave the way for viable technical implementations of legally sufficient consent mechanisms in the IoT context, we propose a lightweight, tripartite approach consisting of (1) a policy specification service running on edge devices with sufficient user interaction capabilities, (2) a policy provider persistently storing user-specified preferences and previous versions thereof, and (3) a policy proxy applying the preferences to concrete, purpose-specific data requests. All these components function and interact on the basis of a preference language that is capable of codifying consent in line with GDPR requirements.

Contributions: The design and specification of this preference language—named YaPPL—is the primary subject of this paper. Through conscious integration of legal requirements into the language design from ground up, YaPPL allows to codify legally sufficient consent and thus provides a valuable basis for GDPR-compliant consent management. In a nutshell, YaPPL is a message and file format that, in combination with the proposed service architecture,

(a) fulfills legal requirements for technically mediated consent provision
(b) can act as an archive for expired preferences for auditing purposes
(c) provides an enhanced user-centric access control model for future or unforeseen data processing requests.

Furthermore, YaPPL is explicitly designed to suit constrained execution environments like those typically present in the IoT context. Besides the specification, we also implemented a prototypical YaPPL software library and, on this basis, the three above-mentioned components. We then instantiated these components in a concrete, realistic setting consisting of constrained IoT devices and multiple cloud services. Preliminary experiments conducted in this setting strongly point towards YaPPLs practical viability, vividly demonstrating the potential of consequently designing technology to address currently unsolved legal challenges.

Structure: The remainder of this paper is organized as follows: In Sect. 2, we analyze the requirements for legally sufficient consent, explore constraints given by IoT environments and briefly sketch our assumed overall architecture. In Sect. 3, we develop a formal representation of consent and identify functional as well as non-functional requirements resulting from the previous considerations. On this basis we then provide the language specification for YaPPL and explain its core functionalities. Finally, we discuss YaPPL in the light of related work (Sect. 4) and conclude.

2 Consent in the IoT Context

Consent is one of the cornerstones of modern privacy regulations, following the idea that individuals should be able to determine who knows what about them or, respectively, what facts about their private life are communicated to others [27]. This fundamental understanding has not only influenced legislative procedures [6], it is also reflected in numerous privacy principles [3], guidelines [2] and frameworks/standards [4].

Under the legal regime of the GDPR, consent must fulfill certain criteria in order to provide lawfulness for the collection or processing of personal data. To establish a sound foundation for technically representing consent in a form that satisfies legal requirements, we therefore briefly analyze these criteria below. In addition, we shortly explore constraints given by IoT environments and sketch a technical architecture facilitating the technically mediated provision of legally sufficient consent in IoT scenarios for which the preference language to be developed herein shall serve as the underlying basis.

2.1 Legal Requirements for Consent

According to the *Principles relating to processing of personal data* provided in Article 5 of the GDPR [6], "personal data shall be [...] processed lawfully, fairly and in a transparent manner [...]". *Lawfulness* can be assumed if "the data subject has given consent to the processing of his or her personal data for one or more specific purposes". Article 7 (*Conditions for consent*) stipulates additional conditions that consent has to fulfill in order to be legally sufficient. In particular, given consent has to be easily retractable at any time and the party that initially collects the personal data has to ensure that it is able to demonstrate that a specific data subject has actually consented to the processing of his or her data [6, Article 7 (1)].

Furthermore, the legal sufficiency of consent is subject to form-related requirements. Besides the fact that it must be freely given, consent particularly must be a "specific, informed and unambiguous indication of the data subject's wishes" and needs to be provided "by a statement or by a clear affirmative action" according to Article 4 of the GDPR [6]. Specificity, the quality of being informed, and the need for a clear affirmative action therefore deserve closer examination.

Specificity. In the GDPR itself it is not explicitly specified how *"specific consent"* is to be interpreted. However, it is at least declared that consent has to be given for "one or more specific purposes" [6, Article 6 (1 a)]. Furthermore, the Article 29 Data Protection Working Party (Art. 29 WP) comments that consent, to be specific, "should refer clearly and precisely to the scope [...] of the data processing. It cannot apply to an open-ended set of processing activities. [...] In other words, blanket consent without specifying the exact purpose of the processing is not acceptable" [8]. If data should be processed for more than one purpose, the controller "should provide a separate opt-in for each purpose, to allow users to give specific consent" [10]. Any technical representation of consent must therefore allow to codify specific purposes at a sufficient level of detail.

Informedness. There are clear explanations within the GDPR itself about the meaning of *"informed consent"*. In recital 42 of the regulation [6], it is stated that "[f]or consent to be informed, the data subject should be aware at least of the identity of the controller and the purposes of the processing for which the personal data are intended". Thus, legally sufficient consent does at least require that the data subject knows who intends to processes their personal data for what reason. Again, any viable technical representation of (requested and given) consent must allow to codify this information.

Clear Affirmative Action. Finally, a controller has to ensure that consent is provided in an unquestionable manner. Acceptable forms, according to recital 32 of the GDPR [6], are oral or written statements, including by electronic means, but also "ticking a box when visiting an internet website" or "choosing technical settings for information society services". As opposed to such clear affirmative actions, "[s]ilence, pre-ticked boxes or inactivity should not therefore constitute consent" [6, Recital 32]. Even though this requirement primarily regards user interfaces, the explicitly mentioned choice of technical settings is of particular relevance for us, as it allows for more technical approaches of consent provision, which is particularly necessary in the IoT context.

2.2 IoT—Systems Perspective

As noted by the Article 29 Data Protection Working Party (Art. 29 WP) [9] the Internet of Things raises several new challenges regarding the legally compliant provision and withdrawal of consent. In particular, sensor devices like fitness trackers or personal weather stations are often not designed to provide extensive information by themselves and also do not contain any interfaces sufficient to obtain individual consent.

Beside this lack of useful interfaces, components of an IoT environment are often constrained in their computation, storage and communication capabilities [22]. For our consent management architecture proposed in the next section, we classify components into three different categories: (1) sensors devices, (2) edge-devices and (3) cloud components.

Of these, sensor devices usually have none or only few computational and storage capabilities. Interfaces for interacting with the device itself are also missing. Edge-devices, in contrast, offer resources to communicate with users as well as with sensors and higher level services, to cache or store and (pre-) process sensor data before sending them to the respective cloud service components [24], but are semi-constrained with regard to their computational power and/or storage space. Cloud components, in turn, have virtually unlimited computational and storage capabilities.

Thus, from an IoT systems perspective, tasks involving substantial processing and/or storing sensor or other data, like privacy preferences [23], can only be performed either in the cloud or on the networked edge devices—bridging the transfer of measured data between sensor devices and the cloud—considering the semi-constrained characteristics of the latter ones.

2.3   Scenario and Architecture

Because of the lack of interaction possibilities on sensor devices, the provision or revocation of consent needs to be performed on another device under the control of the sensor owner. In most cases, sensor devices use the owners' desktop computers, home routers or mobile computing devices to synchronize their data with the cloud backends of associated service providers. These edge-devices are therefore promising points of operation for the management of consent statements [23].

The Art. 29 WP suggests the use of *Privacy Proxies* in the context of IoT applications. By employing such a *Privacy Proxy* for "executing" technically codified consent statements, "data requests are confronted with predefined policies governing access to data [...]. By defining sensor and policy pairs, third parties requests for collection or access to sensor data would be authorized, limited or simply rejected" [9, p. 21, note 30].

Picking up the idea of edge devices as configuration points for a *Privacy Proxy* governing access to personal data, Fig. 1 shows our generalized IoT architecture with sensors, edge-devices and cloud storage systems, supplemented by a *Policy Provider* and a *Policy Proxy*. Users of sensor devices can specify their preferences regarding the further use of their sensor data on their edge-device before the upload to the cloud storage system of the respective service provider is triggered. To avoid the necessity of a new consent provision for every new data processing activity by the service provider, the *Specification Service* on the user-controlled edge-device is used for "choosing technical settings" (see Sect. 2.1). These are then stored in the form of policies by another service, the proposed *Policy Provider*. For incoming requests regarding the sensor data, the *Policy Proxy* ask the *Policy Provider* for an associated policy and answers the request according to the rules and preferences stated by the sensor owner in the received policy.

Thus, our architecture not only implements the recommendations of the Art. 29 WP regarding consent provision in IoT environments, it also can act as an archive for expired preferences for auditing purposes as required by the GDPR. Beyond that, it provides an enhanced user-centric access control model for future or unforeseen data processing purposes. In this model, we give owners of sensor

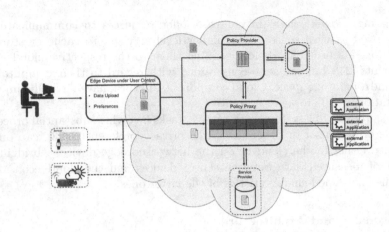

Fig. 1. IoT architecture with a user-controlled edge device running a Preference Specification Service. A Policy-Provider-Service and a Policy-Proxy-Service as a database wrapper guarding the access to data.

devices full control but also the responsibility to manage preferences regarding the future usage of their sensor data by shifting the Policy Administration Point (PAP) as known from usual access control systems completely to the user. While the proposed *Policy Provider Service* acts as a Policy Information Point (PIP), the *Policy Proxy Service* substitutes the Policy Decision Point (PDP) as well as the Policy Enforcement Point (PEP) from conventional access control architectures. If these services are implemented as micro-services, which communicate through standardized interfaces (like REST), the integration into different existing infrastructures is easily manageable. They could be integrated into platforms [26] or deployed as independent distributed (micro-) services.

In order to enable such an architecture, we need (1) a standardized *policy/preference specification language* as well as (2) a respective *message format* to make sure that the three services mentioned above can communicate on the basis of a shared understanding of how to parse, create, evaluate and enforce the policies containing the sensor owners' data processing preferences. Taking into account the legal requirements for consent outlined above, both will be developed below.

3   YaPPL

In this section we will introduce the specification of YaPPL. We start with a formalized representation of consent, formulate requirements and motivate our design decisions to derive the internal structure of a YaPPL policy on that basis. Afterwards we present a concrete example of a policy from our prototypical implementation, illustrate the core functionalities of our software library and discuss our evaluation.

3.1   Formalization of Consent

As a first step towards our language, we need a formal representation of consent in the sense of the GDPR as outlined above. Consent *(C)* as broadly assumed in legal discussions can, on an abstract level, be interpreted as a relation that maps a tuple containing a utilizer[1] *(U)* and a data processing purpose *(P)* specified by the utilizer onto data to be released. Interpreted as permission to process (personal) data *(D)* related to a data subject *(S)*, we get the following function, whereat D_{col} represents all *collected* data and D_{rel} the data to be *released*:

$$c : D_{col} \times C \to D_{rel} \implies D_{col} \times U \times P \to D_{rel}$$

$$c(d_{col}, u, p) := \begin{cases} d_{rel} = d_{col} & \text{if } consent \text{ is given by S} \\ \emptyset & \text{if } consent \text{ is revoked or not present} \end{cases}$$

We strive for an understanding of consent that goes beyond this established conception and allows data subjects to specify transformations T that reflect their wishes for personal data relating to them to be preprocessed before disclosure. The introduced *transformation* can be used to specify computational tasks that have to be performed before the data is transferred. Examples are different types of aggregation, pseudo-/anonymization, or cutting out certain data-points from series of measurements. Thus, T is a transformation from data into other, new data depending on the combination of utilizer and purpose:

$$t \in T : D_{col} \to D_{rel}; \quad \implies t_{up}(d_{col}) = d_{rel}$$

We now can use the specification of t to reflect all kinds of possible consent. If, e.g., consent should be revoked or not be given for certain data, we can specify t in way that $t_{up}(d_{col}) = d_{rel} = \emptyset$. If we generalize this approach towards using transformations as a basic concept for a consent-based privacy preference language, for every single datapoint or whole datasets, a 3-tuple containing a utilizer u, a processing purpose p and a transformation t forms a resulting rule r that describes which data may to what extent be transferred to the requesting institution:

$$r : D_{col} \times U \times P \times T \to D_{rel}$$
$$r(d_{col}, u, p, t) = t_{up}(d_{col}) = d_{rel}$$

Based on this approach, data subjects can define rules that exactly codify their consent regarding which data can be released to a given set of utilizer and purpose. On this formalized basis, we can now proceed defining our aspired language, with rules that act as consent statements.

3.2   Requirements and Design Decisions

Besides the legal aspects outlined in Sect. 2.1, the requirements for the development of a formal language designed to enable specifications of user preferences

---

[1] In the understanding pursued herein, this is the institution that is aspires to collect and/or process personal data – in legal terms: the controller and/or processor.

can be divided into functional and nonfunctional factors. The motivation to develop an own language is particularly rooted in the intention to give domain experts—namely, in the case of a description language for consent-based usage preferences, legal practitioners—the possibility to play a significant role in the design, development, and maintenance of new systems in their domain [20]. For this reason, we consciously chose language constructs and abstract concepts that also non-technologists can easily read, create, and—in the event of audits—evaluate without further utilities. The following requirements will later be addressed and explained in the design decisions section:

Functional Requirements

- **Consent:** distinct representation of consent statements as a combination of processing purposes, potential utilizers and transformations.
- **Purposes & Utilizers:** representation of possible processing purposes and potential utilizers as directed graph to emphasize relationships between entities as well as hierarchies.
- **Transformations:** distinct specification of domain specific transformation functions

Nonfunctional Requirements

- **Readability** should be increased by the usage of appropriate formats that are human- as well as machine readable
- **Extendability** regarding new purposes, utilizers and transformation functions
- **Efficiency** regarding the memory and resource consumption on limited IoT devices

Design Decisions. In our language, we address these functional and nonfunctional requirements as follows:

Functional. As deduced in Sect. 3.1, any single preference rule has to contain at least the three mentioned and obligatory components, *utilizer*, *purpose*, and *transformation*. As they must be adjustable for different domain specific needs, all of these are represented by plain strings within a rule. In our prototypical implementation, we codify the directed graphs containing available utilizers, processing purposes, and generalized categories thereof in JSON configuration files that are integrated at runtime, which allows to easily adjust the respective available vocabularies to, e.g., domain-specific purpose hierarchies.

Since we want to be able to give and codify conditional consent for different circumstances (like, e.g., "Utilizer A is allowed to process my data for purpose X without any restrictions, but for utilizer B only weekly aggregates should be released although it is for the same purpose X"), multiple independent *rules* can be combined in a single *preference*. It is thus possible to assign different transformations to be applied for different utilizers and/or purposes.

To facilitate legally sufficient consent provision also for future and unforeseen purposes and utilizers, we allow the nested attributes "permitted" and "excluded" to be provided for both, utilizer and purpose. With this extension, it is possible to explicitly exclude purposes and utilizer, allowing to make statements like "my data can be used for all future purposes except ..." or "my data can be used by anybody except ...".

*Remark 1 (**Conflicting Rules**).* Even if we can try to prevent the establishing of conflicting rules by carefully checking the creation or update processes inside the *Preference Specification Service*, one should be aware of conflicting rules. Thus, in the *Policy Proxy Service*, which acts as a Policy Enforcement Point (PEP), mechanisms have to be in place that ensure the proper execution. To comply with the basic idea of a prohibition with a reservation of authorization, which constitutes all data protection regulations, rules preventing data transfers should always have higher priorities than the ones allowing them.

To address the fact that a single sensor device often collects multiple measurands (e.g. smartwatches can record heart-rates, sleep phases, etc.), we designed the *transformation* field of a rule as a list of transformation objects, each containing a transformation function and the sensor attribute to which it refers. So far, we only implemented simple examples — like an *average* and a *minmax* function with the possibility to assign different time intervals — in our prototype. However, additional names of available transformation functions can be subsequently added through configuration files as soon as they are specified and implemented in the *Policy Proxy Service* to be enforced in operation.

*Remark 2 (**Revocation & Archiving**).* We decided to integrate two timestamps into each rule, represented by the *'valid_from'* and the *'exp_date'* attributes. The *'valid_from'* value is initialized with the current timestamp of the moment the rule is created, whereas the *'exp_date'* value is initialized with a zero value ("0000-00-00T00:00:00.00Z"). Thus, we can easily determine whether a rule is (or was at a given time) valid by evaluating this attribute. The value of *'exp_date'* is only changed under two conditions: (1) when the sensor owner decides to delete the rule — which means withdrawing this specific consent statement. In this case, the *'exp_date'* is set to the current timestamp and thus renders the rule invalid. Noteworthily, invalidated rules are not deleted but rather kept *archived*. The other case of *'exp_date'* being changed is (2) when a sensor owner updates the rule with different values for utilizers, purposes or transformations. In this case, the *'exp_date'* is also set to the current timestamp, the respective rule renders invalid and thus is *archived*. Simultaneously, a new rule with the old values is created which can then be updated to the user's changed intentions. This procedure makes sure that it is always possible to track back the evolution of the preference as a whole and thus to fulfill the legal requirement from Article 7 (1) of the GDPR [6], which obligates a utilizer to be able to demonstrate that a data subject has consented to the processing at a given moment.

Nonfunctional. To address the aforementioned nonfunctional requirements regarding readability in combination with the efficiency criteria that has to be considered in IoT environments, we chose JSON[2] both as file- and as message-format, because policies in the JSON format are human- as well as machine-readable. As an alternative, we also considered the more generic YAML[3] format. Besides the pro-YAML-argument that YAML is slightly easier to 'parse' for humans [14], technical arguments led to the decision against YAML. In particular, benchmarks have shown that the processing time for serializing and deserializing YAML files can be up to 10–20 times longer than the processing of the same data codified in JSON [1,14]. Furthermore, because of the structure of JSON messages, it is easy to decide if a data transmission has failed, as an interrupted transmission will automatically render to invalid code. For a message format to be used in communication between different web-services, this is a significant advantage.

As a further alternative to JSON, we also considered XML because of its also widespread use in the service domain. But if we take the requirements in IoT contexts seriously and compare XML and JSON with regard to resource consumption for parsing and evaluating data or the storage footprint of data files, JSON is faster to process [21] and more efficient in resource consumption both at rest and 'on the wire'. Thus, JSON is the better fit in an IoT context [16]. Also with respect to human readability JSON has advantages over XML.

*Remark 3 (**Extendability**).* Regarding the last nonfunctional point we decided that the fundamental structure of policies and rules has to be stable and consistent. Besides the timestamps, every rule therefore must have declarations for processing purposes, utilizers and transformation functions, as these are essential for sufficient consent statements. However, and as already mentioned above, it is possible to adapt our design to different domains just by adjusting or modifying the options available for these three obligatory components into a domain-specific variation simply by using different configuration files.

3.3 Policy Format Specification and Example

A YaPPL policy itself contains two first-level attributes: an *id*, which is used to link specific sensor data to a corresponding policy, and a *preference*-block which contains a list of one or more *rules*. These rules codify consent-based usage preferences to regulate the access to the values measured by the respective sensor. A *rule* consists of the three main building-blocks we have derived from our formalized consent model in Sect. 3.1, namely *purpose*, *utilizer* and *transformation*. As delineated in the design decisions Sect. 3.2, the *purpose* part as well as the *utilizer* part of a rule are both divided into a *permitted* and a *excluded* block.

In Listing 1.1 a snippet representing such a *rule* part of a policy is extracted out of the complete BNF for YaPPL, which will be accessible online later on. The aforementioned mandatory building-blocks of every rule (*purpose*, *utilizer*, *transformation*) are complemented by a pair of additional attributes, which obviously are timestamps. The *valid_from* value is set at (and to) the time of the rule

---

[2] https://json.org/.
[3] http://www.yaml.org/.

creation, whereas the value of the *exp_date* attribute is initialized with a "zero" value and an alteration can be triggered for different reasons like the revocation of the represented consent statement or the update of the respective rule with new settings regarding *purpose*, *utilizer* or *transformation*, as illustrated in the design decisions in Sect. 3.2.

Listing 1.1. "Rule" snippet from BNF Policy Specification

```
<rule> ::= '{'
           <purpose> ','
           <utilizer> ','
           <transformation> ','
           <valid_from> ','
           <exp_date>
           '}'

<purpose> ::= '"' 'purpose' '"' ':' '{'
              <permitted_purpose> ','
              <excluded_purpose>
              '}'

<utilizer> ::= '"' 'utilizer' '"' ':' '{'
               <permitted_utilizer> ','
               <excluded_utilizer>
               '}'
```

The policy shown in Listing 1.2 is an example from our prototypical implementation in an IoT testbed. It is used to specify user preferences regarding an indoor environmental sensor which is capable to measure temperature, illumination, air pressure and light spectrum.

Listing 1.2. Example Policy with only one Rule

```
{
  "_id": 4493,
  "preference": [
    {
      "rule": {
        "purpose": {
          "permitted": ["statistics", "planology"],
          "excluded": ["commercial"]
        },
        "utilizer": {
          "permitted": ["wikimedia", "tu_berlin"],
          "excluded": ["netatmo", "gate5"]
        },
        "transformation": [
          {
            "attribute": "temperature",
            "tr_func": "minmax_hourly"
          }
        ],
        "valid_from": "2017-10-09T00:00:00.00Z",
        "exp_date": "0000-00-00T00:00:00.00Z"
      }
    }
  ]
}
```

The ensuing *transformation* block is organized as a list of transformation objects, which represents the conditions for the processing of specific values. Due to the *attribute* field, it is possible to assign different transformation functions to each measurand of a multi sensor device. This is especially useful for the adoption of YaPPL in the wearables sphere, where sophisticated swartwatches capture multiple body- and health-related values like heartrate, sleep phases or the gps route of the last training run. As examples for these transformation functions, we implemented an average as well as a minmax function. While the first one calculates the arithmetic average of a bulk of passed values, the latter returns a minimum and a maximum value of the passed data. Both functions can be triggered with different time intervals like daily, monthly and so on to aggregate values as desired by the sensor owner.

3.4   Core Functionalities Based on YaPPL

On the basis of the aforementioned structure and characteristics of YaPPL policies, the implementation of services which enable consent-based data sharing or data processing activities is straightforward. To showcase the possibilities of YaPPL, we developed a prototypical software library that is integrated into the three services mentioned above to manage legally sufficient consent provision in an IoT testbed. Besides the necessary parser, a validator for the policies, and the usual and obvious CRUD methods (Create, Read, Update and Delete) for rules, this library provides two essential functionalities needed to fulfill the preferences codified in a YaPPL policy: First, we need to know all excluded entities to prohibit further data transfers, and second, we must be able to extract explicit transformation rules in order to customize the sensor values according to the wishes of the sensor owner.

getExcludedEntities. The *excluded* blocks in both, the *purpose* and the *utilizer* part of the rules are intended to explicitly prevent data transfers to specific institutions, generalized categories of potential utilizers (like, e.g., the military or advertising companies), specific processing purposes or categories thereof (e.g., all commercial purposes). There are two methods in our YaPPL library which return the respective lists by traversing all valid rules inside a given policy. If the *policy proxy* receives a request from *'Institution_G'* to provide sensor values for *'Purpose_R'*, it fetches all respective *policies* from the *policy provider* and decides if a transfer is allowed. If neither *'Institution_G'* nor *'Purpose_R'* is in the returned lists, the proxy will extract the *TransformationRules* (as described in the following section) to preprocess the sensor values according to the rules.

getTransformationRules. If a requesting institution with a specific data processing purpose is not excluded from data transfer by the respective rules, the policy proxy will extract a list of transformation objects, each containing a list of (concrete or generalized categories of) permitted utilizers, a list of permitted processing purposes and corresponding transformation functions. Thus, every transformation object can be interpreted as a users consent to the processing of her sensor data for the covered purposes by the contained utilizers under the given conditions (aka. transformations). The proxy passes all original sensor data to the appropriate transformation function, catches the aggregated results and responds to the original request.

3.5   Evaluation

To test our concept we have developed a library, as mentioned above, implemented all components of the consent management architecture as introduced in Sect. 2.3 and integrated the services into a real world IoT application. As this application is a participatory sensing platform, we implemented the specification service for adjusting preferences on a small sensor device that transfers the measured data — supplemented by an extra metadata field which contains the URL of the respective policy — to the platform and sends the appropriate policies to our *policy provider*, which runs inside a container on a cloud server. The *privacy proxy*, also running on a cloud server, mirrors the API of the sensing platform and monitors the requests. When values of a sensor with the aforementioned metadata field are requested, the request is intercepted, the appropriate policy is fetched from the *policy provider* and evaluated. If the data transfer is permitted, the sensor values are pre-processed according to the transformation rules and transferred to the requesting utilizer.

While performance considerations are left to future work, our prototype performs well as a proof of concept and fulfills the requirements deduced in the previous sections.

4   Related Work and Discussion

Some of the ideas presented herein are inspired from previous works on *purpose based access control* [11,15,18]. The original concept of the division of purposes into *'prohibited'* and *'intended'* purposes, which we also use for utilizers, was proposed by Byun, Bertino and Li [11].

Furthermore a vast amount of languages for privacy-, security- and access control-policies exists (see [19] for a comprehensive overview). The most prominent one in the area of privacy policy languages regarding websites and -services is P3P [13] and its companion for user preferences named APPEL [12]. P3P has a limited vocabulary with predefined values for purposes and recipient. While the predetermined purposes hinder an adaption to other or unforeseen processing purposes, the preassigned values for potential recipients of the respective data are not explicit but characterize the relation to the data controller that originally collected the data. In addition, even if the P3P vocabulary is limited, the correct formulation of user preferences in APPEL to match them with P3P policies is difficult and error prone [7].

As a standard for the formulation of attribute based access control policies, XACML [5] has been established over the last decade. Since it was designed to be used by institutions to regulate the access to data and resources within organizations or federations thereof, the usability as preference language for end users seems at least questionable. Thus, while XACML is capable of representing fine-grained access control policies, for the usage as preference language it needs extensions: the PrimeLife Policy Language pursues a similar approach to specify preferences for the future use of specific data like YaPPL. The idea of *Downstream Usage* describes the definition of conditions for the usage of data by third parties after the initial collection and storage. Also obligations are available as a counterpart to YaPPL *transformations* [25]. But since it is an extension to XACML, based on XML and with an extensive ruleset for the formulations of policies, it inherits all the shortcomings mentioned in Sect. 3.2 and policies are by far not human readable or auditable by legal practitioners without the help of additional tools or technicians.

Besides these examples numerous other approaches for privacy preference languages exits. Some are lightweight enough for the usage in IoT environments but use strong compression or binary formats and are therefore not human read- and auditable (e.g. [17]). Most others try to achieve human readability by using XML dialects with the aforementioned drawbacks. Most importantly, however, none of them is explicitly designed to fulfill the legal requirements regarding the provision of consent, acts as an archive for expired preferences for auditing purposes and provides an enhanced access control model for future or unforeseen data processing requests.

While we worked on YaPPL, several open questions arose, which are out of scope of a technical solution, but nonetheless important to discuss for real world use cases. Some examples are:

- Who is responsible for the initial state of the utilizer and purpose graph?
- How should the extension of these graphs be organized?
- Who is responsible for adding new graph entries into appropriate categories?

Beside these more or less organizational problems, also operational questions have to be answered. Dependent from the deployment of the proposed services varied communication patterns have to be established. If, e.g., the *Policy Proxy Service* is operated by another institution than the original service provider, a transfer of all data to the proxy with a subsequent execution of the *transformation* functions is not feasible. In this case, the policy evaluation should lead to a query modification. Thus, the proxy would not see any data not intended for release. Such questions are strongly related to operator models and matters of trust.

These and several further questions will need to be addressed during future developments and, in particular, through implementing our concept in real use cases with practitioners.

5   Conclusion and Outlook

As we have outlined in this paper, technical representations of consent must meet certain requirements in order to be legally sufficient under the GDPR. In particular, this regards the specificity in matters of utilizer and purpose as well as form-related requirements for informedness and clear affirmative actions. In the IoT context, especially the form-related requirements can, however, hardly be met without novel mechanisms and approaches of technical support.

Based on a legal analysis and a formalization of consent, we therefore designed and specified YaPPL, a Privacy Preference Language explicitly designed to fulfill consent-related requirements of the GDPR as well as to suit constrained execution environments like those typically present in the IoT context. We implemented YaPPL in a reusable software library and successfully employed this library to achieve technical consent awareness in a realistic IoT scenario, thus demonstrating the practical viability of our approach. Besides legally sufficient consent provision in IoT environments, the presented file- and message-format in combination with the proposed architecture can also act as an archive for expired preferences and provide a user-centric access control model for future or unforeseen data processing purposes. YaPPL is therefore a valuable contribution to paving the way for sustainable technical implementations of legally sufficient consent mechanisms in the IoT context.

Beyond this, we explicitly foresee YaPPL and the underlying approach to be also applied to IoT scenarios that do *not* fall under the GDPR but still call for the possibility to technically represent and implement differentiated usage preferences. For instance, this could refer to scenarios of participatory environmental sensing, where participants might also be empowered to explicitly govern the use of data provided by them with regard to utilizers and purposes based on the technologies presented herein. The mere fact that certain data are not "personal data" in the sense of the GDPR does of course not invalidate the general validity of consent principles materialized therein.

The YaPPL language specification as well as the mentioned library will shortly be released under an open source license and can thus be used and extended in other projects as well.

References

1. Serializing data speed comparison: Marshal vs. JSON vs. Eval vs. YAML. http://www.pauldix.net/2008/08/serializing-dat.html
2. OECD Guidelines on the Protection of Privacy and Transborder Flows of Personal Data (1980)
3. Online, Privacy: A Report to Congress. Technical report, FTC, June 1998
4. ISO/IEC 29100:2011 - Information technology - Security techniques - Privacy framework (2011)
5. eXtensible Access Control Markup Language (XACML) Version 3.0. OASIS Standard (2013)
6. Regulation (EU) 2016/679 of the European Parliament and of the Council of 27 April 2016 on the protection of natural persons with regard to the processing of personal data and on the free movement of such data, and repealing Directive 95/46/EC (General Data Protection Regulation). Official J. Eur. Union L 119/1, pp. 1–88, April 2016
7. Agrawal, R., Kiernan, J., Srikant, R., Xu, Y.: XPref: a preference language for P3P. Comput. Networks 48(5), 809–827 (2005)
8. Article 29 Data Protection Working Party: Opinion 15/2011 on the definition of consent. Technical report, July 2011
9. Article 29 Data Protection Working Party: Opinion 8/2014 on the on Recent Developments on the Internet of Things. Technical report 14/EN WP 223, September 2014

10. Article 29 Data Protection Working Party: Guidelines on Consent under Regulation 2016/679. Technical report WP259 rev.01 (2018)
11. Byun, J.W., Bertino, E., Li, N.: Purpose based access control of complex data for privacy protection. In: Proceedings of the Tenth ACM Symposium on Access Control Models and Technologies, SACMAT 2005, pp. 102–110. ACM, New York, NY, USA (2005). https://doi.org/10.1145/1063979.1063998
12. Cranor, L., Langheinrich, M., Marchiori, M.: A P3P preference exchange language 1.0 (APPEL1.0). Technical report, World Wide Web Consortium (2002)
13. Cranor, L.F.: Web Pivacy with P3P. O'Reilly Media, Sebastopol (2002)
14. Eriksson, M., Hallberg, V.: Comparison between JSON and YAML for data serialization. Technical report, The School of Computer Science and Engineering Royal Institute of Technology (2011)
15. Ghani, N.A., Selamat, H., Sidek, Z.M.: Credential purpose-based access control for personal data protection. J. Web Eng. **14**(3&4), 346–360 (2015)
16. Guinard, D., Trifa, V., Mattern, F., Wilde, E.: From the Internet of Things to the web of things: resource-oriented architecture and best practices. In: Uckelmann, D., Harrison, M., Michahelles, F. (eds.) Architecting the Internet of Things, pp. 97–129. Springer, Heidelberg (2011). https://doi.org/10.1007/978-3-642-19157-2_5
17. Henze, M., Hiller, J., Schmerling, S., Ziegeldorf, J.H., Wehrle, K.: CPPL: compact privacy policy language. In: Proceedings of the 2016 ACM on Workshop on Privacy in the Electronic Society, WPES 2016, pp. 99–110. ACM, New York(2016). https://doi.org/10.1145/2994620.2994627
18. Kabir, M.E., Wang, H., Bertino, E.: A role-involved purpose-based access control model. Inf. Syst. Front. **14**(3), 809–822 (2012)
19. Kasem-Madani, S., Meier, M.: Security and privacy policy languages: a survey, categorization and gap identification (2015)
20. Mernik, M., Heering, J., Sloane, A.M.: When and how to develop domain-specific languages. ACM Comput. Surv. (CSUR) **37**(4), 316–344 (2005)
21. Nurseitov, N., Paulson, M., Reynolds, R., Izurieta, C.: Comparison of JSON and XML data interchange formats: a case study. In: Proceedings of the ISCA 22nd International Conference on Computer Applications in Industry and Engineering, CAINE 2009, pp. 157–162, San Francisco, California, USA (2009)
22. Reinfurt, L., Breitenbücher, U., Falkenthal, M., Leymann, F., Riegg, A.: Internet of Things patterns, pp. 1–21. ACM Press (2016)
23. Satyanarayanan, M.: The emergence of edge computing. Computer **50**(1), 30–39 (2017). https://doi.org/10.1109/MC.2017.9
24. Shi, W., Dustdar, S.: The promise of edge computing. Computer **49**(5), 78–81 (2016). https://doi.org/10.1109/MC.2016.145
25. Trabelsi, S., Sendor, J., Reinicke, S.: PPL: primelife privacy policy engine. In: 2011 IEEE International Symposium on Policies for Distributed Systems and Networks, pp. 184–185, June 2011. https://doi.org/10.1109/POLICY.2011.24
26. Ulbricht, M.-R., Pallas, F.: CoMaFeDS - consent management for federated data sources. In: Proceedings of the 2016 IEEE International Conference on Cloud Engineering Workshops, pp. 106–111. IEEE, Berlin (2016). https://doi.org/10.1109/IC2EW.2016.30
27. Westin, A.F.: Privacy and Freedom. Atheneum, New York (1967)

PrivacyGuard: Enforcing Private Data Usage with Blockchain and Attested Execution

Ning Zhang[1]([✉]), Jin Li[2], Wenjing Lou[1], and Y. Thomas Hou[1]

[1] Virginia Polytechnic Institute and State University, Blacksburg, USA
ningzh@vt.edu
[2] Guangzhou University, Guangzhou, China

Abstract. In the upcoming evolution of the Internet of Things (IoT), it is anticipated that billions of devices will be connected to the Internet. Many of these devices are capable of collecting information from individual users and their physical surroundings. They are also capable of taking smart actions, which are usually from a backend cloud server in the IoT system. While IoT promises a more connected and smarter world, this pervasive large-scale data collection, storage, sharing, and analysis raise many privacy concerns.

In the current IoT ecosystem, IoT service providers have full control of the collected user data. While the original intended use of such data is primarily for smart IoT system and device control, the data is often used for other purposes not explicitly consented to by the users. We propose a novel user privacy protection framework, PrivacyGuard, that aims to empower users with full privacy control of their data. PrivacyGuard framework seamlessly integrates two new technologies, blockchain and trusted execution environment (TEE). By encoding data access policy and usage as smart contracts, PrivacyGuard can allow data owners to control who can have what access to their data, and be able to maintain a trustworthy record of their data usage. Using remote attestation and TEE, PrivacyGuard ensures that data is only used for the intended purposes approved by the data owner. Our approach represents a significant departure from traditional privacy protections which often rely on cryptography and pure software-based secure computation techniques. Addressing the fundamental problem of data usage control, PrivacyGuard will become the cornerstone for free market of private information.

1 Introduction

The emergence of the Internet of Things (IoT) is the result of rapid advancement in technology in multiple fields. In the past two decades, we have witnessed an explosive deployment of *communications and networking technologies*, especially wireless technologies. At the same time, *mobile devices* have transformed from limited embedded systems to highly capable general purpose computing platforms. A variety of *mobile devices* with increased capability and intelligence are

© Springer Nature Switzerland AG 2018
J. Garcia-Alfaro et al. (Eds.): DPM 2018/CBT 2018, LNCS 11025, pp. 345–353, 2018.
https://doi.org/10.1007/978-3-030-00305-0_24

being introduced at a speed of approximately half a billion each year in recent years [1]. New life-changing *mobile apps* are being introduced every day.

IoT promises a more connected and smarter world. However, as a wide variety of things are increasingly embedded around us and more and more data about us are collected, shared, and analyzed, there is an increased concern on privacy. Individuals share personal information with people or organizations within a particular community for specific purposes. For example, individuals may share their medical status with healthcare professionals, product preferences with retailers, and real-time whereabouts with their loved ones. When information shared within one context is exposed in another outside of the intended context, people may feel a sense of privacy violation [2]. This *contextual nature of privacy* implies that privacy protection techniques need to address at least two aspects: (1) what kind of information can be exposed to whom, under what conditions; and (2) what is the "intended purpose" or "expected use" of this information.

Much research has been done to address the first privacy aspect. There has been a large body of research work on *data access control* that aims to ensure that only authorized data consumers can access private user data [3–11]. Another line of research is *data anonymization* that tries to ensure if sensitive data needs to be published, it is published anonymously, i.e. the personal identifiable information is removed from the data and the linkability between the published data and individual users is carefully eliminated [12–16]. Only recently, there have been a few works that attempted to address the second aspect of privacy, i.e., data used only for the intended purposes [17,18]. In fact, with the current practice, once an authorized user gains access to the data, how this user would use the data, whether or not he/she would use the data for purposes not consented by the user, or simply pass the data to another party (i.e., data monetization) is up to this new "data owner." Legal or regulatory measures may be taken to put some constraints on this, but technical approaches that allow users to specify and enforce the intended use of their data are lacking in general.

In this paper, we propose *PrivacyGuard*, a private data utilization framework, to address this very challenging privacy problem in IoT – how to empower a data owner in an IoT system to have full control over how his/her personal data is used. The data owner should not only be able to control who can have what access to his/her data, but also be ensured that the data is used only for the intended purposes. To realize the envisioned functionality of PrivacyGuard, there are three key requirements.

- User shall be able to define his/her own data access policy concerning to whom she will share the data at what time for what purpose and at what price. The framework shall also support rich encoding of different data utilization conditions.
- There shall be strict enforcement on the data policy set forth by the data owner. Each usage of the user data shall have a verified proof that it is compliant with the policy and data content is well protected during the utilization.
- Each data usage shall be recorded on a platform that offers non-repudiation and transparency.

In PrivacyGuard, users' privacy policies are embedded as smart contracts on a blockchain platform. In recent years, blockchain, the technology behind *Bitcoin* [19] and *Ethereum* [20], has emerged as a popular technology for distributed public repository of data. Bitcoin [19], exploiting the blockchain as a public ledger to store cryptocurrency exchanges (called transactions), is the first implementation of blockchain technology. Other emerging platforms also using the blockchain are quickly gaining popularity, such as Ethereum [20], Hyper-Ledger [21], IOTA [22]. *Smart contract*, a program that runs on the blockchain and has its correct execution enforced by the consensus protocol, has seen fast adoption and increased use in the Ethereum platform. In PrivacyGuard, smart contracts are used to facilitate the transactions of private data utilization on the private data market, providing access control, tamper-resistant record of data utilization.

Smart contract provides a mechanism to ensure desired privacy protection at the protocol level. However, when the program is running on a third party computer (such as in the Cloud) which is not fully trusted by the data owner, the confidentiality of user data as well as the faithful execution of the protocols can no longer be guaranteed. Pure software-based approaches, such as homomorphic encryption and secure multi-party computation, for secure computation in the cloud have been investigated extensively in the past decade. However, the heavy overhead on generic constructions of secure computation makes practical adoption infeasible with the current computing power. In this project, we take a different approach to support generic computation. We will develop a system level security mechanism exploiting Intel SGX enclave technology, which provides a hardware-isolated secure execution environment. In this third thrust, we will focus on the system design of *iDataAgent* running in Intel SGX enclave so that data confidentiality can be ensured and intended data usage is enforced through secure contract execution in the cloud.

2 PrivacyGuard Overview: A Framework Enabling User Control on IoT Data Usage

Things in IoT can take many different forms, from simple RFIDs attached to merchandises, smart thermostats installed in the classrooms, to wearable medical devices on patients and video cameras at home.

Some powerful devices, such as IP cameras and smart TVs, can connect directly through the Internet to the backend application server in the cloud. Some other IoT systems, such as Samsung smart things, make use of something like a smart hub to orchestrate communications between heterogeneous things. However, in most cases, the intelligence of the system is hosted at a cloud backend, therefore all the data generated from the system is stored within the vendor cloud. Data collected by IoT devices could be used directly by the vendor IoT applications. They could also be shared with other services, including various big data analytics tasks.

The huge amount of data collected by IoT and the desire of broad information sharing raise serious privacy concerns.

- **Confidentiality Protection on User Data** When data is generated under the current paradigm, it is stored in the vendor's cloud storage. The data is often stored in plaintext, and the access control on user data relies on the vendor system. Even when the data is stored in an encrypted storage, the user does not control the encryption key. When the data is less sensitive such as video from a driveway camera, plaintext storage might be acceptable. However, video from a camera in the bedroom can contain sensitive private information and would require an appropriate level of protection, and such data should not be exposed even to the service provider. Therefore, user-controlled, rather than service provider-controlled, encryption/decryption is fundamental in IoT data privacy.
- **Verifiable User-controlled Fine-grained Data Access** Under the current paradigm, once the data is uploaded to the vendor cloud, it belongs to the vendor under a service agreement. A user could grant access to his data to someone. But there is no way for the user to find out who actually accessed his private data, not to mention for what purpose. Lack of transparency and verifiability on data access often prompts users to choose the most restrictive data sharing agreement. This is evidential in a recent study on data sharing practice among windows error reporting users, where most people choose not to share data when they do not know how the data may be used. A public service that keeps track of user data usage and makes it auditable by data owners is therefore essential to not only protect user privacy but also promote data sharing in the community.
- **Provable Legal Binding on User Data Usage** Service level agreements and legal contracts are the only control over how data is stored, shared, and mined under the current IoT ecosystem. As more and more devices are connected to the network, we are witnessing an economic drive of intelligence collected from mining the IoT data. On one hand, the intelligence reaped from mining IoT data could help provide quality service, increase convenience, lower the cost of operation, etc. On the other hand, misuse of such information could lead to injustices, such as a patient being denied of health insurance due to a health condition inferred from his medical IoT system. To realize the grand vision of a more connected and smarter world, the capability to provide flexible and provable legal binding over the use of user personal data is the utmost capability our society needs in the era of Internet of Things.

2.1 PrivacyGuard Architecture

As shown in the left half of Fig. 1, an IoT system can be divided into four layers based on the technical supports they provide. The lowest layer is the *Thing/Device layer,* which is made up of various smart objects integrated with sensors and actuators. This is the IoT system's interface to the physical world. The sensors and actuators will interact with their physical environment, allowing real-time information to be collected and processed (mostly signal processing). Layer 2 is the *Network layer* which provides interconnectivity of various wireless access technologies, and supports routing functions. The highest is the *Cloud*

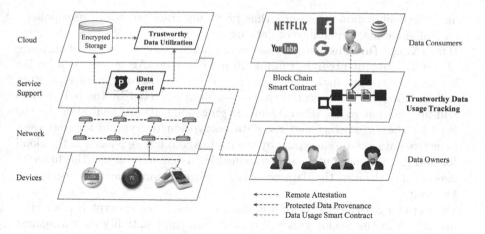

Fig. 1. IoT system architecture and proposed PrivacyGuard framework

layer, which is where the backend services/applications reside. It is a data concentration point and where most of the data analytics happens.

Between the cloud layer and the network layer is what we call the *Service Support layer*. This layer has more computation and storage capability and is capable of carrying out some important information processing tasks, possible through data analytics. From a security and privacy point of view, security control and device management, process modeling and information flow control, such as data filtering, aggregation, can all happen at this layer. The placement of this layer depends on the network architecture of an IoT system. For a Cloud-based IoT system, the layer would be in the Cloud. For an IoT system that adopts a Device-Gateway-Cloud architecture by leveraging edge computing, this layer could be at the edge node.

Figure 1 shows the system architecture of the proposed *PrivacyGuard* framework. Although we have been using the term *users* to refer to individuals or organizations who are using an IoT system, in what follows, we differentiate two roles that an IoT user can take. We refer to the individual or organization that owns the IoT devices and produces IoT data as *data owner* and the entity that needs to access and use IoT data as *data consumer*.

Main Components. There are three main components in the PrivacyGuard architecture.

– **Blockchain:** We employ an external blockchain (such as Ethereum) to enable an accountable distributed data repository for publishing access policy and facilitating data use recording. For data access control, a data owner can encode the terms and conditions regarding the access to his/her personal data as a smart contract. Data uses are recorded as transactions that interact with the smart contract. Here the blockchain serves as a public, auditable, and irreversible data repository, thus providing transparency of user policies as well as public verifiability of data usage.

- **iDataAgent (an Enclave):** iDataAgent is a trusted entity and is an instance of the iDataAgent program running in a TEE. iDataAgent acts as a broker for user data. Any data that goes in and out of the user data repository will go through iDataAgent. Private user data collected by the IoT devices will first be sent to the iDataAgent for processing. iDataAgent manages the keys for the data owner and the data encryption/decryption for that user. Sensitive data will be encrypted by the iDataAgent before pushed to the cloud for storage. iDataAgent is also responsible to remotely attest the function execution enclave in the data consumer before passing the data decryption key to it.
- **Encrypted Storage:** Private user data will always be encrypted when they are at rest in the cloud. This will ensure data confidentiality at rest against the cloud service provider.

2.2   Workflow

In what follows we outline the workflow of the proposed PrivacyGuard. We separate the workflow into three stages: data generation (encrypting user data), data access binding generation (contract negotiation), and data utilization (contract execution).

- **Data Generation and Key Management** In this stage, user data is collected and uploaded to the cloud storage. We propose to build a trusted entity, iDataAgent, at the service support level using Intel SGX secure enclave technology. The framework allows individual data owners to manage the keys used to encrypt/decrypt their data before uploading to the cloud storage through iDataAgent. A straightforward solution to initialize the master secret between a data owner and his iDataAgent enclave is to bootstrap it when a data owner first signs up for the service. Upon successful remote attestation of the iDataAgent enclave, the data owner can transmit his secret key to iDataAgent through the secure channel established along with the remote attestation. This key can then be used to derive data encryption/decryption and integrity check keys for this user. When the user data is generated, it is transmitted to iDataAgent instead of directly to the service provider such as Samsung smart home cloud. iDataAgent encrypts user data using the derived keys before pushing them to the cloud for storage. There are multiple ways to secure the communications between user IoT devices and iDataAgent. This problem is not the focus of this project. To minimize the changes necessary to the current IoT system implementation, we assume that the IoT devices can be reconfigured to connect to iDataAgent rather than Samsung Smart Home server, and rely on existing SSL/TLS implementations to establish the secure channel.
- **Policy Generation and Contract Negotiation** Our framework allows a data owner to define the access policy for the data he generated. The policy

is encoded in a smart contract and committed to the blockchain. A smart contract involves at least the following information, *Policy = [data type, data range, operation, consumer, expiration, cost]*, where the "intended use" of data of certain *type, range* is coded as *operation*, which can be arbitrary computer programs attestable by iDataAgent.

- **Data Utilization - Contract Execution** Smart contract, by design, can only embed some simple logics (functions) and the trustworthy execution of those functions is enforced by the consensus protocol. The "intended use" of the data can be arbitrary computer programs. Thus, it is impractical to embed them into a smart contract and have their trustworthy execution results enforced by the consensus protocol. In PrivacyGuard, we propose to use smart contract and blockchain for trustworthy bookkeeping of user access policy, consumer data usage record, and secure payment transfer. We use the trusted entity iDataAgent to ensure that only programs for the "approved use" can have access to the data and that the program will be executed in a remotely attested separate TEE for contract execution.

When a data consumer app requests the use of the data, iDataAgent remotely attests the contract execution environment and the function to be executed on data. Only when both the environment is trustworthy and the function to be executed is as specified in the smart contract, will iDataAgent pass the data decryption key to the contract execution enclave. Encrypted data can be obtained by the execution enclave from the Cloud storage. Note that an additional layer of defense can be built on the Cloud storage to grant access only to encrypted data as specified in the data access contract. When the contracted operation is finished, the contract execution enclave will commit a transaction to the blockchain to certify that the contracted operation is finished, thus finalizing the final transaction and recording the instance of data usage. In addition, it will clean up all the key materials as well as data inside the enclave to prevent data reuse.

3   Conclusion

In this position paper, we propose *PrivacyGuard*, a novel user privacy protection framework that aims to empower data owners with full privacy control of their data. Two important aspects of data privacy shall be addressed: (1) how to allow data owners to control who can have what access to their data, and be able to maintain a trustworthy record of their data usage; and (2) how to ensure that data is only used for the intended purposes approved by the data owner. To accomplish the afore-mentioned privacy goals, the proposed PrivacyGuard framework seamlessly integrates two new technologies, *blockchain* and *trusted execution environment (TEE)*.

The proposed approaches are novel, representing a significant departure from traditional privacy protection researches that rely on cryptography and pure software-based secure computation techniques. Hardware-assisted approaches will provide a more powerful and more practical solution to the very challenging privacy problem. The unique combination of blockchain and TEE technologies will enable new privacy protection capabilities, i.e., verifiable data usage tracking and data use compliance enforcement. We believe PrivacyGuard framework is a foundational technology for user privacy control in the era of Internet-of-things and data intelligence.

Acknowledgment. This work was supported in part by US National Science Foundation under grants CNS-1446478 and CNS-1443889.

References

1. Cisco visual networking index: Global mobile data traffic forecast update, 2016–2021 white paper. https://www.cisco.com/c/en/us/solutions/collateral/service-provider/visual-networking-index-vni/mobile-white-paper-c11-520862.html
2. National privacy research strategy. https://www.nitrd.gov/PUBS/NationalPrivacyResearchStrategy.pdf
3. Goyal, V., Pandey, O., Sahai, A., Waters, B.: Attribute-based encryption for fine-grained access control of encrypted data. In: Proceedings of the 13th ACM Conference on Computer and Communications Security, CCS 2006, pp. 89–98. ACM, New York (2006)
4. Sahai, A.: Ciphertext-policy attribute-based encryption. In: Proceedings of the IEEE Symposium on Security and Privacy, pp. 321–334 (2007)
5. Chase, M., Chow, S.S.M.: Improving privacy and security in multi-authority attribute-based encryption. In: Proceedings of the 16th ACM Conference on Computer and Communications Security, CCS 2009, pp. 121–130. ACM, New York (2009)
6. Desmedt, Y., Shaghaghi, A.: Function-Based Access Control (FBAC): from access control matrix to access control tensor. In: Proceedings of the 8th ACM CCS International Workshop on Managing Insider Security Threats, MIST 2016, pp. 89–92. ACM, New York (2016)
7. Bates, A., Mood, B., Valafar, M., Butler, K.: Towards secure provenance-based access control in cloud environments. In: Proceedings of the Third ACM Conference on Data and Application Security and Privacy, CODASPY 2013, pp. 277–284. ACM, New York (2013)
8. Bacis, E., di Vimercati, S.D.C., Foresti, S., Paraboschi, S., Rosa, M., Samarati, P.: Mix&Slice: efficient access revocation in the cloud. In: Proceedings of the 2016 ACM SIGSAC Conference on Computer and Communications Security, CCS 2016, pp. 217–228. ACM, New York (2016)
9. Wang, G., Liu, Q., Wu, J.: Hierarchical attribute-based encryption for fine-grained access control in cloud storage services. In: Proceedings of the 17th ACM Conference on Computer and Communications Security, CCS 2010, pp. 735–737. ACM, New York (2010)
10. Yu, S., Wang, C., Ren, K., Lou, W.: Achieving secure, scalable, and fine-grained data access control in cloud computing. In: IEEE INFOCOM 2010, San Diego, CA, USA, March 2010
11. di Vimercati, S.D.C., Foresti, S., Jajodia, S., Paraboschi, S., Samarati, P.: Encryption policies for regulating access to outsourced data. ACM Trans. Database Syst. (TODS) **35**(2), 12 (2010)

12. Dwork, C.: Differential privacy. In: Bugliesi, M., Preneel, B., Sassone, V., Wegener, I. (eds.) ICALP 2006. LNCS, vol. 4052, pp. 1–12. Springer, Heidelberg (2006). https://doi.org/10.1007/11787006_1
13. Machanavajjhala, A., Kifer, D., Gehrke, J., Venkitasubramaniam, M.: L-diversity: privacy beyond k-anonymity. ACM Trans. Knowl. Discov. Data 1(1) (2007)
14. Sweeney, L.: K-anonymity: a model for protecting privacy. Int. J. Uncertain. Fuzziness Knowl.-Based Syst. 10(5), 557–570 (2002)
15. Li, N., Li, T., Venkatasubramanian, S.: t-closeness: privacy beyond k-anonymity and l-diversity. In: IEEE 23rd International Conference on Data Engineering, 2007, ICDE 2007, pp. 106–115. IEEE (2007)
16. Samarati, P.: Protecting respondents identities in microdata release. IEEE Trans. Knowl. Data Eng. 13(6), 1010–1027 (2001)
17. Zyskind, G., Nathan, O., Pentland, A.: Decentralizing privacy: using blockchain to protect personal data. In: Security and Privacy Workshops (SPW). IEEE (2015)
18. Zyskind, G., Nathan, O., Pentland, A.: Enigma: decentralized computation platform with guaranteed privacy. arXiv preprint arXiv:1506.03471 (2015)
19. Nakamoto, S.: Bitcoin: a peer-to-peer electronic cash system (2008)
20. Ethereum: Blockchain app platform. https://www.ethereum.org/
21. Cachin, C.: Architecture of the hyperledger blockchain fabric. In: Workshop on Distributed Cryptocurrencies and Consensus Ledgers (2016)
22. Divya, M., Biradar, N.B.: IOTA-next generation block chain. Int. J. Eng. Comput. Sci. 7(04), 23823–23826 (2018)

DPM Workshop: Privacy and Cryptography

A Performance and Resource Consumption Assessment of Secret Sharing Based Secure Multiparty Computation

Marcel von Maltitz[✉] and Georg Carle

Chair of Network Architectures and Services, Department of Informatics,
Technical University of Munich, Munich, Germany
{vonmaltitz,carle}@net.in.tum.de

Abstract. In recent years, Secure Multiparty Computation (SMC) advanced from a theoretical technique to a practically applicable cryptographic technology. Several frameworks were proposed of which some are still actively developed.

We perform a first comprehensive study of performance characteristics of SMC protocols using a promising implementation based on secret sharing, a common and state-of-the-art foundation. We analyze its scalability with respect to environmental parameters as the number of peers and network properties – namely transmission rate, packet loss, network latency – as parameters and execution time, CPU cycles, memory consumption and amount of transmitted data as variables.

Our insights on the resource consumption show that such a solution is practically applicable in intranet environments and – with limitations – in Internet settings.

Keywords: Cryptography · Secure Multiparty Computation
Privacy · Performance · Resource consumption · Measurement

1 Introduction

While the foundations for Secure Multiparty Computation (SMC) were laid about forty years ago [30], the topic experienced a revival in the last decade: Starting as mere theoretic considerations, improvements in hardware performance made practical implementations and productive use of SMC possible. In consequence, a number of SMC frameworks emerged and its practical application was considered in research [8,9,12,32].

Most publications in this context have in common that they focus on singular events of orchestrated or manually triggered computations. With Smart Buildings and the Internet of Things (IoT), a new type of use case for privacy-preserving data processing becomes relevant: Recurrent and automated processing of data streams will be carried out on commodity or even low-end hardware.

© Springer Nature Switzerland AG 2018
J. Garcia-Alfaro et al. (Eds.): DPM 2018/CBT 2018, LNCS 11025, pp. 357–372, 2018.
https://doi.org/10.1007/978-3-030-00305-0_25

Host nodes will be constrained devices and communication might happen via restricted or unreliable connections. [23, 24]

It is hence vital to understand the resource requirements and performance characteristics of a productively usable SMC solution in order to assess it applicability in this context. Our work provides these insights by performing a thorough performance evaluation of a selected SMC framework based on secret sharing, a common mathematical foundation.

The remainder of the paper is structured as follows: In Sect. 2, we give an overview of SMC in general and argue for the framework we select for further examination. Section 3 presents the related work regarding practical evaluation of SMC. We present preliminary theoretical performance considerations for round based SMC protocols in Sect. 4. Section 5 contains the description of our evaluation setup; the results are presented and discussed in Sect. 6. We elaborate the practical implications in Sect. 7 and conclude our paper with Sect. 8.

2   Secure Multiparty Computation

Secure Multiparty Computation enables multiple communicating parties to collaboratively compute a function while being able to keep their respective input value completely confidential. Yao initiated this field of research by presenting the Millionaire's Problem and the idea of Secure Function Evaluation [30, 31]. While many single purpose protocols were proposed, the main interest was in the creation of a general purpose framework which allows the computation of arbitrary functions. Basic concepts were identified which allowed approaching this aim, most notably *garbled circuits* [31], *homomorphic encryption* [27] and *secret sharing schemes* [5, 28]. Its theory flourished early in the 80's (cf. [3, 5, 15, 16, 19, 26]) while implementations have only been developed in the last decade. Among them, many have been proposed as proof of concept but were not publicly available [9] or have not been developed further since then [12] [18] [4]. Currently, Sharemind [6], SPDZ-2 [17, 20] and FRESCO [1] constitute the state-of-the-art of actively developed SMC frameworks[1].

All of these solutions are secret sharing based. Hence, a similar performance behavior depending on the investigated parameters can be expected. However, for our use case we need a solution which is able to support computations with a theoretically arbitrary number of participants. This is not given by Sharemind. Furthermore, Sharemind is closed-source which further obstructs assessment. SPDZ-2 is currently still work in progress on a level of fundamental changes and consequently not ready for a thorough performance measurement. Our choice is therefore FRESCO, which aims for production-ready application:

Framework for Efficient Secure Computation. FRESCO [1] aims for being a non-prototypical, productively applicable generic SMC framework written in Java.

---

[1] There are further frameworks for the special two-party case, but they are not applicable in this multiparty context.

At the time of writing, FRESCO mainly supports the Ben-Or–Goldwasser–Wigderson (BGW) [5] protocol based on Shamir's secret sharing using polynomials. This allows computations which are secure in the honest-but-curious adversary model.

3   Related Work

The newly gained interest in SMC during the last years resulted in a multitude of publications, which propose successive improvements or applications of established approaches. By contrast, the body of research is missing thorough performance measurements of SMC solutions.

Most of these publications do not provide performance data or merely a single result for their exact setting of application [8–10,29]. Others typically only evaluate overall execution time and to some lower degree transmitted bytes measured while at most varying the number of parties and the amount of input data [6,7,11,12,21,22,25,32]. Only few include further parameters like the transmission rate [20] and technology-dependent factors like circuit size and depth [4] and evaluate further parameters e.g. throughput.

For assessing feasibility in distributed systems and the Internet of Things, it is necessary to perform more thorough measurements including further factors. It is vital to understand the influences of the network characteristics and to further examine the impact on host resources.

We aim to provide the necessary insights by assessing the parameters *number of peers, transmission rate, network latency,* and *packet loss,* while measuring the variables *execution time, CPU cycles, stack* and *heap memory consumption,* and *transmitted bytes.*

4   Preliminary Execution Time Considerations

A computation model for secret sharing based SMC protocol foundations like BGW "is a complete synchronous network of n processors" [5]. The protocol itself is dissected into rounds. "In one round of computation each of the players can do an arbitrary amount of local computation, send a message to each of the players, and read all messages that were sent to it at this round" [5]. A message typically contains a share of a private local value – e.g. a polynomial in the BGW protocol – held by the sender.

From this point of view the protocol becomes an alternating sequence[2] of local computation and network communication:

$$comp_1, comm_1, \ldots, comp_{m-1}, comm_{m-1}, comp_m \qquad (1)$$

The communication steps are also synchronization points providing shares for the next computation step.

---

[2] We consider recombining the shares to be the last step $comp_m$. Hence, there are only $m-1$ communication steps.

We denote the time costs for a step $comp_i$ as $cost_{comp_i}$. The message sent from player P_k sent to P_l during $comm_i$ is referred to as $msg_{i,k \to l}$. Two phases are typical for all SMC protocols: During the *input phase* – a single round – the own private input is transformed into shares and distributed among the players. In the *output phase* the shares of the computed result are exchanged among all players. Their recombination yields the plaintext result. In FRESCO this also takes a round[3]. The round complexity of the basic arithmetic operations in the BGW protocol varies. Addition does not need any communication. Multiplication requires rerandomization of the polynomial and the reduction of its degree [5]. This requires a step of communication, and hence, a round.

The communication cost of the ith round $cost_{comm_i}$ depends on the number of messages sent. As every player sends an individual share to every other player, the overall number of shares sent is $\mathcal{O}(n^2)$. Every player p_i typically contributes its own input v_i for the computation. Hence, a single multiplication step normally means that the product of all input values should be computed: $\prod_{i=1}^{n} v_i$. In such a case, $n - 1$ single multiplications are necessary; consequently the costs for such an array multiplication are $\mathcal{O}(n^3)$. However, analysis of FRESCO shows that sending and receiving for every player can happen in parallel[4]: Sending is a non-blocking action for the computation layer which hands over the messages to be sent to the communication layer of FRESCO. Receiving is blocking on the computation layer, however, the communication layer is able to receive all messages simultaneously.

When a host has sent out every share and it has received all other players' shares, the next computation step can be performed. So, in spite of the theoretical complexity and due to parallelization the communication cost per round mainly depends on the slowest pair of hosts:

$$cost_{comm_i} = \max_{1 \leq k,l \leq n} cost_{msg_{i,k \to l}} \tag{2}$$

While every round is practically performed in constant time, the number of rounds per array multiplication increases linearly. A further approximative simplification of the communication costs can be made: Communication between two peers is always identically structured and of comparable length. Hence, we can simplify that

$$\forall i \in \{1, \ldots, m-1\} : cost_{comm_i} = cost_{comm} \tag{3}$$

---

[3] Some solution perform a resharing in order to make the final shares independent from the shares obtained in the computation. This is, e.g., necessary when the shares should be reused to perform further calculation. Then, another round becomes necessary during this phase.

[4] One exception is the initial input sharing phase. Here, sending of shares is only performed by a single host at a time.

Note that Eq. 3 does not hold for computation steps, as each phase performs different tasks. Combining Eqs. 1 and 3 the overall costs of time can be estimated by

$$cost_{overall} = \sum_{i=1}^{m} cost_{comp_i} + (m-1) * cost_{comm} \qquad (4)$$

Applying the model of the alternating sequence, the influences on the duration are twofold: The computation performance depends in the properties of the players, the communication performance depends on the properties of their network links. Due to the synchronizing behavior of rounds, the costs of both sides add up to the overall costs.

Performance Comparison

Conceptually, SMC replaces a Trusted Third Party (TTP) by providing a secure protocol. Canetti [13] used this understanding to propose a now well-established method to prove secrecy and correctness of SMC protocol designs.

We can also apply this understanding to assess the performance penalty that SMC introduces. Using a TTP for computation can here be used as a performance baseline. In fact, in today's productively used systems, TTP solutions are the established standard; hence, the comparison with a TTP is also practically relevant. In order to do so, we align the necessary actions when using a TTP with the phases of an SMC computation. In a TTP setting, the input phase can be understood as providing the input data to the TTP. The output phase comprises sending the result from the TTP to the participants. Computation steps can be directly adapted. The whole comparison applied to the BGW protocol is shown in Table 1.[5]

Table 1. Performance comparison SMC vs. TTP. Computations are counted in basic (arithmetic) operations, communication in number of messages.

Phase	SMC		TTP	
	Computation per host	Communication (overall)	Computation on TTP	Communication (overall)
Close	Generation of polynomial, calculation of n shares	$n^2 - n$	—	n
Addition	$n - 1$ additions	—	$n - 1$ additions	—
Multiplication	$n - 1$ multiplications, $Comp_{Close}$, $Comp_{Open}$	$n^2 - n$	$n - 1$ multiplications	—
Open	Lagrange interpolation	$n^2 - n$	—	n

---

[5] Common computations are omitted: E.g. the running sum has to be turned into a current average by a single division. As both solutions have to do the same step, it is not reflected in the table.

Presenting our results in Sect. 6, we add – where applicable – an estimation how a TTP solution would perform. In these cases we approximate the communication performance as described before while neglecting the low influence of the computation steps.

5 Evaluation Setup

In the following section we describe our test setup. We refer to a real-world use case performed at our lab; the functionality being similar to other real-world systems. In the methodology, we document the measurement environment in terms of used software, hardware and measurement tools.

5.1 Scenario

Our scenario is inspired by MeasrDroid [14], a smartphone app which allows insights into the sensor data of the device and comparison to other users. Assuming a set of moving devices, a property of interest is their summed and averaged travel distance. Without SMC, the functionality is realized as follows: Each client derives a stream of distances from the GPS coordinates. They connect to a common trusted server which holds a running sum and transmit the travel distance since their individual last connection. Anytime, the average distance can then be computed by the server.

In order to apply FRESCO, the input has to be organized in synchronous sessions. In every session, each device contributes its distance since the last session, whereas the statistics server inputs the current value of the running sum (starting with 0). During computation, each host synchronously follows the predefined algorithm. Between computation steps, messages are exchanged between each pair of hosts (cf. Table 1). These messages exclusively contain secret shares of intermediary computation results. The final result of each session is saved by the statistics server.

With regard to the privacy of the system, it is uncritical that the total sum is calculated privately while the division step to retrieve the average is performed without SMC. Under the premise that the number of participants is known (which is necessary to perform the sharing correctly) the total sum would always be derivable from the average value. Consequently, the total sum does not leak any more information than the average does.

Knowing that communication between the peers is the typical bottleneck for SMC [32] [8] [11], the choice of the use case is beneficial for our performance measurement: The computational part is comparatively low so that performance effects caused by communication and their relationship to the named parameters become clearly visible. This allows better assessment of the communication bottleneck of SMC based solutions with negligible influence by the local computations.

Input Data: We used real world data retrieved from MeasrDroid, yielding five traces consisting of 20000 GPS tuples each. Since the data itself does in no way influence the performance of the system, we could duplicate the inputs when scaling beyond 5 parties without loss of application and closeness to reality.

5.2 Methodology

For our tests we had 15 physical hosts available. Each host has an Intel Xeon CPU with eight cores at 2.50 GHz and a cache size of 8192 KB. They have 15.780 MB RAM and a 1 Gbit networking interface each. They are arranged using a star topology, all hosts are connected via a single switch. The default link latency is around 0.18 ms and there is no packet loss. The test hosts use Debian Jessie (8.5) and a 3.16 Linux kernel. Our Java application was executed by the Java VM from the OpenJDK 1.8.0_111. For assessing influence of network latency we added artificial delay to the communication round-trip while equally distributing the delay to both hosts of each link using tc. For this purpose, tc delays every outgoing packet by the half of the desired additional delay. Packet loss is also simulated via tc.

We use an orchestration layer which configures all client-side parameters and starts the target application. The Java application itself locally loads GPS coordinates. In a preprocessing step the GPS coordinates are transformed into travelling distances by calculating the distance between consecutive GPS locations. During each measurement, each peer p provides 1000 distance values $v_{p,n}$ with $1 \leq n \leq 1000$ and correspondingly 1000 computations are performed. During secure computation c_n each peer p contributes $v_{p,n}$ as numerical input while the host representing the statistics server provides the result of c_{n-1}. The provided values are used to update the running average of the overall travelling distances. Since every computation is short in time, its measured duration can fluctuate randomly. In order to get stable results, 1000 computations are carried out per measurement. Furthermore, each measurement itself has been repeated 50 times if not noted otherwise. The above described realization of the secure computation stays identical over all measurement performed during this study.

Profiling is performed using *perf* from the linux-tools (version 3.16+63) for counting CPU cycles, *BTrace* (version 1.3.8.3 (20160926)) for assessing memory consumption and execution time and *tshark* (version 2.2.4) from wireshark for collecting the raw transmitted data.

6 Results

In the next subsection we focus on the host resources *heap memory* and consumed *CPU cycles*. Afterwards we analyze the amount of *transmitted data* representing the network resource. Then the *execution duration*, most directly affecting the user, is discussed.

6.1 Host Resources

In our context, RAM is separated in stack and heap memory. Our measurements showed that stack memory constantly was between 16 and 20 MBytes. Therefore, we focus completely on heap memory consumption. During our baseline

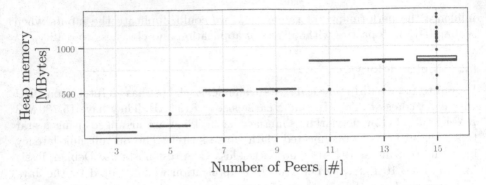

Fig. 1. Impact of the number of peers on the maximum allocated heap memory. Heap memory does not increase directly and proportionally with increasing peers but in distinct plateaus which are shared among an interval of peer counts.

execution with 3 peers the standard memory consumption is around 69 MBytes. This is only negligibly influenced by networking parameters. However, we identified a strong correlation when scaling the number of peers. Heap memory consumption then gradually diverges step-wise (cf. Fig. 1): The application uses around 70 MBytes during a computation with 3 to 5 peers, which increments to 530 MBytes for 7 to 9 peers and increases again to 840 MBytes for 11 to 15 peers. The reason is that data about current connections as well as intermediate results like the shares of all other participants are stored on the heap. We deduce a linear trend from Fig. 1 where the notable amount of outliers at x=15 already foreshadows the next step of heap increment. This factor rapidly becomes critical: With 15 peers, FRESCO already starts exceeding the memory resources of a Raspberry Pi [2] 3 B (1 GByte RAM) and uses a considerate amount of the memory of a current smartphone (2–4 GByte).

During the CPU measurements we noticed that there are major differences when comparing the values of different nodes of the same computation. This difference is found in the setup phase of FRESCO. In an initial step the hosts have to establish connections with every other participant. This is achieved by listening for incoming connections and performing own connection attempts to other hosts in parallel, driven by busy waiting. Starting the application on all hosts sequentially with a little delay between them, the first nodes performs considerably more busy waiting than the last. This understanding is necessary to interpret our results.

Our baseline is around $21.5 * 10^9$ cycles for the first and $16.5 * 10^9$ cycles for the last node. When reducing network performance consumption drops to approximately $12.5 * 10^9$. This effect is best depicted in Figs. 2 and 3. It can be attributed to the startup phase: Impeded transmission slows down polling, making it less CPU intensive. Additionally, Fig. 2 shows a slight increase in CPU cycles when increasing the network latency further. As the number of instructions did not increase during the same measurements, we expect this effect to be caused by IO waiting time during the delayed protocol execution.

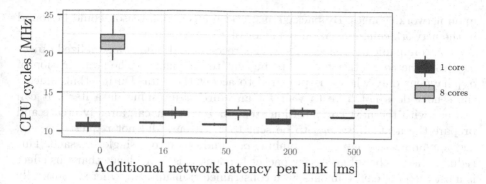

Fig. 2. Impact of network latency on the CPU cycles. With increasing network latency, CPU spends more time waiting for data, slightly increasing the amount of CPU cycles. The high amount of CPU cycles when using 8 cores and having no additional latency is an artifact of busy waiting as described in Sect. 6.1.

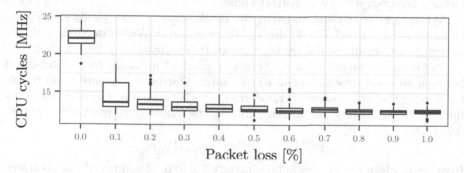

Fig. 3. Impact of packet loss on the CPU cycles. Increased packet loss slows down the busy waiting phase at connection setup. In consequence, the amount of CPU cycles converges to the value actually needed for carrying out the secure computation.

On the side of number of participating nodes, the number of consumed CPU cycles depends strictly linear on it. For the first node we get (mean squared error (MSE): 2.9451)

$$(5.16 + 5.83556 * n) * 10^9$$

and for the last node (MSE: 1.74056)

$$(15.263 + 0.69823 * n) * 10^9$$

We see that the amount of CPU cycles used in the startup phase heavily outweighs the increase of participating nodes.

6.2   Network Resources

Our baseline of transmitted data for three peers is 5.35 MBytes per peer. We identified that the amount of transmitted data per peer varies around 400 KBytes upon network changes. By package inspection a common reason could be found in the network communication behavior of FRESCO:

The communication layer of sender s receives and buffers a serialized object $o_{r,1}$ from the computation layer to be sent to recipient r. The transmission of $o_{r,1}$ happens only when r is prepared to accept the data. During that time, if the sender does not have to wait for any further incoming data itself, it can proceed with the next computation step. As a result it can already create and prepare the next object $o_{r,2}$ to be sent to r. Given r did not request $o_{r,1}$ yet, the communication layer will combine $o_{r,1}$ and $o_{r,2}$ into a single message. This reduces the number of necessary packet headers. It is coincidence that this effect is most useful in environments with constrained transmission, where it naturally also happens most often.

The measurements of two network parameters reflect this behavior up to some degree: When reducing the transmission rate to 1 MBit, a drop to 5.10 MBytes can be detected. A similar behavior occurs when adding artificial network latency, however, without a distinct trend.

While these deviations undercut the baseline, packet loss yields an increase of transmitted data (cf. Fig. 4) due to retransmissions. With a maximum of 10% packet loss, transmitted data was increased by approximately 400 KBytes.

Regarding the number of peers, the number of messages to be exchanged between all peers depends quadratically on it. Our measurements support this by showing that the amount of transferred bytes between *a pair of hosts* increases linearly. In our setting, the increase follows the following regression line (MSE: 0.03332):

$$(-2.743 + 2.69419 * n) \,\text{MBytes}$$

In other words, for each peer approximately 2 MByte of additional data is transmitted *per host*.

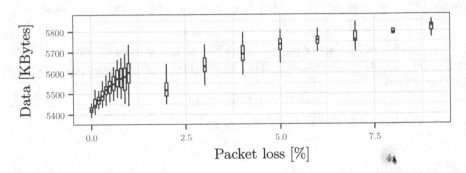

Fig. 4. Impact of packet loss on the transmitted KBytes. Packet loss makes retransmission of data necessary which in turn increase the overall amount of transmitted data. Tests beyond 10% of packet loss could not be performed due to repeatedly dropping connections.

6.3   User Resource: Time

The computation duration is the most interesting variable from the user's perspective. Our baseline is 5.35 s for 1000 calculations, i.e. each computation costs around 5 ms, whereas the startup of the Java VM is not included.

Time is heavily and differently influenced by the evaluated parameters: The increase in time is strictly linear when adding more participants, although the number of exchanged messages increases quadratically. In Sect. 4 we already elaborated how parallel execution of communication can reduce the complexity by n. As a regression function (cf. Fig. 5) we yield (MSE: 0.24894):

$$(-1.086 + 2.01883 * n)\,\text{ms}$$

As comparison, the communication delay of a TTP solution does not notably depend on the number of participants since sending and receiving messages can happen in parallel.

Network latency also causes a linear increase, which is notably stronger in absolute terms. The following regression function (cf. Fig. 6) holds for three participating peers (MSE: 15415.50432):

$$47.327ms + 4.61851 * network\ latency$$

Execution inside an intranet takes around 4 s for 1000 computations. Via the Internet (50 ms to 300 ms), the computations already cost 5 to 25 min. The duration can be roughly estimated as follows: During the input phase with $n = 3$ participating hosts, $n * (n - 1) = 6$ messages must be exchanged. Each participant sequentially waits for $n-1 = 2$ messages. The performed addition operation is free of communication. During the output phase, again 6 messages must be exchanged, while waiting in parallel[6]. Consequently, every participant sequentially waits for $n = 3$ messages, which can consist of one to two packets each.

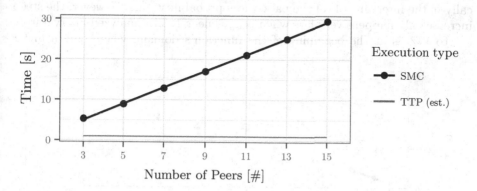

Fig. 5. Impact of number of peers on the execution time. With increasing number of peers, execution time increases strictly linearly in our use case. In comparison, a solution using a trusted third party is practically independent from the number of peers since communication can happen in parallel.

---

[6] Using Eq. 2 we count this as a single message.

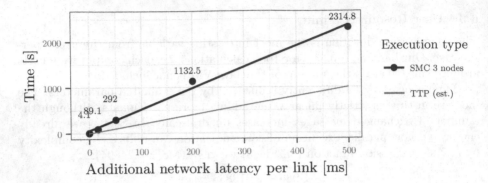

Fig. 6. Impact of network latency on the execution time. A setup featuring SMC is heavier influenced by network latency than a trusted third party. The reason is the higher amount of messages sent during SMC, since each message is slowed down by network latency. The full comparison is performed in Sect. 6.3.

While one packet costs a single network delay, two packets cost three network delays as the second packet is only sent after receiving an acknowledgement. In consequence, we gain an interval of $[n * \text{network latency}, 3n * \text{network latency}]$ per protocol execution.

With a TTP solution, all hosts send their data during a single network delay. The computation itself is performed locally. Another network delay is added for sending the results to all participants (in parallel). While it seems that the performance of the SMC solution is acceptably worse in comparison, it is important to note that the TTP does not depend on the number of peers as a factor at all (cf. Fig. 5).

Packet loss implies repeated retransmissions. Due to this, we expect the execution time (Fig. 7) to constitute a geometric row and to increase hyperbolically in the interval $[0, 1[$ of the packet loss probability p_{loss}. However, the steep increase only happens very late when p_{loss} is near 1. The analyzed interval from 0% to 10% is at the beginning of the function's domain, where only a linear

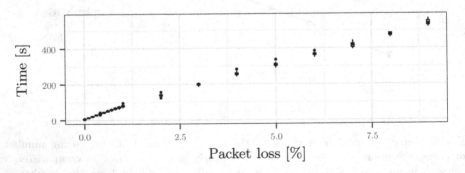

Fig. 7. Impact of packet loss on the execution time. In the tested interval, packet loss yielded linear increase of the execution time of the protocol.

increase becomes visible. The sessions started failing due to timeouts at a packet loss rate of 10%.

Comparatively weak constraints are given by the transmission rate (cf. Fig. 8). A very low rate of 1 MBit influences execution time negatively, but already between 10 MBit and 100 MBit all rate-induced impediments are resolved. A transmission consists of an exchanged share, encompassing one to maximally two packets, having only a length between 100 and 1000 Bytes each. This is the reason why network latency has stronger influence than the transmission rate.

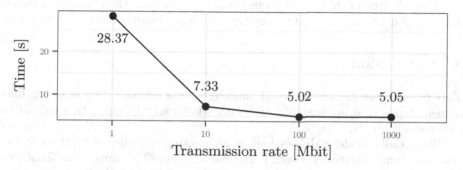

Fig. 8. Impact of transmission rate on the execution time. A low transmission rate highly impacts execution time of SMC. However, already with 10 Mbit the bottleneck of transmission is nearly resolved, so that further increase of transmission rate only provides small improvements.

In conclusion, each single computation has a low duration; the overall duration increases linearly with the number of peers. While this influence is comparatively small, the network parameters have the highest influence on the execution time. In the ranges of the practically relevant intervals we saw that the transmission rate can influence the execution time by factor 5, packet loss has an influence up to a factor of approximately 110 and network latency can slow down the computation even by factor 550. These impediments already occur at network configurations which are realistic on the Internet or the mobile Internet at least.

7 Practical Implications

We showed that FRESCO's performance and resource utilization behavior allows practical application. In intranet settings computations are efficient. The execution time is around 2 to 3 ms per session and peer. This allows batch processing of data and interactive use cases. Performance might, however, not be sufficient for the realization of real-time applications depending on the type of computation. Regarding the host systems, memory consumption can become critical when a multitude of peers participates in the computations. This must be considered upon productive use. However, regarding all identified performance results, we deem the memory consumption to be more related to Java than to secret sharing or SMC in general. With memory-constrained devices, a more economical programming language might be necessary.

In wide area networks as the Internet and mobile Internet, network latency is the most influential constraining factor. Execution time degrades strongly with increasing latency. In these contexts, currently the only use case seems to be batch processing: Given it is acceptable to wait several minutes for a computation result, SMC can be utilized. Further improvement of the situation would require to reduce the amount of transmitted packets. This could be possible by stricter orchestration of computations running in parallel, where packets between different peers would be used for multiple sessions simultaneously.

8   Conclusion

This paper presents the results of thorough measurements to assess the fundamental practical applicability of Secure Multiparty Computation (SMC) in real-world contexts.

We initially model SMC sessions as alternating sequence of local computation and communication between participating peers. This unveils the existence of two individual performance bottlenecks whose delay is typically strictly summative during a single execution.

In our measurements, we examine how network latency, transmission rate and packet loss, as well as the number of peers influence the execution time, the CPU utilization, memory allocation and the amount of transmitted data. Here, we focus on the communication overhead by choosing a scenario which is computationally simple. This yields a baseline of performance behavior of secret sharing based SMC.

Interpreting our findings, we conclude that SMC is practically applicable with weak limitations in intranet settings. Here, requirements for participating host systems are in ranges of today's commodity hardware. Furthermore, SMC seems to be applicable to some (lesser) degree in Internet settings. Here, network latency has the biggest negative influence on performance. However, as performance of SMC protocols continues to increase, we expect that feasibility of SMC over the Internet will also improve in the next years.

Acknowledgements. This work has been supported by the German Federal Ministry of Education and Research, project DecADe, grant 16KIS0538 and the German-French Academy for the Industry of the Future. We would like to thank Daniel Raumer and Florian Wohlfart for their valuable feedback on the initial versions of the paper. Equally, we are very grateful for the constructive feedback given by the anonymous reviewers.

References

1. A FRamework for Efficient Secure COmputation. https://github.com/aicis/fresco
2. Raspberry Pi Models. https://www.raspberrypi.org/products/
3. Beaver, D., Micali, S., Rogaway, P.: The round complexity of secure protocols. In: Proceedings of the 22nd Annual ACM Symposium on the Theory of Computing, pp. 503–513 (1990)
4. Ben-David, A., Nisan, N., Pinkas, B.: FairplayMP: a system for secure multi-party computation. In: Proceedings of the 15th ACM Conference on Computer and Communications Security, pp. 257–266 (2008). https://doi.org/10.1145/1455770.1455804
5. Ben-Or, M., Goldwasser, S., Wigderson, A.: Completeness theorems for non-cryptographic fault tolerant distributed computation. In: Proceedings of the 20th Annual ACM Symposium on the Theory of Computing (STOC), pp. 1–10 (1988). https://doi.org/10.1145/62212.62213
6. Bogdanov, D., Laur, S., Willemson, J.: Sharemind: a framework for fast privacy-preserving computations. In: Jajodia, S., Lopez, J. (eds.) ESORICS 2008. LNCS, vol. 5283, pp. 192–206. Springer, Heidelberg (2008). https://doi.org/10.1007/978-3-540-88313-5_13
7. Bogdanov, D., Niitsoo, M., Toft, T., Willemson, J.: High-performance secure multi-party computation for data mining applications. Int. J. Inf. Secur. 11(6), 403–418 (2012). https://doi.org/10.1007/s10207-012-0177-2
8. Bogdanov, D., Talviste, R., Willemson, J.: Deploying secure multi-party computation for financial data analysis. In: Keromytis, A.D. (ed.) FC 2012. LNCS, vol. 7397, pp. 57–64. Springer, Heidelberg (2012). https://doi.org/10.1007/978-3-642-32946-3_5
9. Bogetoft, P., et al.: Secure multiparty computation goes live. In: Dingledine, R., Golle, P. (eds.) FC 2009. LNCS, vol. 5628, pp. 325–343. Springer, Heidelberg (2009). https://doi.org/10.1007/978-3-642-03549-4_20
10. Bogetoft, P., Damgård, I., Jakobsen, T., Nielsen, K., Pagter, J., Toft, T.: A practical implementation of secure auctions based on multiparty integer computation. In: Di Crescenzo, G., Rubin, A. (eds.) FC 2006. LNCS, vol. 4107, pp. 142–147. Springer, Heidelberg (2006). https://doi.org/10.1007/11889663_10
11. Bonawitz, K., et al.: Practical secure aggregation for privacy preserving machine learning. In: Proceedings of the 2017 ACM SIGSAC Conference on Computer and Communications Security, vol. 2017, pp. 1175–1191 (2017)
12. Burkhart, M., Strasser, M., Many, D., Dimitropoulos, X.: SEPIA: privacy-preserving aggregation of multi-domain network events and statistics. In: Proceedings of the 19th USENIX Conference on Security, p. 15 (2010)
13. Canetti, R.: Security and Composition of Multi-party Cryptographic Protocols (1999)
14. Chair of Network Architectures and Services; TUM: MeasrDroid. http://www.droid.net.in.tum.de
15. Chaum, D., Crépeau, C., Damgård, I.: Multiparty unconditionally secure protocols. In: Proceedings of the 20th Annual ACM Symposium on Theory of Computing, pp. 11–19 (1988). https://doi.org/10.1007/3-540-48184-2_43
16. Chaum, D., Damgård, I.B., van de Graaf, J.: Multiparty computations ensuring privacy of each party's input and correctness of the result. In: Pomerance, C. (ed.) CRYPTO 1987. LNCS, vol. 293, pp. 87–119. Springer, Heidelberg (1988). https://doi.org/10.1007/3-540-48184-2_7

17. Damgård, I., Pastro, V., Smart, N., Zakarias, S.: Multiparty computation from somewhat homomorphic encryption. In: Safavi-Naini, R., Canetti, R. (eds.) CRYPTO 2012. LNCS, vol. 7417, pp. 643–662. Springer, Heidelberg (2012). https://doi.org/10.1007/978-3-642-32009-5_38
18. Geisler, M.: Cryptographic protocols: theory and implementation. Ph.D. thesis, Aarhus University (2010)
19. Goldreich, O., Micali, S., Wigderson, A.: How to play ANY mental game. In: Proceedings of the Nineteenth Annual ACM Conference on Theory of Computing - STOC 1987, pp. 218–229. ACM, New York (1987). https://doi.org/10.1145/28395.28420
20. Keller, M., Orsini, E., Scholl, P.: MASCOT. In: Proceedings of the 2016 ACM SIGSAC Conference on Computer and Communications Security, pp. 830–842 (2016). https://doi.org/10.1145/2976749.2978357
21. Kerschbaum, F., Biswas, D., De Hoogh, S.: Performance comparison of secure comparison protocols. In: Proceedings of International Workshop on Database and Expert Systems Applications, DEXA, October 2009, pp. 133–136 (2009). https://doi.org/10.1109/DEXA.2009.37
22. Kerschbaum, F., Dahlmeier, D., Schröpfer, A., Biswas, D.: On the practical importance of communication complexity for secure multi-party computation protocols. In: Proceedings of the 2009 ACM Symposium on Applied Computing - SAC 2009, pp. 2008–2015 (2009). https://doi.org/10.1145/1529282.1529730
23. von Maltitz, M., Carle, G.: Leveraging secure multiparty computation in the Internet of Things. In: MobiSys 2018: ACM Open IoT Day, p. 3. ACM, New York (2018). https://doi.org/10.1145/3210240.3223569
24. von Maltitz, M., Smarzly, S., Kinkelin, H., Carle, G.: A management framework for secure multiparty computation in dynamic environments. In: NOMS 2018 - IEEE/IFIP DOMINOS Workshop, Taipei, Taiwan (2018)
25. Pinkas, B., Schneider, T., Smart, N.P., Williams, S.C.: Secure two-party computation is practical. In: Matsui, M. (ed.) ASIACRYPT 2009. LNCS, vol. 5912, pp. 250–267. Springer, Heidelberg (2009). https://doi.org/10.1007/978-3-642-10366-7_15
26. Rabin, T., Ben-Or, M.: Verifiable secret sharing and multiparty protocols with honest majority. In: Proceedings of the 21st Annual ACM Symposium on Theory of Computing, pp. 73–85 (1989). https://doi.org/10.1145/73007.73014
27. Rivest, R.L., Adleman, L., Dertouzos, M.L.: On data banks and privacy homomorphisms. Found. Secur. Comput. 4, 169–180 (1978)
28. Shamir, A.: How to share a secret. Commun. ACM (CACM) 22(11), 612–613 (1979). https://doi.org/10.1145/359168.359176
29. Thoma, C., Cui, T., Franchetti, F.: Secure multiparty computation based privacy preserving smart metering system. In: 44th North American Power Symposium (NAPS), pp. 1–6 (2012)
30. Yao, A.C.: Protocols for secure computations. In: Proceedings of the 23rd Annual Symposium on Foundations of Computer Science, pp. 1–5. IEEE, Washington, DC (1982). https://doi.org/10.1109/SFCS.1982.38
31. Yao, A.C.: How to generate and exchange secrets. In: Proceedings of the 27th IEEE Symposium on Foundations of Computer Science, pp. 162–167. IEEE Computer Society Press (1986). https://doi.org/10.1109/SFCS.1986.25
32. Zanin, M., et al.: Towards a secure trading of aviation CO_2 allowance. J. Air Transp. Manag. 56, 3–11 (2016). https://doi.org/10.1016/j.jairtraman.2016.02.005

Privacy-Preserving Trade
Chain Detection

Stefan Wüller[1,2($\boxtimes$)], Malte Breuer[1], Ulrike Meyer[1], and Susanne Wetzel[2]

[1] RWTH Aachen University, Aachen, Germany
{wueller,meyer}@itsec.rwth-aachen.de
[2] Stevens Institute of Technology, Hoboken, NJ, USA
swetzel@stevens.edu

Abstract. In this paper, we present a novel multi-party protocol to facilitate the privacy-preserving detection of trade chains in the context of bartering. Our approach is to transform the parties' private quotes into a flow network such that a minimum-cost flow in this network encodes a set of simultaneously executable trade chains for which the number of parties that can trade is maximized. At the core of our novel protocol is a newly developed privacy-preserving implementation of the cycle canceling algorithm that can be used to solve the minimum cost flow problem on encrypted flow networks.

1 Introduction

Bartering refers to the direct exchange of goods or services for other goods or services [9]. Nowadays, traded goods and services include books, rental cars, apartments, production surpluses, or idle times of employees. The attractiveness of bartering stems from the fact that it does not suffer from shortcomings of currencies such as foreign exchange problems, inflation, liquidity problems of banks, or concentration of economic power.

Today, a large fraction of bartering transactions is carried out via centralized (online) platforms which support their users in finding suitable trade partners. Since bartering involves sensitive personal data (e.g., negotiation ranges), a main objective of prior work [14–16] is to replace these central platforms by decentralized privacy-preserving protocols which allow a fixed number of parties to privately barter their commodities thus eliminating the risk that a platform operator may not only learn sensitive personal data but (to some extent) can also control and manipulate which parties eventually trade their commodities.

Specifically, in the considered bartering setting, the privacy-preserving multi-party protocols of [14–16] allow each party to specify a quote that includes an offered and a desired commodity along with the corresponding quantity ranges at which a party is willing to trade. The protocols then obliviously detect a trade which consists of disjoint *trade cycles* (of lengths greater than or equal to two). These trade cycles encode how the parties can exchange their commodities (in a cyclic fashion) such that each one of the trade partners is satisfied with the

J. Garcia-Alfaro et al. (Eds.): DPM 2018/CBT 2018, LNCS 11025, pp. 373–388, 2018.
https://doi.org/10.1007/978-3-030-00305-0_26

trade. From participating in such a protocol, a party only learns its *local view* of a trade, i.e., its direct trade partners and what to exchange with them. Yet a party's quote remains private at all times.

Besides trade cycles, a *trade chain* is another exchange structure which is widely studied in the literature (see, e.g., [4,5]). Specifically, trade chains are of importance when so-called *donor parties* are considered which are altruistic parties that give their offered commodity away for free (i.e., without receiving another commodity in return). Analogously to a trade cycle, a trade chain indicates how the parties can exchange their commodities, with the difference that the first party in a chain is a donor party and the last party in the trade chain does not have to give away its offered commodity. The analysis of the impact of considering trade chains (instead of considering only trade cycles) in the context of conventional (i.e., non privacy-preserving) bartering is an active field of research (see, e.g., [4,5]). Recent results show that considering trade chains can lead to a significant increase of the overall number of parties that can trade. However, to the best of our knowledge, to date there is no privacy-preserving bartering protocol yet that was explicitly designed for the detection of trade chains (or a combination of trade chains and trade cycles).

In this paper, we present a first step to close this gap by introducing an efficient bartering protocol that enables the distributed detection of trade chains in a privacy-preserving fashion. Our protocol detects an optimal set of simultaneously executable trade chains so that the number of parties that can trade is maximized while the parties' quotes are kept private at all times. Furthermore, we formally prove that from participating in our novel protocol, a party only learns its direct trade partners and what to exchange with them. At the core of the protocol is a novel privacy-preserving protocol implementing the *cycle canceling algorithm* that allows multiple parties to solve the minimum cost flow problem on encrypted flow networks.

2   Preliminaries

Let $e \leftarrow_\$ S$ indicate that e is drawn uniformly at random from S and let $\mathbb{N}_b := \{1, \ldots, b\}$. For a logical statement B (e.g., $0 \wedge 1$ or $5 < 6$), the *Iverson Bracket* $[B]$ evaluates to 1 if B is true and to 0 otherwise. The index set of parties $P_1, \ldots, P_\iota$ ($\iota \in \mathbb{N}$) that participate in a multi-party protocol is defined as $\mathscr{P} := \{1 \ldots, \iota\}$.

A *directed graph* is a graph $G = (V, E)$ where each edge $(v, w) \in E$ with $v, w \in V$ is directed from v to w. For a directed graph $G = (V, E)$, a tuple $(v_1, v_2, \ldots, v_l)$ with $v_i \in V$ and $(v_i, v_{i+1}) \in E$ ($\forall i \in \mathbb{N}_{l-1}$) is referred to as *path* (of length l). If additionally $(v_l, v_1) \in E$, tuple $(v_1, v_2, \ldots, v_l)$ is referred to as *cycle* (of length l). A (directed) graph $G = (V, E)$ is often represented by means of an *adjacency matrix* $A := (a_{i,j})_{|V| \times |V|}$ where for all $i, j \in V$ $a_{i,j} = 1$ if $(i, j) \in E$ and $a_{i,j} = 0$ otherwise.

Let $G = (V, E)$ be a directed graph and let $h : E \to S$ be a function that maps each edge $(v, w) \in E$ to a value in S. For convenience, we sometimes encode h as a matrix $H := (h_{i,j})_{|V| \times |V|}$ where for all $i, j \in V$ $h_{i,j} = h(i, j)$ if $(i, j) \in E$ and $h_{i,j} = 0$ otherwise.

The following definitions are based on [6] (extended by a cost function) and are essential for the formalizing of our approach for the detection of trade chains.

Definition 1 (Flow Network). *A flow network is a directed graph* $G = (V, E)$ *with a capacity function* $u : V \times V \to \mathbb{R}^{\geq 0}$ *and a cost function* $c : V \times V \to \mathbb{R}$ *such that* $u(v, w) = c(v, w) := 0$ *in case that* $(v, w) \notin E$. *Furthermore, if* $(v, w) \in E$ *then* $(w, v) \notin E$. *A flow network has one so-called* source *node and one so-called* sink *node where the source* $s \in V$ *has no incoming edges and the sink* $t \in V$ *has no outgoing edges.*

Definition 2 (Flow). *A flow* f *in a flow network* $G = (V, E)$ *with capacity function* $u(v, w)$ *and cost function* $c(v, w)$ *is a function* $f : V \times V \to \mathbb{R}$ *such that* $0 \leq f(v, w) \leq u(v, w)$ *and for all* $w \in V \backslash \{s, t\}$ $\sum_{v \in V} f(v, w) = \sum_{v \in V} f(w, v)$. *The value of a flow* f *is defined as* $|f| := \sum_{v \in V} f(s, v)$. *A maximum flow* f *is a flow in* G *where* $|f|$ *is maximized. The cost of a flow* f *is given by* $\sum_{(v,w) \in E} c(v, w) \cdot f(v, w)$. *A minimum cost flow* f *is a flow with minimized cost.*

Definition 3 (Residual Network). *Given a flow network* $G = (V, E)$ *and a flow* f, *the* residual network $G_f = (V, E_f)$ *with residual capacity* u_f *and residual cost* c_f *is defined as* $E_f := \{(v, w) \in V \times V : u_f(v, w) > 0\}$ *and*

$$u_f(v, w) := \begin{cases} u(v, w) - f(v, w) & if \ (v, w) \in E \\ f(w, v) & if \ (w, v) \in E \\ 0 & otherwise \end{cases}, \quad c_f(v, w) := \begin{cases} c(v, w) & if \ (v, w) \in E \\ -c(v, w) & if \ (w, v) \in E \\ 0 & otherwise \end{cases}$$

2.1 Paillier Threshold Cryptosystem

Our privacy-preserving bartering protocol for trade chain detection relies on the additively homomorphic Paillier cryptosystem which has been proven to be semantically secure [12]. More precisely, we make use of the (τ, ι) threshold variant of the Paillier cryptosystem from [10] where the private key is distributed among ι parties such that at least τ parties have to cooperate in order to decrypt a ciphertext. Figure 1 gives a brief overview of the corresponding key generation procedure, the encryption function, and some homomorphic properties. In the remainder of this paper, we omit the public and private key from our notation, define $\llbracket m \rrbracket := E(m)$, and represent negative integers by the upper half $[\lceil n/2 \rceil, n-1]$ of the plaintext space $\mathbb{P}$ (cf. Fig. 1). With $\mathbb{C}$ we denote the corresponding ciphertext space (see Fig. 1). For convenience, we write the encryption of a matrix $A = (a_{i,j})_{m \times n}$ as $\llbracket A \rrbracket := (\llbracket a_{i,j} \rrbracket)_{m \times n}$ and define $\llbracket A[i, j] \rrbracket = \llbracket a_{i,j} \rrbracket$.

2.2 Secure Multi-Party Computation

Secure multi-party computation (SMPC) allows a set of ι parties to compute an ι-input functionality $\mathcal{F}$ such that each party only learns its prescribed output and what can be deduced from it in combination with its private input—even in the presence of an adversary. In this paper, we consider a semi-honest adversary that

---

Key Generation:
- Generate two primes $p = 2p' + 1, q = 2q' + 1$ of bit length $k/2$ s.t. p', q' are also primes
- Set $n := pq$, $n' := p'q'$ and select $\beta \leftarrow_\$ \mathbb{Z}_n^*$, $(a, b) \leftarrow_\$ \mathbb{Z}_n^* \times \mathbb{Z}_n^*$
- Set $g := (1 + n)^a \cdot b^n \bmod n^2$ and $\Theta := an'\beta \bmod n$
- Public key: (g, n, Θ), Private key: (τ, ι) sharing of $\beta n'$
- Plaintext space: $\mathbb{P} := \mathbb{Z}_n^*$, Ciphertext space: $\mathbb{C} := \mathbb{Z}_{n^2}^*$

Encryption:
- $m \in \mathbb{P}$, $r \leftarrow_\$ \mathbb{Z}_n^*$, $E(m) := g^m r^n \bmod n^2$

Homomorphic Properties:
- $E(m_1) +_h E(m_2) := E(m_1) \cdot E(m_2) = E(m_1 + m_2)$ (homomorphic addition)

  shorthand notation: $\sum_{i=1}^{l}{}_h [\![m_i]\!] := [\![m_1]\!] +_h \cdots +_h [\![m_l]\!]$
- $E(m) \times_h a := (E(m))^a = E(a \cdot m)$ and $E(m) \times_h 0 := E(0)$ with $a \in \mathbb{Z} \setminus \{0\}$ (hom. scalar mult.)
- $E(m_1) -_h E(m_2) := E(m_1) +_h (E(m_2))^{-1} = E(m_1 - m_2)$ (homomorphic subtraction)

Fig. 1. Overview of the threshold Paillier variant from [10].

corrupts and controls a fixed set of parties following the protocol specifications but trying to learn as much as possible about the inputs of the honest parties.

Let $\overline{x} := (x_1, \ldots, x_\iota)$ and let $\mathcal{F} : (\{0,1\}^*)^\iota \rightarrow (\{0,1\}^*)^\iota, \overline{x} \mapsto (\mathcal{F}_1(\overline{x}), \ldots, \mathcal{F}_\iota(\overline{x}))$ be a multi-party functionality where P_ℓ ($\ell \in \mathscr{P}$) provides input x_ℓ and obtains output $\mathcal{F}_\ell(\overline{x})$. Furthermore, let π be an ι-party protocol allowing to compute $\mathcal{F}$. With $I := \{i_1, \ldots, i_\kappa\} \subset \mathscr{P}$ we denote the index set of $1 \leq \kappa < \iota$ corrupted parties controlled by the semi-honest adversary.

Informally, party P_ℓ's *view* on the execution of a protocol π on input $\overline{x}$ consists of the messages received during the protocol execution as well as the party's internal random coin tosses. Let $\overline{x}_I$ and $\mathcal{F}_I(\overline{x})$ denote the κ-tuples $(x_{i_1}, \ldots, x_{i_\kappa})$ and $(\mathcal{F}_{i_1}(\overline{x}), \ldots, \mathcal{F}_{i_\kappa}(\overline{x}))$, respectively. A protocol π is said to *securely* (i.e., correctly and privately) compute functionality $\mathcal{F}$ if there exists a probabilistic polynomial time simulator S which on input I, $\overline{x}_I$, and $\mathcal{F}_I(\overline{x})$ simulates a protocol transcript that is computationally indistinguishable from the view of the corrupted parties resulting from an actual protocol execution. For the sake of clarity, we enclose simulated values with angle brackets $\langle \cdot \rangle$.

A gate ρ (resp., a gate functionality $\mathcal{G}$) is a special type of protocol (resp., functionality) which obtains encrypted input and/or returns encrypted output. In general, these ciphertexts come from a higher-level protocol (resp., functionality) and the corresponding plaintext values are not known to any party. We write $(o) \leftarrow \mathcal{G}(x)$ (resp., $(o) \leftarrow \rho(x)$) to indicate that all parties provide the same input and obtain the same output.

3   Overview

3.1   Bartering Related Terminology

We consider multiple parties $P_1, \ldots, P_\iota$ where each party specifies one offered and one desired commodity. In particular, given a finite set $\mathscr{C}$ of commodities $c_1, \ldots, c_{|\mathscr{C}|}$, each party P_ℓ ($\ell \in \mathscr{P}$) specifies one quote $\mathbf{q}^{(\ell)} := (\mathbf{o}^{(\ell)}, \mathbf{d}^{(\ell)})$ where

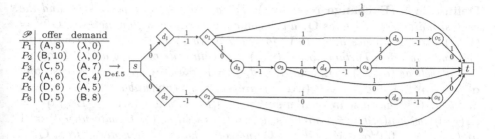

$\mathscr{P}$	offer	demand
P_1	(A, 8)	(λ, 0)
P_2	(B, 10)	(λ, 0)
P_3	(C, 5)	(A, 7)
P_4	(A, 6)	(C, 4)
P_5	(D, 6)	(A, 5)
P_6	(D, 5)	(B, 8)

Fig. 2. Example for transforming a set of quotes **Q** into an exchange network. The source and the sink are represented by square nodes, the offer and the demand of donor parties are represented by diamond nodes, and the offer and the demand of ordinary parties are represented by round nodes. Each edge is annotated with its capacity (above) and its cost (below).

$\mathbf{o}^{(\ell)}$ refers to P_ℓ's offer and $\mathbf{d}^{(\ell)}$ refers to P_ℓ's demand. The offer $\mathbf{o}^{(\ell)} := (c_o^{(\ell)}, \overline{q}_o^{(\ell)})$ indicates that P_ℓ offers a quantity of at most $\overline{q}_o^{(\ell)} \in \mathbb{N}$ of commodity $c_o^{(\ell)} \in \mathscr{C}$. Similarly, the demand $\mathbf{d}^{(\ell)} := (c_d^{(\ell)}, \underline{q}_d^{(\ell)})$ of P_ℓ specifies the minimum quantity $\underline{q}_d^{(\ell)}$ at which it desires commodity $c_d^{(\ell)} \in \mathscr{C}$. A quote $\mathbf{q}^{(\ell)}$ indicates that party P_ℓ is willing to give at most $\overline{q}_o^{(\ell)}$ units of commodity $c_o^{(\ell)}$ iff it receives a least $\underline{q}_d^{(\ell)}$ units of commodity $c_d^{(\ell)}$. We distinguish a special type of a party P_ℓ, called *donor party*, with quote $\mathbf{q}^{(\ell)} := ((c_o^{(\ell)}, \overline{q}_o^{(\ell)}), (\lambda, 0))$ that is willing to give away at most $\overline{q}_o^{(\ell)}$ units of commodity $c_o^{(\ell)}$ where symbol λ indicates the absence of P_ℓ's demand. A party P_ℓ is referred to as *endowed party* in case that P_ℓ receives a specific quantity of its desired commodity without having to give away anything to another party in return. The quotes $\mathbf{q}^{(\ell)} = (\cdot, \mathbf{d}^{(\ell)})$ and $\mathbf{q}^{(\ell')} = (\mathbf{o}^{(\ell')}, \cdot)$ of two parties P_ℓ and $P_{\ell'}$ ($\ell \neq \ell'$) are *partially compatible* iff for $\mathbf{d}^{(\ell)} = (c_d^{(\ell)}, \underline{q}_d^{(\ell)})$ and $\mathbf{o}^{(\ell')} = (c_o^{(\ell')}, \overline{q}_o^{(\ell')})$ it holds that $[(c_d^{(\ell)} = c_o^{(\ell')}) \wedge (\underline{q}_d^{(\ell)} \leq \overline{q}_o^{(\ell')})] = 1$. The set of quotes of all parties $P_1, \ldots, P_\iota$ is denoted as $\mathbf{Q} := \{\mathbf{q}^{(1)}, \ldots, \mathbf{q}^{(\iota)}\}$.

Definition 4 (Trade Chain). *For parties $P_1, \ldots, P_\iota$ and their corresponding set of quotes* **Q**, *a trade chain of length m is a tuple $(P_{\ell_1}, P_{\ell_2}, \ldots, P_{\ell_m})$ (with $\ell_i \neq \ell_j$ for $i \neq j$) such that $\mathbf{q}^{(\ell_1)} = (\mathbf{o}^{(\ell_1)}, (\lambda, 0))$ and $\mathbf{q}^{(\ell_2)} = (\cdot, \mathbf{d}^{(\ell_2)})$ as well as $\mathbf{q}^{(\ell_i)} = (\mathbf{o}^{(\ell_i)}, \cdot)$ and $\mathbf{q}^{(\ell_{i+1})} = (\cdot, \mathbf{d}^{(\ell_{i+1})})$ are partially compatible ($i = 2, \ldots, m - 1$). Two trade chains are called* disjoint *and are simultaneously executable in case they have no parties in common.*

3.2 Approach

The goal of this work is to design an efficient privacy-preserving bartering protocol to determine an optimal set of disjoint trade chains (that when executed simultaneously maximize the number of parties that can trade). Our approach is to first transform the parties' private quotes into a special type of flow network, referred to as *exchange network* (see Fig. 2).

Definition 5 (Exchange Network). *For a given set of ι parties $\mathscr{P}$ and the corresponding set of quotes $\mathbf{Q}$, an* exchange network *is a flow network $G^{EN} = (V, E)$ with two nodes $d_\ell, o_\ell \in V$ for each party P_ℓ ($\ell \in \mathscr{P}$) representing its demand and offer. Furthermore, $(d_\ell, o_\ell) \in E$ with $u(d_\ell, o_\ell) := 1$ and $c(d_\ell, o_\ell) := -1$ as well as $(o_\ell, d_{\ell'}) \in E$ with $u(o_\ell, d_{\ell'}) := 1$ and $c(o_\ell, d_{\ell'}) := 0$ in case that $\mathbf{q}^{(\ell)} = (\mathbf{o}^{(\ell)}, \cdot)$ and $\mathbf{q}^{(\ell')} = (\cdot, \mathbf{d}^{(\ell')})$ are partially compatible ($\ell, \ell' \in \mathscr{P}$). In addition, G^{EN} has a source and a sink node $s, t \in V$ where $(s, d_\ell) \in E$ iff $\mathbf{q}^{(\ell)} = (\cdot, (\lambda, 0))$ with $u(s, d_\ell) := 1$ and $c(s, d_\ell) := 0$ as well as (o_ℓ, t) with $u(o_\ell, t) := 1$ and $c(o_\ell, t) := 0$ ($\forall o_\ell \in V$). $G^{EN} \sim \mathbf{Q}$ indicates that G^{EN} is deduced from $\mathbf{Q}$.*

A maximum flow of minimum cost f in $G^{EN} = (V, E)$ encodes an optimal set of disjoint trade chains for $P_1, \ldots, P_\ell$ where an edge $(o_\ell, d_{\ell'}) \in E$ with $f(o_\ell, d_{\ell'}) = 1$ indicates that a party P_ℓ has to give away some specific amount (to be negotiated after all parties learned their trade partners) of its offered commodity to party $P_{\ell'}$ ($\ell, \ell' \in \mathscr{P}$). A sequence S of edges $(s, d_{\ell_1}), (d_{\ell_1}, o_{\ell_2}), \ldots, (o_{\ell_m}, t)$ in G^{EN} with $f(v, w) = 1$ ($\forall (v, w) \in S$) encodes a single trade chain corresponding to $(P_{\ell_1}, P_{\ell_2}, \ldots, P_{\ell_m})$ where $\ell_1, \ell_2, \ldots, \ell_m \in \mathscr{P}$. This correlation is due to the construction of an exchange network: Each party P_ℓ is represented by two nodes in G^{EN} (with an edge of capacity 1 in between) where one node is associated with P_ℓ's demand and the second node is associated with P_ℓ's offer.[1] This ensures that there is at most a flow of 1 "through" each party enforcing that each party is involved in at most one trade chain. There are directed edges of capacity 1 between the source node and the demand nodes of all donor parties to ensure that each trade chain is initiated by a donor party. Furthermore, there are directed edges of capacity 1 between the sink node and the offer nodes of all parties so that in principle each party can become the end of a trade chain. Our cost encoding is motivated by the fact that for each additional party that is added to a trade chain, the cost of the flow is decreased by one such that determining a maximum flow of minimum cost f in G^{EN} is analogous to determining a set of disjoint trade chains maximizing the number of parties that can trade.

The problem of computing a (maximum) flow of minimum cost is known as the *minimum cost flow problem* (for a maximum flow).

Definition 6 (Minimum Cost Flow Problem). *Given a flow network $G = (V, E)$, a capacity function u, a cost function c, and a maximum flow f in G, the* minimum cost flow problem *is to find a flow f' of minimum cost with $|f| = |f'|$.*

One direct and efficient approach for solving the minimum cost flow problem (for a maximum flow) is to use the *cycle canceling algorithm* [11] (cf. Algorithm 1). This algorithm takes a flow network $G = (V, E)$, a capacity function u, as well as a cost function c as input and first computes a (maximum) flow f in G. Then, it iteratively eliminates directed cycles with negative cost (i.e., cycles for which the sum of the costs associated with its edges is negative) in the residual network arising from G (together with u and c) and f. To this end, the flow along the

---

[1] Note that there is also a demand node for each donor party in order to ensure that no information about them (e.g., the number of all donor parties) is leaked in our privacy-preserving bartering protocol.

Algorithm 1. Cycle Canceling Algorithm for Minimum Cost Flow.

Input : Flow network $G = (V, E)$ with capacity function u and cost function c.
Output: A maximal flow f in G with minimum cost.

Initialization Phase
1 $f \leftarrow \texttt{MaximumFlow}(G, u)$;
2 **if** $|f| = 0$ **then**
3 $\quad$ **return** $\perp$
4 $(G_f, u_f, c_f) \leftarrow \texttt{ResidualNetwork}(G, u, c, f)$;

Main Phase
5 $N \leftarrow \texttt{NegativeCostCycle}(G_f, u_f, c_f)$;
6 **while** N exists **do**
7 $\quad$ $u^* \leftarrow \min\{u_f(e) : e \text{ is an edge of } N\}$;
8 $\quad$ $f \leftarrow \texttt{AugmentFlow}(G, f, N, u^*)$;
9 $\quad$ $(G_f, u_f, c_f) \leftarrow \texttt{ResidualNetwork}(G, u, c, f)$;
10 $\quad$ $N \leftarrow \texttt{NegativeCostCycle}(G_f, u_f, c_f)$;

11 **return** f;

---

negative cost cycle is augmented by the minimum value of the residual capacities of the edges belonging to the cycle. This operation does not change $|f|$. The algorithm terminates once all negative cost cycles are eliminated. According to the *negative cycle optimality condition* [2], this approach allows the computation of a maximum flow with minimum cost.

The maximum flow f in G (Step 1, Algorithm 1) can be computed by using the *push-relabel algorithm* (see, e.g., [6]). A negative cost cycle (Steps 5 and 10, Algorithm 1) can be computed by an extension of the *Bellman-Ford algorithm* (see, e.g., [6]) that not only determines whether a negative cost cycle exists but also computes the edges belonging to such a cycle. After computing the negative cost cycle N, the minimum residual capacity u^* in the cycle is determined and the flow is augmented accordingly (Step 8, Algorithm 1).

At the core of our novel privacy-preserving bartering protocol for the detection of an optimal set of disjoint trade chains (Sect. 5) is a newly developed privacy-preserving implementation of the cycle canceling algorithm.

4 Gates

In the following, we review gates secure against semi-honest adversaries which are used as building blocks for our novel privacy-preserving bartering protocol.

4.1 Secure Basic Operations

Definition 7 ($\mathcal{G}_{\mathrm{Mult}}$: **Secure Multiplication**). *Let* $P_1, \ldots, P_i$ *hold ciphertexts* $[\![x]\!]$ *and* $[\![y]\!]$. *Then, gate functionality* $\mathcal{G}_{\mathrm{Mult}}$ *is given by* $([\![x \cdot y]\!]) \leftarrow \mathcal{G}_{\mathrm{Mult}}(([\![x]\!], [\![y]\!]))$.

A gate ρ_{Mult} implementing $\mathcal{G}_{\text{Mult}}$ for the semi-honest model can be derived from the multiplication gate presented in [7,8] which has communication and round complexities in $\mathcal{O}(\iota k)$ and $\mathcal{O}(1)$, respectively, where k refers to the security parameter of the Paillier cryptosystem.

Definition 8 ($\mathcal{G}_{\text{LT}}$: Secure Less Than Comparison). *Let* $P_1, \ldots, P_\iota$ *hold ciphertexts* $[\![x]\!]$ *and* $[\![y]\!]$*. Then, gate functionality* $\mathcal{G}_{\text{LT}}$ *is given by* $([\![b]\!]) \leftarrow \mathcal{G}_{\text{LT}}(([\![x]\!], [\![y]\!]))$ *with* $b := [x < y]$.

A gate ρ_{LT} implementing $\mathcal{G}_{\text{LT}}$ for the semi-honest model has been presented in [13]. This gate has communication and round complexities in $\mathcal{O}(\iota k)$ and $\mathcal{O}(\iota)$, respectively. Based on gate ρ_{LT} it is straight-forward to derive the corresponding greater than (GT), less than or equal (LTE), greater than or equal (GTE), and equality test (ET) variants as sketched, e.g., in [13].

4.2 Secure Negative Cost Cycle Computation

We use an adaptation of the *Bellman-Ford algorithm* (see, e.g., [6]) for the computation of negative cost cycles in exchange networks.

In general, the Bellman-Ford algorithm can be used to solve the *single-source shortest-paths* problem on a weighted directed graph $G = (V, E)$ for a given source node $s \in G$ where the weights of the edges are defined by a cost function $c : E \rightarrow \mathbb{R}$ (cf. [6]). The single-source shortest-paths problem is to find a shortest path (i.e., the path with the lowest cost) from the source node to all other nodes in G. Since the Bellman-Ford algorithm supports negative edge costs, there can be negative cost cycles in G implying that no shortest path can be found. In this case, the Bellman-Ford algorithm indicates that no solution exists. Otherwise, the algorithm provides a solution to the single-source shortest-paths problem. In particular, the Bellman-Ford algorithm iterates $|V|$ times over all edges $(v, w) \in E$ and for each node maintains the current lowest cost from the source node as well as the associated predecessor node. In case that the current solution can still be improved in the $|V|$-th iteration step, then G contains at least one negative cost cycle. Since we are not only interested in learning whether a negative cost cycle exists in G but also have to determine the edges of a negative cost cycle, the Bellman-Ford algorithm has to be slightly adapted such that, e.g., the node for which the last cost update is obtained is used in combination with the currently stored predecessors for all nodes to find the nodes of the negative cost cycle that induced the last cost update.

Definition 9 ($\mathcal{G}_{\text{NCC}}$: Secure Negative Cost Cycle Computation). *Let* $P_1, \ldots, P_\iota$ *hold the encrypted adjacency matrix* $[\![A]\!] \in \mathbb{C}^{|V| \times |V|}$ *of a directed graph* $G = (V, E)$ *and the encrypted cost matrix* $[\![C]\!] \in \mathbb{C}^{|V| \times |V|}$ *encoding the cost function of* G*. The index of the source node* s *of* G *is publicly known. Then, gate functionality* $\mathcal{G}_{\text{NCC}}$ *is given by* $[\![\mathcal{N}]\!] \leftarrow \mathcal{G}_{\text{NCC}}(([\![A]\!], [\![C]\!]), s)$ *where* $[\![\mathcal{N}]\!] \in \mathbb{C}^{|V| \times |V|}$ *is an encrypted adjacency matrix encoding a negative cost cycle in* G.

In [3], a secure protocol implementing the Bellman-Ford algorithm is proposed. It is straight-forward to modify this protocol to additionally extract the encrypted adjacency matrix $[\![\mathcal{N}]\!]$ encoding a negative cost cycle in G. The communication and round complexities of the adapted protocol from [3] are in $\mathcal{O}(\iota^4 k)$ and $\mathcal{O}(\iota^4)$ where k refers to the security parameter of the Paillier cryptosystem.

5   Protocol

In this section, we now present our novel privacy-preserving bartering protocol for the detection of trade chains.

Definition 10 ($\mathcal{F}_{\text{OTCD}}$: Optimal Trade Chain Detection). *Let P_ℓ hold private input $\mathbf{q}^{(\ell)}$ ($\forall \ell \in \mathscr{P}$). Then, protocol functionality $\mathcal{F}_{\text{OTCD}}$ is given by $(T^{(1)}, \ldots, T^{(\iota)}) \leftarrow \mathcal{F}_{\text{OTCD}}(\mathbf{q}^{(1)}, \ldots, \mathbf{q}^{(\iota)})$ where $T^{(\ell)} := (T_{\text{send}}^{(\ell)}, T_{\text{rec}}^{(\ell)})$ refers to the indices of P_ℓ's direct trade partners w.r.t. the detected trade chains derived from a maximum flow f^* with minimum cost in $G^{EN} \sim \mathbf{Q} := \{\mathbf{q}^{(1)}, \ldots, \mathbf{q}^{(\iota)}\}$ where f^* is chosen uniformly at random from all maximum flows of minimum cost in G^{EN}.*

5.1   Intuition

Intuitively, our novel protocol π_{OTCD} (securely implementing functionality $\mathcal{F}_{\text{OTCD}}$ in the semi-honest model) can be divided into four phases (see Algorithm 2). In the first phase, the parties compute the encrypted capacity matrix $[\![\mathcal{U}]\!]$ and the cost matrix $[\![\mathcal{C}]\!]$, encoding the capacity function and the cost function of the private exchange network $G^{EN} = (V, E) \sim \mathbf{Q}$. These matrices are computed in an oblivious fashion such that no party learns any information about the quote of another party. In the second phase, a maximum flow f (not necessarily having minimum cost) is computed in an oblivious fashion where the result is encoded in an encrypted matrix $[\![\mathcal{F}]\!]$. Based on $[\![\mathcal{F}]\!]$, the encrypted capacity matrix of the residual network of G^{EN} is computed in an oblivious fashion. The third phase uses gate ρ_{NCC} (see Sect. 4) to iteratively find a negative cost cycle (where in ρ_{NCC} the order of the edges to be processed is chosen uniformly at random) in the current residual network of G^{EN} in a privacy-preserving fashion. In order to eliminate the negative cost cycles, the flow as well as the residual capacities are updated by performing homomorphic operations on $[\![\mathcal{F}]\!]$ and $[\![\mathcal{U}_f]\!]$. At the end of the third phase, a maximum flow f^* with minimum cost is encoded by means of $[\![\mathcal{F}]\!]$ (which in turn represents an optimal set of trade chains). In the fourth phase, the parties jointly extract the identifiers $T_{\text{send}}^{(\ell)}, T_{\text{rec}}^{(\ell)}$ of the trade partners of each party P_ℓ from $[\![\mathcal{F}]\!]$ such that a party only learns its own trade partners as prescribed by Definition 10. The identifiers indicate that party P_ℓ has to give away some quantity of its offered commodity to party $P_{T_{\text{send}}^{(\ell)}}$ (receiver) and is to receive some quantity of its desired commodity from party $P_{T_{\text{rec}}^{(\ell)}}$ (sender). An identifier of value 0 is used to indicate that a sender (resp., receiver) does not exist. For example, $T_{\text{rec}}^{(\ell)} = 0$ for a donor party P_ℓ and $T_{\text{send}}^{(\ell')} = T_{\text{rec}}^{(\ell')} = 0$ for a party $P_{\ell'}$ that is not part of a trade chain.

The main challenge of designing a protocol that securely implements functionality $\mathcal{F}_{\text{OTCD}}$ is to keep the parties' quotes $\mathbf{Q}$ (and with that the structure of the resulting exchange network $G^{\text{EN}} \sim \mathbf{Q}$) private. Consequently, it is necessary to design a data oblivious protocol (i.e., the protocol flow is independent of the parties private input) that provides individualized output (i.e., each party only learns its local view of the detected trade chains). Algorithm 1 (see Sect. 3.2) is not data oblivious because the while loop in the main phase terminates once there are no further negative cost cycles. Furthermore, it cannot be used to provide individualized output as it is designed to operate on a public flow network. By fixing the number of iterations for finding negative cost cycles to $|\iota|$, we ensure that all negative cost cycles are found while the protocol flow becomes data oblivious. In case that there are no further negative cost cycles, our protocol obliviously operates on encrypted dummy cycles that do not influence the already computed encrypted maximum flow of minimum cost. Finally, we adopt a technique from [16] to extract the local view of each party from the computed optimal set of trade chains represented by the encrypted maximum flow of minimum cost.

5.2   Protocol Description

In the following, we present the details of protocol π_{OTCD}. For convenience, we associate the 2ℓ-th and the $(2\ell + 1)$-th row (resp., column) of the encrypted adjacency matrices used for the protocol specification of π_{OTCD} with node d_ℓ and node o_ℓ of G^{EN} ($\forall \ell \in \mathscr{P}$), respectively. The first and the last row (resp., column) are associated with the source node s and the sink node t, respectively.

1. Exchange Network Construction Phase: The purpose of the first phase is to compute the encrypted matrices $[\![\mathcal{U}]\!], [\![\mathcal{C}]\!] \in \mathbb{C}^{|V| \times |V|}$ with $|V| = 2\iota + 2$ in an oblivious fashion. These matrices encode the capacity and the cost function of the exchange network $G^{\text{EN}} = (V, E)$ resulting from the parties' private input quotes $\mathbf{Q}$ (see Definition 5) and represent $G^{\text{EN}} \sim \mathbf{Q}$.

First, P_1 initializes the entries at position $(2\ell, 2\ell + 1)$ of the matrices $[\![\mathcal{U}]\!]$ and $[\![\mathcal{C}]\!]$ which encode the directed edge from nodes d_ℓ to o_ℓ representing the demand and offer of party P_ℓ ($\forall \ell \in \mathscr{P}$). In particular, P_1 sets these entries in $[\![\mathcal{U}]\!]$ to $[\![1]\!]$ and in $[\![\mathcal{C}]\!]$ to $[\![-1]\!]$. Additionally, the entries $[\![\mathcal{C}[2\ell + 1, 2\ell]]\!]$ representing the corresponding reverse edges from o_ℓ to d_ℓ (which are not in G^{EN} but may exist in the residual network) are set to $[\![1]\!]$ for later use. Furthermore, party P_1 sets the capacity of the edges from each node o_ℓ ($\forall \ell \in \mathscr{P}$) to the sink node t appropriately by $[\![\mathcal{U}[2\ell + 1, t]]\!] := [\![1]\!]$. All other entries of $[\![\mathcal{U}]\!]$ and $[\![\mathcal{C}]\!]$ are set to $[\![0]\!]$ before they are broadcasted by P_1 (see Steps 1–6, Algorithm 2). Subsequently, all parties obliviously determine the donor parties and update the capacities of the edges between the source node and the demand nodes of the donor parties in $[\![\mathcal{U}]\!]$ to $[\![1]\!]$. Finally, for all pairs of parties $(P_\ell, P_{\ell'})$ with $\ell, \ell' \in \mathscr{P}$ it is obliviously checked whether $\mathbf{q}^{(\ell)} = (\mathbf{o}^{(\ell)}, \cdot)$ and $\mathbf{q}^{(\ell')} = (\cdot, \mathbf{d}^{(\ell')})$ are partially compatible. If this is the case, the encrypted capacity matrix is obliviously updated by setting $[\![\mathcal{U}[2\ell + 1, 2\ell']]\!] := [\![1]\!]$ (see Steps 7–10, Algorithm 2).

Algorithm 2. π_{OTCD} for optimal trade chain detection.

Input : Quote $\mathbf{q}^{(\ell)}$ of party P_ℓ ($\forall \ell \in \mathscr{P}$).
Output: Tuple $T^{(\ell)} \in \mathscr{P} \cup \{0\} \times \mathscr{P} \cup \{0\}$ for party P_ℓ ($\forall \ell \in \mathscr{P}$).

Exchange Network Construction Phase

1 Party P_1:
2   Initialize $[\![\mathcal{U}]\!], [\![\mathcal{C}]\!]$ of size $|V| \times |V|$, $|V| := 2\iota + 2$ by $[\![\mathcal{U}[v,w]]\!] = [\![\mathcal{C}[v,w]]\!] := [\![0]\!] \ \forall v, w \in V$;
3   **foreach** $\ell \in \mathscr{P}$ **do**
4   Set $[\![\mathcal{U}[2\ell, 2\ell+1]]\!] := [\![1]\!]$ and $[\![\mathcal{U}[2\ell+1, t]]\!] := [\![1]\!]$;
5   Set $[\![\mathcal{C}[2\ell, 2\ell+1]]\!] := [\![-1]\!]$ and $[\![\mathcal{C}[2\ell+1, 2\ell]]\!] := [\![1]\!]$;
6   Broadcast $[\![\mathcal{U}]\!], [\![\mathcal{C}]\!]$;
7   **foreach** $\ell \in \mathscr{P}$ all parties **do** Jointly compute $([\![\mathcal{U}[s, 2\ell]]\!]) \leftarrow \rho_{\text{ET}}(([\![c_d^{(\ell)}]\!], [\![\lambda]\!]))$;
8   **foreach** $\ell, \ell' \in \mathscr{P}$ $(\ell \neq \ell')$ all parties **do**
9   Jointly comp. $([\![cond_1]\!]) \leftarrow \rho_{\text{ET}}(([\![c_o^{(\ell)}]\!], [\![c_d^{(\ell')}]\!]))$,
           $([\![cond_1']\!]) \leftarrow \rho_{\text{GTE}}(([\![\overline{q}_o^{(\ell)}]\!], [\![\underline{q}_d^{(\ell')}]\!]))$;
10   Jointly compute $([\![\mathcal{U}[2\ell+1, 2\ell']]\!]) \leftarrow \rho_{\text{Mult}}(([\![cond_1]\!], [\![cond_1']\!]))$;

Flow Initialization Phase

11 Party P_1:
12   Initialize $[\![\mathcal{F}]\!], [\![\mathcal{U}_f]\!]$ of size $|V| \times |V|$ by $[\![\mathcal{F}[v,w]]\!] = [\![\mathcal{U}_f[v,w]]\!] := [\![0]\!] \ \forall v, w \in V$;
13   **foreach** $\ell \in \mathscr{P}$ **do** Set $[\![\mathcal{F}[s, 2\ell]]\!] = [\![\mathcal{F}[2\ell, 2\ell+1]]\!] = [\![\mathcal{F}[2\ell+1, t]]\!] := [\![\mathcal{U}[s, 2\ell]]\!]$;
14   Broadcast $[\![\mathcal{F}]\!], [\![\mathcal{U}_f]\!]$;
15 **foreach** $v, w \in V$ $(v \neq w)$ all parties **do**
16   Jointly compute $([\![cond_2]\!]) \leftarrow \rho_{\text{ET}}(([\![\mathcal{F}[v,w]]\!], [\![1]\!]))$;
17   Jointly compute $([\![\mathcal{U}_f[v,w]]\!]) \leftarrow \rho_{\text{Mult}}(([\![cond_2]\!], [\![\mathcal{U}[v,w]]\!] -_h [\![\mathcal{F}[v,w]]\!]))$
        $+_h \rho_{\text{Mult}}(([\![1]\!] -_h [\![cond_2]\!], [\![\mathcal{U}_f[v,w]]\!]))$;
18   Jointly compute $([\![\mathcal{U}_f[w,v]]\!]) \leftarrow \rho_{\text{Mult}}(([\![1]\!] -_h [\![cond_2]\!], [\![\mathcal{U}_f[w,v]]\!])) +_h [\![cond_2]\!]$;

Cycle Canceling Phase

19 **Repeat** ι many times
20   All parties jointly compute $[\![\mathcal{N}]\!] \leftarrow \rho_{\text{NCC}}(([\![\mathcal{U}_f]\!], [\![\mathcal{C}]\!], t))$;
21   **foreach** $v, w \in V$ $(v \neq w)$ all parties **do**
22   Jointly compute $([\![cond_3]\!]) \leftarrow \rho_{\text{Mult}}(([\![\mathcal{N}[v,w]]\!], [\![\mathcal{U}[v,w]]\!]))$;
23   Jointly compute $([\![cond_3']\!]) \leftarrow \rho_{\text{Mult}}(([\![\mathcal{N}[v,w]]\!], [\![\mathcal{U}[w,v]]\!]))$;
24   Jointly compute $([\![\mathcal{F}[v,w]]\!]) \leftarrow \rho_{\text{Mult}}(([\![cond_3]\!], [\![\mathcal{F}[v,w]]\!] +_h [\![1]\!]))$
           $+_h \rho_{\text{Mult}}(([\![1]\!] -_h [\![cond_3]\!], [\![\mathcal{F}[v,w]]\!]))$;
25   Jointly compute $([\![\mathcal{F}[w,v]]\!]) \leftarrow \rho_{\text{Mult}}(([\![cond_3']\!], [\![\mathcal{F}[w,v]]\!] -_h [\![1]\!]))$
           $+_h \rho_{\text{Mult}}(([\![1]\!] -_h [\![cond_3']\!], [\![\mathcal{F}[w,v]]\!]))$;
26   **foreach** $v, w \in V$ $(v \neq w)$ all parties **do**
27   Jointly compute $([\![cond_4]\!]) \leftarrow \rho_{\text{ET}}(([\![\mathcal{F}[v,w]]\!], [\![1]\!]))$;
28   Jointly compute $([\![\mathcal{U}_f[v,w]]\!]) \leftarrow \rho_{\text{Mult}}(([\![cond_4]\!], [\![\mathcal{U}[v,w]]\!] -_h [\![\mathcal{F}[v,w]]\!]))$
           $+_h \rho_{\text{Mult}}(([\![1]\!] -_h [\![cond_4]\!], [\![\mathcal{U}_f[v,w]]\!]))$;
29   Jointly compute $([\![\mathcal{U}_f[v,u]]\!]) \leftarrow \rho_{\text{Mult}}(([\![1]\!] -_h [\![cond_4]\!], [\![\mathcal{U}_f[v,u]]\!])) +_h [\![cond_4]\!]$;

Output Extraction Phase

30 **foreach** $\ell \in \mathscr{P}$ **do**
31   Party P_ℓ:
32   Compute $[\![T_{\text{send}}^{(\ell)}]\!] := \sum_{i=1}^{\iota} {}_h (i \times_h [\![\mathcal{F}[2\ell+1, 2i]]\!])$, $[\![T_{\text{rec}}^{(\ell)}]\!] := \sum_{i=1}^{\iota} {}_h (i \times_h [\![\mathcal{F}[2i+1, 2\ell]]\!])$;
33   Broadcast $[\![T_{\text{send}}^{(\ell)}]\!], [\![T_{\text{rec}}^{(\ell)}]\!]$;
34   All parties jointly decrypt $[\![T_{\text{send}}^{(\ell)}]\!]$ and $[\![T_{\text{rec}}^{(\ell)}]\!]$ s.t. only P_ℓ learns the result;
35   Party P_ℓ sets $T^{(\ell)} := (T_{\text{send}}^{(\ell)}, T_{\text{rec}}^{(\ell)})$;
36   Party P_ℓ outputs $T^{(\ell)}$;

---

2. Flow Initialization Phase: The purpose of the second phase is to obliviously compute a maximum flow f in G^{EN} which is encoded by the encrypted matrix $[\![\mathcal{F}]\!] \in \mathbb{C}^{|V| \times |V|}$. Based on $[\![\mathcal{F}]\!]$, the residual capacities of G^{EN} are initialized and encoded by the encrypted matrix $[\![\mathcal{U}_f]\!] \in \mathbb{C}^{|V| \times |V|}$. Instead of using a (privacy-preserving) variant of the *push-relabel algorithm* for computing a maximum flow in G^{EN} (see Sect. 3.2), we follow a more efficient approach that exploits G^{EN}'s particular structure: A flow of value 1 is sent from source node s to each demand node associated with a donor party. Then, the flow continues on to the corresponding offer node of the donor party and from there on directly to the sink node t. Note that such a flow is maximal since the maximum flow in G^{EN} is upper bounded by the number of donor parties. Furthermore, from the construction of an exchange network (see Definition 5) it follows that there always is such a flow in G^{EN}. In protocol π_{OTCD}, party P_1 obliviously determines this flow locally by setting $[\![\mathcal{F}[s, 2\ell]]\!] = [\![\mathcal{F}[2\ell, 2\ell + 1]]\!] = [\![\mathcal{F}[2\ell + 1, t]]\!] := [\![\mathcal{U}[s, 2\ell]]\!]$ $(\forall \ell \in \mathscr{P})$. In Steps 15–18 of Algorithm 2, the parties jointly compute the entries of $[\![\mathcal{U}_f]\!]$ based on $[\![\mathcal{U}]\!]$ and $[\![\mathcal{F}]\!]$. More precisely, in Step 16 it is obliviously checked whether or not there is a flow between two nodes v, w $(\forall v, w \in V, v \neq w)$. Based on the result, $[\![\mathcal{U}_f]\!]$ is obliviously updated according to Definition 3 (see Steps 17–18).

3. Cycle Canceling Phase: In the conventional cycle canceling algorithm (see Algorithm 1), the while loop in the main phase is executed until all negative cost cycles are eliminated. In order to leak no information on the structure of the private exchange network G^{EN}, protocol π_{OTCD} has to be data oblivious and thus the number of searches for negative cost cycles has to correspond to the upper bound of necessary searches (to eliminate all negative cost cycles) which is equal to $\iota := |\mathscr{P}|$ (see Theorem 1).

At the beginning of each iteration of the cycle canceling phase (see Step 20, Algorithm 2) gate ρ_{NCC} is used to obliviously compute a negative cost cycle in the residual network of G^{EN}. In gate ρ_{NCC}, the order of the edges to be processed is chosen uniformly at random. First, assume that such a cycle exists. This cycle is encoded by the encrypted matrix $[\![\mathcal{N}]\!] \in \mathbb{C}^{|V| \times |V|}$ which constitutes the output of gate ρ_{NCC}. In Steps 21–25, for each edge $(v, w) \in E$ that is part of the determined negative cost cycle, the flow is obliviously updated in the following way: In case that the edge under consideration is part of the exchange network, the corresponding entry in $[\![\mathcal{F}[v, w]]\!]$ is obliviously incremented by one (see Step 24, Algorithm 2). Otherwise, the edge results from a residual flow over (w, v) and thus entry $[\![\mathcal{F}[w, v]]\!]$ is obliviously decreased by one (see Step 25, Algorithm 2). Based on the updated flow $[\![\mathcal{F}]\!]$, in Steps 26–29, the residual capacities $[\![\mathcal{U}_f]\!]$ are updated analogously to the flow initialization phase.

In case that there is no (further) negative cost cycle before the end of the ι-th iteration, then all entries of $[\![\mathcal{N}]\!]$ correspond to a fresh encryption of 0 and thus the privacy-preserving computations performed on $[\![\mathcal{F}]\!]$ and $[\![\mathcal{U}_f]\!]$ are just re-randomizations of the existing encrypted entries. Consequently, in each iteration of the cycle canceling phase it is kept private whether a (further) negative cost cycle exists.

4. Output Extraction Phase: At the end of the cycle canceling phase, the encrypted matrix $[\![\mathcal{F}]\!]$ encodes a maximum flow of minimum cost in G^{EN} that in turn represents an optimal set of trade chains for the participating parties. The purpose of the output extraction phase is to extract the parties' local views w.r.t. the computed trade chains from $[\![\mathcal{F}]\!]$. In particular, party P_ℓ ($\forall \ell \in \mathscr{P}$) locally computes the encryption of $T_{send}^{(\ell)}$ (resp., $T_{rec}^{(\ell)}$) as the homomorphic sum of the ℓ-th row (resp., ℓ-th column) where each encrypted entry is multiplied with the corresponding column (resp., row) index by using the homomorphic scalar multiplication operation of the underlying cryptosystem (see Step 32, Algorithm 2). Party P_ℓ broadcasts the resulting encrypted values $[\![T_{send}^{(\ell)}]\!]$ and $[\![T_{rec}^{(\ell)}]\!]$ which are jointly decrypted by all parties in such a way that only P_ℓ learns the indices of its direct trade partners.

Complexity. The complexity of the exchange network construction phase is dominated by the $\mathcal{O}(\iota^2)$ calls of gates ρ_{ET}, ρ_{GTE}, and ρ_{Mult} (see Steps 8–10, Algorithm 2). The flow initialization phase has the same communication and round complexity which results from the iteration over all pairs of nodes in G^{EN} in order to compute the residual capacities (see Steps 15–18). The ι executions of gate ρ_{NCC} dominate the cycle canceling phase since the communication complexity (resp., round complexity) of protocol ρ_{NCC} is in $\mathcal{O}(\iota^4 k)$ (resp., $\mathcal{O}(\iota^4)$). Finally, the output extraction phase has a communication complexity (resp., round complexity) in $\mathcal{O}(\iota k)$ (resp., in $\mathcal{O}(1)$). The overall complexity of protocol π_{OTCD} is dominated by the cycle canceling phase, i.e., the communication complexity (resp., round complexity) of π_{OTCD} is in $\mathcal{O}(\iota^5 k)$ (resp., in $\mathcal{O}(\iota^5)$).

Theorem 1. *Let party P_ℓ hold private input $\mathbf{q}^{(\ell)}$ ($\forall \ell \in \mathscr{P}$). Then, protocol π_{OTCD} securely computes functionality $\mathcal{F}_{OTCD}$ in the semi-honest model.*

Proof. Correctness (sketch): In the following, we show that on input $\mathbf{Q} = \{\mathbf{q}^{(1)}, \ldots, \mathbf{q}^{(\ell)}\}$, protocol π_{OTCD} computes functionality $\mathcal{F}_{OTCD}$ (see Definition 10).

In the exchange network construction phase, $\mathbf{Q}$ is obliviously transformed into an exchange network $G^{EN} \sim \mathbf{Q}$ represented by the encrypted matrices $[\![\mathcal{U}]\!]$ and $[\![\mathcal{C}]\!]$. These matrices are constructed according to Definition 5 based on local as well as distributed computations on the parties' private input quotes.

In the flow initialization phase, an initial maximum flow (not necessarily with minimum cost) from the source node through the donors' demand and offer nodes to the sink node is computed locally by party P_1. This flow (with a flow value equal to the number of donor parties) always exists due to the construction of an exchange network (see Definition 5). This flow is also maximal since each edge (with capacity 1) leaving the source node is incident to a donor's demand node. The capacity of the residual network of G^{EN} w.r.t. to the initial flow is computed according to Definition 3 (the cost function of the residual network was already set during the exchange network construction phase).

The correctness of the cycle canceling phase can be reduced to the correctness of Algorithm 1 and the correctness of gate ρ_{NCC}. This phase essentially implements Steps 5–10 of Algorithm 1 in a privacy-preserving fashion. After determining a negative cost cycle in the current residual network of G^{EN} by using gate ρ_{NCC}, the flow along the negative cost cycle is augmented by 1 and the residual network is updated accordingly. Unlike Algorithm 1, the number of iterations of the while loop (see Step 6, Algorithm 1) in Algorithm 2 is fixed to ι in order to achieve data obliviousness. First, it is important to note that ι iterations are sufficient to eliminate all negative cost cycles because there are ι edges with negative costs in G^{EN} and in each iteration the flow along at least one edge with negative cost is increased by 1. Furthermore, in case that there are no negative cost cycles before the last iteration of the loop has terminated, the encrypted adjacency matrix $[\![\mathcal{N}]\!]$ (see Step 20, Algorithm 2) merely consists of fresh encryptions of 0 and the maximum flow of minimum cost in G^{EN} that is already computed and encoded by $[\![\mathcal{F}]\!]$ is not modified by the operations performed in Steps 21–29 of Algorithm 2.

The last phase of protocol π_{OTCD} extracts each party's trade partners from $[\![\mathcal{F}]\!]$ which encodes an optimal set of trade chains. In Step 32 of Algorithm 2, $[\![T_{send}^{(\ell)}]\!]$ (resp., $[\![T_{rec}^{(\ell)}]\!]$) corresponds to the encryption of index $2i$ (resp., index $2i+1$) of the $(2\ell+1)$-th row (resp., 2ℓ-th column) where $[\![\mathcal{F}[2\ell+1,2i]]\!] := [\![1]\!]$ (resp., $[\![\mathcal{F}[2i+1,2\ell]]\!] := [\![1]\!]$). From the computation of $[\![\mathcal{F}]\!]$ it follows that $T^{(\ell)} = (T_{send}^{(\ell)}, T_{rec}^{(\ell)})$ provides party P_ℓ $(\forall \ell \in \mathscr{P})$ with the indices of its trade partners w.r.t. the computed optimal set of trade chains.

Privacy (sketch): In the following, we describe a simulator S which, given $\mathbf{q}^{(i_1)}, \ldots, \mathbf{q}^{(i_\kappa)}$ and $(T_{send}^{(i_1)}, T_{rec}^{(i_1)}), \ldots, (T_{send}^{(i_\kappa)}, T_{rec}^{(i_\kappa)})$, simulates the view of the corrupted parties $P_{i_1}, \ldots, P_{i_\kappa}$ $(I := \{i_1, \ldots, i_\kappa\} \subset \mathscr{P})$ that are controlled by a semi-honest adversary.

The initialization of $[\![\mathcal{U}]\!]$ and $[\![\mathcal{C}]\!]$ which is computed and broadcasted by P_1 in Steps 1–6 (Algorithm 2) can be computed in the same way by S. The following steps of the exchange network construction phase are simulated by using the subsimulators of ρ_{ET}, ρ_{GTE}, and ρ_{Mult} and by setting $\langle [\![\mathcal{C}[s, 2\ell]]\!] \rangle \leftarrow_\$ \mathbb{C}$, $\langle [\![cond_1]\!] \rangle \leftarrow_\$ \mathbb{C}$, $\langle [\![cond_1']\!] \rangle \leftarrow_\$ \mathbb{C}$, and $\langle [\![\mathcal{C}[2\ell+1, 2\ell']]\!] \rangle \leftarrow_\$ \mathbb{C}$. The flow initialization phase can be simulated analogously to the first phase of protocol π_{OTCD}. In order to simulate the ι iterations of the cycle canceling phase, S uses the subsimulator of ρ_{NCC} and sets $\langle [\![\mathcal{N}]\!] \rangle \leftarrow_\$ \mathbb{C}^{|V| \times |V|}$. The remaining steps can be simulated in the same way as described for the exchange network construction phase. The broadcasts sent in the output extraction phase (see Step 33, Algorithm 2) are simulated as $\langle [\![T_{send}^{(\ell)}]\!] \rangle \leftarrow_\$ \mathbb{C}$ and $\langle [\![T_{rec}^{(\ell)}]\!] \rangle \leftarrow_\$ \mathbb{C}$, respectively. The output of the individual decryption operations is simulated based on the corrupted parties' protocol output which is given to S as input.

6   Related Work and Discussion

To the best of our knowledge, in the literature there are only privacy-preserving multi-party protocols that allow the detection of trade cycles:

The authors of [15] propose a privacy-preserving bartering protocol (secure in the semi-honest model) by means of which multiple parties can compute a set of trade cycles based on their private input quotes. In this protocol, the parties' private quotes are transformed into logical formulae which are evaluated in an oblivious fashion. From participating in the protocol, a party only learns its direct trade partners. The protocol in [15] has two interesting features: First, it allows to put arbitrary restrictions on the lengths of the trade cycles to be detected. Depending on the bartering context an upper bound on the trade cycle lengths is essential in order to reduce the impact of a dropout and to facilitate simultaneous exchanges preventing that a party gives away its offered commodity but does not receive its desired commodity in return (cf. [1,4]). Second, the protocol supports the integration of arbitrary selection strategies for the detection of trade cycles (e.g., a strategy that maximizes the number of parties that can trade their commodities). However, the complexity of the protocol can grow exponentially in the number of participating parties which is inevitable as soon as a restriction on the trade cycle length (greater than 2) is supported because the underlying decision problem is NP-complete [1].

Another privacy-preserving bartering protocol for the detection of trade cycles has been presented in [16]. This protocol follows a completely different approach compared to the protocol from [15]. The parties' private quotes are transformed into a private weighted bipartite graph. At the core of the protocol is a privacy-preserving variant of the *Hungarian algorithm* which is used to obliviously compute a maximum weight matching in the weighted bipartite graph which encodes an optimal set of trade cycles maximizing the number of parties that can trade. The communication and the round complexities of this protocol are in $\mathcal{O}(\iota^6 k)$ and $\mathcal{O}(\iota^6)$, respectively. A restriction of the trade cycle lengths is not supported and thus the number of applications is limited.

In contrast to trade cycles, there is no need to restrict the length of trade chains in order to prevent that a party gives away its offered commodity without receiving its desired commodity: By conducting the trades in the order specified by a trade chain (starting with the donor party), in the worst case the trade chain is just aborted prematurely. Obviously, it is possible to reduce the problem of the privacy-preserving detection of trade chains to the privacy-preserving detection of trade cycles by setting the demand of a donor party to a dummy entry that matches with all offers. Then, it is straight-forward to use the protocol from [16] for the privacy-preserving detection of trade chains in time polynomial in the number of participating parties. However, using our novel *direct* approach (see Sect. 5) it is possible to reduce the communication complexity (resp., the round complexity) from $\mathcal{O}(\iota^6 k)$ (resp., $\mathcal{O}(\iota^6)$) to $\mathcal{O}(\iota^5 k)$ (resp., $\mathcal{O}(\iota^5)$). Based on these theoretical results, we expect that our novel protocol yields a significant performance improvement over the existing (more general) protocols for the privacy-preserving detection of trade chains.

Acknowledgments. In part, this work was supported by NSF grant #1646999 and DFG grant ME 3704/4-1. This work was carried out while one of the authors was at the National Science Foundation. Any opinion, findings, and conclusions or recommendations expressed in this material are those of the author(s) and do not necessarily reflect the views of the National Science Foundation.

References

1. Abraham, D.J., Blum, A., Sandholm, T.: Clearing algorithms for barter exchange markets: enabling nationwide kidney exchanges. In: Proceedings of the 8th ACM Conference on Electronic Commerce, pp. 295–304. ACM (2007)
2. Ahuja, R.K., Magnanti, T.L., Orlin, J.B.: Network Flows: Theory, Algorithms, and Applications. Prentice-Hall, Inc., Englewood Cliffs (1993)
3. Aly, A., Cuvelier, E., Mawet, S., Pereira, O., Van Vyve, M.: Securely solving simple combinatorial graph problems. In: Sadeghi, A.-R. (ed.) FC 2013. LNCS, vol. 7859, pp. 239–257. Springer, Heidelberg (2013). https://doi.org/10.1007/978-3-642-39884-1_21
4. Anderson, R., Ashlagi, I., Gamarnik, D., Kanoria, Y.: A dynamic model of barter exchange. In: Proceedings of the Twenty-Sixth Annual ACM-SIAM Symposium on Discrete Algorithms, pp. 1925–1933 (2014)
5. Anderson, R., Ashlagi, I., Gamarnik, D., Kanoria, Y.: Efficient dynamic barter exchange. Oper. Res. **65**(6), 1446–1459 (2017)
6. Cormen, T.H., Leiserson, C.E., Rivest, R.L., Stein, C.: Introduction to Algorithms. The MIT Press, Cambridge (2009)
7. Cramer, R., Damgård, I., Nielsen, J.B.: Multiparty computation from threshold homomorphic encryption. Technical report (2000)
8. Cramer, R., Damgård, I., Nielsen, J.B.: Multiparty computation from threshold homomorphic encryption. In: Pfitzmann, B. (ed.) EUROCRYPT 2001. LNCS, vol. 2045, pp. 280–300. Springer, Heidelberg (2001). https://doi.org/10.1007/3-540-44987-6_18
9. Encyclopedia Britannica. www.britannica.com
10. Fouque, P.-A., Poupard, G., Stern, J.: Sharing decryption in the context of voting or lotteries. In: Frankel, Y. (ed.) FC 2000. LNCS, vol. 1962, pp. 90–104. Springer, Heidelberg (2001). https://doi.org/10.1007/3-540-45472-1_7
11. Klein, M.: A primal method for minimal cost flows with applications to the assignment and transportation problems. Manag. Sci. **14**(3), 205–220 (1967)
12. Paillier, P.: Public-key cryptosystems based on composite degree residuosity classes. In: Stern, J. (ed.) EUROCRYPT 1999. LNCS, vol. 1592, pp. 223–238. Springer, Heidelberg (1999). https://doi.org/10.1007/3-540-48910-X_16
13. Wüller, S.: Privacy-preserving electronic bartering. Ph.D. thesis, RWTH Aachen University (2018)
14. Wüller, S., Meyer, U., Wetzel, S.: Privacy-preserving multi-party bartering secure against active adversaries. In: Fifteenth Annual Conference on Privacy, Security and Trust. IEEE (2017)
15. Wüller, S., Meyer, U., Wetzel, S.: Towards privacy-preserving multi-party bartering. In: Brenner, M., et al. (eds.) FC 2017. LNCS, vol. 10323, pp. 19–34. Springer, Cham (2017). https://doi.org/10.1007/978-3-319-70278-0_2
16. Wüller, S., Vu, M., Meyer, U., Wetzel, S.: Using secure graph algorithms for the privacy-preserving identification of optimal bartering opportunities. In: Proceedings of the 2017 on Workshop on Privacy in the Electronic Society, pp. 123–132. ACM (2017)

FHE-Compatible Batch Normalization for Privacy Preserving Deep Learning

Alberto Ibarrondo[✉] and Melek Önen

EURECOM, Sophia-Antipolis, France
{melek.onen,ibarrond}@eurecom.fr
http://www.eurecom.fr

Abstract. Deep Learning has recently become very popular thanks to major advances in cloud computing technology. However, pushing Deep Learning computations to the cloud poses a risk to the privacy of the data involved. Recent solutions propose to encrypt data with Fully Homomorphic Encryption (FHE) enabling the execution of operations over encrypted data. Given the serious performance constraints of this technology, recent privacy preserving deep learning solutions aim at first customizing the underlying neural network operations and further apply encryption. While the main neural network layer investigated so far is the activation layer, in this paper we study the Batch Normalization (BN) layer: a modern layer that, by addressing internal covariance shift, has been proved very effective in increasing the accuracy of Deep Neural Networks. In order to be compatible with the use of FHE, we propose to reformulate batch normalization which results in a moderate decrease on the number of operations. Furthermore, we devise a re-parametrization method that allows the absorption of batch normalization by previous layers. We show that whenever these two methods are integrated during the inference phase and executed over FHE-encrypted data, there is a significant performance gain with no loss on accuracy. We also note that this gain is valid both in the encrypted and unencrypted domains.

Keywords: Fully Homomorphic Encryption · Privacy
Deep Learning · Encryption · Cryptography · Neural networks
Batch normalization

1 Introduction

Deep Learning has recently become increasingly popular mainly due to the unprecedented computing capabilities promised by the cloud computing paradigm and the exponential increase on the size and amount of available datasets. Problems such as speech recognition, image classification, object detection/recognition or prediction have experienced major breakthroughs thanks to the use of highly complex Deep Neural Networks (DNN). DNN have two different phases: *training*, where a DNN model is optimized sequentially using large

© Springer Nature Switzerland AG 2018
J. Garcia-Alfaro et al. (Eds.): DPM 2018/CBT 2018, LNCS 11025, pp. 389–404, 2018.
https://doi.org/10.1007/978-3-030-00305-0_27

amounts of known and categorized data, and *inference* (often referred to as classification), where the optimized, trained DNN model is employed to process new data. While training poses an open challenge for academic and industrial actors alike, it is when performing inference that the real worth of DNN unfolds, generating substantial added value to organizations using them. It is common nowadays to reuse highly optimized DNN models by slightly adjusting them to fit particular needs (also known as transfer learning and fine tuning [16]), and then deploying them.

With the advent of cloud computing, the expensive computations required by DNN are being pushed to the cloud. Nevertheless, such an outsourcing poses a risk to the privacy and security of the data involved. When targeting problems where sensitive data is used, such as predicting illness using a database of patients or forecasting the likelihood of an individual to commit fraud by inspecting his bank movements, both the input data and the outcome require data protection.

Traditional data encryption solutions unfortunately fall short in ensuring the confidentiality of the data and taking advantage of cloud computing capabilities, i.e. to apply the DNN model over encrypted data. While Fully Homomorphic Encryption (FHE) [5] allows any operation over encrypted inputs, obtaining the corresponding result in the encrypted domain, it unfortunately suffers from serious performance limitations. Some efficient versions of FHE, for instance Leveled Homomorphic Encryption (LHE) [3], have been later proposed encompassing additions and a limited number of multiplications, that is, low-degree polynomials.

The use of LHE for DNN inference purposes, immediately preserves the privacy of input and output data. However, given that LHE only supports polynomials, implementing DNN with LHE imposes the linearization of all the DNN operations or their approximations into low-degree polynomial equivalents. While some of the DNN operations such as fully connected and/or convolution layers are already linear, other functions, namely activation functions, pooling and batch normalization require some transformation in order to support LHE.

Most of recent privacy preserving neural networks mainly focus on the linearization and, in fact, on the approximation of the sigmoid activation function [4,6,13]. This paper studies the batch normalization layer which mainly consists of subtraction of the mean and division by the standard deviation for intermediate values in the network. As also observed by [4], this additional layer significantly improves the accuracy of the model. In this paper, we study this new layer and show how to adapt it in order to compute inference in LHE-encrypted inputs. In short, we observe that computations in the layers preceding batch normalization (namely fully connected or convolution) can be easily tweaked while remaining linear, and therefore propose to reformulate their parameters in a way that these layers mathematically absorb the BN layer. Thus, during the inference phase, instead of relying on two separate layers, the DNN only implements a single layer that inherently applies batch normalization.

This paper is organized as follows: Sect. 2 covers background knowledge on Fully Homomorphic Encryption, Deep Neural Networks, and Batch Normalization (BN). Section 3 reviews related work on privacy preserving neural networks and further describes the conflict between BN and LHE. Section 4 describes the details of the proposed re-parametrization method that allow convolution or fully connected layer to absorb the batch normalization and hence support the use of LHE. Section 5 analyzes the impact of the proposed method on accuracy and performance. Finally, Sect. 6 provides conclusive remarks, exploring the implications of this technique and foreseeing future research based on it.

2 Background

Notation. In the rest of this paper we use the following notation:

- v: Scalar,
- $\mathbf{v}$: Vector,
- $\mathbf{V}$: Matrix or higher dimension tensor,
- $\langle \mathtt{d} \rangle$: Data $\mathtt{d}$ (scalar/vector/matrix) encrypted using FHE.

2.1 Fully Homomorphic Encryption (FHE)

Homomorphic encryption is the main cryptographic building block for outsourcing/delegating data and computation to an untrusted third party such as the cloud server. By definition, an encryption scheme E_k is defined as being "homomorphic" with respect to a function f, if given some inputs $(x_1, x_2, .., x_n)$, one can obtain $f(x_1, x_2, ..., x_n)$ by performing some operations over the individually encrypted inputs $(c_1, c_2, .., c_n)$ and decrypting the resulting value. While initial homomorphic encryption schemes named as partially homomorphic encryption schemes were supporting only additions [15] or multiplications [17], in 2009, Gentry introduced the first fully homomorphic encryption scheme (FHE) [5] which allows the execution of any arbitrary function over encrypted inputs. Unfortunately, this initial scheme and some of its subsequent improvements suffer from poor computation efficiency and prohibitive growth of ciphertext size. Therefore, researchers investigate leveled homomorphic encryption (LHE) solutions [3] that can handle polynomials over encrypted inputs. The encryption operation includes some noise in the encrypted output, which grows when performing some computations. Performance-wise, LHE slows down computations in a factor of 1000 or more. More concretely, while addition is rather fast and does not increase the noise meaningfully, multiplication is slow and it increases the noise considerably [7]. There is a limit on how many multiplications can be performed over the encrypted data due to high noise. Above this limit decryption of the ciphertext becomes impossible. A bootstrapping procedure can be used to control the noise growth and hence support higher degree polynomials. In that case, the encryption scheme becomes fully homomorphic. The bootstrapping procedure unfortunately remains very costly in terms of computation. LHE schemes which do not involve any bootstrapping operation but handle polynomials only, remain much more efficient. To sum up, the two main requirements for LHE in privacy preserving Deep Neural Networks are **transforming all operations into polynomials** and **avoiding** as many **multiplications** as possible while keeping high accuracy. The two popular libraries that implement leveled homomorphic encryption are "SEAL"[1] and "HELib"[2], which support additions and multiplications over encrypted operands ($\langle a \odot b \rangle = \langle a \rangle \odot \langle b \rangle$) and unencrypted operands ($\langle a \odot b \rangle = \langle a \rangle \odot b$).

2.2 Deep Neural Networks (DNN)

DNN are a particular type of machine learning techniques, where sequential transformations called layers are applied to the input. Neural Networks fall into the category of *supervised learning*, where the data used to train the model is labeled: if the neural network is being trained to recognize handwritten digits (e.g.: MNIST dataset[3]), then it requires the dataset with images containing the handwriting samples and the corresponding real value (from 0 to 9). Modern DNN are composed of several kinds of layers:

– **Fully Connected (FC)** is the classical layer present in legacy Neural Networks [2]. Also known as Dense layer, it consists of a vector to vector transformation, where the input $\mathbf{x}$ is multiplied by a matrix $\mathbf{W}$ of weights and subtracted a vector of biases $\mathbf{b}$. Conventionally, each value in input and output vectors is denominated as neuron. The FC layer is expressed as:

$$\mathbf{y_{FC}} \equiv FC(\mathbf{x}) = \mathbf{x} * \mathbf{W} - \mathbf{b} \tag{1}$$

– **Convolutional Layer (Conv)** applies spatial convolution to a matrix $\mathbf{X}$ (Fig. 1), multiplying the values of a filter $\mathbf{W}$ to contiguous sub-regions in $\mathbf{X}$ and then adding a bias $\mathbf{B}$ to the result. By convention, all values in $\mathbf{B}$ are the

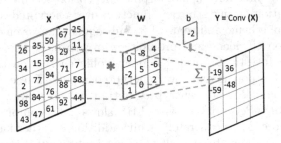

Fig. 1. Spatial convolution in conv layer

---

[1] https://www.microsoft.com/en-us/research/project/simple-encrypted-arithmetic-library.
[2] https://github.com/shaih/HElib.
[3] http://yann.lecun.com/exdb/mnist/.

same. The spacing between sub-regions is named *strides (s)*, and the border appended to $\mathbf{X}$ in order to maintain the same size between $\mathbf{X}$ and $\mathbf{Y}$ is defined as *padding (p)*. The Conv layer is formulated as:

$$\mathbf{Y_{Conv}} \equiv Conv_{s,p}(\mathbf{X}) = \mathbf{X} \oplus \mathbf{W} + \mathbf{B} \tag{2}$$

Although the process of applying the filter to sub-regions is iterative and slow, by appropriately vectorizing both the input $\mathbf{X}$ and the filter $\mathbf{W}$, as well as replicating the latter one, spatial convolution can be expressed as a matrix multiplication (similar to FC layer). Alternatively, applying FFT to the whole layer turns convolution into a multiplication.

- **Activation Function** is a mathematical function applied to individual values of a tensor, therefore it is easily parallelizable. It is generally non-linear, constituting the main non-linearity of Deep Neural Networks: this allows DNN to solve non-linear problems. Activation functions are located after FC and Convolutional layers. The most common variants are sigmoid σ, hyperbolic tangent *tanh* and Rectifier Linear Unit *ReLU* (see Fig. 2).
- **Pooling layer (Pool)** computes a reduction function over sub-regions of the input image $\mathbf{X}$, thus reducing its size while maintaining the number of dimensions. Most typical reduction functions are *max* and *average*.
- **Batch Normalization (BN).** Due to its relative importance for this paper, we will dive deep in its understanding in the next subsection.

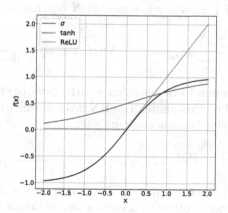

Fig. 2. Common activation functions around their non-linearity at $x = 0$

2.3 Batch Normalization (BN)

Batch Normalization [11] is a layer that is trained over batches of input data. The BN layer reduces internal covariance shift by 'normalizing' each data point with respect to the batch $\mathbf{B}$: subtracting mean of the batch and dividing by standard deviation of the batch. It is generally applied before activation functions, since it packs the values in a small interval around $x = 0$, obtaining a distribution that makes smarter use of their non-linearities. This prevents the model training from getting stuck in saturated modes, also helping to handle gradient explosion. During the training phase, a BN is computed using the following operations over each batch $\mathbf{B}$ of size m and each training step k:

$$\mathbf{Input} \rightarrow \mathbf{B} = \{x_0, x_1, ..., x_m\}$$

$$\mu_{\mathbf{B}} \leftarrow \frac{1}{m} \sum_{m}^{i=1} x_i$$

$$\sigma_{\mathbf{B}}^2 \leftarrow \frac{1}{m} \sum_{m}^{i=1} (x_i - \mu_{\mathbf{B}})^2 \tag{3}$$

$$\hat{x}_i \leftarrow \frac{x_i - \mu_{\mathbf{B}}}{\sqrt{\sigma_{\mathbf{B}}^2 + \epsilon}}$$

$$y_i \leftarrow \gamma \hat{x}_i + \beta \equiv BN_{\gamma,\beta}(x_i)$$

$$\mathbf{Output} \rightarrow \{y_0, y_1, ..., y_m\}$$

In a Batch Normalization layer there are two trainable parameters γ and β, optimized using backpropagation. β is a shifting parameter, while γ is a scaling parameter. Mean μ_B and variance σ_B^2 of each batch are calculated and stored. To avoid zero division, BN also includes a very small constant $\epsilon \approx 10^{-9}$.

Once the network has been trained, "the values of the mean and variance are fixed during inference" (see [11] p. 4). This is accomplished computing the unbiased estimators for μ_B and σ_B^2 across all N batches B of size m:

$$\mathbf{E(x)} \equiv \mu_{\mathbf{T}} = \frac{1}{N} \sum_{k=1}^{N} \mu_{\mathbf{B_k}} \qquad \mathbf{Var(x)} \equiv \sigma_{\mathbf{T}}^2 = \frac{m}{m-1} \frac{1}{N} \sum_{k=1}^{N} \sigma_{\mathbf{B_k}}^2 \tag{4}$$

This allows **inference** to be performed with static parameters: no mean or variance is calculated on this phase. The BN layer during inference uses μ_T and σ_T^2 to perform the scalar transformation:

$$y_{BN} \equiv BN_{\gamma,\beta,\mu_T,\sigma_T^2}(x) = \gamma * \frac{x - \mu_T}{\sqrt{\sigma_T^2 + \epsilon}} + \beta \tag{5}$$

In practice, BN has become part of de-facto standard architectures such as ResNet [9], and its contribution to accuracy improvement is more than established in the Deep Learning community.

3   Problem Statement

3.1   Encrypting Deep Neural Networks

As mentioned in Sect. 1, our goal is to protect data when performing inference using DNN. Indeed, the cloud who performs the inference operation, is considered as an honest-but-curious adversary. Hence data needs to be encrypted

Applying FHE to encrypt data during inference phase leads to executing all operations inside each layer over encrypted data. Regarding their compatibility with LHE, DNN layers can be regrouped into two categories:

- *Linear layers*: their internal operations are intrinsically linear/polynomial. FC and Conv layers fall within this category. Encrypting these layers using LHE is completely straightforward:

$$\langle \mathbf{y_{FC}} \rangle \equiv \langle FC(\mathbf{x}) \rangle = \langle \mathbf{x} * \mathbf{W} - \mathbf{b} \rangle = \langle \mathbf{x} \rangle * \langle \mathbf{W} \rangle - \langle \mathbf{b} \rangle$$
$$\langle \mathbf{Y_{Conv}} \rangle \equiv \langle Conv(\mathbf{X}) \rangle = \langle \mathbf{X} \oplus \mathbf{W} - \mathbf{B} \rangle = \langle \mathbf{X} \rangle \oplus \langle \mathbf{W} \rangle - \langle \mathbf{B} \rangle \qquad (6)$$

- *Non-linear layers*: Activation functions, pooling and Batch Normalization are non-linear: They include non-polynomial functions/operations. In order to be compatible with LHE, activation functions have been subject to many previous research papers (see Sect. 3.2) which use techniques to approximate them such Taylor or Chebyshev polynomials. Furthermore, in [6], pooling layers were proven to have decent approximations when substituting *max* and *mean* functions by *scaled mean*. On the other hand, batch normalization (non-linear due to division and square root) has not yet been studied to become compatible with LHE. Authors in [4] mention this layer without giving further information on how to adapt it to the encrypted domain.

3.2   Related Work

Existing solutions that ensure data privacy for neural networks usually are based on either homomoprhic encryption [4,6] or secure two-party computation [13,14]. Early solutions such as the one in [1] leave the server with the execution of the linear operations over encrypted data only and require the data owner to locally perform the non-linear operations over intermediary decrypted data. More recent solutions apply approximation of the non-linear functions (the activation functions, like sigmoid or hyperbolic tangent) with low-degree polynomials over which homomorphic encryption can be performed more efficiently. Initially, Gilad-Bachrach et al. [6] proposed CryptoNets, a convolutional NN for data encrypted with LHE and suggest to approximate the activation function with x^2 and the max pooling function with mean pooling. This inherently causes some loss in terms of inference accuracy. Later on, solutions such as [4] mainly focused on the improvement of this accuracy. On the other hand, [13,14] define a two-server model whereby the data owners distribute the shares of their data among two non-colluding servers that further perform classification on the joint (but private) data using secure two-party computation.

Among LHE solutions approximating activation functions, Chabanne et al. [4] attempt to improve the accuracy of the inference model by introducing a batch normalization layer before activation functions, similarly to our work. Unfortunately, the paper does not give any detail on the integration of this function when combined with LHE. Our proposed solution not only makes use of BN to improve the accuracy of the model but also integrates the underlying

BN operations within FC or Conv in order to have linear operations only and easily support FHE. Hence, BN is not considered as a separate layer, and we show that the number of operations is noticeably reduced. Furthermore, this new solution does not have any impact on the accuracy of the model and increases the performance of the inference phase (see Sect. 5, for more details).

3.3   BN vs. LHE: How to Address Conflicting Requirements

The targeted problem is how to preserve privacy of data (input and output) when performing inference in Deep Neural Networks. In a context where Deep Learning is being pushed to the cloud, we consider a scenario where a data owner initially gets his hands on a trained DNN model, either by training it himself (be it from scratch, be it from applying transfer learning [16]) or by obtaining an already trained model. Benefiting from cost savings, ubiquity and high availability, this DNN model is then outsourced to the cloud to run the inference phase. In order to ensure data privacy against the cloud while enabling DNN inference calculation, data encryption becomes mandatory.

In our solution, as in previous solutions, this is achieved by applying LHE thanks to its homomorphic nature. Notwithstanding that most layers (FC, Conv, pooling and activation functions) have already been implemented in the LHE encrypted domain, batch normalization remains outside the scope of LHE-encrypted DNNs. The operations included in batch normalization include a division and a square root, which cannot be directly implemented with LHE. In order to linearize it, given that Taylor or other polynomial approximations are clearly inefficient in the sense that they require several multiplications while yielding poor approximations, we suggest a different approach: considering BN during inference as a linear transformation, we first reformulate their parameters, and then combine it with preceding linear layers (Fully Connected or Convolutional), expressing the concatenated layers as a single layer.

We hereafter propose a re-parametrization trick for BN which allows batch normalization layers to be included in privacy preserving DNN while remaining linear and thus compatible with the use of LHE.

4   Solution

4.1   A First Approach: Reformulating Batch Normalization

Firstly, provided that σ_T^2 is the only parameter in BN layers that is operating with functions other than sums and multiplications, we propose a small reformulation inside BN layers for all the operations to be compliant with the two requirements identified in Sect. 2, for the compatibility with LHE. We start with encrypting the formula in Eq. 5 which corresponds to the BN layer and we obtain the following equation:

$$\langle y_{BN}\rangle \equiv \left\langle BN_{\gamma,\beta,\mu_T,\sigma_T^2}(x)\right\rangle = \left\langle \gamma * \frac{x - \mu_T}{\sqrt{\sigma_T^2 + \epsilon}} + \beta\right\rangle$$

$$= \langle\gamma\rangle * (\langle x\rangle - \langle\mu_T\rangle) * \left\langle \frac{1}{\sqrt{\sigma_T^2 + \epsilon}}\right\rangle + \langle\beta\rangle \tag{7}$$

We cannot easily compute the square root and the division in the LHE encrypted domain. However, we realize that we may not need to compute them and instead, we take σ_T^2 from the freshly trained DNN and compute the inverse of its square root over plaintext values. This newly transformed parameter denoted by ϕ is stored to be used in encrypted inference. We can take advantage of:

$$\phi \equiv \frac{1}{\sqrt{\sigma_T^2 + \epsilon}} \rightarrow \langle y_{BN'}\rangle \equiv \langle BN_{\gamma,\beta,\mu_T,\phi}(x)\rangle = \langle\gamma\rangle * (\langle x\rangle - \langle\mu_T\rangle) * \langle\phi\rangle + \langle\beta\rangle \tag{8}$$

We can push this reformulation even further, and minimize the number of operations performed inside an encrypted BN layer by grouping parameters:

$$\left.\begin{aligned} v &\equiv \frac{\gamma}{\sqrt{\sigma_T^2 + \epsilon}} \\ \tau &\equiv \beta - \frac{\mu_T * \gamma}{\sqrt{\sigma_T^2 + \epsilon}} \end{aligned}\right\} \rightarrow \langle y_{BN''}\rangle \equiv \langle BN_{v,\tau}(x)\rangle = \langle v\rangle * \langle x\rangle + \langle\tau\rangle \tag{9}$$

This way, the batch normalization layer can be computed in the LHE-encrypted domain by performing only one addition and one multiplication.

4.2 The Re-parametrization Trick: Absorbing BN Layer

Despite the reformulation of BN detailed in the previous section, BN still involves some computations. We will now show how to make these computations completely disappear while keeping the effect of BN. We start with a trained DNN with BN layers. Our only requirement for the DNN is to have a linear layer (FC or Conv) right before the BN layers, which is indeed the standard case for existing DNN architectures [8,10]. The idea is to absorb the BN operations using the parameters from FC and Conv ($\mathbf{W}$ and $\mathbf{b}$). With this setup, we can merge FC/Conv Eqs. (1 and 2) with Batch Normalization (Eq. 5). For the FC layer we would obtain:

$$\mathbf{y_{BN\&FC}} \equiv BN(FC(\mathbf{x})) = BN(\mathbf{W} * \mathbf{x} - \mathbf{b})$$

$$= \gamma * \left(\frac{(\mathbf{W} * \mathbf{x} - \mathbf{b}) - \mu_T}{\sqrt{\sigma_T^2 + \epsilon}}\right) + \beta \tag{10}$$

By rearranging all the parameters we obtain:

$$
\begin{aligned}
\mathbf{y_{BN\&FC}} &= \gamma * \left(\frac{(\mathbf{W}*\mathbf{x}) - (\mathbf{b}+\mu_T)}{\sqrt{\sigma_T^2 + \epsilon}} \right) + \beta \\
&= \gamma * \left(\frac{\mathbf{W}*\mathbf{x}}{\sqrt{\sigma_T^2 + \epsilon}} - \frac{\mathbf{b}+\mu_T}{\sqrt{\sigma_T^2 + \epsilon}} \right) + \beta \\
&= \frac{\gamma * \mathbf{W} * \mathbf{x}}{\sqrt{\sigma_T^2 + \epsilon}} - \frac{\gamma * (\mathbf{b}+\mu_T)}{\sqrt{\sigma_T^2 + \epsilon}} + \beta \\
&= \left(\frac{\mathbf{W}*\gamma}{\sqrt{\sigma_T^2 + \epsilon}} \right) * \mathbf{x} - \left(\frac{\gamma * (\mathbf{b}+\mu_T)}{\sqrt{\sigma_T^2 + \epsilon}} - \beta \right)
\end{aligned}
\tag{11}
$$

We now define the reparametrized weights and biases for the FC layer as follows:

$$
\mathbf{W_{new}} = \mathbf{W} * \frac{\gamma}{\sqrt{\sigma_T^2 + \epsilon}} \qquad \mathbf{b_{new}} = (\mathbf{b}+\mu_T) * \frac{\gamma}{\sqrt{\sigma_T^2 + \epsilon}} - \beta \tag{12}
$$

With these new weights and biases we have absorbed the BN layer into the preceding FC layer, while still performing mathematically equivalent operations:

$$
\mathbf{y_{BN\&FC}} \equiv BN(FC(\mathbf{x})) \equiv FC_{new} = \mathbf{W_{new}} * \mathbf{x} - \mathbf{b_{new}} \tag{13}
$$

Since spatial convolution is also linear, the same reparametrization trick can be applied to Conv layers followed by a BN layer:

$$
\mathbf{Y_{BN\&Conv}} \equiv BN(Conv(\mathbf{X})) \equiv Conv_{new} = \mathbf{W_{new}} \oplus \mathbf{X} - \mathbf{B_{new}} \tag{14}
$$

The re-parametrization trick allows us to completely absorb BN layers, whereas reformulation of BN layers only reduced the number of operations. Applying LHE to Eqs. 13 and 14 is just as straightforward as it was in Eq. 6.

4.3   Integration with Neural Networks

In this section, we finally study how the re-parametrization trick is integrated within the actual neural network. As an overview, the training phase of the DNN remains unmodified, allowing all previous DNN to be trained as they were before, as well as obtaining already trained networks. Before using the trained DNN to perform inference over encrypted data, we apply both the reparametrization and the reformulation transformations. First of all, the blocks of $[FC \rightarrow BN]$ and $[Conv \rightarrow BN]$ present in the DNN are **reparametrized** into FC_{new} and $Conv_{new}$ respectively using Eq. 12. Secondly, for the remaining BN layers that are not preceded by a FC/Conv layer, we **reformulate** them employing Eq. 9: $BN_{\gamma,\beta,\mu_T,\phi}(x) \rightarrow BN_{v,\tau}(x)$.

Whilst the NN is transformed, the overall mathematical computations remain equivalent, thus having theoretically zero impact on the accuracy of the DNN while conserving the properties of BN layers. At this point we could perform inference over LHE-encrypted data at the untrusted (honest-but-curious) cloud, preserving privacy of data. The process is depicted in Fig. 3. Note that, when **deploying the model** to the cloud, thanks to the available operations in the LHE domain, we can choose to **either encrypt** the model (degrading performance), **or leave it as plaintext** (unsafe but substantially faster for computations). It should be noted that existing privacy preserving neural network solutions consider that the cloud knows the model (the model is not encrypted) but cannot discover the inputs and outputs of the inference phase (the data is encrypted).

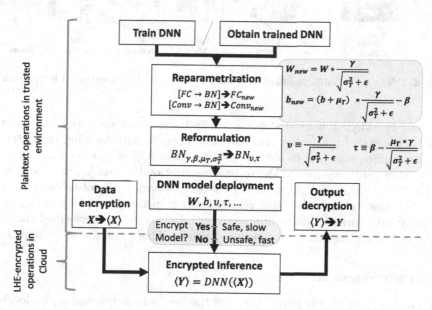

Fig. 3. Encrypted DNN inference with BN reformulation & reparametrization

5   Evaluation

5.1   Impact on Accuracy

In this section we test the zero impact of re-parametrization and reformulation on the overall accuracy of the DNN **during inference**. In order to test the veracity of this statement, we have implemented two unencrypted DNNs in Tensorflow[4], one with more than 15M parameters (Fig. 4, top) and one with less than 200k parameters (Fig. 4, bottom). Both DNN possess one BN layer that could fuse with a Conv layer and one BN that could fuse with a FC layer. In both cases we use ReLU as activation function. Details can be found in Appendix I.

---

[4] Code available in https://github.com/ibarrond/reparametrization-BN.git.

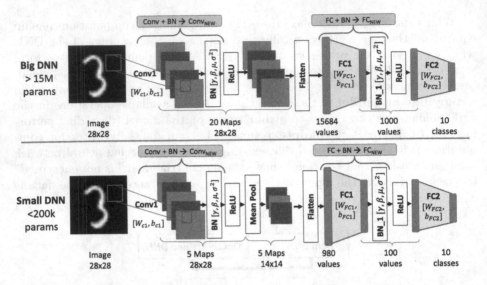

Fig. 4. DNNs with Batch Normalization after Conv and FC layers used for testing.

Using the MNIST dataset [12], we briefly trained each network (Adam optimizer, 5 epochs with learning rate 0.01 and 5 epochs with learning rate 0.001), then performing inference to obtain 99.02% and 98.80% of test accuracy respectively. Afterwards, we applied the re-parametrization trick on $[Conv + BN]$ and $[FC + BN]$ blocks, and re-evaluated the test accuracy. We observed that we indeed obtained exactly the same results for both networks. Finally, we applied the proposed reformulation technique to both BN layers and performed the test again, obtaining the exact same accuracy scores. This validates our approach.

5.2 Performance Analysis

This section analyzes the performance of the new solution, revealing noticeable computational savings with respect to a NN with standard BN.

Case with No Privacy. Empirically, we propose to measure the time taken to perform inference over 10.000 images for the two networks described in Sect. 5.1. We then compare it with the time that the re-parametrized and reformulated versions take. Table 1 shows the total inference time (in ms) for 10,000 images averaged over 30 executions and in two different settings (with a CPU and a GPU).

As shown in this table, we can conclude that the proposed solution significantly improves the performance of the inference within the plaintext domain. Indeed, in average, reformulation of BN layers yields a 9% performance boost, while re-parametrization with FC/Conv layers shows a 21% performance boost.

Table 1. Performance of DNN with reparametrization and reformulation without any privacy protection

Platform	CPU Intel i7 6700HQ		GPU Tesla V100	
Network	15M par.	200K par.	15M par.	200K par
Original	48.1 ms	34.6 ms	11 ms	10.2 ms
Reformulated	43.2 ms	31.8 ms	10.1 ms	9.4 ms
Reparametrized	38.0 ms	27.2 ms	8.6 ms	7.93 ms

Case Where Data Is Encrypted with LHE. In order to evaluate the cost of integrating privacy, we have followed an incremental approach. We have first considered that the model remains in plaintext and the data is encrypted only. Further on, we have encrypted the model as well and applied it over the encrypted data. We have used a small DNN and have implemented it with naive algorithms each of the DNN layers using the LHE open source library *HElib* [7], an implementation of the BGV encryption scheme developed purely over CPU. Similarly to existing solutions, we have used Taylor polynomials of degree 2 to approximate ReLU activation functions around $x = 0$. We have performed inference over one single image employing the trained 200k model. The results, shown in Table 2, testify the large overhead present when dealing with LHE operations. Nonetheless, the performance gain observed in plaintext is still perceivable, although it has decreased in magnitude: using re-parametrization, we observe a 14% of increased performance with the unencrypted/plaintext model and a 12% with the encrypted DNN model. This is due to the fact that we're already avoiding calculation of square root and division by applying the ϕ reformulation. Additionally, we also notice the x7 drop in performance when encrypting the DNN model.

Table 2. Performance of DNN (LHE-encrypted or not) for inference over a single encrypted image

DNN model	200K unencrypted model	200K LHE-encrypted model
Original (ϕ)	6.48 min	47.4 min
Reformulated (τ, υ)	6.16 min	45.2 min
Re-parametrized	5.54 min	41.7 min

6   Conclusion

This paper has studied the problem of privacy preserving Deep Neural Networks when the inference phase is outsourced to the cloud and is executed over data encrypted with LHE. While existing work mostly focus on the compatibility of activation functions with FHE/LHE, we investigated the batch normalization layer and propose a new solution that is suitable to the use of LHE. We hence propose to reformulate the BN layer, linearize the operations and further integrate within the convolution or fully connected layers. The proposed techniques show a performance gain of 21% over plaintext data, and 12%–14% over encrypted data using an encrypted - unencrypted model respectively; all of this without any drop in the model accuracy.

Thanks to the proposed solution, complex modern DNN models that make heavy use of Batch Normalization are now compatible with FHE. This allows the execution of inference models over encrypted data by an untrusted powerful server such as a cloud service provider. Furthermore, even in the unencrypted domain, the proposed re-parametrization shows significant performance results and can be useful if data cannot be outsourced and therefore remain in plaintext. Thus, the novelty and the performance gains of the proposed solution holds both on the encrypted and on the plaintext domain.

As future work, we plan to implement reformulation and reparametrization tricks using well known Deep Learning frameworks such as Tensorflow or PyTorch, automatizing its computation in order to apply it more efficiently.

Acknowledgments. The authors would like to thank the anonymous reviewers for their valuable feedback and comments. This work was partly supported by the PAPAYA project funded by the European Union's Horizon 2020 Research and Innovation Programme, under Grant Agreement no. 786767.

Appendix I: DNN architectures used for Sect. 5

- **Input:** 28×28 greyscale images.
- **Output:** [0–9] Single digit with the class the image belongs to.
- **Layers in order:**

    See Table 3.

Table 3. DNN architectures used for performance study

DNN architecture	15 M	200k
Conv1	20 filters 5×5, stride 1	5 filters 5×5, stride 1
BN	$20(\beta, \gamma, \mu, \sigma^2)$	$5\ (\beta, \gamma, \mu, \sigma^2)$
ReLU	No parameters	No parameters
Mean Pool	-	stride 2×2
FC1	15684*1000 neurons	980*100 neurons
BN1	$1000(\beta, \gamma, \mu, \sigma^2)$	$100\ (\beta, \gamma, \mu, \sigma^2)$
ReLU	No parameters	No parameters
FC2	1000*10 neurons	100*10 neurons

References

1. Barni, M., Orlandi, C., Piva, A.: A privacy-preserving protocol for neural-network-based computation. In: 8th ACM Workshop on Multimedia and Security (2006)
2. Bishop, C.M.: Neural Networks for Pattern Recognition. Oxford University Press, New York (1995)
3. Brakerski, Z., Gentry, C., Vaikuntanathan, V.: (leveled) fully homomorphic encryption without bootstrapping. ACM Trans. Comput. Theory **6**(3), 13:1–13:36 (2014). https://doi.org/10.1145/2633600. http://doi.acm.org/10.1145/2633600
4. Chabanne, H., de Wargny, A., Milgram, J., Morel, C., Prouff, E.: Privacy-preserving classification on deep neural network. In: ePrint Archive (2017)
5. Gentry, C.: Fully homomorphic encryption using ideal lattices. In: Proceedings of the Forty-first Annual ACM Symposium on Theory of Computing, STOC 2009 (2009)
6. Gilad-Bachrach, R., Dowlin, N., Laine, K., Lauter, K., Naehrig, M., Wernsing, J.: CryptoNets: applying neural networks to encrypted data with high throughput and accuracy. In: International Conference on Machine Learning (2016)
7. Halevi, S., Shoup, V.: Algorithms in HElib. In: Garay, J.A., Gennaro, R. (eds.) CRYPTO 2014. LNCS, vol. 8616, pp. 554–571. Springer, Heidelberg (2014). https://doi.org/10.1007/978-3-662-44371-2_31
8. HasanPour, S.H., Rouhani, M., Fayyaz, M., Sabokrou, M.: Lets keep it simple, using simple architectures to outperform deeper and more complex architectures. CoRR abs/1608.06037 (2016). http://arxiv.org/abs/1608.06037
9. He, K., Zhang, X., Ren, S., Sun, J.: Deep residual learning for image recognition. CoRR abs/1512.03385 (2015). http://arxiv.org/abs/1512.03385
10. Huang, G., Sun, Y., Liu, Z., Sedra, D., Weinberger, K.Q.: Deep networks with stochastic depth. In: Leibe, B., Matas, J., Sebe, N., Welling, M. (eds.) ECCV 2016. LNCS, vol. 9908, pp. 646–661. Springer, Cham (2016). https://doi.org/10.1007/978-3-319-46493-0_39
11. Ioffe, S., Szegedy, C.: Batch normalization: accelerating deep network training by reducing internal covariate shift. In: International Conference on Machine Learning, pp. 448–456 (2015)
12. LeCun, Y., Cortes, C., Burges, C.J.: The MNIST database of handwritten digits. Technical report (1998). http://yann.lecun.com/exdb/mnist/

13. Liu, J., Juuti, M., Lu, Y., Asokan, N.: Oblivious neural network predictions via minionn transformations. In: ACM CCS 2017, pp. 619–631. ACM (2017)
14. Mohassel, P., Zhang, Y.: SecureML: a system for scalable privacy-preserving machine learning. In: IEEE Symposium on Security and Privacy (SP) (2017)
15. Paillier, P.: Public-key cryptosystems based on composite degree residuosity classes. In: Stern, J. (ed.) EUROCRYPT 1999. LNCS, vol. 1592, pp. 223–238. Springer, Heidelberg (1999). https://doi.org/10.1007/3-540-48910-X_16
16. Pan, S.J., Yang, Q.: A survey on transfer learning. IEEE Trans. Knowl. Data Eng. **22**(10), 1345–1359 (2010)
17. Rivest, R.L., Shamir, A., Adleman, L.: A method for obtaining digital signatures and public-key cryptosystems. Commun. ACM **21**(2), 120–126 (1978). https://doi.org/10.1145/359340.359342. http://doi.acm.org/10.1145/359340.359342

DPM Workshop: Future Internet

A General Algorithm for k-anonymity on Dynamic Databases

Julián Salas[1][(✉)] and Vicenç Torra[2]

[1] Internet Interdisciplinary Institute (IN3), Universitat Oberta de Catalunya (UOC),
Center for Cybersecurity Research of Catalonia (CYBERCAT), Barcelona, Spain
jsalaspi@uoc.edu
[2] School of Informatics, University of Skövde, Skövde, Sweden
vtorra@his.se

Abstract. In this work we present an algorithm for k-anonymization of datasets that are changing over time. It is intended for preventing identity disclosure in dynamic datasets via microaggregation. It supports adding, deleting and updating records in a database, while keeping k-anonymity on each release.

We carry out experiments on database anonymization. We expected that the additional constraints for k-anonymization of dynamic databases would entail a larger information loss, however it stays close to MDAV's information loss for static databases.

Finally, we carry out a proof of concept experiment with directed degree sequence anonymization, in which the removal or addition of records, implies the modification of other records.

Keywords: Big data privacy · k-anonymity · Graph anonymization
Geo-spatial data anonymization · Microaggregation
Dynamic data privacy

1 Introduction

Dynamic publication of databases and combining data from diverse sources increases privacy risks, any privacy model must satisfy requirements such as linkability, composability and computability to be useful for big data anonymization [1,2]. Composability means that the privacy guarantees of the model are preserved (possibly to a limited extent) after repeated independent application of the privacy model. In [3], it was proved that linking two k-anonymous datasets does not imply that the obtained data set is k-anonymous for any $k > 1$. That is, k-anonymity in general does not guarantees composability.

However, in this paper we show that composability may be achieved considering that the data is managed by only one central holder as in the case of a dynamic database. Thus, providing a general algorithm for k-anonymity of dynamic data.

© The Author(s) 2018
J. Garcia-Alfaro et al. (Eds.): DPM 2018/CBT 2018, LNCS 11025, pp. 407–414, 2018.
https://doi.org/10.1007/978-3-030-00305-0_28

The concept of k-anonymity was defined in [4] and [5]. This model assures that any individual in the dataset is indistinguishable from at least other $k - 1$ individuals in terms of quasi-identifier attributes values (QI).

The definition of k-anonymity for graphs can be restated considering that the attacker knows a specific property $\mathcal{P}$ of a graph, see [6]. In this case, the structural property $\mathcal{P}$ of the graph is the equivalent to a QI in a database. An example of this property $\mathcal{P}$ is the degree of the nodes [7].

Graph modifications to guarantee k-degree anonymity have additional restrictions, for example, the k-anonymous degree sequences must be graphic, i.e., they must correspond to the sequence of degrees of a graph. Some theoretical conditions for degree sequences to be graphic and applications to k-degree anonymization and edge randomization can be found in [8,9].

In this paper we provide a general algorithm based on microaggregation, considering that the tuples of dynamic databases are represented as points in metric spaces, and the databases are updated and published several times. We present examples of the application of our algorithm for databases and degree sequences of directed graphs.

1.1   Related Literature

There are several papers that provide k-anonymity for multiple publications of databases by means of generalizations. In [10], k-anonymity is guaranteed on incremental updates. The authors use generalization as the method for aggregation of the records and reduce the generalization granularity as incremental updates arrive. Their approach guarantees the k-anonymity on each release, and also on the inferred table using multiple releases, by full-domain generalization, using multidimensional partitioning with Mondrian algorithm [11].

Sequential anonymization of a given release T_1 in the presence of a previous release T_2 is considered in [12]. So, the authors consider the case when releasing new attributes associated to same set of individuals. They use generalization/specialization to guarantee (X, Y)-anonymity on sequential releases by leveraging the fact that generalizing join attributes makes more matches, cf. [12].

Shmueli et al. [13] extended the framework that was considered in [12], considering also k-linkability and k-diversity, and achieve them by local recoding (in contrast to Wang et al. global recoding). They expressed the constraints for k-anonymization in sequential release with continuous data publishing scenario, as an R-partite graph, where R is the number of releases. Then, to compute properly the level of linkability or diversity, it is needed to identify all the R-cliques that are part of a perfect matching in the R-partite graph. This was shown to be NP-hard for $R > 2$ in [13].

These approaches were improved in [14] with the guarantee that an adversary cannot link any quasi-identifier tuple with any sensitive value with probability greater than $1/\ell$. Their application scenario is of sequential release publishing in which the set of tuples is fixed, while the set of attributes changes from one release to another.

Byun et al. [15] consider record insertions and provide guarantees of ℓ-diversity, by delayed publishing and maintaining published histories on dynamic databases.

The first study to address both record insertions and deletions in data re-publication, is proposed in [16]. It proposes a new privacy notion called m-invariance, if a record r has been published in subsequent releases $R_1, \ldots, R_i$, then all QI groups containing r must have the same set of sensitive values. They add "counterfeit tuples" and use generalization for anonymization. Moreover, Bu et al. [17] show that the same guarantee of m-invariance, may be used for attribute disclosure.

The problem of k-anonymization of data streams was studied in [18], in which a data stream is modeled as an infinite append-only sequence of tuples with an incremental order that stores also information about when the data have been collected. In that case, the delay in which data is published is relevant, hence they add a constraint that considers the maximum allowed time of a tuple staying in memory before its output.

It is important to note that in all previous cases the method for anonymization was based on generalization, while we will consider microaggregation, which to our knowledge, has not been used before for k-anonymizing dynamic data, except for k-anonymization of documents in [19]. Moreover, our method may be used for additions, suppressions and updates.

2   Proposed Method

We represent by D_t the publication of database D at timestamp t.

To maintain the generality, we denote the elements of the database as pairs (x_j, t), in which x_j represents the QIs of individual j at timestamp t. Thus, x_j are vectors in a metric space of QIs.

Our algorithm for dynamic anonymization (Algorithm 1) works as follows:

From database D we obtain a k-anonymous database $\tilde{D}$, by applying the MDAV microaggregation method [20,21]. We obtain the groups $C_1, \ldots, C_m$ with $k_1, \ldots, k_m$ elements (all $k_i \geq k$) and centroids $c_1, \ldots, c_m$.

Now, each element x of the database D is represented by some c_i with $i \leq m$ in the anonymized database $\tilde{D}$. Since we are assuming that the space of QIs is a metric space, then we can obtain the Voronoi tessellation of the set of points, that is, we partition the space with respect to the points $C = c_1, \ldots, c_m$ as follows: $P_i = \{x \in D : d(x, c_i) \leq d(x, c_j) \text{ for all } j \leq m\}$ therefore we obtain the partition $P = P_1, \ldots, P_m$ of the space D.

Starting from this partition, when modifying the database by adding a record x in timestamp t, denoted as $add(x, t)$, we calculate the centroid with minimum distance to x, $d(x, c_i) \leq d(x, c_j)$, assign x to the corresponding set P_i, and update the count k_i to $k_i + 1$. If $k_i + 1$ equals $2k$, then all the elements in P_i are used to recalculate new cluster centroids c'_i and c_{m+1} to replace former centroid c_i. Note that, the other assignments of records in groups $P_j \neq P_i$ remain unchanged.

If a former element $x \in D$ is removed on timestamp t, denoted $remove(x, t)$ $= \emptyset$, the count k_i of the partition P_i that contained x is updated ($k_i = k_i - 1$), whenever $k_i = 0$ the centroid c_i is removed.

For updating an element at timestamp t, we are removing the original value $remove(x, t)$ and adding the updated value $add(x, t)$. When making several updates at the same time, the algorithm works in a similar way.

A simple example is depicted in Fig. 1. We consider k-anonymization of data on two variables and $k = 2$. In this example, adding the green nodes allows us to update the centers (red triangles) in the right partition. Note that the left size center is not updated, otherwise this will give information about the newly added point.

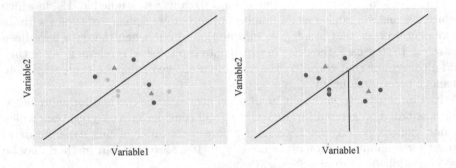

Fig. 1. Improving utility by adding records

3   Empirical Evaluation

If an individual's record belongs to multiple databases, even when it belongs to k-anonymous groups on each of them, his anonymity may be reduced to a value lower than k when the following property does not hold.

Property 1. *In the case of multiple releases of the same database, if an individual x is known to belong to a set S_1 of k-elements on release t_1 and is also known to belong to a set S_2 of k-elements on release t_2, then x is known to belong to a set of $|S_1 \cap S_2|$ which may be less than $|S_1|$ and $|S_2|$, unless $S_1 \subset S_2$ or vice versa.*

When we add records to a database, following our Dynamic algorithm we guarantee that this property holds by assigning the new records to groups of at least k records. Only when a set S_1 has at least $2k$ elements, we can divide it in sets $S_2, S_3 \subset S_1$ without breaking Property 1. Hence, our Dynamic algorithm maintains k-anonymity.

Deleting records may be more problematic because if a group has k records, deleting one node and publishing the remaining would decrease the anonymity set to $k - 1$, this is the reason of not deleting any node until the entire group of k has been deleted in our approach.

Algorithm 1. Algorithm for dynamic k-anonymity

Input: k-anonymous database D, centroids $C = c_1, \ldots, c_m$, partitions
    $P = P_1, \ldots, P_m$, counts $\mathcal{K} = k_1, \ldots, k_m$, timestamp t, operation σ.
Output: k-anonymous database D_t, updated centroids C_t, and counts K_t
if $\sigma = add((x, t), D)$ **then**
    $b = argmin_i d(x, c_i)$ (Add x to group C_b)
    $k_b = k_b + 1$
    if $k_b + 1 = 2k$ **then**
        $(P_b', P_{m+1}) =$ Apply MDAV to the points in P_b
        $C = C \setminus c_b$
        $C = C \cup \{c_b', c_{m+1}\}$
        $P_b = \emptyset$
    end
end
if $\sigma = remove((x, t), D)$ **then**
    $b = argmin_i d(x, c_i)$ (assign b to buffer of removals R_b)
    $k_b = k_b - 1$
    if $k_b = 0$ **then**
        $C = C \setminus c_b$
        $R_b = \emptyset$
    end
end
return (D_t, C_t, K_t, P_t)

For measuring the information loss, we use the average Euclidean distance to the anonymized records:

$$IL(D, \tilde{D}) = \frac{1}{n} \sum_{1 \leq i \leq n} d(x_i, \tilde{x}_i)$$

Here we are considering x_i the original record, $\tilde{x}_i$ its corresponding anonymized record, and d the Euclidean distance.

We apply our method to a database and a graph, to test it under two different assumptions, only adding records, or deleting and updating. Since there is no other microaggregation algorithm for dynamic data, we must compare our algorithm to MDAV that is designed for static data.

We use a subset of 4000 records from the census-income dataset from UCI repository [22] which has 40 attributes. We choose these 4000 records such that at least 5 of their 7 continuous attributes are different from 0. These 7 attributes correspond to age, wage per hour, capital gains, capital losses, dividends from stocks, number of persons that worked for employer and weeks worked in the year.

We start with the first 2000 records, obtain a k-anonymous version of the database and the centroids $c_1, \ldots, c_m$. Then, we add the records one by one and recalculate the information loss measure IL every time we add a record. In Fig. 2, we plot dynamic k-anonymizations for $k = 2, 5$ and compare them to applying the MDAV algorithm for the static dataset with $2000, 2250, 2500, \ldots, 4000$ records.

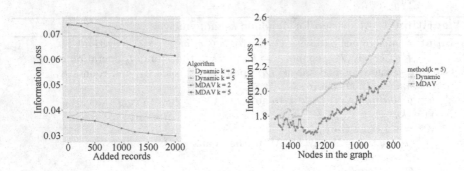

Fig. 2. Comparison of MDAV and dynamic algorithms when adding or updating nodes in a database and a graph

It is interesting to note that our Dynamic algorithm is not monotone since the subdivision step happens only when $2k$ values have been gathered on the same group, it increases the information loss locally until the subdivision, that improves it, see Fig. 2.

Next, we apply our method to the degree sequence of the polblogs directed network [23], which has 1490 nodes and 19090 edges, that represent political blogs in the US. In this case, deleting a node implies that all its relations are deleted, hence the degrees of its neighboring nodes are updated and consequently their corresponding records. The degrees of the nodes are represented as points in a 2-dimensional space where the coordinates represent the in-degree and the out-degree, and it is this set of coordinates that we anonymize. We deleted iteratively 7 nodes, until deleting 700 and remaining with a graph with 790 nodes, and made a comparison between MDAV and our algorithm for $k = 5$, see Fig. 2.

Note that the information loss is worse for Dynamic algorithm than for MDAV as the updates may generate additional nodes. Using microaggregation for degree anonymization has additional subtleties, for example, not all the degree sequences are graphic. More details and methods to obtain k-degree anonymous directed graphs are explored in [24].

4   Conclusions

We defined a general dynamic k-anonymity algorithm, that uses microaggregation and guarantees k-anonymity in a database with additions, deletions and updates of records. We compared our algorithm with the well-known MDAV algorithm, and found out that MDAV performs slightly better, suggesting that the restrictions of k-anonymity for dynamic databases, do not damage considerably the information loss.

As future work, we will apply our dynamic k-anonymity algorithm for anonymizing geolocated data and documents. Also, we would like to integrate further constraints such as ℓ-diversity or t-closeness to the algorithm.

Acknowledgements. Julián Salas acknowledges the support of a UOC postdoctoral fellowship. This work is partly funded by the Spanish Government through grant TIN2014-57364-C2-2-R "SMARTGLACIS". Vicenç Torra acknowledges the suport of Vetenskapsrdet project: "Disclosure risk and transparency in big data privacy" (VR 2016-03346, 2017-2020).

References

1. Soria-Comas, J., Domingo-Ferrer, J.: Big data privacy: challenges to privacy principles and models. Data Sci. Eng. **1**(1), 21–28 (2016). https://doi.org/10.1007/s41019-015-0001-x
2. Torra, V., Navarro-Arribas, G.: Big Data Privacy and Anonymization, pp. 15–26. Springer International Publishing, Cham (2016). https://doi.org/10.1007/978-3-319-55783-0_2
3. Stokes, K., Torra, V.: Multiple releases of k-anonymous data sets and k-anonymous relational databases. Int. J. Uncertain. Fuzziness Knowl.-Based Syst. **20**(06), 839–853 (2012). https://www.worldscientific.com/doi/abs/10.1142/S0218488512400260
4. Samarati, P.: Protecting respondents identities in microdata release. IEEE Trans. Knowl. Data Eng. **13**(6), 1010–1027 (2001)
5. Sweeney, L.: k-anonymity: a model for protecting privacy. Int. J. Uncertain. Fuzziness Knowl. Based Syst. **10**(05), 557–570 (2002). https://www.worldscientific.com/doi/abs/10.1142/S0218488502001648
6. Chester, S., Kapron, B.M., Ramesh, G., Srivastava, G., Thomo, A., Venkatesh, S.: Why waldo befriended the dummy? k-anonymization of social networks with pseudo-nodes. Social Netw. Anal. Min. **3**(3), 381–399 (2013). https://doi.org/10.1007/s13278-012-0084-6
7. Liu, K., Terzi, E.: Towards identity anonymization on graphs. In: Proceedings of the 2008 ACM SIGMOD International Conference on Management of Data, ser. SIGMOD '08, pp. 93–106. ACM, New York, NY, USA (2008). http://doi.acm.org/10.1145/1376616.1376629
8. Salas, J., Torra, V.: Graphic sequences, distances and k -degree anonymity. Discrete Appl. Math. **188**(C), 25–31 (2015). https://doi.org/10.1016/j.dam.2015.03.005
9. Salas, J., Torra, V.: Improving the characterization of p-stability for applications in network privacy. Disc. Appl. Math. **206**, 109–114 (2016). http://www.sciencedirect.com/science/article/pii/S0166218X16300129
10. Pei, J., Xu, J., Wang, Z., Wang, W., Wang, K.K.: Maintaining k-anonymity against incremental updates. In: 19th International Conference on Scientific and Statistical Database Management (SSDBM 2007), p. 5, July (2007)
11. LeFevre, K, DeWitt, D.J., Ramakrishnan, R.: Mondrian multidimensional k-anonymity. In: 22nd International Conference on Data Engineering (ICDE'06), p. 25, April (2006)
12. Wang, K., Fung, B.C.M.: Anonymizing sequential releases. In: Proceedings of the 12th ACM SIGKDD International Conference on Knowledge Discovery and Data Mining, ser. KDD '06, pp. 414–423. ACM, New York, NY, USA (2006). http://doi.acm.org/10.1145/1150402.1150449
13. Shmueli, E., Tassa, T., Wasserstein, R., Shapira, B., Rokach, L.: Limiting disclosure of sensitive data in sequential releases of databases. Inf. Sci. **191**, 98–127 (2012). (Data Mining for Software Trustworthiness). http://www.sciencedirect.com/science/article/pii/S0020025511006694

14. Shmueli, E., Tassa, T.: Privacy by diversity in sequential releases of databases. Inf. Sci. **298**(C), 344–372 (2015). https://doi.org/10.1016/j.ins.2014.11.005

15. Byun, J.-W., Sohn, Y., Bertino, E., Li, N.: Secure anonymization for incremental datasets. In: Jonker, W., Petković, M. (eds.) SDM 2006. LNCS, vol. 4165, pp. 48–63. Springer, Heidelberg (2006). https://doi.org/10.1007/11844662_4

16. Xiao, X., Tao, Y.: M-invariance: towards privacy preserving re-publication of dynamic datasets. In: Proceedings of the 2007 ACM SIGMOD International Conference on Management of Data, ser. SIGMOD '07, pp. 689–700. ACM, New York, NY, USA (2007). http://doi.acm.org/10.1145/1247480.1247556

17. Bu, Y., Fu, A.W.C., Wong, R.C.W., Chen, L., Li, J.: Privacy preserving serial data publishing by role composition. Proc. VLDB Endow. **1**(1), 845–856 (2008). https://doi.org/10.14778/1453856.1453948

18. Cao, J., Carminati, B., Ferrari, E., Tan, K.-L.: Castle: continuously anonymizing data streams. IEEE Trans. Dependable Secur. Comput. **8**(3), 337–352 (2011)

19. Navarro-Arribas, G., Abril, D., Torra, V.: Dynamic anonymous index for confidential data. In: Garcia-Alfaro, J., Lioudakis, G., Cuppens-Boulahia, N., Foley, S., Fitzgerald, W.M. (eds.) DPM/SETOP -2013. LNCS, vol. 8247, pp. 362–368. Springer, Heidelberg (2014). https://doi.org/10.1007/978-3-642-54568-9_23

20. Domingo-Ferrer, J., Torra, V.: Ordinal, continuous and heterogeneous k-anonymity through microaggregation. Data Min. Knowl. Disc. **11**(2), 195–212 (2005). https://doi.org/10.1007/s10618-005-0007-5

21. Domingo-Ferrer, J., Mateo-Sanz, J.M.: Practical data-oriented microaggregation for statistical disclosure control. IEEE Trans. Knowl. Data Eng. **14**(1), 189–201 (2002)

22. Dheeru, D., Karra Taniskidou, E.: UCI machine learning repository (2017). http://archive.ics.uci.edu/ml

23. Adamic, L.A., Glance, N.: The political blogosphere and the 2004 u.s. election: divided they blog. In: Proceedings of the 3rd International Workshop on Link Discovery, ser. LinkKDD '05, pp. 36–43. ACM, New York, NY, USA (2005). http://doi.acm.org/10.1145/1134271.1134277

24. Casas-Roma, J., Salas, J., Malliaros, F., Vazirgiannis, M.: k-degree anonymity on directed networks. Knowl. Inf. Syst., (2018, to appear)

On Security of Anonymous
Invitation-Based System

Naoto Yanai[✉] and Jason Paul Cruz

Osaka University, 1-5 Yamadaoka, Suita, Osaka 565–0871, Japan
yanai@ist.osaka-u.ac.jp

Abstract. In an anonymous invitation-based system, a user can join a
group by receiving invitations sent by current members, i.e., inviters, to
a server anonymously. This kind of system is suitable for social networks,
and a formal framework with the anonymity of inviters and the unforgeability of an invitation letter was proposed in DPM 2017. The main
concept of this previous system is elegant, but the formal security definitions are insufficient and weak in a realistic application scenario. In this
paper, we revise formal security definitions as attacks representing a realistic scenario. In addition, we define a new aspect of the security wherein
an adversary maliciously generates an invitation letter, i.e., *invitation
opacity*, and the security for guaranteeing that an invitee with a valid
invitation letter can always join the system, i.e., *invitation extractability*. A secure and useful construction can be expected by satisfying the
security definitions described above.

Keywords: Anonymous invitation-based system · Anonymity
Unforgeability · Opacity · Extractability · Formal definition
Social networks

1 Introduction

Backgrounds. An invitation-based system consists of a *server*, a group of members, i.e., *inviters*, and a new member called *invitee*, who can join the system by
receiving invitations from a certain number of inviters. Invitation-based systems
provide many advantages; for example, a limited number of server resources can
cover an unlimited number of users and such systems can often resist registration
of fake users. Invitation-based systems have many historical examples, such as
Gmail and Google Wave, and have been discussed in some recent works [3–5],
but these do not consider the *anonymity* of users. To the best of our knowledge, only the work of Boschrooyeh et al. [2] considered anonymity of users and
introduced an *anonymous invitation-based system*.

An anonymous invitation-based system mainly aims to preserve the privacy
of users. In general, when an invitee wants to join a system, he/she may ask an
invitation letter from a known current member of a system, e.g., friends or family.
However, in such scenario, the invitations may contain privacy risks that can leak

© Springer Nature Switzerland AG 2018
J. Garcia-Alfaro et al. (Eds.): DPM 2018/CBT 2018, LNCS 11025, pp. 415–421, 2018.
https://doi.org/10.1007/978-3-030-00305-0_29

affiliations and locations according to common features. To avoid this kind of risks, Boschrooyeh et al. [2] formalized the security of an anonymous invitation-based system and proposed a concrete construction called *Inonymous*. Their main concept is elegant, but their security definitions are not defined well and are far from realistic threats. Well-defined security definitions including realistic threats are important because they can support in understanding the security of our proposed protocol and of subsequent works.

In this paper, we reconsider the work of Boschrooyeh et al. and formalize stronger security containing realistic attacks. We believe that our security definitions can help create realistic and effective constructions of anonymous invitation-based systems.

Contribution. In this paper, we formally define the security of an anonymous invitation-based system that captures realistic threats by revisiting the security of a previous anonymous invitation-based system. The previous definition includes the anonymity of inviters, i.e., *inviter anonymity*, and the unforgeability of invitation letters sent to a server, i.e., *invitation unforgeability*. In our definitions, we give generation of secret information for each user and oracle access for an adversary with respect to invitation letters. These definitions were not captured in the previous system, and we are able to discuss the security even against an adversary who obtains knowledge of invitation letters via our definitions. Moreover, we define *two new security definitions with respect to an invitee*. The first definition considers whether only an invitee can receive a valid invitation letter, i.e., *invitation opacity*, allowing the discussion on security against an adversary who maliciously generates invitation letters. The second definition considers that an invitee can always join the system as long as he/she can obtain a certain number of invitation letters, i.e., *invitation extractability*, allowing an invitee to join the system correctly. This work is ongoing, and we leave the construction of a concrete scheme following our definitions as an open problem and future work.

2   Preliminaries

Threshold Secret Sharing. We recall a definition of a threshold secret sharing scheme [6]. Let participants in this scheme be a set of n players. A set of values $(s_1, \cdots, s_n)$ is said to be a (t, n)-*threshold secret sharing* of the value s if the following conditions hold: any subset with $k (< t)$ values does not reveal any information about s; and there exists an efficient algorithm which takes any t values from the set and outputs s.

Inonymous. We briefly recall the work of Boschrooyeh et al. [2] called Inonymous, which includes three entities, namely, a server, an invitee, and inviters. When an invitee wants to join the system, he/she first requests a token for user invitation from a server. The invitee then sends the token to inviters, who generate an invitation individually. If the invitee can receive invitations more than some threshold value specified in advance, then he/she can get an invitation letter to join the system. Boschrooyeh et al. also defined the anonymity of inviters and the unforgeability of an invitation letter. Our definitions are continuation of the framework described above.

3   Anonymous Invitation-Based System

In this section, we formalize a syntax and new security notions. Boschrooyeh et al. [2] did not provide a syntax although they proposed security definitions of inviter anonymity and invitation unforgeability. Therefore, we first formally define our syntax and then define new security definitions.

3.1   Our Syntax

An anonymous invitation-based system is defined as follows:

Setup Given a security parameter 1^k as input, output a public parameter $para$.

ServerKeyGen Given $para$ as input, output a pair (msk, mpk) of a master secret key and a master public key.

UserKeyGen Given $para$ and two security parameters $(t, n) \in \mathbb{Z}$ such that $t \leq n$ as input, output shares s_i for (t, n)-secret sharing and its corresponding user public key upk, where a secret recovered from at least t output shares s_i is identical to a user secret key usk.

TokenGen Given $para, msk, mpk$, and an index j as input, output a token $token$.

InKeyGen Given $para$ as input, output a pair (isk, ipk) of an inviter secret key and an inviter public key.

InvGen Given $para, token$, a share s_i for the ith user, mpk, upk, and ipk as input, output an individual invitation Inv_i for the ith user or an error symbol $\bot$.

InvColl Given $para, token, mpk, upk, isk$, and t invitations $\{Inv_i\}_{i=1}^n$ as input, output an invitation letter $InvLet$ or an error symbol $\bot$.

InvVer Given $para, token, mpk, upk$, and $InvLet$, output $\top$ or $\bot$.

The correctness of the scheme is defined as follows: for any security parameters $(1^k, t, n)$, $para \leftarrow \textbf{Setup}(1^k)$, $(\{s_i\}_{i=1}^n, upk) \leftarrow \textbf{UserKeyGen}(para)$, $token \leftarrow \textbf{TokenGen}(para, msk, mpk)$, and $(isk, ipk) \leftarrow \textbf{InKeyGen}(para, isk, ipk)$, we say the scheme is correct if the following equation holds:

$$\top = \textbf{InvVer}\left(\textbf{InvColl}\left(\begin{array}{c} para, token, mpk, upk, \\ para, token, mpk, upk, isk \\ \{\textbf{InvGen}\,(para, token, s_i, mpk, upk, ipk)\}_{i \in U} \end{array} \right) \right),$$

where U is any subset of $[1, n]$ such that $|U| \geq t$.

3.2 Inviter Anonymity

In Inonymous, inviter anonymity does not allow an adversary to access oracles for invitations, i.e., invitation generation and invitation collection. The adversary may obtain knowledge about inviters, and thus considering access to such oracles is necessary. In addition, Inonymous' inviter anonymity does not include generation of shares while a pair of a master secret key and a master public key is generated by an adversary. These information should be generated by a challenger to prove the security clearly. We define a new security definition by introducing these points. Our definition is a game-based definition between a challenger $\mathcal{C}$ and an adversary $\mathcal{A}$ as follows:

Initial Phase Given security parameters 1^k and $(t, n) \in \mathbb{Z}$ as input, a challenger $\mathcal{C}$ generates a pair (msk, mpk) of a master secret key and a master public key via the setup algorithm, a pair of shares $\{s_i\}_{i=1}^n$ and a user public key upk via the user key generation algorithm, and a pair of an inviter secret key isk and an inviter public key ipk via the inviter key generation algorithm. Then, $\mathcal{C}$ sets a set U of indexes such that $|U| = n$ and initializes a list $Corr = \emptyset$ for corrupted inviters. $\mathcal{C}$ then runs an adversary $\mathcal{A}$ with $(para, msk, mpk, upk, ipk)$ as input.

Corrupt Oracle $\mathcal{A}$ queries an index $i \in U$, and $\mathcal{C}$ sets $Corr = Corr \cup \{i\}$. $\mathcal{C}$ then returns s_i as a share for the inviter corresponding to i.

InvGen Oracle $\mathcal{A}$ generates a token $token$ and chooses an index $i \in U$ as an inviter. $\mathcal{C}$ then generates an individual invitation inv_i for the inviter corresponding to i.

InvColl Oracle $\mathcal{A}$ generates a token $token$ and a set $\{inv_i\}_{i \in U' \subseteq U}$ of indexes, and then $\mathcal{C}$ returns an invitation letter $InvLet$.

Random Oracle $\mathcal{A}$ queries any input x to a hash function, and $\mathcal{C}$ returns the response y of the hash function.

Challenge $\mathcal{A}$ generates $token^*$, a set $\{in_i\}_{i \in U^* \subset U}$ where $|U^*| = t - 1$, and chooses two indexes $(u_0, u_1) \in U \backslash (U^* \cup Corr)$ as a challenge. Then, $\mathcal{C}$ chooses $b \in \{0, 1\}$ and generates an individual invitation inv_{u_b} via the invitation generation algorithm with $token^*$ and s_{u_b}. $\mathcal{C}$ then generates $InvLet^*$ via the invitation collection algorithm with $token^*, isk$, and $\{inv_i\}_{i \in U^*} \cup \{inv_{u_b}\}$ and returns $InvLet^*$.

Guess $\mathcal{A}$ outputs a guess $b' \in \{0, 1\}$ indicating which of the users u_0^*, u_1^* is used as the inviter. $\mathcal{A}$ wins the game if $b = b'$ holds. Otherwise, $\mathcal{C}$ wins the game.

Definition 1. We say that an anonymous invitation-based system satisfies $(q_r, q_i, q_c, q_h, t, n, \epsilon)$-inviter anonymity if there is no probabilistic polynomial-time adversary $\mathcal{A}$ who wins the game described above with a probability greater than ϵ. Here, $\mathcal{A}$ can access the corrupt oracle at most q_r times, the invitation generation oracle at most q_i times, the invitation collection oracle at most q_c times, and a random oracle at most q_h times, t is a threshold value, and n indicates the number of users.

3.3   Invitation Existential Unforgeability

We define invitation existential unforgeability below. In the invitation unforgeability of Inonymous, an adversary is not allowed to receive individual invitations and verification results of invitation letters. Moreover, a token utilized by an adversary for forging an invitation letter has to be designated in advance. Our definition removes these restrictions for an adversary. Our definition is a game-based definition between a challenger C and an adversary A as follows:

Initial Phase C generates $(msk, mpk, \{s_i\}_{i=1}^n, upk, isk, ipk)$ and a set U of indexes in a similar manner as in the game described in the previous section. However, C owns two additional lists, T and IT, and initializes $T = \emptyset$ and $IT = \emptyset$. C then runs A with $(para, mpk, upk, isk, ipk)$ as input.

Corrupt Oracle This step is the same as in the game in the previous section.

TokenGen Oracle A chooses an index $i \in U$ as user information, and C generates a token $token_i$ via the token generation algorithm with msk and i. Then, C sets $T = T \cup \{token_i\}$ and then returns $token_i$.

InvGen Oracle A generates a token $token$ and chooses an index $i \in U$. Then, C sets $IT = IT \cup \{token\}$ and generates an individual invitation inv_i via the invitation generation algorithm with $token$ and s_i. C then returns Inv_i for i.

Random Oracle This step is the same as in the game in the previous section.

Output A outputs a token $token^*$ and an invitation letter $InvLet^*$ as a forgery. A wins the game if the following conditions hold: the invitation verification algorithm with $token^*$ and $InvLet^*$ outputs $\top$; $token^* \in T$, $|\{token \in T | token = token^*\}| + |Corr| \leq t - 1$; $|Corr| \leq t - 1$; and $token^* \in IT$, $|\{token \in IT | token = token^*\}| + |Corr| \leq t - 1$. Otherwise, C wins the game.

Definition 2. We say that an anonymous invitation-based system satisfies $(q_r, q_t, q_i, q_h, t, n, \epsilon)$-invitation existential unforgeability if there is no probabilistic polynomial-time adversary A who wins the game described above with a probability greater than ϵ. Here, A can access the corrupt oracle at most q_r times, the token generation oracle at most q_t times, the invitation generation oracle at most q_i times, and a random oracle at most q_h times, t is a threshold value, and n indicates the number of users.

3.4   Invitation Opacity

We define invitation opacity below. This definition guarantees that only an invitee can generate an invitation letter from individual invitations generated by inviters. In this setting, an adversary can corrupt several inviters and obtain tokens and invitation letters. In this definition, an adversary can be a malicious inviter or an external attacker and its goal is to generate an invitation letter for an invitee. Our definition is a game-based definition between a challenger C and an adversary A as follows:

420   N. Yanai and J. P. Cruz

Initial Phase $\mathcal{C}$ generates $(msk, mpk, \{s_i\}_{i=1}^n, upk, isk, ipk)$, a set U of indexes, and two lists, $\mathcal{T}$ and $\mathcal{IT}$, similar to the game in the previous section. However, $\mathcal{C}$ then runs $\mathcal{A}$ with $(para, mpk, \{s_i\}_{i=1}^n, upk, ipk)$ as input.

TokenGen Oracle This step is the same as in the game in the previous section.

InvColl Oracle $\mathcal{A}$ generates a token $token$ and a set $\{inv_i\}_{i \in U' \subseteq U}$ of indexes, and $\mathcal{C}$ generates an invitation letter $InvLet$. Then, $\mathcal{C}$ sets $\mathcal{T} = \mathcal{T} \cup \{token\}$ and $\mathcal{IT} = \mathcal{IT} \cup \{InvLet\}$ and then returns $InvLet$.

Random Oracle This step is the same as in the game in the previous section.

Output $\mathcal{A}$ outputs a token $token^*$ and an invitation letter $InvLet^*$ as a forgery. $\mathcal{A}$ wins the game if the following conditions hold: the invitation verification algorithm with $token^*$ and $InvLet^*$ outputs $\top$; $token^* \notin \mathcal{T}$; and $InvLet^* \notin \mathcal{IT}$. Otherwise, $\mathcal{C}$ wins the game.

Definition 3. We say that an anonymous invitation-based system satisfies $(q_t, q_c, q_h, t, n, \epsilon)$-invitation opacity if there is no probabilistic polynomial-time adversary $\mathcal{A}$ who wins the game described above with a probability greater than ϵ. Here, $\mathcal{A}$ can access the token generation oracle at most q_t times, the invitation collection oracle at most q_c times, and a random oracle at most q_h times, t is a threshold value, and n indicates the number of users that generate an invitation letter.

3.5   Invitation Extractability

We define invitation extractability below. This definition guarantees that the invitation verification algorithm with an invitation letter always outputs $\top$ when the invitation collection algorithm outputs the invitation letter. In this setting, information that an adversary can obtain is the same as that in the game in the previous section. However, the goal of the adversary is to output individual invitations whose resultant invitation letter is rejected. Our definition is a game-based definition between a challenger $\mathcal{C}$ and an adversary $\mathcal{A}$ as follows:

Initial Phase $\mathcal{C}$ generates $(msk, mpk, \{s_i\}_{i=1}^n, upk, isk, ipk)$, a set U of indexes, and a list $\mathcal{T}$, but does not generate $\mathcal{IT}$. Then, $\mathcal{C}$ runs $\mathcal{A}$ with $(para, mpk, \{s_i\}_{i=1}^n, upk, ipk)$ as input.

TokenGen Oracle This step is the same as in the game in the previous section.

InvColl Oracle This step is almost the same in the game in the previous section, except that $\mathcal{C}$ sets only $\mathcal{T} = \mathcal{T} \cup \{token\}$.

Random Oracle This step is the same as in the game in the previous section.

Output $\mathcal{A}$ outputs a token $token^*$ and a set $\{inv_i\}_{i \in U^* \subseteq U}$ of individual invitations, where $|U^*| \geq t$. $\mathcal{A}$ wins the game if the following conditions hold: the invitation collection algorithm with $token^*$, $\{in_i\}_{i \in U^* \subseteq U}$, and upk outputs $InvLet^*$; and the invitation verification algorithm with $token^*$ and $InvLet^*$ outputs $\bot$. Otherwise, $\mathcal{C}$ wins the game.

Definition 4. We say that an anonymous invitation-based system satisfies $(q_t, q_c, q_h, t, n, \epsilon)$-invitation extractability if there is no probabilistic polynomial-time adversary $\mathcal{A}$ who wins the game described above with a probability greater than ϵ. Here, $\mathcal{A}$ can access the token generation oracle at most q_t times, the invitation collection oracle at most q_c times, and a random oracle at most q_h times, t is a threshold value, and n indicates the number of users that generate an invitation letter.

4   Conclusion

In this paper, we presented new security definitions of an anonymous invitation-based system from four standpoints, namely, invitation anonymity, invitation unforgeability, invitation opacity, and invitation extractability. The first two definitions are presented in Inonymous [2] and we introduced oracle access related to invitations. The last two definitions are for invitee's security and have never been discussed in previous work. We believe that a scheme that satisfies these definitions can be used for many applications.

Although we did not discuss a specific construction in this paper, we consider that a scheme may be constructed by combining verifiably encrypted signatures (VES) [1] with Inonymous. VES are digital signatures wherein a signer encrypts its signatures under a public key of a trusted third party to confirm that the signer has truly signed a certain object. We consider that a trusted third party in VES is similar to an invitee in our proposed system. We will construct a scheme using such an approach and prove its security as future work.

References

1. Boneh, D., Gentry, C., Lynn, B., Shacham, H.: Aggregate and verifiably encrypted signatures from bilinear maps. In: Biham, E. (ed.) EUROCRYPT 2003. LNCS, vol. 2656, pp. 416–432. Springer, Heidelberg (2003). https://doi.org/10.1007/3-540-39200-9_26
2. Boshrooyeh, S.T., Küpçü, A.: Inonymous: anonymous invitation-based system. In: Garcia-Alfaro, J., Navarro-Arribas, G., Hartenstein, H., Herrera-Joancomartí, J. (eds.) ESORICS/DPM/CBT -2017. LNCS, vol. 10436, pp. 219–235. Springer, Cham (2017). https://doi.org/10.1007/978-3-319-67816-0_13
3. Gong, N.Z., Wang, D.: On the security of trusted-based social authentications. IEEE Trans. Inf. Forensics Secur. 9(8), 1251–1263 (2014)
4. Malar, G.P., Shyni, C.E.: Facebookfs trustee based social authentication. Int. J. Emerg. Technol. Comput. Sci. Electron. 12(4), 224–230 (2015)
5. Parameswari, M., Sukumaran, S., Kalaiselvi, S.: Trustee based authentication. Int. J. Latest Res. Sci. Technol. 4(5), 84–88 (2015)
6. Shamir, A.: How to share a secret. Commun. ACM 22(11), 612–613 (1979)

Probabilistic Metric Spaces for Privacy by Design Machine Learning Algorithms: Modeling Database Changes

Vicenç Torra[1(✉)] and Guillermo Navarro-Arribas[2(✉)]

[1] University of Skövde, Skövde, Sweden
vtorra@ieee.org
[2] Department of Information and Communications Engineering, CYBERCAT-Center for Cybersecurity Research of Catalonia, Universitat Autònoma de Barcelona, Barcelona, Spain
guillermo.navarro@uab.cat

Abstract. Machine learning, data mining and statistics are used to analyze the data and to build models from them. Data privacy for big data needs to find a compromise between data analysis and disclosure risk. Privacy by design machine learning algorithms need to take into account the space of models and the relationship between the data that generates the models and the models themselves. In this paper we propose the use of probabilistic metric spaces for comparing these models.

Keywords: Data privacy · Integral privacy
Probabilistic metric spaces

1 Introduction

Machine learning and statistics are powerful tools to extract knowledge from data. Knowledge is expressed in terms of models or indices from the data. Nevertheless, as it is well known, these models and indices can compromise information and can lead to disclosure [14].

Differential privacy [4] and integral privacy [13,16] are privacy models provided to avoid inferences from models and statistics. Other tools are to evaluate the analysis of disclosure risk from models. For example, membership attacks are about inferring the presence of a record in the database that was used to generate a model.

Machine learning and statistics build models from data, which are analyzed and compared by researchers and users, for example, with respect to their accuracy. Privacy by design machine learning algorithms [15] need to take into account additional aspects. In particular, the space of models, and how these

Partial support from the Vetenskapsrådet project "Disclosure risk and transparency in big data privacy" (VR 2016-03346, 2017-2020), and Spanish project TIN2017-87211-R is gratefully acknowledged.

J. Garcia-Alfaro et al. (Eds.): DPM 2018/CBT 2018, LNCS 11025, pp. 422–430, 2018.
https://doi.org/10.1007/978-3-030-00305-0_30

models are generated. We consider that there are two additional aspects to take into account besides just applying an algorithm and deliver the resulting model.

One is the direct comparison of the models. For example, there are works that study regression coefficients and how the regression coefficients are modified when data is perturbed by a masking method (e.g., microaggregation [3,9] or recoding [10] are applied to achieve k-anonymity [12]).

Another is the comparison of models with respect to the similarity of the databases that have generated them. Up to our knowledge, this aspect has not been studied in the literature until now. This topic is of relevance because databases are dynamic and it is usual that changes are applied to them. Changes can be due to different causes. E.g., the GDPR (e.g., right to rectification or deletion) can require businesses to update their data. When databases change, we may need to revise the models. Therefore, it is useful to know when two models can be generated with similar databases. I.e., how changes in the database are propagated to the models.

In this paper we propose the use of probabilistic metric spaces for modeling the relationships between machine learning models and statistics. This type of spaces define metrics in terms of a distance distribution function, which permits us to represent randomness. We will define the distance between two models in terms of distances between the databases that generate the models. Randomness permits us to represent the fact that the possible modifications that are applied to a database are not know. As we will see, in the context of data privacy, these distances can be applied to measure similarities between models with respect to their training set, or to define disclosure measures on anonymized models.

The structure of the paper is as follows. In Sect. 2 we discuss distances and metrics. In Sect. 3 we introduce a definition of probabilistic metric spaces for machine learning models. The paper finishes with a discussion.

2   Distances and Metrics

Metric spaces are defined in terms of a non-empty set and a distance function or metric. Let (S, d) be a metric space, then $d(a, b)$ for $a, b \in S$ measures the distance between the two elements a and b in S. It is known that d needs to satisfy some properties: positiveness, symmetry, and triangle inequality. Also, that if a and b are different then the distance should be strictly positive. Naturally, triangle inequality is that $d(a, b) \leq d(a, c) + d(c, b)$ for any a, b, c in S. When the distance does not satisfy the symmetry condition, (S, d) is a quasimetric space. If the distance does not satisfy the triangle inequality, (S, d) is a semimetric space.

2.1   Metrics for Sets of Objects

Given a metric space (S, d), its extension to a set of elements of S is not trivial. Several distances have been defined on sets but not all of them satisfy the triangle inequality, thus, do not lead to metrics. For example, with

$dm(x, A) = \min_{y \in A} d(x, y)$ we can define the Hausdorff distance, dH, and the sum of minimum distances, ds, as

$$dH(A, B) = \max\{\max_{y \in A} dm(y, B), \max_{y \in B} dm(y, A)\}$$

$$ds(A, B) = \frac{1}{2}\left(\sum_{y \in A} dm(y, B) + \sum_{y \in B} dm(y, A)\right).$$

However, these distances are not metrics (triangle inequality does not hold).

Eiter and Mannila [5] introduced a way to define a metric. It is based on considering a finite sequence $P = (P_1, \ldots, P_m)$ with $m \geq 2$ and $P_i \subseteq S$ for all $i \in \{1, \ldots, m\}$. The cost of such P is $c_d(P) = \sum_{i=1}^{m-1} d(P_i, P_{i+1})$. The distance $d^w : \wp_\emptyset(S) \times \wp_\emptyset(S) \to \mathbb{R}^+$ is defined as follows where $\wp_\emptyset(S)$ is the power set of S without the emptyset, and $P(A, B)$ denotes all paths between A and B.

$$d^w(A, B) = \min\{c_d(P) : P \in P(A, B)\}.$$

The authors prove in [5] that this definition is a metric when d is a distance.

2.2 Probabilistic Metric Spaces

Probabilistic metric spaces generalize the concept of a metric. Informally, they are based on distribution functions. So, the distance is not a number but a distribution on these numbers.

Definition 1. [11] *A nondecreasing function F defined on $\mathbb{R}^+$ that satisfies (i) $F(0) = 0$; (ii) $F(\infty) = 1$, and (iii) that is left continuous on $(0, \infty)$ is a distance distribution function. Δ^+ denotes the set of all distance distribution functions.*

We can interpret $F(x)$ as the probability that the distance is less than or equal to x. In this way, this definition is a generalization of a distance.

We will use ϵ_a to denote the distance distribution function that can be said to represent the classical distance a. This ϵ function is just a step function at a.

Definition 2. [11] *For any a in $\mathbb{R}$, we define ϵ_a as the function given by*

$$\epsilon_a(x) = \begin{cases} 0, & -\infty \leq x \leq a \\ 1, & a < x \leq \infty \end{cases}$$

Probabilistic metric spaces are defined by means of distance distribution functions. In order to define a counterpart of the triangle equality we introduce triangle functions. They are defined as follows.

Definition 3. [11] *Let Δ^+ be defined as above, then a binary operation on Δ^+ is a triangle function if it is commutative, associative, and nondecreasing in each place, and has ϵ_0 as the identity.*

Triangle functions has close links with t-norms [2]. If T is a t-norm, then $\tau_T(F,G)(x) = T(F(x),G(x))$ is a triangle function. See Def. 7.1.3 and Sect. 7.1 in [11]. The maximal triangle function is τ_{min}.

We are now in conditions to define probabilistic metric spaces.

Definition 4. [11] *Let $(S,\mathcal{F},\tau)$ be a triple where S is a nonempty set, $\mathcal{F}$ is a function from $S \times S$ into Δ^+, τ is a triangle function; then $(S,\mathcal{F},\tau)$ is a probabilistic metric space if the following conditions are satisfied for all p, q, and r in S:*

- *(i) $\mathcal{F}(p,p) = \epsilon_0$*
- *(ii) $\mathcal{F}(p,q) \neq \epsilon_0$ if $p \neq q$*
- *(iii) $\mathcal{F}(p,q) = \mathcal{F}(q,p)$*
- *(iv) $\mathcal{F}(p,r) \geq \tau(\mathcal{F}(p,q),\mathcal{F}(q,r))$.*

We will use F_{pq} instead of $\mathcal{F}(p,q)$ and, then, the value of the latter at x by the expression: $F_{pq}(x)$.

3   Probabilistic Metric Spaces for Machine Learning Models

In this section we define a probabilistic metric space for machine learning models based on the databases that permit to build these models. So, we are considering two spaces. On the one hand we have the space of databases. In this space we can consider transitions from one database to another. These transitions correspond to changes in the database. Naturally, they correspond to record deletion, record addition, and record modification. On the other hand we have the space of models. Each model can be generated by one or more databases in the space of databases. Figure 1 represent these two spaces and some relationships between them.

Formally, the space of databases is a graph. Note that each possible database can be considered the vertex or node in the graph; and that any type of database transformation is represented in terms of an edge (transforms a database into another one). In the figure, we only include directed edges that represent deletions.

Definition 5. *Let $\mathcal{D}$ represent the space of possible databases. I.e., $db \in \mathcal{D}$ are the possible databases we may encounter. Let $\mathcal{O}$ represent the possible minimal set of modifications. More particularly, $\mathcal{O}$ will typically include erasure of a single record, addition of a single record, and rectification of a value of a variable in a record. Then, given $db \in \mathcal{D}$, we have that o_{db} are the operations in $\mathcal{O}$ that are valid for db. For each $o \in o_{db}$, we have that $o(db) \in \mathcal{D}$ and $o(db) \neq db$.*

With these definitions, we can define the graph associated to a space of databases as follows. We assume that the construction leads to a proper graph. That is, there are no multiedges. Formally, $o_1(db) \neq o_2(db)$ for any $o_1, o_2 \in \mathcal{O}$ with $o_1 \neq o_2$.

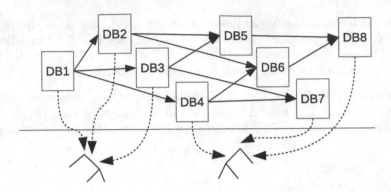

Fig. 1. Space of databases (top) and space of models (bottom) generated from the databases (dotted lines). Some transitions between databases (DB) are represented in the figure (arrows). For the sake of simplicity, we only consider directed transitions (e.g., as the only allowed transition is deletion of a single record) between databases.

Definition 6. *Let $\mathcal{D}$ be a space of databases, and $\mathcal{O}$ be the minimal set of considered modifications. Then, we define the graph for the space $\mathcal{D}$ inferred from $\mathcal{O}$ as the graph $G_{\mathcal{D},\mathcal{O}} = (V, E)$ with the set of vertices defined by $V = \mathcal{D}$ and the set of edges defined by*

$$E = \cup_{db \in \mathcal{D}} \cup_{o \in o_{db}} \{(db, o(db))\}.$$

We say that the set $\mathcal{O}$ is reversible if for any $o \in \mathcal{O}$ such that $db' = o(db)$ with $db \in \mathcal{D}$, we have an $o' \in \mathcal{O}$ such that $db = o'(db')$. If $\mathcal{O}$ is reversible, the graph $G_{\mathcal{D},\mathcal{O}} = (V, E)$ can be seen as an undirected graph. When $\mathcal{O}$ contains only deletions, it is not reversible; while with deletions and additions, it is reversible.

Given a space of databases and an algorithm that generates a model for each database, we can build a space of models. The definition of the space of models is based on a deterministic algorithm A. That is, the algorithm always returns the same model when the same database is used.

Definition 7. *Let $\mathcal{D}$ be a space of databases, and let A be a deterministic algorithm that applied to any $db \in \mathcal{D}$ builds a model m. Then, $\mathcal{M}_{\mathcal{D},A}$ is the space of models that can be inferred from $\mathcal{D}$ using A. Naturally,*

$$\mathcal{M} = \cup_{db \in \mathcal{D}} \{A(db)\}.$$

Now, let us consider a pair of models. As stated above, our goal is to define a distance between pairs of models in terms of the similarities between the databases that have generated them. Then, it is relevant to us how these models are constructed. In our context, this means finding pairs of databases that can generate our pair of models. We formalize this below.

Given two models m_1 and m_2, we define $t(m_1, m_2)$ as the pairs of databases that permit us to *transit* from m_1 to m_2. That is, pairs of databases (db_1, db_2)

such that m_1 is the model generated from db_1 and m_2 is the model generated by db_2:

$$t(m_1, m_2) = \{(db_1, db_2)|A(db_1) = m_1, A(db_2) = m_2\}$$

Then, for each pair (db_1, db_2), we consider all paths from db_1 to db_2 and the corresponding lengths. We define $l(m_1, m_2)$ as the multiset of these lengths. Let $paths(db_1, db_2)$ represent all paths from db_1 to db_2. Then, $l(m_1, m_2)$ is the following multiset:

$$l(m_1, m_2) = \{length(path)|path \in paths(db_1, db_2) \text{ for } (db_1, db_2) \in t(m_1, m_2)\}.$$

Note that this is a multiset as when there are several paths for a pair of databases, it is possible that several of these paths have the same length. For example, there are two paths of length two between $DB1$ and $DB5$ in Fig. 1. When edges represent record deletion, we can find several paths between two databases as records can be removed in different order.

Finally, we define $l^*(m_1, m_2)(x)$ as the function that counts how many elements in $l(m_1, m_2)$ are less or equal to x. That is,

$$l^*(m_1, m_2)(x) = \sum_{d \in l(m_1, m_2) \& d \leq x} count(d). \qquad (1)$$

Here $count(d)$ is the function that gives the number of occurrences of d in the multiset. This function is also known as multiplicity.

We now introduce a distance distribution function.

Definition 8. *Let $\mathcal{D}$ be the space of databases, and let $\mathcal{O}$ be the set of minimal modifications. Let $G_{\mathcal{D},\mathcal{O}} = (V, E)$ be the graph on $\mathcal{D}$ inferred from $\mathcal{O}$. Let l^* be defined as in Eq. 1 above. Let K be a constant such that $K > 0$, then, we define F as follows:*

$$F(m_1, m_2)(x) = \begin{cases} \epsilon_0 & \text{if } m_1 = m_2 \\ \min\left(1, \frac{l^*(m_1, m_2)(x)}{K}\right) & \text{if } m_1 \neq m_2 \end{cases} \qquad (2)$$

We can prove the following result.

Proposition 1. *Let $\mathcal{D}$ be the space of databases, $\mathcal{O}$ be the set of minimal modifications, A be a deterministic algorithm, $\mathcal{M}_{\mathcal{D},A}$ be the space of models inferred from $\mathcal{D}$ and A, $G_{\mathcal{D},\mathcal{O}} = (V, E)$ be the graph on $\mathcal{D}$ inferred from $\mathcal{O}$, and let l^* and F defined as in Definition 8. Then, the following holds:*

- *$F(m, m) = \epsilon_0$ for all $m \in \mathcal{M}$,*
- *$F(m_1, m_2) \neq \epsilon_0$ for all $m_1, m_2 \in \mathcal{M}$ such that $m_1 \neq m_2$,*
- *$F(m_1, m_2) = F(m_2, m_1)$ when $\mathcal{O}$ is reversible.*

Proof. The proof that $F(m, m) = \epsilon_0$ is by construction.

Let us now consider the proof of $F(m_1, m_2) \neq \epsilon_0$ for $m_1 \neq m_2$. In this case, if $m_1 \neq m_2$, we will have that there are at least two different databases db_1 and

db_2 that generate m_1 and m_2, respectively, and $db_1 \neq db_2$. Therefore, there will be at least a path with a distance at least one between db_1 and db_2. Therefore, if $K > 0$, $F(m_1, m_2)(0) \neq 1$, which proves the equation.

Let us now consider the proof of the third condition. In this case, we have that for each path $path$ in $paths(db_1, db_2)$ we will have a path in $paths(db_2, db_1)$. This naturally follows from the fact that if $path = (db_1 = db^1, db^2, \ldots, db_2 = db^r)$ with $o^i = (db^i, db^{i+1}) \in \mathcal{O}$ for $i = 1, \ldots, r-1$, then by the reversibility condition there are $o'^i = (db^{i+1}, db^i) \in \mathcal{O}$ so that $path' = (db_2 = db^r, \ldots, db^2, db^1 = db_1)$, and $path' \in paths(db_2, db_1)$. $\qquad\qquad\Box$

As a corollary of this proposition, we have that the distance in Definition 8 leads to a probabilistic semimetric space when $\mathcal{O}$ is reversible.

Corollary 1. *Given $\mathcal{D}, \mathcal{O}, A, F$ as in Definition 8, then $(\mathcal{M}_{\mathcal{D},A}, F)$ is a probabilistic semimetric space.*

In general, $(\mathcal{M}_{\mathcal{D},A}, F)$ is not a probabilistic metric space because condition (iv) in Definition 4 does not follow. A counterexample of this condition for three models m_1, m_2 and m_3 is as follows: Some databases generating m_1 are connected to databases generating to m_3, and some generating m_3 are connected to databases generating m_2. This implies that $F(m_1, m_3)(u) + F(m_3, m_2)(v)$ is finite. When there is no connection between databases generating m_1 and those generating m_2, the direct distance will be ∞.

4   Discussion and Conclusions

Machine learning is about building models from data. Given a data set, the goal is to find a model that represents the data in an appropriate way. This problem is usually formulated as finding a model that has a good accuracy.

Nevertheless, this is not the only aspect taken into account in machine learning. As the bias-variance trade-off explains, one may have a high accuracy at the expenses of over-fitting. To avoid this over-fitting, we may select a model with less accuracy but with a good bias-variance trade-off.

In addition to that, other aspects are often taken into account. E.g., explainability [8]. We may be interested in a model with less accuracy if decisions are better explained. The same applies to fairness [7] and no-discrimination [6].

Within the privacy context, models need to avoid disclosure, and this requirement can be formally defined into different ways. Differential privacy [4] is one way, that is that the model does not differ much whether a record is present or not. Integral privacy [13,16] is another way, that is that the model can be generated by a sufficiently large number of possible data sets. Resistant to membership attacks is another way. This means that we cannot infer that a particular record was present in the training set.

Under this perspective, it is relevant to compare the models and their similarities with respect to the training data sets. To do so, we need to define a distance for models based on a distance on the training data sets. In this paper we have proposed the use of probabilistic metric spaces for this purpose. We have proposed a first definition in this direction.

More broadly, in the privacy context, these distances can also be used to define disclosure or information loss metrics (see e.g. [1]). By measuring the differences between a privacy preserving model and the original model, one can establish the information that has been lost in the anonymization process.

Further work is needed in this direction. Actual computation of distance distribution functions can only be done easily for small data sets. So, we need to develop solutions for larger data sets. Secondly, we have assumed in this work that A is an algorithm that builds a model deterministically. This assumption does not always apply. On the one hand there are machine learning algorithms that include some randomness. This is the case, precisely, of some algorithms for big data based on sampling. On the other hand, there are randomized algorithms as the ones used in differential privacy. Appropriate models need to be developed to deal with this situation.

We have shown that our distance does not satisfy Equation (iv) in Definition 4. Definition of d^w in Sect. 2.1 satisfies triangle inequality for a distance d, so d^w could lead to a probabilistic metric space (see Definition 8.4.1 in [2]), but we need to explore if this distance is actually computable with actual data. Its cost, based on the set of all paths $P(A, B)$, seems too costly in our context.

References

1. Abril, D., Navarro-Arribas, G., Torra, V.: Supervised learning using a symmetric bilinear form for record linkage. Inf. Fusion **26**, 144–153 (2016)
2. Alsina, C., Frank, M.J., Schweizer, B.: Associative Functions: Triangular Norms and Copulas. World Scientific, Singapore (2006)
3. Domingo-Ferrer, J., Torra, V.: Ordinal, continuous and heterogeneous k-anonymity through microaggregation. Data Min. Knowl. Disc. **11**(2), 195–212 (2005)
4. Dwork, C.: Differential privacy. In: Bugliesi, M., Preneel, B., Sassone, V., Wegener, I. (eds.) ICALP 2006. LNCS, vol. 4052, pp. 1–12. Springer, Heidelberg (2006). https://doi.org/10.1007/11787006_1
5. Eiter, T., Mannila, H.: Distance measures for point sets and their computation. Acta Informatica **34**, 109–133 (1997)
6. Hajian, S.: Simultaneous discrimination prevention and privacy protection in data publishing and mining, Ph.D. Dissertation, Universitat Rovira i Virgili (2013)
7. Hardt, M., Price, E., Srebro, N.: Equality of opportunity in supervised learning. In: Advances in Neural Information Processing Systems, pp. 3315–3323 (2016)
8. Knight, W.: The Dark Secret at the Heart of AI. MIT Technology Review, April 11 2017
9. Laszlo, M., Mukherjee, S.: Iterated local search for microaggregation. J. Syst. Softw. **100**, 15–26 (2015)
10. LeFevre, K., DeWitt, D.J., Ramakrishnan, R.: Multidimensional k-anonymity, Technical report 1521, University of Wisconsin (2005)
11. Schweizer, B., Sklar, A.: Probabilistic Metric Spaces. Elsevier-North-Holland, New York (1983)
12. Samarati, P.: Protecting respondents' identities in microdata release. IEEE Trans. Knowl. Data Eng. **13**(6), 1010–1027 (2001)

13. Senavirathne, N., Torra, V.: Approximating robust linear regression with an integral privacy guarantee. In: Proceedings of PST 2018 (2018, to appear)
14. Torra, V.: Data Privacy: Foundations, New Developments and the Big Data Challenge. Springer, Cham (2017). https://doi.org/10.1007/978-3-319-57358-8
15. Torra, V., Navarro-Arribas, G.: Big data privacy and anonymization. In: Lehmann, A., Whitehouse, D., Fischer-Hübner, S., Fritsch, L., Raab, C. (eds.) Privacy and Identity 2016. IAICT, vol. 498, pp. 15–26. Springer, Cham (2016). https://doi.org/10.1007/978-3-319-55783-0_2
16. Torra, V., Navarro-Arribas, G.: Integral privacy. In: Foresti, S., Persiano, G. (eds.) CANS 2016. LNCS, vol. 10052, pp. 661–669. Springer, Cham (2016). https://doi.org/10.1007/978-3-319-48965-0_44

Lifelogging Protection Scheme
for Internet-Based Personal Assistants

David Pàmies-Estrems[1,2]($\boxtimes$) (iD), Nesrine Kaaniche[3,4] (iD), Maryline Laurent[3,4] (iD),
Jordi Castellà-Roca[1,2] (iD), and Joaquin Garcia-Alfaro[3] (iD)

[1] Department of Computer Science and Mathematics,
CYBERCAT-Center for Cybersecurity Research of Catalonia,
Universitat Rovira i Virgili, Tarragona, Spain
david.pamies@mail.com
[2] UNESCO Chair in Data Privacy, Tarragona, Spain
[3] Télécom SudParis & CNRS/SAMOVAR, Université Paris-Saclay, Evry, France
[4] Chair Values and Policies of Personal Information,
Institut Mines-Télécom, Paris, France

Abstract. Internet-based personal assistants are promising devices
combining voice control and search technologies to pull out relevant
information to domestic users. They are expected to assist in a smart
way to household activities, such as scheduling meetings, finding locations, reporting of cultural events, sending of messages and a lot more.
The information collected by these devices, including personalized lifelogs
about their corresponding users, is likely to be stored by well-established
Internet players related to web search engines and social media. This
can lead to serious privacy risks. The issue of protecting the identity of
domestic users and their sensitive data must be tackled at design time,
to promptly mitigate privacy threats. Towards this end, this paper proposes a protection scheme that jointly handles the aforementioned issues
by combining log anonymization and sanitizable signatures.

1 Introduction

Most of the time, we use tools created by third parties to access the information
we need from the Internet. Traditionally, people have been using web search
engines, as the main gateway to the Internet. As time goes by, we can find
other alternatives. New proposals are trying to reduce the barriers to access
information even more, and to make it accessible to everyone. As a consequence of
these innovations, today we can find a multitude of technological tools that have
been developed precisely for this reason, leading towards Internet-based personal
assistants, consolidated by technologies such as smartphones, smartwatches and
smartgateways.

For reasons of economics of scale, the development of this type of devices is
only available to a few technological organizations [8]. These few organizations
can have access to all the data generated using their devices, such as user queries
and usage statistics [17]. It is often easy to forget that all of our usage data is

J. Garcia-Alfaro et al. (Eds.): DPM 2018/CBT 2018, LNCS 11025, pp. 431–440, 2018.
https://doi.org/10.1007/978-3-030-00305-0_31

stored on Internet servers. In this case, the situation is even more accentuated, since the user is not in front of a computer. Users tend to establish more relaxed relationship with the device, sometimes without even knowing if it is working or sending information to another site, and mostly seeing it as a friend or an extension of its person.

The reality is that these devices are usually interconnected to other services. When we make a request to them, the organization that created them performs an information request on their servers. Apart from fulfilling the request, several other data gets registered in the form of a log. Anyone who uses these services is constantly generating logs and providing personal information to the organization. Additionally, searches made on most modern devices often send the user location and the local time as two additional parameters when it comes to finding the most convenient information in each situation. Therefore, user, location and local time are also registered in the logs of the servers.

Lifelogging, i.e., the recording of information about our everyday lives using smart devices, involves the collection of a huge volume of sensitive information [20]. It can lead to very serious privacy risks of personal data disclosure, as these data can be exploited in isolation, as well as combining the information generated between several of these devices. In addition, the widespread development of technologies such as Artificial Intelligence and Big Data, make the task of extracting information or relevant relationships easier every day [6]. To protect the identity and sensitive users' data, there are some techniques that allow to eliminate direct users' identifiers. However, a specialized type of attack, called Record Linkage attack, allows to link different user records, which contain seemingly harmless information, but when all the data can be mapped, it can end up revealing sensitive information from the users [15].

In this paper, we address the issue of transforming raw user's data from lifelogging data streams generated by Internet-based personal devices like Google Home and Amazon Echo [13]. We study the relation of such devices with other data information actors in terms of EU data protection directives and propose a protection solution via anonymity transformation and malleable signatures. Our proposal takes into account the role of the organizations and their needs to monetize generated data. Our protection scheme aims at limiting the risk of privacy disclosure, while maintaining an adequate level of data utility. The paper is organized as follows. Section 2 reports related work. Section 3 provides the background. Section 4 presents of our proposal. Section 5 closes the paper.

2   Related Work

Early methods to transform raw user's information to a set of privacy protecting data started with batch processing methods. Batch processing methods rely on executing match processing techniques (e.g., via statistic or semantic matching techniques) to remove the interactions that disclose user's identity from a series of stored user logs. Some methods would simply remove old sets of interactions assuming that the logs will not be large enough to enable identity disclosure [5].

This lead to flawed techniques given the likelihood of highly identifying inter-actions. Even the removal of highly identifying data, such as credit cards or addresses [4], are prone to record linkage attacks [2].

The use of *statistical disclosure control* methods can help to reduce the number of deleted records [12]. They group together sets of similar logs. Then, they use prototypes of interactions, instead of the original interactions, making them indistinguishable from each other. Users are still conserved and the interactions are transformed to minimize the risk of information disclosure. Such methods can be improved to include real-time processing, to minimize and avoid the storage of large sets of data requiring *a posteriori* treatment. Open problems using *statistical disclosure control* methods include data mining processing of large network data streams [11].

The work presented in this paper extends an anonymization scheme for web search logs using *statistical de-identification* [14]. The original scheme allows to web search engine providers to share user's raw data with third party organizations with a high degree of privacy and a relatively low decrease of data utility. The extension allows more complex data structures based on lifelogging logs, resulting on an increase of data attributes, such as spatial location of the queries and the processing of user commands. It combines *sanitizable signatures* [1] with probabilistic *k-anonymity* privacy preservation [14,19].

Sanitizable signatures are malleable mathematical schemes that allow a designated party, the *sanitizer*, to modify given parts of a ciphertext c, created by the *signer*. The sanitizer can modify parts of c in a controlled way. The signer divides $c \in \{0,1\}^*$ into N blocks $m_1, \cdots, m_N$, and provides a subset ADM $\subseteq \{1, N\}$ to the sanitizer. The subset ADM represents the description of the admissible modifications. In the end, the signer signs c using a key related to the sanitizer. Using the aforementioned key, the sanitizer is able to modify the admissible parts of c defined in ADM, in a way that keeps the resulting signature valid, under the public key of the signer. The scheme can satisfy *unlinkability*, to guarantees that it is unfeasible to distinguish between sanitized signatures that have been produced from the same ciphertext or by the same sanitizer. It is also possible to limit the set of all possible modifications on one single block and to enforce the same modifications on different messages blocks [3].

The combination of sanitizable signatures and probabilistic k-anonymization in our approach satisfies indistinguishability and real-time (e.g., streaming) data processing [10]. Indistinguishability in k-anonymity methods guarantees that each record in the dataset that has been k-anonymized is indistinguishable from at least $k - 1$ other records. Probabilistic k-anonymity relaxes the indistinguishability requirement of k-anonymity and only requires that the probability of re-identification is the same as in k-anonymity, i.e., users cannot be re-identified by record linkage attacks with a probability greater than $1/k$. In addition, anonymized logs are generated using real user queries, i.e., they are not modified, but distributed among other users with similar interests, leading towards quasi-identifiers that get dispersed between several users and thus preventing record linkage attacks, while maintaining data utility as well [14].

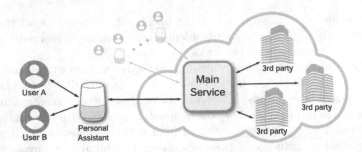

Fig. 1. Architecture for existing Internet-based personal assistants. *Users* represent the data subject, authorized to interact with the *Personal Assistant* devices, by submitting queries and commands. *Personal Assistant* devices send those commands to the *Main Service* that take the role of data collectors. Finally, *Third Parties* are the entities acting as data processors. They represent the parties with interest on legitimately accessing the anonymized logs.

3 Problem Statement

3.1 EU Data Protection Actors

EU Directive 95/46/EC, nowadays superseded by the new General Data Protection Regulation (GDPR) [16], to which we will refer during the rest of the paper, defines different roles that are relevant to the protection of general-case lifelogging environments. First, it defines the *Data Controller* as *"the natural or legal person, public authority, agency or any other body which alone or jointly with others determines the purposes and means of the processing of personal data"* [7]. Lifelogging environments need to clearly identify who is the *Data Controller*, since it determines which national law is applied. The data controller is responsible to determine which data must be processed, which third parties can access this data and when this data must be deleted.

Moreover, the figure of the *Data Processor* has the responsibility to ensure the security in the processing of personal data. The directive states that it is the *"natural or legal person, public authority, agency or any other body that processes personal data on behalf of the controller"*. It is also necessary to determine the *Data Processor*, as it also sets the national law to be applied. It is also necessary to consider the *Data Subject*, as the person who is generating the data and from which we need the consent. The directive also requires to guarantee a set of basic rights to the *Data Subject*, such as the right to access their information or to oppose to the data processing.

Figure 1 depicts a lifelogging environment which involves several actors, namely: *Users, Personal Assistant devices, remote Main Services* and *Third Parties*. Users represent the actors related to data subject, i.e., they represent the entities that are authorized to interact with the Personal Assistant devices, by submitting queries and commands. The Personal Assistant devices receive both queries and commands from associated users. Queries and commands are sent and processed by the Main Services for customized results. The remote Main Services take the role of data collectors. They have direct access to the original queries and command and control logs, sent by the Personal Assistant devices. Third Parties are the entities acting as data processors. They represent the parties that express interest on legitimately accessing the anonymized query and command logs, to eventually process and use them.

3.2 Data Structure

Personal Assistant devices may receive three different types of queries: (1) general search queries, (2) location based queries and (3) commands. They are transferred to the Main Servers for processing. Hence, the Main Service stores all the original logs for each Personal Assistant device with respect to its different associated Users. Queries and commands are defined as follows:

- **General search queries** — Traditional web search-like queries. These queries help users to find what they are looking for, from Internet websites. Users just have to ask a question and the system returns the main result they are looking for.
- **Location based queries** — Use of spatial and temporal data. They can be classified on two main categories: elementary queries and derivative queries. *Navigation and search for Point of Interests* are typical elementary location based queries. Derivative queries are mainly processed for *guiding* or *tracking* to provide customized results to users.
- **Commands** — Allow users to request direct actions that affect their own environment. Actions are usually related to home automation, multimedia control and alarms. Although these actions usually only have a local repercussion, all the data they generate is also stored together with the rest of the logs.

3.3 Privacy and Utility Trade-off

The proposed scheme aims at fulfilling two main requirements (scalability and performance requirements will be addressed in future versions of the work). First, privacy requirements, in terms of user data protection. Second, data utility requirements, in terms of log monetization. These two requirements together allow that non-sensitive user information can be sold to Third Parties, allowing Third Parties to extract user characteristics from the data they acquire. Since query and command logs together can reveal sensitive information, a trade-off between anonymizing logs and keeping them useful to extract information through data mining processes must be guaranteed. Therefore, the main challenge related to data utility is to anonymize sensitive user data removing as few information as possible in order to have enough interesting information to be analyzed. To do so, the proposed scheme aims to build fake logs and user profiles, which should maintain users' interests and break quasi-identifiers that could allow to identify a user. Queries should be anonymized to not relate sensitive information to a user identity. It should be as difficult as possible to relocate queries in order to build original user's profile. In the end, the proposed system should generate those fake logs and profiles with other users' queries.

4   Our Proposal

We extend the initial architecture presented in Sect. 3 to handle the aforementioned goals in terms of privacy regulation, security and functional requirements. Figure 2 depicts the extended architecture. An entity named the Identity Screener ensures the compliance with the legal constraints and requirements to settle, e.g., privacy prevention algorithms, based on criteria set by EU regulation directives [7,16]. It acts as a container of privacy filters to enforce data protection and control any misuse between any other parties. A second entity, the Auditor, acts as a dedicated agent which is responsible of auditing the Identity Screener and the Main Service activities, with respect to accountability and users' consent requirements. In the sequel, we describe more in depth the working properties of our extended architecture and its idealized Identity Screener conducting sanitizable signatures and pre-anonymization of logs.

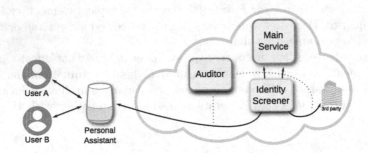

Fig. 2. Extended architecture. It includes an Identity Screener ensuring the compliance of privacy; and an Auditor, responsible of auditing accountability and users' consent requirements.

4.1   Working Properties of the Extended Architecture

To elaborate on the operations of the extended architecture, we refine and examine more in depth the internal components that the full system requires to handle requests and responses. Figure 3 depicts the proposed system. It shows the interactions of a User and its Personal Assistant, and the eventual generation of queries. The queries are sent through the network for treatment. Once treated, the resulting logs become properly anonymized. Then, it becomes possible to provide the anonymized logs to third parties, e.g., to monetize them. Next, we describe the main steps performed at each stage.

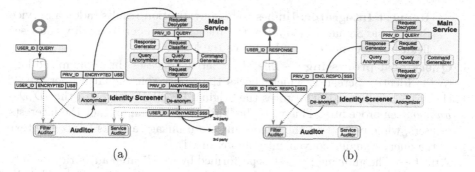

(a)   (b)

Fig. 3. (a) Request architecture: a User interacts with its Personal Assistant, generating a series of queries that are sent through the Identity Screener (which sanitizes the user identity) to a Main Service that anonymizes the queries, and redirect them back through the Identity Screener to the Third Parties. (b) Response architecture: Main Service creates and signs the response for the User, via the Identity Screener, which restores the User identity and redirects the response to the Personal Assistant (i.e., decrypts and provides the result to the User).

1. **System initialization** — As a prior step to the start of the system execution, it shall be ensured the distribution of the key pairs to create and check the User Sanitizable Signatures and the Service Sanitizable Signatures, as well as the public key of the Main Service to all the Personal Assistants.

2. **Query pre-processing** — Two steps are conducted. **First**, in a local step, the User sends a question to its Personal Assistant, which recognizes who has formulated the question and transforms it into text. Once transformed, the query is encrypted using the public key of the Main Service and gets signed using the User Sanitizable Signature. The signature allows the Identity Screener to modify some data about the user (e.g., its real identity), but keeps the remainder elements of the query. **Second**, the query is sent to the Identity Screener (e.g., a distinct administrative entity than the Main Service). A specific module replaces the original User identifier (cf. *USER_ID* in Fig. 3) with a pseudonymous (cf. *PRIV_ID*), preventing the Main Service from knowing the real identity of the user that generated the original query (the Identity Screener does not have access to the original query, which remains encrypted).

3. **Anonymization** — Procedures conducted at the Main Service:
   - **Request Decrypter:** Verifies the signature of the query and decrypts the body of the query with the Main Service private key.
   - **Request Classifier:** Determines the log class (w.r.t. the three classes in Sect. 3.2) and decides how the log shall be treated. General search queries are redirected to the *Query Anonymizer* procedure [14], location-based queries to the *Query Generalizer* procedure [18] and command-based queries to the *Command Generalizer* procedure [9] (conducting k-anonymity and data perturbation treatment tailored for each class).

- **Request Integrator:** Unifies the anonymization results, adds a Service Sanitizable Signature (to allow the Identity Screener to modify the User field, but not the rest) and releases the logs.

4. **Query post-processing** — The Main Service releases the anonymized logs to the Identity Screener, which checks the Sanitizable Signature Service. If the check is validated, it restores the original USER_ID, through the *ID Deanonymizer* procedure. This way, the Third Parties can extract the interests of users, while protecting the logs from record linkage attacks (since the text of the query remains conveniently anonymized).

5. **Audit** — The auditing process is performed by a dedicated authority, mainly relying on the verification process of Service Sanitizable Signature. That is, the auditor has to verify the consistency of signed queries and responses, generated by the User, the Identity Screener and the Main Service, such as:

    - **Identity Screener activities auditing** — Verification of Identity Screener signed queries consistency. Honestly generated signatures (using *signing correctness*) and sanitized signatures (using *sanitizing correctness*) have to be accepted by the verifier. Honestly generated proofs on valid signatures (*proof correctness*) have to be accepted by the Service Sanitizable Signature algorithms [1].

    - **Main Service activities** — Verification of the consistency of signed original queries' responses and anonymized query logs, generated by the Main Service. Each anonymized query has to be sent through the Identity Screener in order to retrieve the USER_ID query identifier, before transmitting to Third Parties. Hence, the auditor may check the signatures after the Main Service and the Identity Screener processing, as well as to verify if transfer actions are allowed with regard to each user authorization vector.

4.2   Discussion

Some limitations in our approach remain open. First, w.r.t. Users's communication, it must be ensured that the Personal Assistant does not send information to the Main Service directly, therefore escaping the treatment of the Identity Screener. On the contrary, the communication with the Third Parties does not have this problem. If they want to recover the original USER_ID, all messages must go through the Identity Screener. In this case, the possible privacy problem would appear if any of the Third Parties send the data back to the Main Service once it has been processed by the Identity Screener. If this situation arises, the Main Service would have access to the anonymized query and the original USER_ID. If the Main Service stores the correspondence between the original query and the anonymized query, it could fetch the original Query and User pair. Solutions to handle these limitations are under investigation.

5   Conclusion

Internet-based personal assistants can lead to serious privacy risks. They may release sensitive information about the identity of domestic users and their sensitive data. The issue must be tackled by jointly addressing anonymization by organizational roles in terms of *Data Controller*, *Data Processor* and *Data Subject*. Towards this end, we have proposed an architecture that combines lifelogging anonymization and sanitizable signatures, to promptly mitigate privacy threats. Future work includes a more exhaustive analysis about the cooperation of the different elements of our architecture, as well as to provide further investigations about the current techniques included in the architecture with a specific brand of Internet-based personal assistants. Ongoing code for the implementation of our proposal is available at github (cf. http://j.mp/lps-ipa).

References

1. Ateniese, G., Chou, D.H., de Medeiros, B., Tsudik, G.: Sanitizable signatures. In: 10th European Conference on Research in Computer Security, ESORICS 2005 (2005)
2. Barbaro, M., Zeller, T.: A Face Is Exposed for AOL Searcher No. 4417749 (2006). https://www.nytimes.com/2006/08/09/technology/09aol.html
3. Canard, S., Jambert, A.: On extended sanitizable signature schemes. In: Pieprzyk, J. (ed.) CT-RSA 2010. LNCS, vol. 5985, pp. 179–194. Springer, Heidelberg (2010). https://doi.org/10.1007/978-3-642-11925-5_13
4. Center for Democracy and Technology: Search privacy practices: a work in progress (2007). http://www.cdt.org/privacy/20070808searchprivacy.pdf
5. Cooper, A.: A survey of query log privacy-enhancing techniques from a policy perspective. ACM Trans. Web (TWEB) **2**(4), 19 (2008)
6. Danezis, G., Domingo-Ferrer, J., Hansen, M., Hoepman, J.-H., Metayer, D.L., Tirtea, R., Schiffner, S.: Privacy and data protection by design-from policy to engineering. arXiv preprint arXiv:1501.03726 (2015)
7. European Parliament and Council of the European Union: Directive 95/46/EC of the European parliament and of the council (1995)
8. Grimes, J.M., Jaeger, P.T., Lin, J.: Weathering the storm: the policy implications of cloud computing (2009)
9. Gruteser, M., Grunwald, D.: Anonymous usage of location-based services through spatial and temporal cloaking. In: International conference on Mobile Systems, Applications and Services, pp. 31–42. ACM (2003)
10. Guo, K., Zhang, Q.: Fast clustering-based anonymization approaches with time constraints for data streams. Know. Based Syst. **46**, 95–108 (2013)
11. Krempl, G., et al.: Open challenges for data stream mining research. ACM SIGKDD Explor. Newsl. **16**(1), 1–10 (2014)
12. Navarro-Arribas, G., Torra, V.: Tree-based microaggregation for the anonymization of search logs. In: 2009 International Joint Conference on Web Intelligence and Intelligent Agent Technology, Washington, DC, USA, pp. 155–158 (2009)
13. Nijholt, A.: Google Home: experience, support and re-experience of social home activities. Inf. Sci. **178**(3), 612–630 (2008)

14. Pàmies-Estrems, D., Castellà-Roca, J., Viejo, A.: Working at the web search engine side to generate privacy-preserving user profiles. Expert Syst. Appl. **64**, 523–535 (2016)
15. Poblete, B., Spiliopoulou, M., Baeza-Yates, R.: Website privacy preservation for query log publishing. In: Bonchi, F., Ferrari, E., Malin, B., Saygin, Y. (eds.) PInKDD 2007. LNCS, vol. 4890, pp. 80–96. Springer, Heidelberg (2008). https://doi.org/10.1007/978-3-540-78478-4_5
16. Regulation (EU): 2016/679 of the European parliament and of the council of 27 April 2016 on the protection of natural persons with regard to the processing of personal data, OJEU l 119/1 of 4.05.2016. In: Elementary Particle Theory (2016)
17. Sarconi, P., Calore, M.: OK, house: get smart. How to make the most of Amazon Echo and Google Home. Wired **25**(6), 39–41 (2017)
18. Shankar, P., Ganapathy, V., Iftode, L.: Privately querying location-based services with SybilQuery. In: 11th International Conference on Ubiquitous Computing. ACM (2009)
19. Soria-Comas, J., Domingo-Ferrer, J.: Probabilistic k-anonymity through microaggregation and data swapping. In: 2012 IEEE International Conference on Fuzzy Systems, pp. 1–8. IEEE (2012)
20. Wang, P., Smeaton, A.: Using visual lifelogs to automatically characterize everyday activities. Inf. Sci. **230**, 147–161 (2013)

Author Index

Ahmed, Mohiuddin 140
Al-Bassam, Mustafa 94
Al-Shaer, Ehab 140
Alshammari, Majed 209
Avarikioti, Georgia 76

Bissias, George 155
Boiten, Eerke 225
Bösch, Christoph 188
Boyd, Colin 130
Bracciali, Andrea 38
Breuer, Malte 373
Brito, Felipe T. 279
Brown, Anthony 313

Cabot-Nadal, Miquel A. 20
Carle, Georg 357
Carr, Christopher 130
Castellà-Roca, Jordi 431
Chepurnoy, Alexander 57
Crabtree, Andy 313
Cruz, Jason Paul 415

Drăgan, Constantin Cătălin 242

Engelmann, Felix 188

Franke, Martin 263

Galal, Hisham S. 3
Garcia-Alfaro, Joaquin 431
Gladbach, Marcel 263

Hartenstein, Hannes 85
Hou, Y. Thomas 345

Ibarrondo, Alberto 389

Janssen, Gerrit 76
Judmayer, Aljosha 197

Kaaniche, Nesrine 431
Kargl, Frank 188

Kharin, Vasily 57
Klomp, Rick 38
Koens, Tommy 113

Laurent, Maryline 431
Leal, Bruno C. 279
Levine, Brian N. 155
Li, Jin 345
Lodge, Tom 313
Lou, Wenjing 345

Machado, Javam C. 279
Mandal, Avradip 296
Manulis, Mark 242
Meiklejohn, Sarah 94
Meshkov, Dmitry 57
Meyer, Ulrike 373
Mitchell, John C. 296
Montgomery, Hart 296
Mut-Puigserver, Macià 20

Navarro-Arribas, Guillermo 422
Nobre, Juvêncio S. 279
Nowostawski, Mariusz 67

Önen, Melek 389

Pallas, Frank 329
Pàmies-Estrems, David 431
Payeras-Capellà, M. Magdalena 20
Piatkivskyi, Dmytro 67
Poll, Erik 113

Rahm, Erhard 263
Roy, Arnab 296

Salas, Julián 407
Schindler, Philipp 197
Sehili, Ziad 263
Simpson, Andrew 209
Stengele, Oliver 85
Stifter, Nicholas 197

Thibodeau, David   155
Torra, Vicenç   407, 422

Ulbricht, Max-R.   329

Vidal, Israel C.   279
von Maltitz, Marcel   357

Wagner, Isabel   225
Wang, Yongge   140
Wang, Yuyi   76
Wattenhofer, Roger   76

Wei, Jinpeng   140
Weippl, Edgar   197
Werman, Shira   175
Wetzel, Susanne   373
Wüller, Stefan   373

Yanai, Naoto   415
Youssef, Amr M.   3

Zhang, Ning   345
Zohar, Aviv   175

Printed in the United States
By Bookmasters